PRAISE FOR *EVOLUTIONARY PSYCHOLOGY*

"Superbly written, the best introduction to the subject I've ever read."
Paul Abramson, UCLA

"This is a truly intelligent, delightful, and humorous presentation of the concepts and findings of evolutionary psychology. The book avoids common pitfalls in the way it presents this body of work. It strikes a great balance between serious scholarship and a personal perspective, and offers many provocative thoughts about the implications of this field's findings for the problems we humans face. I have no doubt that undergraduates will love this book and be stimulated by it – and that their parents and grandparents would enjoy and learn from it as well."
Jeff Greenberg, University of Arizona

"Witty and wise, this quirkily personal telling of evolution's contribution to human nature is as likely to persuade the skeptic as it is to delight the already initiated."
Curtis Hardin, Brooklyn College

"My students loved it! This book is both hilarious and scholarly, and it covers important material not covered by other textbooks."
Martie Haselton, UCLA

"I love this book like a brother. This is to say that although I'd quibble with some of the smaller points, the big picture is spot-on. And also that I got a big kick out of it even when I disagreed. It's insightful and engaging, it focuses on interesting and controversial topics, and it's playful and intelligent at the same time. It's also the only textbook I've ever read that shares my juvenile sense of humor. If I were you, I'd buy it and read every word."
Bill von Hippel, University of Queensland

EVOLUTIONARY PSYCHOLOGY

GENES, ENVIRONMENTS, AND TIME

BRETT PELHAM

First published 2019 by
RED GLOBE PRESS

Red Globe Press in the UK is an imprint of Springer Nature Limited, registered in England, company number 785998, of 4 Crinan Street, London, N1 9XW.

Red Globe Press® is a registered trademark in the United States, the United Kingdom, Europe and other countries.

ISBN 978-1-352-00294-2 paperback

This book is printed on paper suitable for recycling and made from fully managed and sustained forest sources. Logging, pulping and manufacturing processes are expected to conform to the environmental regulations of the country of origin.

A catalogue record for this book is available from the British Library.

A catalog record for this book is available from the Library of Congress.

DEDICATION

To two of my favorite ancestors, Bill and Dottie Pelham, neither of whom believed at all in evolution but both of whom believed wholeheartedly in all six of their children.

BRIEF CONTENTS

CONTENTS

ABOUT THIS BOOK

This book is a playful introduction to evolutionary psychology. It explains, for example, why those who routinely help others live longer than their more selfish counterparts, and why it is such a big insult to call someone a liar. It also offers a view of birth, death, and everything in between from an evolutionary perspective. From astronomy to anthropology, a lot of very different scientific disciplines inform evolutionary psychology.

This book is also pretty contrarian, and I hope that it digs a bit more deeply into some controversial topics than most other textbooks do. Saying this book is contrarian means at least two things. First, evolution often provides a contrarian perspective on many things we tend to view unquestioningly, from sex to swimming. I make a cognitive evolutionary argument about swimming, for example, that will surely offend many avid swimming fans. The gist of the argument is that swimming is an extreme form of athletic affirmative action for rich White people. However, the way our brains work (because of the way they evolved) prevents most people from seeing this.

The second way in which this book is contrarian is that I am a little more critical than most other evolutionary psychologists when it comes to a few very popular evolutionary ideas. For example, despite my argument that understanding genetics is absolutely essential to understanding evolution, I offer a highly critical analysis of genetic studies of twins, including studies of twins separated at birth. The gist of this argument is that, as important as they are, twin studies are very poorly designed to separate the true effects of genes from the powerful effects of stereotypes based on traits like height, skin tone, and physical attractiveness.

Having said all this, I hope readers will quickly see that my critical nature is balanced by my tremendous enthusiasm for science in general and for evolutionary psychology in particular. I believe that psychology can change the world for the better. But if we wish to make tomorrow better, we had better be willing to take a hard look at both yesterday and today. There is no field of scientific inquiry that better connects the past, the present, and the future than evolutionary psychology.

ABOUT THE AUTHOR

I'm the second of six children and a first generation high school graduate. I grew up in rural northwest Georgia, living on a few dollars per day. Most of my childhood role models were lovable, deeply religious, and sometimes brilliant rednecks. My transformation from bumpkin to behavioral scientist is a work in progress, but it began in Louise Boyd's first grade classroom, where I learned to love learning. My next serious mentor was the irreverent Dennis Selvidge, who taught me high school physics. The earnest genius Julian Shand then taught me physics at Berry College. At Berry I learned philosophy from the wry and lovable David McKenzie and then learned psychology from the devoted mentors Dan McBrayer and Ed Vatza. Eventually, I got to study social psychology at UT Austin with Bill Swann and Dan Gilbert. My first professorship was at UCLA, where Bernie Weiner, Shelley Taylor, Barney Schlinger, Curtis Hardin, Bill Grisham, David Boninger, and Paul Abramson patiently trained me for ten years. When I moved to Buffalo in 1999, Derek Taylor, Gretchen Sechrist, Sandra Murray, Gail Mauner, and Shira Gabriel patiently continued my training.

This is my third book, and it's the one I most enjoyed writing. I'm also an author on about 50 empirical research papers. In addition to evolution, my research interests include birth, climate change, close relationships, culture, death, gender, health psychology, human development, marketing, religion, the self-concept, social judgment, stereotypes, and wellbeing. I love carpentry, cooking, card games, juggling, sculpting, writing, and almost all kinds of music. I aspire to become fluent in Spanish, although I am only about a third of the way there. As a highly unlikely psychological scientist, I hope this book will contribute to the scientific education of many other psychological scientists – unlikely and otherwise.

ACKNOWLEDGEMENTS

Many little people contributed to this book. My daughter, Brooklyn, for example, is only 53" tall. My large, dear, and old friend Curtis Hardin read the entire book and offered his brilliant feedback on every chapter. Curtis also helped me make some of the humor a little less juvenile. My smaller, just as dear, and even older friend David Boninger strongly encouraged me to write this book in the first place. David Myers and Bill von Hippel barely know me, and yet these two altruists read a first draft of the entire book and offered me plenty of encouragement as well as thoughtful and critical feedback. Speaking of altruists, two of my brothers, Jason and Barry Pelham, read the book and gave me thoughtful and encouraging feedback.

My two mentors, Bill Swann and Dan Gilbert, also endured early drafts of the book and suggested many improvements. Because I claim not to know David Myers, they are the two best writers I know. They were very, very patient with me in grad school – when I was resisting their efforts to teach me to write. Speaking of patience, my most patient reviewer was Steve Crabtree, who made many constructive suggestions on the book. This ranged from correcting my grammar and making my humor less offensive to helping me trim parts of the book that had gotten badly out of control.

Other experts who generously reviewed parts of the book for me or offered me advice on it include Paul Abramson, Jeff Greenberg, and Martie Haselton. Martie even tested out an early draft of the book for me in one of her advanced undergraduate courses at UCLA. I collectively thank Martie and these 20 UCLA students for helping me improve the book. Craig Anderson, one of the world's leading experts on aggression, was kind enough to provide me with his detailed and extremely thoughtful feedback on the chapter on evolution and aggression. Someone this helpful should probably be studying altruism rather than aggression.

My beloved wife LJ Fletcher Pelham was a fantastic test audience for the book because she is one of the most brilliant people I know. Further, LJ is not a psychologist, and so she offered an invaluable layperson's perspective on the book. She also endured (that's how you spell "enjoyed" in New Jersey) many lonely days while I was obsessed with the book.

I would be remiss if I did not note that many evolutionary scientists inspired me to write this book. To thank just a few – including a couple with whom I pretty often disagree – I'd like to express my thanks to David Buss, Leda Cosmides, Martin Daly, Richard Dawkins, Frans de Waal, Jared Diamond, William Hamilton, Martie Haselton, Olivia Judson, Douglas Kenrick, Steven Pinker, Neil Shubin, John Tooby, Robert Trivers, Bill von Hippel, E.O. Wilson, and Margo Wilson. I thank these scientists (including a couple who are no longer with us) whose work I found so irresistible that I chose writing about it over tending to basic needs such as sleeping, eating, and playing Crossy Road with my two favorite descendants, Brooklyn and Lincoln.

I am also deeply indebted to the Red Globe Press team who patiently endured both my quirkiness and my stubbornness and worked tirelessly to make the book you see here much better than the book I originally sent them. This includes my editor Luke Block, my copyright and image expert Stephanie Farano, my production editor Amy Brownbridge, and my copy editor Maggie Lythgoe.

Finally, without a doubt, the person who has done the most to nurture my abiding interest in evolution (including human evolution) is the brilliant, witty, and exceedingly patient evolutionary biologist Derek Taylor. My deepest thanks, Derek.

FIGURE CREDITS

Figure 1.1 by Michael H.W. Figure 1.2 by Jerry Crimson Mann. Figure 1.3, motor-cycle photo by Dennis Mojado, snake photo by Steve Jurvetson. Figure 1.4, photo by Calistemon. Figure 1.5 photo by Denise Chan, Figure 1.6, photos clockwise from upper left by John Ruble, Jon Richfield, Popovkin, and Klaus Roggel. Figure 1.7, images (left to right) courtesy of Stan Shebs, Vassil, and Adityamadhav83.

Figure 2.1, image by Brett Pelham, Figure 2.2, elephant photo by Phoenix Lumbre, cat photo by Cliff.

Figure 3.1, images clockwise (from top left) courtesy of: Fir0002, Holger Brandl et al., Hartmanga, Weltenbummler84, Copyright © 2005 Richard Ling, Jatin Sindhu and Fir0002 (all images adapted by Brett Pelham). Figure 3.2, credit: Yassine Mrabet. Figure 3.4, foot selfie by Barry Pelham. Figure 3.7, DNA double helix drawing by Brooklyn and Brett Pelham. Figure 3.8, clockwise from top right, original images courtesy of Roland Hale, © Getty Images, Eva Rinaldi and James Woodson © Getty Images. Figure 3.9, all faces generated in Alex Todorov's laboratory. Figure 3.11, original image courtesy of Jatin Sindhu, adapted by Brett Pelham. Figure 3.12, left image: Bonnie U. Gruenberg, right image: Agriflanders, adapted by Brett Pelham. Figure 3.13, Canada Lynx image courtesy of Keith Williams and Iberian Lynx image courtesy of Programa de Conservación Ex-Situ del Lince. Figure 3.14, sketch by Brett Pelham (based on fossil images from the Smithsonian collection).

Figure 4.1, left image courtesy of Harry Winston, Inc., 1958. Figure 4.2, respective photos by Francis Franklin, ChrisO, Mathias Kabe, and Museum of Toulouse. Figure 4.3, seahorse photo by Florin Dumitrescu, phalarope photo by a devoted U.S. government employee. Figure 4.4, reprinted with STM permission from SAGE, Lieberman et al. (2011), Kin Affiliation Across the Ovulatory Cycle Females Avoid Fathers When Fertile, *Psychological Science*, 22, 13–18. Figure 4.5, photo by Harald Olsen.

Figure 5.1 is from Haeckel's (1874) *Anthropogenie*. Figure 5.3, chimp photo by Richard from Canton, gorilla skull photo by Didier Descouens, dog photo by Tom Bjornstad. Figure 5.4, images are based on tests used by Brown and Yamamoto (1986) and Leat et al. (2009). Figure 5.5, photo by James Neill. Figure 5.6, photo by Charles J. Sharp. Figure 5.7, images from *Gray's Anatomy* (1918). Figure 5.8 from Pelham (2017a).

Figure 6.1, image stills taken from a video of Harlow's experiment (1958) available at: www.youtube.com/watch?v=hh9tJnlkHwk.

Figure 6.2, all images in the public domain (and courtesy of Wikipedia). Figure 6.3 created from data in Packer (2001). Figure 6.4 from Pelham (2017b). Figure 6.5 created using data from figure 9 of Sotherland and Rahn (1987).

Figure 7.3a created using figures from Kitaoka and Ashida (2003). Figure 7.3b is an optical illusion created by Edward H. Adelson (1995).

Figure 7.7, constructed from data in Haselton and Buss (2000). Figure 7.10, Iraqi boy photo courtesy of Max Pixel, infant photos by Brett Pelham.

Figure 8.2, photo courtesy of National Oceanic and Atmospheric Administration. Figure 8.3, photo by Donar Reiskoffer. Figure 8.4, white rhino photo by Ikiwaner, bush elephant photo by Lee R. Berger. Figure 8.5, photo credits: Ringed seal by NOAA; elephant seal by Michael L. Baird; gibbon by Diego Lapertina; gorilla by Dave Proffer. Figure 8.7, elephant seal photo by Hullwarren, Donald Trump photo by Michael Vadon. Figure 8.8, images offered via Creative Commons by Svenson et al. (2016). Photography credits: (a) Matthew Nochisaki, (b) Jason Zhu, (c) Adrian Kozakiewicz, (d) Stefan Engelhardt, and (e) Andrew Mitchell. Figure 8.9, image credits (left to right): right image a video still of the incident, courtesy of ViralHog YouTube channel. Figure 8.10, Arnold Schwarzenegger photo by Staff Sergeant Stacee McCausland.

Figure 9.1, monument photo by Dwight Burdette. Figure 9.2, reprinted courtesy of STM permission from the American Psychological Association, Aron, A., Aron, E.N., & Smollan, D. (1992).

Figure 10.10, anemone and clownfish photo by Nick Hobgood.

Figure 11.1, photo courtesy of NASA.

Figure 12.1, image courtesy of Wikipedia. Figure 12.2, top image: Muir Glacier, Alaska, 1941 vs. 2004. Middle image: Pederson Glacier, Alaska, 1917 vs. 2005. Bottom image: Imja Glacier, Himalayas, 1956 vs. 2007.

Chapter opener images: Chapter 2 courtesy of H.Krisp, Chapter 4 courtesy of Hermanus Backpackers under the following licence: https://creativecommons.org/licenses/by/2.0/uk/, Chapter 6 courtesy of Hiroya Minakuchi / Minden Pictures, Chapter 7 courtesy of N'golo, Chapter 12 opener courtesy of iStock.com / schuie.

All chapter epigraphs reprinted with permission from the respective authors and publishers: Bernard (2006) of AltaMira publishers, from *Research Methods in Anthropology Qualitative and Quantitative Approaches*, 4th edition, © 2005; via Copyright Clearance Center, Inc., Tumulty et al. (2014) of Oxford University Press from *The biparental care hypothesis for the evolution of monogamy: Experimental evidence in an amphibian*, Georgiev, Klimczuk, Traficonte, and Maestripieri (2014) from their free-to-access article *When Violence Pays: A Cost-Benefit Analysis of Aggressive Behavior in Animals and Humans*, Robert Kurzban and Mark R. Leary with STM permission from the American Psychological Association from the article *Evolutionary Origins of Stigmatization: The Functions of Social Exclusion*, Psychological Bulletin, Vol. 127, No. 2, 187–208, Adrian V. Bell (2010) with STM permission of Taylor & Francis from *Why cultural and genetic group selection are unequal partners in the evolution of human behaviour*, Communicative & Integrative Biology 2(3), 159–161.

Approximately twenty-nine (29) words from HOW THE MIND WORKS by Steven Pinker Copyright © 1997 by Steven Pinker. Used by permission of W. W. Norton & Company, Inc. and (Allen Lane, The Penguin Press, 1998) Copyright © Steven Pinker, 1998.

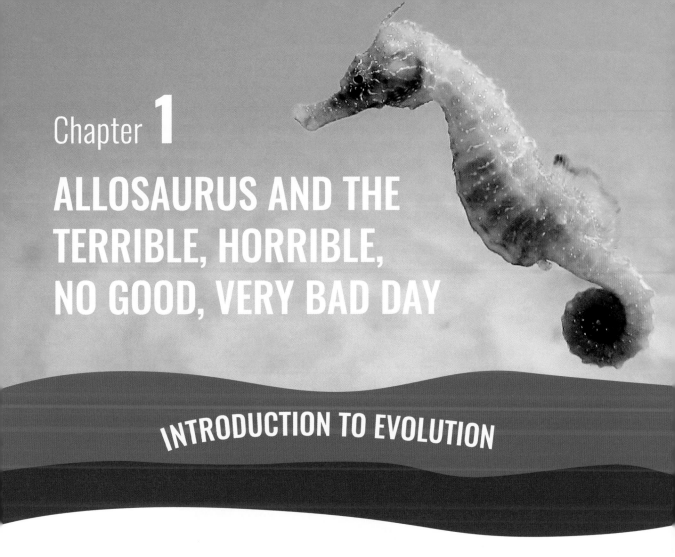

Chapter 1

ALLOSAURUS AND THE TERRIBLE, HORRIBLE, NO GOOD, VERY BAD DAY

INTRODUCTION TO EVOLUTION

"I don't see how we're ever going to agree if you suggest that natural laws have changed. It's magical [thinking]."

— *Bill Nye (2014), the science guy, in a debate about evolution vs. creation*

About 66 million years ago, I'm pretty sure it was on a Tuesday, something truly terrible happened in modern-day Mexico. An extremely large meteorite (10 km wide) obligingly obeyed the laws of physics and smashed into the planet we have since come to adore and abuse. Striking in the Yucatan Peninsula, the massive meteorite created a blast some 30 billion times more powerful than the sum of the atomic bombs that destroyed Hiroshima and Nagasaki in World War II. In an instant, a tropical paradise became a smoldering crater 20 km deep and 160 km wide. Massive tsunamis, earthquakes, and volcanoes were triggered worldwide. Climate change, forest fires, and acid rain must have occurred on an unimaginable scale. Some scientists think it may have taken a decade just for the thick clouds of ash and dust to settle. For the first time in millions of years, it became a terrible time to be a dinosaur. As thick clouds of dust choked the planet, even the cleverest and most resourceful dinosaurs proved to be unprepared to survive on a burning-then-freezing planet practically devoid of plant life (Brusatte et al., 2014). Lloyds of London was not answering any phone calls.

Virtually all evolutionary biologists believe this epic tragedy for dinosaurs became a wonderful opportunity for mammals like me and you. Actually, the typical mammals who were lucky enough to survive in the wake of this planetary disaster resembled a chipmunk a lot more than they resembled me and you. Beginning with descendants of the chipmunkish **Morganucodon** (aka Morgie), many ancient mammals survived the cosmic disaster and then evolved to become the incredibly diverse family of always warm and usually fuzzy creatures that zookeepers and preschoolers know and love. Post-asteroid, most of Morgie's mammalian descendants had some huge advantages over most dinosaurs. For starters, having fur and being good at staying warm probably helped small mammals survive the harsh nuclear winter that helped extinguish all the big dinosaurs. It was probably an even bigger advantage for small mammals that they could live in small places, away from the fire, snow, and acid rain. Morgie, for example, was only about 10 cm long, roughly as big as you see her in Figure 1.1. If you're paleontologically sophisticated enough to know that many birdlike dinosaurs also survived this mass **extinction**, you probably know one likely reason why many of them were able to do so. It's a lot easier to survive a lengthy global famine when you eat like a bird than when your idea of dinner is half a ton of fresh grass, or filet of Triceratops.

Figure 1.1 *Artist Michael H.W.'s impression of Morgie, one of the first known proto-mammals. Morgie's fur, special jaws, and mammalian inner ear bones set her apart from dinosaurs or reptiles. You share quite a bit of her DNA (her genome).*

HOMOLOGY, PALEONTOLOGY, AND PSYCHOLOGY

In the millions of years since the massive asteroid strike, the earth's inhabitants have slowly but dramatically diversified. About 15–20 million years after the strike, some of Morgie's mammalian descendants gradually returned to the oceans that spawned all life on earth, eventually evolving into modern whales and dolphins. Incidentally, one of the many reasons we know that whales and dolphins evolved from land mammals is that their skeletons strongly resemble those of other mammals. For example, as you can see in Figure 1.2, dolphins have forelimb ("flipper") bones that strongly resemble the front limb bones of virtually all mammals. Dolphins even have five "finger" bones just like we do, despite the fact that dolphins look totally ridiculous in gloves. The tendency for animals that share a common ancestor to share traits with one another is known as **homology**, and it occurs because animals that have an ancestor in common have genes in common. Some whales and dolphins have vestigial (tiny, left over) rear leg bones that never emerge from their bodies. In addition to breathing air, nursing their young, and having special mammalian ear bones, dolphins and whales also share a much greater percentage of their genome with you than they do with the sharks or other large fish that they more closely resemble on the outside. Finally, another piece of evidence strongly suggesting that dolphins and whales evolved from land mammals has to do with the way they swim. Unlike fish, which propel themselves by moving their tails side to side, whales and dolphins move their spines up and down to swim. As a wolf or lion runs, the same thing happens to its spine. Notice that mode of swimming is a behavioral trait grounded in a whale's skeletal structure. It's important to note that homology applies to behavioral as well as physical traits, and many of these behavioral traits are grounded in the brain as well as the body. Numerous arguments in this book involve ways in which human beings behave like other mammals, because of their mammalian bodies and/or brains.

It would be another 20 million years after some mammals returned to the oceans (about 25–30 million years ago) before the common ancestors of monkeys and apes split into these two different groups. The apes, by the way, are the ones without tails, and one particular species of great ape, the hominid *Homo sapiens* (you and me), emerged only about 200,000 years ago (Ermini et al., 2015). So our species has only been around for about a fifth of a million years. In fact, it was only 11,000 years ago that we made the agricultural – and then cultural – leaps that have made us the most successful and destructive animals on the planet (Diamond, 1997). I'll say more about that later. For now, it seems safe to say that no human leaps of any kind would have ever happened if the dinosaurs still ruled.

If you're wondering what this paleontology lesson has to do with psychology, the beginning of the answer is that you and I are mammals. Mammals and proto-mammals lived alongside dinosaurs for more than 100 million years without becoming a very diverse family. Seventy million years ago there were no bats, whales, giraffes, or gorillas. They did not exist because tens of millions of years before mammals hit the scene (or exploded in the Pliocene), dinosaurs had cornered the market on the ecological niches needed to support such highly unusual modern-day mammals. Morgie and most of her ancient mammalian cousins filled a unique environmental niche by eating bugs and being agile enough to stay out of the way of T. rex (or T. rex's tinier cousins). Although there were some notable exceptions to this rule of tiny rat-likeness among ancient proto-mammals, mammals never became diverse and populous until the dinosaurs became extinct (Meng et al., 2011; O'Leary et al., 2013).

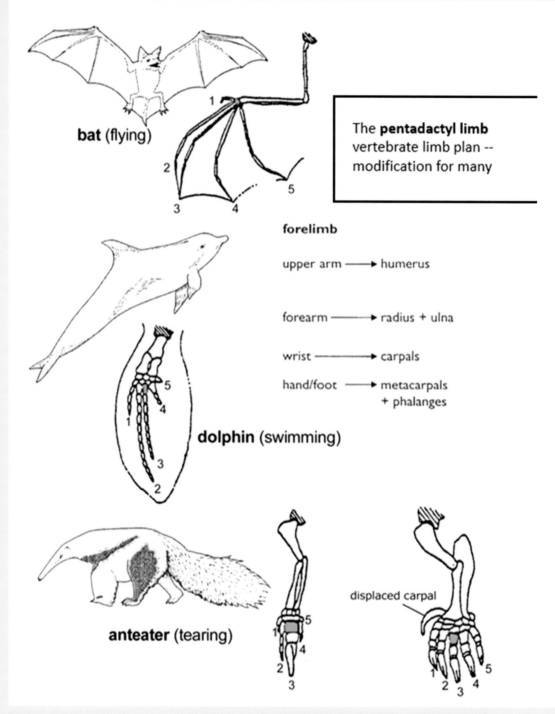

bat (flying)

The **pentadactyl limb**
vertebrate limb plan --
modification for many

forelimb

upper arm ⟶ humerus

forearm ⟶ radius + ulna

wrist ⟶ carpals

hand/foot ⟶ metacarpals
              + phalanges

dolphin (swimming)

anteater (tearing)

displaced carpal

Figure 1.2 *Jerry Crimson Mann's illustration of homology, which is the idea that related species often share common traits, because they share genes derived from a common ancestor. Despite their extreme diversity, mammals all have amazingly similar forelimb and hind limb bones.*

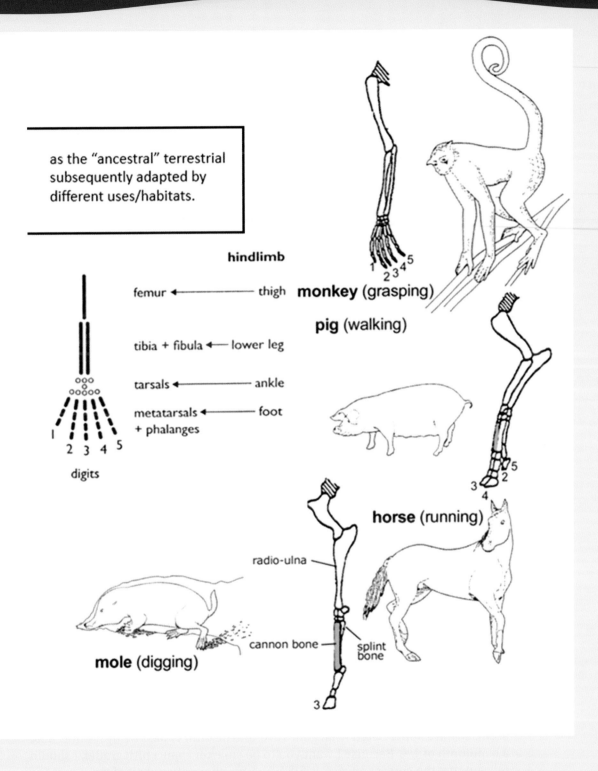

as the "ancestral" terrestrial subsequently adapted by different uses/habitats.

hindlimb

femur ← thigh

tibia + fibula ← lower leg

tarsals ← ankle

metatarsals + phalanges ← foot

digits

1 2 3 4 5

monkey (grasping)

pig (walking)

radio-ulna

cannon bone

splint bone

horse (running)

mole (digging)

Thus, in the absence of that deadly meteorite strike, the chances are virtually zero that any species of dinosaur would have ever evolved into a quirky, brainy, highly social creature that cares for its young for a couple of decades, sings *Ave Maria*, conducts psychology experiments, and is susceptible to both yellow fever and Bieber fever.

Consider a whole class of animals that are even more ancient than the family loosely known as dinosaurs. Insects were around well before the dinosaurs, and they will probably be here long after human beings are extinct. But it's exceedingly unlikely they will ever create art or write poetry. In contrast, you and I can do these uniquely human things, as well as a long list of simpler things done only by mammals. There is also a list of things done almost exclusively by vertebrates, by the way, but this discussion would take us back at least 500 million years rather than 66 million years (Kolbert, 2014; Shubin, 2008). Suffice it to say that because we are mammals, we have a lot more in common with our mammalian relatives than most people appreciate (de Waal, 1996; Diamond, 1992).

We're not *that* special

You may have heard that we share more than 98% of our genes with chimpanzees. Perhaps that's not so shocking. Consider the following thought experiment, adapted from Jared Diamond (1992). Take a male chimpanzee, and sedate him (so he doesn't rip anyone's arms off – chimps are incredibly strong). Now shave his entire body, put a Boston Red Sox cap on him, and drop him onto a New York City subway seat – making sure the train is headed to the Bronx. On second thoughts, replace the Red Sox cap with a Yankees cap – so no one rips the poor chimp's arms off. More than 98% of subway passengers will see an ugly old man who should be arrested for indecent exposure. Chimps are a lot like human beings. This is why zookeepers who want to control their chimpanzee birth rates can simply give their female chimps human birth control pills. And it's presumably why chimpanzees make tools, deceive each other, organize themselves into social groups, go to war, inspect the genitals of newborns to assess their sex, have sex face to face, and sometimes shake hands to greet one another – all very much like we do. According to experts such as Frans de Waal and Jared Diamond, we have way more in common with chimps than most people could imagine.

Speaking of chimps, both people and chimps also have a little something in common with bananas. What percentage of our genes, if any, do you think we share with bananas? Bananas are in a whole different kingdom than animals, but they are life forms, after all. When I asked my son this question, when he was a fifth grader, his answer was an impressive 10%. It was impressive because he seems to have appreciated what genes are, and he didn't guess a tiny number, like a bajillionth of 1%. Because I want you to be smarter than a fifth grader, I should tell you that the correct answer is 50%. Yes, we share about half of our genes (or our genome, to be a little more precise) with bananas. These shared genes go back to a time about 1.6 billion years ago when plant and animal life seem to have diverged from a common, very primitive ancestor (Meyerowitz, 2002). I know that sounds weird, but science is weird, and aside from particle physics, there is probably no scientific topic weirder than evolution. Our surprising similarity to chimps and bananas, including the ancient point in our planet's history when plants and animals diverged, suggests at least **five key features of evolution**.

FIVE IMPORTANT FACTS ABOUT HOW EVOLUTION WORKS

Evolution is slow

First, evolution typically operates on a very long timescale. Both people and banana plants possess successful genes that have been in the global gene pool for 1.6 billion years. So, if I were to say that something evolved "very quickly" in people, I'd probably be talking about tens of thousands of years rather than a few centuries. Quite a few modern problems exist in large part because we have not yet had time to evolve solutions (adaptations) to living in a different world than the plains of ancient Africa, or the valleys of ancient Turkey.

Evolution is conservative

Second, when something works (like a gene that contributes to basic cell metabolism, eye formation, or sperm production), nature almost never abandons it to start over from scratch. Apparently, the single gene *boule* is necessary for sperm production in males of all species (Shah et al., 2010). It seems to have first appeared about 600 million years ago. It has been promoting evolutionarily effective male orgasms ever since. Without this gene, no male mountain goat, mountain lion, or mountain gorilla will ever produce even a mole hill of sperm. Did I mention male slippery dicks? Yes, that's a real fish, and, no, they can't make sperm without boule. Sperm whales? You already knew about them, but they couldn't make any sperm without the boule gene. Without the action of this crucial gene, no male creature on earth is likely to produce any offspring, no matter how much action he gets. As another example of this principle, consider how eyes are positioned. The same PAX6 gene determines eye location in a wide range of animals from octopi to ocelots (Glaser et al., 1992). On the other hand, it looks like eyes themselves evolved independently in vertebrates (like ocelots) and invertebrates (like octopi). Homology strongly suggests this because virtually all invertebrates share one kind of eye structure, whereas virtually all invertebrates share another. These eye structures mean, for example, that vertebrate eyes have blind spots. Invertebrate eyes do not.

Evolution comes with baggage

A third important fact about evolution is that organisms possess millions of years of evolutionary heritage and all the baggage that always comes with heritage. For example, most people, like many of our primate cousins, are born absolutely adoring sugar. The running joke at my house when my daughter was three was "You better finish that cupcake or you won't get any broccoli next time!" Even a three-year-old who was riding the first wave of a sugar high knew this was a joke. This human preference for sweets was surely adaptive in an ancient world where sugary foods like honey or ripe bananas were precious commodities. Ripe fruit is usually more nutritious than sour fruit. But in a modern world where most people are constantly surrounded by sugary foods, this natural craving for sweets contributes to obesity epidemics. And if sugar doesn't get you, fatty or salty foods may get you for evolutionarily similar reasons.

Figure 1.3 *Be very afraid of motorcycles. But don't worry about the coastal garter snake, unless you're a mole.*

Along the same lines, we also inherited several kinds of **preparedness** from our ancient mammalian ancestors. Preparedness is a readiness or predisposition to learn some things very easily. It's much easier to teach people to fear spiders or snakes, for example, than to teach them to fear guns or motorcycles. I don't like guns, but I like the insanely dangerous machines called motorcycles so much that I keep one right in my driveway. About once a week I hop on it and cruise gleefully down the highway next to 18-wheelers that could squash me like a bug. In fact, even a speeding VW Beetle could squash me like a bug. In contrast, I don't keep any spiders or snakes at home, at least not on purpose. In today's world, though, guns and motorcycles kill many more people than spiders and snakes do.

As a final example of preparedness, have you ever noticed how easily kids learn to talk? We'll come back to this topic in later chapters, but I hope you can see this represents a wonderful kind of preparedness. We seem to be predisposed to learn and use language. Unlike craving sweets, however, craving conversation rarely gets us into trouble. In fact, using language helps connect us to other members of our species in ways that are simply unheard of in other animals. As sociobiologist E.O. Wilson (1978) noted, evolutionary pressures have guaranteed that we are not the "tabula rasa" (blank slate) that British philosopher John Locke once suggested.

Psychologist Dan Gilbert (1989) put this third evolutionary principle (that of evolutionary baggage) colorfully when he said: "the human brain itself is essentially a reptilian weenie, wrapped in a neocortical bun." By this, Gilbert mainly meant that people often stick with simplistic social judgments (e.g., first impressions) when it might be wiser to abandon them. E.O. Wilson (1978, p. 68) seems to have put a little more stock in instincts, arguing that: "Because the brain can be guided by rational calculations only to a limited degree, it must fall back on the nuances of pleasure and pain mediated by the limbic system and other lower centers of the brain." Where these two Harvard professors clearly agree is that the big brains that mammals enjoy are not quite as different from the brains of other animals as we might like to assume. A neocortex is an evolutionary add-on. I'm really delighted to have one, but it's not absolutely necessary. Take away my neocortex, and I stop writing this book. Take away my hindbrain and I stop breathing. I'm quite sure, then, that some of the genes we share with birds and reptiles allow us to breathe. Banana trees simply don't have these genes – either because they don't need to breathe like we do, or because they can hold their breath for a very, very long time.

Evolution implies continuity

A fourth important fact about evolution is that it implies continuity across species, especially species that are closely related. For this reason, evolutionary psychologists tend to emphasize the traits and adaptations we share with other animals. For example, Frans de Waal (1996) argued that we are not as cognitively or morally superior to other animals as we like to assume. In fact, many of the cognitive and social skills we thought were uniquely human are not quite as special as we once thought. Naked mole rats use tools – which help keep them from choking – when they dig elaborate underground burrows with their front teeth (Shuster & Sherman, 1998). Moving from the terrestrial to the celestial, there is strong evidence that crows and magpies can identify and long remember individual human faces. They are particularly good at remembering the faces of researchers who have trapped them (later to release them, of course). This holds true even when the researchers change their hats and clothing in an effort to disguise their identities. Ravens also make and use tools. So you might just as well discard that scarecrow you put up in the Eastside Community Gardens. It won't fool any crows or ravens for very long.

"Well, first of all, Robert, I believe I speak for crows everywhere when I say that by just coming here to meet with me today, you've already answered one of our most important and long-standing questions."

Chimps are even more adept at making tools than ravens are. Very few aquatic animals have the fingers or beaks needed to make tools, but quite a few aquatic animals certainly use them. This includes fish and octopi that spray jets of water as tools, crabs that carry stinging anemones for protection, and octopi that strategically carry broken coconut shells for the same reason (Mann & Patterson, 2013). Further, like ospreys, cheetahs, and perhaps even some ants, chimpanzees engage in teaching. Mother cheetahs even scaffold their older cubs by bringing back live prey to their dens and releasing the live prey so that the cubs can do the killing. Scholars disagree, for example, about whether ants ever truly teach, but there can be no doubt that some ants engage in communication (e.g., compare Franks & Richardson, 2006, with Leadbeater et al., 2006). Both dogs and parrots have problem-solving skills that rival or exceed those of human toddlers, at least in some domains. Likewise, chimps, dolphins, and even magpies (a large-brained bird in the crow family) can readily do what we once thought only people could do – recognize themselves in mirrors (Prior et al., 2008). Some octopi also seem to be able to learn the solution to a complex, unfamiliar problem in a matter of moments – by watching another octopus solve the problem.

This last point is worthy of a little more attention. We once thought only human beings engaged in **social learning** (aka **observational learning**). Psychologist E.L. Thorndike (1911) looked for evidence of social learning in monkeys of the genus *Cebus*, and concluded that: "Nothing in my experience with these animals ... favours the hypothesis that they have any general ability to learn to do things by seeing others do them." To his credit, Thorndike was quick to add that this question was not settled by a mere handful of studies. But others latched boldly onto his cautious conclusion that human beings may be special in this way (see Mackintosh, 1974). It wasn't until about 50 years later that some clever experimenters showed that rhesus monkeys could learn just by watching. Darby and Riopelle (1959) set up pairs of rhesus monkeys so that one monkey could always watch another monkey trying to get food – by choosing one of two arbitrarily marked food cup covers. After the chance to observe just one trial of this monkey game show, observer monkeys who watched the other contestant succeed usually tried a similarly marked cup in their own separate cages. This worked just as well, by the way, when the clueless other monkey made the *incorrect* choice. That is, a monkey who watched another monkey screw up by picking the wrong cup usually tried the *unselected* cup. Fast forward another five decades or so, and now we know that a hungry octopus can do something equally impressive. She can watch another octopus unlock the lid on a clear acrylic container to retrieve a delicious crab and immediately copy this novel and highly unusual behavior. "Octopus see. Octopus do."

Evolution is (pretty) orderly

A fifth important fact about how evolution works has to do with how individual organisms develop over time, and it, too, suggests a way in which we are very much like both chimps and bananas. It is this. There are many useful and important adaptations that do not exist at all at the beginning of an organism's life. Organisms develop, and development is almost never willy-nilly. Instead, things that are metabolically costly or biologically complex rarely develop until – and if – they are needed. Banana trees do not – and cannot – produce fruit until they have produced trunks and then fronds (leaves).

Moving closer to people, imagine how inefficient things would be if mammals were born sexually mature, with long horns, or with a full set of adult teeth. Things that are *needed* first *develop* first, and things that aren't needed until later almost always wait. Of course, what is needed first varies radically across the animal (and plant) kingdom. On average, mammals get a great deal of care and protection from their mothers, and many mammals are born blind and helpless. Baby kangaroos do not need to see or hop when they are in their mothers' pouches, for example, and they are born unable to do either. In contrast, most reptiles get little or no care from their parents, and most of them can see, move about, and search for food shortly after hatching. Making comparisons across mammals, gazelles can run within hours of birth because if they could not do so they would quickly become a meal for large predators. In contrast, lion cubs are born blind and helpless because few predators wish to deal with a protective mother lioness, to obtain an otherwise easy meal.

EVOLUTIONARY PRINCIPLES IN PSYCHOLOGY

It's precisely because of the importance of principles such as baggage, continuity, and orderliness that evolutionary psychology has done so much to enrich modern psychology. But what is evolutionary psychology? As I hope you've begun to see, **evolutionary psychology** is an interdisciplinary science that combines insights from evolutionary biology and psychology. More specifically, it's the scientific study of how our thoughts, feelings, and behavior (**psychology**) are influenced by processes such as adaptation and natural selection (**evolution**). It's the scientific study of how we evolved to be who we are.

In the remainder of this book, I introduce readers to the fascinating interdisciplinary topic of evolutionary psychology. I conclude this chapter with an introduction to two key evolutionary concepts: adaptation and natural selection. In Chapter 2, I offer a tour of evolutionary psychological research methods. In Chapter 3, I discuss crucial evolutionary concepts such as genetics, sexual selection, and speciation. In Chapters 4–11, I discuss specific areas of psychological research that were directly inspired by – or have proven to be highly relevant to – an evolutionary perspective. The topics studied by evolutionary psychologists are as diverse and fascinating as the whole field of psychology, but the topic that has probably gotten the most attention in evolutionary psychology is sex. Chapter 4 covers human sexuality and mating, including specific topics such as mate preference, estrus, incest avoidance, sexual jealousy, and mate retention. Chapter 5 discusses the implications of evolution for lifespan human development. Chapter 6 examines the joys and pitfalls of parenting, grandparenting, and stepparenting, and Chapter 7 examines how we evolved to think and communicate. Chapters 8–11 provide an evolutionary perspective on (8) the nature and functions of aggression, (9) prosocial behavior,

(10) sociocultural processes, and (11) how we respond to death and dying. Finally, Chapter 12 focuses on the biological and cultural evolution of major social problems. For example, it examines how our evolved human nature may contribute to problems such as overincarceration, helicopter parenting, and climate change. Evolutionary psychologists provide surprising insights about all these important topics.

Adaptation and natural selection

This book will dig into an evolutionary perspective on sex in later chapters. For now, let's discuss why sex exists at all. From an evolutionary perspective, sexual reproduction is at the heart of adaptation and natural selection. **Adaptation** refers to the ways in which species change over long periods to cope with the basic problems of survival and reproduction in specific environments. It's the way a specific gene, or set of genes, ends up sticking around inside one or more species. A close cousin of this idea is **natural selection**, which is the process by which genes that promote successful reproduction become more likely to be passed on to one's offspring – compared with genes that confer no such reproductive advantage. A turtle's strong, bony shell, like the turtle's ability to pull all its extremities completely inside it, is a specific adaptation to the problem of predators who like to make quick meals of slow-moving targets.

*"**Really**, Terry, all-in, **again?!**"*

A snake's venom is a very different reptilian adaptation. This adaptation solves two problems – by serving both as a defense against predators and as an efficient method of killing one's own prey. It is probably no evolutionary accident, then, that snake venom is not a stomach poison. If it were, how would highly venomous snakes stomach a meal into which they had just injected a generous dose of the stuff? Snake venom is only deadly when it gets into your bloodstream, which is why venomous snakes have special venom-injecting adaptations known as fangs. So yes, the next time you want to win a large bar bet, go ahead and drink the certified king cobra venom. Just be sure you don't have an ulcer and be careful not to bite your lip before you swallow. To get back to the point, adaptation is a specific consequence of natural selection, and natural selection is the engine that drives evolution. If this reminds you of the phrase "survival of the fittest," please try to rid yourself of this notion, unless you mean the long-term *evolutionary* survival of the fittest *genes*.

Excuse my French, but I need to emphasize this. Natural selection doesn't give a darn about an organism's survival. It's all about successful reproduction – passing on specific genes to future generations. To be sure, it's hard to reproduce if you don't survive long enough to mate. But once some animals have mated successfully, they seem content to die. Consider salmon that tirelessly swim a marathon upstream – to the place where they themselves were spawned. After reaching their destinations, they "mate" in the peculiar way Bill Clinton says he did – without actually having sexual relations – and then they die. (To clarify this technical point, female salmon deposit their eggs in the water and male salmon squirt their sperm in the general direction of the eggs. The salmon then die rather than narrowly escaping impeachment.) One poor animal, the male honey bee, actually dies in the process of having sex. When male honey bees have successfully delivered their sperm to a queen bee, their genitals literally explode with a pop and are ripped away from their bodies (Judson, 2002).

I'm not sure how that feels as it is happening, but I'm guessing it sucks afterward. Male honey bees die almost immediately after their explosive orgasms. If you're wondering how this could ever be a good reproductive strategy, let me remind you that the genitals explode after the delivery of sperm and that queen bees are pretty promiscuous. Even more important, the exploded bee penises remain inside the queen and act as partial chastity belts, making it harder for other male honey bees to get their sperm past the carnage. This means that the gene or genes that created exploding genitals right after successful mating became common in male honey bees. If this still sounds crazy, you should know that the percentage of male honey bees who ever get to mate at all is ridiculously low (less than 1%). So the strategy of saving your penis for a second one-minute stand would almost never pay off. Natural selection promotes successful reproduction – not the survival of specific organisms.

Love, *prey*, eat

Allow me to say it again. Natural selection may promote reproduction even at the expense of an organism's survival. Another dramatic example of this comes from Australia's **redback spider**. These deadly predators have been known to take down mice and small lizards, and they love houses and sheds. Because they're highly venomous and love the indoors, they're responsible for many painful bites to Australia's human population. Back before hospitals acquired the right anti-venom, the bites of redbacks occasionally killed people. Like many other arachnids (and most insects), female redbacks are much bigger than males. In fact, males often live on the edge of a female's web and scavenge whatever leftovers they can safely grab. And here's where it gets really weird. When a scrawny male redback mates with a big, strapping female, which only a lucky 20% of males ever get to do, he almost invariably somersaults right into her fangs after copulation. Of course, this puts him in a vulnerable position, and about 65% of the time the female redback rewards this acrobatic feat by consuming the male just as eagerly as she consummated with him.

Figure 1.4 *This female redback spider has just taken out a small lizard. There's a good chance she'll also take out and consume any male redback spider who mates with her. Unlike lizards, however, male redback spiders seem to sacrifice themselves quite willingly. What's more, those who do so are usually rewarded with more offspring.*

Why would male redbacks throw themselves into the mouths of their mates? Offering oneself up for self-sacrifice seems even crazier than accepting the offer. But studies of redback mating outcomes show that male redbacks who are eaten produce more offspring than the ones who escape being eaten (Andrade, 1996, 2002). The reason for this extra success is simple. When male redbacks are in the jaws of the females, they are not just hanging out. They are busily depositing extra sperm they would not otherwise have been able to deposit. Evolutionarily speaking, then, sex is just the way successful genes make their way into future bodies. A gene that promotes self-sacrifice will be passed on precisely to the extent that the self-sacrifice promotes *reproductive* selfishness (e.g., lots of offspring). And this will happen even at the cost of the body of the unfortunate animal that happens to carry the gene for self-sacrifice. By the way, I hope this bizarre story also illustrates that natural selection seems to happen mainly (if not exclusively) at the level of the **gene** rather than the species. Evolution is about genes. Genes are little bits of deoxyribonucleic acid (DNA) that exist at specific sites on specific chromosomes and code for specific proteins. Organisms just happen to be the vessels that carry thousands of specific genes around and do their bidding.

Play dead, keep living

After saying all this, I hasten to add that male redback spiders constitute a clear exception to the usual rules of natural selection. It's normally highly adaptive for genes to promote the survival of the organisms that carry them around. The list of specific adaptations that promote survival is endless. In any one species, moreover, hundreds of genes all do their separate parts to promote survival in that particular animal's specific environment. Camels, for example, are extremely well adapted to desert life. Their extra eyelids protect their eyes from the blowing desert sand. They're also furry on top (to create shade) with very thin fur elsewhere – to promote heat loss. Their feet are wide to help them avoid sinking in the hot desert sand, and their legs are long and thin – to keep them far away from it. Camels also have a great deal of surface area relative to their total volume. A camel is shaped more like a radiator than a thermos. Speaking of radiators, a large camel can drink about 50 gallons (400 pounds) of water in only a few minutes, and they are great at holding onto any water they do consume (Schmidt-Nielsen et al., 1957; Wilson, 1989). In fact, camel poo is so dry that you can burn it, which desert dwellers sometimes do as a handy source of fuel. I hope it goes without saying that none of these specific desert adaptations would be useful for a raccoon, a bird, a fish, or a poison dart frog. In contrast, a couple of these specific adaptations can and do work well for other desert animals. Both camels and gerbils, for example, have really efficient kidneys.

Figure 1.5 *Camels are extremely well adapted to life in the desert.*

In contrast to highly unusual desert adaptations, some adaptations are adaptive in almost any environment, and the genes responsible for these adaptations are commonplace if not universal. Remember boule? Sperm production is important enough that nature seems to have taken no chances with it. Some pretty quirky adaptations are also more widespread than you might think. Consider **tonic immobility**, also known as "playing possum." For many animals, from ants and birds to frogs and opossums, appearing to be dead seems to turn away many would-be predators. As it turns out, most predators strongly prefer freshly killed prey. In contrast to road kill, a healthy animal you just killed yourself is probably free of deadly viruses and bacteria. In fact, the minority of carnivores who don't mind eating dead things have special adaptations of their own that allow them to do so safely. Thus vultures have highly souped-up immune systems. Even more important, they have stomach acid that is hundreds of times stronger than ours, stronger, in fact, than battery acid (Houston & Copsey, 1994; and see especially Smallwood, 2014). It is so acidic that it can kill virtually any pathogen a vulture consumes, including things like Ebola or anthrax.

But if you're not a vulture, you should usually steer clear of day-old sushi, and even day-old frogs or birds. This seems to be why many different animals have evolved to "play possum" as a method of last resort against a deadly predator. As you can see from Figure 1.6, possums are not the only animals that play possum. What I find most interesting about these images is how convincing they are. These animals don't just look dead. They look like they've been dead a while.

Figure 1.6 *A possum, a common swift, a leaf frog, and a brown widow spider, all illustrating tonic immobility in response to severe threat.*

If you're not so sure that playing possum could deter a hungry predator, I should note that, in the specific case of possums, tonic immobility is not a conscious effort to deceive. Instead, the extremely threatened possum instinctively enters a highly unusual state that truly resembles death. The possum's breathing slows down to become almost undetectable. The possum's limbs become somewhat stiff, as they might be if rigor mortis were beginning to set in. It all looks very real. It certainly looked real enough to fool me about six years ago. This was when an unlucky possum found itself in my backyard at the precise moment when I released the beloved canine ball of teeth and muscle I called Liberty. In the aftermath of Liberty's attack on the possum, I shoveled what appeared to be a dead possum into a metal trash can and drove it at 5:15 a.m. to the nearest park (so I could still make my early morning flight). Let me just say that I'm happy that I got the possum out of the trash can before he really got pissed off. What followed still wasn't very pretty, but both the possum and I survived.

"In closing, Faith G. Possum, devoted mother, skilled scavenger, and friend to us all. Now at this crucial time, David, if you could get that bucket of cold water and pour it on her face, just to be really sure."

If you're still not convinced that playing possum could ever be a useful adaptation, consider the results of a clever study of red flour beetles by Takahisa Miyatake and colleagues (2004). To see if tonic immobility could really ever turn away predators, Miyatake et al. painstakingly bred ten generations of red flour beetles in the laboratory. These pesky beetles are ideal for scientific study because they reproduce quickly and in large numbers. To see if playing possum could save a flour beetle's life, Miyatake et al. checked to see how well possum-playing versus non-possum-playing beetles would do when trapped in close confines with a hungry predator. The researchers began with a group of 200 healthy flour beetles (100 male and 100 female). They then put each individual beetle to the test to see exactly which ones responded to a threat by playing possum (by "feigning death" as they put it) and for exactly how long. From each group of 100 beetles, they chose the 10 of each sex that became immobile for the *longest* period during the artificial threat test and the 10 of each sex that became immobile for the *briefest* period. They then bred the 10 male and 10 female beetles that played possum the *longest* and the 10 male and 10 female beetles that played possum the *least*.

After this, they lovingly raised each group of pedigree beetle offspring to adulthood, always making sure to keep the two genetically distinct groups separate. They repeated this selective breeding process for 10 generations, always sampling 100 adults and always choosing the top and bottom 10% of possum players in each successive group. In the end, they had two very different groups of beetles. Almost all the beetles in the group bred to be good at playing possum responded to an artificial threat by playing possum, for about two full minutes. The beetles in the other group hardly responded at all to the artificial threat. Either they never played possum at all or they did so for just a few seconds and then got right back to the usual business of looking for human crops to pillage.

Finally, Miyatake et al. (2004) took each of these carefully bred 10th generation beetles and locked each one up, one at a time, in a clear plastic petri dish for 15 minutes – with an adult female Adanson's jumper spider. They used a different spider for each beetle, and each spider had always been starved for a full week. Almost all the beetles did what they had been bred to do. In the group bred to play possum, 12/14 did so. In the other group, only 1/14 did so. More importantly, as hungry as these spiders were, they rarely ate a beetle that had feigned death. In total, 13 of the 28 beetles feigned death. The hungry spiders spared all but one of them. The beetles who failed to play possum were not so lucky. Nine of these 15 beetles became a delicious meal for their hungry hosts.

Of course, it's hard to imagine that a single gene is responsible for all the variations in tonic immobility that exist across the animal kingdom. Instead, tonic immobility in these different species is a good example of **convergent evolution**. Convergent evolution happens when much the same physical or behavioral trait evolves independently in species that do not share any recent ancestors. It usually happens because the ancestors of the different species who came to resemble one another faced similar problems of survival and/or reproduction. Another example of convergent evolution is flight, which evolved separately in bats, birds, and mosquitos – presumably because it's a really great way to get around quickly. Thorns, quills, and spines are an even more obvious example of convergent evolution. As you can see in Figure 1.7, cacti, chestnuts, and porcupines all

Figure 1.7 *Convergent evolution in three very different species: a barrel cactus, a chestnut, and the Indian crested porcupine.*

evolved similar protective structures that make them undesirable to other animals who would otherwise love to consume them.

Whatever the exact genetic basis of tonic immobility is, species by species, it is clear that a quirky instinct that makes animals look dead when they are in dire trouble can sometimes be the key to staying alive. Like the genes that promote self-sacrifice in male redback spiders, genes that promote tonic immobility can, in the right species and the right environment, remain in the gene pool for a very long time. That's natural selection – even if it took highly unnatural genetic experiments on playing possum to uncover it.

FOR FURTHER READING

» Diamond, J. (1992). *The third chimpanzee: The evolution and future of the human animal.* New York: HarperCollins.

» Duchaine, B., Cosmides, L. & Tooby, J. (2001). Evolutionary psychology and the brain. *Current Opinion in Neurobiology*, 11(2), 225–30.

» Shubin, N. (2008). *Your inner fish: A journey into the 3.5-billion-year history of the human body.* New York: Pantheon Books.

» Tiger, L. & Fox, R. (1971). *The imperial animal.* New York: Holt, Rinehart & Winston.

SAMPLE MULTIPLE-CHOICE EXAM QUESTIONS

On the companion website you will find a multiple choice quiz for every chapter in this book. Each multiple choice quiz focuses on a single chapter and consists of 15–20 questions on key findings and concepts from that chapter. We encourage you to begin with four sample questions after you finish reading each chapter, and then move on to the full-blown on-line quiz for that chapter. You can find the chapter quizzes at: www.macmillanihe.com/evolutionary-psychology

1.01.   Which statement best summarizes the connection between natural selection and adaptation?

   a. natural selection is the general evolutionary process that leads to specific adaptations

   b. homology drives adaptations, which lead to natural selection

   c. natural selection happens over millions of years whereas adaptations usually happen very quickly

1.02.   In which pair of animals below are you most likely to observe many examples of homology?

   a. tigers and sharks because they are both predators

   b. birds and dinosaurs because birds evolved from dinosaurs

   c. zebras and horses because they share many genes

1.03.   The fact that people share about half their genes with many plants strongly suggests that evolution is:

a. orderly

b. conservative

c. capricious

1.04.   Why are the mating behaviors of Australia's redback spiders interesting to evolutionary psychologists?

a. because these spiders mate for life, and we once thought only a handful of mammals and birds did this

b. because they illustrate behavioral homology with spiders all across the globe

c. because at first blush the behavior of the male spiders seems to violate the basic rules of evolution

Answer Key: a, c, b, c.

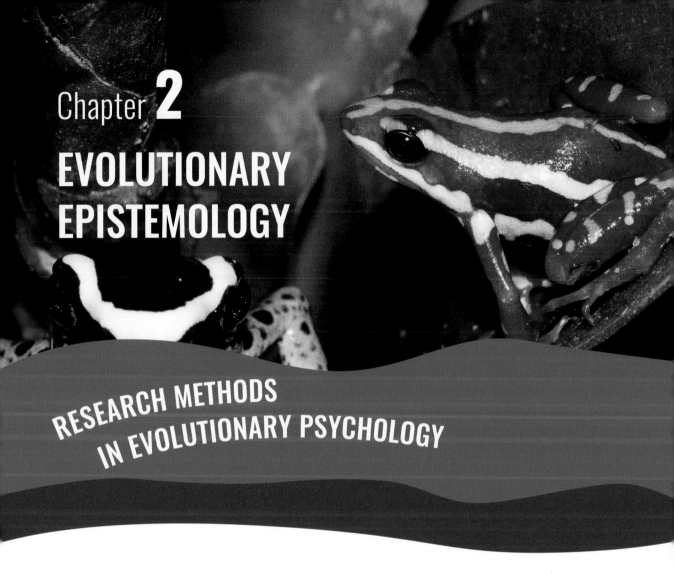

Chapter 2
EVOLUTIONARY EPISTEMOLOGY

RESEARCH METHODS IN EVOLUTIONARY PSYCHOLOGY

"Failure to understand which of two variables depends on the other is the source of endless shenanigans."

— *Bernard (2006, p. 34)*

"You can observe a lot just by watching."

— *Yogi Berra (source unknown)*

"So the other disciples told him, 'We have seen the Lord!' But he said to them, 'Unless I see the nail marks in his hands and put my finger where the nails were, and put my hand into his side, I will not believe.'"

— *John 20: 25, NIV (regarding doubting Thomas, the empiricist)*

About 2,600 years ago, the Greek philosopher **Thales** became very annoyed with some of his materialistic critics. Thales was one of the first people in recorded history to address questions about the basic nature of the world without relying on magical explanations. Although Thales cared little for money,

21

he apparently cared a great deal about being viewed as intelligent. So Thales got pretty annoyed when his jealous critics asked him (translated loosely from the Greek): "If you're so smart, why ain't you rich?" Thales decided to accept his critics' questionable definition of intelligence and prove to them that being smart can make you rich – if that's what you care about. Because Thales had been making careful meteorological observations for years, he had an excellent understanding of weather. According to Asimov (1964), Thales capitalized on his knowledge of the weather by cornering the market on olive presses (the machines that press oil from olives) in a year in which he predicted it would be perfect weather for olive trees. During that year's bountiful olive harvest, Thales charged bountiful rates for the use of his presses. He thus became an instant olive oil baron. Having met his critics' questionable definition of intelligence, he went back to inventing a little something we call "science." Why do some people consider Thales the first true scientist?

The broad answer is that Thales addressed important questions in a way that few people had previously considered. A more specific answer is that Thales seems to have been a firm believer in all four of the modern canons of science. In this chapter on research methods in evolutionary psychology, I'll begin by discussing those four scientific canons. I'll then address the important methodological question of how to know whether one thing causes something else. Next, I'll provide a selective review of some of the basic research methods used by evolutionary psychologists, with an eye toward how they are grounded in the four canons of science or how they help us establish causality – and thus help us test evolutionary theories. Along the way, I'll briefly discuss bits and pieces of the history of evolutionary psychology – to clarify that it's an interdisciplinary field that necessarily relies on a wide variety of research methods. Finally, I'll discuss a useful heuristic – the OOPS! heuristic – for critically analyzing the external validity of research in evolutionary psychology. My broader points in this chapter apply not only to all psychology but also to all science. My more specific points (e.g., how scientists analyze genetic information, how they date fossilized remains) apply more heavily to the evolutionary aspects of evolutionary psychology. Putting it all together, I hope you'll see that evolutionary psychologists make use of an incredibly diverse array of careful research techniques to decide how we got to be the way we are. For those who wish to delve more deeply into the question of how science works (e.g. the four canons of science), I shamelessly recommend Pelham and Blanton (2018), from which I've adapted a few portions of this chapter.

THE FOUR CANONS OF SCIENCE

To gain a fuller appreciation of what it means to study human behavior scientifically, it's useful to consider exactly how all scientists go about their business. This is because the specific methodological rules and techniques that are staples of the trade to evolutionary psychologists can be derived from the broad principles that most all scientists take for granted. Fundamental principles that are accepted largely on faith are often referred to as **canons**. At least four such fundamental principles appear to be accepted by almost all scientists.

Determinism

One hallmark of scientific thinking is the assumption of **determinism**. This is the doctrine that the universe is orderly – that all events have meaningful, systematic causes. Our old friend Thales parted ways with many of the Greek philosophers who preceded him by assuming that everything has a physical – rather than a mystical – cause. Everyone seems to endorse the principle of determinism up to a point. For example, most astrologers seem to believe that something about the motions and positions of celestial bodies causes people to behave in predictable ways. They can't (or won't) tell us exactly what it is about Neptune's rising or Venus's falling that caused Serena to have bad luck last Wednesday, but it is presumably something. Otherwise, why not assign people to astrological signs at random? Whereas there may be some deterministic slippage in astrology, there's no room for such slippage in science. Many psychologists have even argued that people are predisposed to think in causal terms. Even if we are not predisposed to do so, plenty of evidence suggests that we are wont to do so.

As an example, research in social psychology suggests that people are constantly trying to identify the causes of other people's behavior. Consider the following sentences: "Nicole helped the little old lady across the street." "Nicole served the homeless at the soup kitchen." When Winter and Uleman (1984) asked people to read (and then later remember) sentences such as these, they found that the best retrieval cues they could give people to jog their memories for the sentences were *trait* words. In the case of the sentences you just saw, the most useful trait words would be words like "kind" or "helpful." This research suggests that it's impossible to observe another person do a nice thing without jumping to the conclusion that a personality trait caused that nice behavior. Your search for causes might continue after your initial impressions. Suppose you learned, after observing Nicole, that her kind actions were part of her court-ordered community service – and that the people she had swindled were homeless seniors, with cancer. To know if you can trust Nicole, you don't just need to know what she did, you need to know why she did it.

In fact, Fritz Heider (1958), the father of modern attribution theory, referred to laypeople, like your great aunt Shirley, as **naive scientists**. By this he meant that laypeople search pretty systematically for the causes of human behavior. Behaviorist B.F. Skinner (1948) documented an extreme sensitivity to causality in pigeons, when he showed that they often behave as if they have identified causes – even when they really haven't. Like people, pigeons can be "superstitious." It's thus easy to trick pigeons into behaving as if they can cause something that they can't really control. In other words, animals, people included, seem to be constantly on the lookout for causes. They want to know what to do, for example, to get food pellets from a Skinner box, sodas from a vending machine, or votes from a bunch of constituents. It wouldn't be very fruitful to pay attention to if-then contingencies in a world lacking in systematic causes. As you will see in Chapter 7, research in evolutionary psychology suggests that we're hardwired to be especially good at figuring out and testing certain kinds of causal hypotheses. As Nicole would be quick to remind you, we often need to do so – to be sure we aren't being cheated.

The principle of determinism has a close scientific corollary. This is the idea that science is all about theories. A **theory** is a statement about the causal relation between two or more variables. It is typically stated in abstract terms, and it usually has some empirical support. Theories wouldn't be very useful in the absence of determinism, of course, because in the absence of determinism, orderly, systematic causes wouldn't exist. In this regard, scientists are much like laypeople; they make important assumptions. A scientist accepts the canon of determinism largely on faith, in much the same way that a rabbi accepts the Torah largely on faith. To be anti-Torah in any serious way would surely mean being something other than a rabbi. Similarly, to be devoutly anti-deterministic would surely mean being something other than a scientist.

One of the big challenges Charles Darwin faced in convincing his fellow scientists of the validity of his radical new theory was that when Darwin published his theory in 1859, there was no solid, widely accepted scientific theory of inheritance. Ironically enough, in 1859, an Austrian monk named Gregor Mendel had already been working for three years on just such a theory – the theory of modern genetic inheritance. In Chapter 3, you will get a close look at Mendel's work, as well as a close look at some modern work on genetics. For now, though, I'd simply like to argue that the modern theory of evolution didn't really take off in biology until scientists could put their fingers on a precise, testable *causal* mechanism for processes such as natural selection. Incidentally, the important point in scientific history when Darwin's theory of evolution was integrated with a modern understanding of genetics is known as the **modern synthesis** (e.g., see Dawkins, 1976; Hamilton, 1964a, 1964b). If scientists had not discovered a plausible causal (genetic) mechanism that could account for natural selection, the theory of evolution would never have become the most important organizing principle in all biology. So, evolutionary psychology, like biology and particle physics, is deeply deterministic. But it takes more than a belief in determinism to be a scientist. To be a card-carrying scientist, you need to believe in at least three other things.

Empiricism

Scientists not only assume that the universe obeys orderly principles; they also assume that there are good and bad ways of figuring out these orderly principles. The best method, according to scientists, is to follow the canon of **empiricism**, that is, to make observations. Like astrophysicists and psychophysicists, evolutionary psychologists assume that the best way to find out how the world works is to collect data about it. It may seem patently obvious to you that making observations is a great way to find things out, but this is a relatively modern assumption, even among philosophers and scientists.

As brilliant as they can be, philosophers have not always appreciated the canon of empiricism. The phrase "I got it straight from the horse's mouth" illustrates this point. The phrase apparently originated when a group of philosophers were debating the number of teeth a horse should have (Rensberger, 1986). I don't know exactly how many teeth a horse should have, and apparently the philosophers didn't either – because they spent a long time debating the question. At one point, an exasperated philosopher put a quick end to the debate. He suggested that if they really wanted to know how many teeth a horse has, they should just go out, find a horse, and count its teeth. Empiricism has some big advantages over other reasonable ways of knowing.

What horses think about while philosophers count teeth.

As long as we are discussing popular phrases involving horses, let me remind you that the phrase "Don't look a gift horse in the mouth" also reflects an appreciation of empiricism. In the days before solid paperwork, clever horse buyers would carefully examine a horse's teeth for physical signs of aging – to be sure the horses were as young as the sellers insisted. It's pretty rude, then, to treat a gift horse as if it were a potential purchase. Sophisticated indirect measures much like this one are staples of research in archaeology and paleontology. For example, microbiological analyses of both the teeth and the dried-up poo of **Neanderthals** have told us a great deal about their diets. Researchers used to think Neanderthals were extremely carnivorous. But microbiological analyses of Neanderthal poo, while confirming that the Neanderthal diet surely included a lot of meat, also revealed that Neanderthals were not averse to eating plants (Sistiaga et al., 2014). Analyzing ancient poo may not be very appetizing, but it can tell us a lot about ancient appetites.

Throughout scientific history, there have been plenty of empiricists. One of the things that distinguished Aristotle from many of his contemporaries was his emphasis on systematic observation. Recall that Thales, too, was a big fan of empiricism. He made his profitable meteorological predictions based on some careful observations. Similarly, Galileo's biggest claim to fame is a legendary experiment in which he simultaneously dropped a heavy and a light cannonball from the Leaning Tower of Pisa. As the famous story goes, the two balls obligingly fell at precisely the same rate, invalidating the Aristotelian theory that heavier objects always fall faster than lighter ones. This is a great example of Galileo's deep faith in empiricism. However, this example has a bit of a problem. Galileo seems to have never performed this celebrated experiment (see Asimov, 1964; Glenn, 1996; Rensberger, 1986). Instead, he challenged his detractors to do so. They apparently declined the invitation.

Evolutionary scientists also place a great deal of stock in observation. In fact, the most common way in which they try to resolve debates is by making systematic observations. The key to the canon of determinism, however, is the word *systematic*. Systematic observations are different from casual observations. Everyone knows that "the proof of the pudding is in the eating," but not everyone knows how to find out whether men are inherently more sexually promiscuous than women, or whether people are more likely to help others with whom they share genes. Many of the specific research techniques I'll review in this chapter are useful precisely to the degree that they foster systematic, unbiased observation. Psychological scientists know that if you really want to know if one pudding is truly more delicious than another, you'll need to make sure that the folks who taste the two puddings don't know who prepared them. Believing that a master chef created a pudding, or merely serving the pudding in a very fancy dish, can have a huge impact on how delicious people think it is. The proof of the pudding *is* in the eating, but to answer a question as simple as whether a pudding is delicious, we need to be extremely careful about the way the eating happens.

Parsimony

A third basic assumption of science is a sort of scientific tiebreaker. Virtually all scientists agree that if we're faced with two competing theories that do an equally good job of handling the results of a study, we should prefer the simpler of the two. This is the canon of **parsimony**. As the word "parsimony" is commonly used by nonscientists, it refers to extreme stinginess or frugality. This is good to remember because this canon says we should be extremely frugal in developing (and choosing between) theories. Mechanics and engineers surely appreciate parsimony because it's implicit in the idea that it's preferable to make machines that have few moving parts (because this leaves fewer parts to break down). Thales, too, valued parsimony, in the sense that he preferred simple explanations based on a few basic physical laws rather than fanciful explanations involving social interactions between hundreds of deities.

One of the first people to make a potent argument for parsimony was the medieval English philosopher William of Occam. For this reason, parsimony is sometimes referred to as "Occam's razor." The essence of Occam's advice was to avoid making any unnecessary assumptions (Duffy, 1993). In the late 1800s, another famous Englishman, animal psychologist C. Lloyd Morgan, made a similar point. "Lloyd Morgan's canon" stated that we should avoid making too many assumptions when we try to understand the behavior of animals. Morgan is best known for the version of this point that he emphasized in his debates with animal psychologist George Romanes. Morgan was frustrated with Romanes' elaborate anthropomorphic explanations for animal behavior. For example, Romanes (1882) frequently assumed that animals possess complex ideas, engage in reasoning by analogy, and make use of the "logic of feelings."

Morgan's advice was that whenever one can explain animal behavior in terms of simple mental activities such as conditioned associations, it's inappropriate to explain these behaviors in terms of higher mental functioning.

At the risk of undermining arguments for parsimony, I'd like to note that it certainly is not always parsimonious to explain human and animal behavior using different theories. In the case of explaining how a housecat opens a door, for example, it's surely not reasonable to assume that a cat's thoughts and feelings about doors are as complex as an engineer's. But what if you were trying to explain why chimpanzees do some of the sophisticated things they do? For example, like people, chimpanzees make and use tools, and they appear to engage in strategic deception and cooperation. Consider an example. Frans de Waal (1996) observed an amorous but low-ranking male chimpanzee who conspicuously displayed his erect penis to a desirable female. However, when the alpha male in this troop wandered by, the low-ranking chimp quickly and strategically placed his hand over his penis – and casually looked away. Is it more parsimonious to explain this behavioral sequence using the principles of operant conditioning or to describe it using words such as fear and deception? Considering how genetically similar we are to chimps, de Waal (1996) suggested that it's often more parsimonious to explain similar behaviors in people and chimps using a single theory rather than using two completely different theories. This example illustrates that whereas there is clear consensus concerning the basic canons of science, there's a bit less consensus regarding exactly how and when to apply them.

Testability

The final canon of science is the assumption that scientific theories should be testable (disconfirmable) using currently available research techniques. The canon of **testability** is closely related to the canon of empiricism because the techniques that scientists typically use to test their theories are empirical techniques. It's hard to be a firm believer in empiricism without also being a firm believer in testability. After all, empirical tests of an idea very often reveal that the idea is not as correct as its proponents had originally assumed. This means that testability is closely associated with falsifiability. The idea behind **falsifiability** is that scientists should put their theories to the test by actively seeking out tests that could prove their theories wrong. During the period of tremendous scientific advancement that occurred in the early to middle part of the 20th century, Karl Popper became famous for espousing this idea.

In his book *Unended quest*, Popper ([1974] 1990) described his adoption of a philosophical and scientific school of thought known as **logical positivism**. Logical positivists believe that science and philosophy should be based solely on things that can be observed with absolute certainty. Many of them also believe that the way to go about testing scientific theories and hypotheses is to try to disprove them. Popper ([1974] 1990, pp. 38–9) described a crucial step in his conversion to this critical school of thought by explaining his delight at the way Einstein wrote about his general theory of relativity:

> But what impressed me most was Einstein's own clear statement that he would regard his theory as untenable if it should fail in certain tests. Thus he wrote,

for example: "If the red-shift of spectral lines due to the gravitational potential should not exist, then the general theory of relativity will be untenable." ... This, I felt, was the true scientific attitude.

Perhaps the most important thing scientists can do to make their theories testable (falsifiable) is to develop **operational definitions**. Operational definitions are definitions of theoretical constructs that are stated in terms of concrete, observable procedures. We need operational definitions in all branches of psychology because much of what we wish to understand (e.g., hunger, fear, sexual arousal) is experienced privately by the person and thus is not directly observable. Operational definitions solve this tricky problem by connecting otherwise subjective experiences to things that are directly observable. Operational definitions can sometimes solve problems such as self-deception or dishonesty. For example, an evolutionary psychologist interested in sex differences in sexual arousal might be worried that social norms regarding gender would bias people's self-reports of their sexual arousal in response to erotic stimuli. Perhaps the average man would exaggerate his reports of sexual arousal. One possible way around this problem – when studying men, at least – is to use a **penile plethysmograph**. Plethysmographs come in several forms. One is like a flexible C-shaped bracelet that fits around the base of the penis. It measures increases in the diameter of the base of the penis as the penis becomes filled with blood. Another type of plethysmograph is more like a clear glass bottle, which fits snugly on the base of the penis and is airtight. As the penis grows, it forces air out of the top of the device (see Figure 2.1). By carefully measuring exactly how much air is forced out of the tube, the device records exactly how much a penis grows. By whatever physical mechanism it uses, then, a plethysmograph assesses a man's degree of sexual arousal by assessing whether and to what degree his penis grew.

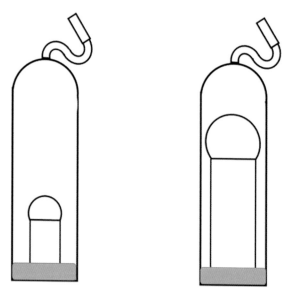

Figure 2.1 *A simplified image of a volumetric penile plethysmograph. The gray ring at the bottom forms an airtight space between the glass dome and the base of the penis. The image on the right indicates increased sexual arousal.*

Needless to say, the use of a penile plethysmograph raises ethical and practical questions. For many men, wearing a plethysmograph would surely be both embarrassing and intrusive. Having acknowledged this potential problem, though, imagine that a study using a plethysmograph showed that physical increases in the size of men's penises were highly correlated with the men's self-reported levels of increased sexual arousal while viewing sexually explicit images. This would suggest that, even if the measurement process is pretty awkward, changes in penis size do serve as a useful indicator of men's sexual arousal.

Research using this technology has led to some interesting insights. For example, a study by Henry Adams and colleagues (1996) assessed the association between **homophobia** and sexual arousal. Adams et al. assessed homophobia using self-reports (e.g., "I would feel nervous being in a group of homosexuals"). But, rather than relying on people's self-reported sexual responses to observing gay sex, they assessed sexual arousal physically – using a plethysmograph. They found that, relative to less homophobic men, more homophobic men showed bigger increases in sexual arousal (bigger increases in penis diameter) when viewing an erotic film depicting two men having sex. It was not merely the case, by the way, that the homophobic men had stronger than usual sex drives. Their physiological responses to an erotic film clip involving heterosexual sex were substantial but ever so slightly weaker than those of the less homophobic men. I hasten to add that this interesting result is open to more than one interpretation. Freud might call this **reaction formation** – developing a conscious attitude that is the opposite of your own feared unconscious desires. Shakespeare might add "homophobic man thou doth protest too much!" But Dan Wegner (1994) might argue that the homophobic men got aroused when viewing other men having sex precisely because they knew their level of arousal was being measured in response to homoerotic stimuli – and thus did exactly what they were highly motivated not to do.

Of course, a huge drawback of penile plethysmography is that it only provides a good operational definition of sexual arousal in men. In the past decade or so, however, researchers have solved this problem by developing a measure that relies on heat (based on blood flow) rather than volume. This is called **thermography** or thermographic stress analysis (TSA), and it involves high-tech temperature assessment. A thermography camera can detect changes of about 1/14 of a degree Celsius in a very brief period. Thermography also has the advantage of being much less intrusive than plethysmography. People do have to be undressed from the waist down to have their genital temperature recorded using TSA, but there's no skin contact with any mechanical equipment. More important, thermography allows researchers to assess sexual arousal in women as well as in men. And it seems to work. In a sample of college students and an older and more ethnically diverse community sample, Tuuli Kukkonen and colleagues (2007, 2010) found that increases in genital temperature when people were watching erotic videos correlated well with people's subjective reports of how sexually aroused they became while watching the videos – for women as well as for men. So Kukkonen et al. could presumably confirm objectively what Mick Jagger sang about many years ago: "I'm so hot for her; she's so cold."

To summarize this section, everyone – scientists included – makes assumptions. Unlike most laypeople, however, scientists are quite willing to articulate and debate their assumptions. In this section, I hope you've also seen that because scientists adhere to basic canons such as testability, they must always be willing to abandon their old beliefs in favor of beliefs that are more consistent with careful scientific observations. As B.F. Skinner (1979, p. 346) advised, scientists must "change and be ready to change again." Skinner also had some concise advice for how to figure out and refine what is true. It was this: "Accept no eternal verity. Experiment."

THE THREE REQUIREMENTS FOR ESTABLISHING CAUSALITY

So, evolutionary psychologists, like astronomers or chemists, take a few important things for granted. But evolutionary psychologists do not adhere to the axioms of science just for the fun of it. They do so with the specific goal of uncovering the causes of human behavior. Scientific research is almost always conducted with the goal of understanding causes. Recall that theories are formal ideas about what causes what. I suppose one could argue that the canon of determinism trumps all the other scientific canons because most scientists are obsessed with causes. After all, if you know *why* something is true, rather than just knowing *that* it is true, you are in a much better position to predict and control whatever you're studying. John Stuart Mill would have strongly agreed with this idea. Mill cared so much about understanding causality that he laid out a precise logical system for how to do so.

Covariation

Most researchers who wish to understand causality rely heavily on the framework proposed by philosopher John Stuart Mill. If I may simplify Mill a bit, he proposed five methods (that can be distilled down to three requirements) for establishing that one thing causes another (see Copi, 1978, for a detailed treatment of the five original methods). The first of Mill's requirements, **covariation** (short for concomitant variation), is probably the easiest. For one variable to cause another, Mill argued, changes in one variable must correspond with changes in the other. As an example, many people strongly believe that the "male" hormone testosterone causes aggression. However, a problem with this argument is that there is surprisingly little evidence that increasing a person's testosterone levels increases that person's tendency to behave aggressively. If testosterone levels aren't really *correlated* with aggression, it's pretty hard to argue that testosterone levels cause aggression. On the other hand, research suggests that even though testosterone may not automatically foster aggression, high levels of testosterone are associated with a desire for competition and social status. That argument seems much safer (Boksem et al., 2013).

Across animal species there is also a sizable correlation between total body mass and skeletal robustness (bone thickness). Elephants have much thicker bones – even relative to their total body size – than cats or mice. And the largest land-dwelling dinosaurs had bones proportionally thicker than those of elephants.

This is a requirement of physics. The total weight of any animal increases as a cubed function of its linear size, because the mass of the animal increases as its height and width and depth increase. Consider a normal and a gigantic man with identical proportions. If the 6' tall man weighed 200 lbs., his 9' tall proportional equivalent would weigh 675 lbs. This is because the giant would be 50% taller and 50% wider and 50% deeper (200 x 1.5 x 1.5 x 1.5 = 675). If elephants didn't have extra stocky bones, their skinny bones would snap under their own weight. Notice that a predictable exception to the rule is the elephant's wispy tail (see Figure 2.2).

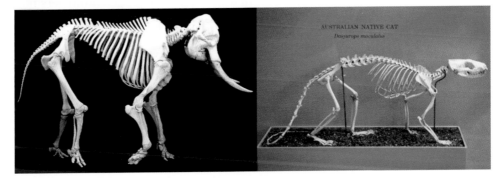

Figure 2.2 *An elephant skeleton and a cat skeleton. The cat's weight-bearing bones are proportionally much thinner than those of the elephant.*

All of this is about covariation. But covariation by itself is not enough to establish causality. Does having thick bones make an animal bigger or does being bigger require an animal to have thick bones? The second option seems more likely. Genes that programmed land mammals to get really big without having thicker bones would surely have fallen by the wayside.

Temporal sequence

This leads us to Mill's second requirement, **temporal sequence**. To argue that changes in one variable cause changes in a second, the changes in the first variable must *precede* the changes in the second. This is not always easy to know. For instance, researchers – evolutionary and otherwise – often measure a wide range of variables at the same time to see if different variables covary with one another in ways predicted by a particular theory. With this kind of cross-sectional research design, it's often impossible to establish temporal sequence, and thus it's often impossible to know what caused what. In light of this problem, researchers sometimes measure variables over time (in **prospective studies** or longitudinal studies) to see if changes in one variable do, in fact, precede changes in a second. At other times, scientists can rely on the scientific dating of ancient artifacts or the remains of ancient life forms.

A detour: radiometric dating

It's because of concerns over temporal sequence that evolutionary biologists often care a great deal about time and dates. To argue that two living animals share a common ancestor, you'd ideally want to know exactly when all the animals in question first evolved. When animals die and are fossilized, no one places a little tag on them to tell us when they lived. So how do we know? One elegant answer to this question is **radiometric dating**. The idea behind such dating is that every living animal on earth is a ticking clock. Consider radiometric dating based on carbon (otherwise known as **carbon-14 dating**). You may recall from a basic chemistry class that all known life forms contain carbon. An organic chemistry course, then, is a course in carbon chemistry. But carbon atoms come in more than one variety. Most carbon atoms are ^{12}C atoms, which means that they have the six protons and six neutrons that give normal carbon its atomic weight of 12 ($12 = 6 + 6$). But every once in a while, a ^{14}N nitrogen atom gets bombarded by cosmic radiation and is turned into a carbon **isotope** – an unstable variation on the usual form of carbon.

Carbon isotopes behave just like regular carbon atoms (by making their way into the bodies of animals when they eat food, for example). But carbon isotopes are predictably unstable. Eventually, every ^{14}C carbon atom loses its two extra neutrons and becomes a normal ^{12}C atom. The half-life of ^{14}C is 5,730 years. This means that, on average, any dead batch of carbon atoms will lose half of its ^{14}C isotopes in 5,730 ($\pm$ 40) years – because animals stop taking in carbon of any kind when they die. So, a freshly dead animal will have the normal tiny ratio of ^{14}C to ^{12}C carbon atoms. An animal that died 5,730 years ago will have half of that tiny ratio. An animal that died 11,460 (5,730 x 2) years ago should thus be down to ¼ of its ^{14}C atoms. By carefully assessing the exact ratio of ^{14}C to ^{12}C atoms in a sample of an animal's remains, scientists can estimate when the animal died with a surprising degree of accuracy. The same thing holds, of course, for an ancient wooden axe handle. All wood contains carbon.

Everything has its limits, and there are some limits to carbon-14 dating. For animals that died more than 60,000 years ago, the amount of remaining ^{14}C is so small that accurate carbon-14 dating is a problem. Carbon-14 dating is also based on the assumption that the proportion of ^{14}C in the earth's atmosphere has been constant over the past 50–60 millennia. It has not. However, this variation has proven to be the difference between thinking something is 10,000 years old when it might really be 11,000 years old. Further, a research team led by C. Bronk Ramsey (2012) found a way to correct this ^{14}C variation bias – by determining just how much ^{14}C has been in the atmosphere every year for the past 52,000 years.

Luckily, there are also isotopes of other atoms that allow scientists to estimate the ages of much older specimens. To be sure, things get trickier as samples get older. For example, because fossils no longer contain the carbon-based bodies of the animals whose features they immortalized, and because some kinds of rocks do not lend themselves well to radiometric dating, scientists may have to date the igneous (easy to date) rocks that exist just above and just below any fossil whose age is in question. This is why age estimates for fossilized dinosaur bones are less precise, for example, than age estimates for ancient human artifacts. Because many things can be dated in more than one way, scientists can sometimes come up with accurate dating for very old things by using multiple methods.

Finally, it is worth noting that one way of determining ancient ages is reliable. Well before the discovery of radiometric dating, scientists were – and still are

– able to perform a reliable form of relative dating. Because the earth's surface is constantly filling up with sediment, deeper layers of the earth are almost always older layers of the earth (with cataclysmic events such as earthquakes sometimes throwing a wrench into the picture). After millions of hours of painstaking paleontological excavation worldwide, no one has ever discovered any human, ostrich, or dolphin fossils in any layer as deep as – or deeper than – that of the most recently living dinosaurs. Instead, millions of hours of expert excavations have confirmed that deeper and deeper digging gets you to older and older fossil records – and that life on earth began very, very simply and then got progressively more complex. Here's how Neil Shubin (2008, p. 8) put it:

> Hundreds of years of fossil collection have produced a vast library, or catalogue, of the ages of the earth and the life on it. We can now identify general time periods when major changes occurred. Interested in the origin of mammals? Go to rocks from the period called the Early Mesozoic; geochemistry tells us that these rocks are likely about 210 million years old. Interested in the origin of primates? Go higher in the rock column, to the Cretaceous period, where rocks are about 80 million years old.

> The order of fossils in the world's rocks is powerful evidence of our connections to the rest of life. If digging in 600-million-year-old rocks, we found the earliest jellyfish lying next to the skeleton of a woodchuck, then we would have to rewrite our texts. That woodchuck would have appeared earlier in the fossil record than the first mammal, reptile, or even fish – before even the first worm.

For those who do not mind getting their hands dirty, the earth itself is one big, well-layered time machine.

Back to temporal sequence. Of course, when most psychologists worry about temporal order, they are worried about minutes, hours or perhaps years rather than millions of years. So documenting temporal sequence does not always require digging. For example, if a researcher finds that, on average, men take greater physical risks than women, we do not have to worry that taking risks (or failing to do so) caused people to become male or female. Sometimes, temporal sequence is obvious.

Eliminating confounds

Even when covariation and temporal sequence are both obvious, though, researchers can't be sure they've established causality until they also address John Stuart Mill's third requirement for knowing when one variable causes another. This third requirement is **eliminating confounds**. By this, Mill meant that we must systematically rule out all the competing causes of an outcome that happen to be correlated with the cause we think we have identified. Did those risk-taking men take risks because of evolved sex differences or because of socialization? **Confounds** can be tough to resolve. To illustrate confounds, let's look at one that's pretty easy to debunk. Consider the finding that as the national levels of ice cream sales increase, national homicide rates also increase. Do ice cream sales cause murders? Should we outlaw the production and distribution of ice cream as a way of lowering homicide rates? Probably not. In this case, it seems extremely likely that both ice cream sales and homicide rates are influenced by a third variable, namely seasonal temperature variation. When it's hot out, people buy more ice cream. In addition, when it's hot out, people become more easily frustrated. Frustration is known to be a strong predictor of violence, including murder. By the way, the problem of confounds is also known as the **third-variable problem**. In this case, the third variable – besides ice cream sales and murder rates – is heat. Heat causes changes in both ice cream sales and murder rates, and so the two variables covary with one another – and give the false appearance of a causal relation.

So far, so good. We figured out, and logically eliminated, the confound in which ice cream sales masqueraded as heat. Now we know that frustration, specifically the frustration of being overheated, is the true cause of homicide. Or do we? Unfortunately, it's possible that frustration, heat, and ice cream sales are all confounded with something else that is the true cause of homicide. Worse yet, this true cause may be a lot less interesting than frustration. Perhaps people simply drink more alcohol, socialize more, or get out of doors more when it is hot out. All these variables are likely to be confounded with temperature. Furthermore, any or all of these variables could conceivably contribute to homicides. If homicides are more likely to occur when people are drinking, socializing, or just hanging, this is a triple threat to our explanation based on frustration.

There's a very good way to eliminate all possible confounds. The solution is to create two identical groups of research participants, manipulate the causal variable you care about (by treating the two groups differently in one and only one way), and then check to see if the two groups behave differently. To do this is to conduct a **true experiment**. To put it more methodologically, a true experiment is a design in which the researcher randomly assigns participants to two or more conditions, enacts a manipulation, and then assesses whether the different experimental groups behave differently. As you may recall, the variable that is manipulated in an experiment is known as the **independent variable**, and the variable that is measured (under the assumption that it is caused by the independent variable) is known as the **dependent variable**. If you believe frustration causes aggression, frustration is your independent variable, and aggression is your dependent variable. The key to eliminating all possible confounds in a true experiment is **random assignment**. It's hard to overstate the importance of random assignment if you want to eliminate confounds.

In the modern research era, the person who did the most to popularize experimentation (and thus random assignment) was one of the earliest evolutionary social scientists. His name was R.A. Fisher and he wrote two landmark books that dramatically shaped the way all social scientists think about research (Fisher, 1925, 1935). Fisher was a scientific genius who spent much of his time obsessing about issues such as buttercups and horse manure. As a scientist deeply interested in agriculture, Fisher wanted to answer practical questions such as what kind of manure would maximize crop yields. Fortunately for psychologists, plants are a lot like people. Every plant is different, and this makes it difficult to know with any certainty whether a given plant grew large because it was fertilized, because it was otherwise well tended, or because it was blessed with good genes. This meant that if Fisher wanted to study the influence of fertilizer on plant growth, he had to figure out how to create two identical groups of plants.

He did so by popularizing the use of random assignment. Using random assignment means placing people in different conditions in an experiment on a totally arbitrary basis. It means that every participant has exactly the same chance as every other participant of being assigned to any given condition of the experiment. Common ways of carrying out random assignment include assigning people to conditions by flipping a fair coin or using a random number generator. If you do this for a large enough group of people, you are virtually guaranteed to end up with two nearly identical groups. The most impressive thing about random assignment is that it equalizes two or more groups on practically every dimension imaginable. This is the magic methodological bullet John Stuart Mill didn't know about. So, if you create two groups of people – or spiders, or warthogs – by using random assignment, you can rest assured that the two groups are identical in age, gender, and body mass. And if you happen to be studying people, you can rest assured that the two groups are identical on important psychological variables such as history of aggressive behavior or ice cream consumption.

Notice that I said that randomization equalizes *groups*. This was Fisher's great insight. He realized that he could not make two specific seeds grow at exactly the same rate, but he could use random assignment to create two large groups of seeds that should grow at the same average rate. This same principle applies in psychological research. Two groups of people can be virtually identical as groups, even though each group is made up of completely different people. I hasten to add that if you are studying people rather than plants or seeds, another great way to create two identical groups of people is to make each person their own control. **Within-subjects designs** expose the same group of people to two or more experimental conditions – to see if people behave differently in the two conditions. If they do (and if you control for important things such as the order in which people experienced the two experimental conditions), you will have fulfilled all three of John Stuart Mill's conditions for establishing causality. But can researchers ever study evolution using experiments?

Consider a clever lab experiment by Joshua New and Tamsin German (2015). These researchers were interested in seeing whether people really are predisposed to detect spiders. After reviewing evidence that venomous spiders used to be a serious threat to human life and limb, New and German argued that if we're evolutionarily predisposed to stay away from spiders, spiders should be "detected, localized, and identified" more readily than other things, including other scary things that have not been around for very long in human evolutionary history. To test their hypothesis, they gave people the task of staring at the center of a circle on a computer screen. People were told that a cross-hair (+) pattern would very briefly appear in the middle of the circle on each of eight trails. Participants had to press a button as quickly as possible to indicate that (a) the horizontal line was longer, (b) the vertical line was longer, or (c) the two lines were equal in length. This judgment task was more difficult than it might seem because a mask (a stimulus that competes with what came before it for short-term visual storage) replaced the crucial cross-hair image after just 200 ms (see the right-hand column in Figure 2.3).

After making this judgment for three quick trials, participants repeated the task for a fourth trial. On this crucial trial, though, they were exposed not just to the circle and cross-hairs but also to an unexpected stimulus – whose location in one of the four quadrants of the circle was determined at random. For some randomly chosen participants, the unexpected peripheral stimulus was a spider (middle row of Figure 2.3). For others, the unexpected stimulus was a harmless housefly (not shown). For still others, the unexpected stimulus was a scary but evolutionarily irrelevant hypodermic needle (bottom row). Pretest participants had reported that the hypodermic needle was just as scary as the spider. But this is a fear that's learned rather than hardwired. (Ancient hominids didn't have controversial things like healthcare and so they never got their inoculations.) As soon as participants made the line length judgments for the fourth trial, the experimenter interrupted them and asked them (a) whether they had seen anything at all other than the expected cross-hairs, (b) in which of the four quadrants any unexpected stimulus had occurred and (c) what that unexpected stimulus might have been. Participants had to choose from eight different stimuli, only one of which was correct.

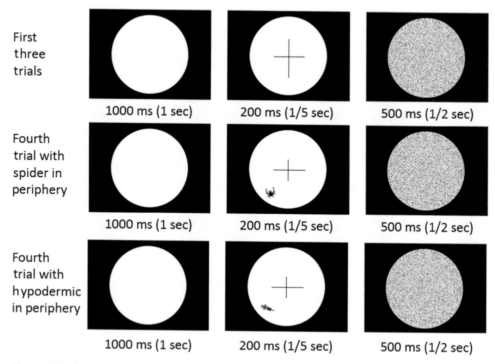

Figure 2.3 My approximation of New and German's (2015) experimental stimuli. Note that the original unexpected stimuli were better drawn than my versions. Sometimes the unexpected stimuli were also presented closer to the center of the cross-hairs, but this distance variable was held constant across types of stimuli.

Averaging across two variations on this experiment, more than half (53%) of those who'd been exposed to the unexpected spider were able to detect it, locate it, and identify it. In contrast, only 11% of those exposed to an unexpected hypodermic needle were able to pass all three of the same visual tests. Results for the natural but harmless housefly were much like those for the unnatural but scary hypodermic needle. Only 10% of participants were able to detect, locate, and identify it. Notice that we do not have to worry, for example, that 53% of the participants were able to pass all three visual tests for the spider because they were much more attentive or thoughtful than the other participants. Variables such as attentiveness (a potential confound) should have been identical in all the randomly assigned experimental groups. Further, imagine that people happen to see things better than usual when they appear in the upper-right-hand quadrant of their visual field. That's not a problem either because the experimenters randomly varied the location of all the stimuli. Spiders, houseflies, and hypodermic needles all appeared equally often in all four quadrants. Experiments allow researchers a great deal of control over possible confounds. In fact, they're the only research design that controls completely for every conceivable confound involving individual differences.

Of course, it's not always easy to conduct true experiments in research on evolutionary psychology. But when a researcher properly conducts a true experiment, you can rest assured that the manipulated independent variable is the real reason why two or more groups of participants behaved differently. I hasten to add that doing experiments cannot take us back in time to ultimate evolutionary origins. A great deal of research in evolutionary psychology has to rely on passive observations of ancient phenomena. Much the same thing is true in other scientific research on origins. Consider **cosmology**, which is the study of the origin and formation of the universe. Cosmologists interested in the formation of stars cannot do experiments to create new solar systems with different physical properties. Instead, they rely heavily on careful observations (many of which involve ancient events) and mathematical simulations, which are essentially highly formal thought experiments – in which astronomers try to model what may have happened with sophisticated computer programs.

Even if we limit ourselves to the here and now, evolutionary psychologists can't always conduct experiments. For example, many evolutionary psychologists are interested in sex differences. It would obviously be highly unethical to manipulate sex experimentally – or to dictate what a person's culture teaches them about sex. But this doesn't stop researchers from studying sex differences. As you'll see in subsequent chapters, those who study sex differences, sexual promiscuity, kin selection, language acquisition, or sensitive periods in human development often have to make clever use of non-experimental techniques – which often use statistical rather than experimental control – to try to rule out confounds.

Another detour: the Human Genome Project

When it's not possible to test evolutionary research hypotheses experimentally, a wide range of non-experimental research techniques come into play. Every year researchers refine and improve non-experimental research techniques. For example, in 2003, two different teams of researchers cracked the entire human genetic code. According to the National Human Genome Research Institute (n.d.), the **Human Genome Project (HGP)** was:

> an international research effort to sequence and map all of the genes – together known as the genome – of members of our species, Homo sapiens. Completed in April 2003, the HGP gave us the ability, for the first time, to read nature's complete genetic blueprint for building a human being.

Before we delve a bit into the HGP, it might be good to establish a framework for thinking about this remarkable achievement. As you already know, genes are the basic units of genetic information that code for proteins, and thus program an organism's development. Each gene is a specific set of instructions to build a certain feature of an organism. If I may use an automotive metaphor, a specific gene would be analogous to a specific set of instructions about how to build a brake cable, or exactly where to place it. In contrast, the term **genotype** is much broader; it refers to all the versions of all the specific genes possessed by a specific organism. I apparently have an allele for blue eyes and an allele for brown eyes. Because brown eyes are dominant, my eyes are brown. It's no surprise, though, that my daughter's eyes are blue because her mom's eyes are blue. She must have gotten my recessive allele for blue eyes as well as either of her mom's recessive alleles for blue eyes. But these two alleles for eye color are just one tiny sliver of my daughter's entire genotype. A person's genotype is like the entire set of detailed instructions for making a specific make, model and color of car, complete with instructions about whether there is a satellite radio system and exactly what color the seats should be. A 2016 Toyota RAV-4 and a 1961 Volvo P1800 were manufactured using very different instructions, but they both have wheels and axles, for example, and the axles always connect the wheels.

An organism's **genome** is even broader than its genotype. It's the genetic equivalent of the entire library of every possible way to make any specific make and model of any car. Now, genes don't come in as many variations as steering wheels or brake systems. In fact, there are quite a few genes that are fixed. Only one form of the gene exists, and thus all (or virtually all) members of a species have identical versions of that gene. If this were true in the case of cars, for example, all cars might have one and only one style of headlight, or come in one and only one color. This was actually the case in the early days of Ford Motors. Henry Ford (Ford & Crowther, 1922) noted that: "Any customer can have a car painted any colour that he wants so long as it is black." But there are plenty of genes for which there are variations across people, and multiple genes sometimes work together in complex ways – the way different mechanical or electronic systems in a car must work together.

Before I review a few important things we've learned from the HGP, I should mention that the HGP would never have been possible without the development of modern methods of genetic amplification. Almost every cell in a person's body contains that person's entire genotype. So, a single hair or a drop of saliva includes everything there is to know about a person's specific genetic makeup. To determine an organism's genotype, though, you need a lot of genetic information. In fact, millions of copies of a person's DNA are necessary to perform sophisticated genetic testing. Kary B. Mullis and Michael Smith solved this daunting problem, and in 1993 they received a Nobel Prize for developing a genetic amplification technique affectionately called "molecular photocopying." Otherwise known as **polymerase chain reaction (PCR)**, it begins with a single strand of a person's (or an animal's) DNA. Paraphrasing the description of PCR from the National Human Genome Research Institute website, this technique begins with a small DNA sample, taken – for example – from a person's saliva or from a cheek swab. Technicians then heat up the sample so that the original strand of DNA splits down the middle of the "rungs" of the twisted DNA ladder. The enzyme "Taq **p**olymerase" (the P in PCR) creates two complete strands of DNA from the two halves. The keys to the technique – besides starting with a pure DNA sample – are the polymerase enzyme and the ability to change the temperature in a very precise way. At higher temperatures, DNA splits down the middle, and at lower temperatures the special enzyme goes to work making copies. A thermocycler – programmed by computer – automatically changes the temperature of all the material in well-timed cycles to make many, many copies of the original DNA. After just 30–40 cycles, the result is billions of exact copies of a DNA sample. For more details, go to www.genome.gov and search for "PCR Fact Sheet."

As your friend Dory, the lovable blue tang fish, might say: "Got it. Something about the polymerase." But what's so important about PCR? First, this new technique has revolutionized genetic testing – making it quicker, more accurate, and much less expensive than anyone could have imagined 30 years ago. About a year ago, I spent $100 to confirm what my parents had always told me – that about half of my ethnic heritage is British and Irish. But I also learned that I am about 21% Norwegian, about 5% Spanish, and about 2% Middle Eastern. In fact, there seems to be almost no European country from which I do not have at least a little ancestry. It's fun to know exactly where your ancestors lived. Of course, if you're not into genealogy, this may be no big deal. But **DNA fingerprinting**, which also relies on PCR technology, has now been used to overturn a large number of erroneous murder convictions. This can happen, for example, when tests show that the DNA found at a crime scene does not match the DNA of the person to whom it was long assumed to belong – prior to the availability of modern genetic testing. PCR is a major high-tech tool of the well-known "Innocence Project."

Focusing on the scientific as well as the practical, the Human Genome Project relied heavily on PCR technology. And we've learned a great deal about genetics and evolution from the HGP. Here are a few practical and scientific highlights:

1. We don't have nearly as many genes as scientists long assumed. Experts are still tinkering with the fine details of the HGP, but it looks like the final figure for the number of human genes is going to be less than 20,000 – rather than the 50,000–140,000 scientists once estimated. In fact, some worms have more genes than we do. Feeling any less important than you used to? I sure am.

2. Much of the genetic information in our genome seems to be "junk DNA," meaning that we have no idea what – if anything – it does. I suppose this

means that the "non-junk" genes that do code for proteins must be pretty darn busy.

3. As a species, human beings are much less diverse genetically than chimps – despite our tremendous dispersal across the globe.

4. Many genes do exactly the same thing for us that they do for much simpler organisms. Homology runs deep. Remember boule? It's the sperm gene for worms and snakes as well as for people.

5. We have some very close genetic cousins. Recall that we human beings share more than 98% of our genome with chimpanzees. This explains why we share so many behavioral and physical traits with chimps. Yet it also suggests that even very small genetic differences between species can sometimes lead to dramatic differences in behavior. Chimps can learn to ride a bike, but try teaching one to change a flat tire or play cribbage.

6. The HGP has helped researchers identify specific genetic risk factors for many diseases with a strong genetic basis. This includes devastating diseases such as Alzheimer's and schizophrenia. We now know, for example, that more than 100 genes each play at least a small role in a person's susceptibility to schizophrenia.

7. The HGP promises to lead to treatments – some of which will surely be controversial – for once-untreatable genetic diseases.

BEYOND PCR: OTHER NON-EXPERIMENTAL METHODS AND TECHNIQUES

Like most other psychologists, evolutionary psychologists make use of many different research techniques. In fact, because evolutionary psychology is an interdisciplinary field – overlapping with fields as diverse as biology and anthropology – evolutionary psychology arguably makes use of a wider array of methods than any other area of psychology. Like clinical psychologists, evolutionary psychologists sometimes rely on interviews or case studies. Like cognitive psychologists, evolutionary psychologists often conduct lab experiments. Like social psychologists, they conduct prospective studies of close relationships. Like sociologists and cultural anthropologists, they often rely on fieldwork such as ethnographies. Finally, like primatologists and ethologists, they often observe the behavior of animals in their natural habitat. In the remainder of this chapter, I briefly review some popular non-experimental research techniques used by evolutionary psychologists. I then discuss the important issue of tradeoffs in research and introduce a heuristic (the OOPS! heuristic) for critically analyzing the external validity of almost any research study involving people.

Passive observational methods

I've always been a little unhappy with the term passive observational studies, but the word "passive" is technically correct when you can't experimentally manipulate the variable or variables you are studying. I came to like the term a little more when I remembered that being passive aggressive can be just as harmful as being actively aggressive. Using passive observational methods, like being passive aggressive, often requires practitioners to be creative to achieve their goals. So, the term **passive observational methods** refers to a wide variety of non-experimental techniques for studying behavior, whether this means interviewing people, observing people unobtrusively, tabulating archival records of homicide rates, or conducting careful ethnographies. Let's take a quick peek at a few of these passive observational research techniques.

Surveys and interviews

Consider research activities as diverse as conducting a national census, asking married vs. unmarried romantic couples detailed questions about their sexual habits, conducting a structured interview that probes for symptoms of depression, and asking people to answer three questions about a video game on their iPhone, in exchange for some helpful clues to playing that same video game. These are all types of **surveys and interviews**. Researchers of all stripes often try to figure out what people think, feel, and do by simply asking them. In Chapter 3, you'll learn about an impressive 48-country survey of people's attitudes about sexual promiscuity (Schmitt, 2005). More often, though, researchers have to be content to ask a smaller group of people who happen to be handy what they've been up to lately. Surveys and interviews are incredibly useful. Who knows more about you than you? You and you alone can tell me, for example, whether you ate a lot of fruit as a child, whether you physically punched anyone last week, and whether you had the fruit punch at Lara's crazy holiday party. This being said, there are some problems with surveys and interviews. The two biggest problems are probably that people are not always able to report honestly (because of fallible memories or language barriers) and that people are not always willing to report honestly (because of guilty consciences or legal barriers).

There are some obvious ways to minimize problems with surveys and interviews. People can better remember exactly what they did yesterday than exactly what they did as children. People also respond more honestly when they know that their answers will be kept completely confidential (Schroder et al., 2003). But some ways of increasing honest responding are not so obvious. The **bogus pipeline** is a good example. Jones and Sigall (1971) convinced participants that they had invented a sophisticated "lie detector" that could detect people's true attitudes. This deception worked, by the way, because – unbeknown to the participants – Jones and Sigall already had access to the participants' true attitudes on several issues. Thus, when Jones and Sigall were presumably just "calibrating" the machine, participants observed what seemed to be striking evidence for the machine's accuracy at lie detection. When White men believed that researchers could truly read their minds, they reported attitudes about Black Americans that were significantly more negative than those reported by White men who just responded to a traditional written survey. Incidentally, attention to detail is important when using the bogus pipeline technique. As Neal Roese and David Jamieson (1993) showed in their review, fake lie detectors work best when you ask people what the machine will say about their attitudes – not when you simply ask people to report what their true attitudes are (while they're hooked up to the machine). Ironically, then, one of the best ways to get people to tell the truth about a sensitive subject is to lie to people.

Of course, bogus pipelines are a real pain to use. Are there any easier ways to increase honest responding in surveys? There are, and one of these ways becomes especially important when you're assessing things like potential sex differences in risky sexual behavior. Kerstin Shroeder and colleagues (2003) found that the specific mode of conducting a survey can matter a lot. People appear to give much more honest answers when they fill out self-administered questionnaires than when they do face-to-face interviews, for example. Arguably, the growing trend toward collecting survey data on the web – to the extent that it relies on self-administered questionnaires – could be a positive development. For researchers who still like to bring people into the lab, things as simple as putting a mirror in the room where people are filling out their surveys can also increase accurate responding (Duval & Wicklund, 1972). A full review of all the ways to avoid bias in survey responses is beyond the scope of this text. Suffice it to say, though, that there are pretty good solutions to most problems with surveys and interviews. This is good because this popular approach to data collection is not going away any time soon.

Unobtrusive observation

When a behavior is sensitive enough, or when it's so mundane that people don't remember it well, the best way to figure out what people do may be to observe them – when they don't know you're doing so. This can be ethically tricky, of course, but if a person is in a public place with no expectation of privacy, most ethicists would say it's OK to observe the person, especially if the observer follows the usual ethical rules for making sure no harm or embarrassment comes to the person being observed. The two main keys to making good **unobtrusive observations** have to do with keeping them unobtrusive. Observations are truly unobtrusive only if researchers don't interfere in any way with people's natural behavior and people don't know they're being studied.

A great example of unobtrusive observational research is a study by Collett and Marsh (1974). Collett and Marsh were interested in gender differences in how people squeeze by strangers. To assess this, they placed a video recorder on the seventh floor of a building overlooking a busy walkway – focusing the camera on a spot where people had to squeeze past one another to get where they were going. They found that 75% of the men in their study faced their fellow pedestrians as they squeezed by them. In contrast, only 17% of the women did so. Of course, Collett and Marsh couldn't say for sure why men and women used different techniques to slip past strangers. But a second look at their observations provided a big clue. They found that in those rare instances in which women did slip past others in a facing direction, they often engaged in a very telling behavior: they covered their breasts by folding their arms across their chests.

Another example of an unobtrusive observational study also involves getting from one place to another, and it also involves gender. But this study had to do with zipping through instead of squeezing past. McKelvie and Schamer (1988) made unobtrusive observations of whether drivers obeyed posted stop signs. Specifically, they made 600 unobtrusive observations at stop signs, coding for whether people (1) stopped completely, (2) did a "slow stop," or (3) failed to stop at all. They also coded for driver gender and whether each driver was carrying any passengers. Finally, they made observations both during the day and at night. Time of day mattered a great deal. When a driver was alone in the car and there was no oncoming traffic, rates of both complete stops and complete failures to stop increased at night. However, these transformations at night depended very much on gender. Solo male drivers who approached intersections at night were just as likely to disregard the stop sign altogether (36%) as they were to stop completely (also 36%). On the other hand, solo female drivers who approached the same intersections at night were much more likely to do the right thing (62% stopped completely and only 16% disregarded the sign). The shroud of night seems to have made women more concerned than usual about safety. It seems to have made men less concerned than usual about getting caught blowing a stop sign.

Archival research

Speaking of getting caught, a great deal of research in evolutionary psychology is **archival research**, which is research that uses existing public records to test research hypotheses. The public records that seem to have been used most commonly in research on evolutionary psychology are records of homicide rates. In Chapter 6, for example, I'll review a great deal of archival research that focuses on who most often kills children (e.g., see Daly & Wilson, 1994). As you will see, a distressing fact about child homicide is that parents who do not share any genes with the children for whom they care (stepparents) are much more likely to kill children than are parents who do happen to share genes with the children. On a happier note, a great deal of archival research by Manuel Eisner (2003) has shown that over the past several centuries, we human beings have become much less likely to murder one another. This radical change in murder rates seems to be the result of many different processes, including the development of economic and political systems that allow people to profit without taking the land or possessions of others (see Pinker, 2011). But evolutionary thinkers such as Pinker have been quick to point out that it wouldn't be so easy to civilize people if there weren't some sense in which we are inherently predisposed to civility (under the right circumstances).

Ethnographies

Archival research is great – when you can gain easy access to reliable archival data. But one can only do archival research on topics that have been archived. There are plenty of records about who marries whom and who kills whom. But no one keeps public records of exactly how people reason about conflict, how close people stand to one another as they speak, or how respectful people are of their elders. When researchers want an in-depth look at how people think, feel and behave, especially in cultures about which researchers know very little, they conduct ethnographies. As Bernard (2006) put it, an **ethnography** is simply "a narrative that describes a culture or a part of a culture." But as Bernard would be quick to add, there are many different kinds of ethnographies – ranging from those in which ethnographers are careful not to influence those they are observing at all (think Jane Goodall, who initially did not interact at all with the chimps she observed) to *participant ethnographies* in which ethnographers truly embed themselves in the cultures they are studying – under the assumption that experiencing something yourself is the best way to understand it.

In many ways, good ethnographies are the opposite of good archival research. For example, ethnographies often require a lot of behavioral coding on the part of the ethnographers. In archival research, someone else has always done the coding for you (like it or not). Because they're in the physical presence of those they observe, ethnographers also have to go to great lengths not to change what they are observing. Otherwise, all they have is a good account of what people do when they know a stranger is watching them. This is not an issue in archival research. Ethnographers may also have to spend months, if not years, to learn the language and customs of those they study. In contrast, archival researchers just need to be sure they have gotten hold of the right records. As a final example, archival research often focuses on very large groups of people, such as entire nations. In contrast, by necessity, most ethnographies focus on one small group, whether it is a small tribe of people living in Papua New Guinea or a small group of American consumers (Mariampolski, 2006). Archival research often tells you just one thing about a huge and familiar group of people. Ethnography often tells you many different things about a tiny and unfamiliar group of people.

I hasten to add that in this chapter I have only scratched the surface of research methods in evolutionary psychology. But I hope this selective list of a few different techniques, from experiments to ethnographies, shows off the diversity in the methodological toolkits of evolutionary psychologists. I hope it's also clear that tools that are great for doing one thing can be terrible for doing something else. Furthermore, even the best and most versatile tools come with tradeoffs. Crescent wrenches make terrible screwdrivers. With this in mind, I'd like to close this chapter by discussing an important tradeoff in research methods. This is the tradeoff between internal and external validity.

INTERNAL VS. EXTERNAL VALIDITY AND THE OOPS! HEURISTIC

The **internal validity** of a research finding refers to the degree to which the finding lets you know what caused what. If a study fulfilled John Stuart Mill's three requirements for establishing causality, then that study would be high in internal validity. Lab experiments are usually very high in internal validity. But some of the features that make lab experiments high in internal validity tend to make them low in a second kind of validity – external validity. **External validity** has to do with generalizability – the question of whether it really happens this way in the real world. Questionnaires involving diverse samples, archival studies, and ethnographies can go a long way toward establishing external validity. But, of course, the price we pay for using these passive observational techniques is often a weakness when it comes to internal validity. That's the tradeoff.

The concerns methodologists raise when they question the external validity of any research finding – evolutionary or otherwise – seem to fall into only four categories. With this in mind, I like to organize these four concerns by referring to the **OOPS! heuristic**. Each letter of the acronym stands for a different specific concern about external validity.

Operationalizations

As you know very well, we can only study things scientifically if we come up with clear and precise operational definitions of those things. But there are many different ways to operationalize most hypothetical constructs. Recall that, in men at least, one operational definition for sexual arousal is based on volumetric changes in the penis. Another is based on genital temperature, based on blood flow. A third is based on simple self-report. When multiple operational definitions of something are all reasonable, we can place greater confidence in a finding when the finding holds up well across all these different operational definitions of the thing in question. Homology, for example, can be defined physically as well as behaviorally. Altruism could be defined in terms of either (a) giving food or physical resources to a fellow organism or (b) risking your own safety to protect a fellow organism from predators. Nursing fits the first definition of altruism. Making an alarm call ("There's a hawk up there!!!") fits the second. As you'll learn in Chapter 9, there's good evidence for something called **kin selection** regardless of which definition of altruism we adopt. Evidence for anything is more impressive when this evidence holds up across many different operational definitions. One reason why Steven Pinker's (2011) argument that human violence has declined over the past few centuries is so convincing is the fact that Pinker uses many, many different operational definitions of violence, from killing people or cutting off their noses to enslaving or imprisoning people. He also includes war, child abuse, burning witches, and hurting animals. Across a vast range of operational definitions, violence has dramatically declined.

Occasions

"To everything there is a season." Indeed, human behavior has always varied greatly across the day-night cycle, across the different seasons of the year, and across the millennia. Thus, the second aspect of external validity has to do with generalization across different **occasions**. Roberto Refinetti (2005) found that college students who had a regular sexual partner were much more likely to report having sex late at night than at any other time of day. About half of all the sexual interactions his participants reported in a three-week-long daily diary study took place during the two-hour window between about 11 p.m. and 1 a.m. Many other things, including people's hormone levels, vary naturally over time. And this natural variation often has important evolutionary consequences. For example, Lisa Welling and colleagues (2008) showed that men's rated attractiveness of highly feminine as opposed to less feminine female faces was stronger than usual on days when the men's testosterone levels were higher than usual.

Looking at timing over a broader window, American women are more likely to get pregnant in December than in other months of the year. Weddings and funerals also vary dramatically with the season. As you must have already known, June is the most popular month for weddings. As you probably did not know, people are also more likely to get married during the month of their own birthdays than other months (Pelham & Carvallo, 2015). Finally, the number of children the average American woman has today is much lower than it was 100 years ago. My grandmother was one of 17 children. My aunt Patsy had 12, I was one of 6, and my children are each one of only 2. This trend may save me a lot of money someday on gifts for my grandchildren.

So time matters. For this reason, when evaluating any research finding, we have to ask ourselves if that finding would hold true at other times. Showing that something interesting is true is impressive. Showing that it was also true 150,000 years ago – and documenting a likely reason why – is even more impressive. The issue of time and timing is particularly important in evolutionary psychology because this is a field in which issues of stability or change over time are of great importance. How have hominids changed over the past million years? How does a man's sperm production vary over the course of his lifetime? When does menopause usually happen? To offer a more detailed example, it's a popular belief – supported by research – that men are more interested in sexual opportunism than women. However, research by Steven Gangestad and colleagues (2010) shows that women's degree of sexual opportunism varies across their ovulatory cycle. When women in committed relationships are at the most fertile point in their ovulatory cycles, they're more likely than usual to endorse sexually "opportunistic" attitudes such as "I believe in taking my sexual pleasures where I find them." So we cannot fairly compare men and women in this way without thinking carefully about the question of timing (see also Bodenhausen, 1990).

Populations

Almost no research finding, psychological or otherwise, applies to every imaginable **population**. People see colors much more vividly than dogs, and dogs smell things people can barely imagine. Even if we limit ourselves to people, the external validity of a specific research finding can vary dramatically depending on the population. Presumably, very few devout nuns would believe in "taking their sexual pleasures where they could find them," even if they were currently ovulating. But if a study of nuns asked them if they ever had any regrets about their vows of sexual chastity, and if nuns were a little more likely to answer this question affirmatively when they were ovulating, this would constitute some pretty impressive support for the external validity of Gangestad's perspective on ovulation (I know of no such studies, but maybe they're on the horizon). Most findings become more impressive when we learn that they hold up across many different populations. And the more diverse the population, of course, the better the evidence in support of external validity across populations. Bob Zajonc (1965) evaluated his evolutionary hypotheses about social facilitation in ants, cockroaches, parakeets, puppies, and monkeys as well as in people. That's a pretty diverse overall population.

Situations

A final aspect of external validity has to do with generalization across different **situations**. All research takes place in a specific context, and that context can dramatically influence what researchers observe. The way people think and reason seems to vary based on the way in which an experimenter dresses. When experimenters talk and dress more casually, people seem to think more casually – more intuitively and less logically (see Simon et al., 1997). And when people dress more formally, others are much more likely to obey them (Bickman, 1974). As we will see in Chapter 10, both the specific situation in which people find themselves (e.g., a synagogue vs. a singles bar) and the chronic situations in which people live (culture) can have a huge impact on how people think, feel, and behave. Situations can be hard to separate from occasions (in a sense, time of day is a situation), but situations are not the same as occasions because situations can vary independent of time (experimenters can be formally or informally dressed in January or July). To know how robust a research finding is, you need to know how well it holds up in a wide variety of situations.

IS EVOLUTIONARY PSYCHOLOGY JUST A BUNCH OF "JUST SO" STORIES?

Now that you've had a crash course in research methods in evolutionary psychology, I'd like to address a common methodological criticism of evolutionary psychology. Scientists and laypeople alike have often argued that evolutionary psychology is not very scientific because it's just a bunch of **just so stories**. Ironically enough, this criticism seems to have begun with the famous evolutionary biologist Stephen Jay Gould. The phrase has its origins in Rudyard Kipling's (1902) famous and intentionally fanciful stories for children. Kipling's stories occasionally pretended to explain how animals got to be the way they are (e.g., how leopards came to have spots). Critics thus use the pejorative phrase "just so stories" to suggest that evolutionary hypotheses are often generated after the fact – as fanciful explanations for something we already knew – or that evolutionary hypotheses are so vague and flexible as to be unfalsifiable.

The "just so stories" criticism sounds pretty damning, but in my opinion, it's just not so. On the whole, scientists who study evolutionary psychology are just as scientific as those who study microbiology or the formation of galaxies. As I hope you now know, what makes a theory or hypothesis scientific has almost nothing to do with its content or whether it tries to explain a lot or a little. Unlike intuitions, political opinions, or deeply held religious beliefs (which all have their proper place in human affairs), scientific hypotheses must be testable and thus falsifiable (Popper, [1974] 1990). This is what makes a theory or perspective scientific.

I suspect that one reason why critics offer the "just so" criticism of evolutionary psychology is grounded in the fact that evolution is a "big picture" theory that might seem unfalsifiable. The theory of evolution has fueled a great deal of research because it's very complex. I think of evolutionary psychology as a perspective rather than a theory per se. As I hope you will see in the rest of this book, there are many theories in evolutionary psychology – just as there are many theories in social, developmental, clinical, or cognitive psychology. But all the theories I will cover here have something in common. They're all scientific.

I hate to admit this, but I suspect that a second reason why some people offer "just so" criticisms of some evolutionary theories is that avid fans of evolutionary psychology – like avid fans of string theory, or avid fans of Johnny Depp – sometimes overstep their reach. In the case of evolutionary psychology, avid fans may occasionally do so (or appear to do so) by trying to explain everything as the product of evolution. At other times, avid fans of evolution may draw solid inferences from evolutionary theories and treat these inferences more like facts than inferences. As I hope you'll see throughout this book, I try hard to avoid that approach.

If I may pick on one of my favorite evolutionary thinkers, I disagree with Richard Dawkins (2006) that evolution virtually guarantees that there cannot be a God. This is a reasonable inference that could be drawn from research on evolution, but it's still an inference. I'm not quite an atheist myself, but my specific brand of agnosticism certainly situates me much closer to atheism than religious fundamentalism. Despite my personal lack of deep religious faith, though, I disagree with Dawkins' clever argument that people who believe in God are delusional. Certainly, evolution offers an interesting perspective on why religion exists (as we will see in Chapter 11), but it is just that, a perspective. In my view, a firm belief in evolution is not wholly and incontrovertibly incompatible with the existence of any kind of God (Myers, 2008). On the other hand, as we will see in Chapter 9, I strongly agree with Dawkins that one does not need to believe in God to be a good person, or to be sincerely motivated to help others (de Waal, 2014). Finally, I should add that I personally find evolutionary theories most useful and interesting when they fly in the face of beliefs most of us take for granted. These beliefs could be religious beliefs, but they could also be beliefs based on competing psychological, sociological, or economic theories. It is precisely when a theory or perspective provides novel insights into human behavior that it fosters productive debate, leads to empirical research, and thus enriches our understanding of human nature. As much as possible in this book, I will emphasize what is unique and surprising about evolutionary psychology, always realizing that, as E.O. Wilson (1978) put it: "I could be wrong."

Getting back to the core scientific principle of falsification, falsification means that those who propose evolutionarily inspired theories and hypotheses, whether biological, psychological, or both, must always be willing to subject their ideas to critical analysis, empirical verification, and revision in the face of uncooperative findings. I know of no evolutionary scientists who do not endorse this basic axiom of science. In light of the axiom of falsification, let's revisit Miyatake and colleagues' (2004) study of tonic immobility in red flour beetles. It's important to note that, after all that rigorous red flour beetle breeding, these researchers could have easily found that spiders are never fooled by possum-playing flour beetles. In fact, they could have even found that spiders strongly prefer them. If I were a spider, I think I might strongly prefer a flour beetle that didn't fight back. Miyatake et al. (2004) had a specific evolutionary hypothesis, and they put it to a rigorous empirical test. Some scientists might prefer a different explanation for the same findings, and still others might not be happy with every aspect of this specific research design. But this kind of healthy scientific debate is common in every branch of science.

For this reason, anyone with some solid methodological training can easily generate reasonable criticisms of almost any empirical study. Can we be sure that reverse causality wasn't possible? Would the effect hold up in other populations or situations? How can we be sure that the same thing that happened in a highly artificial lab setting would hold up in nature? As almost any philosopher or methodologist would be happy to remind us, the answer is that, strictly speaking, we can't. No matter how many careful observations we make in support of any theory or hypothesis, there is always a chance that the next careful observation we make will invalidate the hypothesis – in a never-before-studied context, a never-before-studied species, or a never-before-studied way of operationalizing the variables of interest. This is called the **problem of induction**. And this, of course, is why it's often worth doing more research to follow up on any clever or provocative research finding. But this kind of thoughtful criticism applies to studies of chemistry and particle physics just as well as it applies to studies of evolution, psychology, or evolutionary psychology.

Unlike fortune tellers, evolutionary psychologists aren't afraid to be specific, or to test their predictions critically. In my view, the fact that the theory of evolution generates a great number of testable predictions is arguably a strength. That being said, the trouble that often arises from rich theories (like evolution) is that the same broad theory or perspective can occasionally be used to derive opposing predictions. When this happens, it does not make the theory or perspective unfalsifiable. It just means that it's not so clear which of two opposing predictions one should make. In my book, that's often when things get scientifically interesting.

"I was hoping you could tell me something mildly favorable – yet vague enough to be believable."

If evolutionary psychology really were just a bunch of just so stories, then theories in evolutionary psychology would never need to be revised. But researchers are constantly revising evolutionary theories. As an example, Charles Darwin believed that evolution is a slow and incremental process. In the grand scheme of things, he certainly proved to be right about the slowness. But over the past few decades, we've learned that things aren't nearly as incremental as Darwin assumed. About 40 years ago Stephen Jay Gould and Niles Eldridge (1977) proposed the theory of **punctuated equilibria**. As we'll see in Chapter 3, this theory states that evolution often looks more like a radical revolution than a gradual refinement. Long periods of relative stability in a species are followed by occasional periods of rapid and dramatic change. During the early stages of such changes, you often see a dramatic proliferation of variations on a theme in closely related species. Perhaps an animal that once lived on land becomes semi-aquatic. This doesn't happen overnight, of course, but from the perspective of evolutionary timescales, the change is rapid. Imagine that a river changes course. An area that was once dry is now wet. An organism whose body structure happens to lend itself well to swimming does better in the water than an organism that does not. Furthermore, particular members of that species that happen to be better swimmers – because of random genetic variation – do better than members of the species that happen to be poor swimmers. If the landlubber variation of the species sticks to the land over the millennia and the water-loving variation sticks with the water, members of the species may eventually move so far apart genetically that they could no longer breed and produce fertile offspring. At this point, these genetic cousins would certainly continue to resemble one another (remember homology?), but each would now represent a separate **species**.

The main point behind the theory of punctuated equilibrium is that speciation does not usually happen in the slow and gradual fashion that Darwin strongly believed. There's a lot of evidence that's consistent with the idea of brief periods of rapid speciation followed by relative stability. There's only limited evidence in support of Darwin's original idea of gradualism. If Darwin had known (as we now do) how often dramatic, if not calamitous, environmental changes have taken place in the earth's long history, he would surely have revised some of his otherwise reasonable conclusions about evolutionary gradualism. Modern experts in evolution believe in punctuated equilibria because the fossil record strongly supports it; not because it's a nice story.

Incidentally, you're already pretty familiar with a good example of punctuated equilibrium. It's the dramatic, post-asteroid changes that occurred in mammals once those pesky dinosaurs were all out of the way. Ancient mammals coexisted with dinosaurs for millions of years without changing very much. But once the dinosaurs all bit the dust, mammalian evolution became turbo charged. **Speciation** (the evolution of separate species) happened at a very rapid rate. As we'll see in Chapter 3, many evolutionary experts also think that you and I are the result of punctuated equilibrium. Every year or so researchers discover a new species of (now extinct) bipedal hominid. As I use the term **hominid** here, it refers to a wide variety of bipedal (upright walking), large-brained primates, only some of whom were direct ancestors of modern human beings. (Others use the term hominid more broadly, by the way, to include the "knuckle walkers" or modern great apes, which include chimpanzees, gorillas, and orangutans.)

We now know that there was no simple and gradual transition from an ancient primate ancestor to *Homo sapiens*. We are the one particular bipedal hominid among many "experiments" that has survived in a window of only a few million years of rapid hominid evolution. If you want to explore the tremendous diversity that has existed in bipedal hominids over the past couple of million years, make it a point to visit the Smithsonian Museum's Hall of Human Origins. If you can't get to Washington, DC easily, you can take a virtual tour of this highly engaging exhibition. One of my favorite virtual exhibits is a video clip that shows artist John Gurche at work sculpting some very realistic hominids. Gurche's sculptures range from the tiny *Homo floresiensis* (aka the hobbit), who lived in modern-day Indonesia as recently as 18,000 years ago, to the more familiar, and much more muscular, *Homo neanderthalensis* who flourished in places like Northern Europe between about 500,000 and 30,000 years ago. To see the video, in which Gurche explains his sculpting technique and his forensic skills, go to: http:// humanorigins.si.edu/exhibit/reconstructions-early-humans. In this exhibition, you'll learn that as recently as 30,000–40,000 years ago there were several – rather than only one – fully human species on this planet. Neanderthals, for example, had brains that were slightly larger than our own, so we can be pretty sure that their intellectual capacities made them truly human.

To return to the "just so" criticism, what makes evolutionary psychology a science is the fact that evolutionary psychologists play by the rules of science. They do so, for example, by testing their theories empirically rather than just speculating about them. I hope you now have a solid appreciation of the fact that evolutionary psychologists go about their scientific business in very much the same way that other scientists do. As you will see in Chapter 3, a great deal of that business has to do with understanding things like genetics, natural selection, sexual selection, and speciation.

FOR FURTHER READING

» Ketelaar, T. & Ellis, B.J. (2000). Are evolutionary explanations unfalsifiable? Evolutionary psychology and the Lakatosian philosophy of science. *Psychological Inquiry*, 11(1), 1–21.

» Pelham, B.W. & Blanton, H. (2018). *Conducting research in psychology: Measuring the weight of smoke* (5th edn). Los Angeles, CA: Sage.

SAMPLE MULTIPLE-CHOICE EXAM QUESTIONS

Here are four sample quiz questions for Chapter 2. You can find the Chapter 2 quiz at: www.macmillanihe.com/evolutionary-psychology

2.01.   Like chemists, anthropologists, and physicists, evolutionary psychologists prefer a specific "way of knowing." What is it?

a. observation

b. parsimony

c. induction

2.02. Why is using thermography usually better than using a plethysmograph to measure sexual arousal?

a. because only thermography involves objective measurement

b. because thermography works equally well for both women and men

c. because using a plethysmograph requires much more intensive coding

2.03. What kind of validity does random assignment usually maximize?

a. external

b. construct

c. internal

2.04. The OOPS! heuristic offers suggestions for maximizing:

a. external validity

b. testability

c. internal validity

Answer Key: a, b, c, a.

Chapter 3

HOW DID WE GET HERE?

GENETICS, NATURAL SELECTION, AND SPECIATION

"It looks as if the offspring have eyes so *that* they can see well ... but that's an illusion. The offspring have eyes because *their parents'* eyes *did* see well."

— *Steven Pinker (1997, p. 157)*

"Evolution is the fundamental idea in all of life science."

— *Bill Nye, the Science Guy*

"Evolution isn't true, because if we evolved from monkeys, how can they still be here?"

— *Stephen Baldwin, American actor*

About 13.7 billion years ago, all the matter and energy in the observable universe was apparently condensed into a very tiny space. This tremendously compact, extremely hot proto-universe expanded at unimaginable speeds. Fittingly, this theory of the origin of the universe is known as the **Big Bang**. Eventually, this cosmic explosion cooled and created the regular rules of physics that led to the formation of at least a couple of trillion galaxies (Conselice et al., 2016; Howell, 2017). Since the Big Bang, many, many stars have come into existence in these two trillion galaxies. Some of the tiniest stars that formed early in the history of the universe are still burning today. But the very big ones – the **supergiants** – had enough mass to fuse silicon into iron as they aged. They then exploded dramatically in **supernovas**, and sent all kinds of matter, iron included, all over the universe. In 1987, astronomers captured spectacular images of a supernova that occurred 168,000 years ago. Although the star that had died was 11 billion times as far away as our own sun, the supernova was still visible to the naked eye. Supernovas are important. The leftover matter they scatter about becomes the raw material for new solar systems. This cosmic recycling process was crucial to the formation of our own solar system because big stars create iron, and supernovas disperse it. Our sun has lots of iron in its core, and this gives it some nice properties for fostering life. Further, only rocky, iron-rich planets like the earth appear to be suitable homes for the evolution of life as we know it. So, in a very real sense, we earthlings owe our existence to distant supernovas that occurred billions of years ago – and thus became the seeds of our own life-friendly solar system.

Several different dating systems converge to suggest that about 4.5 billion years ago, a bunch of leftover matter from some supernovas coalesced into our own solar system. A series of lucky coincidences allowed the earth to become a planet that currently harbors an estimated 8.7 million distinct life forms. Incidentally, this is true despite the fact that an estimated 99.9% of life forms that have ever existed on earth are now extinct (Newman, 1997; Raup, 1986). At different points in the earth's history, then, it has been a very different place – with very different inhabitants. You got a glimpse of that in Chapter 1. But it doesn't take a massive asteroid strike to change the face of life on earth. More mundane events, like drifting continents and changing climates, can have similar effects, although usually over longer windows. How did the earth go from being a bunch of molten supernova leftovers to being the six sextillion (10^{21}) ton terrarium that keeps us all alive? How could life evolve from inanimate matter? Further, how could the tiny, ancient proto-organisms that came into being on earth about 4 billion years ago have evolved into organisms as diverse as people and petunias? This chapter addresses such intriguing questions (Bell et al., 2015; Dawkins, 1976).

As shown in Figure 3.1, the earth is home to an amazing array of life forms, only one of which is able to post fake news on its Facebook pages. But it was not always this way. For the first 0.5 billion years of the earth's 4.5-billion-year history, there was little or no life. Molten rock, volcanoes, and the paucity of oxygen in the atmosphere meant that the earth would have been unfriendly to most modern life forms. It also looks like a proto-planet about the size of Mars slammed into the earth very early in its history. This is why we have a very large moon whose rocky composition is distinct from that of the earth. In the short term, this moon-creating impact certainly didn't help nudge life along. However, once the moon settled into a stable earth orbit, and once things cooled off, the same ancient conditions that would have been so hostile to carrots or karaoke singers appear to have become highly favorable to the evolution of tiny, single-celled **prokaryotes**. Prokaryotes are really simple. Unlike the **eukaryotic** (nucleated) cells with which most people are more familiar, prokaryotes lack a nucleus (loosely speaking, a cell brain). This means that DNA just floats around freely in the cell rather than being contained in the nucleus. Prokaryotes also usually lack any organelles (loosely speaking, cell organs). So, unlike eukaryotes, they have no endoplasmic reticulum.

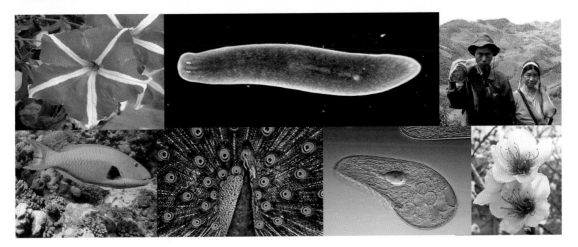

Figure 3.1 *About 99.9% of all species that ever existed on earth have gone extinct. Nonetheless, the earth is still home to an estimated 8.7 million species. This includes the species you see here as well as at least 250,000 known species of beetle. Images (clockwise from upper left) (colloquially): petunia, planarian, people, peach tree, protozoan, peacock, and parrot fish.*

Prokaryotes are simple but evolutionarily successful. Plenty of them still exist today. Natural yogurt, for example, is made using prokaryotic bacteria. I hope it's obvious that no one knows for certain exactly how inanimate matter became prokaryotes (or their precursors). I hope it's even more obvious that cacti and coyotes didn't pop into existence all at once. That's even harder to explain than prokaryotes (Dawkins, 1976). As Buss et al. (1998) put it: "Natural selection is the only known causal process capable of producing complex functional organic mechanisms." Further, every year, evolutionary scientists make new discoveries that illustrate plausible ways in which the basic building blocks of life (e.g., replicating material like DNA and RNA) could have come into existence. But before we examine some modern findings regarding the possible origins of life, let's examine a classic finding.

THE LIKELY ORIGINS OF LIFE ON EARTH

In 1953, Stanley Miller published a provocative paper showing how the conditions on ancient earth could have converted four simple inorganic (non-biological) molecules into amino acids, which are the basic building blocks of life. What has been dubbed the **Miller-Urey experiment** was remarkably simple (well, for a chemistry experiment). In a sterile device like the one depicted in Figure 3.2, Miller combined ammonia (NH_3), hydrogen (H_2), carbon monoxide (CO), methane (CH_4), and water (H_2O). All he added was a little heat and some electrical sparks (as a stand-in for lightning). In just a day, the liquid that condensed down into a water trap became pink. After a week, it became bright red. Chemical analyses of what had formed in this simulated ancient earth system revealed at least nine different amino acids. It's a lot easier for inorganic molecules to become amino acids than Miller had probably imagined. Over the decades, many scientists have replicated and extended this basic finding. Add energy to any of several unremarkable inorganic molecules, and you'll often get things like amino acids. Earth does not appear to be the only place where this can happen. Many asteroids contain amino acids, and some of the amino acids in some meteorites may have formed in outer space, using energy from cosmic collisions (Friedrich et al., 2016).

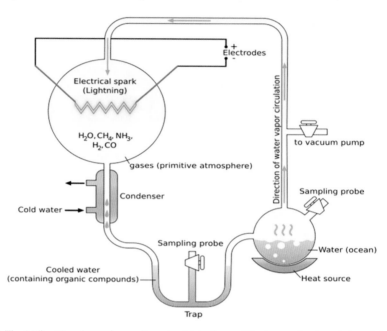

Figure 3.2 *The Miller-Urey (1953) experiment, which showed that some heat and electricity (a stand-in for lightning) can convert inorganic molecules into organic ones.*

I should note that studies like the Miller-Urey experiment have raised some tough questions. For example, the original experiment only yields a lot of amino acids in a hydrogen-rich environment. But, as far as we know, the earth of 4 billion years ago was not a very hydrogen-rich place. Another thorny problem is a variation on the "chicken or egg" question. Normally, it takes DNA to create proteins, and it takes protein-rich organisms to create DNA. Imagine that it took fire to make matches and that matches were the only known way to start a fire. That's a genuine biological puzzle. At least it was until pretty recently.

In the past decade or so, John Sutherland and colleagues have documented some very plausible ways in which one of the crucial ingredients of life – ribonucleic acid (RNA) – could have formed on the ancient earth. For example, Patel et al. (2015) showed that the abundance of meteors known to have crashed into the ancient earth would have created a lot of hydrogen cyanide. All you need to add to this is hydrogen sulfide (H_2S) and ultraviolet light to get the precursors of RNA. In case you slept through your junior biology class, RNA is a close cousin of DNA (deoxyribonucleic acid). Unlike hydrogen, then, all three of the key ingredients needed to create the known precursors of RNA were quite common on the primordial earth. Service (2015) summarized an interview with Sutherland as follows: "the conditions that produce nucleic acid precursors also create the starting materials needed to make natural amino acids and lipids. That suggests a single set of reactions could have given rise to most of life's building blocks simultaneously." A key word here is "simultaneously." You need to get several building blocks of life together at the same time to kick-start life. Sutherland's work is uncovering some very plausible ways in which this could have happened on ancient earth. All it may have taken to bring these building blocks together is some rain, some mud puddles, and a little help from volcanoes. There was presumably no shortage of any of these on ancient earth (van Kranendonk et al., 2017).

Some scientists have argued that the first organic matter on earth probably came from elsewhere in the universe. Critics of this idea have argued that this idea merely replaces one riddle with two others. How did organic matter come to exist elsewhere – and then make its way here? If I may criticize this common criticism, a variation on an old theory known as **panspermia** strikes me as plausible. According to this theory, there were surely ancient places in the universe that had conditions even friendlier to the formation of life than earth did. If life first evolved there, perhaps these cosmic hothouses seeded life in other places – where life otherwise might not have evolved on its own. When you consider that the earth harbors creatures (water bears or tardigrades) that can survive both the freezing conditions of deep space and being boiled (Miller, 2011), panspermia doesn't sound quite so far-fetched. We know for sure that some of the meteorites that strike the earth today come here containing amino acids formed elsewhere. Thus, in my view, we can't completely dismiss the possibility of panspermia.

When it comes to understanding how life emerged on earth, there are still plenty of mysteries. I'm sure chemists and biologists will continue to unravel them. But I don't want to overstate all the uncertainty. There are many biologically plausible ways in which life could have first formed, and there are no biologically plausible ways in which it appeared magically all at once. Further, we know quite a few things about the history of life on earth. For example, Higgs and Pudritz (2009) took some of the mystery out of early evolution by showing that amino acids seem to have emerged in an orderly fashion – with the simpler ones emerging first, for thermodynamic reasons. In fact, one thing we know with great certainty about the evolution of life on earth is that very simple organisms existed for a very, very long time before anything more complicated emerged. Scientists now have a pretty good idea of which organisms evolved when on earth. If I may simplify a lot, single-celled prokaryotes were followed by eukaryotes and then by multicellular organisms. These in turn were followed much later by sea-dwelling trilobites, land-dwelling T. rexes, and Tasmanian devils (in that order) (Shubin, 2008).

To simplify a little bit less, imagine you converted the entire 4.6-billion-year history of the earth's existence to a 100-m timeline (slightly less than the length of a World Cup soccer field). The first half of the line would be pretty barren. The mark where eukaryotes first appear would be at 54 m. Sexually reproducing organisms don't appear until the 76-m mark. The first fish don't appear until 88.5 m, and forests don't appear until 91.6 m. The lengthy window when dinosaurs existed would only cover 95.1–98.6 m. You'd need a magnifying glass to mark the emergence of the first human beings (200,000 years ago). The mark would be at 99.9957 m, meaning that we only appeared 0.43 cm ago. So our portion of the 100-m timeline of the earth is roughly the width of a pea. For an interactive and much more detailed version of this earth timeline, visit www.bbc.co.uk/nature/history_of_the_earth. Of course, all these dates are subject to scientific revision, but the main point is that there had to be a point long ago at which very simple living creatures first appeared on earth. Richard Dawkins (1976) calls the first life forms that could reproduce the "replicators." As he argued, once replicators evolved, the rules of natural selection took over and radically changed the planet. Presumably, the **last universal common ancestor** (the last organism to be an ancestor to everything now alive) eventually led to all living things (Theobald, 2010). The rest of this chapter is about how this amazing transformation appears to have taken place.

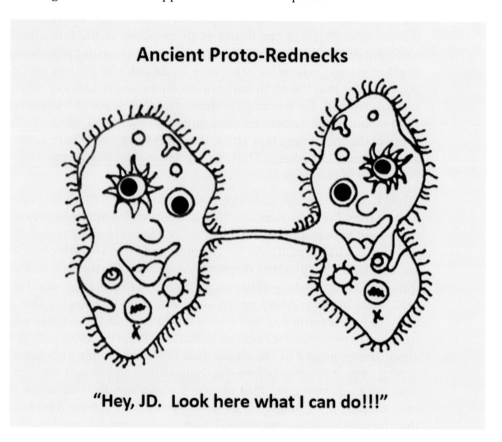

Ancient Proto-Rednecks

"Hey, JD. Look here what I can do!!!"

As suggested by the title of this book, once you have living, gene-wielding organisms, and some major variations in physical environments, all you need is a lot of time to populate a planet with millions of different species. To understand how earth got to be the way it is, then, we need to understand the details of natural selection. I have already touched on natural selection in Chapters 1 and 2. In this chapter I'll expand on natural selection. Before doing so, however, I'll examine the genetic transmission of inherited traits that makes natural selection possible in the first place.

In *On the origin of species by means of natural selection*, Darwin (1859) proposed the bold idea that parents who have specific traits pass them onto their offspring. He further argued that because some traits promote survival more than others in specific environments, the accumulation of very different traits over long periods produced different species (as Darwin's title suggested). But, like everyone else on earth in 1859, Darwin had no idea how offspring come to resemble or differ from their parents. Darwin made no secret of his ignorance. As he put it (1859, pp. 45–6), variability within and between species "is governed by many unknown laws." Darwin further conceded that "Something must be attributed to use and disuse. The final result is thus rendered infinitely complex." Darwin was probably engaging in hyperbole with the word "infinitely." So let's not take him literally. As complex as genetics has proven to be, it is not infinitely complex. Thanks to the work of Gregor Mendel, the first true geneticist, we now know that parents pass on their physical and psychological traits to their offspring because they pass on some of their genes. Genes are long strings of protein-coding nucleotides (pieces of DNA) that are typically considered the basic unit of biological inheritance. Unless my memory fails me badly, though, you won't find the word "gene" in Darwin's famous book (although you will find words like "heritable").

THE BIOLOGICAL MECHANISM OF EVOLUTION: GENETICS

Basic Mendelian inheritance

While Darwin was putting the finishing touches on his famous book on evolution, Mendel was working feverishly on his painstaking genetic studies of 29,000 pea plants. Mendel began his genetic work in 1856 and did not complete data collection until 1863. Recall that in 1859, roughly the midpoint of Mendel's data collection window, Darwin published *On the origin of species*. It probably wouldn't have mattered much to Darwin if Mendel had finished his genetic work more quickly because Mendel's work (published in 1866) initially drew little attention. In fact, Mendel apparently sent Darwin copies of his published work. But Darwin doesn't seem to have read it. Sadly, no one would really appreciate Mendel's work on genetics until the early part of the 20th century, after others replicated his work, and after microbiologists had begun to catch up with his innovative ideas. By then Mendel had long given up growing pea plants. In fact, by then Mendel was pushing up daisies.

Mendel wanted to understand inheritance. Why do two tall parents usually – but not always – have tall children? Why do two blue-eyed parents almost always have blue-eyed children? Stranger yet, how can two brown-eyed parents sometimes have a blue-eyed child? In Darwin's day, biologists couldn't answer such questions with any certainty because they knew almost nothing about genetics. **Genetics** is the study of the **heritability** (biological transmission) of physical and psychological traits and tendencies, including how environments interact with genes to influence an organism's development. Mendel's work addressed important genetic questions. His studies paved the way for a biological revolution Mendel could scarcely have anticipated. Incidentally, it was a lucky accident that Mendel studied pea plants. He originally wanted to study mice. But Mendel was a monk, and the boss monk didn't want him studying sex, not even in mice. The boss was OK, though, with Mendel studying pea plants. This proved to have some big advantages over studying mice. First, you can quickly and cheaply raise a lot of pea plants. You also have a lot of control over reproduction. Finally, unlike mice, pea plants can fertilize themselves if you like (they can self-pollinate). All this gave Mendel a lot of useful data.

For the genetically determined traits Mendel studied (e.g., seed color, plant height), some traits were **dominant** over others. When Mendel crossed two heterozygous yellow-seeded pea plants, he got a 3:1 ratio of yellow-seeded to green-seeded plants. **Heterozygous** means carrying two opposing alleles of a gene, each of which came from a different parent. After getting this 3:1 ratio many times, Mendel concluded that, in peas, the **allele** for being yellow-seeded was dominant over the allele for being green-seeded. The left half of Figure 3.3 illustrates this for eye color. If mom and dad both carry a dominant allele for brown eyes and a **recessive** allele for blue eyes (Bb), there is a 25% chance that any one of their kids will have blue eyes. If, on the other hand, mom is **homozygous** for brown eyes (BB) and dad is homozygous for blue eyes (bb), all of their kids (100%) will have brown eyes (as in the right-hand example in Figure 3.3). To make this second example concrete, my mom almost certainly had two dominant alleles for brown eyes. I say this because my dad had blue eyes (meaning he had two recessive blue-eyed alleles). Nonetheless, all six of my mom's children (myself included) have brown eyes. My parents have plenty of blue-eyed as well as brown-eyed grandchildren, however, because several of their brown-eyed children mated with blue-eyed partners. If my siblings and I weren't all carrying a recessive blue-eyed allele from my dad, we couldn't produce any blue-eyed offspring, even with blue-eyed mates.

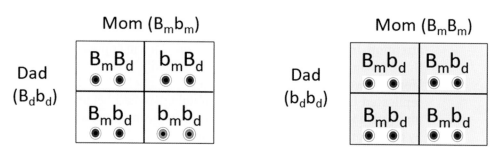

Figure 3.3 *Two examples of dominant-recessive inheritance using **Punnett squares**. These examples simplify reality to assume that eye color is determined by one gene (it's really at least two) and that brown eyes are dominant. B represents an allele for brown eyes, and b represents an allele for blue eyes. Subscripts indicate from which parent (mom or dad) the alleles come.*

In the example on the left, each parent is heterozygous with brown eyes. Across many pairings such as this one, we should observe the same 3:1 ratio of brown to blue eyes Mendel observed for tall vs. short pea plants (tallness being dominant). In the right-hand example, mom is homozygous for brown eyes (with matching dominant alleles), whereas dad is homozygous for blue eyes (with matching recessive alleles). Although dad is blue-eyed, all his offspring should have brown eyes. Note, however, that mom and dad could easily have blue-eyed grandchildren. Perhaps the most important thing Mendel discovered is that there is sometimes a big difference between genotype and phenotype. An organism's genotype is the organism's exact genetic makeup. Because Mendel studied dominant-recessive inheritance, though, he frequently observed that a pea plant could be carrying genes that had no impact at all on the observable physical properties of the plant. The **phenotype** of an organism (its physical properties if it's a plant, its physical and psychological properties if it's an animal) may not be what one would expect from its genotype.

Do dominant traits "dominate" recessive traits?

Many who first learn about dominant-recessive inheritance assume that dominant traits "take over" in natural selection. After all, dominant people often take over conversations and dominant soccer players often take over soccer games. People may also feel that recessive genes get "weeded out of the gene pool" because some well-known genetic diseases, such as Tay-Sachs and sickle cell anemia, occur only when people receive recessive alleles from both parents. But, in genetics, dominant traits are simply those that get expressed phenotypically when a dominant allele co-occurs with a recessive allele. So, dominant traits do not dominate natural selection. Whether alleles are dominant, recessive, or neither, they tend to become more popular in a population when they promote **selective fitness** (e.g., by helping an organism attract a mate, produce hardier offspring, or avoid predation).

If this doesn't make sense, consider the fact that some recessive traits are common and that some dominant traits are rare (in some populations). For our purposes, blue eyes are recessive. But most Norwegians and Estonians have blue eyes. Having a second toe that's longer than one's big toe (aka Morton's toe) is probably dominant (see Figure 3.4). But it's also rare. An even more dramatic example is **polydactyly** – having more than five fingers or toes. This trait is dominant, but I can count on one finger the number of people I've ever known who had an extra digit (my uncle Gary). If this still doesn't sound logical, consider some logic. The right-hand half of Figure 3.4 shows what would be expected if a small population of four people (one of whom was heterozygous for Morton's toe and three of whom were homozygous for "normal" toes) paired up in two couples and produced four children each. Like the parents, 25% of the children would have Morton's toe. Of course, this is just one particular example. But if you run through every logical possibility, dominant alleles simply don't become any more common than recessive alleles. A final way to illustrate this point about how dominant alleles don't outcompete recessive alleles is to recognize that dominant alleles don't obliterate recessive alleles, even when they do show up more often in phenotypes. My mom and dad possessed a grand total of two brown-eyed and two blue-eyed alleles. Their kids possessed a grand total of six brown-eyed and six blue-eyed alleles.

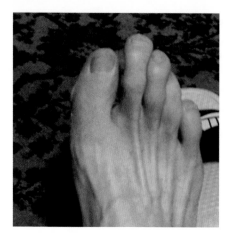

S = allele for second toe longest (Morton's toe). f = allele for first toe longest (normal).

Here's a population of 4 adults: Sf_{d1}, ff_{m1}, ff_{d2}, and ff_{m2}

Sf_{d1} mates with ff_{m1} and has four kids.   And ff_{d2} and ff_{m2} mate, too.

	Dad (Sf_{d1})	
Mom	Sf	ff
(ff_{m1})	Sf	ff

	Dad2 (ff_{d2})	
Mom	ff	ff
(ff_{m2})	ff	ff

Notice that 25% (1/4) of parents and 25% of kids (2/8) have Morton's toe.

Figure 3.4 *Dominant genes do not necessarily become more common over time.*

Post-Mendelian genetics

All this being said, one of the many things we've learned since Mendel published his landmark paper in 1866 is that pea plants don't tell the whole story of genetics. If Mendel had studied mice or people, he might have discovered things like incomplete dominance and codominance. **Incomplete dominance** happens when the alleles we get from different parents produce some kind of average. In the case of incomplete dominance, if you were to cross a homozygous white flower (WW) with a homozygous red flower (RR), the offspring would be pink. Something loosely akin to this happens when a tall parent and a short parent produce offspring of medium height. One complication is that height, like many other human traits, is determined by more than one gene. In fact, as many as 700 genes each appear to play a tiny role in height, although some genes are much more important than others (Marouli et al., 2017). Complicating things even further, some genes appear to influence height in men while having little or no effect in women (Ellis et al., 2001). This could explain why every male first or second degree relative of my old friend Jack is tall (most of them 6'2" to 6'7"). In contrast all of Jack's female first or second degree relatives are of average height (5'3" to 5'7"). That's not infinitely complex, but it's certainly not simple.

Speaking of complexities, inheritance can also happen by means of codominance. **Codominance** happens when two or more alleles express themselves to some degree (yes, many genes have more than two alleles). If codominance were at work in the simple case of flower color, red (RR) and white (WW) parent flowers might produce offspring with a mixture of red and white patches. As it turns out, a lot of human traits, including some major diseases, are determined by multiple genes. The last time I checked, geneticists had identified at least ten genes that increase a person's risk for late-onset Alzheimer's disease. In contrast, a single gene appears to determine whether someone will suffer from a rare form of early-onset Alzheimer's. If a person gets the recessive allele for this rare disorder from both parents, the person will almost certainly develop early-onset Alzheimer's. My wife is a bit worried by this fact because her father died of early-onset Alzheimer's. If her mom proved to be a carrier for this disease (luckily, few people are), my wife would have a 50% chance of developing this form of early-onset Alzheimer's herself (because her dad must have had both recessive alleles).

Quantitative genetics and heritability

Another important thing we've learned since Mendel is that once we move from pea plants to people, a lot of genetics proves to be **quantitative genetics**. Many human traits exist along a continuum. Further, the large majority of such continuous traits are influenced by multiple genes. Recall that as many as 700 genes seem to influence height. A person's risk for schizophrenia and autism both seem to be influenced by multiple genes (Gejman et al., 2010). Most physical and psychological abilities as well as most personality traits also appear to be influenced by quantitative genetics. A good understanding of quantitative genetics requires a lot of math, much of it resembling the math social scientists use to describe and draw inferences about non-genetic data. For example, quantitative geneticists describe the heritability of different traits (the degree to which the phenotype in question is influenced by genes rather than by environments) using a close cousin of r^2 (the coefficient of determination). This genetic statistic is h^2, the **heritability coefficient**. For a given trait, h^2 tells you how much nature typically matters (rather than nurture).

The word *typically* is important because in the case of many important quantitative genetic outcomes (e.g., height, IQ), genes can play a big role in how an organism turns out in highly favorable environments but matter very little in highly unfavorable environments (Turkheimer et al., 2003). The heritability coefficient, h^2, has a maximum value of 1.0 (meaning genes are all that matter) and a minimum value of 0.0 (meaning genes don't matter at all). *If a trait has a low heritability coefficient, natural selection can't act on it much.* This is because the trait is not passed down biologically from parents to offspring. On the other hand, if a trait has a big heritability coefficient, there are plenty of opportunities for the operation of natural selection because organisms who have high or low levels of this trait are very likely to produce offspring who resemble them. Although heritability can be defined many different ways, for example, there is an H^2 statistic that's a bit different from h^2, the simplest way to generate a heritability coefficient is by taking the average value parents have for a trait and using that average parent score across many parents to predict the measured phenotype for that trait in the offspring of all the parents.

The left-hand portion of Figure 3.5 provides a hypothetical example for height, which is known to be strongly genetic (h^2 = 0.81 here). Notice that tall parents almost always have tall children. Conversely, short parents almost always have short children. You can account for about 4/5 (0.81) of the variation in a child's height (within gender, of course) by knowing the average height of the child's parents. Height is highly heritable. The right-hand portion of Figure 3.5 provides a second example. If these hypothetical data were real, they'd suggest that a liking for *SpongeBob SquarePants* cartoons has no genetic component whatsoever (h^2 = 0.00 here). I choose attitudes about SpongeBob, by the way, to illustrate that if you can get the data, you can estimate the heritability of almost anything. As we'll see later, statistical tools such as this one are powerful and elegant, but they raise a lot of complex questions. For example, children don't just get genes from their parents. They also get the physical and social environments that parents often create. For now, though, suffice it to say that there are some clever techniques for disentangling genetic and environmental contributions to almost any observable trait (any phenotype). We'll see later in this chapter that heritability studies of twins separated at birth have some advantages over heritability studies of parents and their offspring, although even twin studies have their methodological limitations.

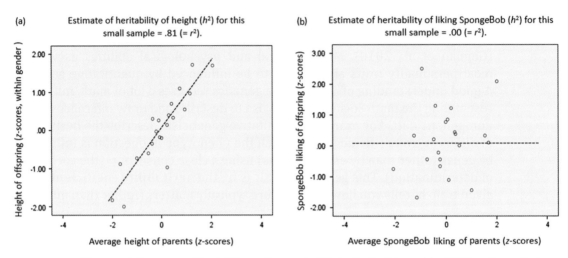

Figure 3.5 *Hypothetical heritability estimates for (a) physical height and for (b) liking SpongeBob SquarePants cartoons in a small sample.*

In both plants and animals, people included, there are lots of continuous traits that seem to be pretty heritable. A recent **meta-analysis** (a study of multiple studies) of hundreds of twin studies revealed that the average heritability coefficient of dozens of traits was 0.49 (Polderman et al., 2015). But heritability varied a great deal across traits. Whereas heritability was very high for height ($h^2 = 0.82$), it was extremely low for "gene expression" ($h^2 = 0.06$).

Modern quantitative genetics can also explain why so many of the traits biologists and psychologists study turn out to be **normally distributed** (following a **bell-shaped curve**). If a trait is influenced by a large number of genes, rather than just one, there are many, many genetic routes by which an organism can turn out about average, but many fewer routes by which the organism can prove to be extremely high or extremely low on the trait. Even if only five genes influence a trait, it will be the rare organism who happens to get only the versions of all five alleles that determine very high or very low levels of the trait in question. This basic idea (which is the quantitative genetic consequence of the *central limit theorem* in statistics) is illustrated in Figure 3.6. All the depicted examples assume that there are only two alleles for a gene and that the two alleles occur with equal frequency in the population. In the far left panel of Figure 3.6, you see the expected distribution of genotypes on a trait determined by a single gene. The distribution is flat. In the second panel, you can see that as soon as just two genes contribute (equally, we're assuming) to a trait, the distribution of scores on that trait begins to resemble the standard normal curve. As we move to the situation in which four and then six genes influence a trait, the frequency distribution becomes increasingly normal. The greater the number of alleles there are for the genes under consideration, by the way, the fewer genes you would need to begin to approximate the normal distribution (Yule, 1902). Notice that none of this logic applied to Mendel's work because he focused on dichotomous (either-or) traits that were determined by single genes.

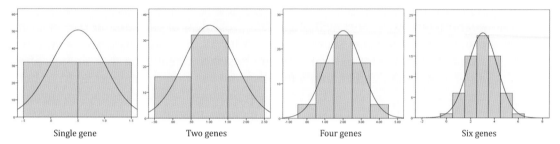

| Single gene | Two genes | Four genes | Six genes |

Figure 3.6 *When many genes influence a quantitative trait, the trait is more likely to be normally distributed. These examples assume all the genes have two equally frequent alleles. But the same logic holds if multiple alleles exist for some genes or if some genes matter more than others. The environment can also smooth out and normalize quantitative phenotypes (e.g., strength, extroversion).*

Mendel could have scarcely anticipated how far modern scientists would extend his basic genetic findings. For example, in Chapter 2, I mentioned that scientists have decoded the human genome. In contrast to genes and genotypes, genomes are much broader. The genome for a particular species refers to all the possible sets of genetic instructions that exist for making specific members of that species. This includes every possible allele that exists for every specific gene, as well as all the billions of possible nucleotides and their locations (e.g., within a specific codon, within a specific gene, within a specific chromosome). If I may recycle an automotive metaphor, the genome for a species is like the specific instructions for assembling every possible variation on a specific make and model of a car. For example, Toyota made 2012 RAV-4s in a variety of possible colors and trim packages, and 2012 RAV-4s probably came with or without sunroofs. In contrast, the size of the steering wheel might have been fixed for the 2012 RAV-4, while its color could have varied. The equivalent of the genome for this particular "species" of Toyota would specify unique potential combinations that don't exist in any actual cars. If we continue with this automotive metaphor, notice that the genotype would be the equivalent of the manufacturing instructions for creating one specific, concrete RAV-4. Further, the phenotype would be the way that specific RAV-4 existed not only as it rolled off the assembly line but many years later, after the battery and tires had been replaced, and after years of city driving had left dings on the body. The phenotype would also include some invisible aspects of this RAV-4. If Togo drove her RAV-4 cautiously and kept up with routine maintenance, the moving parts of the engine and transmission might still be in excellent condition after many years of use. In contrast, if Mitsuru treated his RAV-4 poorly, his particular RAV-4 might be near the end of its useful lifespan when most others were still going strong. Mendel surely knew that environments influence phenotypes. But he could not have known much about the differential role of genotypes versus phenotypes in natural selection.

Natural selection happens via genetic variation

One thing we've learned about genetics since Mendel is that in sexually reproducing organisms, genetic processes pave the way for evolution by guaranteeing that there will often be a great deal of variation in the offspring produced by the same set of parents. After all, if organisms didn't vary, there would be nothing for natural selection to select. One reason why siblings often differ from one another, and why offspring can differ dramatically from both their parents, is based on the way we reproduce. Sexual reproduction involves **meiosis** (sexual cell division), and meiosis magnifies variation because of **crossing over**. Crossing over means that shortly after a sperm fertilizes an egg, sex chromosomes from the father and the mother split down the middle. They eventually reassemble themselves, but for half of these split portions of a chromosome, some of the specific genes that came from your dad swap places with their exact counterparts that came from your mom (thus the term "crossing over").

To most people, crossing over is a pretty unfamiliar concept. So let's consider something more familiar – card games. From the perspective of a card game metaphor, every chromosome you possess is a handful of many genes (many cards) that have been passed down to you from your biological parents (with each parent providing some of the genes). Let's assume your father only has black cards (clubs and spades) and your mother only has red cards (hearts and diamonds). If you could only make new hands (new chromosomes) that took cards from one parent or the other, this would greatly limit your genetic options. During crossing over, however, meiosis creates unique hands (unique chromosomes) that contain a mixture of cards taken from one of your mother's chromosomes as well as cards taken from the "homologous" (matching) chromosome from your father. In these hands that are the results of "crossing over," you'd get a lot of combinations that would have been impossible in the absence of crossing over.

Crossing over during meiosis increases genetic variation among the offspring of sexually reproducing organisms (Wilson, 1978). Because it's often possible for organisms to have novel genotypes that neither of their parents had, there is more for natural selection to select. Imagine that two archaic short-necked giraffe parents produce a longer necked daughter who is able to reach leaves that other members of her species cannot reach. This could happen, for example, if two genes had to co-occur together in a chromosome to lengthen a giraffe's neck in a particular way. If this longer necked daughter outreproduces archaic giraffes with shorter necks, and if this happens for thousands, or even millions of years, giraffes may eventually evolve to be very long-necked. One caveat, of course, is that there would have to be no major changes in the availability of food at the treetops. Another caveat is that the two neck-lengthening genes in question must not be separated by crossing over in future generations of giraffes.

A good way to think about crossing over is that it means you can sometimes create a genetic win–win situation. Imagine that a troublesome allele for one gene and a wonderful allele for a different gene both exist on the same chromosome, say from mom. If crossing over didn't happen, anyone who got the wonderful allele from mom (say, for a great sense of humor) would also be guaranteed to get the troublesome allele (say, for easily fractured bones). But with crossing over, some lucky kid could end up being very humorous while being spared a weak humerus. Of course, some unlucky kids could be born with weak bones as well as a weak sense of humor. But evolution doesn't mind if some kids fall by the wayside. Presumably, the funny and strong-boned winners during meiosis would do well in the highly competitive game of evolution. Crossing over is just one of many examples of how genetics matter in evolution.

Another way to see how genetics matter in evolution is to see what happened to theories of evolution before we had any good theories of genetics. Charles Darwin was not the first person to use the term "evolution." In fact, Darwin's grandfather, Erasmus Darwin, espoused what is known as **Lamarckian evolution**, after French naturalist Jean Baptiste Lamarck. Unfortunately, this theory was as incorrect as it was ingenious. It was built on the flawed idea that animals pass onto their offspring the traits they acquired in their environments. By a Lamarckian account, giraffes evolved their long necks by repeatedly stretching them to reach higher and higher leaves in the trees of the African savannah. Lamarckians might also argue that monkeys who developed strong forearms by **brachiating** (swinging from branch to branch) could pass this acquired trait onto their offspring.

But this is not how evolution normally works. Singing or lifting weights does not usually change your genes in ways that make your children more musical or muscular. The only loose sense in which environments can change genes is that harsh environments can be a source of genetic mutations, which harm organisms more often than they help them. In the interest of thoroughness, I should add that even if environments don't usually change genes, it looks like they sometimes change which genes get expressed. Advocates of **epigenetic inheritance** argue that environments sometimes determine whether specific genes are turned on or turned off. Extreme stress, diet, or long-term drug ingestion, for example, may be capable of changing whether some genes get expressed at all. Epigenetic inheritance is very different than traditional genetic inheritance. For example, it can happen very quickly to large groups of organisms that find themselves in the same unusual environment (Kaati et al., 2002; Vassoler et al., 2013). Because epigenetic inheritance is about gene *expression* rather than actual genetic change, however, it is also less permanent than genetic mutation. Finally, I should say that there is still some controversy about the prevalence of epigenetic inheritance, especially in mammals. Further, even if we assume that epigenetic inheritance is real, the data so far suggest that it's an interesting exception to the usual rule of genetic inheritance rather than proof that Lamarck was correct after all.

It is amazing, then, that Darwin was able to develop the theory of evolution in the absence of a good theory of genetics. In fact, if you read Darwin carefully, you'll find that he occasionally sounds a bit Lamarckian. For example, he noted that domesticated animals often have floppy ears that are rarely seen in their wild equivalents. Instead of concluding that this is due to a genetic mutation, Darwin speculated that living in a world with few predators (and thus rarely having to perk up one's ears) weakened the muscles that would have otherwise kept the ears standing at attention. He then implies that this trait (floppy ears) could have been passed on to the offspring of such predator-inattentive animals. Even avid fans of epigenetic inheritance would reject this environmental explanation in favor of simple genetic mutation and selective breeding. Darwin was a genius, not a soothsayer.

So the main problem with Lamarckian (pre-Mendelian) models of evolution is that these old models proved to be genetically incorrect. Lamarck had no idea, for example, that there is an important difference between genotype and phenotype. Recall that my genotype includes an allele for blue eyes and an allele for brown eyes. But my phenotype is that I have brown eyes, period. As a more obvious example, my dad had the normal genes that code proteins in just the right ways to make ten fingers. But an accident as a teenager left him with nine and a half fingers. His genotype for fingers was normal; his phenotype was not. If Lamarck had been correct, my mom may have had to worry about my dad passing on his mostly missing finger to his offspring. Lamarck tackled an important question in a clever way, but he had the wrong idea about evolution because he had the wrong idea about genetics.

You may recall from Chapter 2 that the modern synthesis occurred when Darwin's theory of evolution was merged with modern genetic discoveries. It wasn't until scientists understood genetics that they could explain exactly how natural selection operates. Consider the boule gene discussed in Chapter 1. It's one thing to speculate that the ability to produce sperm may have been around for a long time. It's quite another to provide evidence that the boule gene has been around for about 600 million years, and to document that male crickets, male shrews, male octopi, and male garter snakes all need this specific gene to produce sperm. We cannot fully appreciate Darwin's theory – nor can we put it to some of its most critical tests – if we do not appreciate the basic principles of genetics.

Mutation and genetic variation

Meiosis is not the only process that creates genetic variation. The genetic process that has the most profound implications for natural selection is **mutation**. There are many forms of mutation, but they all involve some kind of genetic error. Errors mean that parents produce offspring whose genetic information differs a little from their own. The automotive metaphor that applies to genomes and genotypes also applies to mutations. Because of things like bombardment by radiation and copying errors, the genetic information in all living organisms can undergo changes. In long-lived species such as people, quite a few mutations can build up over the course of a lifetime. This is one reason why even the genotypes of identical twins are not absolutely identical. Only mutations that occur in sex cells (sperm and eggs) are passed on to one's offspring, by the way. Mutations in other cells only have obvious implications for evolution in that they can cause a parent to become ill or die. This may happen, for example, if a mutation causes cancer. Most geneticists argue that mutation is the workhorse of evolution. In fact, Nei (2013) has argued that mutation is the one and only driving force behind evolution. E.O. Wilson, who was a big fan of the evolutionary importance of meiosis, would surely disagree. But these two would surely agree that modern theories of evolution are tightly bound to modern theories of genetics. We can't understand evolution without appreciating mutations.

Let's begin with tiny mutations. Genes are long strings of protein-coding **nucleotides**. They contain lots of deoxyribonucleic acid (DNA) (see Figure 3.7). Sometimes, there are uncorrected copying mistakes in nucleotides that mean that a person has a **single nucleotide polymorphism (SNP)** (a variation in that nucleotide), making the person different from other people. Using the RAV-4 metaphor, an SNP (pronounced "snip") would be the rough equivalent of having an accidental word substitution in the instructions for making brake pads. It might replace a high-heat resin with Kevlar. By the way, a single nucleotide variant is called a "snip" only when a non-trivial percentage of the members of a species (say 1% or more) vary for this nucleotide. Sticking with the automobile metaphor, a particular SNP for brake pad construction could have no consequences, it could make the brake pads less efficient, or it could make them more efficient. In this last case, this "mistake" could become the new gold standard for brake pads (the equivalent of producing more surviving offspring in evolution). Despite the fact that mutation is rare, there are lots of snips. In fact, the National Institutes of Health (2018) says that there are about 10 million SNPs in the human genome. Although this figure is proportionately low (only about 1 in 300 nucleotides appear to vary meaningfully across people), recall that 10 million SNPs is way more than the number of genes we possess. SNPs are actually much more common in the genetic sequences between genes than they are in genes themselves. But the fact that they often occur between genes doesn't make them unimportant. SNPs appear to influence health and wellbeing (even when not contained within a gene). SNPs can influence susceptibility to specific diseases, responses to specific medications, and resilience in the face of exposure to specific environmental toxins.

adenine

thymine

cytosine

guanine

Figure 3.7 *A small section of DNA. An SNP would be a change in just one of the base pairs (e.g., from an adenine-thymine pair to a guanine-cytosine pair) in the tiny section of DNA you see here.*

Genetic variation comes about in a variety of ways. SNPs thus represent only one of many sources of genetic variation. Mutations can also produce variation in **multiple nucleotide polymorphisms** (the equivalent of two or more adjacent SNPs). There are also **copy number variations**, in which a string of several nucleotides is accidentally repeated, not to mention genetic errors such as "wobbles" and "transversions." Whatever specific form mutations take, they're important because evolution fueled only by error-free meiosis would surely be less powerful than it is. This doesn't mean we should be wishing for more mutations, by the way. Mutations are very rare, and they are part of a delicate evolutionary balancing act (Dawkins, 1976; Pray, 2008). If mutation ran amuck all the time, life as we know it would be impossible. On the other hand, in the complete absence of mutations, many organisms would quickly cease to exist. Consider Pray's (2008) summary of how accumulating mutations keep many harmful bacteria going in the face of concerted medical efforts to obliterate them:

> This [mutation] is one reason why antibiotic resistance is such an important public health problem; after all, mutations that accumulate in a population of bacteria provide ample genetic variation with which to adapt (or respond) to the natural selection pressures imposed by antibacterial drugs ... Take *E. coli*, for example. The genome of this common intestinal bacterium has about 4.2 million base pairs, or 8.4 million bases. Assuming a mutation rate of 10^{-9} ... every time *E. coli* divides, each daughter cell will have, on average, 0.0084 new mutations. Or, another way to think about it is like this: Approximately 1% of bacterial cells will contain a new mutation. That may not seem like much. However, because bacteria can divide as rapidly as twice per hour, a single bacterium can grow into a colony of 1 million cells in only about 10 hours ($2^{20} = 1,048,576$). At that point, approximately 10,000 of these bacteria will have accumulated at least one mutation. As the number of bacteria carrying different mutations increases, so too does the likelihood that at least one of them will develop a drug-resistant phenotype.

Getting back to sex cell mutations in big animals like us, the reason they're important to evolution is that such mutations are passed onto one's offspring. Some mutations can even lead directly to other mutations. Of course, mutations can sometimes lead to serious problems. I know a young man who has a heart condition that appears to be the result of a mutation (none of his relatives who have been tested have any genotypic or phenotypic signs of his disorder). But mutations may also lead to successful adaptations to particular environments. If *E. coli* bacteria could be thankful, they would surely appreciate mutation. Presumably, dolphins got their blowholes by means of a series of mutations that gradually moved their nostrils to a place that greatly facilitated breathing while swimming. Human beings have speech and an upright posture. Each of these is presumably the lucky result of numerous mutations. When mutations promote survival for a specific organism in a specific environment, they are often passed on. When they do not, they usually disappear. As we will see later, different species exist largely because of inherited mutations.

Genotype-environment correlations

Genes and genotypes do not exist in isolation. Genes build brains and bodies by coding for proteins. But, especially in social creatures such as people, development happens in complex environments. One cannot fully appreciate genetics without appreciating this basic fact. Geneticists have argued that there are typically positive **genotype-environment correlations**, because of three different ways in which genes create environments that tend to support their simple biological effects (Kendler & Baker, 2007; Scarr & McCartney, 1983). In honor of Mendel (and as a memory aid), I refer to this general model of genotype-environment effects as the **PEA model**. Each letter of "PEA" reflects a different way (passive, evocative, and active) in which genes can shape environments.

Perhaps the simplest way in which genes can produce environments that reinforce them is through **passive genotype-environment effects**. Children are typically reared not only by their biological parents but also by close relatives, who share many of their genes. On average, parents and siblings will share half their genes. Biological aunts, uncles, and grandparents (being second degree relatives) share a quarter. Because most of us grow up surrounded by others who share genes with us, we tend to live in worlds that foster the effects of most of our genes. You probably know a family or two in which everyone loves sports. Researchers such as Sandra Scarr would say that Jason didn't just become athletic because he was born with a lot of athletic talent. He also grew up surrounded by nimble siblings and competitive cousins. Any genes he got that predisposed him to be athletic were reinforced by the fact that he lived in a world full of jerseys, cleats, and helmets, usually filled with sweaty people. This doesn't just apply to athletics. My mom was both highly religious and highly empathic. She loved to read Bible stories to her children. But she didn't choose the story of David slicing off Goliath's head or God smiting the toddlers of Gomorrah. Instead, she selected stories such as Jesus healing the sick and the blind, or the Good Samaritan rescuing a stranger in distress. These are called passive genotype-environment effects because the developing person doesn't have to do anything to be exposed to the environment. It comes from others, who share the developing person's genes, and the developing person passively absorbs it.

But people, children included, are not always passive. **Evocative genotype-environment effects** exist because people possess inherited traits and preferences that may habitually evoke responses from other people. A child who is artistically gifted may catch the eye of her art teacher. A child who can sing well may become the teacher's pet in music class. Conversely, a child like me – who was naturally gifted at sinking and flailing in the water – was unlikely to be approached by any swim coaches. Notice that evocative effects may extend beyond the immediate family to include other members of one's tribe. When I was a child I hated hunting, and I was no good at it. You could even say I was a liability, if not a danger, in a two-person hunting team. The last time I remember going hunting, my dad sent me with his friend James, who was an excellent hunter. When I asked my dad why he'd paired me up with the best hunter, he replied, in James's presence: "Well, James ain't kin to us. And besides, he's the only one who's got life insurance." This comment evoked quite a bit of laughter, which is another example of evocative genotype-environment effects. My dad wouldn't have kept making such snide jokes if his friends and relatives didn't encourage him.

Moving beyond evocative effects, people actively choose some of their environments. **Active genotype-environment effects** exist because people with specific inclinations choose specific situations. Just as my brothers all gravitated toward sports, even in novel environments, my sister Rhonda gravitated toward art and music (my other sister gravitated toward privacy, and so I will respect that). I once had to choose between staying on the high school wrestling team and maintaining a high grade point average (GPA). (The wrestling coach gave everyone a low A in the "athletics" class one had to take to remain on the team, which brought down my GPA.) I was a mediocre wrestler, but a very good student. Despite pressure from my dad to stick with wrestling, I chose the academic route. I also actively sought out a sport, track and field, in which I could participate without reducing my GPA. Instead of opposing one another, then, genes and environments often go hand in hand.

A problem with the PEA model

As clever and influential as the PEA model is, I have a criticism of it. I think it's precisely because of the evocative component of the PEA model that **twin studies** sometimes overestimate the heritability of some traits – by overlooking some powerful environmental effects on human development. Consider the fact that twin studies suggest that IQ is highly heritable. Studies of monozygotic (identical) versus dizygotic (fraternal) twins show that **monozygotic twins** tend to have very similar IQs (the twin pair correlations for IQ are very high), whereas **dizygotic twins** have only somewhat similar IQs (the twin pair correlations are much more modest). The logic of twin studies seems airtight. We know that monozygotic twins share virtually all their genes, whereas dizygotic twins share only half their genes. So, if identical twins behave in a more similar fashion than fraternal twins, this would seem to be due to the extra genes shared by identical twins. A few methodologically rigorous twin studies even focus on twins who were separated at birth. Such twins obviously grow up in different places, with different parents, for example. Twin studies are clever but the unusual studies that focus on twins separated at birth are even cleverer.

But there's a problem with the design of twins studies, including studies of twins separated at birth, which is that identical twins look almost exactly alike. In fact, a close look at the heritability of the traits assessed by Polderman et al. (2015) shows that many observable physical traits, such as height, structure of the mouth, weight maintenance functions, and shape of the eyeball (which will determine if a person needs eyeglasses) have very h^2 values (high heritability coefficients). In practice, this means that if Leslie is tall, thin, and beautiful, with olive skin and curly hair, you can be confident that her identical twin sister has all these same physical traits. You can thus be pretty sure that even if Leslie grew up in Sarasota while her twin grew up in Minnesota, the physical appearance of Leslie and her twin would evoke similar responses among teachers, coaches, romantic suitors, police officers, and adoptive parents.

If people accurately judge other people's IQ and personality from their height, weight, and level of physical attractiveness, one could argue that these are valid examples of evocative genotype-environment correlations. The problem, though, is that people strongly assume that many physical traits are associated with psychological traits (IQ, sociability, leadership, etc.) that have little or nothing to do with them. For example, research shows that we judge physically attractive people to be much more sociable, honest, and competent than physically unattractive people (Eagly et al., 1991). All the twins you see in Figure 3.8 are physically attractive. But you can imagine that if they were highly unattractive, their physical appearance would consistently evoke lukewarm – if not negative – reactions from strangers worldwide. And recall that identical twins don't just share the same faces; they also share the same heights, body types, hair colors, skin tones, and often the same shoe sizes and eyeglass prescriptions, not to mention the same biological sex.

Figure 3.8 *Four sets of identical twins. Even if we were to separate these twins at birth, research shows that, for all their lives, the individual members of each twin pair would be treated in similar ways by others, which means that the identical twins were not truly "separated" after all.*

To see how powerful stereotypes about physical appearance can be, consider a few examples. Jennifer Eberhardt studies Afrocentrism – the degree to which people (including those within a specific ethnic group) have features stereotypically associated with African Americans. These include features such as dark skin, large lips, and broad noses. In a group of Black men who had been convicted of killing White victims, Eberhardt et al. (2006) found that the more Afrocentric facial features Black men possessed, the more likely they were to receive the death penalty. This was true after controlling for a long list of known predictors of who receives the death penalty, such as aggravating circumstances, severity of the murder, and even the defendant's level of physical attractiveness. Even after controlling for these important confounds, Black men with a more stereotypically Black appearance were twice as likely as Black men with a less stereotypically Black appearance to be given a death sentence. Notice that all these men self-identified as Black. So this is not a simple matter of ethnic categorization as it's usually defined. Further, I hope it's clear that if any of these men had identical twins, these men and their twins would receive almost identical Afrocentrism scores. Physical appearance is highly heritable. Furthermore, it plays a huge role in social perception, and sometimes in ways that it logically should not.

No one knows this better than Bulgarian psychology professor Alexander Todorov. Todorov has identified the specific facial cues people use to judge traits, such as attractiveness, dominance, extraversion, and trustworthiness (Olivola & Todorov, 2010; Todorov et al., 2015). The gist of this research is that people who live in the same culture share many of the same largely inaccurate stereotypes about physical appearance and personality traits. Figure 3.9 shows four computer-generated human faces (for hands-on demonstrations, go to https://tlab.princeton.edu/demonstrations/), each of which reliably evokes the listed judgment in most people. Almost no one thinks the artificial guy labeled "incompetent" will outrun, outsmart, or outwrestle the artificial guy labeled "competent." Likewise, few people would judge the artificial man labeled "unattractive" as more honest or sociable than the artificial woman labeled "attractive."

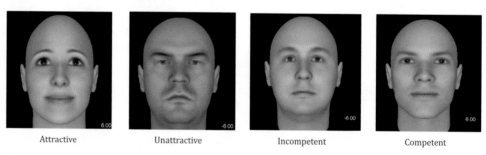

| Attractive | Unattractive | Incompetent | Competent |

Figure 3.9 *Four computer-generated faces that evoke dramatically different judgments of attractiveness and competence.*

We also make strong assumptions about other people's personalities based on their height, especially for men. Taller people are much more likely than shorter people to be elected to leadership positions, and taller people earn more money than shorter people (Rietveld et al., 2015). The average height of male U.S. senators is about 6'2". U.S. presidents also tend to be much taller than average. Furthermore, taller presidents have typically been perceived as stronger leaders than shorter ones – compare Washington, Jefferson, and Lincoln with Carter, Hoover, and McKinley. There is some controversy about whether taller people actually have superior leadership skills or are just perceived that way. My sense of this literature is that taller people have more self-confidence than shorter people, which is certainly one asset when it comes to leadership. However, when it comes to mastery of managerial, organizational, or interpersonal skills, I know of no conclusive data showing that tall people have any big advantages over their shorter peers, although see Schick and Steckel (2015) who would beg to differ.

The fact that we're quick to judge a book by its cover doesn't completely invalidate studies of identical twins. It just complicates them. It means that when we try to disentangle genetic and environmental effects, we must remember that genes strongly influence physical appearances – in ways that could easily masquerade as much simpler genetic effects. For example, because people are quick to judge competence from physical appearance, this raises tough questions about whether identical twins have similar IQs because they have inherited equally beautiful minds or because they have inherited equally beautiful faces. It would be remiss of me if I did not mention that most evolutionary psychologists put a lot more stock in twin studies than I do. For a thoughtful discussion of this issue that favors nature (the heritability of specific traits) over nurture (the power of culturally shared stereotypes), see Pinker (2002).

By the way, assuming I'm correct about the power of stereotypes, there are probably good evolutionary reasons why we rely so heavily on cues such as height and physical attractiveness when judging others. Many thousands of years ago, sheer physical size may have been an extremely important trait to have in a leader. If size didn't matter in physical battles, the biblical story of David and Goliath would be a lot less interesting. It is conceivable that preferring big and tall people as leaders is a leftover from the Pleistocene. It certainly goes back as far as 1 Samuel, 17. Further, as noted in Chapter 1, beautiful human faces have historically been healthier human faces. Thus, evolution may have programmed us to put a lot more stock in physical attractiveness than we need to in the modern world. Now that deadly diseases that once ravaged our appearance are largely under medical control, perhaps we needn't care as much as we once did about beauty.

But, as we will see later in this text, formerly adaptive judgmental biases that have been around for many, many millennia don't disappear in a mere century just because a guy named Fleming invented antibiotics. Haselton and Buss's (2000) **error management theory** could be taken to suggest, for example, that overvaluing attractiveness is probably a better evolutionary bet than undervaluing it. The essence of error management theory is that judgmental biases that promoted survival and reproduction in the world in which we evolved might still be favored today. It might be better, for example, to overestimate anger in unfamiliar human faces than to underestimate it (Haselton & Funder, 2006).

From the perspective of error management theory, the tendency to assume that beautiful people possess many highly favorable personality traits might continue to hold today, especially in places where lots of people still die from communicable diseases. In fact, Gangestad et al. (2006) showed that human preferences for attractive versus unattractive faces are stronger than usual in nations where communicable illnesses are more common. Even in the healthiest nations, however, the preference for attractive faces had not disappeared altogether. Even newborns show a robust preference for looking at attractive as opposed to unattractive faces (Slater & Quinn, 2001). If a preference appears in people who are only a few hours old, it's highly unlikely that the preference is learned. Of course, plenty of other stereotypes are culturally transmitted (and thus learned). But the preference for beautiful faces seems to be hardwired. To the degree that either evolution or culture has programmed us to pay too much attention to physical appearances, genes for traits like height or physical attractiveness (which are both highly heritable) may be hard to disentangle from genes for leadership, sociability, or intelligence (which are probably less so). As clever as twin studies are, they cannot fully separate the effects of genotypes from the effects of stereotypes.

Does the fact that we cannot always separate genotype from phenotype make genetics unimportant? Absolutely not. In fact, genes do strongly influence traits such as height and looks, and we had better appreciate that fact. Further, I'm not saying nothing else is genetic; just that some things may have lower true heritability coefficients than the h^2 values would seem to suggest. Finally, in my view, the most important ways in which genes matter is that they are the stuff of speciation (to be discussed later in this chapter). Many important genes in people are *fixed*, meaning that there is only one version of the alleles for this gene. When this is true, geneticists use the term **fixed allele** to say that this variant of a gene is shared by practically everyone on earth. Many of these fixed genes create important traits we share with all animals, all vertebrates, all mammals, or all primates. Many other fixed genes are what make us uniquely human. For example, the genes for an upright posture, finger dexterity, abstract language use, a huge neocortex, and a relatively low level of sexual dimorphism are fixed in human beings. Even people with severe developmental disorders, for example, usually learn to comprehend and produce speech. All people share 100% of their genome with other human beings. Further, human beings appear to share more than 99% of their exact genetic makeup (nucleotide by nucleotide) with other human beings. Genes make us who we are as a species.

A CLOSER LOOK AT NATURAL SELECTION

Natural selection vis-à-vis artificial selection

So, without the genetic transmission of traits from parents to their offspring, there could be no natural selection and thus no evolution as we know it. But how, exactly, does natural selection work? Before revisiting natural selection, I'd like to address a common critique of it. How could a mindless, disinterested process involving copying errors and competition produce 8.7 million distinct forms of life? It seems odd to many people that natural selection could populate a planet in a completely mindless way. But Darwin argued that natural selection is just another impersonal scientific rule, no different than Boyle's gas laws or the universal law of gravitation. Darwin came to many of his conclusions about natural selection by making careful observations of artificial selection. For example, he devotes most of the first chapter of his 1859 book to animal husbandry (selective breeding). People have been trying to increase the size, health, and milk production capacity of cattle for several thousand years. It's a similar story for dogs and ducks as well as hens and horses, not to mention pigs and pigeons. Darwin argued that animal breeders have long been hijacking natural selection – in a fervent, goal-directed effort to do what natural selection does aimlessly. He further argued that many dramatically different breeds of specific domesticated animals (say, pigeons) probably descended from a single species of wild ancestor, although he was willing to grant an exception for dogs. The pervasive belief at the time was that each distinct breed of a domesticated animal was descended from a different species of wild ancestor. Darwin was more insightful than he realized. We now know that all breeds of domestic dog are merely wolves that have been tinkered with for a few thousand years. All dogs essentially are wolves. Tea cup poodles and wolves could produce healthy, fertile offspring. Darwin also recognized that natural selection – the route by which species evolve – is not mindful the way artificial selection is.

Can a blind system with no intentions or assembly instructions really yield evolution via natural selection? Let's follow Darwin's lead and look at artificial selection. In his book *Adapt*, Tim Harford (2011) describes how, many years ago, evolutionary geneticist Steve Jones helped Unilever develop a highly efficient nozzle to produce powdered laundry detergent. The nozzle Unilever had been using was supposed to create a fine mist of detergent that could be sprayed into the air for drying, and then, once dry, packed into millions of cardboard boxes for use in laundry machines worldwide. But the best nozzle Unilever's engineers could create was woefully inefficient. Instead of trying to outengineer the engineers, Jones capitalized on what he knew about natural selection. He began with the nozzle design that wasn't doing the trick and generated ten random variations on this design. He chose the best of these ten "mutated" designs the way natural selection might choose the best of ten designs for a terrapin shell or a finch beak. Jones kept the one design that functioned best in a spray test, while mercilessly killing off the other nine designs. He then created ten random variations on the winning stage-two design. Next, Jones tested these ten new variations to see how effectively they sprayed detergent into the air. The winner survived; the losers bit the dust. Jones repeated this artificial selection process 45 times. In the end, 449 less-than-optimal designs had all gone extinct, and the design that remained proved to be incredibly efficient. Of course, no one knew why. Notice that Jones didn't need to be a good engineer. A mindless system in which random variations on an original entity competed for survival led to the evolution of a highly efficient species of detergent nozzle. I can think of no better example of how natural selection works than this. The basic principles that make natural selection work can "design" virtually anything, in the complete absence of any goals or intentions.

Not just selective fitness: inclusive fitness

Unlike Unilever's single-function nozzles, living organisms do many different things. They may have to forage for food, avoid predators, mate, find fresh sources of drinking water, and perhaps even care for their young, to name a few. So natural selection in animals can be a lot more complex than it was in Unilever's detergent lab. This means that specific adaptations that promote fitness in some ways (e.g., calls that attract mates) may compromise it in others (e.g., by attracting predators as well). Natural selection is often a balancing act. On the other hand, some seemingly costly traits or behaviors may prove to be highly adaptive as long as they pay evolutionary dividends that make up for their costs. One of the most important evolutionary insights along these lines came from evolutionary biologist Bill Hamilton. Hamilton (1964) argued that Darwin's classic notion of selective fitness needed to be expanded.

Rather than just considering **personal fitness** (the number of viable offspring an animal produces), we need to consider **inclusive fitness** – the number of copies of its genes, or "offspring equivalents," an organism produces. Often there is no practical difference between these two concepts. Male redback spiders who offer themselves up as meals to their mates increase their personal fitness and their inclusive fitness, because they have more offspring when they do so. But consider social insects such as ants, bees, and termites. By virtue of **haplodiploidy**, female workers in these highly social species often share 75% of their genes with one another. This means that a female who sacrifices herself for the good of even two of her sisters looks like a loser in the game of personal fitness but is a winner in the game of inclusive fitness. Hamilton offered **Hamilton's rule** to address the evolution of altruism (seemingly unselfish helping). Hamilton wished to explain how seemingly unselfish behavior one organism directed at another could sometimes prove to be a good evolutionary bet. However, Hamilton's rule applies just as well to routine parenting behavior as it does to helping a niece or cousin in distress. So, nursing your own young or adopting your niece could be examined through the lens of Hamilton's rule just as appropriately as stinging a bear that is raiding your hive's honeycomb or making an alarm call to warn your siblings of an eagle's presence. Hamilton's rule states that costly behaviors are evolutionarily plausible (because they will increase inclusive fitness) when rb > c:

r refers to genetic **relatedness** – the proportion of genes shared by the two organisms in question

b refers to the fitness-relevant **benefits** to the recipient of the helpful action

c refers to the reproductive **costs** to the organism engaging in the apparently altruistic act.

It has been harder than one might think to devise stringent tests of Hamilton's rule. As you can see in Figure 3.10, figuring out relatedness is easy (assuming you know some genealogies or can do genetic testing). But good operational definitions of b (benefits) and c (costs) are very hard to come by. Nonetheless, it's clear that according to this rule, organisms should be most likely to help those with whom they share the most genes. Even if you love your cousin and your sister equally, you should be more willing to donate a kidney to your sister than to your cousin. Further, you should be more likely to loan $500 to your cousin than to an equally trusted acquaintance.

We'll return to Hamilton's rule in Chapter 9 on helping behavior. For now, though, I should note that a few clever researchers have found good ways to test Hamilton's rule. Gorrell and colleagues (2010) studied more than 2,000 litters of red squirrels in the Yukon in Canada for 19 years. They examined adoption of orphaned baby squirrels as a form of extreme helping by nursing mother squirrels. Adoption in red squirrels is rare and thus hard to document. In fact, the

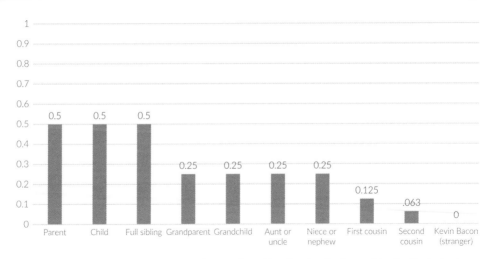

Figure 3.10 *Relatedness coefficients as they apply to Hamilton's rule. For an identical twin (not shown) the relatedness coefficient would be 1.0 (virtually all genes shared). Note that offspring equivalents make relatedness a directional concept. Grandmothers should help granddaughters more than granddaughters help grandmothers, because grandmothers are usually done having offspring.*

researchers could identify only 34 cases in which adoption was possible – and 5 cases in which it happened – in these 19 years of data. Because red squirrels are highly asocial (solitary) creatures, this low adoption rate isn't as surprising as it might otherwise sound. Although the number of adoptions was admittedly small, the study provided a great test of Hamilton's rule.

By virtue of careful observations and genetic testing, Gorrell et al. (2010) knew the relatedness (r) of all the orphaned squirrels and the nursing moms who adopted them. They calculated b as the likelihood that an adopted nursing squirrel would survive post adoption (the likelihood of it surviving otherwise was zero). They calculated c as the reduction in the likelihood of survival of the other squirrels in the litter to which the adoptive mothers had given birth themselves. As an obvious example, if adopting a baby squirrel who was barely related to you meant that even one of your own baby squirrels would likely die, it would be an evolutionarily foolish gamble to adopt the orphan in question. Gorrell et al. found that orphaned squirrels who were lucky enough to be adopted were always adopted by relatives, despite the fact that their deceased moms had lived closer to more non-relatives than relatives. Further, the mothers who adopted these orphans seem to have known when doing so was a good Hamiltonian bet. Adoptive mothers weren't just relatives; they were usually close relatives (e.g., an older sister from a previous litter). Furthermore, the litters of adoptive mothers were small enough that the costs of adoption were low, although certainly not negligible. As Gorrell et al. (2010) put it:

> We found that females did suffer fitness costs of adoption through reduced survival of their own juveniles, but this cost was offset by the inclusive fitness gained when the adopted juvenile was closely related. Further, although females had the opportunity to contravene Hamilton's rule by adopting unrelated juveniles or more than one related juvenile, they never did so.

Apparently, Hamilton's rule rules. Inclusive fitness appears to be even more important than personal fitness, at least in red squirrels.

Notice that Hamilton's rule is pretty consistent with Dawkins' idea that evolution is all about the survival of genes rather than organisms. The r (for relatedness) in Hamilton's rule is the proportion of your genes you share with a potential recipient of your helpful act. Just as organisms may sometimes sacrifice themselves to produce more offspring, Hamilton's rule suggests that organisms may sometimes expose their own living offspring to a little extra risk if they can greatly increase the likelihood that a needy niece or nephew will survive. The bottom line in evolution is that genes become more common in a population when the organisms that carry them around are more likely to pass them on to future generations. And this is why Hamilton's rule is directional. Grandmothers help granddaughters a lot more often than granddaughters help grandmothers. This makes evolutionary sense because grandmothers are usually done producing offspring. This is why Dawkins (1976) said we are all "survival machines" – biological robots that merely do the bidding of our selfish genes. Hamilton's rule means that stinging a hungry bear, even if it kills you, or nursing a hungry daughter, even if it weakens you, can sometimes be considered selfish in a Darwinian sense.

Adaptation vs. exaptation

Recall that an adaptation is a specific physical trait, ability, or preference that presumably helps facilitate reproduction (or inclusive fitness, to be broader) in a particular species in a particular environment. Adaptations are the successful end product of natural selection. Extremely dexterous fingers in people, blowholes in dolphins, and large canines in tigers are all adaptations. More invisible properties such as antibiotic resistance in bacteria, a preference for sweets, the ability to digest acorns, the ability to hibernate, or a preference for attractive faces are also adaptations. Sometimes, though, a trait or ability that evolved as a solution to one problem turns out to be a good solution to a very different problem. An elephant's trunk is an extreme example. Elephants use their trunks to pick up heavy logs, sniff out food or water, greet one another, strip leaves from trees, and spray or transport several liters of water. An elephant's trunk can also serve as a snorkel, making it a lot easier than it would be otherwise for elephants to cross deep bodies of water.

I'm not sure what initially drove the evolution of the elephant's trunk, but I'd be very surprised if it evolved as a snorkel first and then proved to be good for picking things up. So, elephants use their trunks as snorkels when they need to – even though snorkeling pressures are presumably not what drove their evolution. When a useful adaptation is put to a secondary or tertiary use, the later use is considered an **exaptation** (Gould & Vrba, 1982). Trunks have so many good uses that it's hard to know for sure which use (the adaptation) came first. A simpler example of exaptation comes from birds. It looks like feathers first evolved for the same reason fur did – thermoregulation. But the same feathers that served as insulation also proved to facilitate elevation. Because the insulation function came first, this was the adaptation; providing extra lift during flight proved to be the exaptation.

There is a lot of debate about how useful the concept of exaptation is. Daniel Dennett (1993) has argued that because evolution always repurposes things, almost any adaptation can reasonably be considered an exaptation. Are mammalian legs, which appear to have evolved from the fins of fishes, an adaptation or an exaptation? What about the vertebrate eye? Lamb (2011) has shown that the complex vertebrate eye began as a primitive light-detecting device that helped organisms regulate their circadian rhythms. It was essentially a day or night detector. With a few million years of gradual modification, the eye became the much more complex detector of electromagnetic radiation that allows us to know where we are going before we even get there. This, too, would seem like an exaptation, or co-opted adaptation to be more specific (see Buss et al., 1998). Using vision to navigate the environment is dramatically different from merely knowing whether it's daytime.

The story of exaptation is also complicated by the fact that some adaptations are inherently complex. Some adaptations, by their very nature, can do many specific things. Human hands did not specifically evolve to type, thread needles, or play the cello. But the incredible fine motor control the human hand allows appears to have evolved. Many of Gould and Vrba's (1982) prime examples of exaptation involved complex structures and behaviors. Further, focusing specifically on human evolution, Gould (1991) argued that behaviors as diverse as language, art, music, warfare, and religion are likely to be exaptations. Buss et al. (1998) argued that, as intriguing as the concept of exaptation may be, it may not have much **heuristic value**, that is, it may not easily lead to any specific, testable research hypotheses. Buss et al. argued that, in contrast, the original idea of adaptation has led to dozens of major research programs. Pigliucci and Kaplan (2000) framed the exaptation debate a little differently. They noted that Gould's main point about adaptation was that adaptation should not always be taken as a given. In essence, they argued that we must avoid the "just so" stories mentioned in Chapter 2. This idea has many implications.

First, evolution can occur in many ways, not solely via adaptation. For example, because of **bottlenecks**, there may be a dramatic reduction in genetic variation in a particular species when most of them are killed off in a single generation. **Founder effects** are similar. If only seven birds of a particular species make their way to a specific island, and they all have white-tipped feathers, all their offspring may carry this trait. For a variety of reasons, then, some traits may exist more by virtue of chance than by virtue of adaptation to specific environments. Pigliucci and Kaplan (2000) further argued that Gould's analysis of exaptations was meant as a critique of researchers who merely identified what seemed adaptive after the fact – without having done due diligence in setting up competing hypotheses.

I'm not sure there will ever be a resolution to the adaptation-exaptation debate. I take the debate as a reminder that some complex things that might never evolve in a single step could have evolved in intermediate steps. Ideally, of course, a fossil record would clearly reveal those intermediate steps. Sometimes, these intermediate steps provided intermediate levels of the same benefit conferred by the adaptation in question. At other times, the intermediate steps may have conferred very different benefits. Consider the evolution of flight in birds (post-feathers). Before there were eagles or hummingbirds, there were apparently proto-birds that could fly short distances with a running start. Being able to fly even short distances could certainly have helped the first feathered fliers escape a predator (Dial et al., 2008). So half-wings were presumably an inferior version of modern wings, in that they allowed proto-birds to fly a little. In that sense, flight was an adaptation. Grasping arms gradually became flapping wings. And once they were wings, they were no longer any good for grasping. In contrast, as noted previously, the elephant's trunk seems more like an exaptation. This being said, I wonder if some exaptations might seem more like adaptations if we sliced them up a bit. The thing we call an elephant's trunk is actually several distinct things. It includes a highly elongated set of nostrils and a highly muscular lifting device – with two or three finger-like pincers at the tip. Likewise, the human brain contains highly specialized areas for speech (e.g., Broca's area) as well as a highly specialized prefrontal cortex that sometimes keeps us from saying things we'd later regret. To produce speech, we also need the complex vocal apparatus that other primates lack. So, is speech an exaptation, or is it a specific adaptation that took root in an extremely social, big-brained primate – who could already make crude vocalizations?

Sexual selection

One of the most dramatic forms of natural selection is known as sexual selection. In addition to things like staying warm in the snow, or extracting nectar from flowers, many organisms seem to have put a lot of their evolutionary eggs in the mating basket. This is **sexual selection** – the evolution of specific traits or behaviors that serve no purpose other than attracting mates. In fact, some forms of sexual selection may be major liabilities outside the context of mating. Darwin himself seems to have been both delighted and stupefied by the peacock's elaborate tail. It's easy to imagine how evolution could program peahens to prefer males who were healthy and agile enough to grow brilliant and enormous tail feathers. But Darwin also recognized that sporting such an elaborate tail must have compromised the ability of peacocks to forage for food or escape predators. One thing we know for sure, however, is that sexual selection is not just a "just so" story. Experiments with birds that seem to show evidence of sexual selection reveal that some specific physical traits are absolutely irresistible to members of the opposite sex. Here's Jared Diamond's (1992, p. 118) vibrant description of how biologist Malte Andersson documented this in long-tailed widowbirds:

> In this species the male's tail in the breeding season grows to twenty inches long, while the female's tail is only three inches. Some males are polygamous and acquire up to six mates, at the expense of other males who get none. Biologists had guessed that a long tail served as an arbitrary signal by which males attracted females to join their harems. Hence Andersson's test was to cut off parts of the tails from nine males so that their tails were only six inches long. He then glued those cut segments to the tails of nine other males to give them thirty inch tails, and he waited to see where the females built their nests. It turned out that the males with the artificially lengthened tails attracted on average over four times as many mates as the males with artificially shortened tails.

To female widowbirds, size definitely matters. Of course, sexual selection is not always so extreme. The bright red feathers of male cardinals appear to be highly attractive to female cardinals, whose feathers are pretty drab. You may recall from

Chapter 1 that variations on this colorful plumage theme exist for many other birds, although they rarely approach what we see in peacocks or widowbirds. Along similar lines, swollen red rumps (technically, anogenital regions) in female olive baboons let male baboons know when female baboons are getting ready to ovulate. These swellings are literally a pain in the butt, and they expose female baboons to injuries and infections to which they would not otherwise be exposed. But they drive male baboons crazy, and thus their evolutionary costs are offset by the mating advantages they create. Some have argued that features such as permanently enlarged breasts in women and facial hair in men are products of sexual selection. If nothing else, such features advertise that a person has made it through puberty. Along similar lines, the pheromones many animals release when they are sexually receptive and the ability to detect those pheromones (with your trunk, if you're an elephant) seem to be examples of sexual selection.

As another example, male Mormon crickets attract mates by producing large **spermatophores**, nutrient-rich gift packets that also contain their semen. Spermatophores can weigh 25% of the body weight of an adult male Mormon cricket. We'll revisit spermatophores in Chapter 8. For now, suffice it to say that female Mormon crickets strongly prefer males who offer larger gift packets. In cases such as this, an unusual trait or behavior evolves specifically because it attracts mates. Sometimes, it's obvious why the attractive feature would be desirable. Bigger spermatophores provide more nutrition to female recipients. In the case of the peacock, though, it's less obvious why an elaborate tail is a good asset. The sense in which it appears to be so is that males who can survive and maintain gorgeous tails are probably healthier than those who cannot. Johnstone (1995) argued that forms of sexual selection that seem arbitrary at first blush often prove to be based on **honest predictors** – desirable traits that one must usually possess to display the cue that is highly attractive to potential mates. In the case of birds like peacocks and widowbirds, Johnstone argued that if only the fittest male birds can survive while carting along those elaborate tails, then female birds who choose mates based on this cue will maximize their own inclusive fitness (by producing sturdier and healthier offspring).

"Well, if it isn't CJ – with a big bag of sperm and nutrients! How can a lady say no to THAT!?"

Sexual selection also seems to apply to people. The fact that people are somewhat sexually dimorphic is one potential example. On average, men are taller, more muscular, and hairier than women. Most women also prefer tall men over short men, and almost all women prefer men who are taller than they are (Stulp et al., 2013). Dev Singh (1993) also showed that men prefer women with a low **waist-to-hip ratio** (an hourglass shape with a small waist). Further, Singh found that a low waist-to-hip ratio may be an honest predictor of fertility. In a study of patients at a fertility clinic, women with a lower waist-to-hip ratio were more likely to get pregnant over the course of the study. Lewis et al. (2015) note that male preferences for an "angle of lumbar curvature" in women suggests greater female fertility.

Are people really so shallow when judging mates? There is certainly variation in what body shapes people find attractive. However, the waist-to-hip ratio bias appears to be cross-culturally robust and independent of things such as body mass index (Singh et al., 2010). As noted earlier in this chapter, we also know that people are strongly attracted to others with beautiful faces, and this is especially true in harsh environments (Gangestad et al., 2006). Recall that the preference for attractive faces exists even in neonates, for whom culture has not yet kicked in. Singh's cross-cultural data notwithstanding, it's a little harder to know for sure if the preference most heterosexual men have for the hourglass shape is cross-culturally pervasive. Let me add, as usual, that the existence of a bias does not mean that it is fair or good. I don't think it's morally acceptable to bombard shoppers with ads for sugary drinks. Neither is it OK to advertise cars, or women's clothing, using dangerously thin and artificially beautiful faces. In fact, being aware of the inherent appeal of sugary foods and symmetrical faces arguably puts us in a better position than we might otherwise be in to resist the power of such stimuli. Finally, sexual selection in people appears to be less dramatic than it is in animals. It would presumably be a lot easier to find a woman who goes for wimpy, unattractive men than to find a peahen who goes for a peacock without a tail. As you can see in Figure 3.11, a gray peacock without any tail feathers just isn't very sexy.

Figure 3.11 *A healthy, mature peacock loses his avian sex appeal if you take away his fan and his vivid colors.*

It would be surprising if sexual selection in people proved to be as simple as it is in peacocks or Mormon crickets. It would be even more surprising, however, if sexual selection proved not to apply to people at all. When advertisers, cosmetic surgeons, and BMW dealers try to sell us their products and services, they may often capitalize on preferences grounded in sexual selection. Along these lines, some have argued that **conspicuous consumption**, such as buying and showing off fancy cars, homes, clothing, and jewelry, is grounded in sexual selection (de Fraja, 2009). How could I afford this mansion or this Maserati if I weren't bringing in the big bucks?

As suggested by many cases of conspicuous consumption, sexual displays in people may be behavioral as well as physical. In skate parks in Brisbane, Australia, Ronay and von Hippel (2010) asked male skateboarders if they would mind being videotaped while trying an easy and a difficult trick (they also paid the skateboarders for doing so). Their field experiment had one simple manipulation, which was whether the experimenter was a young man or a beautiful 18-year-old woman (who was blind to predictions). Ronay and von Hippel found that the presence of the beautiful female observer increased the skaters' risk-taking behavior. In the presence of the attractive female experimenter, male skaters were more likely to complete a highly challenging maneuver and more likely to bite the dust. Perhaps my favorite part of this study is the author's description of their manipulation check – which they report so readers can be sure these young men really felt the young woman was "hot." In addition to reporting highly favorable ratings of the woman's photo made by men who did not take part in the study, Ronay and von Hippel (2010, p. 59) also reported that "these attractiveness ratings were corroborated by many informal comments and phone number requests from the skateboarders." Although no teenagers were seriously harmed in the making of this research, I hope you can see that sexual selection can sometimes make people try dangerous things.

Finally, in addition to making people behave stupidly, sexual selection may sometimes make people behave splendidly. Farrelly et al. (2016) found that when it comes to long-term mating decisions, women prefer homely men who are described as having behaved altruistically (e.g., jumping in a raging river to save a child, feeding a homeless person) over handsome men who are described as having chosen not to help in the same scenarios. Nice guys may not *always* finish last.

Speciation

As you know, scientists estimate that there are about 8.7 million species of life on earth. The most common definition of a species is a group of organisms whose genome is similar enough that they can interbreed and produce fertile offspring. But based on routine natural selection, exaptation, sexual selection, and less predictable phenomena such as bottlenecks and genetic drift, organisms sometimes change dramatically over time. Sometimes, the same common ancestor can gradually become two or more species. At other times, a single species will gradually morph into only one new species (e.g., as a wet area becomes much drier). As the title of his 1859 book suggested, Darwin certainly appreciated the gist of this basic idea. Darwin made a controversial argument for speciation – the process by which a new species evolves when it had never before existed.

There are several ways in which speciation happens. One common route to speciation is **isolation**. When this happens, members of the same species become physically separated, adapt to very different environments, and eventually become so different that they're no longer considered members of the same species. Despite the fact that the human genome is pretty similar to the chimpanzee genome, people and chimps are clearly distinct species. We have different numbers of chromosomes, for example, and we cannot interbreed. Horses, donkeys, and zebras are even more physically similar than people and chimpanzees, but they, too, are different species. Even though these equids (horse-like mammals) can sometimes mate and produce healthy offspring, their offspring are almost always sterile, meaning they cannot produce offspring of their own. The mating of a female horse and a male donkey, for example, produces a mule. Mules are usually strong and healthy, but they cannot reproduce – even if you try to breed them with other mules. One simple way to think about why mules are sterile is that they have an odd number of chromosomes. Horses have 64 and donkeys have 62. Mules end up with an awkward 63 chromosomes. In contrast to this, if you could arrange a successful date between a miniature horse and a gigantic Clydesdale (see Figure 3.12), the offspring should be fertile.

Figure 3.12 *Clydesdales and miniature horses are different breeds of the same species, colloquially known as the horse. Thus, although Clydesdales may weigh more than 2,000 pounds and miniature horses may weigh less than people, the two breeds (the two subspecies) could mate and produce fertile offspring.*

A similar story holds for many big cats. Consider ligers and tigons, the hybrid offspring of lions and tigers. They're healthy but sterile. Contrast this with dogs and wolves. As different as they look on the outside, they can breed and produce fertile offspring. Thousands of years of selective breeding by people have made many modern breeds of dog look very little like wolves, but without changing their genome much. If one were starting from scratch rather than relying on Linnaeus's ancient taxonomy, dogs and wolves would be just one species. Finally, despite sharing a lot of physical features, and a common ancestor, African and Asian elephants have drifted so far apart genetically that they cannot produce viable offspring at all. They are clearly separate species. In fact, recent genetic studies of African elephants show that the large African bush elephants that live in the savannah are a different species than the smaller African forest elephant (Callaway, 2016). Notice that geographic isolation does not have to involve thousands of miles. It just has to involve very different selection pressures. Genetic studies also show that there are probably four distinct species of giraffe (rather than 9–11 subspecies) (Fennessy et al., 2016).

Isolation can also occur because of simple migration. As animals roam in search of food, shelter, or water, those who venture deeper into new environments may gradually change (via mutations) in ways that make them more likely to survive in new environments. Even if animals always wished to stay put, it's also the case that the earth's continents are moving. If you know about **plate tectonics** and continental drift, you know that about 250 million years ago, all the earth's continents existed as a supercontinent known as **Pangaea**. About 200 million years ago, South America and Africa slowly split apart (at roughly the rate at which your fingernails grow). North America also drifted away from Europe. Continental drift over many millions of years explains, for example, why South America and Australia harbor a lot of marsupial species that seem to have common ancestors. It also explains why similar but distinct species of many animals exist in Europe and North America. American and European bison are considered different species. If you take a peek at the Iberian lynx and the Canada lynx shown in Figure 3.13, you'll see that these two cousins have diverged noticeably from a common ancestor, adapting to very different environments. Notice that as well as being lighter in color and having less distinct spots, the Canadian version of the lynx has bigger paws, a much denser coat, and a

Figure 3.13 *The Canada lynx (top left) adapted to living in the snow. The Iberian lynx (top right) adapted to the warm, arid Iberian peninsula (southern Spain and a bit of Portugal). The common North American raccoon (bottom left) and the South American coati (bottom right) are members of the same family but a different genus as well as a different species. I'm guessing, then, that raccoons and coatis share less of their genome than the two lynxes.*

much shorter tail. In contrast to these two distinct species of lynx, African and Asiatic lions appear to have been separated for only about 200,000 years, in environments that are not so radically different. They're distinct subspecies – but not separate species. This means they look somewhat different, but they could interbreed and produce healthy, fertile offspring.

It's not always possible to tell by looking at two animals if they're different species. In fact, even genetic testing can't always determine for sure whether two closely related species are best considered separate species. Consider polar bears and brown bears. We once thought that polar bears evolved from the brown bears known as grizzly bears. But things appear to be much more complicated than that. It looks like male polar bears can breed successfully with female brown bears, whereas male brown bears cannot breed successfully with female polar bears. The reasons seem to be pragmatic rather than chromosomal. Polar bears simply must be white to hunt effectively. Brown bears can survive just fine if they get a bit lighter. The two bears are still considered different species (Cahill et al., 2015), but if we applied the traditional rule about producing fertile offspring, they could reasonably be considered two different subspecies of brown bear.

Speciation can also result from **specialization**. For example, dramatic changes in the local environment can produce speciation. Recent studies suggest that human beings evolved from an ancient hominid ancestor in Africa during a period when the African climate had become hugely unpredictable. One theory about how we became the extremely adaptable species of primate that we are is that we specifically evolved to adapt to climactic unpredictability. No one believes we evolved from chimps, by the way. Instead, human beings and chimpanzees seem to have evolved from a common ancestor that existed several million years ago. But we now differ in some very dramatic ways from our chimpanzee cousins, and we differ more modestly from many early hominids. There are many fossils of early hominids that shared some features with chimps, while sharing others with *Homo sapiens*. Consider the sketch of skulls, pelvises, and feet in Figure 3.14. The bones on the left come from a modern chimp, those in the middle column come from *Australopithecus africanus* ("Lucy"), and, of course, those on the right belong to a modern human.

Notice that if all you had at your disposal were the three skulls, you might assume "Lucy" was just a chimp species that had lost its huge canines. Like modern chimps, for example, Lucy's brain was only about one-third the size of ours. But even a cursory peek at Lucy's pelvis and her feet reveal that she was bipedal. (An analysis of her leg bones would further confirm this.) So, if I may dramatically oversimplify an incredibly complex comparison, Lucy was a cousin of both chimps and people who was more like us from the waist down and more like a chimp from the neck up. But she was a hominid, because she walked upright. There is also pretty good evidence that she used stone tools.

If you saw the chimp pelvis from the side, you'd see that chimp hips, like gorilla hips, are tilted dramatically forward in ways that hominid hips are not. Figure 3.14 also suggests one important way in which Lucy's skull was pretty different

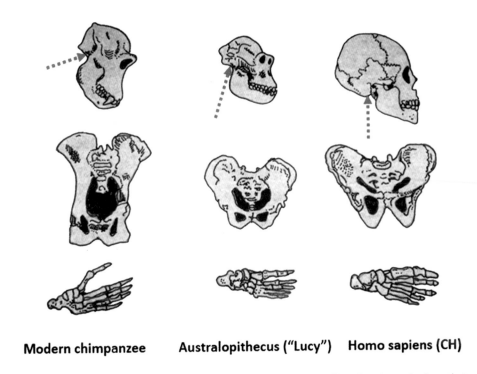

Modern chimpanzee   Australopithecus ("Lucy")   Homo sapiens (CH)

Figure 3.14 *These sketches of skulls, pelvises, and feet from chimps, "Lucy," and people show that Lucy, like people, was well adapted for upright walking. Chimps are not. Also, only the chimp foot is well adapted to tree climbing.*

from a chimp's skull, which is the way it attached to her spinal column. Her skull didn't sit perfectly atop her spinal column as ours does, but it came pretty close. In contrast, the skulls of "knuckle walkers" like chimps and gorillas fit into their spinal columns in much the same way that a dog's skull does. There isn't much guesswork in figuring out if an animal walked principally on four legs or two.

A review of all the routes via which speciation can occur is beyond the scope of this text. However, suffice it to say that speciation happens in many different ways. **Hybridization**, for example, can also produce speciation (Abbott et al., 2013). Occasionally, two different species prove to be able to mate and produce fertile offspring. If the offspring end up with traits that increase selective or inclusive fitness in a particular environment, a new species may emerge, either replacing the common ancestors or coexisting with them. In some cases of hybridization, one species may be "absorbed" by the other via interbreeding. Modern humans (*Homo sapiens*) and Neanderthals appear to have evolved from a common hominid ancestor. Although European Neanderthals have been extinct for about 30,000 years, studies of modern human and ancient European Neanderthal DNA reveal that modern people of European descent often have small amounts of Neanderthal DNA. At least some ancient European *Homo sapiens* appear to have interbred with their more muscular but less verbal cousins.

Punctuated equilibrium

Speciation does not just apply to hominids or even primates. It appears to have happened to beetles much more often than it happened to any mammal. There are 250,000 known species of beetle. Insanely high numbers of beetle species exist, at least in part, because there are so many unique ecological niches that different species of beetles can fill – even within a few square meters of forest. It's difficult to find a modern animal that does not have a long line of ancestors that represented variations on whatever specific adaptive theme best describes that modern animal. This does not mean, however, that speciation is merely a long list of gradual variations and transitions.

Eldredge and Gould (1972) refuted this idea that speciation happens at a slow and constant rate. They pointed out that ancient fossil records often reveal long periods during which there was little or no speciation at all. These periods of the biological status quo, known as **gradualism**, were then followed by short evolutionary bursts during which there were explosions in speciation. Eldredge and Gould referred to this unsteady pattern of speciation as punctuated equilibrium. For example, about 385 million years ago, there was a tremendous explosion in the number and variety of sea-dwelling trilobites. Eldredge and Gould documented a similar phenomenon for land snails (snail bodies don't fossilize well, but snail shells do). Eldredge (2016) argued that Darwin himself amassed some neat evidence for punctuated equilibrium but just couldn't accept it (Darwin's unpublished notes show he was torn about gradualism versus rapid evolutionary explosions). To be clear, modern data show that gradualism can happen, but it appears to be the exception rather than the rule. The reason is simple. When environments don't change much and there is little geographical isolation, there are no powerful new selection pressures to promote high rates of speciation. Evolution happens much more quickly than usual in periods of dramatic environmental change. Consider the asteroid strike that meant the demise of dinosaurs and the well-documented explosion in evolution among mammals.

A metaphor for punctuated equilibrium comes from business. When a new product hits the market, dozens of competing variations on it may quickly appear as well. Those that fill a unique niche often survive and prosper. Others bite the dust – often to be replaced by still other variations, only a few of which succeed. The original product itself may also undergo some tinkering (e.g., a change in screen size). Once a few big winners emerge, you may observe business as usual for a long time in the absence of much radical innovation. After the clunky car phones of the 1990s were replaced by cell phones, the more portable cell phones became all the rage. But when smartphones came along a decade or so later, second-generation cell phones became more or less extinct. Early on there were lots of smartphone designs. Neither the Motorola Flipout nor the Samsung Juke ever caught on. Eventually, the ubiquitous iPhone and the surviving but less popular Android became two of only a few popular smartphones. But what tomorrow will hold in the high-tech world of smartphones is hard to predict. It's also hard to know what tomorrow will hold when it comes to animal evolution on our rapidly changing planet. Many evolutionary biologists have argued that due to anthropogenic problems such as habitat destruction and climate change, we have entered a period of mass extinction – much like the one that allowed mammals to take the reins of the earth from dinosaurs. In Chapter 12, I offer a few suggestions for slowing down this modern mass extinction. Whatever happens next, it is clear that the 4.5-billion-year ride from a barren, rocky planet to the lush and fertile planet we are currently taking for granted has been fueled by evolution.

FOR FURTHER READING

» Eldredge, N. & Gould, S. J. (1972). Punctuated equilibria: An alternative to phyletic gradualism. In T.J. Schopf (ed.) *Models in paleobiology* (pp. 82–115). San Francisco, CA: Freeman Cooper & Co.

» Miller, S.L. (1953). A production of amino acids under possible primitive earth conditions. *Science*, 117(3046), 528–9.

» Ronay, R. & von Hippel, W. (2010). The presence of an attractive woman elevates testosterone and physical risk taking in young men. *Social Psychological and Personality Science*, 1(1), 57–64.

» Van Kranendonk, M.J., Deamer, D.W. & Djokic, T. (2017). Life springs. *Scientific American*, 317(2), 28–35.

SAMPLE MULTIPLE-CHOICE EXAM QUESTIONS

Here are four sample quiz questions for Chapter 3. You can find the Chapter 3 quiz at: www.macmillanihe.com/evolutionary-psychology

3.01. According to cosmologists, what important event happened about 13.7 billion year ago?

    a. the collision of a small planet with the earth, which formed our moon

    b. the formation of our solar system

    c. the explosion that created the modern universe

    d. Stan Lee created the Marvel Cinematic Universe

3.02. The (1953) Miller-Urey experiment suggested that a few inorganic molecules may have provided the building blocks of the first organic molecules. Which elements or molecules listed below served as starting points in the experiment?

    a. ammonia, water, and methane

    b. carbon, water, and sodium chloride

    c. eukaryotes, prokaryotes, and oxygen

3.03. Unlike the traits Mendel's studied in pea plants, many human traits are determined by many different genes. The study of traits that vary along a smooth continuum (most of which are normally distributed) is known as:

a. quantitative genetics

b. quantified inheritance

c. bell curve phenotypes

3.04. The physical trait of having brown eyes is part of a person's:

a. genotype

b. phenotype

c. DNA

Answer Key: c, a, a, b.

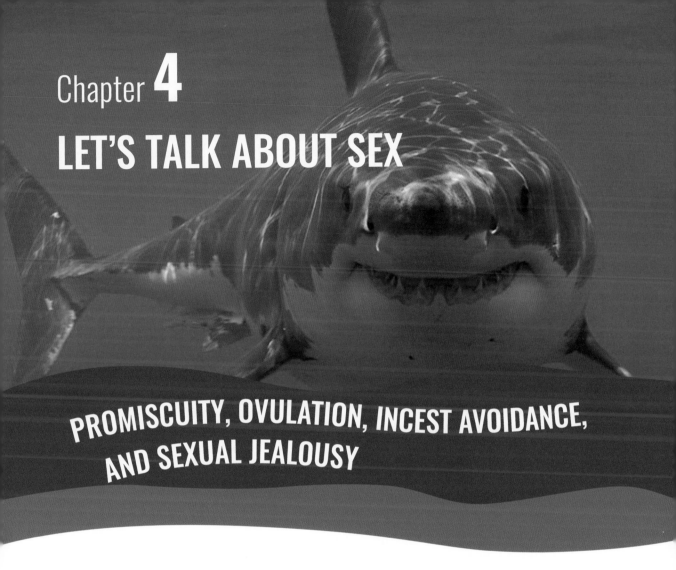

Chapter 4
LET'S TALK ABOUT SEX

PROMISCUITY, OVULATION, INCEST AVOIDANCE, AND SEXUAL JEALOUSY

"– data suggest that ... female orgasm depends on the quality of a female's mate."

— *Puts, Dawood, and Welling (2012, p. 1139)*

"Sex is a part of nature. I go along with nature."

— *attributed to Marilyn Monroe*

About 40 years ago, Richard Dawkins (1976) argued that natural selection happens at the level of genes; organisms are merely the vessels that carry genes around. Everything we do, Dawkins argued, can be thought of as the work of genes that survived over the millennia, because they promoted successful reproduction. On the other hand, it is organisms, not genes, that have orgasms, and an evolutionary perspective on sex suggests that different organisms should have different sexual habits. In this chapter I address four broad questions about sex that get lots of well-deserved attention in evolutionary psychology. First, do men want sex more often (or with more partners) than women do? If so, are there any predictable exceptions to this general rule about sexual promiscuity? Second, does human interest in sex follow any kind of predictable cycle? Experts in human sexuality have long argued that sex in people is completely unrelated to basic biological functions such as female ovulation. But from an evolutionary perspective, this would be pretty surprising. Is human sex cyclical or not? Third, why is incest such a big taboo? How and why do most people avoid it? Fourth, are there sex differences in sexual jealousy? Could they have an evolutionary basis?

SEX DIFFERENCES IN MATING STRATEGIES: PARENTAL INVESTMENT THEORY

Do men want sex more often – and with more partners – than women do? Why, yes; yes, they do. That one sure was easy. I'm just kidding. This serious question deserves a much more serious answer. Most evolutionary psychologists subscribe to some variation on Robert Trivers' (1972) provocative **parental investment theory**. The gist of this theory is that women's relatively greater investment in their offspring usually makes them pickier than men when it comes to mate choice. A close cousin of this idea is that, on average, men are naturally more promiscuous than women (Symons, 1979). This is not a prediction of evolutionary theory across the board, by the way. It's a particular prediction that mainly applies to mammals, especially primates. Eventually, we'll examine why this elegant theory makes different predictions about different animals. But let's begin with people. Like most other sexually mature female primates, women typically produce only one egg (ovum) per month. In contrast, the average man produces about a million sperm every sexual attention span, which for men is about six minutes.

A little math thus tells us that young men produce mature sperm at about three billion times the rate at which young women release mature eggs. As if this weren't dramatic enough, I'll remind you that most men have a great deal of choice about when and where they release their sperm. In contrast, barring medical intervention, women's eggs always stay right inside their bodies. Further, assuming a woman's one mature egg is healthy, it's only available for easy fertilization during a brief window every month, let's say three days. This means that about 90% of the time, most young, healthy, highly fertile women are mostly infertile. These facts about "scarcity" alone imply that perhaps women should be choosier maters than men.

But things get even more lopsided than this. First, when women are born, they possess most, if not all, of the eggs they will ever possess. Unlike even our nearest primate cousins (chimps and gorillas), female human beings also experience a biologically rare thing known as **menopause**. This is the time, at about age 50, when most women stop releasing eggs altogether. This compounds the scarcity principle further because it means that most women are only highly fertile for a couple of decades. In contrast, men continue to produce millions of sperm every hour until they die, although admittedly at somewhat lower rates at 85 than at 25. Would you be more careful with a possession if your mother gave it to you at birth and if you only had access to it once monthly, or if you were constantly making millions of others very much like it?

Figure 4.1 *On the left, the famous Hope Diamond. On the right, a pile of cheap glass beads. With which would you be more careful?*

I hate to sound so much like a banker, but moving from scarcity to investment, which is the key to Trivers' parental investment theory, the arguments continue to suggest that women should be more selective maters than men are. Suppose a woman does become pregnant. If all goes well during her taxing nine-month pregnancy, and if she does not die during childbirth, she will be the proud mother of an adorable but incredibly **altricial** baby. Yes, we're the world's most altricial species. In altricial species, the young require significant parental care and would surely die if left to their own devices. Contrast this with highly **precocial** species such as ducks and crocodiles, whose young can fend for themselves surprisingly well right after hatching. In fact, human beings are highly altricial even in comparison with most other mammals, primates included. Horses can walk, and even run, within hours of birth. We require about a year merely to toddle. Rhesus monkeys mature in a little more than three years. Even chimps and gorillas develop quite a bit more quickly than we do.

The mammalian constraint that prevents men from nursing their offspring is yet another sex difference that has had profound implications for the roles men and women played in childrearing throughout human history. If I might add yet another argument to the mix, let me remind you that in the days before hospitals (and thus an occasional hospital mix-up), women were always absolutely sure of maternity. My mother gave birth to six kids, and she knew for sure that each of us grew from one of her eggs. Despite how devoted to my father my devoutly religious mother was, simple logic dictates that my dad, like every other primate dad who ever preceded him, could never be absolutely sure of his paternity. Men know that their sperm is their own, but they can never be absolutely sure these sperm will be the only sperm that ever fertilize the egg of a woman with whom they have mated. As David Buss (2008) pointed out, there is an old saying for this: "Mama's baby is daddy's maybe."

So human eggs are a much rarer commodity than human sperm. Further, throughout human evolutionary history, women had to invest enormous amounts of time and energy in their children if these children were to have any chance of survival. Throughout human evolutionary history, then, the average mother should have been more invested in her offspring than was the average father. It is thus possible, in principle, for a man to mate with dozens of different women, to ignore them all completely once they've become pregnant, and to rest assured that some of his many offspring will surely survive. A sex-linked gene that promoted such caddish behavior might do well for itself in an evolutionary arms race. In contrast, the argument goes, women do not have the luxury of being so sexually callous. Throughout human history, most mothers gave birth to only a few children, and if they ignored these children, they did so at the evolutionary peril of any genes they carried. If children represent a huge investment to women, then the average woman might be wise to invest in a committed, trustworthy mate. All else being equal, women should gravitate toward the kind of guy who mans up, brings home the bacon, cooks it up, and then cleans the kitchen afterwards. In my own family, several of the adult women insist that the physical trait they look for most in men is dishpan hands. As a guy who used to work as a maid, I do well on that dimension.

"Yes, Brian, I know I'm your soul mate.
The problem is you're not *my* soul mate."

Common concerns about evolutionary theories

Before moving on with a sensitive topic, I should clarify that believing that evolution promotes something – including sex differences in mating preferences – does not mean believing that this thing is good or ethical. This error – the tendency to think something is good because it is natural – is the **appeal to nature fallacy**. Evolution has produced all kinds of natural things, but this naturalness doesn't make them morally acceptable. As Steven Pinker noted in an interview with Steve Sailer (2002), the naturalistic fallacy

> is the idea that what is found in nature is good. It was the basis for Social Darwinism, the belief that helping the poor and sick would get in the way of evolution ... Today, biologists denounce the Naturalistic Fallacy because they want to describe the natural world honestly, without people deriving morals about how we ought to behave – as in: If birds and beasts engage in adultery, infanticide, cannibalism, it must be OK.

Pinker goes on to note that almost any belief system, from old school Marxism to modern capitalism, can be used to justify the abuse of others – without making it right.

I've never read a more honest, or irreverent, evolutionary scientist than Olivia Judson (2002). Judson never shies away from the most taboo topics. She, too, argues that the descriptive rules of evolution and the proscriptive rules of morality, decency, and justice are very different things. One of her points is that if we happened to identify a gene that made some men more likely than others to become rapists, this would not suddenly make rape OK. The same logic holds for other forms of violence. Despite my belief that culture powerfully shapes human behavior, I do suspect that there are innate sex differences in physical aggression. But that doesn't mean we should either encourage or excuse unnecessary aggression in men, or forgive unnecessary violence when committed by women because we assume they are unlikely to repeat it in the future.

In short, no serious evolutionary thinkers tolerate this fallacy (or any of its variations). In sharp contrast, parents and teachers often fall prey to this fallacy when they forgive or reward behaviors in boys that would be wholly unacceptable in girls. ("Boys will be boys," after all – unless we sometimes require them not to be.)

If there is a group that's even worse than parents like me, it's advertisers like me. Many shamelessly capitalize on the appeal to nature fallacy to promote their products – presumably because they know the fallacy is so seductive. Ads for not-so-healthy foods often imply that the foods are healthy because they're "all natural." But to paraphrase the famous skeptic James Randi, tobacco and bird droppings are all natural, but no one thinks they are good for you. Have I told you about my line of fat-free all-natural colas? What about my all-natural, sugar-free heroin? I was working on a line of organic cigarettes, but American Spirit beat me to the punch. (No, I don't *really* promote heroin, and yes, that *really* is a brand of cigarettes. They target young, earth-loving hipsters like your friend Zack.)

Having said all this, I must add an important caveat. The fact that evolutionary scientists can thoughtfully avoid the appeal to nature fallacy does not guarantee that regular consumers of evolutionary psychology will always be able to do the same. Does learning about evolutionary theories of sex differences in mating strategies make regular men more accepting of male sexual violence against women? The answer seems to be no, but I must add a subtle qualification to that no. Dar-Nimrod and colleagues (2011) asked some men to read a scientific article about evolved sex differences in mating strategies while asking others to read about a neutral (control) topic. Men who had just read about evolutionary psychology did not become more lenient in their attitudes toward a defendant accused of criminal sexual behavior. But Dar-Nimrod et al. included a third condition in their studies. A third group read a non-evolutionary social scientific account of sexual behavior that emphasized the role of culture, roles, and socialization in gender differences. Relative to either the neutral control condition or the condition in which men read about evolution, this third condition made men much more critical, for example, of a man accused of a sex crime. I think a fair take on this important study is that learning about evolution certainly doesn't make things worse, but it also doesn't make things better. The results of this study should be a challenge to us all. How can we educate the world about the truths of our evolved nature while doing our best to make the world a better place for future generations? Understanding evolution without also appreciating the power of socialization may not be enough to pave the way to a better future. I'll return to this important topic in later chapters.

Back to natural selection. Getting back to the key theme of natural selection, you learned in Chapter 1 that evolution seems to have promoted selfless sacrifice among male redback spiders and selfish cannibalism among females of the same species. But this does not make it nice – or even OK – to eat your lover, at least not in the manner of redback spiders. Incidentally, the redback spider also offers us another lesson in evolution: many female insects are quite happy to mate with many males, and they are not always very picky. One likely reason why is that many female insects produce hundreds, thousands, or even millions of eggs (Wilson, 1975). As Brueland (1995) noted, the world egg-laying champions are probably African driver ants – a queen can lay several million eggs per month. Like most other ant moms, these prolific queens do little or nothing to care for their young. They don't have to, of course, because lots of devoted nannies (worker ants) take care of this duty for them.

Back to sex differences in sexual interest

Getting back to people, there are good evolutionary reasons to think that, if men and women were unfettered by pragmatic constraints (e.g., the availability of a handy, receptive partner), the average man would be more willing than the average woman to mate indiscriminately. Psychologists have tested this idea many different ways. I'll share just two. One approach is simply to ask men and women how interested they would be in having casual, uncommitted sex. An impressive cross-cultural study by Schmitt (2005) surveyed people in 48 countries from all over the world. In one portion of the study, people reported their attitudes about casual sex. Specifically, they reported whether they agreed with statements such as "Sex without love is OK" and "I can imagine myself being comfortable and enjoying 'casual' sex with different partners." In all 48 countries Schmitt sampled – from Argentina to Zimbabwe – men were significantly more likely than women to agree with such statements. As much as I admire this painstaking and carefully crafted study, it did necessarily rely on that useful but imperfect technique known as "self-report." Do men and women really possess fundamentally different attitudes about sex? Or is it simply more socially acceptable for men than for women to admit that they'd like to get it on with a stranger? I don't want to be too hard on a brilliant and hard-working researcher, but it would be nice to see whether men are more likely than women to act – or try to act – on their sexually lax attitudes.

Are men really more sexually permissive, and less sexually choosy, than women? Let's consider **Clark and Hatfield's (1989, 2003) studies.** In each of these studies, which Clark and Hatfield ran in 1978 and then in 1982, they trained average-looking, young male and female confederates to approach attractive, opposite-sex strangers on the Florida State University campus. In the most interesting condition of these interesting studies, confederates made a very forward pass: "I have been noticing you around campus and I find you to be very attractive. Would you go to bed with me tonight?" Now that you've picked your jaw up off the floor, let me add that this jaw-dropping line may have been a little less jaw-dropping when the studies were run than it would be today. First, this was a college campus in Florida, not a meeting to elect a new pope. Second, even in 1982, the American "sexual revolution" had not yet petered out, and there was almost no public awareness of the dangers of AIDS. How would you respond to this surprising come-on? According to Clark and Hatfield, I might just as well have asked you whether you are male or female.

Averaging across the two studies, more than 70% of men accepted the confederate's offer. Furthermore, many of the men – but not as many of the women – who refused the offer politely explained that they would have accepted it, except for the fact that they were currently in a monogamous relationship. Almost all men seem to have felt the woman had made them an offer no single man could refuse. Maybe no single man could. But plenty of single women could. And they did. Averaging across the two studies, the number of women who agreed to have sex with the male stranger was 0%. That's right; nil, nada, nobody. So let's generously round that soccer score of zero up to 10 (%) and say that college-aged men were at least seven times as likely as college-aged women to agree to have casual sex with a stranger. To be sure, real life can be a little more complicated than this. For example, when Clark and Hatfield replaced their jaw-dropping request with a more socially acceptable request ("Would you go out with me tonight?"), the huge gender differences they observed almost completely disappeared. Averaging across the two samples, 53% of all men and 50% of all women accepted the offer to go out on a date.

Gender differences also disappear, even for a purely sexual request, if a target is attractive enough. Conley (2011) asked women to consider a hypothetical situation much like this one – but in which the stranger was rich, famous, and exceedingly hot. In one study it was Johnny Depp, in another Brad Pitt. Many young women said they'd have a hard time saying no to a sexual request from Brad Pitt or Johnny Depp. Evolutionary psychologists probably wouldn't be too disturbed by these results. According to Buss and Schmitt's (1993) **sexual strategies theory,** women have a few evolutionarily acquired strategies of their own. Accordingly, some of the things heterosexual women value most in a mate include good looks, physical health, social status, and material resources (wealth). In light of this, both Johnny Depp and Brad Pitt would seem to represent a perfect evolutionary storm of hotness. Or maybe it's a trifecta of hotness. The point is that they are both really, really hot. No one said women were made of stone. To say this a little differently, it's not a problem for parental investment theory that both men and women are highly attracted to highly attractive mates. The main sex difference suggested by parental investment involves our attraction to not so wonderful mates, not our attraction to the rich, hot and famous.

"You had me at 'billionaire.'"

If the world were populated only by men like Johnny Depp, there might be little or no gender difference in people's interest in sex. In a world where most men merely smell like pirates rather than playing them in movies, however, it seems safe to say that, on average, women are less interested in sex – especially casual sex – than men are. Consider a few additional findings and how they have held up to thoughtful criticisms. First, men routinely claim to have had more sexual partners than women do. Mathematically, however, it takes two to tango. With whom are all these men having sex, if not women? One way to sidestep this thorny question is to look at sex among gay men and lesbians. The data are clear. Compared with lesbians, gay men report having sex more often and with more partners (Michael et al., 1995; Symons, 1979). The gender difference in sexual interest also shows up in a wide variety of demographic groups, including different ethnic groups, different age groups, and in blind people as well as sighted people (Abramson et al., 2013).

Ask people whether or how often they have looked at pornography or erotica on the internet, and you get the same pattern. Men consume much more sexually explicit material than women do, and this is true even among men who are not proud of this behavior (Carroll et al., 2008). Analyses of people's right swipe rates ("yes, I'm interested") at a popular "female-friendly" dating website also showed that men swipe right at much higher rates than women do (Bear & Pelham, 2018).

An inconvenient truth of evolutionary psychology is that men and women simply are not identical in every imaginable way. Culture is important, too, of course. It often magnifies evolved sex differences, and sometimes it seems to create gender differences entirely. But the myth that culture is everything is just that, a myth. My personal approach to how to deal with the difficult topic of gender discrimination, for example, is that we should stop working so hard to resocialize women to be more like men. Instead, we might consider spending more time resocializing boys and men to be more like girls and women. Among other things, this might include a diligent effort to socialize boys and men to become less competitive and physically aggressive while becoming more compassionate and nurturing.

Common myths about evolutionary psychology

To be clear, I did not just say that men are from Mars, or that women are from Venus. Both men and women are from places more like Phoenix and Poughkeepsie. It just appears that men and women have evolved a little differently. Popular books about Mars and Venus are reminders, though, that there are many myths about sex, including myths about what evolution suggests about it. This means that it's important to avoid straw man fallacies regarding evolution. As any philosopher will tell you, the **straw man fallacy** refers to discrediting a way of thinking by attacking a weak or ridiculous version of that way of thinking. A famous but scientifically uninformed minister once got a lot of mileage out of the criticism that evolution is impossible because it means that life should be constantly arising from non-life. He asked why life doesn't constantly crawl out of jars of freshly opened peanut butter.

One of the seventeen answers to this nutty criticism is that companies who manufacture peanut butter are required to do so under highly sanitary conditions – that is, conditions designed to prevent contamination by tiny life forms. Another answer is that a jar of peanut butter is very, very far removed from the ancient conditions that are thought to have led to the evolution of life on earth. In a jar of peanut butter, there's not much radiation or lightning, for example, and scarcely any ammonia or methane. To put this second answer a little differently, the peanut butter is usually in aisle seven, next to the jams and jellies. The primordial soup is in a completely different aisle, next to the nucleotides and amino acids.

Many of the common criticisms of evolutionary theories are really criticisms of straw versions (weak versions) of these theories. In fact, a study by Winegard and Deaner (2014) showed that authors of popular textbooks in gender and human sexuality often misrepresent evolutionary theories. Winegard and Deaner identified eight kinds of errors, and the most common of these errors was the straw man fallacy. For example, evolutionary sociobiologists have been criticized by some textbook authors for ignoring the rampant sexual promiscuity of female chimps. But this point has been duly noted for many decades, and is a point of healthy evolutionary debate.

In fact, female promiscuity among chimps is a big reason why male chimps have embarrassingly small penises but very big testicles (Diamond, 1992; Shackelford & Goetz, 2007). So in chimps, size apparently matters a lot. But it's the size of the *ejaculate* (the amount of sperm) that helps a male chimp win the evolutionary battle known as sperm competition. **Sperm competition** is not quite as juvenile, or X-rated, as it may sound. It refers to a battle for fertilization between the sperm of different males, and it happens inside the female chimp's vagina and Fallopian tubes. One simple way to win the competition is to make more sperm than your rivals (thus the large chimp testicles). Another way is to produce sperm that swim faster and/or longer than other sperm. In the 1980s, some researchers even suggested that men produce special sperm that are designed not to fertilize eggs but to hang out in a woman's reproductive tract and destroy the sperm of any competitors. Despite a lot of subsequent searching for them, no one has yet been able to uncover clear evidence for these **kamikaze sperm**. They just don't seem to exist. I mention this as a reminder of the principles of empiricism and falsification. The way scientists find out what's true is by making careful observations – even if it means having to sift carefully through many ejaculations. This being said, sperm competition does exist in people as well as in many other animals. Shackelford and Goetz (2007) reviewed several lines of evidence attesting to the importance of sperm competition in men. For example, men who have greater reason to worry that their female partners could have recently had sex with another man produce larger than usual ejaculations when they have sex with their partners – but not when they masturbate (Baker & Bellis, 1993).

To identify another straw man, evolutionary psychologists don't argue that women don't enjoy sex. In fact, genes that make sex highly pleasurable, like genes that make sugar taste good, are a huge reason why both men and women are highly motivated to have sex (Abramson & Pinkerton, 2002; Puts et al., 2012). Sex differences in behavior are almost never absolute. Even if we take it as a given that the average man is more interested in sex than the average woman, this still leaves a lot of room for individual differences, including some highly sexual women and some asexual men. As my friend Christine used to put it: "My sexual preference is often."

Yet another straw man criticism of evolutionary theories is that they are inherently racist or sexist. The idea that "biology is destiny" can be offensive, and it can surely be misused to justify unfairness. To be sure, many racist ideas are explicitly or implicitly based on the idea that one race is superior to another. But there are some big problems with this criticism of evolutionary psychology. One of the biggest problems is that "race" is a social invention rather than a biological reality. Like almost all anthropologists and sociologists, most evolutionary biologists and psychologists realize that race is a socially constructed idea. I'd go a step further to say that the main sociopolitical function has been to justify treating some ethnic and/or religious groups unfairly. The average Black woman shares almost as many of her genes with a randomly sampled White woman as she does with a randomly sampled Black woman. The small proportion of genes she is very likely to share with another Black woman happen to be genes that affect aspects of our appearance to which we've attached the label of race, such as dark eyes, skin, and hair. As noted in Chapter 3, physical appearance is often the basis of powerful stereotypes, which is the main reason why "race" plays an important role in daily life. But rather than basing race on a person's ancient geographical origins, we could just as easily have created "races" of tall versus short people, people who can or cannot digest milk, or people who can or cannot roll their tongues. Likewise, the same genes that make the skin of native Africans very dark also create very dark skin in most Australian Aborigines and many Asian Indians. The common denominator here is not race, it's having ancestors who lived where it is very, very sunny.

Along these lines, you might be interested to know that sex is modestly linked to skin color. On average, even within any "racial" group, men are a little darker than women (Jablonski & Chaplin, 2000). An evolutionary view of this little known fact may be linked to one of the likely reasons why skin color varies across the planet in the first place. Dark skin protects people from the harmful ultraviolet rays of the sun. The mutations that produce lighter skin were only adaptive in places (like Norway) where it isn't very sunny. They were adaptive there – and in other less sunny places – because lighter skin allows a person to make the hormone we call vitamin D easily using sunlight. In an ancient world without multivitamins, making vitamin D was pretty useful, but not so useful that it would make up for the cost of being chronically sunburned if you lived in the Australian outback. Getting back to sex, if it is more important to women than to men to avoid a vitamin D deficiency (e.g., because of the need for vitamin D during pregnancy or women's greater susceptibility than men to bone diseases such as osteoporosis), it would make evolutionary sense for the average woman to be a little better than the average man at making vitamin D from sunlight. On the other hand, if men across the planet generally get out in the bright sun more often than women do (e.g., to hunt), naturally dark skin would also serve them well by giving them a little extra skin protection relative to women. Incidentally, I am not usually big on vitamins, but one vitamin I do take regularly, especially in the winter, is vitamin D. Given how religiously I try to protect myself from the harmful ultraviolet rays of the sun, I'm happy to ingest this hormone daily if it protects my aging bones.

Evolutionary scientists don't always agree with one another

In the interest of fairness, I should note that not all evolutionary thinkers buy into this account of human skin color variation based mainly on ultraviolet (UV) radiation and vitamin D production. Some have argued that sexual selection is the main reason, or at least an additional reason, why people across the globe look so different on the outside. The idea of sexual selection is as old as Darwin's (1859) original theory. As you learned in Chapter 3, sexual selection is just a specific kind of natural selection. It's the natural selection of specific physical traits or behavioral tendencies that make an organism attractive to members of the opposite sex. Remember the peacock's beautiful tail? Remember the experiments with widowbirds?

Evolutionary experts such as Jared Diamond have argued that features such as skin tone, hair color, eye color, and whether people have epicanthal eyelid folds (almond-shaped eyes rather than round eyes) may have evolved via sexual selection. Facial hair or deep voices for men and enlarged breasts or curvy hips for women might qualify as additional examples. All else being equal, most women prefer men with deep voices. And remember Dev Singh's research on the waist-to-hip ratio we discussed in Chapter 3? Likewise, some have argued that women's permanently enlarged breasts evolved via sexual selection. Other female primates only have enlarged breasts when they are nursing. In contrast, women may have evolved enlarged breasts to demonstrate their health and sexual maturity all the time. From this perspective, a woman who has breast augmentation surgery (or a man who has pectoral implants) will attract more mates for the same reason that male widowbirds with artificially lengthened tails did. The gist of the sexual selection argument for human hair, eye, and skin color variation is that the correlation between historical human skin color variation and distance from the equator is not perfect (Diamond, 1992). Further, there are some places within the same latitudinal band, especially in Europe, where there is enormous variation in eye, skin, and hair color. Fans of this theory do not deny that pale skin would serve a person poorly in the desert, but they argue that theories based on skin protection and vitamin D alone don't explain everything.

Figure 4.2 *Clockwise from top left: a male and female mandarin duck, a female and male pheasant, a male and female gibbon, and a male and female December moth. Among gibbons, however, males and females come in both shades.*

My take on this controversy is that you can account pretty well for how much melanin people have in their skin by knowing the amount of sunlight to which the person's ancestors were routinely exposed. The fact that the correlation is not absolutely perfect just means that UV radiation is not all that matters. Prior to the invention of things like air travel and sunscreen, you practically never found fair-skinned, blue-eyed native people in extremely sunny places because the cost of chronic sunburn and vision problems (blue eyes are easily damaged by the sun) would have been too great to offset any positive effects of sexual selection. But in ancient Sweden or Norway, there was some wiggle room – meaning some room for sexual selection – because dark eyes or skin do not pose the enormous cost there that fair skin would pose in the African savannah or the outback.

Blending the two evolutionary perspectives, people the world over have hair, skin and eyes of so many different colors for two different reasons. Dark skin protects you well from the sun, and fair skin lets you manufacture vitamin D easily. Any color of skin, eyes, or hair allows you to attract people who find that particular feature attractive, perhaps because of exposure to specific features early in one's life (see Diamond, 1992). Notice that both of these evolutionary theories – one based on UV exposure and one based on advertising one's unique looks to others – suggest that dark-skinned and light-skinned people are no different inside than are dark-furred and light-furred gibbons. Like Dr. Seuss's star-bellied and plain-bellied Sneetches, we are all one species. In my view, few myths are more powerful, or more harmful, than the **myth of race**. But this popular myth was not invented by devotees of evolution, and modern research on human evolution has clearly disconfirmed it.

Evolution and the myth of race

So, there's nothing inherently racist or sexist about evolutionary theories. In fact, evolutionary theories offer some novel insights into how to reduce stereotypes and discrimination. Here's one such insight. One reason why we discriminate against others is that, much like other primates, we are inherently hierarchical creatures, adapted for group living (de Waal, 1982). People are wary of unfamiliar groups for much the same reason that chimps are wary of unfamiliar troops (yes, a group of chimps, like a group of Boy Scouts, is fittingly called a troop). Unlike chimps, however, we can self-consciously work to broaden our perception of groups to which we do not belong. In so doing we can sometimes let go of our distrust of outgroup members. Consider what evolutionary psychologist Nigel Barber (2004, p. 12) had to say about racism and intergroup conflict:

> One of the toughest conclusions of this book is that in-group altruism can translate into out-group aggression. A soldier supports his own nation by killing the sons of an enemy nation. This irony is all the more remarkable given that group allegiances can be so easily, and so arbitrarily, formed. Just about any distinguishable feature of a group, such as wearing red buttons rather than blue, can promote in-group identification and social hostility against other groups ... Such instant groupishness means that we are very good at transcending our groups of origin and assimilating in new ones, whether they are commercial companies, new countries, fan clubs, or religions. Ultimately, such flexibility will be important in the forging of a world community in which nations can cooperate to ... solve environmental problems, fight AIDS, and confront hunger and poverty.

An influential theory of discrimination and intergroup conflict, known as **social dominance theory**, builds on the basic assumptions of evolutionary ideas – such as those emphasizing our inherent "groupishness" – to suggest a powerful way to reduce stereotypes and discrimination in a multicultural society. According to theories such as social dominance theory (Pratto et al., 2006), and specific ideas such as the **contact hypothesis** (Allport, 1954a; Pettigrew, 1998), one of the best ways to reduce stereotyping and discrimination is to create opportunities for equal status contact among the members of groups who dislike or distrust one another. It gets a lot easier to appreciate Sera as a unique individual when you work, play, or worship with her on a regular basis. Better yet if you have come to depend on her, and she on you. The list of ways in which evolutionary psychology can inform our understanding of prejudice and discrimination does not end here. Neuberg and Schaller (2014) offer many other examples, ranging from how we perceive people with baby faces to how emotions such as fear and disgust promote specific stereotypes.

Back to parental investment theory

Getting back to parental investment theory, it has been tested in a few species in which males make huge parental investments. Many female insects can lay enormous numbers of eggs. Most of them, like queen bees, aren't very picky maters, and many of them are downright loose. There are also a few fish and birds in which the males of the species are much more invested in their offspring than the females are. Let's begin with fish. In many pipefish and seahorses, males make huge investments in their offspring. Examples include males who carry the eggs they've fertilized in a sealed pouch and – in some species – even nourish the developing eggs. It is female pipefish and seahorses who often compete for picky males. And it's these same females who begin searching for new mates shortly after mating. Some male water birds are also highly invested fathers. Male **red-necked phalaropes** make a huge investment in their offspring by incubating their eggs without any help from the mothers. Furthermore, the fathers dutifully care for their chicks for weeks after the little ones hatch, while the red-necked mothers are out shamelessly looking for new lovers. In seahorses, pipefish, and phalaropes, then, males invest heavily in their offspring, and it's the males who treat mating as a heavy decision.

Figure 4.3 *A seahorse of unknown sex and a female red-necked phalarope (male phalaropes are less colorful). Males of both species make huge investments in their offspring, and males of both species are very picky maters.*

It is worth noting that there is more than one way in which mothers can "invest" in their offspring. At a minimum, investment may be biological or behavioral. Beginning with biological investment, it varies widely across species. Animals with very few predators seem to be able to keep their genes in the gene pool while producing few offspring. Whales, Galapagos tortoises (which have no natural predators), elephants, and lions all produce very few offspring. In contrast, rabbits, frogs, sea turtles, and most insects produce many, many offspring. In some frog species, mothers can produce 10,000 eggs in a single clutch. If you are a female frog or a sea turtle, you're programmed to invest heavily in your offspring by laying many, many eggs – and then hitting the road. Most of your offspring will prove to be food for predators, but the sheer numbers will make up for this drawback. Your investment is more biological (in the form of laying more eggs) than behavioral. On the other hand, if you are a bear, dolphin, or lion mother, the bulk of your investment is not very bulky – because your main maternal investment is a long-term behavioral one. You're unlikely to produce more than one or two offspring at a time. But you make up for this by sticking around for a long time – to feed and nurture any offspring you do produce.

THE TIMING OF SEXUAL DESIRE

A second basic question about evolution and sex is why human beings seem to have sex at almost any time of the day, week, month, or year. In contrast, many other animals have periods of total sexual apathy followed by periods of tremendous sexual interest. Sexually mature male elephants (bulls) enter musth about once a year. During this one- or two-month window, they become both extremely interested in sex and extremely aggressive. Their hormone levels soar. Testosterone, in particular, can be 50 times higher than normal. How sharply do we differ from other animals on this dimension? Do we differ even from other primates or other great apes? Is there any sense at all in which human sexual interest waxes and wanes in a predictable way?

Let me begin by noting that as recently as the turn of the 21st century, most psychologists believed that human beings are completely different from other animals when it comes to our interest in mating. Let's begin with other animals, focusing on mammals. Most female mammals enter a cyclical period of sexual receptivity that is closely linked to **ovulation**. When a female dog, mouse, or kangaroo is about to release her eggs, she gives off physical and olfactory cues that tell male members of her species that she is ready to conceive. Likewise, in some primates, sexually receptive females both smell and look different than usual. Thus, like many other Old World monkeys, female olive baboons who are getting ready to ovulate (more colloquially, who are "in heat") develop bright pink swellings on their behinds that serve as unmistakable cues that they are sexually receptive. Remember sexual selection?

In contrast, we long believed that human beings have sex whenever they please. Likewise, until pretty recently, many psychologists assumed that natural body smells play little or no role in human sexual attraction. Finally, until pretty recently, many researchers assumed that, unlike other female mammals (including other great apes), female human beings were equally interested in sex during all phases of their ovulatory cycles. From an evolutionary perspective, this pattern would be a big break from millions of years of successful mammalian evolution. In contrast to this assumption, Martie Haselton and Kelly Gildersleeve (2011, pp. 87–8) argued:

> Like other mammals, women can only conceive by having intercourse on the day of ovulation … Throughout evolutionary history, these were the crucial few days when women's sexual decisions had the greatest reproductive consequences and the only days when men could produce offspring by having sex.

Accordingly, they suggest that ovulation does influence human mating preferences.

From an evolutionary perspective, it would be pretty surprising if human beings were ovulationally clueless. This would mean that neither men nor women have any idea whatsoever when women are ovulating. In contrast to this idea, Haselton and Gildersleeve suggested that women do, in fact, emit cues regarding their ovulatory status. Moreover, the average heterosexual man seems to be pretty good at picking up on these cues. Before I borrow liberally from Haselton and Gildersleeve's review of men's ability to detect women's ovulatory cues, it might be useful to remind you that, in principle, there are many cues women could give off to advertise (unconsciously, I assume) that they are about to ovulate. These cues include how a woman dresses, how she smells, how she walks, how rosy her cheeks are, or how dilated her pupils are when she speaks to a potential suitor. Furthermore, some of these cues (clothing) are likely to be clear to almost anyone, whereas others (body odors) are likely to be available only to those who are physically very close to a woman – and perhaps not even to them if the woman chooses to hide the cues.

Let's begin with cues you can only detect with your nose. To study such cues, researchers have developed the **stinky T-shirt paradigm**. Randy Thornhill and colleagues (2003) convinced young women to go to bed wearing a clean, odorless T-shirt – without doing anything that could influence their natural body odors during sleep. The women were forbidden, for example, from applying perfume, anti-perspirant, or deodorant. Thornhill et al. then recruited male judges to come into their lab, sniff the empty but recently slept-in T-shirts, and judge how pleasant and how "sexy" the shirts smelled. If you know how powerfully Americans have been socialized to think that human body odor is undesirable, you won't be surprised to learn that the men were not too crazy about the **smell** of these T-shirts. However, the question is not whether dirty T-shirts smelled like fresh cut flowers, it is whether they smelled sexier than usual when they had just been worn by women on the most fertile days of their ovulatory cycles. Of course, Thornhill et al. wanted to know if the perceived pleasantness of the carefully stunk up T-shirts would be correlated with the fertility of the women who had recently worn them. This is exactly what they found. The T-shirts that had been worn by women who were at their most fertile were rated as both more "pleasant" and more "sexy" than the T-shirts worn by women who were not at their most fertile.

So, some stinky T-shirts have provided a colorful thread of evidence that women smell better than usual to potential mates when women are highly fertile. Women may also sound better than usual when they are highly fertile. Pipitone and Gallup (2008) recorded women counting to ten at four different points in their ovulatory cycles. If it strikes you that counting to ten is not a very sexy pick-up line, you're absolutely right. The researchers wanted to control for the content of the women's speech so that only nonverbal cues (voice cues) could differ at different times of a woman's ovulatory cycle. Both male and female judges who were kept blind to the women's ovulatory status agreed that the women sounded more attractive than usual – that's right, when counting to ten – when recorded during the high fertility phases. Bryant and Haselton (2009) replicated this effect, having female UCLA undergrads record the simple phrase "Hi, I'm a student at UCLA." Acoustical analyses revealed that the pitch of the women's voices became higher (more stereotypically feminine) when they were recorded closer to the windows of greatest fertility.

In yet another study along these lines, researchers examined whether women look sexier than usual when they are at their most fertile. Haselton and colleagues (2007) took full-body photographs of 30 women when (according to a hormonal test) the women were either highly fertile or not fertile. Male and female judges who were kept blind to hypotheses viewed the photo pairs with the women's faces covered. Judges simply picked the photo in which the woman was "trying to look more attractive." About 60% of the time they chose the photos taken when women were highly fertile. In a follow-up study, Durante et al. (2008) observed similar findings when they asked women who were either at the most or least fertile window of their ovulatory cycles to draw a picture of what they would like to wear to a party that evening. Women who were ovulating drew sexier and more revealing outfits.

It's worth adding that variations on the stinky T-shirt study have also revealed that women differ in how they respond to cues given off by men at different times of their fertility cycles. A classic study by Rikowski and Grammer (1999) exposed women to what must have been some very stinky T-shirts. These T-shirts had been worn by sleeping men for three nights in a row (and carefully cooled and sealed up every day while the men went about their stinky daily lives). Compared with women who were in a less fertile phase of their ovulatory cycle, women who were in the fertile phase rated the men's stinky T-shirts as sexier than usual. Further, when women were in the fertile part of their cycles, they considered stinky T-shirts even sexier still when they had been worn by handsomer men (as judged by independent raters of the men's photos). Somehow, without knowing how they were doing it, reproductively receptive women preferred the smells of hotter men. Of course, men don't have an ovulatory cycle. But yes, Rikowski and Grammer studied men's reactions to stinky T-shirts, too. Men also judged T-shirts to have sexier smells when the shirts had come from more physically attractive women. Sometimes, the nose really knows.

"And for *this*, I shaved my legs, feet, back,
butt, chest, stomach, arms, hands, and neck?"

If your methodological senses are as refined as your olfactory senses, you may have noticed that the studies summarized here focused on a highly artificial situation – the laboratory, where very few human beings actually mate. Do these kind of findings replicate outside the lab? They do. Guéguen (2009) conducted a field study in a place that is essentially the opposite of the lab – a dance club. Specifically, Guéguen exposed women at a dance club to the same carefully controlled stimulus. It was always an attractive young man who invited them to dance, and he always used the same well-rehearsed protocol. Women who happened to be in the fertile phase of their ovulatory cycles were substantially more likely to say yes to the same request for a dance.

Field studies have also examined how men respond to women at different phases of women's ovulatory cycles. Miller et al. (2007) convinced exotic dancers at a Dallas strip club to participate in an online daily diary study. In this study, the dancers recorded exactly how much money they earned in tips for each of 60 days (minus their days off). Because Miller et al. studied the women day by day, they were able to count backwards from the point of the dancers' periods to identify the days on which the dancers were at their peak fertility. Further, they were able to make separate comparisons for dancers who were on the pill (whose hormones were being artificially regulated) and dancers who were not. They found that dancers who were not on the pill earned an extra $15 per hour in tips on high fertility days as compared with low fertility days. Because these are the same dancers working at the same club with the same motivation to make as much money as possible every night, it is hard to come up with any great alternative explanations for these findings. Putting all these lab and field studies together, it becomes hard to dismiss the evolutionary idea that human ovulation is a more powerful factor in human mating than most people realize (Miller & Maner, 2010).

SEXUAL REPULSION: INCEST AVOIDANCE

So, where mating is concerned, men aren't generally as picky as women. And where the timing of human interest in sex is concerned, timing isn't everything, but it is something – and it is something to men as well as to women. An evolutionary perspective on sex suggests a second area where men and women are generally in agreement. Both men and women should usually avoid harmful or truly indiscriminate mating. Thus, men and women seem to be in agreement that it's a bad idea to mate with cacti or with bald eagles. That's patently obvious, of course. I hope it's almost as obvious that almost all men and women avoid mating with close relatives. In fact, in cultures worldwide, incest is considered morally deplorable. If you want a reminder of how morally deplorable incest feels, consider the uncomfortable sexual scenario studied by evolutionary psychologist Jon Haidt (1995, p. 814):

> Julie and Mark are brother and sister. They're traveling together in France on summer vacation from college. One night they are staying alone in a cabin near the beach. They decide that it would be interesting and fun if they tried making love. At the very least, it would be a new experience … Julie was already taking birth control pills, but Mark uses a condom too, just to be safe. They both enjoy making love, but they decide never to do it again. They keep that night as a special secret, which makes them feel even closer to each other. What do you think about that? Was it ok for them to make love?

Almost everyone who hears this story agrees that there is something deeply yucky about sex between siblings, even when there is no chance at all it could lead to any offspring, even when it is not illegal, and even when it seems to have brought these two siblings closer together. Why? In contrast to purely logical or rational models of morality, evolutionary models assume that certain things are inherently yucky because they were not generally a good idea in human evolutionary history. There's no conscious calculation involved in this kind of instinctive reaction. It comes from millions of years of indirect genetic programming (aka, natural selection). Genes that make incest feel gross – however they do it – are likely to remain in the gene pool. But why?

It is well established that in almost all animals, people included, siring offspring with a close genetic relative has terrible genetic consequences for the offspring. This is because first degree relatives, such as siblings, are likely to share harmful recessive traits that neither healthy sibling would be likely to share with an unrelated stranger. Thus, those who have sex with close relatives court genetic disaster. Because this is true, most animals seem to have ways of identifying and sexually ostracizing others who share a lot of genes with them. Simply recognizing, consciously or unconsciously, that you grew up with another person could be at the root of **incest aversion (incest avoidance)**. After all, siblings almost always grow up together, and one or more aspects of sibling familiarity (facial cues, smell, etc.) could be reliably used to avoid mating with someone who might be genetically dangerous. A classic study of Israeli kibbutzim yielded support for this idea. In kibbutzim, genetically unrelated kids are reared collectively. So they grow up as if they were siblings even though they are not genetically related. Shepher (1971) studied records of more than 2,700 marriages recorded among people who grew up in Israeli kibbutzim. He was unable to find even a single record of a marriage between unrelated people who had grown up together since birth. That's right; zero, zilch, nada. It's important to note that this was true despite the fact that there were no cultural or religious rules of any sort prohibiting this kind of mating. So someone doesn't have to be your actual sibling to feel sexually repugnant; they just have to feel familiar the way siblings do (Fessler & Navarrete, 2004). Elephants don't live in kibbutzim. Thus, we can't know what they would think of mating with a highly familiar but genetically unrelated age-mate. But genetic studies show that wild elephants, like even the wildest people, avoid mating with close relatives. This being said, Archie and colleagues (2007) found that incest avoidance in elephants isn't quite as powerful as it seems to be among people, perhaps because in some small populations, it's hard to avoid relatives. Marrying your bald and prickly cousin might sometimes beat marrying an eagle or a cactus.

Although we can't claim to know all the cues people use to avoid the risks of incest, it's clear that one of them is probably olfactory (based on smell). In support of this idea, I'm sorry to say that your close opposite-sex relatives stink. That's right. The same stinky T-shirt paradigm that has been used to study human sensitivity to ovulation has also been used to show that we really dislike the smells of first degree relatives. In fact, a study by Weisfeld and colleagues (2003) showed that people were actually OK with the smells of their same-sex siblings. It was only the smell of people's opposite-sex siblings that both men and women found repulsive.

A brief detour on the human sense of smell

Because I've talked about smell a lot, I can't resist adding that our sense of smell is pretty wimpy compared with that of some other mammals. A dog can smell things that would have to be concentrated at least 10,000 times, some say 100,000 times (see Walker et al., 2006), to be detectable by me or you. If dogs had this same proportional advantage in the area of vision, they could see an object that was 40 miles away as well as you and I see it at 20 feet. And the noses of dogs aren't nearly as good as those of bears, who can smell food 18 miles away. These comparisons notwithstanding, the human sense of smell is nothing to sneeze at. We can detect the pleasant odor from just one drop of perfume in a space the size of six rooms (Galanter, 1962). In fact, we go to great lengths to remove most of our natural body odors, and most of us are very careful about when and where we release natural odors. Caring about smell is in our genes. Our sense of smell exists for reasons other than sex; two of the most important of which must be locating food and identifying people.

"Hey, isn't that ole' Rex Conley over there? Why I haven't smelled him in years!"

There are plenty of cultures that place a great deal of stock in smell, and I suspect that people living in most modern cultures could be trained to pay a lot more attention to smell. Newborns certainly care about smell. This is one of the main ways in which they find out where to nurse. In one very elegant study, researchers asked nursing mothers to carefully wash only one of their breasts and then offer both to their hungry infants. Most infants clearly preferred the breast that had not been cleaned. Apparently, mom smelled a lot better than soap.

So, if you thought smell only mattered when it comes to sex and homemade chocolate chip cookies, you'd be wrong. Smelling another person is visceral and deeply emotional. It makes you feel you are in that person's presence. Think about someone you love. Now picture that person. I could even show you a picture of that person, and you probably wouldn't feel that the person was in the room with you. But if you smelled the person's scent, I suspect you'd feel like the person was right there. There hasn't been much research on this topic, but studies do show that smells can trigger powerful emotional memories. You can find a heartbreaking example of this in an interview Dave Davies (2015) conducted with journalist Jill Leovy. Leovy had the painful job of writing about the families of murder victims. Here's how she described an interaction between Barbara, mother of murder victim Dovon, and a detective assigned to return some of Dovon's possessions:

> He's brought her the shoes of Dovon that have been sitting in an evidence locker, and he gives her the shoes. And Barbara does what I've seen other mothers do, which is she puts the opening of the shoe against her face to get the scent of her son. The scent of these victims – scent lingers on their clothes and on their shoes. And when she smells him, she collapses and slides down the wall on the floor. And Skaggs [the detective] stands there, and she sobs. And that's all that

happens. They just stay in that position, and it's the kind of thing that happens to you a lot if you're a homicide detective.

Scents are emotionally powerful, to people as well as to dogs. The likely reason why is suggested in a report from the UK's Social Issues Research Centre:

> Our olfactory receptors are directly connected to the limbic system, the most ancient and primitive part of the brain, which is thought to be the seat of emotion ... by the time we correctly name a particular scent ... the scent has already activated the limbic system, triggering more deep-seated emotional responses. (Fox, 2009, p. 4)

When a sense is so intimately linked to sex, eating, and identifying those you love, it stands to reason that the scent will be the source of some strong emotions. Smell is as powerful as it is ancient.

From smell back to incest avoidance

Smells matter. But smell alone can't be the whole story of incest avoidance, at least not for women. Lieberman et al. (2011) wondered if women might avoid even talking to a close male relative when they were at the most fertile points of their ovulatory cycles. To see, Lieberman et al. tracked the cell phone calls female UCLA students made to their mothers and their fathers during a monthly cell phone billing cycle. By establishing a fertile (ovulatory) and an infertile (non-ovulatory) window for each woman, and by tallying the frequency and duration of each woman's cell phone calls, these researchers were able to see if the women avoided communicating with their dads when the women were highly fertile. Women were about half as likely to call their fathers on days when the women were fertile as on days when they were not fertile. And when women did call their dads on the days when they were highly fertile, they kept these conversations much briefer than usual. The same women showed the opposite pattern when it came to phoning their mothers. When women were at their most fertile, they were more likely than usual to call their moms, and they spoke to their moms a bit longer than usual.

It's hard to explain these findings without reference to ovulation and some kind of father-specific aversion. Figure 4.4 summarizes these findings. When they were ovulating, and only when they were ovulating, women avoided talking to those otherwise lovable, middle-aged men who were making 167,000 sperm during a typical one-minute, father–daughter phone call.

This is a good time to note that evolutionary psychologists do not think people self-consciously try to promote the survival of their genes. I'm pretty sure that none of the ovulating participants in the cell phone study said to themselves: "Hmmm ... I'd kind of like to call my dad today – to see if he got that big promotion. But I'm just too hot and sexy right now. Yeah, I'll like totally wait until I'm less fertile." Phenomena such as incest avoidance, ovulation detection, and preferences based on parental investment, much like preferences for sweet or fatty foods, are driven largely by innate or easily learned preferences. It's unlikely that people have much conscious access to the instinctive, emotional processes that drive them.

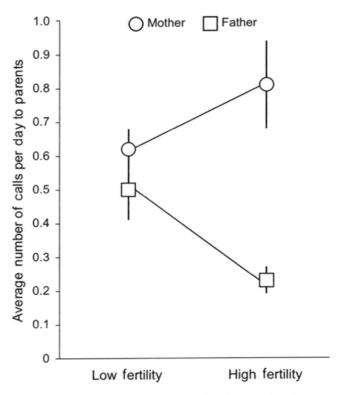

Figure 4.4 *Young women were less likely than usual to call their dads when they were highly fertile. The same women were more likely to call their moms when they were highly fertile. This same pattern held up for length of calls made in addition to likelihood of calls.*

SEXUAL JEALOUSY

Perhaps you're wondering if evolutionary psychologists study anything other than pick-up lines or stinky T-shirts. They do. They also study the lipstick on people's collars. Sexual jealousy is another hot topic in evolutionary psychology. Every culture in the world has rules about who can have sex with whom, and people often get hot under the collar when they suspect their romantic partners of having sex with someone else. This is especially true when two people have agreed to have sex only with one another. People get jealous. They probably should. Sexual infidelity exists in every culture on earth, even in those in which it carries the risk of public disgrace or stoning. There is a sense in which infidelity is more worrisome for men than for women because, as you should recall, men can never be absolutely sure of paternity. Remember "daddy's maybe"? If I spend years caring for a kid I believe to be my own, when, in fact, he was fathered by the milkman, that's a big reason for me to cry over spilled milk. Duping another man into caring for a child you fathered is known as **cuckoldry**. Likewise, the man who becomes the victim in such a sexual scam is known as a **cuckold**.

The terms cuckold and cuckoldry get their names from **cuckoo birds**, who often lay their eggs in the nests of other birds, allowing the victims to incubate and then dutifully raise the cuckoo chicks. If you're wondering how another bird could be so easily duped, you shouldn't assume that the victims are all bird-brains. First, male and female cuckoos often work as a team – just like many of the best human con artists. Among some of the sneakier cuckoo species, the male strongly resembles a hawk when he is overhead. So it's easy for him to scare small birds out of their nests. Cuckoos are invariably bigger than their victims; that helps, too. Once the male cuckoo scares the victim from her nest, the female cuckoo swoops in, throws exactly one existing egg out of the nest, lays her own egg in about 10 seconds, and departs. And in some cuckoo species, the cuckoo's egg looks very much like the eggs of the victims. In these cases, the more difficult it is for a human observer to tell the cuckoo's egg from the victim's, the less likely the victim is to notice the swindle and cast out the cuckoo's egg (Payne, 2005).

Figure 4.5 *A mother reed warbler is raising a common cuckoo, who will likely grow up to continue the con on other generations of hapless reed warblers. I know, it looks crazy to an outsider, but you and I would surely fall for it, too.*

It doesn't stop there. Female cuckoos have evolved to retain their own eggs for an extra 24 hours once the eggs are fully formed. This gives the cuckoo's eggs a 24-hour head start over most of the victims' eggs. I'm still not done. Once all the chicks have hatched, the cuckoo chick uses its sheer size to evict all the mother bird's real offspring (as in "Whoopsie! Have a nice flight, little guys without any feathers yet"). I mean, how can a mother be expected to feed a huge cuckoo chick if she has to feed her own chicks as well? That's just not going to fly. The backstabbing, double-dealing villains in reality TV shows have nothing on the cuckoo. No wonder people used to lock them up in clocks (see also Adams, 2009).

Of course, this sweet deal for the cuckoos is a bitter rip-off for the cuckoo's unsuspecting victims, who go on to feed the chicks of the sneaky cuckoo birds until the chicks can barely fit in the victims' tiny nests. I guess the cuckoo's victims have one advantage over cuckolded human dads, which is that the birds never seem to know they've been conned. In the case of people, being repeatedly lied to and screwed over can be a source of great misery – and thus, of course, it is the subject of many jokes. Here's one I've adapted from David Buss (1995, p. 15).

Bill came home one night and announced to his parents that he was marrying the woman of his dreams. Her name was Molly, she was lovely, she lived five houses down, and they would marry in June. Later that night Bill's dad pulled him aside and made a confession: "When I was young, I was a bit of a scoundrel. I screwed around on your mom. I'm sorry to say you can't marry Molly. She's your half-sister." Bill was devastated, and he never forgave his father. Eventually, however, Bill met a woman named Holly, they fell deeply in love, and they planned to marry. Again Bill shared the good news with his parents. Again his dad pulled him aside: "I was really quite a scoundrel when your mom and I were first married. I'm sorry to say Holly is also your half-sister." Bill was furious. This time, he pulled his mother aside and ratted his dad out, pointing out that his philandering father had once again ruined his chances of marriage. His mother remained calm: "I wouldn't worry about what that asshole says, honey. He's not your real father."

Cuckoldry rates in people and sexual jealousy

Estimates of the rates of cuckoldry in people vary widely by detection method, and across cultures. But a review by Anderson (2006) suggested that, even among men who reported feeling highly certain that they were the biological fathers of their children, rates of cuckoldry were nothing to sneeze at. Rates seem to have ranged from less than 1% in some countries and regions to more than 10% in others. Some argue that this is a pretty low rate, but remember that this is what is happening in an age of birth control, private investigators, and some awareness of DNA testing. It's very hard to know how to convert a 5% cuckoldry rate into rates of extramarital affairs. But to state the obvious, at least some people who have extramarital affairs work hard to be sure that the affairs do not lead to extramarital pregnancies. Rates of infidelity are almost certainly much higher than rates of cuckoldry. So, in a place where 5% of all married men's children are being fathered by the butcher or the baker, most candlestick makers have good reason to worry about whether the children they are rearing are truly their own.

So cheating happens. And in the evolutionary history of hominids, it probably happened more than it does now. In light of this enormous inconvenience, evolutionary psychologists have argued, men and women should both worry a lot about sexual cheating but in predictably different ways. Recall the assumption from parental investment theory that, on average, women are likely to be more invested in their offspring than men are. Further, in altricial creatures like us, our offspring require many years of parental care. What a typical woman might wish for, then, would be a reliable, committed partner who is emotionally committed to her. The long-term emotional bond would presumably keep him around long enough to develop those irresistible dishpan hands we talked about earlier. In contrast, from an evolutionary perspective, a typical man should wish for a partner who is sexually faithful (rather than emotionally committed). After all, if his partner has even one well-timed tryst with a sexual cheater, this could lead to a case of cuckoldry that is a terrible deal for the male victim.

David Buss and colleagues (1992) have put gender differences in **sexual jealousy** to many tests. In the simplest test, they merely asked people which specific kind of infidelity would bother them more. Remember, people were choosing between a rock and a hard place. The rock was having their partner become deeply and emotionally attached to another person. The hard place was having their partner enjoy passionate sex with that person. No one was crazy about either option, but when asked which was worse, 60% of men but only 17% of women said the sexual infidelity would bother them more. Buss and colleagues (1999) replicated this sex difference in Korea and Japan. Finally, follow-up studies have shown that sexual jealousy plays out in real life much as it did in Buss's scenario studies. In a review of research on sexual jealousy, Buss (2013) summarized how people respond to real sexual indiscretions. Women are more likely to dump men because of perceived emotional infidelity. Men are more likely to dump women because of perceived sexual infidelity. These breakup patterns are consistent with the evolutionary ideas that men desire women who will be sexually faithful (so the men won't be cuckolded), whereas women desire men who will be emotionally faithful. This way women won't get stuck doing all the driving – whether this means driving all the predators away or driving all the kids to school.

Good reason to be jealous: mate poaching

Research also shows that both men and women engage in mate poaching and mate guarding. **Mate poaching** refers to trying to attract a sexual or romantic partner who you know to be in an existing relationship. **Mate guarding** is taking measures to prevent this kind of romantic or sexual thievery, and it can get ugly. People are not the only animals to engage in mate poaching or mate guarding. As you'll see in Chapter 8 (on aggression), many male animals (especially alpha males who try to maintain a harem of desirable females) must be constantly on the lookout for mate poachers (those who would gladly mate with members of a harem if the alpha male did not guard them). Male baboons, for example, are known to limit their foraging ranges because of concerns about mate poachers (Alberts et al., 1996).

In people, women as well as men admit to having tried to poach a mate who they knew to be "taken." In a study of people in 53 nations, Schmitt (2004) found that 35% of women and 57% of men admitted that they had "attempted to attract someone who was already in a relationship." Of course, this gender difference is highly consistent with parental investment theory. It's also consistent with parental investment theory that this gender difference grew smaller when people were asked about long-term mate poaching. For men, the value didn't change at all; it was still 57%. But rates for women increased from 35% to 43%. Gender differences in mate poaching are thus smaller for long-term poaching than for short-term poaching. Culture matters, too. Gender differences in self-reported mate poaching were smaller than usual in regions of the world where women enjoy greater social power. In Western Europe, for example, 56% of men and 46% of women admitted to having engaged in long-term mate poaching.

People's efforts to prevent mate poaching also follow predictable rules. For example, people who are jealous engage in more fervent mate guarding efforts, whether they have good reason to be jealous or not (Buss, 2013). Unfortunately, jealousy surrounding one's mate can also beget physical violence, especially when the jealous person is a man (Daly & Wilson, 1988a). On a less violent note, people often take much more subtle steps to guard their mates. Inspired by work showing that women become more attractive when they are ovulating, Krems et al. (2016) showed that women involved in heterosexual romantic relationships are very sensitive to cues of ovulation in other women.

In one study, Krems et al. (2016) showed women photos of other women "taken during either their ovulatory or nonovulatory menstrual-cycle phases." Without knowing exactly why, of course, women reported that they would socially avoid ovulating women more than they would avoid non-ovulating women. However, this was true only for women who rated their current romantic partners favorably. Another study revealed that showing women photos of ovulating women increased their desire to have sex with their own partners. Again this was true only for women who rated their current partners as highly desirable. Krems et al. (2016, p. 551) argued that "women can be sensitive to subtle cues of other women's fertility and respond (e.g., via social exclusion, enhanced sexual attention to own mate) in ways that may facilitate their mate retention goals while not thwarting their affiliative goals."

Sela and colleagues (2015) have documented conceptually similar effects. They argue that providing one's romantic partner (male or female) with oral sex may be best conceptualized as a "mate retention strategy." For example, they've shown that both men and women who report greater interest in holding onto their romantic partners spend more time performing oral sex on their partners. They have also shown, by the way, that people higher in the personality traits of agreeableness and conscientiousness give their romantic partners more oral sex.

If this research finding ever makes its way to the masses, I envision a lot of personal ads that say things like "SWF seeks SWACM," where everyone knows that the A and the C stand for agreeableness and conscientiousness. At any rate, when it comes to retaining a mate, it looks like some people would rather "make love, not war." Notice that this research suggests that both men and women often engage in mate retention strategies. Of course, oral sex is just one of many such strategies. More obvious mate retention strategies range from being highly vigilant when a stranger appears to be flirting with one's partner to holding a highly public wedding ceremony. As my friend Yon-Say (personal communication) put it: "If you liked it, then you should've put a ring on it!" Of course, "putting a ring on it" should help reduce mate poaching whether your partner is male or female, although no mate guarding strategy is absolutely foolproof. Even more than is the case for most other primates, then, people are both highly social and highly sexual creatures.

We are born highly social, by the way, even though we are not born highly sexual. But both human sexuality and human sociality develop in ways that are virtually unprecedented in the animal world. Chapter 5 is about how we develop and change over the course of our lives.

FOR FURTHER READING

» Buss, D. M., Larsen, R. J., Westen, D. & Semmelroth, J. (1992). Sex differences in jealousy: Evolution, physiology, and psychology. *Psychological Science*, 3(4), 251–5.

» Haselton, M.G. & Gangestad, S.W. (2006). Conditional expression of women's desires and men's mate guarding across the ovulatory cycle. *Hormones and Behavior*, 49(4), 509–18.

» Judson, O. (2002). *Dr. Tatiana's sex advice to all creation*. New York: Metropolitan Books.

» Kenrick, D.T., Sadalla, E.K., Groth, G. & Trost, M.R. (1990). Evolution, traits, and the stages of human courtship: Qualifying the parental investment model. *Journal of Personality*, 58(1), 97–116.

» Lieberman, D., Pillsworth, E.G. & Haselton, M.G. (2011). Kin affiliation across the ovulatory cycle: Females avoid fathers when fertile. *Psychological Science*, 22(1), 13–18.

» Sela, Y., Shackelford, T.K., Pham, M.N. & Euler, H.A. (2015). Do women perform fellatio as a mate retention behavior? *Personality and Individual Differences*, 73, 61–6.

SAMPLE MULTIPLE-CHOICE EXAM QUESTIONS

Here are four sample quiz questions for Chapter 4. You can find the Chapter 4 quiz at: www.macmillanihe.com/evolutionary-psychology

4.01.   From the perspective of parental investment theory, the average human mother is usually more invested in her offspring than is the average human father. Why?

   a.   women carry developing babies inside their bodies

   b.   women only produce about one egg per month

   c.   unlike men, women can nurse their offspring

   d.   A–C are all correct

4.02.   The opposite of precocial is:

   a.   altricial

   b.   bipedal

   c.   delayed

4.03. The peacock's vividly colorful and hard-to-maintain tail feathers are a good example of:

a. exaptation

b. sexual selection

c. an evolutionary trap

4.04. What do most evolutionary experts say about the concept of race?

a. the idea of race has little or no biological basis

b. the five most common races separated about 500,000 years ago

c. different racial groups are best thought of as different subspecies of *Homo sapiens*

Answer Key: d, a, b, a.

Chapter 5

WILL YOU NEVER GROW UP?

HUMAN DEVELOPMENT

"In genetic epistemology, as in developmental psychology, too, there is never an absolute beginning."

— *Jean Piaget (1970, p. 19)*

"You aren't just the age you are. You are all the ages you have ever been."

— *Kenneth Koch (source unknown)*

For several decades now, evolutionary psychologists have studied sex, but they aren't quite as obsessed with sex as you might think. In addition to ovulation, sperm competition, and cuckoldry, they also care about things like nipples, conception, pregnancy, and breastfeeding. Hmmm. Maybe evolutionary psychologists are a little preoccupied with sex, but remember that sex is a huge force in natural selection. This includes the fact that sexual reproduction in and of itself is a sort of genetic insurance program. As E.O. Wilson (1978, p. 124) put it, sexual reproduction is a way of hedging one's genetic bets in a changing world:

> When the two gametes unite in fertilization they create an instant mixture of genes surrounded by the durable housing of the egg. By cooperating to create

zygotes, the female and male make it more likely that at least some of their offspring will survive in the event of a changing environment. A fertilized egg differs from an asexually reproducing cell in one fundamental respect: it contains a newly assembled admixture of genes.

So sexual reproduction itself evolved to create novel combinations of traits. Further, sexual reproduction apparently works so well that very few living animals get by without it. If sex goes well, of course, this leads to the physical development of the fertilized egg (the zygote) that E.O. Wilson found so biologically intriguing. With this in mind, let's take an evolutionary peek at human development, beginning with pregnancy and prenatal development. Human prenatal development is evolutionarily telling. In fact, I'd like to argue that two of the most interesting things about prenatal development are how telling it is when it goes right and how telling it is when it goes wrong.

So what happens when it goes right? One of the most interesting things that happens in successful embryonic development is based loosely on an idea proposed in the early 1800s. Writing 31 years before Darwin proposed his theory of evolution, German embryologist Karl Ernst von Baer (1828) vaguely hinted that the embryonic development of a specific organism mirrors the ancient history of that organism. About 40 years later, shortly after Darwin proposed the modern theory of evolution, another German guy named Ernst, Ernst Heinrich Philipp August Haeckel, made an even bolder proclamation: "**ontogeny recapitulates phylogeny.**"

HAECKEL'S TIME MACHINE

Haeckel believed that the development of an embryo over the course of days or weeks (ontogeny) revealed, in detailed ways, what had happened in the ancient evolutionary history of that organism (phylogeny). It's easy to see why Haeckel got excited when he compared images of the embryos of different animals. As shown in Figure 5.1, which is taken from Haeckel's (1874) *Anthropogenie*, animals as different as fish, turtles, and people do look surprisingly similar when they first begin to develop. Then they dramatically diverge. In fact, early in our own embryological development, we have pretty obvious gill pouches (Gould, 1977). The same pouches that become gills in fish become part of our necks and heads. In fact, one human adult in ten still retains a tiny vestigial gill hole (Shubin, 2008).

You will also notice that when we first begin to develop we have a very obvious tail. In fact, we have retained a vestigial (small, left over) tailbone. A few people are even born with short external tails. Having said this, Haeckel was accused, pretty fairly, of taking some artistic liberties with some of his technical drawings. In more technical terms, there was probably a bit of **experimenter bias** (seeing what he was looking for) in some of Haeckel's observations. His famous proclamation proved to be something of an oversimplification. More than 100 years of embryological research has revealed that embryonic development is not quite the faithful evolutionary time machine that Haeckel had believed. To

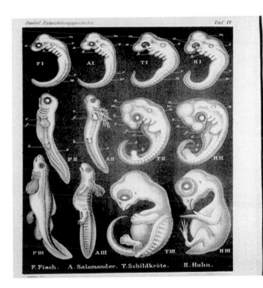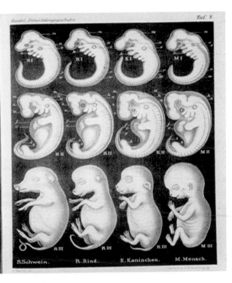

Figure 5.1 *Haeckel's (1874) original technical drawings of prenatal (or pre-hatching) development in six different animals.*

add some detail, Kalinka and Tomancak (2012) argued that the middle period of embryonic development tells us much more about an organism's phylogenetic history than does the beginning period. Presumably, the reason is that the middle (phylotypic) period is when the details of an animal's body structures are really beginning to take shape.

On the other hand, as suggested by paleobiologists such as Neil Shubin, there is one aspect of von Baer and Haeckel's shared view that has held up pretty well. It seems fair to say that sometimes ontogeny *sort of* recapitulates phylogeny. This is closely related to the idea that there's a lot of conservation in embryonic development. Out of all the millions of possible ways to build a goat from a zygote, nature has recycled a few basic ways across millions of species. According to Kalinka and Tomancak (2012), you always begin with fertilization, which gives us E.O. Wilson's amazing genetically admixtured zygote. This is followed by the development of two of the physical axes of the body (front to back and internal to external). The developing zygote for an organism with a meaningful top and a bottom as well as a left and a right must have an orientation before it can begin to have a specific shape. A few steps and a great deal of cell division later, and we've made it from zygote to early embryo. Now we have the nearly universal arrangement of the three cell layers that reliably become certain parts of all animals that exhibit **bilateral symmetry**.

In all bilaterally symmetrical animals, from crickets to cricket players, the ectoderm will become the nervous system, whereas the mesoderm will become the muscles. In mammals, the mesoderm will also become the skeleton, whereas the ectoderm will become the skin. Of course, insects don't have bones or flexible skin, and so the parallels between human and insect development are fewer than those between people and other mammals. However, the basic strategy of

Figure 5.2 *Leonardo da Vinci's famous* Vitruvian Man *illustrates bilateral symmetry. Like dogs, butterflies, robins, and turtles, we have a top and a bottom as well as a left and a right. If you divide us laterally (head to toe), our left and right halves are mirror images of one another.*

beginning with the three layers (endoderm, ectoderm and mesoderm) exists in millions of animal species, and is conserved very well (used over and over again) in all vertebrates (Keller et al., 2003).

WHAT CAN GO WRONG SOMETIMES DOES

Where does all this leave us? It leaves us developing in much the same way that many other animals do, and in a highly predictable fashion. To be more specific, the window of about 15–60 days of human development is known as **organogenesis**. It is so named ("organo" and "genesis") because this is when all the major organs begin to develop. This makes it a crucial window for a pregnant woman to be concerned about **teratogens**. To paraphrase Kimmel (2001), a teratogen is anything to which a mother and developing baby are exposed that causes abnormal development. As the term is normally used, then, a teratogen is an insult to the mother during pregnancy that leads to an injury to the developing embryo. Teratogens range from nicotine and alcohol, both of which cross the placenta when a mother-to-be smokes or drinks, to psychological stress, which creates a strong risk of low birth weight (Lobel et al., 1992).

Perhaps the most dramatic example of a teratogen is the drug thalidomide, which pregnant women used to prevent morning sickness in Germany and other parts of Europe beginning in the late 1950s (LaBarba, 1981). Unfortunately, thalidomide also prevents the embryo's arms and legs – and some internal organs – from developing normally. Until the medical community realized the potent teratogenic effects of thalidomide, thousands of European babies were born suffering from very serious deformities. About half of them did not survive to adulthood.

In light of the chilling consequences teratogens can have for the developing embryo, it is obviously important for pregnant women to avoid teratogens, especially during the first trimester of a pregnancy. It seems to be no accident, then, that **morning sickness** (the nausea and vomiting that many women experience when pregnant) is most common during the first trimester of a woman's pregnancy. In fact, Flaxman and Sherman (2000) reviewed a lot of evidence suggesting that morning sickness is yet another price many mothers-to-be pay to protect their developing embryos. Flaxman and Sherman summarized four lines of evidence suggesting that morning sickness is an evolved, and perhaps uniquely human, adaptation that protects the developing embryo:

1. As I already noted, morning sickness is most likely to occur at precisely the window of pregnancy when teratogens pose the greatest risk to the embryo.

2. Women who have morning sickness are less likely to have miscarriages than are women who do not.

3. Studies show that vomiting – not nausea – is the key symptom that protects the developing embryo. This is informative because there is no known benefit to the embryo to having mom feel nauseated, but plenty of benefit to having her puke her poor guts out – to be absolutely sure the embryo isn't being exposed to any teratogens.

4. During their first trimester, many pregnant women develop distastes for specific foods and drugs, such as meats, caffeine, and alcohol, all known to pose a risk to the developing embryo. Bitter foods such as broccoli often become intolerable. This is probably no accident; many teratogens and poisons are naturally bitter.

If you are thinking that it can't really be good for an embryo when its mother is puking her guts out for many weeks, remember that women who suffer from morning sickness do not starve; they are almost always able to keep some food down (usually the bland, teratogen-free stuff like rice crackers, or oatmeal). Further, remember that during the first trimester of pregnancy the embryo is still teeny and does not yet require that many calories to develop normally. Just as evolution has little pity for male redback spiders or male praying mantises, it seems to have little pity for mothers who get sick as a dog, so long as it doesn't kill them and it confers a meaningful benefit – or used to – to the developing baby.

EVOLUTION AND EARLY POSTNATAL DEVELOPMENT

Got milk? Not for long

Additional examples of how evolutionary forces shape early human development come from what happens during infancy and early childhood. If you recall that we are the world's most altricial (slow to mature) species, you might be surprised to learn that we wean our little ones pretty young. This is true even if we take the natural human time of **weaning** from traditional human cultures, where it usually happens much later than in modern cultures (a little after the age of two is pretty common). Considering both how wimpy our teeth are and how slowly we develop, then, you'd probably expect us to wean very late. After all, we have nothing but our "milk teeth" until we are about six years old. At the other extreme, domestic dogs have formidable teeth as adults, and they reach adulthood in about a year. Many dogs naturally wean their pups when the pups reach four to five weeks for a couple of obvious reasons – the most obvious of which is that it must hurt like crazy to have a predator's teeth sinking into your nipples.

As you can see in Figure 5.3, adult chimps have huge **canine teeth (canines)**. However, these canines do not begin to replace a chimp's baby teeth until chimps are about seven or eight years old (Bolter & Zihlman, 2011). Devoted chimp mothers often nurse their offspring until the youngsters are four or five. Gorillas, too, have huge canines as adults. They also mature slowly, and they hold off on weaning until their young are about four years old. So, given that we human beings are even slower to develop than either of our primate cousins, that we have huge brains, and that we have pretty harmless teeth, you might expect us to breastfeed our children until we're sure they're pretty good at calculus – so we know they can get high-paying jobs. Instead, women in most traditional cultures wean their children at about the age of two. Why so soon?

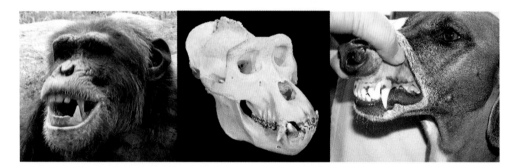

Figure 5.3 *Chimps and gorillas have large, aptly named canine teeth ("fangs"), but canines make their appearance much sooner in dogs than in primates. Unsurprisingly, dogs wean their young much sooner than chimps or gorillas.*

To answer this developmental riddle, Psouni et al. (2012) carefully analyzed average weaning times for a veritable zoo full of mammals (e.g., cats, mice, chimps, deer, bears, goats, camels, and elephant shrews). Across these 67 different mammals, there was wide variation in weaning times. Further, Psouni et al. could predict these weaning times extremely well from one species to another – from three things. First, bigger brained animals weaned their young later. Can you say altricial? If you can't, start practicing. Second, animals that walked later weaned later. Go ahead, say altricial again. If I can't yet walk, you can be pretty sure I can't yet find my own food. Third, animals with lots of meat in their diets weaned sooner. This probably has as much to do with the protein requirements of building big brains as it does with scary fangs, because people have much more meat in their diets than either chimps or gorillas. Gorillas are strict vegetarians. Their huge canines are for fighting and scaring off – not for eating. Chimps are delighted to eat meat whenever they can hunt it down. But our superior tool and weapon use, combined with our mastery of fire, means that we typically get way more meat in our diets than chimps do.

In a nutshell, then, our extraordinary ability to provide our toddlers with protein seems to have freed up human mothers from six or seven years of nursing. For better or worse, this freedom from extended nursing also seems to have allowed human mothers to have kids in closer succession than would otherwise have been possible. This is because nursing serves as a natural form of birth control, reducing the likelihood of ovulation. Coming back to the naturalistic fallacy we discussed earlier, let's assume Psouni and colleagues are absolutely correct. There are evolutionarily predictable reasons why human beings eat a lot of meat and don't nurse very long. This does not mean that meat-eating is ethical or that early weaning is healthy for babies. I must admit that I love meat myself, but as I have aged I have begun to eat less ridiculous amounts of it, for both ethical and environmental reasons. Along the same lines, the fact that we wean our young at an early age does not mean that human babies would not benefit from a longer period of breastfeeding. Breastfeeding has well-documented benefits, which include boosting children's intellectual development, strengthening their immune systems, and strengthening the psychological bonds between mothers and their children (see Kramer et al., 2008). To paraphrase Steven Pinker, evolution can provide a compelling picture of how we got here, but it doesn't have to dictate where we go next.

Slow to see, quick to taste

Another unusual aspect of early human postnatal development is how long it takes us to see well. So I can put something in bold for you, I'll refer to this as **altricial visual development**. At birth we are almost blind, and every aspect of human neonate vision is seriously flawed relative to normal adult vision. In fact, a newborn's sensitivity to light is only one *fiftieth* that of an adult – which is one reason newborns have no difficulty sleeping at any time of day. A newborn's visual acuity is also about 20/800 – at 20 feet they see about as well as we do at 800, yes, eight hundred, feet (Brown & Yamamoto, 1986). Newborns also have poor sensitivity to contrast and thus have difficulty detecting edges and boundaries. Finally, they lack the ability to track moving objects, and they have little or no color vision. Our vision isn't fully developed until the age of five. So, you can probably see better than your three-year-old niece can, and your grandmother can probably see better than your five-month-old nephew can.

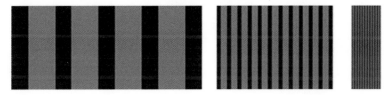

Figure 5.4 *Babies should not be left in charge of UPC barcodes. The left image represents the limits of the visual acuity of a typical week-old infant. Make the stripes any narrower and a week-old baby can't tell that there are any stripes at all. The middle image shows what a typical eight-month old can barely see. The right image is the adult standard. If you can't tell that there are stripes there, please see your optometrist, you big baby.*

In comparison with newborn humans, precocial birds such as chickens and geese can see in vivid colors immediately after hatching. Their visual acuity only a week after hatching allows them to forage for food. At birth, Old World monkeys are just as blind as newborn humans are, but their vision develops four times as quickly as ours does (Boothe et al., 1985). None of these human visual limitations get in the way of normal human functioning for the first few years of life, however, because of the prolonged attention and protection we receive from our principal caregivers, usually our moms. In stark contrast to their terrible vision, human newborns have a well-developed sense of taste. At birth, they recognize all five basic flavors except for saltiness, and they respond favorably to sugars and glutamate (both of which are found in human breast milk). Conversely, newborns show a strong aversion to most sour and bitter tastes. Newborns also hear much better than they can see. In fact, babies often learn to tell the difference between their mother's voices and other voices while still in the womb. They even prefer the cadence of stories their mothers read them shortly before birth to the cadence of unheard stories (DeCasper & Spence, 1986).

This combination of one horribly developed sense (sight) and one highly developed sense (taste) at birth may seem quirky, but recall that a basic principle of evolution is that natural selection is pretty efficient. Things rarely develop in the life history of an organism before they are needed, especially when these things are biologically complex or metabolically costly. Recall that we also have a pretty good sense of smell at birth. This comes in handy for nursing. Recall further that there are differences in the rate of development across predators and prey, as well as big differences between reptiles (which are highly precocial) and mammals (which are generally altricial). Birds go both ways, depending on the species. But even the most helpless birds grow up in weeks or months rather than years. Although we're a highly altricial species on the whole, we are most helpless in the domain of vision, where we can most easily get away with it. We're much more highly developed at birth in the domain of taste, because being able to taste is crucial to our early survival.

Figure 5.5 *Like most other songbird chicks, these chicks are blind and helpless just after hatching, but they already have well-developed chirping systems. They won't need to see well, or fly, for example, until they get so big that their parents can't keep up with their appetites.*

Extremely quick to do what's instinctive

To wind down this discussion of early development, it's worth noting that there are also several reflexes that are highly predictable from an evolutionary perspective. A **reflex** is an innate (instinctive, hardwired) behavior that occurs reliably in specific situations, without any need for learning or insight. Let's begin with two neonatal reflexes. The **palmar (grasping) reflex** is the innate tendency for neonates to grab firmly onto anything you place in their palms. This reflex is probably a lot more useful to primate babies whose moms carry them on their hairy backs than it is to human babies, whose moms need slings or strollers (pushchairs) to transport them. But this grasping reflex seems to have hung on pretty well even after we became so hairless. Another highly adaptive neonatal reflex is the **rooting reflex**, which is the tendency for newborns to turn their heads and suck when you lightly stroke their cheeks. This promotes successful breastfeeding, and I'd be surprised if some variation on this reflex doesn't exist for almost all mammals.

Neonatal reflexes disappear during infancy, but there are a few human reflexes that remain intact for life, and most of these seem to promote survival. Such reflexes include blinking, sneezing, and coughing, which all occur when different parts of your body are highly irritated. Blinking protects your eyes, and both sneezing and coughing protect your airways. Shivering when you are cold – to conserve heat – is another reflex that seems pretty adaptive. It's probably less useful to get goose bumps when you are scared or threatened, but if you've ever seen a dog, cat, or chimp whose hair stands up on end in a scary situation, you can guess that goose bumps are a form of baggage that stuck around even after we lost most of our body hair. In almost all mammals other than people, having your hair stand up on end makes you look bigger and more threatening than usual. I'd love to know if dolphins get goose bumps when they get scared. Finally, consider the potent reflex of pulling your hand away from a source of intense pain, such as a hot stovetop. This reflex is so simple that it doesn't even require a brain. As Marshall Hall (1833) demonstrated long ago, freshly decapitated animals show a version of this **hot stove reflex**. This rapid response to a painful stimulus requires only functional limbs and an intact spinal cord (including the crucial medulla oblongata). If you had to mull it over before pulling your hand from a flame, you'd be an unhappy camper at almost any campfire.

THE EVOLUTION OF CRITICAL AND SENSITIVE PERIODS

Human development is all about timing, and one of the most interesting topics in human development has to do with the specificity of this timing. Are we equally able to learn or develop at all phases of life? Or are there certain crucial windows of opportunity for specific kinds of development, after which the doors close forever? Even if a specific door never closes forever, are there periods after which specific doors become a lot more difficult to open? Developmental psychologists refer to specific periods that are the only opportunities for something to develop normally as **critical periods**.

Anyone familiar with **life history theory** would be quick to note that there are plenty of critical periods in both human and animal development. I discussed critical periods earlier in this chapter, without using this term, when I summarized the impact of teratogens on prenatal development. But even in the absence of teratogens, aspects of an animal's developmental trajectory can become set early in life. For example, juvenile water fleas who molt in the presence of chemical clues indicating the presence of predators become armored. They develop a large helmet and/or a sharp spine on their tails. They fail to develop this protective armor, though, if the chemical composition of their liquid neighborhood yields no signs of lurking predators (Weiss et al., 2012). If lots of predators move in after they have molted, they are simply out of luck. The critical period for triggering the development of armor has passed. On the other hand, if they were to produce the armor when it was unnecessary, they would be wasting a lot of biological resources. Armor must be built and then it must be maintained. Life history theory addresses the ways in which developing animals balance costs and benefits. Critical periods can be, well, critical, to which of two or more specific developmental route an organism takes.

It was embryologist Charles Stockard who seems to have been the first person to use terms like "critical moment" and "sensitive period." Stockard studied the crucial importance of timing in prenatal development, and he knew very well that different human organs and tissues develop at different times. As Stockard (1921, p. 139) put it: "when an important organ is entering its initial stage of rapid proliferation or budding, a serious interruption of the developmental progress often causes decided injuries to this particular organ, while only slight or no ill effects may be suffered by the embryo in general." We now know that many teratogens have terrible consequences for specific organs, including the brain, because they mess things up precisely when that organ is first beginning to develop. During the unimaginably rapid period of growth and development known as pregnancy, then, there seem to be lots of critical periods.

The idea of critical periods gained momentum many years after Stockard, based on clever studies of critical periods in highly precious birds such as geese and ducks (which leave their nests quickly after hatching). For example, Konrad Lorenz (1952) showed that shortly after hatching, geese enter a critical period for **imprinting**. During their first hour out of the shell, goslings become very strongly attached to any large moving object that happens to be nearby. This bonding – like the incredibly cute following process it produces – is rigid and fixed. Of course, in the evolutionary history of precocial birds such as geese, as well as the life history of any specific goose, the large, moving object that was most likely to be handy shortly after hatching was mom (Lorenz, 1952; Wilson, 1975). This automatic bonding process makes evolutionary sense in precocial birds that produce many chicks because in such birds all the eggs in a clutch hatch at about the same time. If this impressive feat of synchronized hatching did not happen in the first place, imprinting may not have proven to be very adaptive. So how is synchronized hatching accomplished?

Even a city slicker like yourself probably knows that a chicken or goose cannot lay ten eggs at once. Even highly prolific geese and hens produce barely an egg a day. So, in a clutch of eight eggs, the first egg mom lays might be seven to ten

Figure 5.6 *This mother duck need not worry about her ducklings wandering away. Each of them imprinted on her shortly after hatching.*

days older than the last. How do they all hatch together? The main answer is that freshly laid eggs enter a state of stasis, facilitated in part by a special protective film that the mother bird places on the eggs when she lays them. This means that the eggs do not begin to develop until they are incubated, and moms who lay many eggs are careful not to begin incubation until they've laid an entire clutch. It's also worth adding that, unlike people, many mother birds can store sperm for a long time until it is needed. Finally, once hatching and imprinting take place, mother birds are programed to take great care of the fuzzy little cheeping objects that follow them around (Fox, 1973).

In short, a lot of things had to go right in evolution for Robert McCloskey (1941) to be able to write the classic kids' story *Make way for ducklings*. Lorenz showed that this imprinting process is all instinctive. He demonstrated, for example, that when he was the only large moving object that was around when a group of goslings hatched, they dutifully imprinted on him and followed him everywhere, as if they had joined a marching band. This must surely have made for some adorable presentations by Lorenz at international ethology conferences. I just hope Lorenz was careful to clean up after the poopy little fuzzballs afterwards.

Are there any critical periods of human development after birth? It's hard to say for at least two reasons. First, it would be highly unethical to conduct the kind of rigorous experiments that would be necessary to settle important questions about critical periods. Second, many people have trouble settling the question of exactly what a critical period is in the first place. Let's address the simpler but more sensitive problem first. Why is it so hard to study critical periods in people?

We're the animal that's hardest to study

We know a great deal about critical periods in animals because it's possible to do some highly informative but ethically sensitive experiments with animals. Until ethologists like Lorenz manipulated the specific objects to which goslings could become imprinted – and the precise window in which these objects appeared to goslings – we didn't know for sure how imprinting worked, or whether there was truly a critical period for it. Consider an even more sensitive experiment by Wiesel and Hubel (1963). They wanted to know if there is a critical period for the development of normal vision in kittens. To find out, they had to deprive some kittens completely of the normal visual experiences necessary for the development of vision. Further, they had to see, for example, if it mattered exactly how long kittens were deprived of visual stimulation, and at exactly what age the deprivation began. Their experiment suggested that there is, in fact, a critical period for the development of certain aspects of normal vision in kittens. The clear evidence of this, however, was some originally healthy kittens who ended up with messed up visual systems. These were the unlucky kittens who had been deprived of all visual stimulation during the critical period. Needless to say, it would be highly unethical to deprive some groups of healthy human infants of visual stimulation, for carefully specified periods and at carefully specified ages, to see for sure if there are critical periods in the development of human vision.

Having said all this about experiments, some natural experiments approximate true experiments. The stage was set for a series of natural experiments on human cognitive and social development in the horrific conditions of Romanian orphanages in the 1980s. Infants in these orphanages were not deprived of visual stimulation, but they were deprived of just about everything else, including anything that even vaguely resembled normal interactions with caregivers. Many of these orphans suffered from abuse as well as neglect. When the news of this horrific maltreatment came to light worldwide in the early 1990s, many of the orphans were quickly adopted to comfortable and loving homes in Canada and the U.K.

How well the orphans fared in their new homes depended dramatically on the exact age at which they happened to have been adopted. In a study of the orphans' intellectual development, Beckett and colleagues (2006) followed a large group of orphans until they were 11 years old. Infants lucky enough to have been adopted before the age of 6 months did very well. Those who had to endure the terrible conditions any longer than 6 months fared much worse. At age 11, the average IQ score of the infants who were adopted before the age of 6 months was a healthy 101. As a group, the infants were perfectly normal. In contrast, the infants who had been in the same orphanages but had languished there between 6 and 24 months before the abuse was discovered had an average IQ of 87, which is well below average. Other studies from the same research team revealed social as well as cognitive deficits – but mainly for the kids who were stuck in the orphanage during (or during and beyond) the sensitive period beginning at about the age of 6 months. Even 9 or 10 years of living in a loving and stimulating home was not enough to compensate for a terrible environment – unless kids were rescued from that terrible environment before a sensitive period of cognitive and social development.

Is being sensitive better than being critical?

Did you notice that I just said "sensitive period" rather than "critical period"? Most researchers who have studied the Romanian orphans have been careful to use this softer and more flexible developmental term, because there is some room for debate about exactly how to interpret most studies of these Romanian orphans. Because studies of people must often be less rigorous than studies of geese, and because people seem to be a bit less susceptible to developmental rigor mortis than geese are, many developmental psychologists now prefer to use the more cautious language of **sensitive periods** – somewhat flexible periods in which we are predisposed to develop specific traits or capabilities more easily than at other times of life.

Even if we accept this more cautious definition, however, there is still plenty of room for developmental debate. Consider the unfortunate Romanian orphans who fared poorly after late adoptions. Did these later-adopted kids suffer from serious cognitive deficits because they were starved of nurturance (social interaction) during a sensitive period? Or did they suffer these deficits merely because they had spent too much time starving? In this study it's hard to separate nurturance from nutrition. Research covered in Chapter 6 suggests that depriving infant monkeys of routine social interaction with a nurturing caregiver produces huge developmental deficits that are independent of the important effects of nutrition. But those who wish to understand the complex, ethically sensitive topic of human development must often draw their conclusions based on multiple sources, including studies of animals.

Clearly, the Romanian orphanage studies do attest to a sensitive, if not critical, period. It's just not absolutely clear exactly which specific aspect of maltreatment was the main ingredient of this complex recipe for cognitive and social disaster. The evidence is a little clearer in the case of what is probably the most extensively studied sensitive period – the sensitive (some would even say critical) period for learning language. In keeping with this idea, toddlers quickly and effortlessly acquire that highly abstract thinking skill known as spoken language. In contrast, the little tykes struggle tremendously with almost any other kind of abstract thinking. Thus, even the most articulate and well-spoken two-year-olds are clueless when it comes to using the simplest possible map or model. Further, researchers have shown that it is precisely their inability to think abstractly (rather than problems with memory, for example) that makes two-year-olds such poor map users (DeLoache et al., 1997).

In contrast to toddlers who soak up a first language effortlessly, adults who have mastered many other forms of abstract thinking usually have great difficulty acquiring a second language. Studies of grammatical proficiency or the ability to speak without an accent also reveal large advantages for those who acquire languages early rather than later in life. Most experts seem to agree that there is a sensitive if not critical period for learning to talk (e.g., see Mayberry et al., 2002).

So, is there anything as extreme as imprinting in people? Are there any critical periods in people after birth? Some have argued that if there's a time outside the womb to expect a critical period, it's shortly after we leave the womb. Unless we count death, it's pretty hard to imagine an event in the human lifespan that represents a more dramatic transition than birth. Perhaps the clearest example of a critical period in people comes from research on sweating. Most everyone knows that sweating is the body's way of staying cool in the heat. But as Jared Diamond (1991, p. 4) noted in his review of the natural history of sweat, sweating doesn't just vary within people, based on current temperature. It also varies greatly across people, based on a critical period for the development of sweat glands:

> The hotter the conditions under which we grow up, the greater the number of our sweat glands that get programmed to function. By age two or three, the programming is as complete as it ever will be. If we grow up in a hot climate, most of our glands become activated, and for the rest of our lives we'll be able to stay comfortable in hot weather by sweating profusely. If we grow up in a cold climate, our body soon decides that that's what it will be like until we die, and barely more than half our glands become programmed.

In the jargon of modern biology, sweat gland function is fixed irreversibly by critical period programming, that is, by conditions prevailing at a certain critical age, usually early in life.

This is not a small difference. People who grow up in the tropics have about twice as many functioning sweat glands as people who grow up in cool climates. Studies also show that it's not where your ancestors grew up that determines how much you can sweat as an adult; it's where you grew up for the first two or three years of your life. After age two or three, the number of sweat glands you have is set for life. Moving from Philadelphia to the Philippines will certainly affect how much time you spend sweating, but it will not have any influence on your capacity to sweat.

Some infant attachment experts also argue that the moments after birth are a critical period for mother and child bonding. On the other hand, others argue that human neonates are a lot less discriminating than goslings. In the first few months of life, human infants don't seem to care much who feeds, bathes, or holds them. In fact, it's not until about five or six months that most infants become distressed when mom or dad passes them off to a stranger (Field et al., 1984). If you recall that human infants can barely see or move at birth, you can probably see why human babies probably don't engage in imprinting per se. A lack of imprinting, though, may not mean a total lack of bonding. As we'll see in Chapter 6, there's plenty of evidence that human infants bond strongly with their caregivers. It just takes them a bit longer than goslings to do so. Finally, even if human newborns do not immediately become strongly attached to their caregivers, this does not mean their caregivers do not immediately become very attached to them. In a species as altricial as we are, parental care involves a lot of devoted parental carrying, down a one-way street.

So there may be only a handful of critical periods of human postnatal development. And the line between critical and sensitive periods is often a matter of our operational definitions of these two constructs. To cite an area where the research is a bit fuzzy, consider the development of vision. Experiments with animals, including monkeys as well as kittens, suggested that there is a critical period for the development of most aspects of normal vision. As Roger Brown (1965) astutely noted many years ago, studies of previously blind adults who had been surgically granted sight for the first time seemed to support the idea of a critical period. As Brown noted, one aspect of vision that develops effortlessly in people with normal vision is size constancy. More specifically, Brown noted that even infants seem to know that things do not magically grow larger as we move toward them (or smaller as we move away). With this in mind, Brown (1965, p. 215) described a previously blind woman who gained her sight as an adult. She was shown unfamiliar cards of various sizes and at different distances: "She thought the nearest of the cards the largest. It was in fact the smallest but was so near as to cast a larger retinal image than any of the others." Brown provided another example of a patient who gained his sight as an adult. This patient judged a nearby candle's flame to be about the size of his arm and judged the sun to be about the size of his hat. Either this newly sighted guy had a fantastically humungous head, or he failed to acquire size constancy.

In contrast to Brown's observations, Ostrovsky and colleagues (2006) studied a woman who had been born virtually blind but gained vision in both eyes at age 12. The woman could see well enough 20 years later to walk without a cane and work as a maid, although she continued to suffer a few subtle deficits. To muddy the waters further, Huber and colleagues (2015) studied a man who lost his vision at age 3, but had it restored at age 46. The man suffered from major visual deficits. More than a decade after his eye surgery, the man had great difficulty recognizing faces and three-dimensional shapes. It's thus hard to know exactly where we stand. Fans of a highly sensitive, if not critical, period for vision might argue that it's hard to know for sure just how blind the woman had been for years when she had her eye surgery at age 12. It could also be crucial that the woman got corrective surgery in both eyes whereas the man got corrective surgery in only one. Given how slowly human vision develops, and how plastic the brains of children are, it's also possible that it's a lot better to get your corrective eye surgery at age 12 than at age 46. On the whole, it seems like there's a highly sensitive period for vision, but whether research on vision in people supports a critical period depends on how critical we are of some of the research on this topic.

Seeing without eyes: Ben Underwood. Then, of course, there's **Ben Underwood**, the boy who learned to see without eyes. After losing his vision to cancer as a 3-year-old, Ben taught himself to see. By the time he was a teenager Ben could skate, ride a bike, navigate stairs without a handrail, and even shoot baskets. When I first heard this story I was highly skeptical. But when I watched an *Extraordinary people* documentary about Ben, I saw for myself what he can do. I watched awestruck as he removed his glass eyes and washed them in his bathroom sink. How the heck does anyone "see" without eyes? Ben learned to do so by painstakingly teaching himself **echolocation**. By emitting a series of distinctive clicks, Ben learned to navigate the world a bit like a dolphin or a bat – by listening carefully to the sound waves that bounced back to him. Of course, this method had its limits. Ben couldn't watch TV or enjoy the sight of a beautiful sunset. But he could "see" in a very real sense, and he was able to function very much like a sighted person. In fact, as Ben was quick to tell people, he didn't consider himself blind. Sadly, Ben died from cancer in 2009, at age 16.

Ben's case is fascinating, but does it tell us anything about sensitive periods? I think it does. The first lesson of Ben's story stands in contrast to the basic idea of sensitive periods, Ben's story is testament to the fact that we are an incredibly flexible species. Even after suffering serious losses or physical traumas, at least some highly resilient people find a way to cope when coping would seem impossible. Ben could not magically grow new eyes, but he could almost magically solve a visual problem by turning it into an acoustical problem. The second lesson of Ben's story is much more in keeping with the idea of critical or sensitive periods. From this perspective, it's probably no coincidence that Ben lost his eyesight when he was very young. One of the strongest lines of evidence in support of sensitive periods is the finding that the brains of children are generally much more plastic than the brains of adults. Children often seem to be able to compensate, neurologically and otherwise, for losses or injuries that would be more likely to devastate adults whose brain development has largely run its course (Knudsen, 2004).

It's a jungle out there: proliferation and pruning

Before I move on to a couple of developmental issues that apply to life post-childhood, I should add that one of the most important lessons of research on human development is the finding that the human body and brain do not simply march forward in a slow and steady fashion to adulthood. Development happens in fits and starts. Things are complicated even further by the fact that our brains have evolved to be very plastic. One interesting indicator of this first complication (involving irregular timing) has to do with the way in which our brains develop during infancy and toddlerhood (the window in which we first become truly self-aware) and then during adolescence (the window in which we first become truly obnoxious). Many people are surprised to learn that when we are toddlers, our brains contain many more synapses (more connections between brain cells) than during adulthood (Webb et al., 2010). Throughout childhood, and especially in adolescence, the highly interconnected brains we had as toddlers are radically transformed by means of synaptic pruning.

The super, highly interconnected brains of toddlers come to be that way during the first two years of life by means of proliferation. **Proliferation** refers to the rapid production of trillions of synaptic connections between brain cells all over the brain. This is surely an oversimplification, but I think of the toddler brain as a dense jungle in which everything is connected to virtually everything else by a huge number of vines and branches – except that the neural vines and branches are all relaying information rather than just fighting for sunlight. Like the vines in a jungle, however, the synapses in the developing brain are truly competing with one another. Those that get used a lot remain and become strengthened. Those that do not get used wither away. This "use it or lose it" brain self-landscaping process is referred to as **synaptic pruning**. The result of synaptic pruning is usually an adult brain that is very well suited to the specific environment in which the person grew up. As you must know, this environment could be a real jungle, a concrete jungle, or the arctic tundra. As far as I know, there is no other animal whose brain is quite as plastic (flexible, adaptable to local conditions) as ours is. This is probably a big reason why human beings have been able to thrive in environments as diverse as Saskatchewan, Sarasota, and the Sahara. It's also a big reason why culture plays such a powerful role in human behavior, which is a major theme of Chapter 10.

Getting back to sensitive periods, the extremely rapid proliferation of synapses during infancy and toddlerhood, not to mention the dramatic growth and development of the brain as a whole during this same window, seems to make the period from birth to about 24 months a sensitive period for brain development. In developing countries, the period immediately after weaning may also represent a sensitive period, in the pragmatic sense that poor children who are no longer breastfed almost invariably receive solid food that is nutritionally and immunologically inferior to highly nutritious breast milk. Although more studies are needed, it looks like starving a toddler has more devastating developmental consequences than starving a five- or ten-year-old (Lenroot & Giedd, 2006; Nyaradi et al., 2013). Finally, it's well established that during that familiar period of rapid development known as puberty, naturally unfolding biological and hormonal changes lead to radical changes in brain development. Challenging or life-threatening experiences during this window could lead to serious problems in achieving adult levels of cognitive, emotional, and interpersonal functioning (Knudsen, 2004).

EVOLUTION, PUBERTY, AND THE CULTURAL EVOLUTION OF ADOLESCENCE

Speaking of speeding trains with conductors who like to disable the brakes, just to see what will happen, adolescence is one of the most challenging aspects of human development. Sticking with train metaphors, adolescence is that poorly engineered bridge we all have to cross – to get from the bliss of childhood to the stark realities of adulthood. Adolescence is not the same as puberty, by the way. **Puberty** simply refers to the biological changes associated with sexual maturation. Once puberty has kicked in, a person can usually produce offspring. In contrast, **adolescence** is psychological and cultural as well as physical. It refers to the psychological window of life when people are getting ready to take on adult roles (Arnett, 2012). I suspect that in the ancient human past, adolescence was a very trying time. There is a sense, though, in which adolescence may be even more trying (or at least more confusing) now than it was 10,000 years ago. There are two different reasons why, and they collectively mean adolescence may be more trying than it used to be simply because it lasts a lot longer than it used to.

First, the cultural and technological revolutions that have taken place in wealthy nations over the past few centuries have meant that puberty (sexual maturation) comes much sooner than it did in the ancient human past. One indicator of puberty for which there are excellent historical data is **menarche** – the appearance of a girl's first menstrual period. Flynn (1999) examined changes in the timing of menarche in six wealthy nations (e.g., Norway, Sweden, Germany) over a span covering 140 years. In every country Flynn examined, the age of menarche declined. Norwegian records were particularly good, going all the way back to 1840. In Norway in 1840, the average girl experienced menarche at about age 17. By about 1970, this age had dropped to about 13. In wealthy countries today, the average age of menarche is about 12.5. The main reason for this dramatic change appears to be diet. If a child's diet is rich enough to allow the person to put on a little extra fat from a young age, the human body seems programmed to take advantage of this opportunity by setting early puberty into motion. We aren't the only species that takes advantage of a favorable environment by kicking development into a higher gear. Mosquitos complete their four-stage life cycles much more quickly in ideal temperatures (roughly 79°F) than in temperatures that are too cool (Beck-Johnson et al., 2013).

Getting back to people, reaching puberty a bit early was probably fine 10,000 years ago when a period of bounty may have allowed some well-fed people to jumpstart their adult lives. But unfortunately, human brains still take just as much time to develop today as they did in ancient history. Crucial areas of the prefrontal cortex (the area of the brain right behind your forehead) don't mature fully until about the age of 25. The prefrontal cortex is crucially involved in decision-making and emotional regulation. This means that in places where people mature physically way before they mature emotionally, there are lots of opportunities for bad decisions. Thus, in wealthy nations, the average 15-year-old is just as capable of producing offspring as the average 30-year-old. However, the adolescent lags way behind the young adult when it comes to assessing things like emotional costs and long-term physical risks. So, things that sound insane to most 30-year-olds (like unsafe sex or driving a motorcycle home at 3 a.m. after a night of drinking) may sound like a blast to many adolescents.

All this is made worse by the second modern problem of adolescence. The amount of formal schooling or professional training required to be economically self-sufficient today is dramatically greater than it was in 1840. So we are living in an odd time to be an adolescent. If things go well for us, we speed into puberty at roughly age 12 and then stay there for at least a decade before we complete college. Graduate or professional training can easily extend this unusual window of life another few years. During much of this long window, many people report feeling trapped in a form of maturational limbo somewhere between childhood and true adulthood. Jeffrey Arnett (2003) calls the modern period of extended adolescence (ages 18–25) **emerging adulthood**. As Arnett would be quick to remind us, there are both pros and cons of stretching out adolescence. But Arnett also argues that one of the key features of an extended window of adolescence is high levels of risk-taking. Fortunately, many parents and legislators are aware of this. This is why states all across the U.S. have enacted **graduated driver's license programs** over the past couple of decades. As Arnett (2012, p. 411) explains, these programs: "allow young people to obtain driving experience gradually, under conditions that limit the likelihood of crashes by restricting the circumstances under which novices can drive." Collectively, such programs have saved many thousands of American lives (McKnight & Peck, 2002). If only we could pass some laws enacting graduated dating programs. I'll come back to this point in a more serious way in Chapter 6.

THE EVOLUTION OF MENOPAUSE

The fact that you are reading this book means that you did not stop developing once you were weaned, or even once you began adolescence. Further, you've gotten this far on a lot more than simple reflexes. Human development is a lifelong process. I would thus be a little remiss if I didn't mention that evolution has implications for the full range of human development. To conclude this chapter, let's go well beyond childhood and adolescence to middle adulthood and beyond. Middle adulthood is an interesting window of human development because we seem to be one of only a few species of mammal, and the only primate species, whose females experience menopause (a complete cessation of ovulation).

Menopause might seem like an evolutionary mistake. After all, evolution is all about producing lots of surviving offspring (inclusive fitness). Why should women become biologically incapable of reproduction once they have finally gotten some wisdom under their belts? This is a hard question to answer, but that hasn't stopped folks from trying. One simple way of dividing up answers to this question comes from Austad (1994), who suggested that there are two good evolutionary ways to think about menopause. First, it may be a quirk of the fact that we currently live a lot longer than we did in the past. Many millennia ago, women had no reason to conceive past the age of about 50 because women rarely lived past age 50. Austad's second option is a little more interesting. Menopause may be a useful adaptation. It may exist because its benefits outweigh its costs.

Jared Diamond (1992) expressed this second idea by noting that, in ancient times, the costs of continuing to give birth throughout the lifespan would have been substantial. One unusual human adaptation is our humungous heads. Our huge heads create unrivaled difficulties for human mothers giving birth. Mother bears that weigh half a ton or more give birth to cubs that weigh ounces. Even chimps, who have huge brains compared with any other primates except us, have a pretty easy time giving birth. Our huge brains simply make it hard, and risky, for human mothers to give birth (see Figure 5.7).

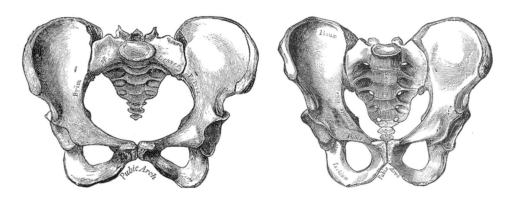

Figure 5.7 *The female pelvis (left) is well adapted for giving birth to babies with huge heads. But birth is still no easy matter. In contrast, the male pelvis (right) is well adapted for being glad it's them and not us.*

When you consider the risks childbirth poses to mothers, especially older mothers, and add to this the fact that we're so altricial, menopause might not be as crazy as it sounds. Given how long it takes us to mature, it certainly would not be a great idea for women in any era of human existence to be giving birth at age 70. Diamond goes further to note that when you consider how social and altricial we are, menopause could be very adaptive. The post-menopausal woman who doesn't die in childbirth at age 50 hangs around to help care for her existing children and grandchildren. She also hangs around to make substantial contributions to collective labor and decision-making. This might also include things like knowing where to get water after an unusually long drought – just like your mom taught you 40 years ago. Grandmothers are a pretty useful human resource.

EVOLUTION AND NATURAL VERSUS ARTIFICIAL CHILDBIRTH

Speaking of childbirth, evolution also has some important implications for modern childbirth practices. This is especially true in places such as the U.S., where childbirth has become extremely medicalized. There is no getting around the fact that childbirth is painful and poses risks to a mother's health and safety. As you already know, human babies have really big heads, which makes birth difficult. So, even in modern, wealthy nations, with excellent healthcare technology, mothers sometimes die during childbirth, or shortly thereafter. And, of course, babies die during or shortly after childbirth much more often than mothers do. Focusing on moms for now, the CIA Factbook reports that in the U.S. in 2015, the maternal death rate was 14 moms per 100,000 births (www.cia.gov/library/publications/the-world-factbook). In the U.K. the figure was 9 deaths per 100,000 births. By way of comparison, the figures for Iceland and Greece are only 3 deaths per 100,000, and those for the Central African Republic are a much higher 852 deaths. So giving birth is a risky business. There's a reason the birth process is called "labor" rather than "leisure."

Although birth in Europe or North America is certainly safer than birth in any of the world's poorest nations, there has been a dramatic global trend in the past few decades toward the unnecessary *medicalization* of birth. Birth is not an illness, after all. As recently as 1900, virtually all births in the U.S. and the U.K. took place at home, supervised by midwives rather than by surgeons. But, as Betrán and colleagues (2016) put it, the rate of birth by Cesarean section worldwide has recently "increased to unprecedented levels." In Latin America and the Caribbean, about 40% of all births happen via Cesarean sections. In the U.K., the rate is 25%. In the U.S., it's 32%. All this is happening despite growing evidence that unnecessarily medicalized births are harmful to mothers and infants (Harper et al., 2006; Lydon-Rochelle et al., 2000; Sandall et al., 2013). To see how medicalized birth has become in the U.S., consider that according to the most recent CDC (Centers for Disease Control and Prevention) data (for 36.5 million recent U.S. births), women in the U.S. are about 70% more likely to give birth on a Tuesday (a convenient day for doctors and hospitals) than on a Sunday, a much less convenient day for doctors and hospitals (Pelham, 2018a).

If you're wondering what all this has to do with evolution, there are several answers. First, when mothers give birth by Cesarean section rather than giving birth naturally (vaginally), they are less likely to breastfeed their newborns. And thanks to millions of years of primate evolution, breast milk is extremely good for an infant's immune system. Cesarean births are also associated with infant breathing difficulties and (among preemies) elevated infant mortality (Grivell et al., 2012). A second evolutionary problem with birth by Caesarean section has to do with **co-evolution** (cooperative evolution between two different species, a close cousin of symbiosis).

Ma et al. (2012, p. 372) argue that the "vaginal ecosystem is thought to have been shaped by co-evolutionary processes between the human host and specific microbial partners." The adaptive result of this co-evolution is that when human infants are delivered vaginally, as they always were for many millennia before the invention of the Cesarean section, the infants pick up healthy biomes as they pass through the birth canal (see also Dethlefsen et al., 2007). These biomes promote the development of a healthy infant immune system. But birth by Cesarean section denies babies this natural (evolved) health benefit (Dominguez-Bello et al., 2010).

Finally, there is even evidence suggesting that the extraordinarily high rates of birth by Cesarean section in places such as the U.S. and the U.K. are leading to an average reduction in the size of the human birth canal relative to the size of infants' heads (Mitteroecker et al., 2016). Before Cesarean sections became so pervasive, strong selection pressures were at work that ensured that infants' heads didn't become too huge and that birth canals didn't become too tiny. Very high rates of birth by Cesarean section appear to have thrown that delicate evolutionary balancing act out of whack. The long-term result could be that whereas very few mothers today truly need Cesarean sections, many more mothers will need them in the not-so-distant future. In extreme environments evolution can happen very quickly.

"Well you're in labor, Brittney. So we have a tough decision here. We *could* just let nature take its course, and you'd almost certainly have a safe and uneventful delivery. But we could *also* pump you full of a lot of drugs that will dramatically accelerate your labor. Then, once this artificial process puts the baby's life at risk, we can cut the baby out of you. It's really up to you."

To be clear, even the most avid supporters of natural childbirth (even radicals like me) recognize that Cesarean sections are sometimes necessary. When there are major birth complications, Cesarean surgeries can obviously save lives. But many modern birth practices artificially create a "need" for birth by Cesarean section. For example, the routine use of the artificial hormone Pitocin (to mimic the effects of the naturally occurring hormone oxytocin) during labor dramatically speeds up and intensifies contractions – and directly causes maternal and infant distress. Likewise, the practice of having moms lie flat on their backs during labor is much like trying to get ketchup from a bottle by laying the bottle on its side. (Variations on squatting or standing are more ergonomically correct.) Artificially messing with millions of years of evolution in ways that are much friendlier to hospitals than to patients does a disservice to both mothers and their infants.

THE MIDLIFE CRISIS AND SOCIOEMOTIONAL SELECTIVITY THEORY

Getting back to middle age and menopause, men don't experience the abrupt changes that are part of menopause, but they do change a lot in middle age. As men reach their forties and fifties, they begin to experience reductions in testosterone levels, and this usually comes with an accompanying reduction in energy and muscle mass. As their metabolism slows, middle-aged men may also put on excess weight. Most of these declines only get worse with age (Arnett, 2012). Like middle-aged women, middle-aged men often see their hair turn gray. And unlike most women, who see only a gradual thinning of their hair with age, many middle-aged men experience male pattern baldness. In light of distressing developmental effects such as these, it would not be surprising if many middle-aged people, women as well as men, experienced an average reduction in wellbeing relative to their youth – and perhaps even relative to their senior years. Long ago, psychoanalyst Carl Jung popularized the idea of a **midlife crisis**, arguing that it was particularly pronounced for middle-aged men. But many contemporary developmental psychologists have argued that the midlife crisis is a myth. For example, in his insightful and popular lifespan human development textbook, Arnett (2013) argued that there is simply no good evidence for a midlife crisis.

In contrast to this idea, Weiss and colleagues (2012, p. 19950) argued that there is, in fact, a midlife dip in wellbeing for women and men. In fact, they argue that, evolutionarily speaking, "there may have been selection for individuals who have higher well-being in youth and old adulthood." This argument gets tricky because back in the Pleistocene, old adulthood was often 40 or 50. Although I agree with Weiss and colleagues that the midlife crisis is genuine, I take a slightly different evolutionary view. I agree completely that it makes evolutionary sense for there to be selection pressures for being happy and optimistic in young adulthood. Who the heck would have children, traipse across the Bering Strait, or go hunting for woolly rhinos if they weren't highly optimistic? But to explain the high level of wellbeing observed among modern seniors, I think we may need a cultural evolutionary perspective. It has really only been in the past century or so of human existence – and only in wealthy nations – that meaningful numbers of people have lived to be 70 or 80 years of age.

Laura Carstensen argues that in response to this unprecedented change in human longevity, seniors have responded by valuing close, established relationships and positive emotional experiences, even more than younger adults do. The logic of **socioemotional selectivity theory** is that "I don't have much time left. So I better enjoy myself." Carstensen et al. (1999) have conducted a great deal of research showing that seniors process and remember information in ways that "accentuate the positive." Research on socioemotional selectivity theory has also shown, for example, that you can make young people think like seniors by asking them to imagine that they are about to make a permanent move to Mars (Chung & Baldwin, 2015). When they believe that time is short, even young people strongly prefer to spend their time with people they already know and love, rather than wanting to get to know new people. As my twice widowed grandmother put it when she was about 75: "I don't need no boyfriend. If I ever go on a date, it'll be a blind date, but only because I'll be too blind to know what I'm doing."

A decent argument against the idea that the midlife crisis is a purely cultural phenomenon comes from Weiss et al. (2012), who provided strong evidence for a midlife dip in wellbeing in a large group (n = 508) of chimps and orangutans. Of course, these researchers had to rely on human judges who could rate the wellbeing of these great apes. This introduces the possibility of bias (judgmental projection from human observers). But conceding this pragmatic necessity, Weiss et al. found that the observer ratings revealed a clear dip in wellbeing among the middle-aged great apes – followed by levels of wellbeing in late adulthood that were almost as high as those observed for the young adults. It seems unlikely these older chimps and orangutans recognized that their days on earth were numbered. On the other hand, the midlife dip in wellbeing is only one indicator of a midlife crisis. Jung conceptualized the midlife crisis as just that – a midlife *crisis* – rather than a mere midlife dip in wellbeing. Jung argued that this is why middle-aged people may take great risks and behave unpredictably. But this is exactly the kind of reckless behavior during middle adulthood that Arnett said was merely a stereotype.

Is there any evidence for a true midlife crisis in people? I recently examined several large datasets to see (Pelham, 2018b). Specifically, I examined five different face-valid indicators of risk-taking or crisis. The five indicators for which I was able to obtain either national or nationally representative data included divorce rates, suicide rates, motorcycle ownership, sports car ownership, and reports of being "way below average" in life satisfaction. As you can see in Figure 5.8, there was a clear bump upward in these indicators of risk-taking and distress in middle adulthood – for women as well as for men.

These data are a little paradoxical. Intuitively, one might expect people to be most likely to experience a psychological crisis when they know death is just around the corner. But in these data, as in much of Carstensen's data, the age group who is doing the best psychologically is the oldest group. If I may add a final evolutionary spin on things, there might be more selection pressure to worry about death when you are 20 or 30 (before you have much inclusive fitness "in the bank") than when you are 80. I'm not saying that a survival instinct applies to the young more than to the old. Very few evolutionary psychologists believe in

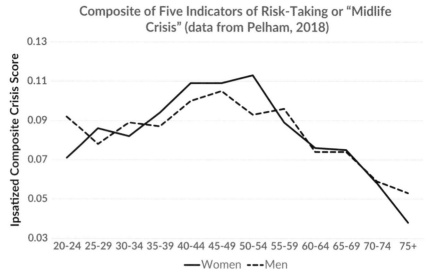

Figure 5.8 *There seems to be a real midlife crisis for American adults.*

anything akin to a "survival instinct." But I am saying that one drawback of being big-brained is worrying a lot about one's own demise (as we'll see in Chapter 11). The big twist on this fact is supported by the data reported in Figure 5.8, as well as a lot of data reported elsewhere (e.g., see Newport & Pelham, 2009). Surprisingly enough, these data points converge to suggest that worrying about death (not to mention worrying in general) is least common among people who are staring death in the face.

"Is there something you wanted to talk about?"

To summarize this highly selective review of human development, much of human development, especially early development, is highly predictable from an evolutionary perspective. Things as different as the time at which our mothers wean us, how quickly different sensory systems develop, and why we possess some useful (and a couple of no-longer-useful) reflexes are all informed by an evolutionary perspective. The difficult question of whether there are critical or sensitive periods in human development is also informed by an evolutionary analysis. Life history theory certainly suggests that one would expect critical periods to be an important part of lifespan human development. Menopause in middle-aged women is even more mysterious than critical periods, but it exists, and we can be sure that it somehow evolved. Whether menopause represents an evolutionary side effect of some other useful adaptation or constitutes a useful adaptation in its own right, it is a universal aspect of lifespan female human development.

It's also possible to view the controversial midlife crisis through an evolutionary lens. For example, I'm not sure I would've bothered to see if there was any evidence for the midlife crisis if I hadn't been aware of the work Weiss and colleagues did with other great apes. It's also worth noting that, in contrast to the cultural stereotype, the midlife crisis is just as robust for women as for men. One cannot fully appreciate socioemotional selectivity theory either without appreciating the fact that there were very few great-grandparents in the Pleistocene. Finally, the finding that wellbeing increases after a dip in middle age in chimps and orangutans as well as in people raises interesting questions about the possible biological basis of socioemotional selectivity theory.

FOR FURTHER READING

- » Huber, E., Webster, J.M., Brewer, A.A., MacLeod, D.I., Wandell, B.A. et al. (2015). A lack of experience-dependent plasticity after more than a decade of recovered sight. *Psychological Science*, 26(4), 393–401.
- » Lamb, T. (2011). Evolution of the eye: Scientists now have a clear vision of how our notoriously complex eye came to be. *Scientific American*, 305(1), 64–9.
- » Lorenz, K. (1952). *King Solomon's ring: New light on animal ways*. New York: Crowell.
- » Weiss, L., Laforsch, C. & Tollrian, R. (2012). The taste of predation and the defences of prey. In C. Bronmark & L.-A. Hansson (eds) *Chemical ecology in aquatic systems* (pp. 111–26). Oxford: Oxford University Press.

SAMPLE MULTIPLE-CHOICE EXAM QUESTIONS

Here are four sample quiz questions for Chapter 5. You can find the Chapter 5 quiz at: www.macmillanihe.com/evolutionary-psychology

5.01.   In human beings, most teratogens pose the greatest threat to the development of a developing baby if the mother ingests the teratogens during:

a. autogenesis

b. organogenesis

c. the third trimester of pregnancy

5.02. Which aspect of human sensation develops most slowly?

a. taste

b. hearing

c. vision

5.03. Getting goose bumps and shivering when you are cold are permanent reflexes, meaning that they are present from birth and never disappear. But a few reflexes (e.g., the tendency to grip things placed in a baby's palm) do disappear during the first year of life. What's the name of the instincts that *do* disappear?

a. infant impulses

b. neonatal reflexes

c. primal constitutions

5.04. Both life history theory and the concept of synaptic pruning are consistent with the idea of:

a. critical periods

b. altricial periods

c. genotype plasticity

Answer Key: b, c, a, a.

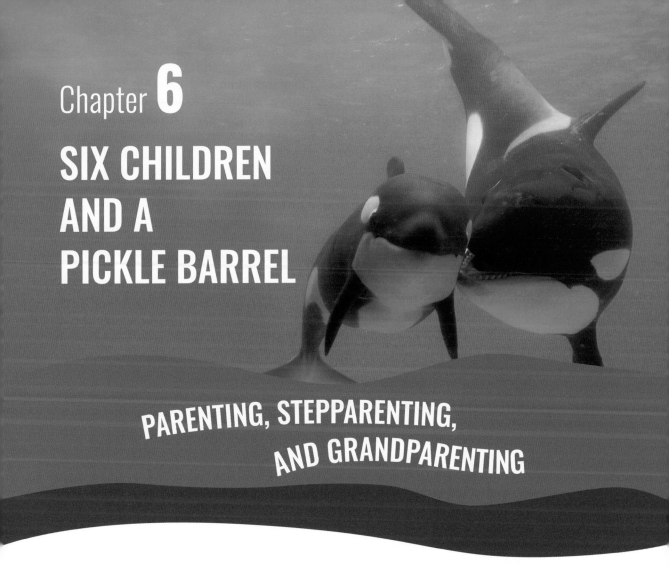

Chapter 6
SIX CHILDREN AND A PICKLE BARREL

PARENTING, STEPPARENTING, AND GRANDPARENTING

"Insanity is hereditary. You get it from your children."

— *Sam Levenson (source unknown)*

"The sole purpose of a child's middle name is so that he can know when he is really in trouble."

— *Justine Vogt (source unknown)*

"Couples that raise tadpoles together stay together."

— *Tumulty et al. (2014, p. 262); lay summary of shared parenting and monogamy in mimic poison frogs*

More than 300 years ago, the badly behaved English poet John Wilmot expressed an interesting view of parenthood: "Before I got married I had six theories about raising children; now, I have six children and no theories." More than 200 years later, the well-behaved American writer Mark Twain expressed a similar view of the demands of parenting, when he advised: "When a youngster turns 13, put him in a pickle barrel, nail the lid shut, and feed him through a knothole. Then, when he turns 16, plug up the knothole." That's right, we've come to the most controversial topic in a field absolutely packed with controversies. That controversial topic is parenting.

Looking at parenting across the animal kingdom, it's amazing how many forms parental care can take. Evolutionary biologists Royle et al. (2012, p. 1) define **parental care** as that which happens "whenever parents increase the survival and growth of their offspring, often at a cost to their own survival and reproduction." If I may paraphrase some of Royle et al.'s technical terms, they note that parental care in non-human animals includes making eggs and sperm, choosing a good place to lay one's eggs, nest-building or burrowing, egg attendance (e.g., incubation and/or nest guarding), carrying one's eggs or one's offspring around on one's body, attending to one's offspring, feeding one's juvenile offspring, and even caring for one's mature offspring (e.g., helping your son scare off a rival male chimpanzee). In mammals, of course, there are additional forms of parental care from gestation to education.

Although we're certainly not the only animals to provide a great deal of care to our offspring, we are arguably the animal kingdom's parental champions. In a highly altricial, hypersocial species like people, long-term care from devoted parents, and often many others, is an absolute necessity.

SOME PERSPECTIVES ON HUMAN PARENTING

Before going any further, I should note that I'll review a good deal of research suggesting that some human parents are much more invested in their children than others. Some parents even go so far as to neglect, harm, or kill the children one would hope they would cherish. But let's stop for a moment to appreciate how odd it is for any creature to make the highly unusual sacrifices parents routinely make for their offspring, and how often human parents go above and beyond the extraordinary parental sacrifices made by other animals. In a highly altricial species like people, most parents make tremendous long-term investments in their children.

In contrast to human parents, many animal parents make no behavioral investments at all in their kids. This is particularly true in fish, insects, and reptiles. Consider leatherback sea turtles. The reproductive adaptation that has proven highly successful for these turtle moms is to produce a lot of offspring. Leatherback moms-to-be build up their biological resources for a few years at sea. They then mate and return to the same shores where they hatched, often laying more than 1,000 eggs in a season (about 100 every 10 days for three to four months). But after making this huge biological sacrifice, leatherback moms provide no care at all for their precocial hatchlings. Although about 90% of leatherback sea turtle hatchlings make it to the sea without being taken by predators, life in the ocean is highly unforgiving. An estimated 96% of leatherback hatchlings never reach the age of one (www.leatherback.org/why-leatherbacks). This means that the large majority of sea turtle hatchlings are destined to become one of three things: breakfast, lunch, or dinner. There are exceptions to this reptilian rule. Many crocodilians, for example, are highly attentive and devoted mothers. For example, many alligator moms do things like nest guarding and carrying their recent hatchlings around, which offers them strong protection from predation. Maybe it really does take one to know one.

"What have *I* ever done for *you*? Well, let me tell you, little missy. Let's start with gamete provision, partner selection, nest site selection, and egg laying. Then there's nest guarding, offspring attendance, offspring transport, and food provisioning. Speaking of food, there's also protection from your great aunt Josephine, who tried to have you for lunch last week."

But contrast the Dickensian story of most reptile or insect mothers with what happens when a typical human mother gives birth, usually to just one child, and always to children that are extremely helpless. Human children require intense and continuous care for the first few years of life, require intense but more intermittent care for five or six more years, and then require a different kind of intense care once they learn to sass their parents. Even the lousiest human caregiver of 50,000 years ago had to nurse an infant many times daily, keep it away from predators, keep it reasonably clean, hunt or forage for the child's food as it got older, and save the kid from routine dangers such as infection, predation, and dehydration. As evolutionary biologists such as Tim Clutton-Brock (1991) have noted, these ridiculous levels of parental investment only make sense if we understand concepts such as inclusive fitness (discussed in detail in Chapter 3) and kin selection (to be discussed in Chapter 9 on helping). Human parents, often without knowing why, typically offer extreme levels of care to their children.

Three unique aspects of human parenting

Costly things like carrying our offspring around everywhere we go only make evolutionary sense because our offspring carry around plenty of our genes. Getting back to people, the sheer amount of time, energy, and nutritional support we provide to our children is mind-boggling. In fact, evolutionary biologist Sigal Balshine (2012) argued that there are three ways in which human parents are different from any other parents on the planet. First, as I have already noted, we hold the record in the animal kingdom for caring for our children the longest. Second, more than any other animal, we share in childrearing. Even relative to the children of other primates, human children receive a great deal of care from relatives other than their mothers, for example aunts, uncles, and grandmothers. Finally, human children receive a great deal of care from their fathers. Human fathers are not as invested in their children as red-necked phalarope dads. But, in every human culture ever studied, human fathers play at least some role in childrearing. As Balshine argued, this is rare, even in mammals. Male members of the species only provide any childcare at all in 9–10% of mammalian genera.

So, in cultures worldwide, men always provide at least some childcare. Further, you might be surprised to learn that if we go far enough back in time, men used to provide a lot more childcare than they do today. In traditional, hunter-gatherer cultures, fathers typically spend more time with their children than fathers in any other kind of culture, from traditional herding cultures to modern agriculturalists. More specifically, Marlowe (2000) studied 186 cultures across the globe using the Standard Cross-Cultural Sample. This is a unique collection of data on 186 cultures spanning the globe. The cultures that are a part of these data were carefully chosen to reflect the earth's cultural diversity and to be statistically independent of one another (see Murdock & White, [1969] 2006). Using these data, Marlowe observed two noteworthy things about fatherhood. First, in all kinds of cultures, dads spent more time with older children than with infants. The fact that men cannot nurse, for example, could help explain this finding. Second, as cultures became more modern and industrialized, the role of men in childrearing decreased rather than increased. Hunter-gatherer dads devoted more time to their children than did dads from any other cultural group. Apparently, men in hunter-gatherer cultures are rarely married to their careers. Recall that for most of human history, hunter-gatherer cultures were the only kind of cultures that existed anywhere on the planet.

Having said this, it is important to note that in every culture ever studied, including hunter-gatherer cultures, mothers spent more time caring for children than fathers did. So, if human fathers are like Olympic sprinters when it comes to parenting, human mothers are more like cheetahs. Furthermore, the extended family members who are most likely to care for children they did not personally beget are aunts more often than uncles, grandmothers more often than grandfathers, and older sisters more often than older brothers. Having said this, it is not unheard of in human culture for people to offer meaningful amounts of care to children to whom they are not genetically related. At least some acts of reciprocal altruism (paying back those who have helped you in the past) involve assistance with childrearing. Furthermore, in other highly social primates, one of the best predictors of whether a newborn will survive the harrowing first year of life is the number of social contacts the infant's mother has (Silk et al., 2003). Human parents devote a lot of effort to childrearing. Some of this effort involves convincing others in their families and communities to help out.

In sum, when I argue later in this chapter that some human parents provide a lot less care to their offspring than other parents do, remember that, as a species, human beings are pretty darned devoted to their kids. To survive that incredibly risky period of life known as childhood, and thus to be in a position to reproduce, we need a lot of help from our primary caregivers. One implication of this fact is that when we are very young we should become very strongly bonded to our primary caregivers – and they to us. Just as attachment and commitment are important in a friendship or marriage, they are all the more important in a mother–child (or father–child) relationship. Speaking of fathers, you may notice in this chapter that I leave dads out of many of the discussions to come. As a father who has changed jobs and moved to new states more than once to be with his family, especially his children, I don't want to shortchange dads. But speaking actuarially, primary caregivers are usually moms. Accordingly, I'll tip my cap to dads when I can fairly do so (as I just did above). But I will usually pay more attention in this chapter to those who have traditionally done more of the attending.

LOVE IS (ALMOST) ALL YOU NEED

In people and other altricial primates, babies should be strongly predisposed to become attached to their moms – and to do things that would make their moms become pretty darned attached to them. Let's begin with what babies do. About 60 years ago, psychologist Harry Harlow (1958) conducted a series of innovative studies that revealed the depth of our need to be cuddled as infants. Harlow separated infant rhesus monkeys from their biological mothers and reared them artificially. In one of his most telling studies, Harlow offered these infants a choice between two very different **surrogate mothers**. A surrogate is a substitute or replacement. Thus, Harlow's infant monkeys had to choose between two substitute moms, which were equally available to the infants but which were always separated by a partition.

Figure 6.1 *Harlow's two surrogate moms, a wire and a terrycloth mom. On the right, you can see which one a typical infant rhesus monkey chose to be with 20 times more often than the other. Infants showed this strong preference for the cuddly mom even when the wire mom provided nutrition and the cuddly mom did not.*

The gist of Harlow's surrogate mother studies is that infant bonding has more to do with the motivation to hold and be held than it does with the basic biological need to be fed – at least when you are a baby. Before Harlow came along, psychologists, especially experimental psychologists, had virtually ignored the strong bonds we forge at birth with our caregivers. Those who addressed topics like love, bonding, and attachment at all assumed that these processes were the results of simple conditioning. I associate mom with food – and maybe safety – and so I love her. Harlow felt there was much more to love and attachment than milk. As he put it in his classic paper (1958, p. 573): "The little we know about love does not transcend simple observation, and the little we write about it has been written better by poets and novelists." Harlow's brilliant work quickly eliminated this blind spot. Poets and novelists, especially the crappy ones, are now jealous of us.

Harlow's studies help explain not only why the market for wire teddy bears is so tiny but also why the market for the fuzzy kind is so huge. In the cartoon strip *Peanuts*, it's no accident that Linus's security blanket, like those of so many real children, is soft and huggable. Both of my children have always been deeply attached to their stuffed animals. When my daughter Brooklyn was barely two she loved a stuffed pink pig so much that when she dropped it into a storm drain, my wife spent an hour on eBay that evening looking for an exact replacement. I'm happy to say she found one. All we had to do to convince Brooklyn that we had rescued Softie was to run the new one through the dryer for three hours with some old running shoes and then remove the left eye. The deep connections many children feel for their security blankets, pillows, and stuffed dinosaurs seem to have ancient roots. I'm considering marketing a line of stuffed animals with built-in dummies ("pacifiers" if you're on the left side of the pond). Why should the poor kids have to choose?

Some have argued from Harlow's findings that the need for contact comfort even trumps the biological need for nutrition. That's a tough call to make because it's tricky to compare two things that are so different. Harlow's more careful claim was that contact comfort matters – a lot – and that infant *bonding* may be rooted more strongly in contact than in simple nutrition. After all, Harlow's infant monkeys did nurse on the wire mom whenever they were hungry. But few of them spent any time at all on the wire mother unless they were in the act of nursing. From an evolutionary perspective, this makes a great deal of sense. An infant monkey who can't nurse for a few hours probably gets pretty hungry. An infant monkey who has no mom to cling to for a few hours probably gets eaten. Harlow's results surprised even him at first, but they are not quite so surprising when you consider the extreme dependence all mammals have had on their mothers for millions of years.

This need for a mother's care seems particularly intense in highly social mammals such as primates. In fact, in some of his lesser known studies, Harlow deprived monkeys of any motherly care whatsoever, whether from a real or surrogate mom. Although the monkeys had plenty of access to food, they had nothing resembling a mom. These socially isolated monkeys were at increased risk of death (Harlow et al., 1965). Further, when those that did survive were later introduced to other rhesus monkeys, they proved to be social misfits and outcasts. It appears to be impossible for primates to develop normally in the absence of routine, loving interactions with a caregiver. As Harlow (1958) put it: "man cannot survive on milk alone." Apparently, man (and woman) also needs social interaction and what Harlow called "contact comfort."

Harlow's studies are all the more remarkable, by the way, when you consider what a pale shadow of the real thing his terrycloth mothers were. The wire mothers did provide truly nutritious infant formula, for example. Except for the fact that the formula was missing some useful antibodies, it rivaled the milk of real mothers. In contrast, the terrycloth moms were not even all that soft and cuddly. A fuzzy wash cloth on a wire frame is a poor substitute for a pair of real arms that actually pick an infant up when it's distressed. Like people, apparently, infant monkeys will cling to the very poorest of substitutes for a warm, soft, and responsive caregiver when the real thing is unavailable.

But do Harlow's findings with monkeys apply to people? It would be highly unethical to offer human babies wire versus terrycloth mothers. (In fact, some argue it was unethical to do this to monkeys.) It would be even more unethical, of course, to see what happens when a human baby never has access to a mother of any kind. On the other hand, some real human mothers aren't all that warm and cuddly. Others are highly lovable but rarely available. According to Harlow (1958), a woman who seemed taken with one of his research talks told him afterwards that it had opened her eyes. As she put it: "Now I know what's wrong with me ... I have been only a wire mother." The distressing Romanian orphanage studies discussed in Chapter 5 also suggest that Harlow's findings probably apply to people.

INFANT ATTACHMENT STYLE

When children have unresponsive caregivers, for whatever reason, this puts them at risk for developing an insecure attachment style. According to attachment researchers Mary Ainsworth and John Bowlby (1965), who were influenced by Harlow as well as by work on primate evolution, an **infant's attachment style** is its characteristic way of relating to and depending on its primary caregiver. The most commonly observed *insecure* infant attachment style is an **anxious** style. Kids with this attachment style behave in ways that reflect chronic worry, especially in unfamiliar situations, as in: "Please, please, please, don't abandon me!" Instead of clinging like a vine, a second way to deal with an unresponsive caregiver is to put up a stone wall. Kids who develop an **avoidant** attachment style are psychologically detached from their primary caregiver, even in unfamiliar situations, as in: "I can take care of myself; I'm cool like that." Luckily, the majority of human infants seem to have pretty responsive caregivers. Thus they develop a **secure** attachment style, which means that they seem to know they can trust their primary caregiver. This means that they use the caregiver as an emotional resource (a secure base) in times of fear or uncertainty, as in: "Mom, I know you've always got my back. That makes life pretty sweet."

To summarize thus far, human beings seem to have a powerful need to bond to their caregivers. Based on how well their primary caregivers meet this basic need, infants develop beliefs (aka **working models**) about when and if they can count on their primary caregivers – and perhaps whether they themselves are worthy of love. These beliefs, both conscious and unconscious, persist and develop throughout life. For this reason, many social, clinical, and personality psychologists study **adult romantic attachment styles**, which have some of their roots in infant attachment (e.g., see Bartholomew & Shaver, 1998; Collins & Freeney, 2004; Fraley & Shaver, 2000). We wouldn't develop these powerful attachment beliefs, as infants or as adults, if a deep attachment to others – especially one's parents – were not an essential aspect of human experience.

Allow me to address the topic of gender again by adding that babies are not predisposed to bond to their mothers per se. They are predisposed to *bond*, and they will bond strongly to any caregiver, regardless of gender, who spends a lot of time caring for them in the crucial first year or two of life. In the first 15 months of my son Lincoln's life, I was able to arrange a flexible work schedule. Because of my theory that newborns are sensitive to how responsive their caregivers are, I also made it a point to pick Lincoln up any time he cried, even at 3 a.m., and then 3:07 a.m., and then again at 3:16 a.m. As a result of my high level of responsiveness, Lincoln became strongly attached to me. I could be kidding myself, but I'm pretty sure that at the age of 14 (at the time of writing), Lincoln has a secure sense of being loved, and we have a solid relationship. He has some of the worries that typically plague 14-year-olds, from acne to algebra. But he doesn't ever seem to worry about whether he is loved.

So most infants become deeply attached to their parents. This obviously helps them survive. But what's in it for the parents? It is parents who do all the work while babies maintain a random schedule of eating, peeing, pooping, and crying. From an evolutionary perspective, the attachment system must be a two-way street. Parents make huge sacrifices to rear their children, and these sacrifices must usually be worth it. Although I hope very few parents sit down and calculate such things, the only payoff for years of parental care is a long-term hope for some grandchildren and great-grandchildren, who often require some care of their own. Any genes that promote parental care and devotion would be weeded out of the gene pool very quickly unless they also promoted careful discrimination, that is, unless they increased inclusive fitness via Hamilton's rule. Parents don't just feed and shelter anything that looks at them with big brown or blue eyes. They show a strong and clear preference for their own offspring, which carry about half of each parent's genes. This raises an uncomfortable question. Do parents, including grandparents and stepparents, do a better job of caring for children when they know the children share their genes?

CINDERELLA, YOU'RE NOT ALONE

More broadly speaking, do children receive better care from those who share their genes than from those who do *not* share their genes? I'm sorry to say that from a purely evolutionary perspective, this is exactly what we'd predict. I'm even sorrier to say it's almost always what we find. Martin Daly and Margo Wilson (1994, 1998, 2001) have investigated this question in great detail. Their evolutionary logic is both clear and chilling. All else being equal, abusive parents, like the fictional stepmother in *Cinderella*, should be more abusive to children who do not share their genes than to children who do. This leads to the uncomfortable prediction that, on average, stepparents should be more likely than biological parents to kill or harm any children left in their care. Let's be clear. Only a tiny fraction of parents of any kind ever kill or seriously abuse their children. But this small but distressing fraction should be bigger and thus more distressing for stepparents.

It is bigger, much bigger. As Daly and Wilson (n.d.) put it: "in several countries, stepparents beat very young children to death at per capita rates that are *more than 100 times higher* than the corresponding rates for genetic parents." Daly and Wilson dubbed this the **Cinderella effect**: the tendency for stepparents to neglect, abuse and even kill their stepchildren at a higher rate than genetic parents. Large-scale studies of child murder records in Australia, Britain, Canada, and the U.S. all converge to support the Cinderella effect. Because of variations in how crime records are kept across countries, it is tricky to make direct cross-cultural comparisons, but in all the countries studied by Daly and Wilson, the Cinderella effect was huge for the tragic statistic of child murder.

Culture matters, too

Daly and Wilson (2001, n.d.) note that there is one carefully studied country in which the Cinderella effect for the murder of toddlers seems to be much weaker than in any of the heavily studied English-speaking countries. In Sweden, the rates of toddler murders by stepparents are only about 8 times (rather than 100 times) higher than for biological parents. Daly and Wilson (2001) suggest that because Sweden has such a generous social welfare system, stepparents may not feel such strong financial obligations to stepchildren and thus may resent them less. This is a reasonable interpretation, but as a social psychologist, my preferred interpretation is more cultural than financial.

Cultural psychologist Geert Hofstede (2001) has rated 67 countries across the globe on several important cultural dimensions. For example, some countries are much more collectivistic (group-focused) than others. Hofstede's ratings also include the cultural dimension of **masculinity vs. femininity**. On Hofstede's cultural website (www.hofstede-insights.com/models/national-culture), he defines masculinity as "a preference in society for achievement, heroism, assertiveness and material rewards for success. Society at large is more competitive. Its opposite, femininity, stands for a preference for cooperation, modesty, *caring for the weak* and quality of life" (emphasis added).

Removing my evolutionary cap and putting on a cultural one, Hofstede's cross-cultural data show that Australia, the U.S., and Britain are all pretty masculine nations (there are no ratings for Canada). The median (typical) global masculinity score is 52, and all three of the English-speaking countries for which there are data have masculinity scores between 61 and 66 – clearly masculine but not downright macho. In contrast, Sweden scores in a decidedly feminine direction. In fact, its score of 5 (yep, five) is the lowest measured masculinity score (or the highest femininity score, if you like) on the planet. In short, Swedes are nicer than the rest of us.

Even in a country with a strong and pervasive culture of caring, though, stepparents are about eight times as likely as natural parents to kill their small children. It's worth adding that I don't think many evolutionary psychologists would be troubled to know there is cross-cultural variation in the strength of the Cinderella effect. Culture is a powerful force that shapes who we are (Markus & Kitayama, 1991; Triandis, 1989). In fact, the tremendous power of culture is highly consistent with two important human adaptations. The first adaptation

Figure 6.2 *Variations on* Cinderella, *always including a cruel stepmother, have existed for centuries worldwide. Ye Xian was a popular version of the story in China around 860 A.D. If you know Walt Disney's animated American version, you may note that Disney replaced the doves and pigeons in the German version (Aschenputtel) with smaller and cuter birds, who didn't poop all over Cinderella's stage coach.*

is that we human beings are extremely flexible; we are *cognitive* creatures who can live by a wide range of rules. For example, there is evidence that whether cultures emphasize individual rights ("individualism") or group connections and responsibilities ("collectivism") depends to a large degree on the disease burden (prevalence of infectious diseases) in a given region. When people around you are dropping like flies, it makes sense to take strength in numbers (Fincher et al., 2008). The second basic adaptation is that we are extremely sensitive to the beliefs of others; we are *social* creatures (see also Gangestad et al., 2006). The idea of culture only makes sense in the first place in a social species.

Getting back to Cinderella, remember that Cinderella's stepmother didn't actually try to kill her (although I can't say the same thing for Snow White's stepmother). Instead, Cinderella's stepmom just treated her badly. If the Cinderella effect is really robust, stepchildren should suffer from more mundane slights and oversights. Yet again, I'm sorry to say that they do. Daly and Wilson (2008) reviewed a series of studies showing that stepparents are less caring and generous to stepchildren than to the fruit of their own loins. This is true when it comes to intangibles such as love and affection as well as tangibles such as time and money. These findings come from a diverse set of studies. They include a survey of American stepparents who often admitted that they didn't have much "parental feeling" for their stepchildren. They also included an anthropological study of Tanzanian dads, who played with the children they had fathered but never with their stepchildren. Stepparents also seem to be less vigilant with their stepchildren than they are with their own offspring. Children under the care of stepparents are at elevated risk for dying or being injured in accidents, such as falling or drowning (Daly & Wilson, 2008).

The child's age also matters

One of the most distressing aspects of the Cinderella effect is the finding that, in the case of children's death by physical abuse, the Cinderella effect gets larger as children get younger. Stepparents kill children of all ages at a higher rate than natural parents do. But the difference between stepparents and natural parents shrinks as children get older. One cruel perspective on those who are cruelest of all to infants is that the total amount of lifelong care a child could require from a stepparent is much greater for younger children. Further, all else being equal, women who have just given birth to a child are more likely to be fertile than those who produced them 10 or 15 years ago. Of course, there could be legal as well as evolutionary reasons why the Cinderella effect is biggest for the youngest victims. Unlike teenagers, for example, infants are unable to fight back, and they never report their abusers to the authorities. All this being said, this pattern of focusing on the most helpless is not unique to people.

Lions live in stable groups called prides, with a coalition of males cooperating together for shared breeding rights with a group of lionesses, who greatly outnumber the males. Pusey and Packer (1994; Packer, 2001) documented that when a coalition of male lions takes over a lion pride by defeating the reigning coalition, their first order of business is often to kill off all the lion cubs. As you can see in Figure 6.3, the younger a cub is, the more likely it is to die after a takeover. In the absence of a takeover, 56% of all lion cubs aged 0–9 months survived at least nine months. After a takeover, only 14% of cubs of this age survived. For older cubs, there was an effect of a takeover on survival, but the effect was much weaker. In the absence of a takeover, 9-month survival rates for cubs aged 18 months or older were in excess of 90%. After a takeover, survival rates for older cubs dropped, too, but only to 70%. Of course, infant mortality does not always mean infanticide. Further, lions are mostly nocturnal, and thus hard to observe directly. However, many cases of obvious infanticide in lions have been well documented. Pusey and Packer (1994, p. 280) provide a chilling description of one such case:

> The most complete observation was made by a film team who had set out specifically to film infanticide. After several weeks monitoring females that we knew were vulnerable to a male takeover, they observed a mother with three cubs aged 3 months being chased by another pride of females. The cubs remained alone in the initial location. A single resident male from the invading pride followed behind the females and stopped in the vicinity of the cubs. After an hour or so, the male noticed the cubs and immediately ran to them, bit the first in the head, dropped it, and then successively picked up and bit each of the remaining two in the abdomen. He then carried one cub to the shade and ate some of it. The killing was over in less than two minutes … The male growled aggressively in a manner that is completely unlike lions' behavior while killing their prey.

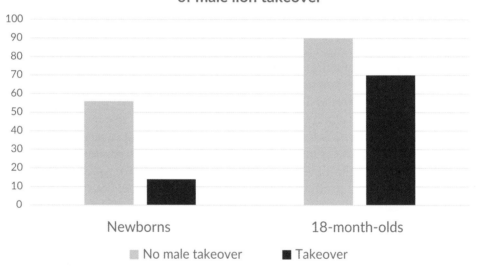

Figure 6.3 *The likelihood a lion cub will die with or without a takeover in a lion pride. The younger the cub, the greater the risk post-takeover. Sadly, the same basic pattern holds for people. Infants are the age group who are the most likely victims of the Cinderella effect in child murders.*

If you think of the villain Scar in the animated Disney movie *The Lion King*, you'll be on the right track, but not far enough down it. Even Scar's behavior wasn't as callous as that of this male lion. Scar was also unrealistic in one other sense. Whereas Scar was content to just eat and be the boss, real thieves of the lion throne are almost always interested in creating a genetic legacy of their own. I'd like to repeat that unlike lions, most stepparents do not make it their first order of business to murder the helpless children who are left in their care. Murdering infants is as rare as it is heinous, but it's more common than usual when children are living with a stepparent. Our species is a little more lion-like than we all might like to believe. Having said that, it would be remiss of me if I did not note that Packer (2001) is cautious about drawing any conclusions about human parents based on this work with lions. Despite the chilling parallels between Packer's work and that of Daly and Wilson, it is unlikely, for example, that there are any particular genes people share with lions that specifically create this form of infanticide.

Methodological concerns about Cinderella. Thoughtful skeptics have leveled many clever criticisms at the Cinderella effect, but the effect seems to have survived such criticisms well. For example, you might worry that if families with stepparents happen to be poor, poverty could be the real reason for the Cinderella effect. As it turns out, however, stepparents are not much more common among poor people. Further, studies that have statistically controlled for this possible bias still yield a robust effect. You might also worry that the kind of people who become stepparents in the first place tend to be emotionally troubled or physically aggressive. However, studies that have looked at the rates at which stepparents kill or ignore their own children yield no support for that criticism. Stepparents are just as kind and loving as the rest of us when it comes to their own offspring. Of course, no field study can ever rule out every possible confound, but there do not appear to be any obvious rival theories that can easily account for all versions of the Cinderella effect.

Where was Cinderella's maternal grandma all that time?

A less controversial cousin of the Cinderella effect has to do with differences in the investments different *grandparents* typically make in their grandchildren. Across a wide range of studies – looking at many different forms of investment – a clear pattern emerges. Focusing on people whose grandparents survived long enough for the kids to get to know them, adults report that they received more attention and affection from some specific grandparents than from others. Blended families aside, everyone has four biological grandparents. Think about your four biological grandparents, if you know who they all are, and ask yourself to whom you feel emotionally closest.

I'm putting my money on your mom's mom. I might not win the bet with you, but if I made the bet to a thousand people, at the appropriate odds, I'd come out way ahead. If you ask people to rank-order how close they feel to all four of their grandparents, or how much they felt loved by them growing up, big samples almost always yield the same pattern. Think of this as the senior Olympics of good grandparenting. The gold medal most often goes to mom's mom. Mom's dad and dad's mom vie closely for the silver and bronze medals. Finally, dad's dad never makes it to the medal stand. In fact, sometimes he doesn't even qualify for the games. So, I'm going to call this robust but (as far as I can tell) unnamed finding the **selfish grandparent effect**. On average, the amount of care grandparents offer to their grandchildren is directly related to the likelihood that they are genetically related to the grandchildren (see Euler, 2011, for an excellent review). Notice that this can't be a simple effect of gender in disguise.

Maternal grandmothers generally offer more care than paternal grandmothers, yet both are female. Likewise, maternal grandfathers generally offer more care than paternal grandfathers, yet both are male.

"In your case, Jeff, we're going to have to go back a little
farther. Tell me about your great great grandmother."

If you recall our earlier discussion of paternal uncertainty, I hope it's obvious that concerns over paternity are greater for daddy's daddy than for daddy himself. Logically speaking, confidence in paternity has to be lower for dad's dad than for dad himself. Further, I hope it's clear that if your mom always knows you are her kid, then her mom always knows you are her grandkid. So, evolutionarily speaking, a maternal grandmother should have nothing to worry about when it comes to making big sacrifices for her grandchild. She knows with absolute certainty that you share about a quarter of her genes. In contrast, your paternal grandfather might want to ask for a genetic test before he agrees to help pay for your college education. Of course that might offend grandma. Maybe he should just fork out the bucks.

PARENTAL INVESTMENT AND LIFE HISTORY STRATEGIES

Another important evolutionary perspective on parenting comes from life history theory (Stearns, 1992). Life history theory is built on the idea that natural selection often involves tradeoffs and contingencies. You may recall from Chapter 5 that water fleas only develop armor and spines if the water in which they live offers chemical cues of the presence of predators. That's a **contingency**, and it's based on a **tradeoff** between safety from predators and metabolic energy consumption.

Life history theory also dictates that animal behavior (not just morphology) can vary greatly with important features of the environment. In the case of parenting, some contingencies can be pretty harsh. Anyone who has ever observed a few litters of kittens or puppies has probably seen that mammalian moms will sometimes reject the runt of the litter. Even the most devoted moms will make no special effort to accommodate the runt's weaknesses. This rejection is presumably based on evolved (and unconscious) mechanisms that serve to promote inclusive fitness. But the harsh logic of this approach is simple. Why keep feeding the little one who will only grow weaker and die? It's better to focus on the healthy ones (Stearns, 1992). This same logic also explains why human mothers do not usually have a great number of children at once. Giving birth to twins, for example, is pretty risky because it increases the chances that one or both will fail to thrive. Even in modern, wealthy nations, human twins are considerably more likely to die in infancy than singletons. Twinning is the exception rather than the rule in human mothers.

Based on predictions derived from life history theory, Bugental et al. (2013) documented a variation on the "runt of the litter" theme in human parents. Their first finding seemed to fly in the face of what mother cats and dogs do when they neglect a runt. Bugental et al. found that in wealthy families (who had access to plenty of medical and educational resources), children who had medical or psychological problems received more parental care and were provided with more resources than those whose development was going swimmingly. Parents gave more care to the kids for whom more care was needed. However, parents who had to cope with the limited resources that come with poverty adopted a different strategy. When facing the dilemmas associated with having a child with special needs, impoverished parents provided the least parental care to their least healthy children – meaning that they gave more care to the children who had a greater chance of surviving and thriving. If cats and dogs could afford to hire nannies and physical therapists, runts of the litter would presumably do just fine. Conversely, when human parents are unlucky enough to live in a world where survival is not a certainty, they appear to behave more like cats and dogs than most people would wish.

Even if all your children are born fit as a fiddle, this doesn't guarantee you can afford violin lessons. Life history theory predicts that, all else being equal, those who live in difficult environments must adopt different parenting strategies than those who live in friendly environments. For parents who live in a world full of disease or predators, for example, it makes a great deal of evolutionary sense to begin having children when you are younger, to have more children over the course of your life, and to provide less care to any specific child. In the language of life history, this is a **fast strategy**, also known as a K strategy (Stearns, 1992). Contrast this with the **slow strategy** (or R strategy) that is more common among parents who live in a safe, resource-rich world. Lucky human parents who can be virtually guaranteed that they and their children will live to a ripe old age can take their time before becoming parents. They can also safely have only one or two children. Finally, they can make big investments in each individual child. Summer robotics camp, swim lessons, and college savings accounts are all part of a slow strategy.

I adopted a slow parenting strategy. I have two children who live safe and comfortable lives. I had just turned 42 when my first child was born. In contrast, my brother Stacy, who is less than a year my senior, had his first grandchild the same year I had my first child. That's a very fast strategy. But it's not nearly as fast as the lightning fast strategy of my parents. My mom gave birth to her fourth child when she was 21 (no twins involved), and she had six who survived to birth. My mom's sister had 12 children, which made my mom feel our family was pretty small. My dad often noted that it would be a small miracle if all his children reached adulthood. When I was 13, I told him that I was seriously worried I could be killed if I took his advice about fighting a bully who was much older and bigger than I was. His response was: "You don't need to worry about that; I could always make a replacement." Likewise, as a young adult, I was moving a large piece of heavy furniture with my dad, and I loudly told him that his favored way of getting the piece through a doorway was protecting the furniture but badly ripping up my knuckles. He quickly retorted: "Skin grows back; furniture don't!" Comments like these were made partly in jest, but there can be no doubt that my parents – who lived in a world of great uncertainty – adopted what life history theorists call a fast parenting strategy. Consistent with life history theory, I must also note that my parents didn't live very long. My mom died at 55; my dad died at 66. Needless to say, this was much too fast for my taste.

Pelham (2017a) tested predictions from life history theory in a global study of environmental harshness and parents' life history strategies – including their level of investment in their children. A study of 150 nations showed that in nations where pathogen loads (communicable disease rates) were higher than average, infant mortality rates were higher than average. Further, pathogen load and infant mortality rates both predicted higher adolescent birth rates (a higher percentage of women who began having kids as teenagers). The same basic pattern held for pathogen load, infant mortality rates, and the average number of children women had over the course of their lives. In nations where things were difficult, the typical mother bore a large number of children. Finally, in nations with higher disease loads and higher infant mortality rates, parents invested less time and energy in each of their individual children, for example by being more willing to allow their children to engage in child labor. This last effect is illustrated in Figure 6.4, which focuses on a composite measure of parental attitudes about child obedience, attitudes about child beating, and objective risks to children (child labor, lack of early education). To be clear, I'm not saying parents who live in a harsh world gleefully adopt more positive attitudes about child beating or happily allow their children to engage in child labor. But in a world in which communicable diseases and infant death are commonplace, many parents seem to feel they have no choice but to expose their kids to risks that would be unthinkable to parents who live in a safe, healthy world.

I'd like to note some methodological strengths of this cross-national study. First, for some of these measures of parenting strategies (but not the one shown in Figure 6.4), I had access to recent as well as historical indicators of parenting strategies. This allowed me to assess changes in these parenting strategies. For example, I found that adolescent birth rates in a given nation increased over a 50-year window if that nation had high historical pathogen loads and high recent infant mortality rates. Second, all these parental investment effects, such

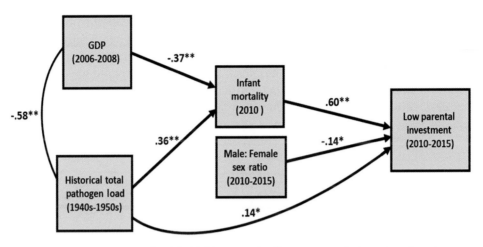

Figure 6.4 *In keeping with predictable life history tradeoffs, parents made fewer investments in their kids (placing them at more risk) in nations with higher disease loads and higher infant mortality rates.*

as having a greater number of kids in nations where there is more disease, held up in this global study after statistically controlling for competing predictors such as GDP (national wealth). Apparently, it's not poverty that directly leads parents to adopt a fast parenting strategy – at least where these indicators are concerned. It's living in an uncertain world where death and disease often rear their ugly heads. Unfortunately, then, even biological parents seem to invest less in their children's development when they know there is a decent chance their children may never make it to adulthood.

Notice that this study illustrates a tradeoff between the level of parental investment in any specific child and the likelihood that any specific child can be expected to survive and reproduce. The higher the chances that one of your offspring will survive, the more time and energy you can afford to invest in that child. Life history theorists have documented many examples of the tradeoffs that animal parents must navigate (Stearns, 1992). One of the more intuitive tradeoffs in life history theory has to do with one's place in the food chain. Predators generally produce many fewer offspring than prey, for example. Contrast eagles and ducks, sharks and sardines, or foxes and rabbits. All else being equal, those who get eaten more often must produce a greater number of offspring. There are many other tradeoffs in life history theory and many of them have to do with parenting.

One such life history tradeoff has to do with the initial biological investments mothers make in their offspring. Stearns (1992) notes that, for birds, there is an ideal clutch size (the number of eggs a mother bird lays) that varies with maternal health and the availability of food. In times of excess, healthy mother birds will often lay more eggs than usual. In times of duress, they will lay fewer. Further, if things get tough enough after mother birds have laid their eggs, mothers may abandon their nests completely. Figure 6.5 illustrates another life history tradeoff that is highly relevant to parenting. Across bird species, mothers of more precocial offspring make larger biological investments in their eggs themselves. In more precocial bird species, mothers lay eggs that are much richer in the nutrients it takes to make a highly capable hatchling (Sotherland & Rahn, 1987). As Sotherland and Rahn note, kiwis hatch fully feathered and highly precocial. In contrast, brown creepers, like most other songbirds, hatch blind, almost bald, and quite helpless. As you probably could have guessed, ruddy duck chicks are pretty precocial, too, but not as precocial as kiwis. They have fuzzy down rather than full-blown feathers, for example.

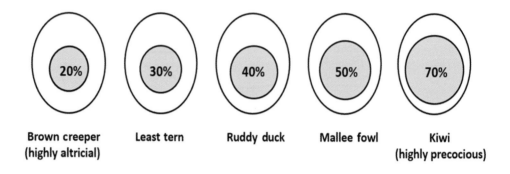

Brown creeper	Least tern	Ruddy duck	Mallee fowl	Kiwi
(highly altricial)				(highly precocious)
20%	30%	40%	50%	70%

Figure 6.5 *The energy-rich yolks of highly precocial birds are much larger than those of more altricial birds.*

To be clear about the specific parental tradeoff that appears to be at work in the case of cross-species egg yolk size variation, it only makes evolutionary sense for a particular species of mother bird to invest a great deal of energy into her offspring up front (by producing eggs that are much more biologically taxing to create) if these eggs are guaranteed to become offspring who will require less of her energy after hatching. As a reminder, no one thinks that mother birds sit down and calculate these contingencies. Instead, genes that cause mother birds to make larger biological investments in their eggs will only remain in the gene pool if these genes – or other genes that activate or accompany them – mean that baby birds can better fend for themselves after hatching.

A parent's main job is conflict management

One of the most interesting implications of evolutionary theory for parenting is based on the idea that evolution is mainly about genes rather than organisms. If evolution happens mainly at the level of genes rather than organisms, which most evolutionary experts believe is the case, then this sets the stage for a lot of familial conflict. Mothers, who are positive their children share half their genes, are somewhat more invested in their children than fathers. Children, who share only half of their genes with either parent, will often be at odds with their own parents. To paraphrase Kilner and Hinde (2012), in sexually reproducing organisms, a mother shares about half her genes with her daughter, but that same mom shares 100% of her genes with herself. So, a daughter should usually want more from a mother than the mother can or should give them. This sets the stage for parent–offspring conflict. For example, it's much more common for human parents to have to say no to their children's nonstop requests than it is for parents to have to ask their children if there is anything else they can do for them. For example, mothers almost always wish to stop nursing their offspring before the offspring wish to stop being nursed.

In contrast to the counterintuitive idea that children are often at odds with their own parents, it's pretty intuitive that siblings are often at odds with one another. Even the most devoted caregivers have only so much time, energy, and resources to go around. The more energy mom invests in my siblings, the less energy she has left to invest in me. Trivers (1972) argued that our present children are even in competition with our potential future children. The longer any mother nurses, for example, the longer she is likely to go without getting pregnant again (because nursing reduces fertility). The better I feed my daughter, the fewer biological resources that leaves for me – for future reproductive opportunities.

ADOPTIVE PARENTS: THE FAIRY GODMOTHER EFFECT?

An exception to some of the harsh evolutionary rules of parenting (e.g., the Cinderella effect, parental *dis*investment in a harsh world) comes from studies of a large group of parents who share no genes at all with their children and yet who seem to behave very differently than stepparents – or even biological parents who take a sink or swim approach to parenting. These parents are **adoptive parents**. If failing to share genes with your kids puts you at risk for being a less than wonderful parent, shouldn't this mean adopted kids would be at higher than average risk for neglect or abuse by their adoptive parents?

I haven't gotten to say this very often in this book, but I'm happy to say the answer seems to be no. On average, adoptive parents seem to take great care of the kids they adopt. Nigel Barber (2004, 2009) is an evolutionary psychologist who has looked closely at this question. Barber points out that the limited amount of research focusing on adoptive parents shows that they offer their adopted children just as much care and attention as do biological parents. (I know of no studies looking at abuse committed by adoptive parents.) In fact, a study by Kyle Gibson (2009) looked at families with at least one adopted child and at least one biological child. This controls for a lot of potential worries involving individual differences between people who adopt and those who do not. Gibson directly compared how much care and attention adoptive parents gave to their adopted children with how much care and attention these same parents gave to own biological offspring. It was the adopted kids who received more care from the parents. This is a bit misleading because the kids who had been adopted apparently had greater needs, on average, than the couple's biological kids. It seems pretty safe to assume, though, that the average adoptive parent goes to great lengths to rear a child with whom they share no genes. Adoptive parents appear to be the real-world equivalent of fairy godmothers (Hamilton et al., 2007).

As Barber (2009) has argued, a likely reason why adoptive parents are so good to their adoptees is that they are carefully screened to be able to adopt kids in the first place. Most adoption agencies reject convicted murderers, psychopaths, and people who say they would change a child's first name to "Supreme Ruler."

Just as important, most adoptive parents adopt newborns, who seem to become just as strongly bonded to them as they do to the infants. Just as a cuckoo chick's adoptive parents usually take great care of it, adoptive human parents – who knowingly take adoptees in rather than being taken in – should have little trouble bonding with their adopted children. In fact, research on what Buckels and colleagues (2015) call the **parental care motivational system** suggests not only that human beings evolved to be predisposed to care for needy infants but also that some people are much more strongly motivated to do so than others. Buckels et al. found, for example, that people who scored higher than average in their index of parental caring (strongly endorsing items such as "Babies melt my heart") reported greater than usual distress at the sight of an unhappy infant. Consistent with the idea that stepparents can be strongly motivated to care for adoptive children, Buckels et al. also found that people who did not yet have children but scored high in their measure of paternal care motivation expressed a much stronger than usual desire to have children in the future. Presumably, those who are strongly motivated to care for infants but learn that they cannot become biological parents would be predisposed toward adoption. This final implication of Buckels et al.'s findings awaits future empirical scrutiny.

Any profound tendencies toward parental nurturance aside, Tracy DeHart and colleagues (2011) argue that parents, adoptive or otherwise, seem to include their children in their own self-concepts. This is important because research shows that the minute something becomes a part of the self, people begin to adore it. Jay Beggan (1992) has shown, for example, that giving a person an object (a coffee mug, a pen) leads the person to evaluate that object much more favorably than usual. Beggan called this robust tendency the **mere ownership effect**. Other studies have shown that the mere ownership effect grows even larger than usual when people get to choose an object, and when people get to touch an object, rather than being told it is theirs without getting to touch it (see Reb & Connolly, 2007). The fact that adoptive parents almost always get to name their children should even further increase their affection for them (Pelham et al., 2005). Putting all this together, the fact that adoptive parents usually get to choose, touch, and name the babies they adopt puts adoptive parents in a much better position than stepparents to become highly nurturing caregivers (e.g., see Festinger, 1957; Gilbert & Ebert, 2002).

In short, it's pretty easy to see why adoptive parents usually behave like devoted fairy godmothers. In addition to the model of the fairy godmother, there may be a second positive message to the story of Cinderella. In almost every version of this timeless story, Disney's version included, there is a happy ending. The uppity stepmother always gets her comeuppance, and Cinderella goes from sweeping up after others to being swept off her feet by a charming prince. The fact that this happy ending is so satisfying says something profound about human nature. We care, and we have a strong sense of social justice (Brosnan & de Waal, 2003). These qualities make it possible for us to engage in acts of caring that extend well beyond adoption. Any person who can feel empathy for someone else is capable of altruism – a topic to be addressed in detail in Chapter 9. But before we discuss the evolution of helpfulness, let's discuss the evolution of thoughtfulness. If there is a single area of research in which evolutionary psychology flies most flagrantly in the face of common sense, this may be it. We may not be nearly as thoughtful as we would all like to think.

"Mom, *please* tell us you brought us something besides puke this time."

FOR FURTHER READING

» Barber, N. (2004). *Kindness in a cruel world: The evolution of altruism.* Amherst, NY: Prometheus Books.

» Daly, M. & Wilson, M.I. (1994). Some differential attributes of lethal assaults on small children by stepfathers versus genetic fathers. *Ethology & Sociobiology*, 15(4), 207–17.

» Harlow, H.F. (1958). The nature of love. *American Psychologist*, 13, 573–86.

» Royle, N.J., Smiseth, P.T. & Kölliker, M. (2012). *The evolution of parental care.* Oxford: Oxford University Press.

» Saraux, C., Chiaradia, A., le Maho, Y. & Ropert-Coudert, Y. (2011). Everybody needs somebody: Unequal parental effort in little penguins. *Behavioral Ecology*, 22(4), 837–45.

SAMPLE MULTIPLE-CHOICE EXAM QUESTIONS

Here are four sample quiz questions for Chapter 6. You can find the Chapter 6 quiz at: www.macmillanihe.com/evolutionary-psychology

6.01.   How do human fathers compare with fathers of other mammals when it comes to the average amount of care they provide for their offspring?

a.   human fathers offer a lot *more* care than do most other mammalian fathers

b.   human fathers are typical of most mammalian fathers, providing a modest amount of care for offspring

c.   human fathers offer a lot *less* care than do most other mammalian fathers

6.02.   Karen studies the details of how and why infants bond to their primary caregivers – and the consequences of this bonding process for later development. Karen is most likely:

a. a socioemotional theorist

b. an attachment theorist

c. a family trait theorist

6.03.   One of the important ways in which Daly and Wilson studied the "Cinderella effect" was by examining.

a. parental ratings of their devotion to their step children versus their biological children

b. inheritance records for people's biological vs. adopted children

c. infant and child homicide statistics

6.04.   The more children a parent produces, the less amount of time and energy that parent can invest in any one child. Along similar lines, having a child at all often means having less time and energy to grow and maintain one's own body. Evolutionarily significant trade-offs such as these are a key aspect of:

a. substitution theory

b. life history theory

c. trade-off theory

Answer key: a, b, c, b.

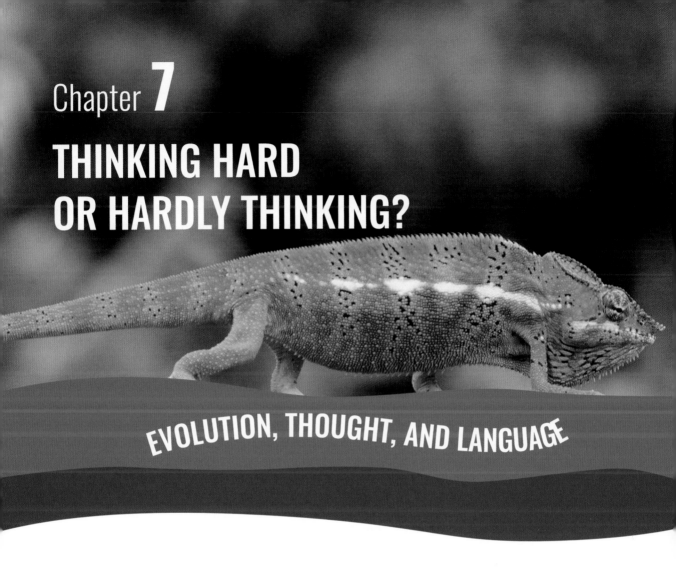

Chapter **7**
THINKING HARD OR HARDLY THINKING?

EVOLUTION, THOUGHT, AND LANGUAGE

I'd give my right arm to be ambidextrous.

— Yogi Berra (source unknown)

For about 200,000 years, modern humans have been doing more than just mating, developing, and taking care of kids. We've also been doing a lot of thinking, or so we'd like to think. In fact, a popular view of human nature is that we're great at abstract reasoning. According to this view, human beings are – perhaps above all else – thinkers. We pride ourselves on being different from other animals, and we point to poetry, the Sistine Chapel, and cell phone towers as proof of our amazing intellect. The moon inspired ancient Theban and Elizabethan poets. Our modern response to the moon is, "Yeah, we've been there." Colleges tell us that they don't just teach specific facts. Instead, they instill "critical thinking skills." I don't want to be too critical of our critical thinking skills, but there appears to be a big gap between what we can be, sometimes, in rare moments of inspiration, and what we typically are.

ARE WE GENERAL PURPOSE REASONING MACHINES?

I'm not saying we're stupid. I'm just saying maybe we're not quite the rational "economic man" (or woman) of classical economics, or even the thoughtful "naive scientist" in which many social psychologists once deeply believed. Socrates may have been right that the "unexamined life is not worth living," but exactly how much examination did Socrates have in mind? How do we do when really put to the test? This is, of course, a complex question, but let me spell out two specific ways in which researchers have put human reasoning to the test. First, when we have to make a complex decision, do we follow our gut instincts, or do we carefully reason our way through it? Second, when a decision is not complex at all, but our guts are pitted directly against our intellects, which usually wins? Recall from Chapter 1 that Gilbert (1989) described the mammalian brain as a reptilian brain wrapped in a neocortical bun. That neocortical bun is proportionately much larger in people than in other mammals. But just how much power does Gilbert's neocortical bun have to overrule the reptilian weenie?

It's just not in the cards

As usual I'm treading on controversial ground. Even big advocates of evolutionary psychology have had some pretty spirited debates about the evolution of thinking, and how we should best study it. With that caveat in mind, let's consider a couple of popular ways of seeing how carefully we reason. In 1968, Peter Wason gave people a test that, he argued, assessed "reasoning about a rule." A variation on the **Wason card task** appears below. Why not test the rule yourself. Your goal is to find out if a specific rule is true or false in a set of only four two-sided cards, all of which have a number on one side and a letter on the other side. The rule is: "If a card has a vowel on one side, then it must have an even number on the other side." I'll simplify things by telling you that – to test the hypothesis – you need to turn over exactly two of the four cards. You're wasting your time if you turn over any more than two, and you can't know for sure whether the rule is really true if you turn over only one. Which two cards would you like to flip over?

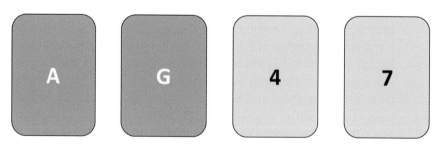

Figure 7.1 *Which two cards should you turn over to test the rule?*

In Wason's original studies and many others since, most people who turn over two cards choose the cards marked A and 4. That was my response the first time I saw the problem. I remember this well because my first-year adviser in grad school, Bill Swann, had just posed the question, and I was anxious to show off my mad reasoning skills. But my answer was much madder than it was reasoned. The truth, I hope you'll agree, is that I should have turned over the A card and the 7 card. Why ignore the 4? Because the rule didn't say consonants couldn't ever have an even number. It clearly said that all vowels must have one. To see if this is really true, you'd need to turn over the 7 – because if the 7 has a vowel on the other side, then the rule is false. Trust me. Turn over that 7, and you'll see an E, which is clearly a vowel. Logically speaking, you absolutely, positively do need to turn over the 7. Don't feel so bad. At least Bill Swann isn't smiling knowingly and asking you if you've considered a career that doesn't require the use of letters or numbers. Bill wasn't just making fun of me. He was also making a point. Most people test abstract hypotheses by looking for what they expect to see rather than putting hypotheses to a more critical test (see Klayman & Ha, 1987). Wason and others refer to this as the **positive test bias**, and it is just one of many hypothesis-confirming biases. For example, both stereotypes about groups and expectancies about specific people can determine what we focus on and what we ignore.

If we are **general purpose reasoning machines**, then we shouldn't fail so badly on the Wason card selection (reasoning) task. On the other hand, one criticism of this particular task is that people don't always interpret it the way a logician like Wason did. That may be a bit of a cop out, but let's try another reasoning task, one that has only one simple interpretation, and one for which I'll accept even a decent approximation of the right answer. Let's move from esoteric cards to a common sheet of copy paper and look at simple numerical estimation rather than "if-then" reasoning.

The paper-folding problem

Imagine that you took an ordinary sheet of copy paper and folded it over upon itself 100 times. I should be very clear that this is not physically possible. But imagine that you could somehow do it. Assume that the original sheet of paper was 0.1 mm thick. After the first fold you'd have a sheet of paper 0.2 mm thick. After the second fold it'd be 0.4 mm, and after the third fold, 0.8 mm. How thick would it be after the 100th fold? Please don't read on until you offer a specific estimate.

Unless you are a truly unusual person, I have some bad news. Your answer is incorrect. It's too low. For now, you're really just going to have to trust me on this. Let me make a strong suggestion for improving your answer. First, take your original estimate and multiply it by ten. Hmmm. Let's see. Nope, that's *still* too low. In fact, it's *much* too low. Try multiplying this second guess by 100! Yes, 100. Hmmm … I'm sorry to say that your third guess is *still* too low.

I'm growing impatient. Do anything you want, but make a fourth guess that is so high that you feel that there is only one chance in a thousand that the true answer is higher than this fourth guess! Go ahead. Take your time. I'm practically giving the answer away now. Hmmm … That's certainly better. Much better, yes. But *still* too low.

OK, by now, *you* must be growing impatient. Allow me to help. For your fifth and final guess, please give your answer in astronomical units. An astronomical unit is the average distance between the earth and the sun. Yes, I'm seriously saying the correct answer is *more than* the distance between the earth and the sun. But how much more? Exactly how *many* astronomical units is it? Go ahead. Make a final guess. Again, take your time. I'm not going anywhere. Really? That's it? I must say I'm pretty disappointed. Unless your last name is Newton and your first name is Sir Isaac, I'm betting that your estimate is *still* too low. The correct answer is a little less than 850 *trillion* astronomical units. That's 2^{100} (2 to the 100th power) x 0.1 mm. Yes, that's 2 x 2 x 2 x 2 x 2 x 2 x 2 x 2 x 2 x 2 x 2 x 2 x 2 x 2 x 2 x 2 x 2 x 2 x 2 x 2 x 2 x 2 x 2 x 2 x 2 x 2 x 2 x 2 x 2 x 2 x 2 x 2 x 2 x 2 x 2 x 2 x 2 x 2 x 2 x 2 x 2 x 2 x 2 x 2 x 2 x 2 x 2 x 2 x 2 x 2 x 2 x 2 x 2 x 2 x 2 x 2 x 2 x 2 x 2 x 2 x 2 x 2 x 2 x 2 x 2 x 2 x 2 x 2 x 2 x 2 x 2 x 2 x 2 x 2 x 2 x 2 x 2 x 2 x 2 x 2 x 2 x 2 x 2 x 2 x 2 x 2 x 2 x 2 x 2 x 2 x 2 x 2 x 2 x 2 x 0.1 mm. And *that* turns out to be 1,267,650,600,228,229,401,496,703,205,376 x 0.1 mm. In scientific notation, it's about 1.2677×10^{29} mm or 1.2677×10^{23} km. That's about 7.8768×10^{22} miles, which is nearly 850 trillion times (8.4697×10^{14} times) the 93 million miles between the earth and the sun. Now that's one *thick* piece of paper. It also makes me feel a little thick to have guessed only 24 miles the first time I heard the question.

The **paper-folding problem** was developed by Scott Plous (1993) to illustrate a basic feature of human judgment and decision-making. This is the tendency to stick too close to an initial starting point when revising a judgment. Researchers refer to this tendency as the **anchoring and adjustment bias** (or the **anchor and adjust heuristic**), with the important warning that the adjustment part is often woefully insufficient. Maybe it's expecting too much of people to serve as human calculators, but when I answered the question myself for the first time, I *knew* that $2^{10} = 1,024$. (My name is Brett, and I am a recovering numbers geek.) If I had merely rounded this down to a thousand and then multiplied that 1,000 by 1,000 nine more times, I would have very quickly realized that the answer was more than a nonillion (10^{30}) of those 0.1 millimeter units. As you now know, that's scientific notation for "ginormously humungous." But I didn't do the math. I felt like my intuitions would surely get me pretty close. I wasn't just way off-base, I was way off-galaxy.

JUDGMENTAL HEURISTICS: FLYING ON AUTOPILOT

The literature in human reasoning, judgment, and decision-making is full of examples such as these. The conclusion Nobel Prize winner Daniel Kahneman (2011) came to after decades of such research is that most of the time we get through life not by means of careful calculations but by means of **judgmental heuristics** – quick and dirty rules of thumb for solving problems of magnitude or likelihood. One frequently used judgmental heuristic is known as the **representativeness heuristic** (Kahneman & Tversky, 1972). We often judge the likelihood of an event on the basis of how much it resembles (represents) some other event, which is often a darn good idea. By the way, I sometimes like to call this heuristic the *similarity heuristic*, because "similarity" is a word I can actually pronounce. Regardless of what we call this, let's consider how it might work. To see, Tversky and Kahneman (1974, p. 1125) asked people a question about two hypothetical hospitals:

> A certain town is served by two hospitals. In the larger hospital, about 45 babies are born each day, and in the smaller hospital, about 15 babies are born each day. As you know, about 50% of all babies are boys. However, the exact percentage varies from day to day. Sometimes it may be higher than 50%, sometimes lower.
>
> For a period of one year, each hospital recorded the number of days on which more than 60% of the babies born were boys. Which hospital do you think recorded more such days? (Circle one letter.)
>
> a. the larger hospital
>
> b. the smaller hospital
>
> c. about the same (that is, within 5% of each other)

Before we discuss the answer options, consider your own hunches about the answer. The large majority of people choose option c. After all, 60% or more of a big number (45) is exactly the same as 60% or more of a small number (15). That intuition is quite correct, but this doesn't mean that a random result that meets or exceeds 60% is equally likely in a big versus a small sample. Results that vary from an expected population value are much more likely in a small sample than in a large sample. Instead of applying this careful, logical (statistical) decision rule, most people use the representativeness heuristic.

If you don't see why the unusual result (60% or more male births) is more likely in the hospital with fewer daily births, consider a simpler version of the question about sample size. When flipping a coin, is it easier to get 80% (4/5) heads when you flip 5 coins or 500 coins? Based on this situation, Pelham and Neter (1995) made a small tweak in the classic version of the hospital problem. Among other things, we just wanted to see if making the math easy enough – or activating the right intuition – might allow people to answer the problem correctly sometimes. We asked people to consider the number of days in a year in which not 60% but all (100%) of the babies born would be boys. Further, we made the small hospital really tiny; it had only about 2 (not 15) births per day. I hope you can see that in the teeny hospital, both babies (100% of them) would be boys fully 25% of the time (0.5 x 0.5 = 0.25). In the big hospital, in contrast, 100% of the babies would be boys about 0 times per millennium. Don't make me break out my powers of 2 again ($p = 1/2^{45}$).

Efrat Neter and I weren't trying to debunk judgmental heuristics. We were just trying to establish some of the conditions under which people are most and least likely to use them. We concluded, for example, that people only seem to apply statistical decision rules to the hospital problem when presented with an extremely hospitable version of this classic problem. We also found, by the way, that when the math is hard rather than easy to do, people are more – not less – likely to use judgmental heuristics when they are highly motivated to find the correct answer.

Before moving on to a couple of other heuristics, I'd like to note that, in real life, math is often tough and decisions are sometimes deadly. In my view, judgmental rules of thumb such as the representativeness heuristic apply to decisions made in real hospitals about as well as they do to abstract decisions in the classic hospital problem. For example, research suggests that one scary reason why medical professionals sometimes overlook the symptoms of heart attacks in women is that heart attacks are perceived as more *representative* (stereotypical) of men than of women. Things as subtle as the color of a sports jersey can have a big impact on important social judgments – by means of representativeness (Frank & Gilovich, 1988). Frank and Gilovich found, for example, that professional U.S. football and hockey teams whose jerseys were black got called for more penalties, because referees and fans associate the color black with aggression.

To touch on another seductive heuristic, if you ask me how frequent or likely something is, I'll often consider how easily that thing comes to mind. Doing so means I'm using the **availability heuristic**. In keeping with the allure of this heuristic, many people think that murder rates in the U.S. are much higher than suicide rates. In reality, suicides slightly outnumber homicides. But murders are more dramatic, of course. As journalists like to put it: "If it bleeds it leads." If we can remember more murders, there must be more of them. In the rush of daily life, what most people don't usually do to estimate murder or suicide rates is to consult an actuary or public health expert (although we might occasionally ask our friend, Siri). Daniel Kahneman won his Nobel Prize in economics for showing that the hypothetical "economic man" (or woman) is not quite what he (or she) is hyped up to be. In case I haven't already annoyed or insulted you enough in this section, let me offer just one more example of how we think. I bet I can make things up to you.

Once I collect my Nobel Prize, I plan to become a philanthropist. So let me start practicing. Would you prefer that I give you $8,000 in cash, guaranteed, or an even (50/50) chance of winning $18,000. The rational economist or investor would quickly do the math and quickly choose the gamble. Economists assess the long-term **expected utility** of gambles by multiplying probabilities by payoffs. The long-term expected utility of the risky option here is ½ x $18,000, which is $9,000. That long-term expected utility is more than $8,000. However, unless you're reading this book at the high rollers table at Caesars Palace, I'm guessing you'd opt for the sure thing – to help out with those pesky student loans. If so, you'd be showing evidence of **loss-aversion**, which refers to being more sensitive to losses than to gains. It would hurt more to *lose* $8,000 than it would feel good to *win* an additional $10,000. Psychologically, losses loom larger than gains, and this can sometimes lead people to do crazy things. Ironically, among gamblers, one of these crazy things is to take unwise risks to try to win their money back once they've lost some of it. At any given time, there are a lot of people in Vegas merely trying to "win it back." It hurts to go home a loser (Belsky & Gilovich, 1999). What happens in Vegas does stay in Vegas, and most of what stays in Vegas is your money.

COULD YOU BE MORE SPECIFIC? GENIUS IS DOMAIN-SPECIFIC

So maybe we aren't quite as thoughtful as we'd like to believe. But there is more to the story than that. In addition to research in judgment and decision-making, there is also research in many other areas of psychology suggesting that we simply aren't general purpose problem-solvers. This includes not being general purpose problem-solvers when it comes to many real-life problems. In fact, this lack of general ingenuity even seems to apply to geniuses. Let me elaborate.

More than 40 years ago, Chase and Simon (1973) conducted a series of clever studies of chess masters. Then, as now, chess masters were the poster children of human genius. **Chase and Simon's (1973) chess master studies** pitted these world-class chess players against regular college students in a study of memory. Specifically, they showed chess masters and students images of chess boards, in the middle of real games. People had five seconds to study the 8 x 8 chess boards before trying to recall the exact locations of all 32 pieces. If you're like me and have trouble remembering the name of those horsey-shaped pieces, you might be impressed to learn that the average college student was able to remember the exact locations of about 7 pieces. The average chess master, though, remembered almost 28 pieces. If you think that's obvious, I'll forgive you. Chess masters are geniuses, right? As one of my students once put it, maybe they even have photogenic memories. They don't – at least not if you mix things up just a little. Consider what happened when the experimenters changed the task slightly by placing the chess pieces on the board at random. This hardly mattered at all for the college students. Their memory dropped from 7 to about 6 pieces. But it made a huge difference for the chess masters. Just like the college students, they now remembered about 6 pieces.

In my view, this **specificity principle** is quite robust. People who stand out as Uber-geniuses in their areas of expertise are no better than the rest of us schmucks when you move to a different domain. In fact, they are often no better than the rest of us when you stick to the same domain but change the rules of the game a little. Despite the popular notion that human beings are reasoning machines, the human mind is not a general purpose problem-solver. Instead, our knowledge and expertise is often highly modular. We become very good – or are born being very good – at certain specific problems, and *we rarely generalize that expert performance to closely related problems*. Let's consider a few examples, beginning with the classic Linda problem (Tversky & Kahneman, 1983):

> Linda is 31 years old, single, outspoken, and very bright. She majored in philosophy. As a student, she was deeply concerned with issues of discrimination and social justice, and also participated in anti-nuclear demonstrations.
>
> Which is more likely?
>
> 1. Linda is a bank teller.
> 2. Linda is a bank teller and is active in the feminist movement.

In study after study, the very large majority of college students given this problem report that option 2 is more likely. Students wrongly conclude that a woman who stereotypically *sounds like* a feminist is more likely to be a feminist bank teller than to be a bank teller. That's called the **conjunction fallacy**, mistakenly reporting that A *and* B can be more likely than A all by itself. It can't be more likely that your dad is a librarian who can juggle than it is that he is a librarian, and it cannot even be more likely that your dad is a librarian who likes books than it is that he's a librarian. I'm sure of this because my high school librarian hated books (although all the other librarians I've known seem to adore them). Although there has been some debate about the exact wording of the Linda problem, and what mindset people adopt when given the problem, I think it's fair to say that many experts on judgment and decision-making agree that this is a fallacy (see Mellers et al., 2001).

To get back to the point about the limits of judgmental expertise, one of the reasons why so many researchers have been impressed by the Linda problem is that a group of statisticians who were given this problem made exactly the same mistake made by the college students (Tversky & Kahneman, 1983). That's right. A group of PhD-holding statisticians who could explain eigenvectors and Poisson distributions in their sleep failed this simple test of statistical thinking just as often as college students did. In fact, it was Kahneman's demonstration of the conjunction fallacy – in conjunction with demonstrations of many other judgmental biases – that helped him win that Nobel Prize.

Baseball great Ted Williams never won a Nobel Prize, but he was a 17-time MLB (Major League Baseball) all-star, and he won the American league batting crown six times. Many baseball experts consider him the greatest hitter ever. On a couple of occasions in the 1960s, Williams accepted a challenge to bat against a woman, Joan Joyce, who had been one of the best amateur female softball pitchers of the 1960s. Williams succeeded in raising big money for charity, but he failed miserably as a fast-pitch softball hitter. In a demonstration Joyce says took more than 10 minutes, Ted Williams never got a hit. The best he could do was to foul away three balls. Hey, Joyce, you go, girl! And you, Williams, you're cut from the girls' softball team. Stick with what you're good at. This same principle applies to wiffle ball by the way. The best MLB batters look like amateurs when hitting against the best wiffle ball pitchers (just Google "wiffle ball pitcher vs. MLB batter" for a fun demonstration). If you're still not convinced that athletic genius is domain-specific, just ask basketball great Michael Jordan how that baseball thing worked out for him. The second greatest basketball player ever was, at best, a mediocre baseball player. Likewise, the late Sir Roger Bannister was an amazing middle distance runner, but he didn't shatter any records in the 100 meters or the marathon. Similarly, if Conor McGregor could stay out of trouble, the controversial mixed martial arts (MMA) fighter would almost certainly beat the aging Floyd Mayweather in an MMA fight. But when the two men fought in late August 2017, they followed the formal rules of boxing. And the aging boxer kicked ass. Expertise in sports is highly domain-specific.

Moving from a memorable athletic event to human memory, consider some of the first memory athletes. Memory expert Dan Schacter (1996) described a man who learned to repeat random 100-digit numbers after looking them over for just a minute or so. The same man performed no better than you or me when asked to remember long strings of letters rather than numbers. Or consider research by Karen Adolph (2000). Adolph found that very young infants will often crawl

"Well *of course* I've heard that story, chromis. ***Everyone's*** heard that story. But as you'd know if you had looked more carefully, this one is not a horse at all. It's a donkey."

right off the edge of a "visual cliff" onto a piece of safety glass that seems to be a drop-off. After they become accomplished crawlers, however, infants learn to respect the edge of the apparent cliff. They stop just short of the edge and stay where it looks safer. However, when Adolph tested the same children a few months later, after they had just begun to walk, most of them walked right off the cliff – as foolishly as Wile E. Coyote in an old Warner Brothers cartoon.

Sticking with development, Roger Brown (1965) noted that it's practically unheard of for three- to four-year-olds to pass a typical Piagetian conservation task. **Conservation** is the recognition that things do not always undergo a real physical change every time they change their appearance. In violation of this logical rule, preschoolers seem to believe that the way things *look* are the way they always *are* (Flavell, 1986). This is why four-year-olds believe that you can make more clay, for example, by dividing one lump into two pieces. However, as Brown noted, the same kids who fail miserably when it comes to a clay conservation task show adult-like levels of conservation when it comes to a visual conservation task. As noted in Chapter 4, even infants and toddlers seem to know that objects do not grow larger as we walk closer to them. Conservation is domain-specific.

So this specificity principle seems to apply to adult chess masters, statisticians, athletes, and children of many ages. It also applies to adult problem-solvers. Gick and Holyoak (1983) asked people to read a story about a military commander who wanted to attack a fortress. But the fortress was well defended against large armies. The commander solved the problem by breaking his army into small units that all converged on the fortress at the same time, from different directions. Those who designed the fortress apparently hadn't thought of this strategy. After reading this story of creative problem-solving, people later had a chance to solve a problem of their own. This one involved medicine. A patient had an inoperable tumor. Doctors had developed a beam of radiation that would kill tumors at high levels of intensity. But this high-intensity radiation also killed healthy tissue. A low-intensity version of the radiation wouldn't harm any healthy tissue, but it wouldn't kill the tumor either. How could doctors destroy the tumor? Only 30% of Gick and Holyoak's participants solved the tumor problem. The solution was to point several low-intensity beams at the tumor from different angles and have them all converge right on the tumor. Even though people had just read about a problem that was logically identical to the tumor problem, only 30% solved it. When people were specifically instructed to use the military solution as a key to solving the medical problem, nearly everyone could do so. After leading a horse to water, you will often need to remind the horse that water is for drinking.

A savant is neither a soap nor a wine

An even more dramatic example of the specificity principle comes from case studies of prodigious savants. **Savants** are people who suffer from serious mental disabilities (often autism) and yet possess incredible intellectual, musical, or artistic talents. The sculptor Alonzo Clemens can spend a few moments looking at a photo of an animal, and then sculpt a realistic version of the animal in motion in 20 minutes. Alonzo does this from memory – without ever needing to look at the model again. The same artistic genius who can craft beautiful and realistic animals from memory has the vocabulary of a small child and requires assistance for routine activities such as eating and getting dressed.

Figure 7.2 *This is one of my favorite sculptures. It took a bright, semi-professional artist about a week to sculpt it, by working painstakingly from several photos and models. Alonzo Clemens could produce a superior sculpture from memory, in less than 20 minutes. The present artist, BP, is very modest and has asked not to be identified.*

In fact, Alonzo's genius is somewhat domain-specific even within the domain of sculpting. He's brilliant when it comes to sculpting animals but so-so when it comes to sculpting people. When it comes to drawing or painting he has no special artistic skills whatsoever. He's on par with a small child.

Speaking of small children, one of my favorite examples of domain-specific genius comes from my nephew Justin. When Justin was about six years old, he was a baseball genius (for a kid, at least). He knew exactly what a balk was, for example, and he knew the complete starting line-up and pitching rotation for the Atlanta Braves. Justin was also a huge fan of the record-breaking home-run hitter Mark McGuire (this was well before anyone knew McGuire was cheating). At one point in 1998 or 1999, Sammy Sosa had pulled ahead of McGuire in the home run race for that season. When I told Justin I thought Sosa was a better home run hitter than McGuire, Justin had a quick retort: "Yeah, but Sosa plays in Wrigley Field, where it's a lot easier to hit home runs. So McGuire's still better." Baseball experts might disagree with Justin's facts about baseball stadiums, but his logic was impeccable. Attribution theorists call this logic "discounting." Later that same day, I asked Justin where he wanted to go for lunch. He begged me to take him to Burger King. This surprised me because he had always preferred Wendy's. When I asked Justin why he wanted to go to Burger King, he explained that he wanted to be rich. Justin had apparently seen a commercial promising a "gold Pokémon coin" with every kid's meal. When I tried to explain to Justin that the coins were just gold-colored plastic, he thought I was pulling his leg. No amount of metallurgical or economic reasoning could rid Justin of this firm belief. Justin's genius was baseball-specific.

Mental modularity

Cognitive evolutionary psychologists such as Jerry Fodor (1983) have argued that these kinds of **dissociations** (disconnections between things that one might expect to be related) illustrate **mental modularity**. This is the idea that, rather than being a general purpose problem-solver, the human mind consists of many separate segments – which are specific, highly insulated information-processing tools. Fodor seems to have gotten the idea that the mind is modular after being struck by how powerful visual illusions are – even when the person viewing a visual illusion knows very well that the illusion is exactly that. Figures 7.3a and 7.3b show two powerful visual illusions. Knowing that they are illusions will do nothing at all to change your perceptual experience. Fodor reasoned that if this is so consistently the case for visual illusions, different parts of your mind must be doing their business in a pretty insulated fashion. Fans of mental modularity argue that just as your car's brakes are separate from the ignition system, your brain consists of many separate systems that each do their own thing, often in complete physical and psychological isolation from other systems.

Evolutionary psychologists have argued that at least some of these **modules** (specific, isolated mental functions) are probably hardwired, because they solve a specific problem of survival or reproduction. Importantly, these modules operate independently of one another, and they are pretty hard to shut down. Knowing they exist, and even knowing how they work, simply does not turn them off. That's not usually problematic because the modules do things that are

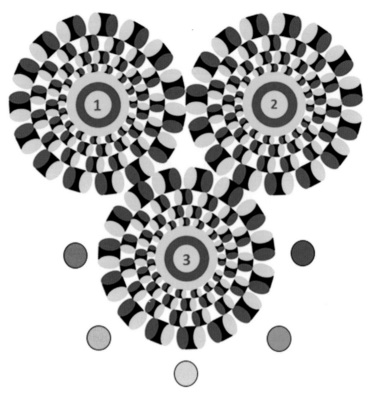

Figure 7.3a *The sneaky circles illusion. The sneaky circles illusion is my variation on the original "rotating snakes" (peripheral drift) illusion created by vision scientists Kitaoka and Ashida (2003). In my version, circles 2 and 3 rotate only when you look at the number 1. Likewise, circles 1 and 2 rotate only when you look at the number 3 (each circle stops rotating as soon as you look directly at it). Of course, they'll all start to rotate as soon as you start to read this description (or scan in half circles back and forth across the five colored dots). Sneaky, huh?*

Figure 7.3b *The checkerboard shadow illusion. In Edward H. Adelson's famous checkerboard shadow illusion, squares A and B are exactly the same shade of grey. Jerry Fodor was struck by the fact that knowing about visual illusions such as these, and even knowing exactly why they occur, does not make the illusions go away. This led Jerry Fodor to come up with the idea of mental modules.*

pretty important, and they are usually very good at what they do. They had to be. The idea of modularity is much like the idea of preparedness discussed in Chapters 1 and 2 (remember the spiders and snakes?). The difference is that some evolutionary psychologists think that many of these mental modules are more complex and precise than a simple readiness to learn. Some of them are much more like an instinct than an inkling. Another apparent example of mental modularity in action is the perception of biological motion from some very specific physical walking or running cues (which may be why wild predators on African game reserves don't attack cars; cars don't move like they're alive). Another example is the automatic perception of emotions from certain facial cues, which we'll briefly address later in this chapter. As you'll also see later, Steven Pinker (1994) has even argued that our natural skill at learning and using language, like a spider's skill at spinning a web, is an instinct.

IS THERE A SOCIAL EXCHANGE OR CHEATER DETECTION MODULE?

Speaking of webs of deception, let's return to an old topic – cheating. In this case I'm talking about something broader than sexual cheating. It's violating the **golden rule of social exchange**. If I give you something, you should almost always give me something in return – especially if you agreed to do so. According to Leda Cosmides (1989), human beings are masters of social exchange, and have been for millennia. This means that there should be such a thing as a **cheater detection module** in people, which means we should be pretty masterful when it comes to figuring out whether someone has screwed someone else over. Concepts such as cheating and stealing are cultural universals, and reasoning well about cheating and stealing should be a cultural universal as well. Cosmides and Tooby (1997) boldly argue that we enjoy the benefits of a cheater detection module, and they've traveled boldly across the globe to put this idea to the test. Let's put a version of it to the test right here. Your goal is to find out if a specific rule of exchange is true or false in the set of four two-sided cards that follow – all of which tell you on one side whether four different people used a friend's car and then on the other side whether each person filled the car's gas tank. So here's the rule: "If a person borrows the car, then she must fill the gas tank." I'll tell you (again) that you only need to turn over two of the four cards. To see if anyone cheated (by taking undue advantage of a friend's generosity with her car), which two cards in Figure 7.4 should you turn over?

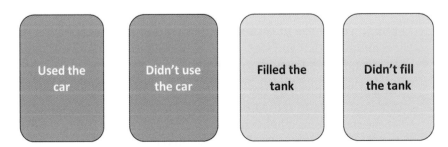

Figure 7.4 *Which two cards would let you test the social exchange rule?*

When faced with this "cheater detection" version of the Wason card task, most people do very well. In fact, the large majority of people correctly state that you should turn over the card that says "Used the car" and the one that says "Didn't fill the tank." This does not seem to be a simple question of being familiar with the situation in question. The "cheater detection" boost in reasoning occurs even for specific social exchanges to which people have never before been exposed. In fact, Sugiyama et al. (2002) showed that even the residents of a remote tribe in the Amazon, who could neither read nor write, performed very well on a variation of this task. There has been some debate about whether Cosmides and Tooby controlled for every conceivable non-evolutionary reason why you might expect to see content effects for this task. Further, some experts have gone so far as to argue that the Wason card task just isn't cut out to evaluate evolutionary hypotheses, because good or bad performance on the task is open to so many interpretations (e.g., see Atran, 2001, but compare Fiddick et al., 2000). However, most experts seem to agree that studies such as the Amazon study strongly suggest that we're really good at reasoning about social rule violations. Presumably this is because being able to do so is highly adaptive in a highly social and imperfectly cooperative species.

One thing that's even more adaptive than catching cheaters is surviving. Cosmides and Tooby (1997) have shown that people also kick butt on variations on the Wason card task that require reasoning about getting one's butt kicked – by nature. Here's a version I like: "Imagine that you are the parent of four teenagers who could all be planning to do separate trips to the desert on a given day. If a child plans to cross the desert that day, then he or she must fill his or her canteen before leaving home." To see if anyone took a dangerous risk on a particular day, which two cards from Figure 7.5 should you turn over? Remember, each card represents a different child.

Figure 7.5 *Which two cards should you turn over to test the survival rule?*

I hope you chose to turn over the first and fourth cards. If you did not do so, I recommend that you steer clear of the Sahara yourself until you've had a chance to consult with Cosmides or Tooby.

Research inspired by the same kind of evolutionary thinking shows that one of the best ways to remember a long list of items is to evaluate how much each of the items would help you survive. Nairne et al. (2007) showed people a list of words one at a time. Some people rated each word in terms of whether it would help them move to a foreign land. Others rated each word for its pleasantness.

A third group rated the words for how well the objects named would help them survive in a wilderness with little food and plenty of carnivores. Those who rated how well the objects would help them survive recalled the words best (see also Fiddick et al., 2000; Klein et al., 2002).

Do other evolved modules influence reasoning about rules?

It would be interesting to see how well people test hypotheses involving other evolutionarily inspired forms of the Wason card task. It would be easy, for example, to create tests for rules involving incest aversion, contamination, or kin selection (the tendency to help those with whom you share genes). One could also see whether modules ever lead us astray. Research suggests that we are hardwired to prefer physically attractive faces over unattractive faces. Alan Slater and colleagues (Slater & Quinn, 2001; Slater et al., 2000) found that even newborns prefer to look at beautiful as opposed to unattractive human faces. Presumably, this innate preference for beauty is grounded – at least in part – in the fact that more attractive people tend to be healthier. So evolutionary pressures on attraction and mate selection seem to be at least partly responsible for the **physical attractiveness stereotype**. This is the widespread assumption that physically attractive people are happier, more honest, and more sociable than their less attractive peers (Dion et al., 1972; Eagly et al., 1991). Finally, research in evolutionary psychology has shown that whereas men care more than women do about finding a physically attractive mate, women care more than men do about finding a mate who is financially secure. With this last finding in mind, suppose we asked people to test the following social rule, assuming that each card represents a different person in a specific culture: "If a man is rich, then his wife must be beautiful." To see if this rule held up in a set of four specific people, which two cards in Figure 7.6 should you turn over?

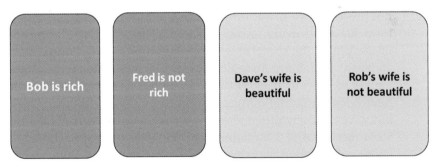

Figure 7.6 *Which two cards should you turn over to test this descriptive rule involving marriage in a specific culture?*

If people received this version of the card task, might they perform even worse than those who were given the abstract (number and letter) version? It's so tempting to conclude that wealthy men and beautiful women go hand in hand that it might not feel right to select the logically necessary "Rob's wife is not beautiful" card. In my own class demonstrations and preliminary studies of the Wason task, this is what I've usually observed. I've also found that people perform almost as well on an "incest aversion" form of the task as they do in a social exchange version – and much better on both versions than on Wason's original (abstract) version (Pelham, 2015). Cosmides and Tooby's (1997) findings appear to apply pretty well to at least a few other evolutionarily relevant judgment tasks.

IS BIAS ALWAYS SO BAD?

Because of the research attention the Wason card task has received in cognitive and social psychology, I have focused pretty heavily on this task in this chapter. However, evolutionary psychology has many other implications for how we reason and make judgments. One such implication is based on the idea that bias is not always bad. Most researchers who study judgmental heuristics argue that heuristics exist precisely because they are adaptive. They usually lead to correct answers. Whether we are predisposed to learn heuristics for evolutionary reasons or whether we have learned them from scratch, heuristics exist because they usually work. No one would decide how common something is based on how easily it is called to mind if this rule of thumb had no validity at all. Allow me to demonstrate. Consider the Siberian tiger and the house cat. Which species is so common we should almost always spay or neuter them? Which is more endangered? Which is more dangerous? By the time you consult Google for the statistical answers, the tiger will have eaten you, and you will never have had the chance to make that donation to the World Wildlife Fund. Worse yet, who's going to feed Toby and Tigger when you're gone?

Error management theory

As you may recall from Chapter 3 on natural selection, Haselton and Buss's (2000) error management theory suggests that even if heuristics and bias do not always work beautifully today, some of them have hung around for a long time for good evolutionary reasons. The **auditory looming bias** makes us overestimate the speed at which things are moving toward us but not the speed at which things are speeding away. The presumed evolutionary value of this bias is to keep us from getting clobbered (Haselton & Funder, 2006). I myself have been clobbered quite a few times by things that were speeding toward me but never once by things that were speeding away from me. Along similar lines, Stefanucci et al. (2008) found that hills look steeper to those who are atop them looking down than they do to those at the bottom looking up. As a former roofer and framer who is a bit afraid of heights, I firmly believe this isn't such a bad way to be biased. At least some judgmental biases are exactly the kind that have been increasing selective fitness (e.g., by keeping people alive) for a very long time.

Because dying usually makes it pretty hard to produce more copies of your genes, error management theory can also help explain prospect theory. The essence of **prospect theory** is that the curve describing our psychological responses to negative stimuli is steeper than the curve describing our psychological responses to positive stimuli. This means that when making decisions about valued objects, people typically weight losses more heavily than gains. Winning $100 does not make us feel twice as happy as winning $50. But *losing* $100 *might* be twice as painful as losing $50, especially if it means you can't make your rent (Kahneman & Tversky, 1979). Prospect theory thus predicts that people should often be loss-averse (systematically biased toward minimizing losses), which sometimes means that people will be unwilling to take very good gambles. Would you rather have $750 with absolute certainty, or have an honest 85% chance to win $1,000? The logical choice is the gamble – because it has a bigger expected value. But most people show evidence of loss-aversion. They say they'd go for the sure thing.

Classic work in psychophysics is also consistent with the evolutionary assumptions of error management theory. **Psychophysics** includes the study of how our subjective sensory experiences ("Wow, that's loud!") change with objective changes in the physical stimuli we are judging (the changing decibel levels of a sound). A rule of diminishing returns describes many perceptual experiences (Stevens, 1961). To make a second light appear twice as bright as a first, you must increase the objective brightness of the first light (the amount of light energy emitted) by a factor of eight. A similar rule applies for the perceived weight of small objects as well as for perceived pitch or loudness. This is Stevens' famous power law. But when it comes to stimuli that could harm or kill us, the basic rules of perception change dramatically. To make one shock feel twice as intense as a standard shock, I would only need to increase the amperage by about a third (Stevens et al., 1958).

A slightly more complex but conceptually similar situation exists for the perception of heat (Green, 1984). There is a specific point at which things stop feeling warm and start feeling painful, and people are very sensitive to small variations in the range of temperatures that hurt. If you have much experience with hot tubs, you know exactly what this means. For most people, the difference between bliss and blistering in a hot tub falls somewhere between 39 and 41°C.

To put all this in the language of survival, we better be more sensitive to things that can harm us than to things that can help us. There are often limits to how much we can benefit from pleasant things. I can only eat so much food before I get full. There's also a limit to how much things can harm us, but unfortunately the name of that limit is death. Most genes that promote death get kicked out of the gene pool (male redback spiders notwithstanding). Life is an inherent asymmetry. No amount of things good or pleasant can ever make up for any amount of badness that kills me. Even that which does not kill me often makes me weaker, and there is strong evidence that most bad things are weighted more heavily by the human brain than most good things. As Roy Baumeister and colleagues put it: "bad is stronger than good." In a review of topics as diverse as sex, food, emotions, parenting, and marriage, Baumeister et al. (2001) note that the psychological impact of bad events almost always outweighs the impact of good ones.

To provide an example of this idea, take my wife … please. At the root of that old joke is an ancient kernel of truth. It's the idea that an unhappy marriage looms large in a person's psychological landscape. In contrast, a happy marriage is almost taken as a given. An old but brilliant man named John Gottman has spent decades studying marriage, and the fact that you surely noticed my jab at Gottman's age is consistent with our sensitivity to badness. The big compliment I added ("but brilliant") doesn't begin to make up for the gerontological insult. I know this because Gottman's brilliant research clearly shows it. Gottman (1994) summarized a key theme in his research by noting that it usually takes a ratio of at least five good events to every one bad event in a marriage to keep it from falling apart. Assuming this 5:1 rule also applies to academic relationships, I offer my apologies to the brilliant, compassionate, creative, charming, and witty John Gottman. There, John, we're even. And I hope we're in agreement. Evolutionarily speaking, it's badness we really have to look out for.

In addition to having implications for perceptions of loss and threats to survival, error management theory makes important predictions about issues relevant to mating and sexual selection. To be more specific, error management theory predicts that there should be gender differences in the perception of sexual interest versus commitment. Recall that, in keeping with parental investment theory, there are large gender differences in people's interest in casual sex. Error management theory predicts that the differing evolutionary realities of mating for men and women should bias men's and women's perceptions of romantic cues in very different ways. Consider what happens when a woman who is out on a first date with a man touches him gently on the shoulder or laughs at one of his jokes. Error management theory predicts that, on average, men are more likely than women to perceive this innocent behavior as a flirtation, if not an outright invitation to sex. Conversely, consider how men and women might differ in their interpretation of what happens on a 14th date, when Ben presents Bridget with an expensive piece of jewelry. Error management theory predicts that, on average, women should be a lot more skeptical than men are about whether this gift is a reliable indicator of romantic commitment. Maybe that beautiful brooch means Ben is committed to Bridget, or maybe it just means he wants to get in her britches.

Research on error management shows that men and women do view the same romantic situations very differently. Haselton and Buss (2000) asked people how they'd interpret numerous romantic cues, including holding hands with a person, kissing a person passionately, or giving someone jewelry. In one study, they asked women and men how much these romantic behaviors reflected a "commitment intent" on the part of the romantic actor in question. As shown in Figure 7.7, when judging a male stranger, women were a little more skeptical than men were that the stranger's romantic behavior reflected a commitment intention. But the biggest error management biases emerged when men reported what these same romantic behaviors would mean if they *themselves* had engaged in them. The same men who had expressed skepticism about whether another man's romantic behavior indicated real commitment reported that if they engaged in these same behaviors, this would be a true indicator of commitment (what Trivers would call an "honest signal" of commitment).

Studies such as this one suggest that error management processes – in this case those grounded in parental investment motivations – play an important role in sexual selection and social perception. One way to think about error

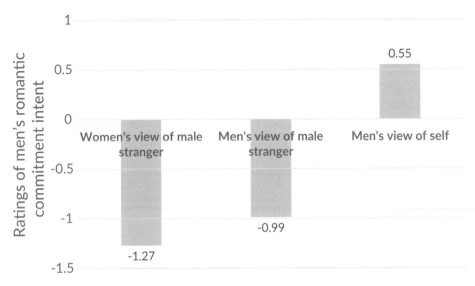

Figure 7.7 *Error management theory and perceived romantic intention.*

management theory is that when it comes to detecting romantic commitment, cheater detection modules may be activated more easily for women than for men. I should also add that, in my view, the useful but imperfect judgmental rules of thumb known as **heuristics** have some of the important features of modules. They're often irresistible, specific to very particular judgment tasks, and sometimes notoriously difficult to train away (Kahneman, 2011).

Human brains don't care for probabilities

Yet another evolutionary perspective on judgmental heuristics suggests that people are not really quite as prone to error and bias as classic work suggests. Gerd Gigerenzer has argued that human brains evolved to solve problems that are expressed differently in day-to-day life than they are in research on judgment under uncertainty. Specifically, Gigerenzer (2008) argued that there is an easy way to reduce or erase many judgmental biases. Just ask people about concrete **frequencies** rather than abstract probabilities, and then let people trust their beautifully evolved intuitions about frequencies.

I hope I already convinced you that abstract thinking is usually tough. Probabilities are surely abstract. Did you ever touch a proportion, or a margin of error? Even a great thinker like Plato wasn't too fond of probabilities. As Plato (1954) put it in *Phaedo*: "theories which rest their proof upon likelihood are impostors, and unless you are on your guard, they deceive you."

Gigerenzer's basic point is that Plato was not alone. He has argued that it's possible to reduce or even eliminate many judgmental biases if you allow people to think about raw frequencies (simple counts, as in 5 apples or 50 accountants) rather than abstract probabilities. Further, he argues that the reason we deal better with frequencies than with probabilities is that we have millions of years of evolutionary history dealing with counting but precious little time, in an evolutionary sense, dealing with the more abstract notion of probability. In my view, this clever point does not render research on judgmental heuristics meaningless, but it does suggest some useful ways to minimize certain reasoning errors. Gigerenzer and Kahneman seem to have pretty different views of the human decision-maker. But they seem to agree, at least implicitly, that we are not as adept at abstract thinking as we might wish. Presumably, a general purpose reasoning machine would deal with probabilities just as comfortably as with frequencies. But that's not how our brains work.

MAYBE WE'RE A LITTLE TOO PREDISPOSED TO THINK ABOUT FREQUENCIES

To perform a little judo on Gigerenzer's frequency hypothesis, recall that evolution's greatest blessings often come with incidental curses, otherwise known as baggage. If we're predisposed to pay special attention to frequency information, this can sometimes get us into trouble. As Pelham and colleagues (1994) showed, people, much like chickens and rats, sometimes overinfer quantity from numerosity. It's an easy and evolutionarily well-trodden path from "many" to "much." Along these lines, we found that when we divided stimuli into multiple pieces, people consistently overestimated the total magnitude ("amount") of the stimuli. We called the tendency to pay too much attention to frequency the **numerosity heuristic**.

Denes-Raj and Epstein (1994) independently documented exactly the same kind of bias, which they referred to as the **ratio-bias phenomenon**. This is the preference for gambles with a greater number of winning possibilities even when such gambles offer no true (abstract) statistical advantage. In one of their studies, Denes-Raj and Epstein gave people a choice between two lotteries. In the first lottery, there was 1 red (winning) jelly bean and 9 white (losing) jelly beans. In the second lottery, there were 10 red (winning) jelly beans but 90 white (losing) ones. The odds were identical in the two lotteries, and everyone knew it because the probability of winning was listed on the bowls. But the majority of people preferred having "ten chances to win." Many people even preferred the lottery with more jelly beans when they knew it offered them a lower chance of winning (e.g., when the researchers blatantly removed one of the winning red jelly beans). There is thus a reason that a box of Kellogg's Raisin Bran brags about having not one but "two scoops of raisins," whatever a scoop is.

If you've ever seen the wonderful 1984 mockumentary film *This is Spinal Tap*, you may recall the lovable but not so brilliant guitarist of the fictitious heavy metal band that was the topic of the film. Nigel had obviously consumed a lot of, let's say, product in his day. The same Nigel was also obsessed with cranking up the heavy metal band's music as loudly as possible to take things "to the next level" during concerts. During a revealing interview, Nigel shows the interviewer some of his favorite musical possessions. Nigel's prized possession is a simple, old school analogue amplifier (the kind with volume knobs you physically turn). However, unlike all the other amplifiers, this "very special" amplifier had knobs that could be cranked up not to 10, but to 11. When the interviewer cynically asks Nigel if this special amplifier is really any louder than any of the others, Nigel confidently replies: "Well, it's *one* louder now, isn't it?"

Numerosity biases are seductive. People overestimate the deliciousness of a box of Kellogg's Raisin Bran for the same reason they overestimate the athletic prowess of Michael Phelps. I've got nothing against swimming, by the way, but a great example of the numerosity heuristic gone wild is all the buzz Michael Phelps received during and after the 2016 Olympics – because he had won so many Olympic swimming medals. Some argued that Phelps was not only the "greatest Olympian ever" but perhaps the greatest athlete ever, and definitely one of the greatest pot-smoking athletes ever. I like Mike, but he's just not *that* great. First, from a global perspective, you have to be pretty rich to have frequent access to a swimming pool. To run, by comparison, all you need is frequent access to something called the outdoors. Michael Phelps had to compete against everybody whose parents could afford frequent indoor winter swimming lessons. Usain Bolt had to compete against everybody who had biological parents. More important, Phelps competed in a lot of essentially identical races – scoops and scoops of them. Have you ever wondered why there are four different, highly specific swim strokes? Sociologically speaking, I feel comfortable saying it's so rich White people can win more Olympic medals (Jost et al., 2011).

Then there are all the swimming relays, including the medley relays in which each of four swimmers uses a different stroke. Oh yeah, and there are also two individual "relays" – the medley events in which the same swimmer swims 50 or 100 m four different times, using a different stroke for each "leg." Do the math and you'll also see that swimmers in short and long events simply are not traveling at very different speeds (sprinters and distance runners are). An easy way to see whether different athletic events are really different is to look at the bodies of those who do them. Gymnasts don't look like shot putters. And sprinters don't look like 10 km runners. In contrast, as you can see in Figure 7.8, short and long distance swimmers are physically very much the same. The same pattern holds for women's world records in running versus swimming. At the time of this writing, the women's world record holder in the 1500 m in swimming was a little taller and heavier than the women's world record holder in the 50 m. Swimmers all have about the same build because swimmers are all doing many tiny variations on the same thing. It's called swimming. If I were Usain Bolt, I'd be bragging not only about my amazing running speed but also about my phenomenal skipping, darting, and scurrying speed. I'd surely get to run the anchor leg on about 16 different sprint relays. And I'd go back to Jamaica with about 18 Olympic medals – per Olympics. In short, concluding that Michael Phelps is "the greatest Olympian ever" because he has won so many Olympic medals is a good example of judgment by numerosity.

If only numbers geeks had designed the Olympics, they'd be fairer. Nice thought, but think again. Exactly the same numerosity bias (frequency bias) exists in a very well-funded affirmative action program at the National Science Foundation (NSF). This program is known as EPSCoR (Established Program to Stimulate Competitive Research), and its goal is to "broaden participation in science and engineering." That's government lingo for affirmative action. As Jerome D. Odom (2006) put it in an NSF report on the history and mission of EPSCoR: "How can we ensure the torch of science shines throughout the nation? Leaving half the states behind is not acceptable national R&D policy." In fact, NSF EPSCoR funding

50 meters men's swimming
César Cielo, 6'5" 194 lbs.

1500 meters men's swimming
Sun Yang, 6'6" 196 lbs.

100 meters men's running
Usain Bolt, 6'5" 207 lbs.

10,000 meters men's running
Kenenisa Bekele, 5'3" 123 lbs.

Figure 7.8 *World record holders in the longest and shortest men's running and swimming events for which there are recognized records.*

dollars are meted out exclusively to U.S. states that have historically received very little total NSF funding. I don't know your attitudes about affirmative action, but I'm guessing that the more you like it, the less you'll like EPSCoR. Here's why. For decades, only the states that have gotten the smallest number of NSF funding dollars have qualified for EPSCoR. However, the folks who set up this rule simply count up how many NSF dollars have recently gone to each U.S. state, period. Notice that I didn't say how many *per capita* funding dollars. That's right, NSF EPSCoR experts seem to have forgotten that fractions have denominators.

As a result of this policy, rich but small U.S. states qualify for and routinely receive EPSCoR funding. Poor but populous U.S. states never do. Because Dartmouth

College is in a state with a population of roughly a million people, Dartmouth has received plenty of EPSCoR money. In contrast, Huston–Tillotson University, a historically black college in Austin, Texas does not qualify for EPSCoR funds. If only 26 million people would move from Texas to New Hampshire, we could fix this science and engineering problem. Or we could try fractions. But we did not evolve to use these. If NSF had been in charge of awarding food stamps or Medicare, I worry they'd be sending extra funding to small but rich states like New Hampshire. By the way, the NSF EPSCoR debacle also happens to be a great example of the specificity principle of expert judgment. None of the brilliant mathematicians who work at NSF would ever fail to use fractions if asked to solve a complex math problem that required fractions. But their mathematical prowess goes out the window when they are wearing their managerial rather than their mathematical caps. (My name is Brett, and I am a recovering former NSF program director.)

A final peek at detecting cheaters

Getting back to cheating, evolutionary hypotheses involving cheater detection modules are not without their critics. In my view, one of the best criticisms of the idea of evolved cheater detection modules is the idea that, rather than relying on modules, people may rely on **pragmatic reasoning schemas**. These schemas are presumably learned rather than hardwired, and they seem to operate somewhere between the very precise level of modules and the taxing but incredibly flexible level of abstract thinking. Pat Cheng and Keith Holyoak (1985) thus showed that people can do well even on an unfamiliar version of the Wason card task if they can activate and use a "permission schema." It is worth noting, however, that even if you don't believe in cheater detection modules, the results of clever studies such as those of Cosmides and Tooby (1997), like the clever studies of Cheng and Holyoak, still reveal powerful and interesting *content* effects. The specific details of a logical question matter – a lot. Details that have a lot of evolutionary meaning seem to make a logical problem easier to solve.

Debates about the Wason card task and the precise nature of human reasoning may never be settled for sure. For example, Ahn and Graham (1999) found that content effects no longer mattered – at least not for students at Yale – when they explained the card task really well. Having duly noted some complexities, though, let me add that there is evidence from other reasoning tasks that supports something akin to a cheater detection module. Research in social psychology shows that arousing **suspicion** about why someone did something greatly increases the sophistication of people's social judgments about the suspicious person – especially with regard to why he or she did that suspicious thing (Fein, 1996). I think it's pretty fair to say that the content of the Wason card task does usually matter. The same logical reasoning task involving four simple cards goes from odious to obvious when you simply change the surface details of the problem. In my view, the bulk of research on cheater detection seems at least somewhat at odds with the idea that we are general purpose thinking machines. If we're general purpose reasoners, then we should be equally good – or bad – at all the logically identical versions of a reasoning task. Clearly we're not.

OTHER EXAMPLES OF EVOLUTIONARY COGNITIVE PSYCHOLOGY

Foraging and the "hot hand"

Evolutionary reasoning can also help explain a robust judgmental bias known as the **hot hand fallacy**. Gilovich et al. (1985) found that people often believe that successes in sports are clumped together. In basketball, players who have made a few shots in a row are often described as having the "hot hand." Most players, coaches, and fans seem to believe strongly in this idea. But Gilovich et al. showed that there simply is no such thing as the hot hand in basketball. If Kevin has just made a clutch jump shot, he is no more likely to make his next jump shot than he would be if he had just missed his last jump shot. The best predictor of whether a player will make any specific jump shot is the player's season shooting percentage for jump shots. Likewise, asking people if they *feel* the hot hand right before taking a shot simply does not predict how likely they are to make that shot. Another way to put this is that a lot of apparent clumping in event sequences (e.g., tossing five heads in a row in a long series of coin tosses) is just randomness rather than hotness. Gilovich et al. argue that people believe in the hot hand because they apply the representativeness heuristic to short event sequences. Specifically, they argued that "even short random sequences are thought to be highly representative." Others argue that a belief in the hot hand in basketball is just overgeneralization. Some things in life do happen in clumps. Due to things like injuries, illnesses, and family crises, for example, athletes certainly have good and bad games, or good and bad seasons.

In contrast to the idea that the hot hand is a purely cognitive illusion, Wilke and Barrett (2009) argue that the biased belief known as the hot hand is probably grounded very deeply in the human evolutionary past. People have been *foraging* (hunting and gathering) a lot longer than they have been tossing coins or shooting hoops. Foragers implicitly know that good things do often come in clumps. It's the rare mango tree that has just one ripe mango. Likewise, many hunted animals can often be found in groups, near food sources (say, mango trees) or watering holes. On the basis of such evolutionary logic, Wilke and Barrett (2009) argued that there might be an evolved default assumption (a bit like the cheater detection module) that desirable things come in clumps. They don't argue that this assumption can't be modified. Experience in a particular judgmental domain might teach us otherwise. But just as it is easy for people to learn to fear snakes, it might be easy for people to learn that one good event is often followed by another. In support of this reasoning, Wilke and Barrett (2009) showed that UCLA undergrads did seem to adopt a hot hand default for a wide range of judgments. Students assumed, for example, that if the nest they just observed had a bird in it, then the next nest they observed would probably have one, too. Likewise, students assumed that if a tossed coin just landed on heads, then the next coin toss would be more likely to land on heads than on tails. This hot hand assumption applied to judgments about nests, fruits, parking spaces, bus stops, and coin tosses (which was every judgment they examined).

Wilke and Barrett (2009) also showed that the hot hand bias was bigger for predictions about natural events than predictions about artificial events. Further, they showed that although the hot hand bias never disappeared completely, it was weakest for coin tosses. They argued that because most undergrads are pretty familiar with the logic of coin tosses, their knowledge of this particular variety of random sequence reduced but did not eliminate the hot hand default. In a second study, Wilke and Barrett (2009) focused on judgments of fruit and coin tosses. More important, they compared the judgments of a separate group of UCLA undergrads with those of a large group of "Shuar hunter-horticulturalists from Amazonian Ecuador." In the student sample, they replicated the finding that the hot hand assumption was weaker for coin tosses than for fruit foraging. For the Shuar, however, they found that the hot hand bias was just as powerful for coin tosses as it was for fruit foraging. The Shuar, of course, had little or no exposure to coins or probability theory. It is also worth noting that for both the UCLA participants and the Shuar participants, taking part in the study itself was a form of foraging. Participants were paid, trial by trial, for each correct prediction they made across numerous trials of the two games (one game involving fruits, the other involving coin tosses).

In a follow-up report, Wilke teamed up with two primatologists to show that there is even a robust hot hand bias among rhesus monkeys (Blanchard et al., 2014). The monkeys received a small squirt of a delicious liquid – rather than money – when they made correct predictions. They assumed that one reward would usually be followed by another. In fact, the researchers were only able to make the hot hand assumption disappear by having the monkeys play a version of the game in which getting a reward on one trial was a very good predictor of not getting a reward on the next trial. Such evolutionarily inspired studies do not invalidate the original work on the hot hand. But they do suggest that the hot hand may be grounded in something even more fundamental than representativeness. Further, consistent with evolutionary approaches such as error management theory, such studies suggest that the hot hand may be a mostly adaptive bias rather than a fallacy.

As Wilke and Barrett (2009) note, an evolutionary perspective on the hot hand bias also suggests some specific conditions under which the bias might be eliminated or even reversed. In some foraging contexts, there is a small and finite resource that will have been depleted if someone just happened across it. The act of hunting a specific grazing animal will usually make the rest of the herd run away from you. Eating all the berries from a small bush means there is no need to return to the same bush tomorrow. As Wilke and Barrett note, there is a well-documented bias among gamblers that is essentially the opposite of the hot hand phenomenon. The **gambler's fallacy** refers to the assumption that if a random outcome has occurred several times in a row, it is less likely than usual that it will occur the next time it's possible (Ayton & Fischer, 2004).

There's at least one situation in which animals behave as if they, too, believe in the gambler's fallacy. If you always reward mice for entering one arm or the other of a simple T-maze (where one enters a straight alley and then must make either a right- or left-hand turn to look for a reward), mice can learn to go to one arm of the maze or the other (because that's where the food pellet always is). However, one well-documented impediment to rapid learning in this kind of

T-maze is known as **spontaneous alternation** (Deacon & Rawlins, 2006). After having just found food in a specific location, mice tend to *avoid* this location in the immediate future. Why? Well, duh, from the foraging mouse's perspective, "I just ate all the food in that location; why the heck would I go back there immediately?" Although there is room for debate about the exact origins of the hot hand bias, it is clear that an evolutionary perspective on judgments that resemble foraging can yield some insights not revealed by a cognitive perspective alone.

Look who's talking

Cognitive psychologists study more than just reasoning, mating, and foraging. Allow me to share just two additional examples of evolutionary cognitive psychology. One of the most interesting and hotly debated topics in psycholinguistics (the psychology of language) has to do with our ability to learn and use language. You already know that we learn language very easily as children. Experts on language love to use their words to debate exactly why this is the case.

Of course, some non-human animals can use language. But none of them can keep up with people. Consider chimps who can develop 100- or even 300-word vocabularies. Chimps can also make some pragmatic use of sign language (Gardner & Gardner, 1969). But compare that with many college students, who can understand 200,000 words. We also learn language effortlessly (as children, at least), whereas most other animals have to work their butts off to master even the simplest linguistic tasks. It's also clear that kids do a lot more than just memorize words. Kids develop **grammar**, which is an appreciation of the deep rules of language use. This includes things such as how to express future versus past tense, how to indicate that there is more than one of something, and how to switch word order to change meaning. (There's a big difference between "Flo bit Al" and "Al bit Flo.") We've long known that kids learn grammar even when they're not explicitly taught it – and without even knowing that they know it.

Wait! So if kids don't even know they know it, how do we know they know it? We know because of clever tests such as Jean Berko's "wug test." Brown and Berko (1960) showed kids of different ages some simple drawings and asked the kids to fill in a missing word. Figure 7.9 shows my adaptation of one of Berko's test questions. As you can see, only kids who understand the English rule for forming plurals can correctly answer the wug question. If you pose this question to two-year-olds, they will answer "There are two wug." But by the age of five or six virtually all kids get plurals, and they will tack on the "s." Another question from the test (complete with another adorable drawing) was: "This wug knows how to fripple. Right now he is frippling. He did the same thing yesterday. Yesterday he _____." Most five- and six- year-olds understand grammar well enough to say "frippled."

Another cute piece of evidence that young children learn grammar comes from the cute mistakes they make. When my daughter Brooklyn was five, she would routinely say things like "We didn't go by ourselves. Uncle Brian goed with us." This is an example of **overregularization**, which is the tendency for young

Here is a wug.

**Now there are two of them.
There are two _____.**

Figure 7.9 *How many wugs does it take to show that little kids understand grammar? Just two.*

children to apply the rules of grammar too stringently. In this case, Brooklyn conjugated an irregular ("oddball") verb as if it were regular. This kind of mistake is very telling because it's obvious that children never hear adults say this kind of thing. Instead, at a very young age, kids seem to have strongly internalized many of the rules of grammar, having completely forgetted that the rules have some very important exceptions.

Did you notice that I might seem to be changing my tune? I previously argued that we are not the brilliant, general purpose thinkers that we'd like to assume. Now I'm arguing that we are really brilliant, at least when it comes to learning and using language. I'm not changing my tune at all. I've just begun a new verse. Remember that we can be really good at things (like cheater detection) if we are preprogrammed to do so, or if we spend many thousands of hours deliberately practicing them (see Ericsson, 2002). That's right; I'm simply parroting Steven Pinker's (1994) argument that we evolved a unique human ability when it comes to language. We are singularly good at that amazing trick called language just as elephants are singularly good at that amazing trick called picking things up with your nose. Many animals have unique adaptations. According to Steven Pinker, our most interesting and important unique adaptation is language.

Speaking of Pinker, I'd like to address one of the more hotly contested questions regarding the presumed evolution of language. For many decades now, linguists, anthropologists, and psychologists have fiercely debated the question of whether and to what degree we are predisposed to use language. It seems hard to deny that we are predisposed to learn language. Children across the globe learn language much more easily than they learn less demanding cognitive skills. But was linguist Noam Chomsky (1986) correct to argue that there is a universal grammar? Do all human languages share a specific set of evolved features, such as action words (verbs), quantification (number words), and extreme flexibility, so that there are an infinite number of ways to say the same thing? Pinker has argued that the answer is yes. As linguist and anthropologist Charles Hockett (1958, 1960) somewhat more cautiously argued, is there a more limited set of basic features of language that are shared by cultures all over the globe? Hockett's arguments are more widely accepted than Pinker's or Chomsky's. Hockett considered language to be a highly refined form of communication, and he thus argued that understanding non-human communication could yield useful insights into the origins of human language. According to Hockett, then, human language shares some very important features with the communication of whales and dogs. It is pretty well established, for example, that both dogs and whales produce different arbitrary sounds to communicate different motivational states. Dogs bark differently to warn about an approaching stranger than they do to express a desire to play or to stake their claim to a desirable piece of food (Hare & Woods, 2013). Whales, monkeys, and elephants, too, use very specific vocalizations to communicate very specific desires. Adult vervet monkeys, for example, emit different warning calls to advertise that they have spotted a leopard, an eagle, or a snake (Diamond, 1992).

"Yes, Helen, get me the employment agency again. This time I'd like to remind those assholes *myself* that I specifically asked for *elves* , tiny little *elves*."

But do all human languages really share certain basic, presumably evolved, features? If language evolved the way big brains and upright posture did, we might expect this to be the case. It would be interesting, for example, if each of the roughly 6,900 human languages that exist today all shared a common set of features. Hockett argued, for example, that one of the unique features of human language is **arbitrariness** – such that sounds have no obvious connection to their meaning. There is nothing inherently carrot-like about the word "carrot" in English; thus the word "zanahoria" in Spanish or the word "wortel" in Dutch will do the very same trick. Of course, this means, for example, that two words that sound very much alike can often have radically different meanings – consider "elves" and "Elvis." Conversely, two words that mean virtually the same thing (two synonyms) can sound nothing alike. I know that sounds both peculiar and bizarre, but it's true as well as correct. According to Hockett, another universal and uniquely human aspect of language is that all human languages allow **displacement**. They allow us to describe things that are not in front of us right now. This allows us to talk about the past or the future, which few other animals do. It also allows us to talk about hypothetical or abstract things that do not exist at all. Along similar lines, Hockett argued that all human languages can be used to engage in **prevarication** (lying) as well as other intentional misrepresentations.

Prior to Hockett's theory, a more popular position in anthropology and linguistics was the **Sapir-Whorf linguistic relativity hypothesis**. This hypothesis states that human thought depends heavily on language, and it implies a great deal of cross-cultural variability in how people think (Sapir, 1929; Whorf, 1956). The argument was that people who speak very different languages must, by necessity, think very differently. An anecdote often cited in favor of this idea is that the Inuit Eskimo language has a hundred words for snow. The idea is that this rich meteorological vocabulary allows the Inuit to make and remember fine distinctions between different kinds of snow – distinctions that people who do not speak Inuit could not make. Like many other anecdotes, this one has been the source of some debate, including debate about whether the Inuit really even have a lot of words for snow in the first place. By one reasonable accounting system, English has just as many words for snow as does the Inuit language. Even if we ignore this complexity, though, my view is that for about 75 years, no one was able to produce any highly convincing evidence in strong support of the linguistic relativity hypothesis (e.g., see Au, 1983; Brown, 1986, for critical accounts of failed or disappointing efforts).

"Actually we only have one word for 'snow.' But we do have about 100 words for 'freezing your ass off.'"

An arguable exception to this rule is that researchers have found that in languages with a greater number of multisyllabic number words, people have a harder time holding a lot of counting numbers in short-term memory. Thus, it is apparently a lot easier to remember "4-8-5-9" in English ("fôr-āt-fīv-nīn" = four syllables) than in Spanish ("kwă-trô-ô-chô-sên-kô-nōo-ĕ-vĕ" = nine syllables). This finding, based on the acoustic length of number words, holds up across quite a few languages, including Welsh and Mandarin Chinese (Chincotta & Underwood, 1996; Ellis & Hennelly, 1980; Naveh-Benjamin & Ayres, 1986). But despite the obvious practical importance of this finding (e.g., for intelligence testing), this is probably not quite what Sapir and Whorf had in mind when it comes to linguistic relativity. They were presumably thinking of something more profound.

In contrast, throughout the second half of the 20th century, things went pretty well for Hockett's evolutionarily inspired theory. Many evolutionary psychologists took the accumulating evidence in favor of linguistic universals as support for the evolved nature of language. Sapir himself conceded (before formally proposing that language shapes thought) that anthropologists and linguists had been wrong to expect people in so-called "primitive" cultures to use primitive forms of language. As Sapir (1921, pp. 21–2) put it:

> There is no more striking general fact about language than its universality. One may argue as to whether a particular tribe engages in activities that are worthy of the name of religion or of art, but we know of no people that is not possessed of a fully developed language. The lowliest South African Bushman speaks in the forms of a rich symbolic system that is in essence perfectly comparable to the speech of the cultivated Frenchman.

Accumulating evidence that people worldwide speak in unique but equally rich and complex ways attested to the fact that we are all one species. The same finding also suggested that certain features of language are hardwired – or at least developmentally favored.

But then, in 2004, all hell began to break loose. First, Peter Gordon (2004) published a provocative paper arguing that the Pirahã, a group of hunter-gatherers in the Brazilian rainforest, spoke a highly unusual language that simply had no words at all for number. As a result, Gordon argued, the Pirahã performed abysmally even at tasks that required the simplest forms of counting. Show Pirahã tribesmen three batteries and ask them a minute later how many objects they saw, and they would be absolutely bewildered – even if you presented the answer options pictorially. It might seem obvious that people who don't have a word for three or four would have difficulty counting, but the depths of the Pirahã's numerical deficits seem to defy common sense. Even many animals have a basic sense of numeracy. Is thinking about frequency or numerosity really so constrained by language?

Gordon's study suggested that the answer is yes. Furthermore, shortly after Gordon published his provocative paper, Daniel Everett (2005) published an even more provocative paper arguing that the Pirahã language violates quite a few of the most important linguistic universals thoughtfully proposed by experts such as Chomsky, Hockett, and Pinker. Everett spent decades living among the Pirahã, and he became fluent in their language. He argued that their language clearly violates several of Hockett's presumably universal (cross-cultural) rules. Most strikingly, Everett suggested that the Pirahã live perpetually in the present and that this cultural orientation toward immediate experience has many powerful consequences for the way the Pirahã talk – and thus the way they think. To cite a few of his points, Everett argued that the Pirahã language has:

» no number words of any kind
» no abstract color words
» a dramatic dearth of pronouns
» the simplest concept of kinship ever documented
» the complete absence of a deep knowledge of the past, including a lack of any kind of meaningful narrative about how the world came to be as it is, or how it will be in the future.

Everett expressed a deep respect for the Pirahã, and noted that some aspects of their culture and language are incredibly rich and complex. Nonetheless, he argued that the ways in which the Pirahã language lacks abstraction simply make certain kinds of abstract thinking impossible. For example, he noted that he spent about eight months earnestly trying to teach the Pirahã how to count to 10 or perform extremely simple calculations (such as 2 + 1) with no success whatsoever. This happened despite their extreme eagerness to learn this specific skill and their extreme ingenuity about complex matters better suited to expression in their language.

Everett's provocative paper was followed by some equally provocative commentaries. Tomasello (2005, p. 641) went beyond even Everett's own position to argue that: "Universal grammar was a good try... [but] ... we must come up with something new." Follow-up studies with the Pirahã have added some balance to this debate. Frank et al. (2008) replicated Gordon's results but also showed that if the Pirahã were allowed to answer questions about quantity that didn't require them to rely on memory, they were quite proficient. They knew, for example, that five deflated balloons is the same quantity as five spools of thread. Frank et al. argued that the use of very precise quantity terms is a cultural invention rather than an evolved aspect of language. Let's assume that some aspects of Pirahã language and thought raise doubts about whether Hockett's list of linguistic universals is truly universal. What's so flawed about nearly universal? And why is it so problematic if large numbers represent an invention rather than an evolved aspect of all languages? In the case of the Pirahã, it appears that no one ever invented specific number words because the Pirahã are so incredibly interconnected with one another that they never needed them. In fact, it was only when the Pirahã traded with dodgy outsiders that their lack of number words got them into trouble.

Cognitive psychologists have long known that it's virtually impossible to come up with a set of necessary and sufficient (universal) conditions to define virtually anything. Should language really be so different? Try to define a car, schizophrenia, or womanhood in a way that leaves absolutely no room for debate. Must a car have a motor? Must it always use fossil fuel? If electric cars are OK, what about three-wheeled pedal cars? Experts on categorization remind us that even the most familiar natural categories are best thought of in terms of family resemblances rather than hard and fast rules. The fact that the Pirahã language seems to fly in the face of some of Hockett's rules to some degree does not require us to discard his account altogether. In fact, I consider the Pirahã language more of an opportunity than a threat to theories of the origins of language. In my view, it is almost like gaining access to a living woolly mammoth or Neanderthal. It stands to reason that the languages biologically modern human beings spoke 80,000 years ago bore a much stronger resemblance to the Pirahã language than they do to modern English or Portuguese. It seems highly unlikely that the very first human proto-language included useful subtleties such as the past perfect or pluperfect. In fact, Hockett argued that in addition to having the property of arbitrariness and allowing for prevarication, all human languages also share a feature he called **productivity**. Productivity means that all languages allow users to create an infinite number of novel utterances and that all languages are constantly evolving. The sheer number of words in the English language has doubled in the last century. It is thus unthinkable that all Hockett's universal rules applied to the very first spoken human language. If the language and culture of the Pirahã can be protected for future generations, studying this unique culture may offer us some insights into ancient spoken languages that cannot be attained any other way. I believe language evolved. But it apparently evolved to be pretty flexible. And there can be no doubt that language sometimes bends itself to the will of culture. The degree to which thought bends itself to the ways of language is a more difficult question.

Speaking yet again of Steven Pinker, I cannot discuss language without noting that, as Pinker and others have argued, written language is very different from spoken language. I'll return to written language in Chapter 10. For now, I'd just like to parrot Pinker again and note that in contrast to how effortlessly almost all children the world over learn spoken language, many have great difficulty learning written language. Spoken language obviously paved the way for written language, but written language did not evolve. Instead, we invented it, and like most other cool inventions, written language requires an instruction manual. Kids require years of careful instruction to learn written language well. Reading teachers, when they are not pulling their hair out, spend a lot of time splitting phonetic and alphabetic hairs. Because I have a brother who is a school teacher, and because I worked part time for about three years at a preschool, I know all too well how hard it is for most kids to master written language. Here's my favorite story that illustrates that point. The names have been changed to protect the guilty.

One of the first things Jennifer Howell noticed when she became an elementary school principal was that children were constantly tattling to her about the misdeeds of their classmates. One warm spring day in South Georgia, first grader Ray Ann approached Jennifer on the playground and said, "Missiz Howell, CH called me the B-word!" Jennifer was at first stunned that CH (a mere first grader) may have used such coarse and sexist language. But then she reminded herself that Ray Ann might not mean the same thing by "the B-word" that an adult might. She was rooting for "butt-head" or "booger." So she reluctantly asked: "Ray Ann, I know that's a bad word, but can you tell me exactly *what* B-word it was, so that I can talk to CH about it?" She replied: "Yeah, but I have to whisper it ... It was ... *asshole*." Learning to speak is as easy as falling off a log. Learning to read and write is more like carrying a log on your shoulders.

Feelings trump thoughts

Even if I haven't convinced you that we're preprogrammed to detect cheaters, or to learn to talk, I hope I can convince you that we are programmed to trust our emotions. In fact, I'd like to argue specifically that **feelings trump thoughts**. Charles Darwin himself was fascinated with emotions, and there is a great deal of evidence that we come into the world ready to express and to decode them – or at least ready to learn to do so. People who are blind from birth and thus have never seen another person smile will spontaneously smile when something very good happens to them (Matsumoto & Willingham, 2009). Likewise, Ekman (1972, 1993) showed that tribesmen from Papua New Guinea who had no exposure to Western culture were very good at reading basic human emotions on the faces on Westerners they had never seen before. As a less formal demonstration of the fact that there are probably some basic human emotions, consider the youngsters in Figure 7.10. Which one of them looks happy? Which is disgusted? Which one is extremely sad?

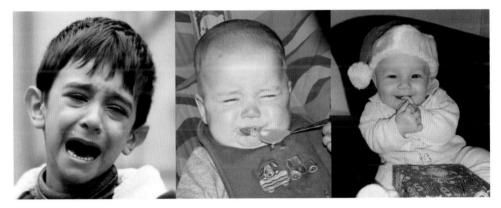

Figure 7.10 *People anywhere on earth would quickly recognize the basic emotions expressed by these three youngsters. Just as there is little doubt that the Iraqi boy on the left is sad, there is little doubt that these two American infants are experiencing the basic emotions known as disgust (center) and happiness (right).*

Darwin (1872) was interested in emotions because he felt they served similar purposes in people and animals (the rapid communication of internal goals and desires). Darwin was also interested in emotions because he felt that emotions drive a great deal of our behavior. If you think emotions are only the icing on the cake of human communication and social interaction, you need to try a new recipe. It is my position that when push comes to shove, emotions almost always trump cognition, even when cognition obviously points to a very simple conclusion. As the poet E.E. Cummings put it, "feeling is first." As Bob Zajonc (1980) put it (having just offered the same poetic quotation), "preferences need no inferences."

That's disgusting!

Even more to the point, Paul Rozin and colleagues (2008) suggest that emotional beliefs in things like "contagion" and "bad magic" often trump cognition. In one study, Rozin et al. (1986) showed this by opening a new, perfectly clean flyswatter, and using it to stir a pitcher of lemonade. To most people the lemonade suddenly became a lot less desirable. No one thought the flyswatter carried any diseases; they just associated the flyswatter with flies, which do sometimes carry diseases. Rozin et al. called this powerful aversion for things that resemble or touch disgusting things the **principle of contagion**. The principle seems to be even stronger for poo than for flyswatters. Making otherwise delicious chocolates shaped like dog poo makes them a lot less desirable. These irrational feelings matter. They're a strong reason why most people are disgusted by the thought of "recycled water." For some people, no amount of evidence documenting the extreme purity and safety of water that was recently sewage makes them willing to drink it. In arid countries like Australia, the public seems much more interested in paying handsomely for desalination plants – that remove salt from seawater – than in setting up plants to make recycled water from sewage. Apparently, people would rather drink water that was recently peed out by fish and whales than water that was recently peed out by their fellow human beings.

I have often carried out a colorful demonstration of this emotional contagion principle. Several times every year, I bring a small carton of milk to my general psychology class and ask the students who is willing to open it and have a sip. Some vegans notwithstanding, a sea of hands goes up. So far so good. Then I take out a sealed condom, open it, and assure everyone that there's nothing in the condom that has any flavor or could possibly make anyone sick. I think you know where I am going with this, and it's not pretty. Next, I carefully pour an ounce or two of milk into the condom and dangle it around a bit. Finally, I offer $5 to anyone who is willing to come to the front of the class and drink the milk directly from the condom. Sometimes, I up the offer to $10 or even $20. I've done this demonstration with many groups of almost universally disgusted students. So far, only one brave student has ever taken me up on the offer. Ray earned a quick $5 in about 10 seconds. On every other occasion, I've had to crank up the collective disgust level by drinking the condom milk myself. There is always a lot of wailing and gnashing of teeth. As I pick up the condom and get ready to drink, some students sincerely beg me not to do it. Of course, I ignore their pleas. People need to learn that emotions usually trump cognitions. No one leaves my class that day failing to appreciate the power of the reptilian weenie, even when – no, *especially* when – you use a condom.

FOR FURTHER READING

» Everett, D.L. (2005). Cultural constraints on grammar and cognition in Pirahã: Another look at the design features of human language. *Current Anthropology*, 46(4), 621–34.

» Hare, B. & Woods, V. (2013). *The genius of dogs: How dogs are smarter than you think.* New York: Penguin.

» Kurzban, R. & Aktipis, C.A. (2007). Modularity and the social mind: Are psychologists too selfish? *Personality and Social Psychology Review*, 11(2), 131–49.

» Pinker, S. (2002). *The blank slate: The modern denial of human nature.* New York: Penguin Books.

» Sugiyama, L., Tooby, J. & Cosmides, L. (2002). Cross-cultural evidence of cognitive adaptations for social exchange among the Shiwiar of Ecuadorian Amazonia. *Proceedings of the National Academy of Sciences,* 99, 11537–42.

SAMPLE MULTIPLE-CHOICE EXAM QUESTIONS

Here are four sample quiz questions for Chapter 7. You can find the Chapter 7 quiz at: www.macmillanihe.com/evolutionary-psychology

7.01. People often perform horribly on the "paper folding problem." One likely reason why is that:

    a. people use the availability heuristic and think about the single sheets of paper they see every day

    b. people anchor on the thickness of a single sheet of paper and stick too close to this anchor

    c. people know that paper is highly flammable but overlook the fact that the sheet of paper in question is wet

7.02. Most economists are geniuses when it comes to answering economic problems but they may perform poorly when asked to solve sociological or anthropological problem. This is consistent with what Jerry Fodor called:

    a. mental modularity

    b. the representativeness heuristic

    c. the availability heuristic

7.03. The gambler's fallacy refers to the belief that:

    a. if an outcome has just occurred it becomes less likely to occur in the immediate future

    b. if an outcome has just occurred it becomes more likely to occur in the immediate future

    c. people think they will be luckier when playing a familiar game than when playing an unfamiliar game

7.04. Which evolutionary theory states that heuristics and judgmental biases may prove to keep people alive and well more often than they tend to get people in trouble?

    a. strategic fitness theory

    b. healthy baggage theory

    c. error management theory

Answer Key: b, a, a, c.

Chapter 8
UNTIL SOMEONE GETS HURT

EVOLUTION AND AGGRESSION

"It's always funny until someone gets hurt. Then it's just hilarious."

— *Bill Hicks*

"From an optimization perspective, organisms in any given species will use a particular competitive [i.e., aggressive] strategy only when its benefits outweigh the costs. If different competitive strategies are available, organisms will tend to use the strategy with the highest benefit/cost ratio."

— *Georgiev, Klimczuk, Traficonte, and Maestripieri (2014, p. 3)*

"Ready, fire, aim!"

— *Iron Man (2008)*

In late July 1945, after Germany and Italy had surrendered to the Allied powers in World War II, Allied leaders still faced a nightmarish dilemma. The final Axis power, Japan, simply was not willing to surrender. In response to devastating losses, Japanese leaders began to employ desperate techniques such as suicide bombing. The infamous kamikaze pilots who flew their planes into Allied aircraft carriers were but one example of this desperate and selfless response to losing a major war. Japanese sailors rammed their miniature, explosive-packed subs into Allied battleships. Japanese foot soldiers armed themselves with backpacks laden with explosives, threw themselves under American tanks, and detonated themselves. They thus evened the odds in ways as clever as horrific. Suicide bombing occurred at every level of the Japanese military effort. Japanese suicide bombers were not rogue heroes. This was a well-planned strategy to avoid unconditional surrender at any cost (Powers, 2011).

The extreme willingness of Japanese citizens to die for their country baffled the Allies, and it only got worse as things went more poorly for Japan. At one point near the end of the war, Japan had planned to enlist child soldiers. As Allied forces began attacking Japan on their home island, some Japanese senior citizens prepared to fight Allied soldiers to the death with bamboo spears. Some Japanese mothers, with their children in their arms, reputedly threw themselves off cliffs rather than surrendering to the Allies (Powers, 2011). Such extreme sacrifices did not emerge in a cultural vacuum. The rules of battle in Japan had long dictated that an honorable death was greatly to be preferred over surrender. Japanese leaders endorsed this ancient tradition. But how many millions of soldiers – and how many Japanese civilians – would have to die before Japan finally conceded defeat? Eventually, American leaders – with the consent of a war-weary Britain – decided that the only way to get Japan to surrender would be to demonstrate that the Allies could destroy Japan entirely. This was the harsh logic that prompted the atomic bombings of Hiroshima and Nagasaki on August 6 and 9, 1945. Collectively, these two American bombing campaigns killed more than 100,000 people in a matter of minutes. Over the next few months, thousands of additional Japanese victims, most of them civilians, died slow, painful deaths after their exposure to intense heat and nuclear radiation.

Figure 8.1 *Left: Japanese corporal Yukio Araki (center, with puppy), the day before he died as a suicide bomber. Right: mushroom cloud from the Nagasaki bombing.*

Historians still debate whether this nuclear attack was the lesser of two necessary evils or was a blatant war crime. But no one would confuse these atomic bombings with an act of charity. The horrific end to World War II, like warfare itself, constitutes a dramatic example of the tremendous human capacity for aggression. We may not be the most aggressive species on the planet, as some have claimed. But the breadth and the scale of human aggression – from slander and playground bullying to armed robbery and nuclear war – is mind boggling. What role did evolution play in human aggression? Conversely, what role did aggression play in human evolution? No matter how we answer these questions, we are not the saintly creatures we might wish to be. Even saints sometimes engage in aggression. Jesus reputedly threw a bunch of greedy moneychangers out of the temple. Muhammad led a military attack on Mecca in 629 A.D. As a less noble example, Saint Teresa seems to have allowed many poor children to suffer under her watch, because of her belief that suffering is good for the soul.

In this chapter, we will explore human aggression, including forms of aggression that we share with other animals and forms of aggression that are distinctively human. But before sorting out different forms of aggression, and providing an evolutionary spin on major theories of aggression, I'm going to make an argument for the pervasiveness of aggression. Aggression is everywhere, and it has been around for a very long time. When Dawkins (1976) wrote about the selfish gene, he was arguing that being a survival machine comes at the expense of other survival machines. Along similar lines, Tennyson's famous phrase "nature red in tooth and claw" is meant to indicate that nature is brimming over with hurting and killing. What is the nature of all this violence? Why does it occur?

THREE FORMS OF AGGRESSION: INFECTION, COMPETITION, AND PREDATION

The pervasiveness of aggression

To understand human aggression, we must understand how it evolved. But what is **aggression**? To paraphrase Berkowitz (1981), who studied people, aggression is anything a person does that's intended to harm another living being (who doesn't welcome it). With an important tweak, this definition applies to animals, too. The tweak is that in the case of animals, we don't usually worry much about intentions. As Sell et al. (2012, p. 31) put it: "aggression is the disordering of another organism's functional machinery – typically in a manner that disrupts that other organism's ability to pursue its fitness interests." From this perspective, behavior that harms another creature is aggression, period. When a lion kills a gazelle, this is aggression. When a bee stings, this, too, is aggression. Getting back to people, notice that a caring nurse who gives a terminal cancer patient a lethal dose of morphine wouldn't be guilty of aggression. The nurse is trying to help rather than hurt. In contrast, a con artist who helps a victim to his feet after an accomplice pushes the man down would be guilty of aggression. Much like the anglerfish who lures in her prey with a fake worm (see Figure 8.2), con artists who pretend to help – so they can later hurt – are aggressors. In its ancient forms, however, aggression bore little surface resemblance to the behavior of con artists. Instead, ancient aggression seems to have taken one of three basic forms, and the key feature they all share is that they are all a nasty way to promote the survival and reproduction of aggressive actors. All else being

Figure 8.2 *A striped anglerfish, with the bioluminescent lure (far left) the fish uses to attract prey.*

equal, genes that promote aggression *without exposing the aggressor to undue risks* are likely to be evolutionarily successful.

Infection

It's hard to know which of the ancient forms of aggression came first. So let's start with the smallest aggressors. For more than a billion years, tiny pathogens such as viruses and bacteria have been attacking larger animals. This form of aggression is known as **infection**. If it seems odd to consider infection a form of aggression, consider a definition. *The Free Dictionary* (2016) defines infection as "the invasion of bodily tissues by pathogenic microorganisms that proliferate, resulting in tissue injury that can progress to disease." I hope words like "invasion" and "injury" make the point. Surely pathogens such as viruses and bacteria don't intend to hurt anyone, but I don't know if lions intend to hurt antelopes. Further, as we will see later, some forms of human aggression do not involve hurtful intentions per se. When a virus infects you, it certainly harms you. Further, infections promote the successful production of additional copies of the infecting agent. Of course, not all infections lead to harm or death. In fact, Huang and colleagues (2011) found that about half the people they infected with the influenza A virus experienced little or no flu symptoms.

A similar story holds for many cold viruses. When a cold virus enters your body, you may fight it off very well, but you have still been attacked. If all goes well for the virus, it grabs onto an unwitting host cell, and then *takes over the cell*. This includes the fact that the virus injects its own DNA into the host cell. After replicating itself inside the cell, the virus often kills the cell, and copies of the virus often spew out of the cellular victim. These copies of the virus promptly attack other healthy cells. This is all possible, by the way, because viruses are very tiny. Viruses (20–400 nm in width) are typically much smaller than bacteria (usually about 1000 nm wide). In fact, some viruses even infect bacteria. A big difference between a bacterial infection and a viral infection is that bacteria reproduce on their own, without using the victim's DNA. Thus the pesky bacteria responsible for tooth decay consume carbohydrates on your teeth, but they don't hijack any of your DNA. But dental caries is, in fact, an infection. In the days before dentists, many ancient hunter-gatherers seem to have suffered horribly from toothaches and broken teeth (Humphrey et al., 2014). As pesky as bacteria are, though, viruses are worse. The large majority of viruses are harmful, with only a few known to be friendly to people (Skwarecki, 2013). In contrast, many bacteria are harmless, and quite a few are very useful. In fact, according to WebMD (www.webmd.com), less than 1% of bacteria are the kind that make people sick.

To summarize, biological entities that *infect* other organisms harm them in ways that promote the survival and reproduction of the attackers. This process occurs microscopically, and so it may fly under the radar of casual observation. But it's a prime example of how evolution is about successful reproduction, regardless of who gets hurt in the process. Throughout the ancient human world, infectious diseases killed many people, especially after people began to live in crowded, unsanitary settlements. The infamous Spanish flu pandemic of 1918 killed between 20 and 40 million people, a number that is unfathomable by today's standards. It's hard to know exactly how often people died of infections in the Pleistocene, but studies of traditional cultures that still existed in the 20th century suggest that infection has long been a common cause of human death. Hill et al. (2007) reported that infectious diseases accounted for 20–85% of the deaths in five different groups of hunter-gatherers. Of course, infection has been at least as unkind to other animals as it has been to people. As Dawkins would be quick to remind us, infection is almost as old as life itself.

Competition

When an organism is much, much smaller than you, it may infect you. If an organism is roughly your size, if it occupies an ecological niche much like your own, or both, the organism cannot infect you. Instead, it's likely to compete with you. **Competition** is another evolutionarily ancient form of aggression. Competition is a very broad term. It includes squaring off against the members of other species to obtain food, water, or a good place to lay one's eggs. It also includes struggling against members of one's own species for the chance to eat, drink, stay warm, or reproduce. In fact, siblings in the same nest or litter often compete fiercely for the protection and nutrition offered by their parents. I hope it's also clear that cuckoos and other brood parasites are competing aggressively with the birds they dupe into caring for their chicks. Competition is rarely friendly.

Aggressive competition is biologically ubiquitous. In 1934, Georgy Gause documented competition among **paramecia**, which are extremely simple, single-celled organisms that have existed for at least 200 million years. Based on this and other work, Gause developed the ecological principle of **competitive exclusion**, which states that two species that require the same resources can't permanently occupy exactly the same biological niche. As Hardin (1960) put it: "Complete competitors cannot coexist." One species will ultimately outcompete the other. Often this means that one of two competing species will go extinct. It is also possible, however, for the two species to evolve in different directions, so that the competition for scarce resources is not quite so fierce.

It's hard to overstate how pervasive competition is. In addition to happening in paramecia, competition even happens in that kingdom of organisms that have no brains and can barely move. Plants that sprout in the vicinity of one another must compete for water, sunlight, space, and the nutrition they extract from the soil (Stearns, 1992). This harsh fact is why gardeners often have to do a lot of weeding. In fact, many plants seem to be able to tell whether the plant residing next to them shares their genes. Although the rules of competition in plants are more complicated than you might expect, the roots of many plants tend to avoid the roots of others. At least some plants also respond to the presence of the roots of other plants by diverting energy that they would normally direct at reproduction to increased root development. The roots of plants compete in other ways, too. When red beets and legumes are planted within a few inches of one another in a restricted area, red beet roots grow more quickly and more deeply than the legume roots (Tosti & Thorup-Kristensen, 2010). In fact, red beets respond very differently to fellow red beets than they do to legumes, dominating the legumes but backing off in their growth when in close proximity to fellow red beets. Legumes, in contrast, are pretty tolerant of their red beet competitors. They survive beside them by occupying the shallower soil, a process plant biologists, like sociologists, refer to as **segregation**. More broadly, Depuydt (2014, p. 1) argued that the roots of many plants "have ways to discriminate non-related roots, kin, and … self/non-self roots." They make these distinctions, Depuydt argued, "to avoid intra-plant competition."

Competition in plants is not limited to beets and legumes. Kunstler et al. (2016) studied more than 2,500 species of trees worldwide and concluded that trees compete with one another for key resources. They argued that three key features of a tree (wood density, maximum tree height, and leaf area) determine how well trees compete both within and across species. Kunstler et al.'s (2016) global study also revealed that trees usually competed more vigorously with other members of their own species than with members of other species. This is a good reminder that **intraspecific competition** (competition between two or more members of the *same* species) is usually more common than **interspecific competition** (competition between *different* species that try to exploit the same resource). By the way, if you have trouble remembering which of these technical terms is which, just think about the form of human competition known as sports. *Inter*collegiate competitions occur between students at *different* colleges. *Intra*mural competitions occur between students at the *same* college. The metaphor also works pretty well for the relative frequency of the two kinds of competition. In American colleges, at least, major intercollegiate competitions occur only once or twice per week. In contrast, intramural competitions can happen many times a day.

If we take the principle of competitive exclusion to its logical extreme, the organisms that compete most vigorously with woodchucks are other woodchucks. They have exactly the same diet, for example, and they inhabit exactly the same environments. Further, in species that occupy unusual niches, there may be very little, if any, interspecific competition. Ignoring people, polar bears historically had no carnivorous rivals. Grizzly bears, for example, are not suited to swim in icy waters, and there simply are no large polar cats. To be fair, many niches that seem highly unusual are not as unusual as you might think. Intuitively, larval dung beetles might seem to have exploited a unique niche. But even most poo-dwelling creatures have to compete with both intraspecific and interspecific rivals (Finn & Gittings, 2003). One animal's poo is another animal's homestead. Perhaps the most obvious reason why intraspecific competition is more common than interspecific competition has to do with mating. It's conceivable that some other scorpion-eating species competes with meerkats for this unusual food source, but when it comes to mating, meerkats only compete with other meerkats.

Figure 8.3 *The trees in this Belgian forest may look peaceful enough, but they made it to the top, middle, or bottom of this temperate forest canopy by competing successfully with rivals.*

As a more intuitive example of competition, consider how carnivores compete with one another on the African savannah. Many predators compete for the same prey. Predators as varied as wild dogs and lions compete to catch gazelles. The more gazelles that lions kill, the fewer that remain for wild dogs, cheetahs, or leopards. This being said, smaller predators tend to focus on smaller prey. A wild dog, weighing only about 25 kg, would be happy to catch a bird or a rodent. But a lion wouldn't bother to go for something so small. A Thompson's gazelle, weighing in at about 23 kg, is fair game for either a wild dog or a much larger female lion. A healthy 600-kg Cape buffalo, on the other hand, is quite safe from wild dogs. In fact, only two or more lions, hunting cooperatively, constitute a threat to a heathy Cape buffalo. Hyenas, too, hunt healthy Cape buffalo, but only in large packs. The more similar two predators are in terms of diet and lifestyle, the more often they compete – as suggested by Gause (1934). Lions and hyenas are thus in greater competition than lions and wild dogs.

An intense form of competition happens when predators steal food from one another. Almost any predator is happy to pilfer the kill of another. This is bad news for many savannah predators because they stand little chance of vanquishing a lion who covets their kills. Cheetahs, for example, are downright frail compared with lions. Further, they are solitary and cannot rely on strength in numbers. In contrast, hyenas, while no heavier than cheetahs, are as robust and muscular as lions, and they are pretty social. A single lion could easily steal a kill from a lone hyena, but a single lion who tries to steal from a pack of hyenas is sure to be sent packing. In the case of lions versus hyenas, stealing thus happens in both directions, depending on which social species has the numerical upper hand. Leopards, like cheetahs, are solitary, but they, too, are much stronger than cheetahs. Further, leopards are great climbers. Leopards often protect a kill from competitors by dragging it up into a tree, where no hyenas, and very few lions can follow. At the risk of anthropomorphizing, I must add that lions and hyenas – who occupy pretty similar ecological niches – behave as if they detest each other. In fact, these apparent enemies will gladly kill each other when the rare opportunity arises (Schaller, 1972).

Predation

Speaking of killing, a third important form of aggression is **predation**. Richard Dawkins' ancient, microscopic proto-carnivores were presumably the first predators. But they have since been joined by lions, tigers, bears, dolphins, eagles, and many other killers who never quite made their way to NFL helmets. As Dawkins noted, the logic of predation is something like this. You did a nice job of capturing energy with all that eating you did. But rather than capture energy the hard way, as you did, I think I'll just capture and eat you. That'll be a real time-saver. In fact, predation is such a clever solution to the problem of selective fitness that even a few hundred plant species engage in it. Much like the anglerfish, the Venus flytrap attracts its prey by presenting what appears to be an easy meal. In the case of the flytrap, the meal is not a fake worm but some very real nectar. But the price many insects pay for sampling the nectar is death and then digestion (which includes recycling the nectar if you're the flytrap). There aren't many predators who actually set traps for their prey. Most predators sniff out their prey, corner them, run them down, swoop down on them from the air, or wait like statues and then strike in the blink of an eye. In all its myriad forms, though, predation is a clever, if unsettling, solution to the problems of survival and reproduction.

Many organisms that occupy the edible part of predator–prey relationships have evolved traits and strategies for protecting themselves from would-be predators. These forms of protection from predation are incredibly diverse. Even single-celled paramecia swim away from attacks, and they increase their swimming speeds when the danger is objectively greater. In cases of extreme danger, they can even engage in a "jumping gait" by relying on "the explosive release of a group of trichocysts in the direction of the hot spot" (Hamel et al., 2011). From the horns of Triceratops to the quills of a porcupine, many other animals poke or pierce those who portend to eat them. Monarch butterflies and poison dart frogs advertise their poisonous nature with bright colors. The distinctive stripes of most skunks advertise their ability to produce a highly obnoxious odor. Many turtles can pull themselves completely into their rock-hard shells. Armadillos aren't quite as well armored as turtles, but at least one species can roll itself completely into a ball, and all armadillos are excellent diggers.

Because almost all plants are food to at least some animals, many plants have also evolved forms of self-protection. Presumably, cacti, rose bushes, and chestnut trees were protecting themselves with thorns and needles long before porcupines independently evolved a somewhat similar strategy. (Recall that this is known as convergent evolution.) Plants, like animals, have evolved to escape the herbivorous equivalent of predation in numerous ways. Tobacco plants produce nicotine as a natural defense to predation from many insects (István, 1999). For at least one species of caterpillar that tolerates nicotine very well, the nicotine they consume protects them from predation by wolf spiders, who have a strong aversion to nicotine (Kumar et al., 2016). In small doses, nicotine may be highly addictive to human beings, but in its natural form, most bugs hate it. For some plants, a very different adaptation to being eaten is to take the opposite approach of a tobacco plant. Many fruit trees advertise how delicious their fruit is with bright colors that indicate ripeness. The same trees that produce nutritious, easily digested fruit usually produce virtually indigestible – if not poisonous – seeds. Animals who eat an apple or a grape often do what the parent plant could never do – which is to transport fertile seeds to a distant location.

As any life history theorist would be quick to remind us, yet another solution to predation – and to a few other problems – is **fecundity**. Plants that get eaten a lot tend to mature quickly and reproduce fervently. The more seeds you produce, for example, the better you can survive living in less than ideal soil, being munched on by herbivores, or failing to receive ideal amounts of rain or sun. Many invasive plant species that outcompete the plants that previously did well in a given region produce a great number of seeds, for example (Jelbert et al., 2015). Strength in numbers thus applies to dandelions as well as to lions, although in very different ways. Getting back to predation in animals, ants, chickens, and rabbits produce many more offspring than anteaters, chicken hawks, and coyotes. This is because those nearer the bottom of the food chain have a much greater chance of being eaten before adulthood than do those nearer the top. Consistent with life history theory, most species who get eaten a lot not only produce many offspring but also produce offspring who mature pretty quickly. Rats and mice are short-lived, and they mature very quickly, for example. At the other extreme, great white sharks occupy a very high place in the marine food chain. Female great white sharks do not appear to reach sexual maturity until about 33 years. They also produce very few offspring, and they can easily live to be 70 (Natanson & Skomal, 2015).

Limitations of the three-category scheme

These three forms of aggression provide a simple, biologically informed framework that covers a lot of evolutionary ground. But they do not cover everything. If you argued that these three categories are better considered as points along a continuum, I'd have a hard time disagreeing. Consider **parasitism** (feeding off the body or nutritional resources of a host). This form of aggression doesn't fit neatly into any of these three categories. But if we construe the categories as points along a continuum, it seems fair to say that parasitism is a neighbor of infection. The main difference is that parasites are usually a bit bigger than pathogens, and they never harness the victim's DNA. To further criticize this scheme – but to emphasize further that aggression is ubiquitous – I should note that in several species of deep sea anglerfish, there is **sexual parasitism**. In some of these species, the parasitic males weigh 1/500,000th as much as mature females. When a tiny male locates a female, he bites into her, usually near her belly. Their tissues then fuse, his eyes degenerate, and he becomes a permanent freeloader, gaining all his nutrition from his female host. Some female anglerfish host as many as eight male parasites (Castro, 2015; Pietsch, 2005). This may sound like a horrible deal for females, but the payoff for the females is that they carry around a continuous source of sperm. If you consider how difficult it must be to find a mate in the bleakness of the deep ocean, I hope you can see that the line between parasitism and **symbiosis** (interaction that yields benefits to each of two different organisms) is pretty gray in the dark world of the anglerfish (Miya et al., 2010).

To return to gray areas for the three-part scheme, one way to conceptualize rape is to think of it as a specific form of violence that falls somewhere between competition and predation. A rapist arguably gains sexual pleasure, a sense of power, or a chance at reproduction by assaulting a victim who did not willingly offer any of these to the rapist. Debates about exactly what motivates rape, and whether it ever confers any evolutionary advantages on perpetrators, are unlikely to end any time soon (c.f. Thornhill & Palmer, 2000, vs. de Waal, 2000). But using the scheme described here, no one would confuse rape with viral infection. One way to frame some of the sensitive debates about rape has to do with whether rape is best considered an unethical form of competition (like doping in sports), an ethically bankrupt but effective form of competition (like cuckoldry), or a form of predation in which the attacker stops short of actually killing the victim, like attempted infanticide (see Abramson, 2017).

To make a less controversial point, it's partly because the three categories described here are so pervasive that they pretty often overlap. As already noted, predators often compete with each other for access to the same prey. Furthermore, no predator is ever powerful enough to defend itself against all possible infections. In fact, one tradeoff of being near the top of the food chain is routine exposure to many of the pathogens that may have weakened or killed one's prey. All this being said, I hope the three-part organizing scheme proposed here makes two useful points. First, aggression takes a variety of very different forms, most of which promote selective fitness. Second, aggression has been a driving force behind evolution for many millions of years, and that cold evolutionary fact shapes a lot of what many animals do. Understanding this helps clarify the roots of human aggression. To appreciate how useful an evolutionary perspective can be, however, we need to appreciate a few other evolutionary ideas that play a key role in almost all forms of aggression, human or otherwise.

KEYS TO AGGRESSION: FIGHT OR FLIGHT, COSTS VS. BENEFITS, AND STATUS-SEEKING

The fight-or-flight response

Long ago, Cannon (1914) proposed that when a mammal encounters a potential threat, the sympathetic branch of the animal's autonomic nervous system automatically kicks into overdrive. This **fight-or-flight response** includes a quick increase in heart rate, and sometimes a dramatic decrease in digestive activity. Sugar is also released into the bloodstream and, in combination with increased blood flow, this rush prepares the highly aroused animal to either beat the heck out of a would-be attacker or get the heck out of Dodge. The coagulating agents that allow blood to clot in the event of an injury are also ramped up during this alarm response (Selye, 1956). Cannon recognized that this rapid reaction to stress had deep evolutionary roots. A century of research on organisms as diverse as people, rats, mollusks, and hydra (the last two of which are invertebrates) suggests that Cannon was really on to something. Animals in danger, especially mammals, prepare to fight or to flee from the source of that danger. This response is powerful and hardwired. In people, the fight-or-flight response is closely connected to two basic human emotions, namely fear and anger. If you feel that you can eliminate or control a threat, you are likely to experience **anger** in response to the threat. Accordingly, you're likely to engage in some form of attack (the fight response). But if you feel that you have little or no power over the threat, you are much more likely to experience **fear**. In this case, you'll be much more likely to try to exit the situation (the flight response).

Recent research suggests that the fight-or-flight response to an acute stressor is counterbalanced by a **rest and digest** response that happens when all is well, especially when an organism encounters food. For about a century, researchers believed that only vertebrates engage in this biological balancing act. However, Shimizu and Okabe (2007) showed that something very much like a fight-or-flight response and a rest and digest response exists in at least three invertebrates: hydra, mollusks, and nematodes. This is remarkable in the case of nematodes because they have no hearts and no vascular system. However, they do circulate "pseudocoelomic fluid," and this happens much more vigorously when they are foraging for food than it does after they have latched onto their prey (often bacteria). At this point, the hydra begins the rest and digest phase. Shimizu and Okabe's findings for hydra are also news because until recently biologists thought that digestion in the hydra happened passively via diffusion. But Shimizu and Okabe showed that the hydra equivalent of fight or flight only occurred in hydra who had intact nerves. Hydra are so simple, by the way, that it is possible to "construct animals [hydra] devoid of neurons and maintain them in a healthy situation." When Shimizu and Okabe did this, the hydras that had no primitive nervous system showed virtually no digestive activity, even when they were handfed. Shimizu and Okabe (2007) conclude that "the roots of mammalian physiology could lie much deeper in the animal evolutionary tree than has been appreciated previously."

Why the big deal about fight or flight – or rest and digest? The main reason is that this perspective suggests that aggression in response to threat has a very long evolutionary history. If this is the case, aggression might not be as easy to control as we might ideally wish. Nathan Azrin and colleagues would probably agree. In animals as diverse as rats, squirrel monkeys, raccoons, and turtles, Azrin and others have shown that if you restrain an animal and then give it a painful electric shock, the victim will reliably bite, attack, or threaten almost anything it can get hold of (Azrin et al., 1968; Fraser & Spigel, 1971). It's also pretty easy to teach animals to flee a situation in which they are shocked (Azrin et al., 1967). Consistent with the basic idea of fight or flight, receiving a shock is particularly likely to lead to biting when an experimenter arranges it so that biting stops the shock. On the other hand, the same shocks are particularly likely to lead to flight when all the animal can do to stop the shocks is flee. To be clear, human aggression certainly is not as automatic as human digestion. No one can swallow a delicious bite of food and then decide not to digest it. But we can sometimes swallow our pride, or redirect our anger in ways that do not involve maiming or killing. On the other hand, the same flexibility that allows us to learn to make peace rather than to fight in response to threat can sometimes allow us to attack in ways that are more harmful than biting or clawing. Suicide bombing, racial profiling, and pyramid schemes are good examples of uniquely human forms of aggression.

The cost–benefit rule

An implicit aspect of the fight-or-flight response reveals another important principle of aggression. Aggression usually happens because it works. Fight usually happens when an organism has some shot at winning an aggressive confrontation. When there is little or no chance of winning, flight is much wiser. If Thomson's gazelles suddenly developed superpowers and kicked the butts of lions, you can be sure that lions would be quick to look for a new source of nutrition. As things stand, of course, lions are much more likely to attack gazelles than to attack elephants. The sheer size and strength of elephants, not to mention their deadly tusks, make them a dangerous choice for a would-be meal. It's hard to find an incidence of animal aggression that does not reflect this basic principle, which I'll refer to as the **cost–benefit rule**. If we flesh out the rule, it's a bit more complicated in social species such as people than in asocial species, but the gist of the rule is that aggression has both costs and benefits. It is only when likely benefits outweigh likely costs that people, or paramecia, are likely to behave aggressively. Georgiev et al. (2014) identified several key variables that are part of this cost–benefit equation. They note, for example, that whether you are an ostrich or an astronaut, behaving aggressively always has costs. Potential costs include expended energy, increased exposure to predation, injury or death from aggressive activity itself, and – in the case of most social animals – the potential for damaged relationships. Let's consider these costs and benefits, beginning with the costs.

Costs. As Georgiev et al. (2014) note, the costs of aggression abound. A single lion would be foolish to attack a healthy adult elephant. But lions are happy to take down sick or badly injured elephants, especially in groups. The major costs associated with trying to kill a giant are reduced when the giant can't fight back as well as usual. The same cold logic dictates that infant elephants are a smarter choice as a victim than adults. All else being equal, it is less costly to attack smaller, less experienced animals. In the case of elephants, though, the trick for lions is separating infants from their highly formidable mothers. Although there is debate about which large animal African lions avoid the most, many have argued that lions attack rhinos even less often than they attack bush elephants. For purposes of comparison, a very large male lion can approach 200 kg. A large male African bush elephant can weigh 6,000 kg. Rhinos are big, too, but much smaller than elephants. A large male white rhino weighs in at about 2,000 kg. But if you take a quick peek at a rhino and an African bush elephant, you'll see that rhinos are much more muscular than elephants (see Figure 8.4). They are also quicker, fiercer, and more territorial. With this in mind, consider this August 1966 entry in the Annual Report for the Ngorongoro Conservation Area (www. ntz.info/gen/b00668.html#03921):

> At 10.30 a.m. a lion tried to kill a rhino, Felicia's eleven-month-old calf. Felicia who lives to the north of Lake Makat is rather hostile normally, and when her off-spring was in danger she was quite fierce. The lion managed to separate the calf from the mother. The calf ran away and the lion gave chase, with Felicia lumbering behind in hot pursuit, bellowing loudly. The calf circled back towards its mother, and Felicia immediately engaged the lion. The lion grabbed her by the hind leg and clawed and chewed her thigh viciously. Felicia wheeled round and gored the lion twice in the centre of the ribs. The lion rolled over paralysed by the tremendous blows. She then gored him in the neck, in the head and trampled him to death in a matter of minutes. Two other lions had sat by during the entire incident and kept a respectable distance. Within forty minutes of the killing the [lion] carcass was eaten clean by hyaenas.

Figure 8.4 *White rhinos may be smaller than bush elephants, but they are also fiercer.*

I'm pretty sure this is what Tennyson meant by "nature red in tooth and claw." So don't mess with a mother rhino, even if you are a lion. Of course, the costs of aggression are not always this high, but there are always costs. Consider the behavior of two of my nephews. When Jonathan was 28 months old, he stole a small toy from his younger cousin, Eric, who was not yet two. The older Jonathan towered over Eric. Jonathan must have felt it was pretty safe to snatch away the small action figure Eric was enjoying. Eric looked befuddled but did not cry or protest. Instead, he calmly marched over to Jonathan, who was enjoying his spoils. Eric then faced Jonathan head on, grabbed Jonathan's head as if he were about to kiss him, and bit Jonathan fiercely on the cheek. I don't believe I've ever heard a toddler cry so loudly. Eric did not draw blood, but he left a very obvious mark. So, as Jonathan quickly learned, don't mess with Eric. To sample just one other variable from Georgiev et al.'s (2014) model, I'm sure you can think of a time when someone hurt you – either physically or psychologically – and damaged your previously close relationship. As Georgiev et al. (2014) argue, social creatures like people and lions often experience not only physical but also interpersonal consequences of aggressive behavior. My apologies, David Hare. I should never have taken your Frito Bandito eraser.

Benefits. So, if there are usually costs to aggression, why is aggression so pervasive? Because there are usually benefits, and sometimes the benefits are huge. Georgiev et al. (2014) argue that access to food, space, and mating opportunities represent three of the key benefits of behaving aggressively. These are not trivial benefits. Just try keeping any of your genes in the gene pool without them. Georgiev et al. also argue that the main reason why human beings are much more aggressive than one might expect is that we are so clever at maximizing benefits – and minimizing costs – of aggressive behavior. As these authors put it: "the benefits of aggression depend on what animals fight about." By this, they meant that, holding costs constant, the better something is, the more likely it is that organisms will fight over it. Consider food. If a food, like grass or leaves, is highly abundant and relatively low in nutritional value, few animals fight over it. At the other extreme, when a highly nutritious food, like meat, is hard to come by, there is likely to be fierce competition for it, as I've already noted. Fruit might seem to fall in between these extremes, but in a natural world devoid of supermarkets, ripe fruit can be as highly coveted as meat. Thus, as Georgiev et al. note, many primates are quite willing to fight over it. Competing troops of chimpanzees appear to engage in a simplified version of warfare. Very often, what they appear to fight over is access to fruit (de Waal, 1989). Of course, fruit exists on territory and many animals fight over territory as well. The more valuable the territory, the more reason there is to fight over it.

Another big benefit worth fighting for is mating. There's often intense intraspecific fighting between males over mating rights. Further, fighting for mates is fiercest in species in which a limited number of males get to mate (when benefits are very high). In species for which this is the case, there are many evolutionary consequences. One of the most important is physical adaptations that maximize fighting success – or minimize injury. Consider bighorn rams. These rams fiercely butt heads for mating rights. This seems crazy. If human males did this with any ferocity, they could easily kill each other. But in bighorn sheep, especially males, genes that make skulls better able to absorb intense shocks have been favored – to be passed on to future generations of aggressors. Growing bigger horns is only one of several evolved ways to win the right to mate. The horns of bighorn rams are pretty flexible, for example, acting a lot like automobile bumpers. Horn size varies across rams, and it appears to matter (Pelletier & Festa-Bianchet, 2006). Rams with bigger horns tend to be higher in social rank. Body mass and age also matter. All else being equal, larger, older rams tend to be higher in social rank. And rams that are higher in social rank enjoy more reproductive success (selective fitness). In a five-year study of a large group of wild bighorn sheep, Pelletier and Festa-Bianchet found that the three highest ranking rams (out of about 25–30) typically fathered at least half of the lambs born to 40–60 ewes in a given year. Rates of intraspecific aggression are higher in bighorn rams than in many other animals because in this species the benefits of fighting can be enormous.

Another animal that has to be hard-headed to behave aggressively is the woodpecker. Woodpeckers do a great job of minimizing costs and maximizing benefits of extracting grubs and insects from trees. Some of the same traits that allow rams to compete successfully without getting concussions protect woodpeckers as well. Strong neck muscles and brains that fit tightly inside the skull have proven to be just as useful for woodpeckers as for rams. Because woodpecker heads have to endure even more punishment than ram heads do, woodpeckers also have several other adaptations that allow them to slam their beaks safely into trees thousands of times per day. Their beaks have features that resemble seat belts and shock absorbers, and their brains fit in their skulls in unique ways that spread out the impact of pecking rather than concentrating it in any single area (Wang et al., 2011; see also Gibson, 2006; Pappas, 2012). Finally, the breaks woodpeckers take between bouts of pecking allow their skulls to cool off a little. The fact that woodpeckers are small and have light brains makes them hardier as well. And the point of all this hardiness is to capture and eat highly nutritious grubs and insects that live in wood. That's a huge benefit if you're a hungry bird – and for woodpeckers it comes at the lowest possible cost to the brain.

Mate hoarding and sexual dimorphism

When animals fight, they do so in ways that reflect cost–benefit dynamics. This applies to specific animals that are more aggressive than their peers and specific species that fight more than others. Consider fights over mating rights. This is a form of **mate hoarding**. In animals that forage together, like gorillas, or hang out in large groups, like elephant seals, highly aggressive males have the opportunity to acquire a harem of females. In contrast, in species that cover a wide geographic area, and in nonsocial species (who often get together only to mate), males simply have no chance to dominate other males to gain greater access to mates. In this second case, rates of intraspecific competition for mates among males are very low. Further, many such animals engage in long-term pair-bonding. This topic gets a little sensitive because, as many have noted, females can be considered a prized resource if you are a male. Further, in keeping with parental investment theory, females are generally pickier maters than males are.

This sets the stage for high levels of male–male intraspecific fighting in species for which mate hoarding is physically and environmentally feasible. Across the evolutionary history of an organism, it also sets the stage for a particular kind of **sexual dimorphism**. Recall that sexual dimorphism refers to physical differences between male and female members of a species. In many birds, males are much more brightly colored than females. In species in which there is a great deal of aggressive male–male competition for mates, there is also a great deal of sexual dimorphism. The specific kind of sexual dimorphism often seen here can be really extreme, and it has to do with physical size and fighting ability. See Figure 8.5 for some examples.

Figure 8.5 *There is no body mass sexual dimorphism in ringed seals (top left). In contrast, male elephant seals can weigh many times as much as the largest females (top right). There's also no body mass sexual dimorphism in most gibbons (bottom left) but there's plenty in mountain gorillas (bottom right).*

In animals for which there is a big payoff to males who maintain a harem, males are often much larger than females, and aggressive contests between males can be very fierce. In many mammalian species, even those that are completely herbivorous, males may also have much more pronounced canine teeth than females. Such is the case for gorillas and hippos. In both of these plant-eating species, fully mature males are much larger than females. In both species, males also have much more pronounced canines. Both species are polygynous, and male mountain gorillas even maintain a stable harem (hippos, in contrast, mate more opportunistically). If you compare the skulls and teeth shown in Figure 8.6, you'll see that the canine teeth of human beings are detectable only by their location. In contrast, both hippo canines and gorilla canines are obvious. Both hippos and gorillas show much greater sexual dimorphism than people. Thus, it shouldn't be surprising that although polygyny (multiple wives) exists in some human cultures, so does polyandry (multiple husbands). In contrast, you won't ever find any polyandrous hippos or gorillas. In species that tend to have harems, males tend to be a lot bigger and fiercer than females (Cullen et al. 2014). Further, just as peahens show a preference for peacocks with extravagant tails, the female members of species in which there is sexual dimorphism in body size often prefer larger males. Koalas are a good example (Charlton et al., 2013). Females prefer larger males, and they can reliably tell a male koala's size from how deep his voice is. Further, male koalas in general have very deep voices (much deeper than any human male, for example). I don't know of any studies of female preferences in bighorn sheep, but recall that, all else being equal, larger rams have more offspring.

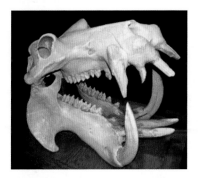  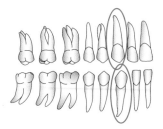

Figure 8.6 *Pronounced canines, especially for males, exist even in some herbivores, like hippos and gorillas. This is often the case when males at the top of a hierarchy in a species have special mating privileges. Although human canines are puny above the gum, the long roots of modern human canines may be a reminder of ancient primate ancestors (who resembled modern chimps and gorillas more than they resemble us).*

At first blush, we don't appear to be a very sexually dimorphic species, and we certainly have pretty wimpy canines. However, we do seem to be holding onto the roots of enlarged canines in two subtle ways. First, even though it has been millions of years since we shared a common ancestor with gorillas or chimps, men do have slightly larger canines than women (Schwartz & Dean, 2005). Furthermore, if you examine the roots of human teeth (see far right of Figure 8.6), you can see that our canines have longer roots than any of our other teeth. This appears to be an interesting, if modest, example of conservation. Further, although we surely are not as sexually dimorphic as gorillas, we are sexually dimorphic in a couple of key ways. When it comes to upper body strength, men are much stronger than women. This is true for male vs. female couch potatoes and male vs. female elite athletes. In fact, a recent large-scale study compared regular men, regular women, and elite female athletes. The elite female athletes had much greater grip strength than the untrained women, but as a group the elite female athletes scored only at the 25th percentile compared with the large group of untrained men (Leyk et al., 2007). This means that three out of four untrained men (75%) in this large study had stronger hands than the average highly trained female athlete. This was true despite the fact that Leyk et al. focused exclusively on elite female athletes in two sports that require strong hands (judo and handball). Based on a review of studies across the social sciences, Sell et al. (2012) listed 26 empirically established ways in which the body of the average man is better adapted for fighting than the body of the average woman. The list includes greater bone density in the arms, thicker jawbones, higher blood hemoglobin levels, and greater heat dissipation ability.

To be fair, sex differences in lower body strength are small once we account for differences in size between men and women. But men are, in fact, larger than women. Further, upper body strength is a much more important requirement for fighting than is lower body strength (Sell et al., 2012). On average, men simply evolved to fight more than women did. I'm not likely to pick a fight with Ronda Rousey (despite her losses in 2015 and 2016), but I don't think she could take Floyd Mayweather Jr. There is also clear evidence that the hands of men and women are shaped differently. If I may be blunt, men's hands more strongly resemble those of our cousins, the chimpanzee. In addition to the obvious fact that men's hands tend to be larger than women's, men tend to have proportionally longer ring fingers, and much longer pinkies than women do (Voracek, 2009). There are many interpretations of this sex difference, but at least one is that women's hands give them advantages when it comes to fine motor skills (like writing or painting), whereas men's hands give them advantages when it comes to fighting and heavy lifting.

So, we are not as sexually dimorphic as gorillas or hippos, but we are somewhat sexually dimorphic in several important ways. Accordingly, many have argued that a lot of male–male violence across the globe is grounded in striving for status (Buss, 2013; Georgiev et al., 2014). Status – even in people – has a clear connection to mating. Very few human males maintain harems, as King Solomon reputedly did. But in cultures worldwide, men with great power and financial resources usually have greater access to more desirable mates. To be clear, I'm not in any way endorsing this pattern as fair or ethical. I'm just describing it. The aggressive ways in which modern human males rise to the top of a social hierarchy are not as gory as those we see in rams, gorillas, or elephant seals. But there can be little doubt that in many cultures, aggressive behavior is often rewarded financially. In my view, failing to pay your fair share of taxes or overcharging consumers for a life-saving drug are both forms of aggression. Both can make people very rich. We'll discuss this idea further later in this chapter. For now, there can be little doubt that many men who do aggressive things often become very powerful. And once powerful men make it to the top of a hierarchy, they usually have little difficulty attracting mates that others find highly desirable. Even an extreme comb-over seems to become forgivable if one is wealthy enough. At my age this gives me very little time to become a millionaire.

Figure 8.7 *Unlike these elephant seals, Donald Trump may not have drawn any blood on his rise to fame, wealth, and political power. But he certainly behaved aggressively. And even many of those who voted for him in the 2016 U.S. presidential election have conceded that his attitudes about exploiting women leave much to be desired.*

Aggression is an equal opportunity employer

I should conclude this section on sexual dimorphism and aggressive competition for mates by noting that this works very differently in different species. In most insects and many birds of prey, females are larger than males. In the case of female insects, being large allows you to produce more eggs. In the case of predatory insects, being larger also makes female insects better hunters (Svenson et al., 2016). Recall that in some species of anglerfish, female fish are half a million times larger than the tiny, parasitic males. Although male mammals are usually larger than female mammals, spotted hyenas are an exception to the mammalian rule (Swanson et al., 2013). In fact, female hyenas are so masculinized that their highly enlarged clitorises are hard to distinguish from penises. Female hyenas also rule the roost. In other animals, including meerkats and topi antelopes as well as many crickets and katydids, female courtiers fight aggressively over desirable male mates (Bro-Jorgensen, 2002; Sharp & Clutton-Brock, 2011). In the species of crickets for which female–female competition is fiercest, male crickets offer very large spermataphores to potential mates. As you may recall, spermatophores contain sperm. But these "nuptial gifts" consist mainly of proteins and other nutrients (Gwynne, 2001). In species in which the males offer the most generous gift packages, these nutritious dowries can easily be a quarter of a male cricket's body weight. That's worth fighting for.

Consider a striking example of extreme female aggression in insects. In most of the 2,300 species of mantis, female mantises are much larger than their male counterparts. To get a sense of how much sexual size dimorphism varies across mantis species, check out the five well-camouflaged mantises appearing in Figure 8.8. For male praying mantises, their petite size makes mating a very risky activity. A male praying mantis often gets eaten by his lover. By the way, this form of **sexual cannibalism** may happen before, during, or immediately after copulation. But even in species in which the female decapitates the male before they have mated, this does not stop him from mating.

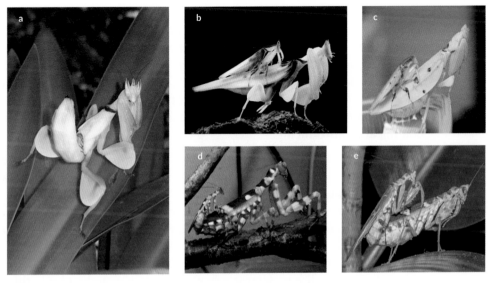

Figure 8.8 *Five species of mantis (Hymenopodini) that vary in sexual size dimorphism. The first two species look like orchids. They use floral camouflage to attract prey.*

Barry et al. (2008) thus hypothesized that sexual cannibalism in mantises might follow a cost–benefit model. They reasoned that if your male partner is big enough to make a nice meal, and if you are pretty hungry, eating your partner would represent a big benefit. They studied a species of mantis with "moderate sexual size dimorphism," and they compared hungry and well-fed female mantises. In *Pseudomantis albofimbriata* (false garden mantis), mature males are about 40% the weight of mature females. To manipulate the benefits of cannibalism experimentally, Barry et al. fed some female mantises much better than others over a seven-day period. At the end of this seven-day period, the females who had eaten smaller meals were thinner – and we can assume hungrier – than those who had eaten well. Barry et al. then set up blind dates on plants favored by this species of mantis. They found that when a female mantis was hungrier, she was much more likely to consume her mate. In fact, 89% (8/9) of the hungry females but none (0/10) of the well-fed female mantises attacked and ate their partners. Furthermore, they found that female mantises who cannibalized their partners produced heavier egg cases. To summarize, when the ratio of benefits to costs for aggression is high enough for the female members of a species, they can evolve to be much more aggressive than their male counterparts.

Status-seeking in social animals

A final evolutionary principle that is highly relevant to human aggression is **status-seeking**. This refers to the idea that social organisms often recognize a hierarchy of dominance and compete with one another to make it to a high position in the hierarchy. Elephant seals and bighorn sheep, for example, operate in a clear hierarchy. In fact, in virtually all social species, both male and female members of the species know very well who is at the top and who is at the bottom of the **social hierarchy**. In social insects like *ants,* members of a colony are born into their fixed social positions. A small number of males (drones) exist only to fertilize princesses who – once they have mated – become queens and start their own colonies. The colony includes many thousands of female workers who are responsible for almost all the daily business of the colony – from finding and gathering food to feeding and cleaning up after the queen (Wilson, 1975). The queen's sole job is to lay eggs. There is no clawing one's way to the top in an ant colony. Instead, in this rigid caste system, each organism knows its place. There is clear variation across ant species in exactly how the hierarchy works (Gill et al., 2009), but there is always a rigid hierarchy. In the case of ants, the thousands of aptly named "worker ants" do all the work, while a privileged few do all the mating and reproducing.

In social mammals, such as people, hierarchies aren't quite so rigid. There is often competition, including fighting, to see which male and female members of a social group will become the **alpha** member (the boss) of the group. You might think of social hierarchies as structures that assure that there will be a lot of fighting. As primatologist Frans de Waal (1996) has noted, however, you'd be wrong. One of the main purposes of a social hierarchy is to prevent needless fighting. If we all know who the boss is, there will be some occasional fights to see if the boss still has what it takes – or to see exactly who is third or fourth in command. But social hierarchies establish clear rules that usually reduce fighting. In social species as diverse as chimps, lions, and meerkats, the alpha males and alpha females usually eat first, for example. In fact, among lions, the alpha male almost always eats first, even when he played no role at all in a kill. The lionesses who did the actual hunting usually eat next, followed by whichever hungry lionesses have the highest rank. There are rankings even among lion cubs, and higher ranking cubs eat first if there is anything left. If there were no established rankings among the members of a pride of lions, for example, there would surely be serious fights between lions after a major kill. In lions, as in rams and meerkats, rankings thus determine daily privileges. This is not limited to eating. In social species, the alpha males almost always have special mating privileges, and they often enjoy territorial privileges as well.

Evolutionary psychologists have argued that a great deal of aggression between people is due to status-seeking. CEOs who rule with an iron fist may tell their underlings to run work-irrelevant errands, and they may insult such underlings with impunity. Members of rival gangs often feel compelled to make an example of a member of a rival gang who has not respected their territorial boundaries. In **honor cultures** – cultures in which a man's social status depends on his willingness to defend himself and his group against physical or psychological threats – boys and men often feel it is their duty to fight someone who has stolen from them, insulted them, or even ventured into their territory. Because I grew up in a very poor neighborhood in the southeastern U.S., I witnessed my fair share of honor-based violence and status-seeking. My father was such a strong believer in the culture of honor that he assaulted his sons if he ever heard that they walked away from a fight. I eventually learned that no bully could hurt me as much as my father could. I do not say this proudly but apologetically. My father was carrying on the sometimes violent tradition he had learned from his forefathers.

But there were times when striving for status in a culture of honor almost got my dad killed. Here's an example shared by my late father's cousin, Joe Carter. When my dad was about 21, already the father of two kids, a very large man came into a bar where Joe worked. The guy was new in town and asked Joe if he knew who "the toughest man in Chattanooga" was. Joe casually answered, "That'd have to be Bill Pelham" as if he were answering a trivia question. The man was not playing games, and he gave Joe a message: "Then when you see Bill Pelham, you tell him I came to Chattanooga to kick his ass." When Joe reported this to my dad, my dad asked Joe to take him to the stranger. Joe did so. The two men wasted no time fighting, and the stranger was, in Joe's words, "beating the shit out of Bill." Joe was already thinking about getting Bill to the hospital after the fight. But Bill didn't give up. Instead, he took punches, gouges, and kicks until he wore down the huge stranger, and he eventually turned the tables on him. According to Joe, after beating the crap out of the would-be king of Chattanooga, Bill apparently didn't let the man go until the stranger answered a question, "Who's the toughest man in Chattanooga, asshole?" When the man replied "Bill Pelham," my dad let him go. I cannot imagine any explanation for this crazy behavior that is not rooted in status-seeking. In the world in which my dad grew up, any threat to a man's status had to be answered swiftly – and violently. Just to be clear, I have no idea who the toughest man in Chattanooga really was back in 1961, but my dad sure thought the title was his, and he was quite willing to defend it.

This culture of honor also required my dad to defend threats to his immediate family members. When my dad was about 19, his younger sister Mary's fiancé (Bobby) pulled a gun on her while she was driving home from a high school dance (my dad was not present). Bobby was impatient to get home, and when Mary stopped dutifully at a red light, Bobby told her to drive through it. When Mary refused, Bobby put a pistol to her head and told her that if she did not go, he would "blow her head off." All this was dutifully observed by my then-13-year-old aunt Shirley, by the way. Mary's defiant response was to tell Bobby to pull the trigger if he was in that big a hurry. Bill's response the next day was to tell Bobby that if he ever put his sisters in danger again, Bill would kill him. According to my aunt Shirley, this quickly put an end to Bobby's aggression against Mary. Bobby knew his place in this hierarchy. Status-seeking and the defense of one's honor do not always play such an extreme role in human affairs, but there can be little doubt that a major source of human aggression is a desire for status. Sidanius and Pratto's (2000) social dominance theory, one of the most heavily studied theories in political psychology, is based on the idea that a lot of intergroup conflict is grounded in the evolved human desire to maintain social hierarchies, ideally with one's own group at the top. One of the most well-established findings in social dominance theory is that, on average, men are more interested in maintaining dominance hierarchies than women are.

APPLYING EVOLUTIONARY PRINCIPLES TO PEOPLE

Thus far in this chapter, I hope I've made four points. First, aggression is both pervasive and evolutionarily ancient. This applies as well to hominids as to arachnids. Second, the ancient fight-or-flight response that often leads to aggression is highly pronounced in mammals. Third, aggression evolved in a world full of costs and benefits. Fourth, aggression works differently in hierarchical, status-seeking species than in asocial species. To understand aggression in people, however, it is not enough to consider these four key evolutionary principles. We must also consider the important ways in which human aggression differs from animal aggression. In the remainder of this chapter, I review some unique distinctions that are crucial to understanding human aggression. I then review some major theories and empirical findings in the area of human aggression, with an eye toward how consistent they are with evolutionary principles. I conclude the chapter by summarizing Steven Pinker's insightful arguments that human beings today are much less aggressive than they have ever been before.

Physical, verbal, and relational aggression

As you may recall, Berkowitz's (1981) famous definition of human aggression includes anything a person does that is intended to hurt another organism. The most intuitive form of aggression is **physical aggression**, such as committing a flagrant foul in basketball, stabbing someone, bombing an enemy outpost. Almost all forms of aggression in animals are physical. But we human beings are much more flexible and creative in the ways in which we hurt each other. In addition to engaging in physical aggression, we also engage in **verbal aggression**. Verbal aggression refers to harming another person using language. Examples include insulting a sibling's taste in clothing, sending a coworker a demeaning text message, and spreading false rumors that a presidential candidate is using a pizzeria as a cover for a child prostitution ring. This last example may sound ludicrous, but in 2016, fake news sites attacked Hillary Clinton in exactly this way. Fueled by concerns over these false claims, 28-year-old Edgar Maddison Welch carried an assault rifle into the Washington pizza restaurant Comet Ping Pong in early December 2016. Welch submitted himself to police questioning without a struggle, and he explained that he was there to "self-investigate" the claims of the child prostitution ring. There is debate about whether Welch fired his gun or pointed it at anyone, but there is no debate that the ensuing chaos did a great deal of harm to the owner of this popular family restaurant. Any possible damage to Clinton's presidential campaign had already been done.

Because we are the only species to use language in highly complex ways, verbal aggression would appear to be uniquely human. Other forms of aggression hold a similar distinction in that they are much more common in human beings than in other animals. Because one of the key benefits of being a highly social species is enjoying social and interpersonal rewards, we often engage in **relational aggression**. This is a form of aggression in which the harm comes in the form of a lost or damaged relationship. Falsely telling a person that she cannot trust a friend, stealing someone's romantic partner, or ostracizing someone from a group because of sexual jealousy are all examples of relational aggression. Divorcing a person who has been unfaithful to you also qualifies. Although verbal and relational aggression often overlap, there are plenty of forms of verbal aggression that are not explicitly relational. Further, it is also possible, in principle, to engage in relational aggression using deeds rather than words. Chimps sometimes engage in what I'd call relational aggression, for example, but they don't ever spread nasty rumors about one another. Finally, notice that physical versus verbal aggression differ behaviorally (in terms of actions versus words), whereas relational aggression refers to the specific type of harm that is inflicted upon one's victim (e.g., interpersonal rather than economic).

The distinction between these three forms of aggression is crucial. For example, these distinctions are necessary to understand gender differences in aggression. Most people think boys and men are simply much more aggressive than girls and women. As I have already noted, there are some important senses in which this is true. Men murder other people, especially strangers, much more often than women do (Kellermann & Mercy, 1992). Likewise, only about 6% of American bank robbers are female. In 2003, in the U.K. and the U.S., men arrested for robbery of any kind outnumbered women about eight to one (Brookman et al., 2007). But men are only slightly more likely than women are to kill people they know very well. In fact, when it comes to killing those we love with knives or blades, wives in the U.S. stab their husbands to death about 50% more often than husbands do the reverse (Kellermann & Mercy, 1992). That's what I'd call an extreme version of relational aggression. The differences between men and women in verbal aggression are also very small. Finally, when it comes to mundane forms of relational aggression that don't involve murder, girls and women have proven to be at least as aggressive as, if not more aggressive than, boys and men (Ostrov et al., 2014). Don't tell anyone I said that, by the way, or I won't be your friend anymore.

Aggression varies not only in the type of behavior and the type of damage it entails, but also in its emotional and motivational origins. There appear to be two very different motivations that fuel human aggression, and it is crucial to understand each of them. What are they?

Hostile aggression

A form of aggression that appears to be common in many social species – and rare if not absent in nonsocial species – is **hostile aggression**. Hostile aggression (also known as **angry aggression**) is motivated by the desire to hurt someone *for the sake of hurting them* (e.g., punching your little brother during a heated argument). Many cases of assault and homicide appear to be motivated by the desire to hurt for the sake of hurting. People sometimes do things in a fit of anger that they would never do if they sat down and calculated the costs and benefits. Especially in cultures that emphasize personal and family honor, many murders seem to happen because the homicide victim did something to belittle or insult the killer. Historically, honor cultures are often places where people had to make a living in a high-risk world. Cattle- and sheep-herders, for example, were constantly on the lookout for rustlers. Farmers, in contrast, rarely had to worry that someone would rustle a field of wheat while they were sleeping (Nisbett & Cohen, 1996). Gladwell (2008, p. 254) summarized research on the culture of honor and violence as follows. In the South, he argued, "violence wasn't for economic gain. It was *personal*. You fought over your honor." I'll return later to whether the existence of hostile aggression flies in the face of an evolutionary cost–benefit analysis. For now, let me acknowledge that a second basic form of aggression is very obviously consistent with a cost–benefit analysis.

Instrumental aggression

Sometimes aggression in people is not personal at all. In contrast to hostile aggression, **instrumental aggression** refers to a harmful action performed to achieve an important, non-hostile goal. In this case, the aggressor's goal is not to hurt for the sake of hurting but to hurt to get something desirable – no matter what the cost to others. Robbing a bank, cheating in a sporting event, and killing a woolly mammoth you plan to eat are all examples. Many examples of corporate greed are more arguably examples of instrumental aggression. In 2015, Turing Pharmaceuticals came under attack after it increased the price of a life-saving drug from $13.50 per pill to $750 per pill, putting it out of reach for many people who needed it to live. In spring 2016, Volkswagen also got caught for engaging in instrumental aggression by designing its cars' computerized exhaust systems to cheat on emissions tests. This made the cars look much more environmentally friendly than they really were. If you are wondering where the harm was in this aggressive activity, just ask someone who paid a lot of extra money for a VW because they thought they were taking better care of the planet in so doing.

These examples qualify as instrumental aggression, if you cast the net as widely as I do, because the goal of Turing and Volkswagen was to make money any way they could make it – not to hurt people for the sake of hurting.

To get a bit technical, I should note that many psychologists who study aggression argue that aggression (including instrumental aggression) must involve an *intent to hurt* the victim, or likely victims. This gets tricky because, in my view, many who engage in instrumental aggression have no intention of hurting others, but they don't mind doing so if this is the only way to get what they want. If we adopt the strictest definition, we couldn't say that Turing Pharmaceuticals engaged in instrumental aggression. But if we flip our psychological caps sideways – which turns them into sociological caps – we could surely say that Turing engaged in **structural violence**. Structural violence is subtle but deadly. It refers to social rules, systems, or structures that facilitate the harm of people – or deny them basic human rights. I have no beef with capitalism. But extreme forms of capitalism that value profits over human welfare are examples of structural violence that also qualify as instrumental aggression. As a teenager, my father worked in a foundry that hired poor, underage workers. They also failed to take basic safety precautions, and this cost my dad one of his fingers. Surely, the owners of the foundry did not *intend* to *hurt* their workers, but their callous emphasis on nine-figure profits left my dad with only nine digits. My dad's response was to feel lucky. Other workers he knew lost arms. At his next place of work, a larger foundry, workers sometimes lost their lives.

Figure 8.9 *Aggression can be humorous (left) or tragic (right). Some tragic acts of aggression are instrumental. The sniper who shot and killed Harambe (May 28, 2016 at Cincinnati Zoo) killed the captive gorilla to save the life of a child who had fallen into the gorilla's pen.*

In short, the distinction between hostile and instrumental aggression can get tricky. This is true not only because intentions are hard to know but also because people can have multiple intentions. Many actors who engage in instrumental aggression are willing to harm others to get what they desire, but harm is not their main intention. Others mean to hurt, but they mean to hurt so that they can achieve something. An athlete who breaks a competitor's legs means to hurt the other person, but the unscrupulous athlete probably cares more about breaking records than breaking femurs. And what if the athlete merely used steroids, and didn't physically hurt anyone? If she robbed another competitor of a gold medal, this can still be considered harm. I raise such points not to muddy the waters but to note that the waters are inherently muddy. U.S. Navy SEALs surely meant to kill Osama bin Laden in May 2011. I suspect that hostile as well as instrumental motivations were behind their actions.

Berkowitz's classic definition of aggression has survived a lot of criticism because it is both nuanced and useful (Geen, 1998). For example, the definition helps clarify that some things that look like aggression at first blush (e.g., punishing a disobedient child) do not qualify as true examples of aggression. Clearly, the parent who took away a coveted privilege from a poorly behaved child knew that this would make the child unhappy. But if the parent's goal was to help the child become better behaved, the parent would surely argue that the punishment was an act of nurturance rather than belligerence. In the 19th century, doctors sometimes sawed off patients' badly infected limbs, without the benefit of modern anesthesia. They did so because they knew this was the only chance they had to save their patients' lives. By the same token, many things that laypeople would not describe as acts of aggression do fit Berkowitz's definition. Failing to protect coal miners from the long-term dangers of exposure to coal dust (because the safeguards are perceived as too expensive) is a good example.

PREDICTORS OF PHYSICAL AGGRESSION

It is precisely because human aggression takes many forms and occurs for many reasons that researchers have documented many predictors of human aggression. There is also no shortage of theories of human aggression. In the next section I review some of the established predictors of aggression – with an eye toward how they fit into the evolutionary perspective I've offered here. I'm going to argue that research on many of the important causes of aggression is pretty consistent with this evolutionary perspective. I begin with research on properties of the aggressor. What personal characteristics make some people more prone to aggression than others? I should note in advance that my review will be biased toward studies of the roots of physical aggression. This is because this particular form of aggression has overwhelmingly garnered the greatest amount of research attention.

PROPERTIES OF THE AGGRESSOR

Poverty and social inequality

Personality psychologists, demographers, and criminologists have long wished to identify which groups of people are most prone to violence. It's a common belief that poor people are more aggressive than wealthy people. Many laypeople believe that poor people are inherently violent. However, sociologists and social psychologists have argued that stereotypes and powerful social forces such as crowding, stress, and a lack of economic opportunity are the real reasons why poor people tend to be more physically aggressive than wealthy people (Barkan, 2012). Without delving too deeply into a debate that has been going on for decades, I should note that recent work in economics, criminology, and sociology suggests that it is actually **social inequality** rather than poverty per se that is the better predictor of violence. It's not so much a lack of income but a *relative* lack of income in disadvantaged groups that seems to promote aggression. In counties, cities, or nations where some people have very little and their neighbors have a lot, people seem to experience **relative deprivation** (having or getting less relative to a salient comparison group). The perceived unfairness that comes with this can apparently foster a great deal of violence (Pinker, 2011). In fact, Hicks and Hicks (2012) argued that it is not just inequality but *conspicuous* inequality (as evidenced by spending on luxury goods) that is the real culprit. People are apparently most frustrated by their own poverty when their neighbors flaunt their wealth with expensive cars, clothing, or trips to nice restaurants.

It's not so clear how well this finding on relative deprivation supports an evolutionary perspective. The basic idea that people with very little might want to hurt those with a lot is pretty consistent with a cost–benefit analysis. But Hicks and Hicks (2012) found, for example, that the highly visible kinds of social inequality they studied better predicted violent crime rates than property crime rates. They argue that a cost–benefit analysis makes the opposite prediction. Perhaps this just means that concerns for social justice sometimes trump a cost–benefit analysis. Anger may sometimes trump economics. On the other hand, even if we accept Hicks and Hicks' arguments, one clever study does not invalidate a great deal of data suggesting that crime follows a cost–benefit analysis (Becker, 1968). CEOs of selfish corporations rarely mug people, for example. This is too costly, and the benefits are trivial. Instead, some CEOs arguably make their killings financially rather than physically.

This raises a broader point. It is precisely because the costs and benefits of aggression are so important, and so different for people in different social classes, that it is hard to compare rates of aggression and violence between the rich and the poor. I feel pretty comfortable saying that Martin Shkreli is more dangerous than the average mugger. Shkreli made a career out of buying up drugs used to treat rare, life-threatening diseases. He then dramatically jacked up the prices of the drugs to make enormous profits. In fact, Shkreli was the founder and CEO of Turing Pharmaceuticals. As mentioned earlier, Turing preyed on patients by dramatically overcharging them for much-needed drugs. Profit-hungry companies may not kill people with knives or guns, but they sometimes kill nonetheless. Having said this, just as it is inappropriate to stereotype all poor people as aggressive, it is inappropriate to stereotype all companies, or all CEOs, as willing to jeopardize human life for financial gain. But whether we are considering muggings or financial killings, the role of costs and benefits in human aggression is of obvious importance.

Youth and maleness

With a couple of exceptions noted previously, two of the strongest predictors of physical violence in people are youth and maleness. As Barkan (2012) noted, according to the FBI's Uniform Crime Reports, men appear to commit about four times as many violent crimes as women do. The rate is closer to two to one for property crime, but as Barkan (2012) put it: "crime is a man's world." Violent crime is, in fact, a *young* man's world. Boys and men between the ages of 15 and 29 committed almost half of all the violent crimes recorded by the FBI in 2004. In fact, men aged 30 and older so rarely commit violent crimes that the official FBI report I examined for 2004 made "30 and older" a single, undifferentiated age group. It's hard to imagine when else researchers might put everyone 30 and older in the same boat. "SWM older than 29 seeks SWF 25–29" wouldn't garner much interest at an online dating site.

When it comes to the most violent crime of all, homicide, the skew toward young male offenders is even more dramatic. According to figures compiled by the FBI for 2011, men committed almost nine times as many homicides as women. Further, men aged 20–24 committed slightly more homicides (2,179) than *men and women together aged 40 and older* (2,124). As David Lykken (1995, p. 93) jokingly put it: "We could avoid two-thirds of all crime simply by putting all able-bodied young men in cryogenic sleep from the age of 12 through 28." Surely, culture and social roles play a role in the strong connection between being a young man and being violent (Barkan, 2012). But costs and benefits surely play a role, too. It would be just as unwise for a typical 9-year-old as for a typical 90-year-old to try to take money from adult strangers by force. If we dig deeper into violent crime, we see that boys who are about 15 are disproportionately responsible for a lot of young male crime. This might seem surprising from a cost–benefit perspective because men reach their peak physical strength in their late twenties rather than their early teens. However, the early teen years are one of the first times that many adolescent males are left unattended long enough to plan and carry out crimes (Arnett, 2012). Even more important, teenage offenders appear to be even more likely than adult offenders to carry and use guns (Zawitz, 1995). It doesn't take big biceps to pull a trigger. Finally, in the case of crimes that pay, the perceived benefits of stealing $20 are almost certainly much greater to the typical 15-year-old than they are to the typical 25-year-old. All things considered, a cost–benefit analysis is highly consistent with many of the demographic facts behind violent crime.

Physical strength and fighting ability

Perhaps the most interesting evolutionary perspective on physical aggression comes from research on the attitudinal importance of **physical strength** and fighting ability. In modern cultures, there is little or no logical reason why physically stronger people should be more prone to anger, should feel more entitled, or should more strongly believe that war is the solution to international conflicts. As Sell et al. (2012) have argued, the world in which most of us live today is dramatically different than the ancestral world in which we evolved. In fact, one of the most common causes of death among men in traditional societies was violence. In traditional societies, as many as 30% of men could expect to die violently. Today, about 5 people per 100,000 can expect to die of violence in a given year. To drive this difference home, Sell et al. (2012) noted that: "if modern Western societies had homicide rates as high as some foraging peoples, a male graduate student would be more likely to be killed than to get a tenure-track position." In the world in which we evolved, men who could not fight well often found themselves on the losing end of social interactions. Conversely, men who could fight well often got what they wanted. According to Sell et al. this hard, cold fact about human evolution strongly shapes thinking and behavior in men in ways that are still with us today.

To be clear, then, personal strength and fighting ability shouldn't influence one's attitudes about group-on-group violence in today's world. After all, we have vanquished predators, invented guns that can instantly incapacitate fierce attackers, and hired professional soldiers and police officers to do the fighting and protecting for us. But personal strength does still matter, a lot. As it turns out, human judges are very good at looking at a man's body or face and assessing his physical strength. More important, men who are stronger than average, or who look so, tend to possess positive attitudes about aggression. They also report being more willing than physically weaker men to use aggression to get what they want. In a clever archival study, Sell et al. (2012) identified a group of 80 well-known Hollywood actors. Judges, unaware of the purpose of the study, categorized the men as action, dramatic, or comedic actors. Sell et al. then categorized the actors as military "hawks" or "doves" based on behavioral criteria such as their political party donations and their public speeches. The late Charlton Heston's speeches in favor of the National Rifle Association, for example, helped earn him a designation as a hawk rather than a dove. Arnold Schwarzenegger was also easy to categorize because he served as a Republican governor of California for many years. As you can see in Figure 8.10, the buff men who were known for action roles were much more likely than dramatic actors or comedians to possess rightwing political attitudes.

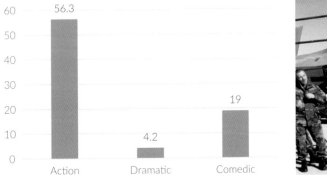

Figure 8.10 *Sell et al. (2012) found that actors who played action roles (and who tend to be physically imposing) are much more likely than other actors to possess militarily conservative (rightwing) political attitudes, despite the fact that real wars don't always guarantee a victory for the good guys.*

The tendency for physically strong men – but not physically strong women – to possess attitudes that promote physical and political aggression is now very well documented. I have no doubt that my father's unusual physical strength contributed to his willingness to behave aggressively. My hands are large enough that I can comfortably palm a basketball, but my hands are pretty wimpy compared with my dad's. Recently, I was trying to explain how huge my dad's hands were to my 13-year-old son, who was lamenting the size of his own hands. "My dad's pinkies were thicker than my thumbs," I told him, trying to offer some hope that he might inherit his grandfather's massive hands. "So did your dad have really big hands – or just regular hands with really fat pinkies?" came Lincoln's facetious reply. Lincoln may not have inherited his grandfather's hands, but he certainly inherited his grandfather's sense of humor. Getting back to how physical strength predicts attitudes about aggression, Sell et al. (2012) showed that "better fighters feel entitled to better outcomes, set lower thresholds for anger/aggression, have self-favoring political attitudes, and believe more in the utility of warfare."

In a study of more than 1,400 Swiss students, Sell et al. (2016) also found that other evolutionarily significant indicators of strength and social value played a role in adolescent aggression. Sell et al. measured aggression using not only teacher ratings of student aggressiveness but also boys' and girls' self-reported aggressive delinquent behavior. In this study, as in others, boys who were physically stronger behaved more aggressively. But the researchers also found that boys who were part of a powerful "clique" or coalition and boys who had greater "mate value" (based on boys' reports of being physically attractive and having had sexual intercourse) behaved more aggressively. These same patterns applied to girls as well as to boys but the effects for girls were usually much weaker. Putting all the existing findings together, it would appear that our evolutionary history of being a pretty aggressive species continues to leave its mark on our current behavior. And it does so in ways that are pretty sensitive to both status-seeking and costs versus benefits. The basic evolutionary logic behind much of Sell et al.'s research is that a cost–benefit analysis of human aggression is so hardwired that men and boys continue to base much of their behavior on cost–benefit calculations that would have mattered in the Pleistocene – even when such calculations are seriously outdated.

PROPERTIES OF THE POTENTIAL TARGET

Costs, benefits, and status-seeking involve properties of potential targets as well as properties of potential aggressors. It would be surprising indeed if properties of the target played no role in aggressive behavior. In fact, many evolutionarily significant features of potential targets can either facilitate or inhibit aggressive behavior. Here are a few examples.

Dangerousness of the target

In our discussion of aggression in animals, I hope it was clear that predators carefully assess the physical prowess of their potential victims before deciding whether to attack. People are at least as sophisticated as lions and hyenas in their decisions about aggression. We need only look to middle school playgrounds to see that bullies usually choose their victims carefully. Bullies are more likely to choose unpopular children who have few friends and who are less physically imposing than their peers (Juvonen & Graham, 2014). Beginning in middle school, bullies are not the dislikable villains we see in movies and cartoons.

Instead, they are often quite popular with their peers, who often admire their physical skills and their high social status. This popularity makes it harder than it would otherwise be to stamp out bullying. In fact, one of the many barriers to stopping bullying is the fact that victims often convince themselves that the bullying they receive was justified (Juvonen & Graham, 2014). Sadly, it is precisely because most bullies have a good implicit understanding of status-seeking, and because they often make implicit cost–benefit decisions when choosing targets, that bullying continues to be a serious social problem. Bullies, like hyenas and bighorn sheep, usually choose targets they believe they can defeat.

Many murderers appear to behave in ways that reflect cost–benefit dynamics. In keeping with a cost–benefit analysis, murderers appear to adjust their choice of method – almost surgically so – in ways that reduce the risks of being killed themselves. Figure 8.11 features U.S. death data from the Centers for Disease Control and Prevention (CDC) to show how this plays out in the case of a victim's age and gender. As you can see in Figure 8.11, murderers almost never use guns to kill the very young or the very old. Further, when killers do use a firearm to kill the very young or the very old, they make only a weak distinction between male and female victims. However, as shown near the center of Figure 8.11, those who shoot and kill teenagers and young adults are much more likely to kill boys and men, rather than girls and women. Why try to strangle someone who might be better at strangling than you are? Killing with a gun is a much safer bet. When possible victims are physically imposing, killers lean strongly toward the use of a weapon that is a great equalizer. Incidentally, I repeated this exact analysis for killing someone with your bare hands. Unsurprisingly, the figures for male and female victims were now much lower in almost all age groups. It's not only risky (and messy) to do hand-to-hand combat; it is simply hard to kill people with one's bare hands. However, the likelihood of dying this way is now higher for adult female rather than for adult male victims. Among victims aged 15–34, for example, women were 86% more likely than men to be killed in physical assaults that did not involve a weapon.

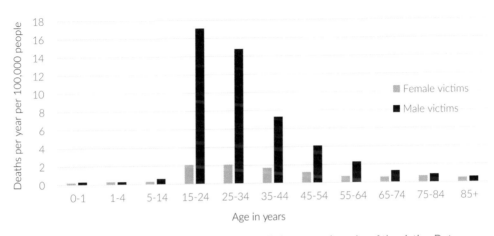

Figure 8.11 *Rates of death by firearm vary dramatically by age and gender of the victim. Data are nationwide deaths per 100,000 people per year, from CDC records for the period 1999–2015.*

It is both striking and chilling that one group of victims was by far the most likely to be killed via assaults that did not involve weapons. This group was infants, those one year of age or younger. In fact, regardless of infant gender, infants were more than five times as likely as toddlers to die when killers assaulted without using a weapon. To be sure, infants are more physically vulnerable than toddlers. Thus, violent acts meant to harm rather than kill might more often kill infants. Nonetheless, the strong tendency for killers to use weapons that greatly reduce the risk of harm to the self *only when it appears to be actuarially advisable* suggests that costs and benefits probably play a major role in homicide. Almost no violent offenders seem to think the way to kill a baby is with a gun. Finally, I'm sure another reason why people rarely shoot babies is that even the most heartless killers realize that juries do not look kindly on those who put bullets in babies. To the degree that this is true, however, one could argue that even the most heinous of killers – baby killers – appear to select the methods of killing that are the least likely to get them the death penalty. That's certainly a major cost.

Of course, archival data like these are open to many interpretations. A competing *evolutionary* explanation for the findings in Figure 8.11 begins with the stark fact that guns are a highly effective way to kill people. It is a short step from the logic of within-species (and within-gender) competition to argue that when competition gets badly out of hand, it is young men who are most likely to be involved. If this is the case, we'd expect to see a lot of young men being murdered with guns (Buss, 2013). This doesn't fully explain why so few young men beat each other to death sans weapon, but perhaps killing another young healthy man with one's hands is a very tall order. Further, if young men often fight over young women, it would not be shocking to learn that a tragic way that these fights occasionally end involves the shooting of the young women about whom boys and/or men are fighting. This is also consistent with the bump up in female deaths by firearm that occurs for those aged 15–34.

Finally, there are surely cultural or legal as well as evolutionary reasons for at least some of these age and gender trends. Teenage boys, especially those younger than 18, are typically treated more leniently than adults in the American legal system. Further, in most U.S. states, teenage boys can legally drive a car at age 16. Access to cars may facilitate access to guns, and victims (who are often about the same age as those who kill them). Although 35- to 55-year-olds surely have greater access to cars and guns than do teenagers, post-adolescent men often have family responsibilities that may reduce their propensity to violence. The last time someone invited me to fight him, I was in the car with two of my young male relatives (aged 12 and 7). An irate driver lost it when I stopped at a crosswalk for a woman who was having difficulty walking. In his defense, I must admit that, with his horn blaring, I waited an additional, wholly unnecessary, 10 seconds to get going again after the woman had safely crossed. The male driver then got out of the car and challenged me to a fight, with my son and nephew watching. Given that I had 50 pounds on him, I think the odds were in my favor. But, in light of what my impressionable family members would have seen (whichever way the fight went), I politely declined the invitation. So the data in Figure 8.11 do not guarantee that murder follows the rules of a cost–benefit analysis. But, at a minimum, they do clearly show that violent crime victimization, like violent crime perpetration, is what Barkan (2012) and Lykken (1995) might collectively call a "young man's world."

Gender of the target

One well-documented demographic fact about victims would seem to fly in the face of a cost–benefit analysis of violent crime. In fact, you just saw this fact in Figure 8.11. Men are much more likely to be shot and killed than women are. The same sex differences in victimization applies to being robbed. Men get mugged much more often than women do. At first blush this would seem to fly in the face of a cost–benefit analysis. All else being equal, it should be a lot safer for muggers to target female as opposed to male victims. However, interviews with male and female muggers reveal that, from the perspective of those who do the mugging, all else is not equal. Men are perceived as better victims than women are. First, muggers strongly assume that men carry more cash than women do. So the perceived benefits of mugging a man are much greater than the perceived benefits of mugging a woman. Second, muggers often indicate that they target a man who is in the company of a woman, because they assume that the presence of a woman makes male victims less likely to resist. Third, female muggers do not prefer male victims. Instead they're more likely to target other women, because they believe they can more easily dominate them. In keeping with a cost–benefit analysis, female muggers also change their choice of a weapon and their physical approach to mugging depending on the gender of their victim.

Female muggers who usually threaten women with knives often switch to guns when mugging men. Female muggers also report being more likely to keep their physical distance when mugging men at gunpoint – to minimize the chances of retaliation or resistance. Finally, status-seeking also seems to work its way into the mugging equation, especially for male muggers. Many male muggers report that they feel like it would be wimpy, or even humiliating, to focus exclusively on female victims. As Brookman et al. (2007, p. 862) put it: "Men use crime to establish their manhood on the streets; many of their assaults, for example, evolve out of perceived status challenges to their gendered reputations." Needless to say, beating up a little old lady and taking her purse is not likely to do much to establish a male mugger's street cred. The only thing worse might be shooting a baby. For male muggers who value status and money, then, the only way to get a lot of both is to focus on male victims.

Genetic relatedness of potential targets

If plants and insects can identify their genetic kin, people can surely do the same. One of the cardinal evolutionary rules of aggression is that, all else being equal, people are less likely to harm those who are genetically related to them than to harm those who are not. You may recall that Hamilton's rule says we should be more willing to help those with whom we share more genes. The converse version of this rule is that the more genes people share with another person, the less likely people should be to harm that person. Of course, people who are genetically related often spend a lot of time together and more time means more opportunity for harm. One way to control for this problem was discussed in Chapter 6 on parenting. Stepparents probably spend less time with their stepchildren than with their biological children. Unfortunately, however, as Daly and Wilson (1994) have shown, stepparents are much more likely than biological parents to harm or kill the children left in their care. All else being equal, people should also be a lot less likely to kill a sibling (with whom they share half their genes) than a cousin (with whom they share only an eighth of their genes). Likewise, people should be less likely to kill or harm a cousin than a complete stranger.

Some researchers have expressed skepticism about this evolutionary idea because in the Pleistocene people may not have always known who their genetic kin were. There were no mirrors in the Pleistocene, for example. Thus, some have argued that people did not know who looked like them and who did not. Further, any tendency to inhibit aggression against kin would have to operate pretty automatically. Evolutionary pressures usually operate well below the surface of any conscious considerations. I am not convinced by the skeptics. First, most traditional cultures have terms like *sister* and *cousin,* and such terms usually correspond to genetic relatedness. People also know very well what their parents and siblings look like, and so if someone looks a lot like my father or my brother, there is a good chance he shares some of my genes. Recall that we discussed work in Chapter 4 suggesting that people have sexual aversions to the smells of their opposite-sex relatives. If we can use smell to decide with whom to mate, we could presumably use smell to decide with whom to cooperate. None of these automatic cues for genetic relatedness require people to use a mirror.

Ingroup versus outgroup status of potential targets

One of the best predictors of whether a male (or a group of males from a tribe or coalition) will attack other males is whether those males are members of one's own social group. Research shows that a hard and cold cost–benefit analysis determines a great deal of male-on-male outgroup aggression. Further, Tooby and Cosmides' (1988) **risk contact theory of warfare** suggests that, sadly enough, going to war against a group with whom you compete for survival can sometimes pay evolutionary dividends. Along similar lines, research on the **male warrior hypothesis** (McDonald et al., 2012) suggests that men are naturally more prone to fight than women are because serving as a soldier in a successful war would yield much greater benefits for men than it would for women.

When a neighboring group has resources your own group desires, you and your fellow male ingroup members may decide to take the resource by force. One of the most disturbing aspects of an evolutionary perspective on warfare is the idea that because one man can impregnate many women (because people are somewhat polygynous), there is a tragic sense in which men are more biologically disposable than women. If a tribe loses half its male members in a war but gains a lot of highly valuable resources, the remaining men can father even more children than the original group of men could have. In fact, the tremendous evolutionary gains to the surviving men may outweigh the risk of death they themselves faced during a war with a rival clan. Hypotheses such as the male warrior hypothesis are controversial because they suggest that our evolutionary history has made men *inherently* predisposed to possess "more xenophobic and ethnocentric attitudes" than women do (McDonald et al., 2012). In fairness to the male warrior hypothesis, McDonald et al. have carefully noted that the tendency of men to favor outgroup derogation and war more than women do is an average tendency, which is also shaped by culture.

If we accept the idea that physically stronger men possess more favorable attitudes about aggression than physically weaker men do, it stands to reason that the sex that happens to be physically stronger would possess more favorable attitudes about aggression, including aggression against outgroups. Recall also that a well-replicated finding from social dominance theory is that men tend to be higher in social dominance orientation than women. Regardless of one's position on the male warrior hypothesis, however, there can be little doubt that, for both women and men, there is a natural tendency to be distrustful of the members of unfamiliar groups. Under the right conditions, such as competition for scarce resources, such distrust can easily turn into aggression (Sherif, 1958).

PROPERTIES OF THE ENVIRONMENT

Both a cost–benefit perspective and the idea that people seek social status imply that properties of the social environment can have a big impact on human aggressive behavior. Likewise, the basic idea of fight or flight is that organisms fight in some situations and flee in others. If you are outnumbered or exhausted from a previous fight, for example, flight would usually trump fight as an immediate response to threat. The idea that environments matter applies to fleeting aspects of the environment, such as whether it is daytime or nighttime, and more enduring aspects of the environment, such as cultural values and whether the city in which you live is well policed or not.

Strength in numbers

As suggested by observers of lions and hyenas, many social organisms become much more aggressive than usual when numbers are on their side. Primates, people included, are no exception to this cost–benefit rule. One of the worst things that can happen to a male chimpanzee who is by himself is to run into a group of two or more male chimpanzees from a rival troop (de Waal, 1982). By the same token, a soldier who becomes trapped alone behind enemy lines will have to be extremely lucky to survive such an ordeal. Likewise, a common strategy among many bullies is to enlist the help of an entourage whose presence adds to the bully's social power (Scaglione & Scaglione, 2006). Even warfare appears to follow the principle of strength in numbers. Lanchester's square law states that the military advantage one army has over another is a function of the squared value of the number of armed soldiers fighting on each side. Assuming neither group is holed up in an easily defended position, and that combat involves single-fire rifles, the group with the larger numbers has an advantage. Further, this advantage grows exponentially as one group's size advantage increases in a linear fashion. A group that outnumbers the enemy 4:1, for example, has a much larger advantage than a group that outnumbers the enemy 3:1 (Adams & Mesterton-Gibbons, 2003). In hand-to-hand battles with spears or canines rather than guns or canons, the advantages to the larger group dictated by Lanchester's law get somewhat smaller. But there can be no doubt that it is always good to outnumber your enemies. The costs of fighting when you outnumber your enemy go way down, usually with little or no changes in the likely benefits.

Culture of honor

I hope it's evident that certain kinds of violence are highly pronounced in honor cultures. In places such as the Deep South (e.g., Georgia, Alabama) – where people historically had to defend their property against others who would gladly take it from them – a culture of honor developed. The norms and values that are central to an honor culture lead people – especially men – to be especially vigilant to threats to their honor and especially willing to fight those who would taint their honor with insults or attacks. One way to conceptualize an honor culture is that it is a culture in which men are more focused than usual on threats to their secure position in a social hierarchy. In my experience of living in an honor culture, however, this is not so much about trying to make it to the top of a hierarchy. Rather, it is about making sure no one, no matter how imposing, drags your honor into the mud. This cultural logic applies just as well to tragic as to trivial forms of aggression. Nisbett (1993) documented that murder rates in the South were notably higher than murder rates in the North. This was only true, however, for murders that arose from arguments. Job prospects for hitmen are thus no brighter in Alabama than in Massachusetts. Relative to those who live in other regions of the U.S., Southerners – especially those from traditional herding regions – more readily endorse violence as a solution to personal insults and as a valid form of self-protection (Nisbett, 1993).

Arguing and even killing one another over very small infractions would certainly seem to fly in the face of the principle of costs and benefits. Why risk one's life to fight a bully who merely insulted your mother, or put a tiny scratch in your car? The answer, in a culture of honor, is that threats and insults are unlikely to end with a mildly insulted mother or a scratched car. Instead, small threats often become litmus tests for whether a belittled person will fight back at all. This is apparently why those reared in a culture of honor are quick to attack others in ambiguous situations. For example, an archival study of more than 57,000 professional baseball games recently showed that when a pitcher, let's say a Chicago Cubs pitcher, hit a player on the opposing team (say, a St. Louis Cardinal outfielder), the Cardinal pitcher whose teammate had just been hit often retaliated by hitting a batter – any batter – from the Cubs during the next inning. This aggressive payback pattern applied much more dramatically to pitchers who had grown up in the South, however, than to pitchers who had grown up in other regions of the U.S. (Larrick et al., 2014). The culture of honor is not about literal costs and benefits. In fact, it often flies blatantly in the face of them. Instead, it is about protecting one's status. Furthermore, it is also clear that lashing out at someone who has threatened your honor is also part of the basic fight-or-flight reaction that all mammals experience in highly threatening situations. Those who grow up in honor cultures learn to see serious threats – and become highly angry – in situations that those from non-honor cultures would perceive as much more benign. The culture of honor is certainly learned, but it is readily learned by an organism that is hardwired to attend to status and threats.

Potential for detection and punishment

Research on the potential for the punishment of aggression provides some of the strongest evidence for the cost–benefit perspective on aggression. For example, **deindividuation**, a state of mind in which people do not feel personally identifiable, can greatly increase the likelihood of human aggression. More specifically, situations such as darkness, being a member of a large group, or wearing a mask – which all make it difficult for others to identify an aggressor – can increase aggressive behavior. In a classic experiment, Zimbardo (1969) randomly assigned some students to wear hoods that shrouded their identities. Others wore name tags that personally identified them. This and other studies like it have shown that shrouding people's identities makes them more willing to hurt others, including others who have done nothing to deserve poor treatment. In an archival study of hundreds of acts of violence perpetrated in Northern Ireland in the mid-to-late 1990s, Silke (2003, p. 493) found that when people wore disguises that shielded their identities, the perpetrators "inflicted more serious physical injuries, attacked more people at the scene, engaged in more acts of vandalism, and were more likely to threaten victims after the attacks." Acts of violence are also more likely to occur at night rather than in the daytime. When people feel they cannot be personally identified, this surely has multiple psychological effects. But one of the most obvious effects is that the potential costs of aggression are lowered, because it becomes less likely that people will be personally identified and punished as the perpetrators of a violent act. As a very famous guy named John once put it: "Everyone who does evil hates the light, and will not come into the light for fear that their deeds will be exposed" (John 3:20, NIV). Cost matters.

AN EVOLUTIONARY SPIN ON FIVE MAJOR THEORIES OF AGGRESSION

This selective review of predictors of aggression reveals that many of the known precursors of aggression are consistent with the evolutionary perspectives I have reviewed here. Many popular theories of aggression, both classic and contemporary, have also yielded findings that are highly consistent with the evolutionary perspective offered here. Let's examine some of the most prominent theories of human aggression and examine how they may be understood via an evolutionary framework.

Realistic group conflict theory

One highly revered theory of aggression and intergroup conflict is based on competition. **Realistic group conflict theory** states that when two human groups are competing for the same desirable resources, conflict almost inevitably ensues. Thus, it would be hard to find a theory that better supports the role of competition in aggression. Social psychologist Muzafer Sherif (1958) showed this by staging small competitions between groups of boys enrolled in his summer camps in Robbers Cave, Oklahoma. Competition between the "Rattlers" and the "Eagles" quickly escalated into tension, distrust, thievery, and assault. After turning these previously peaceful boys into hateful child warriors, Sherif tried making peace between the two groups. His attempted solutions ranged from thoughtful sermons about brotherly love to identifying a common enemy (campers from a nearby camp). The only solution that worked was to require the boys to work together as a single, unitary group. They did so to solve important everyday camp problems, many of which resembled survival problems. It took all the boys working together, for example, to solve a water supply problem and to revive a truck with a dead battery.

Sherif noted that the key to reducing intergroup conflict was the creation of **superordinate goals**. Enacting superordinate goals means that two previously feuding groups must cooperate rather than compete to achieve a joint goal. Just as competition often breeds contempt, cooperation can often undo it. As noted earlier in this chapter, if you observe almost any social species, you will almost invariably observe a great deal of within-group cooperation combined with a great deal of outgroup competition and aggression (Wilson, 1975). In fact, in social species as diverse as ants and chimpanzees, incidental contact between two nearby groups can lead to collective behavior that strongly resembles human warfare. In contrast, within a social group, whether colony or troop, ants and chimpanzees work closely together to do things no single ant or chimpanzee could ever do alone.

The basic idea of realistic group conflict theory is highly consistent with the evolutionary perspective I have offered here. In addition to building on the basic idea of competition, realistic group conflict theory is also built loosely on the idea of status-seeking. People are inherently concerned with status both *within* and *between* groups, and we strongly prefer our own groups over others. Setting up competition between two groups that guaranteed that one group would gain desirable resources at the expense of the other was an excellent recipe for intergroup aggression. Sherif was thus able to manipulate both the need for status and the benefits of aggressing against another group in ways that virtually guaranteed that the Rattlers and the Eagles would come to hate each other. It is no accident that Sherif studied boys rather than girls, for example. He also created feelings of territoriality in these boys by giving them a sense that certain parts of the camp belonged to them, before seeing the boys from a different group "invade" their space. It was only when Sherif merged the two groups of boys into a single, psychologically united group that he was able to stamp out the distrust and aggression that he had so easily ignited.

Frustration and aggression

One of the oldest theories of human aggression is referred to as the **frustration–aggression hypothesis** (Dollard et al., 1939). The original version of this idea assumed, somewhat simplistically, that frustration always leads to aggression. That simply has not proven to be true. On the other hand, Berkowitz (1989, 1990) developed a more realistic version of the hypothesis that suggests that frustration often leads to anger, which does often lead to aggression. Frustration may be a powerful driver of aggression, then, but people are not robots. You can imagine that a frustrated 10-year-old might tell a lie about her brother or even pull her sister's hair (especially if the sibling in question is the reason she is frustrated). But she is unlikely to try to punch out her father or join Isis. Research suggests that frustration can lead to aggression, especially if people believe that the person in question intentionally caused their unhappy state of affairs. Dill and Anderson (1995) tested the frustration–aggression hypothesis by motivating participants to learn to make an origami (paper) sculpture. The experimenter served as the origami instructor, and he either took his time so that anyone could follow his careful instructions, or worked and talked so quickly that it was impossible for participants to succeed at the origami task. In the condition of the experiment that was surely the most frustrating, a (fake) fellow participant politely asked the experimenter to slow down, and the experimenter responded: "I would like to hurry and get this over with. My girlfriend is coming soon to pick me up and I don't want to make her wait."

When the frustrated participants had a chance to make critical ratings of their origami instructor (which they knew would be seen by his supervisor), they seem to have been pretty bent out of shape. Compared with a group who had not been frustrated by the teacher, they gave him more negative ability ratings and assigned him a much lower grade for his teaching skills. Further, although participants seemed reluctant to admit in writing that they were frustrated or wanted to hurt anyone, analyses showed that across all conditions of the experiment, the more frustrated people said they felt, the more harshly they graded the experimenter ($r = 0.40$). Despite the strong intuitive appeal of the frustration–aggression hypothesis, there are plenty of times that frustration leads to non-aggressive responses. In keeping with Berkowitz's reformulation, one reason for this seems to be that frustration does not always lead to the anger that is more directly linked to aggressive behavior. On the other hand, lots of research, on both people and animals, shows that directly causing pain, anger, or discomfort does usually seem to make those who have just been hurt more aggressive than usual. As noted previously, Azrin et al. (1968) found that animals who receive a painful electric shock often attack anyone or anything that is handy. I have observed the same phenomenon pretty often in preschoolers and CEOs.

Research on frustration and aggression is highly consistent with the basic idea of the mammalian fight-or-flight response to threat. Those who frustrate the unwitting participants in research on frustration and aggression always have little or no meaningful power over those who are frustrated. If obnoxious origami instructors had the ability to kill, or even fire, those who failed to whip their papers into shape, for example, you can be pretty sure that frustration would have led to fear and appeasement rather than aggression in these classic studies. On the other hand, in my view, one of the clearest lessons to be taken from laboratory research on frustration and aggression is that even the kind of small, temporary frustrations that can be ethically created in the lab can readily lead to meaningful forms of aggression.

Heat

One painful experience that is a cousin of frustration has been linked closely to aggression in people. In particular, making people uncomfortably hot seems to be a very reliable way to get them to want to hurt others. "Hot under the collar" may be more than just a metaphor. In a classic field study, Kenrick and MacFarlane (1986) found that on hotter days, drivers in Arizona were especially likely to honk their horns at another driver who was taking too long to get going at a green light. This effect was particularly large for drivers who had their windows rolled down (and who presumably were not enjoying the benefits of air conditioning). Plenty of lab experiments, too, have shown that hot temperatures increase both aggression and the aggressive thoughts and feelings that often precede it.

Some of the best evidence that heat causes aggression comes from the world of professional baseball. Reifman et al. (1991) analyzed 862 major league baseball games. The hotter the weather was, the more likely pitchers were to hit batters on the opposing team with "beanballs" (balls thrown deliberately to hit a batter). If you are wondering if heat makes pitchers more aggressive or just makes them less accurate, the answer is clear. On hotter days, pitchers actually walked batters a little less often than on cooler days, and they threw slightly fewer wild pitches. So heat doesn't mess up a pitcher's aim. It just messes with what they are aiming for. Remember the archival study of how baseball pitchers from the southeastern U.S. seem to follow the rules of the culture of honor? This same archival study of more than 57,000 baseball games also showed that pitchers hit batters with "beanballs" more often when it was hotter (Larrick et al., 2014). This was particularly true when it was hot *and* when it was "payback time" – that is, when a pitcher from the opposing team had hit one of their own teammates in the same game. Heat can, by itself, be enough to make people boil over. But heat becomes more dangerous than usual when the **norm of reciprocity** gives it a little extra nudge. It's also worth adding that temperature doesn't increase all kinds of aggressive behavior. It only increases hostile (angry) aggression. In hot weather, rates of assault go up, but bank robberies do not (see Geen, 1998). "Yeah, Richie, I know I promised to rob First National with you today, but it's just too darn hot out! Can I give you a rain check?"

Reciprocity

As a child, I cannot remember many days when my older (and stronger) brother and I did not get into some kind of physical fight. Further, I sometimes claim, only half-jokingly, that the thing I said most often to my mother when I was a child was "He started it!" There can be no doubt that violence begets violence. Israelis and Palestinians have been fighting for a very long time, and each side has often argued that they are merely retaliating for the aggressive actions of the other group. According to Dallas Chief of Police David O. Brown, the killer who took the lives of five Dallas police officers on July 7, 2016 seems to have been engaging in "payback" for the actions of officers in highly publicized killings of young black men all over the U.S.

Summarizing a great deal of research on aggression, Anderson and Bushman (2002, p. 37) argued: "Perhaps the most important single cause of human aggression is interpersonal provocation ... Provocations include insults, slights, other forms of verbal aggression, physical aggression, interference with one's attempts to attain an important goal, and so on." In principle, most of us probably agree with the idea that "an eye for an eye makes the whole world blind." But, in the heat of the moment, many people want revenge. The human desire for justice and fairness is a two-sided sword. As we will see in Chapter 9, for example, the principle of reciprocity dictates that people feel strongly compelled to pay back favors from others. But the same principle ("Do unto others as they have done unto you") often leads people to pay back violence with violence. Breaking cycles of violence between people who have traded injuries with one another in the past is thus one of the biggest challenges in the social sciences. As I suggested in my analysis of the culture of honor, many aggressive acts of reciprocity appear highly irrational from a strict cost–benefit perspective. From the perspective of those who are paying back a perceived wrong, however, the kind of account balance that matters has more to do with justice than economics. Especially in honor cultures, perceived attacks often kick in automatic fight responses that do not obey economic rules.

Modeling

Perhaps the least controversial theory of aggression in psychology is the idea that we often copy aggressive behavior when we have observed other people engage in it. In fact, the only controversy about this robust finding is what we should call it. The idea of copycat aggression has been dubbed **modeling, social learning, emulative violence,** and **vicarious learning.** Because Albert Bandura is the best known advocate of this theory, and because he usually calls copycat violence "modeling," I will use that term here. Please note, however, that terms like "modeling" and "social learning" apply to all kinds of behavior rather than just aggressive behavior. One of the best ways to reduce aggressive behavior, then, is to model prosocial behavior (being nice) especially as a response to provocation.

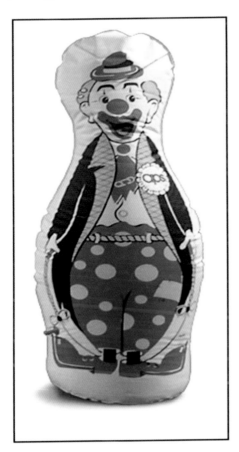

In a classic study of modeling, Bandura et al. (1961) studied some normally delightful little kids at a Stanford nursery school. The children were *all* frustrated, by the way, by being shown some really cool toys and then being told that they could not play with them. Bandura knew very well that frustration could set the stage for aggression. But he also felt that whether frustrated kids behaved aggressively might be heavily influenced by what kind of behavior they had just observed in an adult model. In a control condition, kids who had just been frustrated observed an adult who did not model any kind of aggressive behavior. In an aggressive model condition, however, the frustrated kids watched a video of an adult woman smacking down an inflatable pop-up Bobo doll, much like the one shown in Figure 8.12. In addition to pummeling poor Bobo with a hammer, the woman threw him up in the air, kicked him forcefully, and yelled things like "Sock him in the nose!"

Figure 8.12 *A modern replica of Bandura's Bobo doll.*

By clicking on this link (www.youtube.com/watch?v=dmBqwWlJg8U), you can see a video segment of a boy who not only copied some of the exact behaviors of the aggressive model but also came up with some of his own creative ways to beat up poor Bobo. The aggressive boy was not alone. In Bandura et al.'s (1961) classic experiment, frustrated kids who observed the aggressive model were much more likely than frustrated kids who had not observed an aggressive model to engage in a wide variety of aggressive behaviors.

Is there any evidence that the human tendency to engage in modeling evolved? Evolutionary psychologists certainly think so. They have pointed out, for example, that the tendency to copy the behavior of others emerges at a very young age and is extremely pervasive. Further, Nielsen et al. (2012) have shown that children often engage in what they call "overimitation." Many times, children dutifully copy arbitrary, even highly inefficient, aspects of a modeled behavior, rather than extracting the gist of a good idea and running with it in a more efficient fashion. You surely recall that monkeys engage in modeling. In most animals, however, the tendency to model obeys the basic laws of reinforcement. Recall that monkeys who see another monkey make the wrong choice in a monkey game show usually make the opposite choice. In so doing, they obtain a reward much more quickly than they could via trial-and-error learning. Rats are also good modelers. An otherwise highly curious rat who sees another rat burn her whiskers on a candle usually steers clear of the same candle (Bunch & Zentall, 1980).

Unlike rats and monkeys, both children and adults sometimes copy some pretty ludicrous behaviors. In fact, people sometimes copy behaviors that are strongly punished. In dozens of archival studies of copycat homicide and suicide, Phillips and Carstensen (1986) have shown that when a homicide or a suicide gets a great deal of media attention, homicide and suicide rates increase in the wake of all the media coverage. In fact, the more media coverage a violent event receives in a specific area, the greater the increase in copycat violence (aka modeling) in that specific area. Phillips and Carstensen also found that people are especially likely to copy a homicide or suicide when they resemble the model. In response to Marilyn Monroe's famous suicide, for example, there was a greater increase in suicide rates among young women than among middle-aged men. Copycat violence is most surprising in the case of suicide, of course, because it is harder to imagine a more punishing outcome than death. Just as we seem to be predisposed to pick up language, and to be overly concerned with fairness, we also seem to be strongly predisposed to copy. As I will suggest in Chapter 9, if you had to program an inexperienced social organism to do just one thing, it wouldn't be a bad idea to program the organism to copy its leaders or caregivers.

WE'RE BECOMING LESS VIOLENT: PINKER'S "BETTER ANGELS"

We're getting nicer

After documenting the many reasons why we human beings hurt one another and the creativity and doggedness with which we sometimes do it, I would like to end this chapter with some good news. As I noted in my discussion of the evolution of fighting ability, we appear to live in a much less violent world than at any other time in human history. Daly and Wilson (1988b) made this point many years ago, but Steven Pinker (2011) recently echoed the point in clever ways that leave little doubt that human beings today are much less aggressive than human beings of yesteryear. As Pinker noted, all you have to do to see how aggressive people used to be is to read the Old Testament, or pick up an original version of the fairy tales that parents told their children in the 1800s. Here is an example, from I Chronicles 3:20, recounting what David did to the people of Ammon, whom the Israelites had presumably overthrown: "And he [David] brought out the people that were in it and cut them with saws, and with harrows of iron, and with axes. Even so dealt David with all the cities of the children of Ammon." Likewise, after Joshua toppled the walls of Jericho we learn that: "Then they devoted all in the city to destruction, both men and women, young and old, oxen, sheep and donkeys with the edge of the sword" (Joshua 6:21). It is hard to read the Old Testament without getting the feeling that the authors had a very cavalier attitude about ethnic cleansing. As Pinker notes, there is a good chance that some of these atrocities never really occurred, but the fact that the moral leaders of an ancient generation felt these were reasonable stories speaks volumes about ancient attitudes about violence. There are lots of equally macabre examples of violence in the fairy tales parents used to tell their children. In one old version of Rumpelstiltskin, Rumpelstiltskin becomes so angry when the queen learns his name, and prevents him from taking her child, that he physically rips himself in half. In old versions of Little Red Riding Hood and Goldilocks, the price children pay for not following the rules is being eaten by a wolf or a family of bears. (There are no heroic woodcutters to save the day.)

In addition to offering many bloody and compelling anecdotes, Pinker (2011) also pulled together an ocean of objective evidence that violence has declined, no matter what definition of aggression one prefers. In so doing, Pinker showed that, with very few exceptions, most of us are lucky enough to live in a modern world with levels of violence that are much, much lower than they used to be. This is true whether violence is defined in terms of homicide rates, forms of punishment for criminal violations, the frequency of punitive parenting practices, rates of harming animals while making motion pictures, killing others in warfare, or abortion. Pick your poison, and you'll see that the world has been getting less poisonous. Further, this is true whether you compare us with those who lived 100,000 years ago, 1,000 years ago or even 100 years ago. In fact, the further back we go in human history, the more violent we used to be. The good old days would be more aptly named the gory old days.

Why are we getting nicer?

Pinker (2011) astutely argues that the reasons why we have become less violent over the centuries must be largely cultural. From an evolutionary perspective, there simply has not been enough time for us to evolve in a kinder, gentler direction. Pinker identifies five distinct reasons why "the **better angels** of our nature" have largely won out over our more aggressive impulses in modern times. The first is that in most modern cultures, violence is less often rewarded than it used to be. Now that most nations have well-developed police forces, for example, it is much harder than it used to be to get away with murder. From fingerprint evidence to DNA analysis and the ubiquity of smartphone videos, it is simply a lot harder to kill or hurt another person without detection today than it was in the past. I hope it is clear that this point is highly consistent with a cost–benefit analysis of aggression.

Pinker (2011) also argues that technological developments such as the dramatically increased ease of travel and internet access are shrinking the once narrow definition of "we." It would have been almost unheard of 400 years ago for anyone to conceptualize him- or herself as an Asian or Asian American. Back in the 1600s, your identity would have been something more like the "eldest son of the Kim family who lives by the three great oaks." Sherif's idea that superordinate group membership can reduce aggression is highly consistent with this logic. If you and I both are dog lovers, or fellow members of the European Union, rather than Northern and Southern Irishmen, then we are a lot less likely to fight. As the world shrinks and people cooperate more across ancient group boundaries, we become less interested in harming each other. Pinker cites several other important reasons why we hurt each other a lot less often than we once did. Perhaps the most interesting is that feminization (the growth of female voices in daily life) has led to a cultural sea change as more and more women have gained social and political power. When only men could vote, for example, you can be sure that the voices of women – who lobby for peace and cooperation more often than men do – were heard only faintly, if at all.

Pinker (2011) also notes that technological and scientific developments over the past few centuries, especially the past few decades, have radically changed the ways in which the average person thinks. Compared with our great-grandparents, for example, we are exposed today to a much wider range of worldviews. Settlers on the American prairie in the 1800s didn't read the *New Yorker* or watch documentaries about life in Sweden or Papua New Guinea. Finally, the same kind of technological and scientific developments that fostered a more multicultural view of the world have also fostered an unprecedented appreciation of reason. Today, liberals and conservatives may debate the best solution to modern housing problems, but we no longer place people under house arrest for arguing that the earth orbits the sun. As science and reason have proven their practical utility, we have come to place more faith in them – and less faith in violence and superstition.

CONCLUSIONS

In this chapter I've summarized some basic evolutionary principles that have powerful implications for human aggression. I hope it's clear that understanding how aggression evolved could reduce human suffering – by helping us engineer schools and homes that encourage less aggression and more cooperation. If we agree that social inequality contributes to human aggression, for example, we must consider the fairest and most sensible ways of reducing it. Likewise, if we realize that boys and men have evolved to be more physically aggressive than girls and women, this does not require us to throw up our hands at male violence. Instead, we could carefully consider Pinker's list of reasons why human beings have recently become less violent and apply his ideas to the socialization of our children. It's possible there would be drawbacks as well as advantages of any such efforts, but in my view we must be willing to take such risks if we wish to see murder rates continue to drop. Thomas Jefferson would have surely agreed that we must sometimes be willing to change longstanding traditions. When asked, in 1816, if the Virginia Constitution should be revised, Jefferson first noted that it is risky to revise laws or constitutions. But he quickly added that:

> laws and institutions must go hand in hand with the progress of the human mind. As that becomes more developed, more enlightened, as new discoveries are made, new truths disclosed, and manners and opinions change with the change of circumstances, institutions must advance also, and keep pace with the times. We might as well require a man to wear still the coat which fitted him when a boy, as civilized society to remain ever under the regimen of their barbarous ancestors. (letter to Samuel Kercheval, July 12, 1816)

Because stories about death, dismemberment, and destruction get so much media attention, many Americans believe that we live in a time where aggression is on the rise. As Pinker (2011) argued in great detail, this is simply a myth. America today – like much of the rest of the world – is a much safer and less violent place than it ever was in the past. Thankfully, we are hurting each other much less these days than ever before in human history. Let's hope that if your great-grandchildren ever take a course in evolutionary psychology, they will learn that the robust historical trend for human violence to decline has continued unabated.

FOR FURTHER READING

» Anderson, C.A. & Bushman, B.J. (2002). Human aggression. *Annual Review of Psychology*, 53(1), 27–51.

» Pinker, S. (2011). *The better angels of our nature: Why violence has declined.* London: Penguin Books.

» Sapolsky, R.M. (2005). The influence of social hierarchy on primate health. *Science*, 308(5722), 648–52.

SAMPLE MULTIPLE-CHOICE EXAM QUESTIONS

Here are four sample quiz questions for Chapter 8. You can find the Chapter 8 quiz at: www.macmillanihe.com/evolutionary-psychology

8.01. According to the classic definition of aggression provided by Berkowitz, which of the following qualifies as an example of aggression?

   a. taking out one's frustration by repeatedly hitting a punching bag at the gym

b. spreading a false and nasty rumor about a person who is running against you for school president

c. practicing wrestling moves with your younger brother to help him qualify for the varsity wrestling team

d. A–C all fit Berkowitz's classic definition

8.02.   Your textbook discriminates between three very basic forms of aggression. Which of the three forms is most common when it comes to within-species aggression (e.g., wolf on wolf aggression)?

a. self-defense

b. hierarchical aggression

c. competition

8.03.   In most animals that fight for feeding or mating rights, fights only tend to occur among two animals that have roughly the same fighting ability. A very low ranking male, for example, almost never challenges an alpha male. This tendency to fight only when one has a decent chance of winning can be explained by:

a. the cost-benefit rule

b. predator-prey transition theory

c. social dominance theory

8.04.   Male and female gibbons are almost exactly the same size. What does this imply about the likelihood of mate hoarding in gibbons?

a. it should be common

b. it should be rare

c. it is impossible to predict without knowing about sexual selection pressures in gibbons

Answer Key: b, c, a, b.

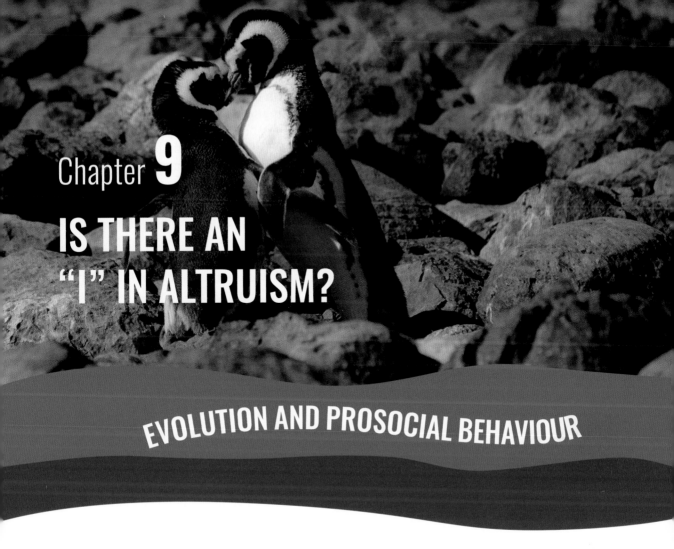

Chapter 9

IS THERE AN "I" IN ALTRUISM?

EVOLUTION AND PROSOCIAL BEHAVIOUR

"A man was going down from Jerusalem to Jericho, when he was attacked by robbers … leaving him half dead. A priest [happened by], and when he saw the man, he passed by on the other side. So too, a Levite, when he came to the place and saw him, passed by on the other side. But a Samaritan, as he traveled, came where the man was; and when he saw him, he took pity on him. He went to him and bandaged his wounds, pouring on oil and wine. Then he put the man on his own donkey, brought him to an inn and took care of him. The next day he took out two denarii and gave them to the innkeeper. 'Look after him,' he said, 'and when I return, I will reimburse you for any extra expense you may have.'"

— *Luke 10: 30–35, NIV*

About 20 years ago, my boss Will sent me on a free five-day vacation to Hawaii. Well, sort of. I had to work for two of the five days, but in addition to paying me well for the work, Will paid all my expenses for five full days. This included the cost of bringing my dear friend Joanne. ("Dear friend Joanne" sounds a lot better than "my wife at the time," doesn't it? Yeah, let's go with that.) It was a sweet deal, especially for Joanne. On the days when I was working, she hung out on a gorgeous beach – slowly sipping Mai Tais. On the days when I wasn't working, she hung out on a gorgeous beach – slowly sipping Mai Tais. On my days off, I, too, had my share of Mai Tais in the evenings. But I spent my mornings hiking and kayaking, both of which were her idea of that place that's the opposite of a tropical paradise – and much, much hotter.

I came to agree with her about the kayaking part. On my second kayaking trip, I had only been out a few minutes when a wave the size of Kansas City took me out. The huge wave was followed by several others, and I was positive I was going to drown. I had lost my kayak after that first hit, and although I frantically searched for it whenever I came up for air, I was unable to find it. Did I mention that I am a really horrible swimmer? To make matters worse, I'd been pulled into a sharp coral reef, which roughed me up quite a bit until I escaped that additional danger. I couldn't have been more than a few hundred meters out, but I was unsure of whether I could swim back, given the conditions. At one point, I saw a couple on a jet ski – who'd obviously been spared by the waves. I wasn't shy about asking for help: "I'm drowning!" I yelled. I wasn't *sure* I was drowning *at that moment*, but I wasn't taking any chances. "He's got a life jacket. He'll be OK," I heard the driver say. They sped away, presumably anxious to get back to their jobs serving Mai Tais to my dear friend Joanne. Eventually, a teenage girl on a kayak made her way to me. She said she had seen part of what had happened, and had come out as soon as she felt it was safe. She had towed an empty kayak behind her, and she offered it to me. I gladly accepted it, awkwardly boarded it in the rough water, and paddled back to shore. I've never been so glad to be on dry land.

Both Will's generous decision to send me to Hawaii and the unnamed teenager's generous rescue mission qualify as examples of prosocial behavior. If the teenager had gone further and had sacrificed her own life to save mine, this evolutionarily puzzling behavior, too, would have qualified as prosocial behavior. **Prosocial behavior** is simply behavior that benefits another person, period. But within that broad category of good deeds, researchers make some important distinctions. Almost everyone agrees that the most interesting distinction is called altruism. Altruism refers to the noblest category of good deeds. To paraphrase experts such as Daniel Batson (2008), **altruism** is prosocial behavior that is also voluntary, costly to the doer, and performed without expecting any reward. Whereas Will's generous offer to pay for my trip was prosocial behavior, he also turned a profit from my work. In contrast, I believe the young kayaker's behavior qualified as true altruism. No one forced her to help me, there was a serious risk to her of so doing, and she seems to have expected nothing at all in return for her good deed. I hope you see the difference. Prosocial behaviors happen constantly. They're often a dime a dozen. They deserve something like a heartfelt thank you. Altruism is the crown jewel of helping. It deserves something more like a Purple Heart.

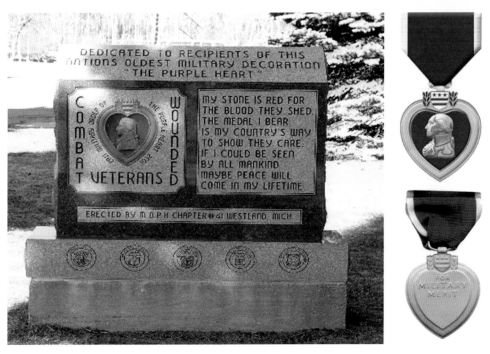

Figure 9.1 *Like my grandfather, J.L. Johnson, anyone wounded or killed while serving in the U.S. military receives the Purple Heart. Since 1917, 1.9 million Americans have earned it. Fully 100% of those I've interviewed said they'd prefer to receive the "wounded" rather than the "killed" version. After all, the two versions of the medal look exactly alike. What you see to the right are merely the front and back sides of the same medal.*

Of course, there are examples of altruism that are more dramatic than the unselfish behavior of the kayaker. People dive into freezing bodies of water or dash into burning buildings hoping to save others, and some would-be heroes never make it out alive. If evolution is all about the success of genes that promote survival, how could any gene ever survive if it promoted self-sacrifice? You saw one answer to this question in Chapter 1 when we discussed male redback spiders. Their seemingly crazy behavior isn't so crazy after all when you consider their dismal future prospects for mating and the fact that their self-sacrifice creates more baby spiders. But no one runs into a burning building to father a few extra children before being burned alive. You also gained some perspective on altruism when we discussed Hamilton's rule in Chapter 3. But Hamilton's rule applies to genetic relatives. Further, when mothers save their own children from burning buildings, this is admirable, but it's not a big challenge to the idea of selective fitness. Something different must be at work when people risk their lives to help total strangers. This chapter is largely about what that something different might be. The question of whether there is any such thing as true altruism is so tricky, in fact, that researchers have identified different kinds of altruism. Before we address the question of the kayaker's apparent act of altruism, we'll need to discriminate it from a couple of less controversial forms of altruism.

BLOOD IS THICKER THAN FACEBOOK FRIENDS: KIN SELECTION

Richard Dawkins weighed in heavily on the issue of true altruism in his classic book *The selfish gene* (1976). Dawkins was not a big believer in a genetic basis for the specific kind of true altruism illustrated by the kayaker. Dawkins firmly believed that the "selfish gene" is the primary unit of evolution. Individual organisms never survive for very long in the grand scheme of things, but genes that strongly promote survival can be practically immortal. Dawkins was quick to concede that certain kinds of altruism make perfect evolutionary sense. In particular, **kin selection** is a great example of altruistic behavior that can prove to be highly adaptive. Kin selection refers to costly helping behavior directed at one of your genetic relatives (Hamilton, 1964a, 1964b; Trivers, 1971). The more closely related you are, the more it is the case that helping the relative is practically like helping yourself. So, if a gene or set of genes nudges me toward helping a close relative, with whom I share many genes, that gene has a good chance of surviving. As E.O. Wilson pointed out (1975), a quirky sex assignment system called haplodiploidy in ants means that female worker ants don't just share half their genes (as human siblings do). Instead, they can share three-quarters of their genes. So if I am a typical female worker ant, saving four of my sisters is like saving three copies of my own genes. Although experts have recently raised some very tough questions about whether haplodiploidy really cranks up kin selection (Gadagkar, 2010), it seems evolutionarily unremarkable that animals, human and otherwise, are more helpful to blood relatives than to perfect strangers. Few people debate this.

We don't have to limit ourselves to the social insects to find dramatic examples of kin selection. They're staring us in the face every time we look at our own, well-cared-for children. Here's how Richard Dawkins (1976, p. 139) put it:

> The truth is that all examples of child protection and parental care, and all associated bodily organs, milk secreting glands, kangaroo pouches, and so on, are examples of the working in nature of the kin-selection principle. The critics are of course familiar with the widespread existence of parental care, but they fail to understand that parental care is no less an example of kin selection than brother/sister altruism.

Many cases of altruistic behavior in animals prove to be examples of kin selection, and there's no doubt that kin selection also applies to people. Remember the red squirrels who became adoptive moms? They provided support for Hamilton's rule by adopting orphaned squirrels – but only one at a time, and only when it was a pretty close genetic relative. If you're not sure if kin selection would apply to you, consider a classic philosophical problem known as the **trolley problem** (Foot, 1967). Here's a version of the problem. A maniac has tied five strangers to a trolley track, and the poor engineer who is driving the trolley is oblivious to this. You can change the trolley's path at the last minute and save the five people by pulling a switch. However, there's a single stranger tied to the alternate track, and you would have to kill him to save the other five. Would you pull the switch? In this particular version of the trolley problem, many people say they would, however reluctantly, pull the switch.

But let's switch things up a bit. Imagine that the one person you'd have to sacrifice to save five strangers was your cousin. When I posed this question to one of my closest friends, his answer was: "Which cousin? I've got a whole bunch of 'em." I replied: "OK, let's switch to your kids. Would you sacrifice the life of one of your own children to save five complete strangers?" His answer? "Which kid? I love them all the same, but as you know, I like some of them a lot more than I like others." I didn't give up: "What about your grandson?" His reply was instantaneous: "No, I could never do that to my own grandson." I hope this story illustrates three things. First, it's hard to get a straight answer out of my friend, unless the topic is grandchildren. Second, most people are more reluctant to harm a close genetic relative, even if it is for the greater good of humanity, than they are to harm a complete stranger. Third, people are more reluctant to harm young people with whom they share genes – sometimes even if it is fewer shared genes – than to harm older people with whom they share genes.

Let's make it personal and keep it simple. *The Titanic* is sinking. The water is freezing. If you could only send your mother or your daughter to the lifeboat, who would it be? They both share half your genes, but only your daughter is likely to put any more of your genes into the gene pool. Consistent with your likely decision to save your daughter, a series of trolley studies conducted by Bleske-Rechek et al. (2010) showed that people were about three times as likely to say they'd sacrifice a 70-year-old adult with whom they shared a quarter of their genes (e.g., an aunt) than to say they'd sacrifice a 2-year-old with whom they shared a quarter of their genes (e.g., a niece). If Darwin were still around today, and if he were your cousin, he'd completely understand why you were willing to throw an old guy like himself under the bus (or out of the lifeboat). He's unlikely to add any of your shared genes to the gene pool. Perhaps the only person who would support you more strongly in your decision to save more "offspring equivalents" would be William Hamilton, who came up with Hamilton's rule.

Of course, this chapter is mainly about who you'd gleefully help rather than who you'd begrudgingly hurt. But I hope it's clear that hurting and helping are often two sides of the same coin (Krebs & Miller, 1985). Kin selection should play a powerful role in both. Remember the distressing stepparent studies? One way to look at them is that biological relatedness is a protective factor against harming a child. The grandparent studies are even more obviously relevant to kin selection. Recall that the grandparents who can be most confident they share a quarter of their genes with you are, on average, more likely to help you. And you're likely to reciprocate by telling them how much you love them. Many people say they would throw themselves in front of the trolley in a heartbeat to save one of their own children. Hamilton would say that you should only do so to save two or three of them – unless you're sure you're done having kids, and you have a pretty decent life insurance policy.

IT'S PAYBACK TIME: RECIPROCAL ALTRUISM

In addition to kin selection, there's a second evolutionarily plausible way in which true altruism can happen. Unlike the first way, though, this second way is almost certainly limited to highly social species. There are a few species of social mammals who figuratively seem to borrow – and then later repay – cups of sugar from their neighbors. This give-and-take process is known as **reciprocal altruism**, which is prosocial behavior directed at another animal with the consequence that this animal repays the favor in the future. The part about the future is pretty important. Scratching my back while I scratch yours is what researchers such as Brosnan and de Waal (2002) call **mutualism**, and it's not quite as impressive as reciprocal altruism. For one thing, mutualism doesn't require any kind of mental scorekeeping. For another, it usually poses little risk (little reduction in selective fitness) to either party. Having sex is supposed to feel good to both parties involved. At least that's what my wife keeps telling me. We don't need the concept of altruism to explain mutualism any more than we need it to explain masturbation.

But we do need it to explain certain kinds of regurgitation. A study of **vampire bats** by DeNault and McFarlane (1995) showed that vampire bats often share food with one another, by regurgitating a portion of a night's blood meal to an unfortunate cave-mate who had no luck finding blood that night. Because vampire bats can only go two or three days without food before starving, genes that promote reciprocal altruism in vampire bats are not just advantageous; they might be a necessity. But is blood sharing among vampire bats really a form of reciprocal altruism? Maybe bats only share blood with blood relatives, which would qualify as a nice example of kin selection but not as an example of reciprocal altruism. One reason to wonder whether vampire bats can really engage in reciprocal altruism is that they are not exactly the sharpest tools in the shed (or in the cave next to it). Many primates seem well qualified to engage in reciprocal altruism because they are great at keeping track of who has done what to whom, and in what frequency. Can vampire bats keep track of past favors – at all?

Apparently they can. In a two-year study of a large colony of vampire bats, Gerald Carter and Gerald Wilkinson (2013) went to great lengths to make some of the bats hungry on some nights. They then compared the effects of several important predictors of food sharing – by conducting the mother of all bat studies to see exactly why bats seem to mother each other. Because they did some genetic testing, they could tell, for example, if bats only shared food with close genetic relatives. Because they knew the sex of every bat in the colony, they could see if female bats were more generous than males. The strongest predictor of whether a potential donor shared blood with a hungry potential recipient was how much blood the current potential recipient had given in the past to the current potential donor. So, if a vampire bat ever asks you for a loan, go ahead and give her the money. She's good for it.

There were several other interesting predictors of blood sharing. One of these was that, on average, female bats were more generous than male bats. In fact, male bats never gave blood to other male bats. They did give blood to female bats, but female bats gave blood to both sexes. So donor sex also mattered. Perhaps some genes for maternal care predispose female bats toward generosity. If this is so, some male bats may routinely take advantage of this fact. This being said, even a mother's generosity wasn't always a one-way street. Mother bats were highly generous to their juvenile and nearly-adult offspring (if the offspring were any younger, mom was freely giving them milk rather than blood). But when the mothers were hungry, these older children freely shared food with their mothers. "Honor your father and mother and love your neighbor as yourself." Vampire bats seem to have paid attention pretty well in Sunday school.

There were three other findings that might increase your admiration – or at least reduce your disgust – for vampire bats. First, they seem to have kept track of long-term giving rather than just what happened yesterday. I don't think the bats were keeping any written receipts, but they were more sensitive to the total food a specific bat had shared with them over a long window than to whether the bat had shared food the night before. Second, there was also a modest effect of genetic relatedness (bats did give a bit more food to siblings than to cousins, for example). But the big reciprocal altruism effect I already noted was dramatically larger than this modest kin selection effect. Third, there were actually two forms of reciprocity at work in the bat colony. Bats not only gave blood to those who had given them blood in the past but also gave blood to those who had groomed them in the past. Unconsciously, of course, the bats were somehow acting as members of an informal bat economy. Like your neighbor who gladly gave you a ride to the supermarket yesterday, knowing that you had loaned her your lawn mower back in July, these vampire bats seem to have exchanged one kind of important favor for another.

Reciprocal altruism and the importance of fairness

It now seems clear that vampire bats engage in a pretty sophisticated form of reciprocal altruism. To me, what's so impressive about reciprocal altruism is that it implies that organisms other than people might have a basic sense of fairness. I doubt that vampire bats have judicial systems, but they certainly behave as if they have some kind of instinctive sense of fairness. How far does a basic sense of fairness go in animals other than people? Sarah Brosnan and Frans de Waal (2003) showed that in female capuchins ("organ grinder monkeys"), fairness is a very big deal. Like any other monkeys, capuchins have little trouble learning a token economy. As long as they're hungry, they will gladly offer little rocks or trinkets to a seemingly gullible experimenter in exchange for food. I give you a useless little rock, you give me a slice of fresh cucumber. Nice doing business with you. This is nothing new. Capuchins will do this until they're stuffed.

But as de Waal has put it in talks and interviews, this token economy begins to look more like a Wall Street protest when the exchange rate becomes patently unfair. All you have to do to see what happens when capuchins get mad is to play this exchange game with two capuchins at once. If you always reward one capuchin with the usual piece of cucumber but always reward the other capuchin with a grape, the cucumber recipient usually gets pretty angry. And she refuses to accept what otherwise would have felt like a sweet deal. Often, the shortchanged capuchins refuse to hand over the token. About as often, they hand over the token and even take the cucumber – but then angrily throw the cucumber back. In a video demonstration of this finding de Waal offered in a TED talk, the shortchanged monkey not only threw the cucumber at the experimenter but shook her cage and banged her hand down in seeming protest. I defy anyone to watch this clip and argue that capuchins have no basic sense of fairness. To see a very angry capuchin, then, just do a quick internet search for "de Waal TED talk."

Reciprocal altruism in other species

Interestingly, most people I've spoken to about altruism have an easier time accepting the fact that monkeys can truly get angry at unfairness than they do accepting the idea that monkeys can truly be fair – or even generous. It's harder to document long-term reciprocal altruism than to document immediate righteous indignation if for no other reason than that it's hard to keep track of exactly what animals do over time. Large-scale studies of reciprocal altruism are a giant pain in the neck, then, even when the bats aren't biting. So there aren't too many of them. Furthermore, it's not always as easy to separate reciprocal altruism from some less sophisticated forms of prosocial behavior, such as subtle forms of mutualism. Finally, those who spend their evenings and weekends thinking about reciprocal altruism sometimes set the bar even higher than I have here. Brosnan and de Waal (2002), for example, make distinctions between three different forms of reciprocal altruism. They astutely note that some forms of reciprocal altruism can be explained by simply hanging out more with those who've been nice to you. Even Carter and Wilkinson (2013) refer to their vampire bat findings as evidence for "reciprocal help" rather than reciprocal altruism per se.

Despite these caveats, it looks like a couple of primate species – and possibly a couple of bird species – engage in some pretty sophisticated versions of reciprocal altruism. Let's stick with primates – if for no other reason than because they stuck with us. As Frans de Waal (1997a) has observed, well-acquainted capuchin monkeys are extremely generous to one another. For this reason, de Waal wanted to see if they would ever engage in reciprocal altruism with each other. In at least a modest way, they do. If you place two of them in adjacent cages, separated by a wire mesh, and you put some delicious apple slices where only one of them could possibly get to them, the lucky winner of the food lottery often makes her way over to the spot where the loser is trying to get closer to the action. The apple lottery winners rarely hand food right over to the losers. After all, these are apple pieces we're talking about. That's practically the crack cocaine of monkey food.

But when the poorly mannered winners drop pieces of apple, they often allow the losers to retrieve and feed on some of these delicious scraps. That doesn't sound as generous as freely sharing blood, but no one said the capuchins were saints. More important, this level of passive sharing among the capuchins fits the predictions of reciprocal altruism. De Waal allowed specific pairs of monkeys to play this apple lottery game on multiple occasions, systematically varying who was the winner. The more food Curtis had passively shared with Simon on one trial, the more food Simon usually shared back with Curtis on a subsequent trial. In case I've been encouraging you to stereotype males as inherently unhelpful, I should also add that in capuchin experiments such as these, it's usually the boys rather than the girls who share more.

As de Waal (1997b) noted, chimps show even more impressive forms of reciprocal altruism. In a study of captive chimpanzees, de Waal kept careful track in the morning of how much time one chimp, say Maxine, spontaneously spent grooming another, say Audrey. In case I haven't clarified this yet, primates love to be groomed. It feels good, and it keeps ticks and other annoying parasites out of your hair. Later in the day, de Waal gave all the Audreys (the chimps who had or had not received a lot of grooming from the Maxines), a delicious bundle of leaves, sometimes with a nice bottle of 2007 Chilean Malbec. The more time Maxine had spent grooming Audrey that morning, the more of the leaves Audrey usually shared with Maxine that afternoon. Furthermore, this generosity wasn't just based on being in a good mood. Well-groomed chimps didn't share more than usual with just anyone – only with the ones that had done the grooming.

Reciprocal altruism and related processes in people

In case most of your friends are people rather than bats, chimps, or capuchin monkeys, you may be wondering about the status of reciprocal altruism in people. There can be no doubt that we keep track of who has helped us in the past, and that we feel compelled to pay back past favors. In fact, the idea of reciprocal altruism – "social exchange" – is so pervasive that it is hard to think of a social science that has not extensively studied it. To select two of my favorites, sociologist George Homans (1958) and social psychologists John Thibaut and Harold Kelley (1959) developed elaborate and influential **social exchange theories**. A core assumption of both versions of social exchange theory is that we keep track of what others have done for us and carefully compare this with what we have done for them. The idea of equitable social exchanges is also a central feature of Cosmides and Tooby's (1997) modern research program on reasoning and cheater detection modules. Caring deeply about being cheated seems to make human beings very good at detecting cheating. Along the same lines, there are very few researchers who study money, marriage, work, or play who do not pay tremendous attention to ideas grounded firmly in reciprocity and social exchange.

Let's consider just two examples. Willer et al. (2012) wanted to see if the tendency to pay back favors is so strong that it would influence people's behavior in a "highly structured group environment … in which reciprocity does not clearly serve individual or group interests." The environment they chose is NBA (National Basketball Association) basketball, and one routine way in which players do favors for one another on the court is referred to as an **assist** – passing the ball to a teammate so he or she can take a high percentage shot. There is nothing irrational whatsoever about earning assists. They help teams win championships, and they make players look good to fans and coaches alike. But the fact that I gave you an assist earlier in the game should not make you more likely than usual to give me an assist later in the same game. On any given play, all offensive players should try to get the ball to the person who happens to be in the best position to take a high percentage shot. But Willer et al. (2012) found that NBA players did pay back assists. Further, they paid them back specifically to the teammate(s) who had given them assists earlier in the game (rather than just "paying it forward" by becoming a more frequent assist-giver). Finally, this tendency to pay back assists was strongest right after a player had just received an assist. Like the tendency to pay back other kinds of favors, the payback of an assist faded with increased time since the last assist was received. People eventually forget who helped them. Perhaps this is why the legendary basketball coach Dean Smith taught his players to point a finger of gratitude to the specific teammate who had just dished out the assist that led to their basket. There's a powerful human tendency to do unto others what they have recently done unto you. Dean Smith wanted to be sure the players, and the fans, did not forget.

As the Dean Smith story suggests, it might not be wholly irrational to pay back favors on the basketball court. Doing so might increase camaraderie or team morale. Being the kind of player who quickly acknowledges a favor might also increase one's clout on the team. However, there is an area of human behavior where paying back favors can only get people into trouble. Perhaps the best indicator of how strongly we are hardwired to pay back favors comes from research on the role of social norms in compliance and persuasion. **Social norms** are powerful but often unspoken rules about how we ought to behave in social situations. The social norm of reciprocity states that when someone does a favor for you, you should try to reciprocate or return the favor. In fact, when someone does you a favor and you can't return the favor, you're bound to feel a bit uncomfortable.

Unscrupulous experts such as salespeople, con artists, and parents often realize the power of this social norm, and they've learned to use it to their own advantage (Cialdini, 1993). Consider sales. Many salespeople know that one of the best ways to get potential customers to buy things they don't need is to do the potential customers a small favor. This compliance technique comes in many flavors. One is the **free sample technique**, which involves giving a consumer a "free" sample of a food, material good, or service – with the goal of getting the person to purchase the real thing. The smiling woman at the mall who offers you a free piece of chicken on a toothpick knows that if you accept the free sample, you'll feel at least a small compulsion to purchase a whole meal – even if your free sample of General Tso's chicken was only so-so. Millions of Americans who spend their free time playing "free" smartphone games are getting outsmarted by marketers who make sure the "free games" come with hidden costs. If you want to play Crossy Road with a more colorful turtle, you can either shell out the 99 cents or watch a lot more of those Magic Piano commercials. They give you a free game, you give them some free time, you play the game, they ask for a little more time. Repeat as necessary.

Finally, the reason that Mazda salesman offered you a bottle of Coke and a hot dog while you were waiting for Lenny to pull the demo model around was not that he was worried about you dying of thirst or hunger before you could sign the deal. Instead, he was doing you a favor. Unless you were thoughtful enough to bring a bottle of water and a candy bar as a gift for the salesman, you were going to feel some pressure to do the salesman a favor as payback. As any compliance expert could tell you, that payback involves Mustangs or pickups more often than it involves mustard or ketchup. We'd never fall for such transparent tricks if we weren't powerfully programmed to feel that we should always pay back favors.

In my view, this imperfectly calibrated, social exchange-based payback system (or should I say *module*) is an important reason why we engage in true altruism, whether that means building houses for Habitat for Humanity or giving blood at a campus blood drive. The same Bob Cialdini who has taught many of us how to save money when buying a car has also taught us how to avoid getting roped into helping – unless we really wanted to help in the first place. The same rules of social exchange that show how salespeople can get us to pay a lot more than we really should also show how more socially conscious change agents can get us to help out a lot more than we otherwise would. Before we examine this idea, though, I need to point out that the powerful social norm of reciprocity has a couple of equally powerful corollaries. One of the most important of these is that we shouldn't agree to do something up front and then back out on the deal when it becomes a little inconvenient. That's cheating – at least that's how it feels. Many social change agents know that's how it feels, and they use this feeling against us.

Let's look at a concrete example. Cialdini et al. (1978) wanted to see if they could convince people to sign up for a 7 a.m. psychology experiment. They strongly suspected that one of the best ways to get people to refuse to sign up for a 7 a.m. experiment was to ask them to sign up for a 7 a.m. experiment. It's just too easy to make an excuse. ("I'd love to help out, but 7 a.m. is when I always drive the orphans to get their much-needed blood transfusions.") So, Cialdini et al. simply asked people to sign up for a psychology experiment. Once most people agreed, the experimenters apologetically sprung the bad news (the clever liars) that there was only one slot remaining, and this slot was – you guessed it – at 7 a.m. But 56% of these participants stood by their agreements and actually showed up for their 7 a.m. appointments. Just thinking about it makes me yawn. In comparison, only 31% of those warned up front about the biorhythmically inconvenient start time agreed to participate. Cialdini et al. dubbed this sneaky compliance technique the **lowball technique**, because that's what car salespeople call it when they make you a wonderful offer – and then apologetically make it a little less wonderful. They know, of course, that once you've agreed to the sweet deal, you'll have a hard time breaking your agreement, even when the deal sours a little. Cialdini et al.'s point is that whether we're deciding on purchasing a new house or agreeing to help a friend move across town, we're reluctant to back out of our initial agreements – even when the cost to us goes up. We often hold up our side of a deal even when the deal becomes pretty one-sided.

In my view, then, a mundane but potent source of altruistic behavior is based on an overgeneralization of an otherwise adaptive social rule. Some altruistic acts (e.g., giving blood) can be byproducts of an otherwise "selfish" adaptation that came about to solve a different problem: "Keep your end of social contracts, so people don't think you're a liar." If you're not convinced that there's a powerful motivation to keep your end of a social bargain, consider a classic study by Norman Anderson. Anderson (1968) was interested in social perception – how we figure out what other people are like. As a starting point, he felt it would be useful to get some baseline ratings of 555 popular trait terms. If you want to understand the calculus of social perception, he assumed, it'd be nice to know the values of all the variables in the equations. If nothing else, Anderson's classic paper helped me become better at complimenting and insulting others. That's because I know which of Anderson's long list of 555 commonly used trait terms are considered the most and least likeable. The six most likeable traits are *sincere, honest, understanding, loyal, truthful*, and *trustworthy*. Are you seeing a pattern? The six least likeable traits are *liar, phony, mean, cruel, dishonest*, and *untruthful*. You'd be lying if you said you still didn't see a pattern. We all love those who do what they say and say what they do. If social exchange were more of an afterthought than an anthem in our species, I feel confident a different set of traits would populate the top and bottom of this huge list. When I was a kid, if I wanted to start a fistfight with my slightly older and much stronger brother, all I had to do was say "liar, liar, pants on fire!" in a serious and accusatory tone. Stacy didn't need Norman Anderson to tell him that breaking one's word leads to dishonor. And I didn't need Norman Anderson to know not to call Stacy a liar unless my mom was in the room (and knew I was telling the truth).

If we wished to use more cynical language, I suppose we could call some forms of altruism a noble form of evolutionary baggage. Returning to the notorious cuckoo birds we discussed in Chapter 3, notice that their scam only works because almost all mother birds engage in an extreme form of kin selection. The beautifully cynical Richard Dawkins (1976, p. 110) referred to this as a "misfiring of the maternal instinct." This is an instinct, he noted, that is normally very adaptive:

> Cuckoos exploit the rule built into bird parents "Be nice to any small bird sitting in the nest which you built." Cuckoos apart, this rule will normally have the desired effect of restricting altruism to immediate kin, because it happens to be a fact that nests are so isolated from each other that the contents of your own nest are almost bound to be your own chicks.

People who trick us into overpaying, or overhelping, based on our overzealous obedience to norms of social reciprocity are a bit like cuckoo birds. They are exploiting a crack in the armor of an otherwise wonderful adaptation. In fact, there is sometimes a turning point in the delicate dance between a salesperson – or even a petitioner for charity – and the target of social influence. This happens when a target suddenly puts on her "cheater detection" cap rather than her "pay back favors" or "keep your word" cap. This is the point when things can quickly go sour, as in "Dude, I agreed to help you move to South *Amherst* – not South America. I'd be fleeing the country, too, if I always lowballed my good friends."

I hope you now know why your aunt Rhonda does so much volunteer work. But the norm of reciprocity still can't explain the behavior of the kayaker who rescued the flailing psychologist. No one promised her a leisurely ocean kayak trip that turned into a rescue effort. She knew exactly what she was doing from the moment she began the rescue effort. So how do we explain the noblest forms of altruism? Why do some people sometimes make big, voluntary sacrifices for strangers who will never be able to pay them back? The key, I believe, involves an overgeneralization of a different highly adaptive social motive. Human beings are inherently social creatures. It is hard for me to overstate how sensitive we are to the needs and wishes of others. Cultures that promote conformity and cooperation reinforce this sensitivity, but it seems likely that we're all programmed from birth not only to care about what others think about us but possibly, if I dare say, to care about others.

THE NEED FOR CONNECTEDNESS AIDS AND ABETS RECIPROCAL ALTRUISM

Let's begin with the easy one – caring about what others think of us. Psychologists call this motivation the **need for connectedness**. Roy Baumeister and Mark Leary (1995) prefer the phrase **need to belong**, but the point is exactly the same. Our deep desire to be connected, both physically and psychologically, to other people begins at birth, and it is only strengthened and refined with development. Consider a few of Baumeister and Leary's points about why the need to belong qualifies as a basic human motive. First, as I just noted, from the moment of birth we are eager to form bonds with others. Remember Harlow's studies of terrycloth moms in Chapter 6? We naturally and unhesitatingly form deep social bonds. Conversely, we are very reluctant to sever social bonds. Sometimes this holds true even when a specific relationship becomes tiresome or abusive. The fact that our need for connectedness begins at birth and shows up in every culture on earth also suggests that this motive is innate rather than learned. The need to belong also functions like other basic needs. Most obviously, the need gets stronger when it goes unmet (e.g., after you've just been rebuffed) and it gets a bit weaker when it has just been satisfied (e.g., after you've just been re-elected).

A couple of dramatic pieces of evidence that the need to belong is truly a need come from studies of the consequences of social deprivation. As Harlow noted, monkeys who are reared in complete social isolation are at a substantially increased risk of death, even in clean, comfortable cages where there is plenty to eat and drink. Likewise, when asked about the worst form of torture he endured as a prisoner of war in Vietnam, Arizona senator John McCain wrote that it was social isolation ("solitary confinement"): "It crushes your spirit and weakens your resistance more effectively than any other form of mistreatment." Even living alone as an adult is a risk factor for death and disease. Kathleen King and Harry Reis (2012) followed men and women who had undergone coronary bypass surgery – to see how they were doing 15 years later. After controlling for many other risk factors, one of the best predictors of recovery was simply being married – better yet being happily married – rather than being single. This benefit of marriage was especially true for men. Even men who reported being in unhappy marriages shortly after their surgeries were more likely than single men to be alive 15 years later.

Studies such as these leave little doubt that we are inherently social creatures, who thrive on social interaction – and who are highly attentive to the needs, wishes, and emotional states of others. Both our powerful need to belong and our highly empathic nature are important human adaptations that come at a cost – at least to the noble few who feel so much empathy for others that they often put others ahead of themselves.

Needing to belong and including others in the self

How might this happen? Evolutionary biologists have long known that social creatures such as primates are quick to cooperate with members of their own social groups. This principle seems to go even deeper in people than in other primates. As Baumeister and Leary (1995) noted, once we enter a close relationship with another person – or once we learn that the person is a member of our own group – the normal boundary between self and other begins to blur. Consider a study of married couples. Art Aron and colleagues (1991) examined husbands' and wives' reaction times to identify words that they (the husbands or wives) had previously identified as self-descriptive. Aron et al. found that husbands and wives both responded especially quickly to self-descriptive words (yep, that's me!) when their spouses also reported considering these words self-descriptive. On the basis of such studies, Aron et al. concluded that an important component of being in a close relationship is **including the other in the self**. In fact, one way in which researchers in this area have measured relationship closeness is to ask people to report how much they include another person in the self. As an even more famous Art (Art Garfunkel) once sang in a Jimmy Webb love song: "We were looking in the mirror at the time. I got confused and thought your eyes were mine."

Bill Swann and colleagues have shown that the "other" who is assessed in the **Inclusion of Other in the Self (IOS) Scale** can be a social group (e.g., Los Angelenos) just as readily as it can be another specific person (e.g., Angelina). Swann et al. (2014, p. 714) refer to this possibility as **identity fusion** – "a visceral sense of oneness with the group." It's worth noting that identity fusion is not the same as strongly identifying with one's group. Instead, identity fusion very intimately connects the self to specific ingroup members. The best way I can describe this is by resurrecting an old *New Yorker* cartoon. A woman who has been pulled over for speeding by a police officer seems to be responding to his accusation that she hates police officers, as a group. "No, officer, I don't hate all of you as a *group*. I hate each and every one of you *individually*." People who are psychologically fused with a beloved group don't just feel connected to the group as a whole, or what it means. They seem to care about each and every group member individually. This is presumably true even for some very large groups. The most commonly studied social group in research on identity fusion is Spaniards, which includes about 47 million people. Fused Spaniards report caring about their fellow Spaniards the way the allegorical Good Shepherd loved all his sheep, individually (Swann et al., 2014). That's one really big flock.

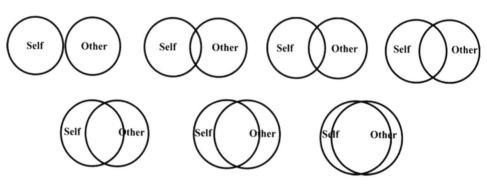

Figure 9.2 *IOS Scale. According to Aron et al. (1992), if you want to know if Ben has truly allowed Jen into his heart, just ask him to circle the image that best describes his relationship with her.*

Speaking of big, identity fusion seems to have big consequences for people's altruistic intentions toward their fellow group members. Although this research is still in its infancy, it's already clear that identity fusion is connected to self-reported altruistic motives and intentions. Using variations on the classic trolley problem, researchers studying identity fusion have observed a number of striking findings. First, identity-fused people are much more likely than unfused people to say they would sacrifice themselves to save the lives of several ingroup members. Saying and doing are two different things, of course. So I should clarify that no Spaniards were harmed in the making of these early identity fusion research papers. It's hard to know from self-reports alone that the effects of identity fusion on self-reported willingness to give up your life for a fellow ingroup member would translate into actual martyrdom. It's notoriously hard to get studies of actual martyrdom past ethical review boards. But the developing identity fusion literature is suggesting some very intriguing answers to some important questions about the causes of altruism in human beings. And one recent identity fusion study, as we will soon see, comes pretty close to studying real martyrs.

Let's examine a few identity fusion findings. First, manipulations of physiological arousal – the laboratory versions of putting people "in the heat of the moment" – show that when identity-fused people are more physiologically aroused, they become *more* – not less – likely to say they'd give up their lives for a group they love. Putting people under time pressure has the same effect. It *increases* the impact of identity fusion on self-reported willingness to make the ultimate self-sacrifice. Findings such as these are important because they begin to answer the difficult question of whether apparent cases of true altruism in people boil down to people making a self-conscious decision to override the impulses of their "selfish genes." Sacrificing oneself for a member of a group to which you are psychologically fused seems to be an automatic rather than a carefully reasoned response. If all helping is ultimately selfish, you might also expect people who've been primed to think about the self to become less self-sacrificing. Instead, priming people to think about themselves as individuals seems to increase self-reported willingness to sacrifice oneself for the group, but only among identity-fused people.

If you're thinking all these trolley studies are just a bunch of false bravado, think again. In a study of Libyan rebels fighting against the Gaddafi regime, Whitehouse et al. (2014) found that frontline fighters reported extremely high levels of identity fusion with their fellow battalion members. In contrast, those who chose to serve in honorable but less risky support roles reported more modest levels of identity fusion. People who are truly identity-fused are often willing to back up their beliefs by putting themselves directly in harm's way. In fact, one striking finding from this study was that those who were fighting on the frontlines reported feeling just as identity-fused to their battalion members as they did to their biological families. In contrast, those who had taken on support roles felt more bonded to their families than to their fellow battalion members. Apparently, our social connections to others we have included in the self sometimes makes us treat them *as if* they were genetic relatives – not biological brothers, of course, but "brothers in arms" as Whitehouse et al. put it.

EMPATHY PROMOTES TRUE ALTRUISM

We're drifting ever closer to the altruistic kayaker, but I'm not sure if we're there yet. There appears to be yet another route to true altruism. This route does not require a chronic state of identity fusion. Instead, it involves a uniquely social, culturally universal emotion called empathy. When we experience true empathy for another person, including a person we just met, we seem to treat the person as if he or she were a member of the family. Before I delve too deeply into the relation between empathy and altruism, I should briefly note that different researchers have used the word "empathy" somewhat differently. When I use the term **empathy** in this chapter, I am referring to what is more technically known as empathic concern (see Marsh, 2017). When you have **empathic concern** for another person, you can feel that person's pain – but you aren't so freaked out by it that you fall apart emotionally. The fabled Good Samaritan presumably experienced this form of empathy for the beaten-up stranger he came across on his travels. The person who has done the most to help us understand this special form of empathy is probably social psychologist Daniel Batson.

Daniel Batson and colleagues (1981) have studied empathy in many contexts, but the first demonstration of how empathy fosters altruism took place in Batson's lab. In Batson et al.'s classic experiment, participants learned that they would be playing the role of observer while another participant, Elaine, performed a task that required her to endure a series of ten mild electric shocks. Before any of the shocking happened, though, the experimenter manipulated how much the participants felt empathy for Elaine. They did so by arranging for participants to learn either that Elaine was very much like them (which is known to promote empathy) or that Elaine was very different from them (which is known to reduce empathy). As you'll soon see, this empathy manipulation proved to be very telling.

As you have probably guessed by now, Elaine was an actress playing the part rather than a real participant – so no Elaines were harmed in the making of this research paper. In fact, very often, Elaines were helped. Here's how. After receiving a couple of electric shocks, Elaine asked for a break and explained to the experimenter that the shocks were very hard for her to take. As it turns out, Elaine had been shocked pretty badly – by an electric fence – as a child, giving her a bit of a shock phobia. But Elaine was a trooper. She asked for a glass of water, and she said she was willing to see if she could make it through the eight remaining electric shocks.

The experimenter was really reluctant to put poor Elaine through this, but he didn't want to have to cancel the experiment. After puzzling over the dilemma a bit, the experimenter happened on an idea. If by any chance the observer participant could trade places with Elaine, she could play the role of observer, and the experiment wouldn't be ruined. Of course, this was a lot to ask, and so the experimenter made it clear that this decision to help was totally up to the real participant. But there was a little more to the experiment than this. First, some participants learned that if they couldn't trade places, the experimenter would cancel the study, and they would be free to go, earning full credit for their partial participation. Woo hoo! Everyone loves free credit. Other participants learned, however, that if they couldn't trade places, they would have to stay and continue to watch poor Elaine suffer. Assuming that none of these participants would have enjoyed watching Elaine suffer, these participants faced a big cost of not helping. Notice that the free credit option offered to some participants made it easy for them to escape the obligation of helping. For participants who probably were not experiencing much empathy for Elaine, this manipulation of cost had a big effect. More than 60% of those told they'd have to watch Elaine suffer agreed to take her place. In contrast, when easy escape was an option, only 20% of participants offered to take her place. In fact, I suspect that many of them just sped off on their jet skis.

People can be so selfish. But they can also be so helpful. Remember that this study was about empathy and helping. Recall that the researchers also manipulated how much empathy participants felt for poor Elaine. Their simple empathy manipulation had a huge effect. People who felt empathy for Elaine almost always helped her. In fact, among those led to feel empathy for Elaine, 90% offered to take the shocks, even when it would have been easy for them to walk away with full credit. The option to be selfish isn't a big temptation when you can feel a victim's pain.

Findings such as these support Daniel Batson's once controversial **empathy-altruism model**. In a nutshell, this model says that experiencing true empathy for another person, putting yourself in his or her emotional shoes, often promotes true altruism, even for a stranger. Research that looks at the emotional consequences of being unable to help – despite one's best efforts – provides further support for the empathy-altruism model. Batson and Weeks (1996) showed that when people unsuccessfully tried to help another person for whom they felt empathy, the would-be helpers felt horrible – even when they later learned it would have been "absolutely impossible" to have helped. Would-be helpers didn't feel bad just because they failed. They felt bad because they failed to help.

It's no secret that some people are more empathic than others, and there is now strong evidence supporting another prediction of Batson's empathy-altruism model. People who are chronically more empathic should be chronically more altruistic. Marsh and colleagues (2014) conducted a clever test of this idea. Taking advantage of modern neuroimaging methods, they compared the brains of 19 people who had donated a kidney with the brains of a matched set of 20 controls (non-donors). In case you're unfamiliar with how researchers study human brains with neuroimaging, let me assure you that no altruists were harmed in the making of this research. Modern technology allows researchers to see what's happening in a living person's brain based on indirect, high-tech (and very safe) measurements of blood flow to different regions of the brain. The only risk of getting an **fMRI (functional magnetic resonance imaging)**, for example, is a little claustrophobia from laying inside a large tube. It's worth noting, by the way, that Marsh et al. knew where to look. That is, they already knew that the right amygdala plays a crucial role in feeling negative emotions, especially fear and sadness. Compared with the rest of us, the kidney donors had larger right amygdalae. Marsh et al. also found that the right amygdalae of the kidney donors became especially active when these altruists were asked to view fearful expressions in strangers. These findings suggest that true altruism in human beings may be as plain as the nose on your face. It's just that it's sitting an inch or so behind it, and a little to your right.

Clever studies such as these have not completely resolved the thorny debate about whether people ever engage in true altruism (e.g., see Maner et al., 2002, for a dissenting opinion). But in combination with many other laboratory and field studies, the weight of the evidence – including the emerging work on identity fusion – has begun to suggest that true altruism isn't quite as evolutionarily puzzling as many once believed. And we *Homo sapiens* do not appear to be the only species to engage in unselfish helping. Nobuya Sato and colleagues (2015) found that rats quickly come to the aid of a cage-mate who appears to be at risk for drowning. What's more, some of the potential rat rescuers in Sato et al.'s main study had recently been dropped themselves into the same "drowning pool" in which their cage-mate was trapped. These rats were even quicker than rats who had never been threatened with drowning to offer help to a cage-mate. Rats seem to be more likely than usual to help a cage-mate when they have walked a mile in that other rat's moccasins. Human beings may not have cornered the market on empathy (de Waal, 1996).

LOTS OF THINGS PROMOTE HELPING

A more indirect line of evidence in favor of human altruism is the simple fact that there are so many ways to get people to help others. After all, if there are a lot of ways to nudge people into something, it seems likely that that something may not fly in the face of human nature. Consider a list of some of the mundane, easily manipulated things known to increase helping. We become more likely than usual to help strangers if we have made eye contact with them, if we have briefly chatted with them, if they have smiled at us, or even if we have just told them that we are not the sibling of one of their acquaintances (Solomon et al., 1981). Learning that another person resembles us, even in ways that do not communicate meaningful group membership, also promotes helping. We're more likely to help another person who happens to share our first name, or even our fingerprint pattern (Burger et al., 2004). Research on unconscious mimicry ("the chameleon effect") shows that we're more likely to help others who subtly mimic our physical gestures (van Baaren et al., 2004).

Nicolas Guéguen and colleagues (2012) have also shown that practically anything that endears us to a stranger increases the likelihood that the stranger will help us out. French motorists are more likely to pick up hitchhikers, for example, if the hitchhikers happen to be holding a bunch of flowers (which gives me a great idea in case I ever decide to write a self-help book for serial killers). A waitress can get customers to fork over more money in tips by simply placing a small flower in her hair (Stefan & Guéguen, 2014). Waitresses who forget to bring their flowers can receive the same boost in tipping by simply giving the customer a friendly touch on the forearm (Guéguen & Jacob, 2005). Bartenders of either gender can increase their tips by merely drawing a smiling sun on the receipt (Guéguen & Legoherel, 2000). Moving on to more costly forms of giving, people are more likely to agree to donate blood if the person doing the asking is wearing a T-shirt that reminds them that "loving = giving" (Charles-Sire et al., 2013).

Guilt works, too. Simply adding the phrase **even a penny will help** to the end of a request for a charitable contribution doubles donation rates, without reducing the size of the donations (Cialdini, 1993). Reminding people that even the smallest amount of help would be helpful seems to increase helping, at least in part, because it motivates people to avoid the guilt associated with refusing to help. Guilt can also motivate people to compensate for having been selfish to a stranger in the past. Ketelaar and Au (2003) showed that reminding people of a time when they had felt guilty or ashamed in the past greatly increased the likelihood that they would make a generous offer to a stranger – especially when they had previously taken economic advantage of that same stranger. A little guilt can sometimes go a long way to curb human selfishness.

Most of these subtle effects on helping are surely unconscious. People who help others because these others have copied their nonverbal behavior do so without ever knowing they were copied – and certainly without knowing that being copied influenced their decision to help. There are many potential interpretations of the fact that helping can happen because of unconscious processes. But my preferred interpretation is this. If helping were as far removed from human nature as some have argued, it would probably be a bit more difficult to get it to happen so often on autopilot. To date, no studies in the voluminous literature in implicit social cognition have revealed any unconscious forces that ever compel people to chop off their arms or jump off tall buildings. That's because, unlike helping, these things just don't come naturally.

A LITTLE HELP HERE, LITTLE GUYS

A very different line of evidence suggesting that true altruism is possible comes from research by Felix Warneken and colleagues. They argue that if we evolved to be altruistic, even toddlers who can barely speak – who are unlikely to have been socialized to put the needs of others ahead of their own – might help others. One trick, though, might be making sure toddlers understand that help is really needed. A second, less obvious, trick might be making sure toddlers are able to do something to help in the first place. One implication of Warneken's (2015) research (see also Warneken & Tomasello, 2006) is that researchers in technologically advanced countries may have underestimated children's natural desire to help simply because it's so unusual for kids to be able to help in a modern world. I know that I myself rarely ask toddlers for their help when I have experienced problems with kurtosis or heteroskedasticity. In contrast, Warneken argues that in tribal cultures, and even in traditional farming cultures, virtually all children routinely help the adults in their small social groups, especially those who rear them. Twenty thousand years ago, six-year-olds could not track a mastodon or start a fire, but they could easily stick close to their caregivers and offer to throw a few sticks on the fire. Any amount of help children could offer, however small, would certainly promote their own survival. Fetching firewood, delivering a simple message, or babysitting one's much younger siblings, for example, could free up one's adult caregivers to do the heavy lifting or skilled labor for which children themselves were not yet well suited.

In keeping with the idea that children may be naturally predisposed to help – even in the absence of any rewards – Warneken (2015) showed that toddlers spontaneously helped an adult stranger as long as the need for help was clear (see also Svetlova et al., 2010). Just as telling, toddlers did not help an adult stranger when it was clear that help was unnecessary (e.g., when the adult discarded an item rather than accidentally dropping it). Warneken and Tomasello (2006) looked at several specific forms of toddler helping (e.g., helping an adult deal with a physical obstacle, helping the adult retrieve a dropped object). They found that toddlers were especially likely to help an adult stranger when the stranger had dropped a useful object and was actively trying to reach it. To at least some degree, these results appear to apply to other primates. In a study of juvenile chimps who had been extensively exposed to people, Warneken found that when the need for help was obvious (when a human adult was actively trying to retrieve something that was out of reach), the young chimps often helped – much as the human toddlers had. In contrast, the young chimps never helped at all when it was harder to see that the adult needed help.

Here's what Warneken (2015, p. 4) concluded:

> I suggest that early helping behaviors are genuinely prosocial and serve an evolutionary function in humans. In support of this claim I ... [argue] that juvenile help might be essential for human subsistence. Although many humans today live in postindustrial societies, it is important to examine the ecology of traditional societies when considering the factors that have shaped human evolution. In traditional societies families depend on help from their offspring ... This might have provided the evolutionarily relevant context in which humans became the precocious helpers they are today.

To connect this to a running theme of this book, one good way to think of the human predisposition toward altruism is that it could be an adaptive compensation for how tremendously altricial we are. As difficult as it is to be a human parent, can you imagine how much harder it would be if our children never offered us any help whatsoever?

As a social psychologist, I hasten to add that a potent mechanism through which some forms of helping might emerge among very young children is social learning (modeling). Anyone who's ever had a toddler in tow while raking leaves or cleaning house knows that toddlers absolutely love to do whatever the adults around them are currently doing. If I had to add a tendency to the gene pool of a social and altricial organism that would make that organism do one thing and only one thing, I'd probably choose a tendency for juvenile organisms to copy the behavior of the older members of their group. An adult and three children, including a toddler, can certainly carry more firewood than the adult alone

(Bandura, 1977; Nielsen, 2012). Further, toddlers who follow the chief while carrying even the most useless pieces of firewood might be less likely than usual to carry out forms of mischief that could only get them in trouble.

HELPING AND RELIGIOSITY: IT'S COMPLICATED

The fact that helping is common, and perhaps even hardwired from an early age, does not mean that it's simple. There are many unresolved complexities regarding prosocial behavior. One tricky question is whether people's self-reported attitudes or personality traits predict their level of helping others. As Galen (2012) has argued, for example, it is unclear whether being religious really promotes helping. More religious people do report helping more, and this has been shown worldwide and for people from every major faith tradition, from Buddhism to Judaism (Pelham & Crabtree, 2008). However, Galen (2012) argues that it is unclear whether religious people really are more chronically helpful, or whether they're just strongly committed to the satisfying belief that they should be – and thus must be – helpful. According to Galen, then, the connection between religiosity and helping may be largely illusory. Although this possibility may be puzzling, it does not mean that there is no such thing as true altruism. In fact, if religiosity proved to be completely unrelated to costly forms of helping, this could be considered weak evidence in favor of altruism (de Waal, 2013). Many highly religious people believe that altruism in this life will be rewarded in the next. If many atheists who do not ever expect to be rewarded for good deeds continue to do them anyway, this could be considered evidence for altruism. After all, recall that altruism is voluntary helping behavior that is costly to the doer and performed without any expectation of reward.

Having said this, if we take Pelham and Crabtree's (2008) cross-cultural findings at face value, they do indicate a modest connection between religiosity and helping. This finding held up, directionally at least, in more than 130 countries worldwide. More in keeping with Galen's thoughtful critique, however, the connection between religiosity and self-reported helping in the Pelham and Crabtree report became smaller and less robust for the presumably spontaneous behavior of "helping a stranger in need." If Batson's empathy-altruism model is correct, however, one would probably expect only a weak connection between religiosity and costly forms of helping. According to this model, religiosity should only lead to altruism when it leads to chronically high levels of empathy. Further, anything else that leads to empathy, including discovering that a stranger deeply values what you value, should also lead to costly forms of helping.

Some of the anecdotes that seem to link religiosity to extreme self-sacrifice seem to go a little beyond mere empathy. Abraham Lincoln, Martin Luther King, Jr., and Gandhi come to mind as people who made tremendous sacrifices for the good of others. As the life stories of these famous people suggest, many who engage in truly courageous forms of helping seem to be deeply committed to a belief in *social justice*. There is plenty of evidence that most people care deeply about fairness and justice (Robinson et al., 2007; Tyler, 2006). Putting together the human concern with fairness and justice with the power of empathy to promote altruism, perhaps it is the unique combination of a profound commitment to social justice and a propensity to put oneself in the shoes of other people that sets the stage for true altruism. This would seem to be a fruitful area for future research. The Dalai Lama seems to represent a more contemporary example of the empathic person who is also strongly committed to social justice. The Dalai Lama expressed this core religious truth very simply: "My religion is kindness." He offered a similar sentiment in the form of advice: "Be kind whenever possible. It is always possible."

Assuming that kindness is the product of empathy, and possibly a concern for social justice as well, the Dalai Lama seems to have been right to assume that we are not wholly and inevitably selfish. Summarizing more than 25 years of research on his empathy-altruism model, here's how Daniel Batson (2008, p. 13) put it. Batson argued that if empathy truly promotes altruism:

> then the assumption of universal egoism must be replaced by a more complex view that allows for altruism as well as egoism. Such a shift in our view of the human motivational repertoire requires, in turn, a revision of our assumptions about human nature and human potential.

According to Batson, we are capable of caring for others in a truly unselfish way.

I can imagine some evolutionary biologists dismissing this "soft science" and noting that we still haven't answered Dawkins' questions about how there could ever be a gene that promotes altruism. As Dawkins (1976, p. 2) put it: "a predominant quality to be expected in a successful gene is ruthless selfishness." On the other hand, even Dawkins (1976) argued it might be possible to nurture altruism: "Let us try to *teach* generosity and altruism, because we are born selfish." In the past four decades, however, studies have begun to suggest that we may not be born quite as selfish as two brilliant British biologists (Darwin and Dawkins) once believed. I cannot speak for famous British guys I've never met, but I think it's fair to say that the evidence no longer points quite so clearly toward Dawkins' ruthless selfishness. In fact, a famous Dutch guy I've only met once has long argued that being "good natured" may be deeply wired into the primate psyche (de Waal, 1996; Horner et al., 2011).

DEFECTORS AND REDUCED SELECTIVE FITNESS MAY NOT BE SUCH BIG PROBLEMS

The defector argument

One popular argument against the evolution of true altruism is the **defector argument** (Dawkins, 1976). Suppose a gene did promote altruism, leading animals to contribute unselfishly to group efforts or help genetically unrelated members of their own species. Surely, many other members of this species could be expected to cheat these do-gooders and become selfish **free-riders**. Free-riders would accept anything others offered without ever repaying the favor. This would be to their advantage, and any genes that promoted this advantage would outcompete any genes that promoted unselfishness. This logic seems airtight, but it's based on some important assumptions. The biggest assumption is that unselfish do-gooders are highly tolerant of cheaters. They aren't. Sometimes they punish them. And even when they don't, they often walk away from them, leaving the cheaters to fend for themselves. In keeping with this idea, Athena Aktipis (2004, 2011) has shown that a very simple "walk away" rule can promote cooperation in species as diverse as single-celled organisms and people. In studies of real people as well as mathematical simulations of the "walk away if things here suck" strategy, Aktipis has shown that this simple rule makes cooperation highly stable in a world where cheating would dominate if cooperators simply tolerated poor outcomes in a group. Aktipis might be too polite to say so, but I think her brilliant work suggests we consider renaming the "defector argument" the "defective argument."

Cheating death

I don't pretend that anyone has completely resolved the riddle of altruism. However, I'd like to make a final point that suggests that it might not be as fanciful an idea as thoughtful critics have argued. Even those who believe in true altruism of the noblest sort admit that when we help others we often reduce our own selective fitness. Selective fitness refers to your overall chances of getting lots of your genes into the gene pool (by surviving, mating, and producing surviving offspring). Kidney donors thus reduce their selective fitness by risking death on the operating table. When I was in high school, my father endured a great deal of pain, and risked a serious infection, when he pulled one of his own teeth with a pair of pliers. His reward was having the money that would have gone to a dentist to pay for food for his six hungry children. I like to think my dad was pretty good at kin selection. Helping sometimes hurts. That's why it's such an evolutionary puzzle. On the other hand, it's possible that social exchange processes, social admiration, or the personal satisfaction altruists get from helping others, can compensate for some of their pain. Could this be true?

Stephanie Brown and colleagues (2003) would probably say so. These health psychologists took the normal finding that social support from other people is good for you and turned it on its head. Specifically, they followed a sample of more than 800 seniors (aged 65+) for five years – to see who survived. Those most likely to survive over the five-year window were those who initially reported offering the most emotional and physical help to other people. This sounds impressive. But it's possible that something other than helping per se was the real reason some of these seniors lived longer than others. Consider two obvious confounds. Women help other people more than men do. Women also live longer than men do. We already knew that. Even more worrisome, younger seniors almost certainly help others more than much older seniors do. Today, I'm delighted when my 69-year-old mother-in-law offers to babysit my 6-year-old daughter. In 20 years, I suspect the babysitting may still be happening, but in the opposite direction. Maybe Brown et al. were merely showing that 69-year-olds are more likely to be around in five years than are 89-year-olds. Again, we already knew that.

So did Brown and colleagues. To rule out as many confounds as possible, they statistically controlled for a long list of them – including age, gender, education, income, exercise level, smoking status, alcohol consumption, subjective wellbeing, health satisfaction, self-rated functional health, interviewer rated health, the kitchen sink, the five basic human personality factors, marital satisfaction, perceived marital equity, receipt of social support, and psychological dependence on one's spouse. OK, you're right. They didn't *really* throw in the kitchen sink, but they sure threw in just about everything else. The result? Those who reported helping others more still lived longer. It's hard to say exactly how much selective fitness helpful seniors got back for their good deeds, but it seems clear that their good deeds were somehow rewarded. In the long haul, those who carried the burdens of other people lived longer. This suggests that the assumption that altruism reduces a person's selective fitness is not always correct.

At least one Belgian population researcher might agree. Michel Poulain (2012) found that Belgian monks and nuns (who, I assume, are a highly prosocial group) lived longer than other people. This included other people matched with the nuns and monks for initial age, gender, marital status, education level, and private vs. collective living conditions. These data are open to other interpretations, but they are certainly consistent with the idea that engaging in prosocial behavior has long-term benefits. Future studies might focus on others whose careers require or promote helping behavior. Despite the stresses and strains of working with the sick and the dying, I suspect that many healthcare professionals find their work deeply rewarding. I'd also hope that the patients who receive care from their professional caregivers would routinely express their appreciation. Feeling appreciated surely fills a basic human need (Baumeister & Leary, 1995). As Lara Aknin and colleagues have now shown in multiple studies, more mundane forms of helping also make helpers feel happier than usual. Both adults and toddlers appear to experience true happiness after giving something to another person (Aknin et al., 2012; Dunn et al., 2008). For example, blind raters reported that toddlers looked more delighted after giving one of their own treats (a coveted Goldfish cracker) to a puppet than they did after receiving eight of these delicious treats themselves.

Helping others is truly rewarding

Perhaps the strongest evidence that people are inherently helpful – at least under the right conditions – comes from work by Naomi Eisenberger and Matt Lieberman. These social neuroscientists are interested in the neurological basis of pain and pleasure. In study after study, they've found that human beings truly crave the acceptance of others, experience pleasure when they see good things happen to deserving others, and experience pleasure when they help others, even when it is at their own expense. In one study, they had people (whose brains were being scanned via fMRI) play Cyberball with two other players (Eisenberger et al., 2003). Cyberball is a simple virtual ball passing game. You just pass the ball to the avatar of one of two other people who are both playing the game with you online. The person controlling that avatar either passes the ball back to you or passes it to the third player. That's it. It's worth adding, though, that participants who played Cyberball in this study did not think they were taking part in a study of social rejection. Instead, they thought they were helping these behavioral neuroscientists understand "how brains coordinate with one another to perform even simple tasks like ball tossing" (Lieberman, 2013).

Figure 9.3 *Like the fabled Good Samaritan, people who feel empathy for a stranger may sometimes engage in true altruism. Further, research in health psychology suggests that doing so may actually promote rather than reduce inclusive fitness.*

In fact, there were no other online Cyberball players, just the one real participant and a computer program that made sure two fake virtual players always threw the ball to the real person at first but eventually iced the person out – by exclusively throwing the ball back and forth to each other. Even in this really simple game – that people thought they were playing with complete strangers – people still reported being hurt by this online rejection. And Eisenberger and colleagues have the brain scans to prove this social pain was real. While participants were being rejected, their brain scans showed a distinctive pattern of activation (in the dorsal anterior cingulate cortex, to be more exact) that is a known signature of physical pain. In a follow-up study, Nathan DeWall and colleagues (2010) repeated the Cyberball experiment but had some participants take Tylenol every day for three weeks prior to taking part in it. Other participants took a placebo that they only thought was Tylenol. The result? Tylenol eradicated the social pain that normally stems from rejection in much the same way that it eradicates physical pain. We are wired to desire social acceptance.

Of course, feeling pain in the wake of social rejection is not the same as being inherently helpful. But in his provocative book *Social,* Matt Lieberman (2014) argues that it is precisely because we are such hypersocial creatures that we have been wired by evolution to feel pleasure when we see good things happen to needy or deserving others. This can even be the case when others benefit at our own expense, and it can motivate us to be truly altruistic. For example, Tricomi and colleagues (2010) scanned the brains of participants who played a game of chance with another participant. Early in the game, participants got really lucky and won $50. The other participant got really unlucky and won absolutely nothing. Unsurprisingly, winning $50 produced activity in areas of participants' brains known to be associated with reward. Surprisingly, there was even more activity in these reward regions on later trials of the game, when the other player finally won some money, even though it was always at people's own expense.

An even clearer example of how it can be rewarding to help others comes from a brain imaging study by Jorge Moll and colleagues (2006). These researchers measured activity in the reward regions of the brain while people had the chance to accept some cash, or while they had a chance to donate some of their cash to charities. When people were simply asked if they wished to receive $5 with no consequences for any charity, people were happy to accept the gift. And sure enough, the fMRI scanner showed that getting paid reliably lit up the brain's reward regions. But these same reward regions lit up even more brightly when participants had the chance to accept some money while also giving some of their money to a charity. For example, giving up $2 so that a charity would receive $5 led to stronger signals of reward than simply receiving $5. Lieberman (2014) reviews many other studies like this one, which all use brain imaging techniques to see what is happening in the brain's reward regions when people help others. People truly feel reward, for example, when they are able to soothe loved ones who are in pain (by touching their arms). Teenagers feel reward when they are able to give some of their winnings in an experimental game to other members of their own families (knowing these family members will not be allowed to give it back, by the way). Lieberman (2014, p. 90) succinctly summarized neuroscientific studies such as these: "Our supposedly selfish reward system seems to like giving more than receiving." Health psychologist Stephanie Brown, as well as the many helpful seniors she studied, would surely agree.

GROUP SELECTION MAY NOT BE SO CRAZY AFTER ALL

To add one final argument to the mix of arguments regarding the possibility of true altruism, I should note that some researchers used to argue that altruism might be functional at the group level, even if it produced disadvantages at the level of the individual organisms that engaged in it. This is highly intuitive. Consider two different species that are competing for the same food source (say, lions and hyenas), or two different groups of the same species (say, two different tribes of hunter-gatherers). If one species or one group is much more altruistic than the other, the tremendous survival advantages that result for the species or group that included a lot of altruistic cooperators might mean that this group survives whereas the other group dies off, or at least becomes less successful. This general argument fell out of favor in the 1960s and 70s, based on the kind of clever arguments proposed by people like Richard Dawkins. As Dawkins (1976, p. 11) put it in his clever critique, the problem with group-level selection is knowing where to draw the line:

> If [group] selection goes on between groups in a species, and between species, why should it not also go on between larger groupings? Species are grouped together into genera, genera into orders, and orders into classes. Lions and antelopes are both members of the class Mammalia, as are we. Should we

then not expect lions to refrain from killing antelopes, "for the good of the mammals"? Surely they should hunt birds or reptiles instead ... But then, what of the need to perpetuate the whole phylum of vertebrates?

This seems reasonable enough, but if lions are not as biologically sophisticated as Dawkins is, we might not expect them to worry much about the good of the antelopes or vertebrates. But we should expect them to recognize other members of their own species (Fan et al., 2013). Further, lions certainly recognize, and behave as if they hate, hyenas, who are in a very real sense their competitors. Lions and hyenas aside, variations on group selection theory have made a big comeback in evolutionary biology in the past two decades. One of the most persuasive voices for a form of group selection is David Sloan Wilson, who has popularized multilevel selection theory. **Multilevel selection theory** states, in a nutshell, that under the right circumstances, groups sometimes behave almost as if they are individual organisms. If the benefits to the group of individual cooperators or altruists greatly outweigh the costs to the individual altruists, group-level selection can presumably occur (Wilson & Sober, 1994).

Along these general lines, many biologists conceive of ant colonies as **superorganisms**. Superorganisms are highly cooperative groups of social individuals who behave almost as if they were a single organism. The Portuguese man o' war is an even more intriguing superorganism because it's made up of several different organisms (different **zooids**). Zooids are biologically distinct organisms, but they are so specialized in their cooperative functions that none of them could survive alone. One zooid is responsible for stinging and catching prey, for example, whereas another is responsible for keeping the man o' war afloat. Thus, whether the man o' war is one organism or several is open to debate (Gould, 1984). Multilevel selection theorists such as David Sloan Wilson and colleagues (2008) point out that the very evolution of multicellular life required separate single-celled organisms to become biologically integrated billions of years ago. Wilson and colleagues argue that life itself became possible because of groups of "cooperating molecular interactions."

From the perspective of multilevel selection theory, Dawkins was still right about evolution the very large majority of the time. Evolution does usually happen at the level of the gene. But every once in a while, at least in highly social species, the rules of evolution may change. The tremendous benefits to the group of ingroup cooperation simply outweigh the possible costs to some highly cooperative individuals. It may be quite a few decades before there is a resolution to this intense debate about group selection. But suffice it to say that some thoughtful evolutionary scientists argue that even if altruism could never evolve at the level of Dawkins' "selfish genes," it could easily evolve at the group level of highly social organisms.

I hope I've finally suggested a couple of plausible answers to the question of why a teenage kayaker risked her own safety to help a complete stranger. Perhaps she saw me not as a stranger but as a fellow kayaker. Or perhaps she was one of those unusual people who feel their identities are fused with everyone – or every kayaker – on the planet. A more likely possibility is that she was just chronically high in empathic concern. Whatever the reason, I expect someone as helpful as she was to live to a ripe old age.

FOR FURTHER READING

»   Batson, C.D., Duncan, B., Ackerman, P., Buckley, T. & Birch, K. (1981). Is empathic emotion a source of altruistic motivation? *Journal of Personality and Social Psychology*, 40(2), 290–302.

»   Brosnan, S.F. & de Waal, F.B.M. (2003). Monkeys reject unequal pay. *Nature*, 425(6955), 297–9.

»   Dawkins, R. (1976). *The selfish gene.* Oxford: Oxford University Press.

»   Eldakar, O.T. & Wilson, D.S. (2011). Eight criticisms not to make about group selection. *Evolution*, 65(6), 1523–6.

»   Marsh, A.A. (2016). Neural, cognitive, and evolutionary foundations of human altruism. *Wiley Interdisciplinary Reviews: Cognitive Science*, 7(1), 59–71.

»   Marsh, A. (2018). *The fear factor: How one emotion connects altruists, psychopaths, and everyone in between.* New York: Basic Books.

»   Wright, R. (2000). *NonZero: The logic of human destiny.* New York: Pantheon.

SAMPLE MULTIPLE-CHOICE EXAM QUESTIONS

Here are four sample quiz questions for Chapter 9. You can find the Chapter 9 quiz at: www.macmillanihe.com/evolutionary-psychology

9.01.   Is it evolutionarily predictable that a woman might give up her own life to save the lives of her three siblings?

a.   yes, because Hamilton's rule says that the three siblings collectively contain 150% of the woman's genes

b.   yes, doing so would qualify as a good example of kin selection

c.   both A and B are correct

9.02.   Helping your aging neighbor with yardwork because she once loaned you money when you were in serious financial need is a good example of:

a.   reciprocal altruism

b.   equity-based helping

c.   the "good neighbor" policy

9.03.   According to your text, true altruism should be more likely to evolve in:

a.   social as opposed to solitary animals

b.   animals that are aware of a hierarchy rather than animals that are not

c.   safe environments as opposed to unsafe environments

9.04.   What emotional state in people appears to promote unselfish helping?

a.   happiness

b.   limerance

c.   empathy

Answer Key: c, a, a, c.

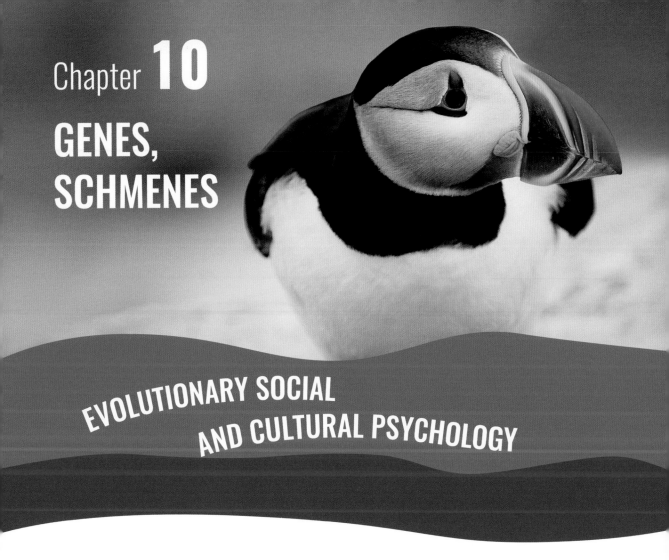

Chapter 10

GENES, SCHMENES

EVOLUTIONARY SOCIAL AND CULTURAL PSYCHOLOGY

"Socialization is assisted by the existence of adaptations."
— *Robert Kurzban and Mark Leary (2001, p. 199)*

"... cultural evolution is a stronger force [than is genetic evolution] in the evolution of large-scale cooperative societies."
— *Adrian V. Bell (2010, p. 159)*

More than fifty years ago, Bob Rosenthal and Kermit Fode (1963) asked 12 bright college students to serve as experimenters in what may have struck the students as a pretty unremarkable study. They learned that they'd be trying to replicate a well-established effect. They'd be trying to show that rats who had been specially bred to excel at learning mazes ("maze-bright rats") learn T-mazes – you guessed it – *faster* than rats specially bred to suck at learning mazes ("maze-dull rats"). Rosenthal and Fode trained the experimenters carefully, setting up clear rules for running the rats in T-mazes for five days. For example, the experimenters deprived all the rats of food for exactly 23 hours before each learning session – to be sure the maze-dull and maze-bright rats were equally motivated to learn to get food. Further, none of the rats had ever been exposed to a maze before. So you can also be sure that the maze-bright rats didn't have any learned advantages prior to the study. Successful performance on this maze-learning task always meant entering the darker of two arms in the T-maze (see Figure 10.1). But it wasn't quite that simple. To be sure the rats weren't just learning to go right or left, the experimenters randomly varied whether the right or left arm on any given trial was the dark one. The dark arm, and only the dark arm, contained the food reward.

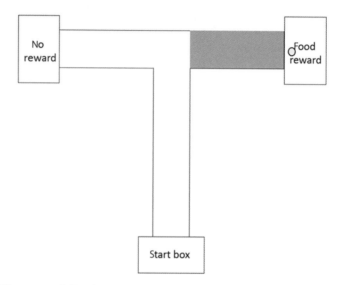

Figure 10.1 *A T-maze much like the one used by Rosenthal and Fode. Half the time the left arm was dark. Whether the dark arm was on the left or right, it always contained the reward.*

As you can see in Figure 10.2, the maze-bright rats learned this task much better than the maze-dull rats did. What makes this seemingly obvious finding so important is the fact that the maze-bright rats were not really maze-bright. In fact, the two groups of rats were identical. Rosenthal and Fode simply got a bunch of maze-average rats and randomly split them into two groups. But the bright, motivated experimenters thought that some of the rats were much brighter than the others. Rats labeled as geniuses performed like geniuses because the experimenters unwittingly treated them like geniuses. On a scale that required experimenters to report how *bright, clean, tame,* and *pleasant* they felt the rats were, the experimenters assigned to the maze-bright rats rated them more favorably. They also reported being more *relaxed* and *pleasant* with the presumably maze-bright rats. Finally, they reported handling the maze-bright rats more gently and being quieter with them. The maze-bright rats became the teachers' pets, even though the teachers themselves didn't seem to realize it.

It's important to note that the experimenters were not consciously trying to cheat. Instead, they just allowed their expectations to get the better of them. Researchers have called this presumably unconscious tendency for experimenters to create (or see) what they expect to see "experimenter bias," and it is but one of a large family of confirmatory biases. In a wide variety of ways, people often find what they expect to find. Confirmatory biases are even more common in

"'Maze-dull,' 'a little slow,' 'maze-impaired.'
It all starts to get to a guy after a while."

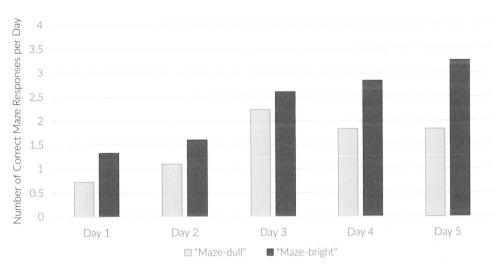

Figure 10.2 *Average number of correct maze responses per day among Rosenthal and Fode's (1963) maze-dull and maze-bright rats.*

studies of people than in studies of rats. This is because human expectations are often a two-way street. Decades of research on **self-fulfilling prophecies** show that when we expect something to happen, this expectation itself may cause that very thing to happen (Merton, 1948). Imagine how bad it would have been for the poor maze-dull rats if they knew they had been negatively labeled. It's so hard to avoid confirmatory biases in research on people that researchers often have to keep themselves and their human participants blind to their real experimental conditions. This is why there's a placebo condition in most drug efficacy studies. A **placebo** is an inert pill containing no drugs of any kind. To see if a drug truly works for pharmacological reasons, we need to see if it works better than a placebo. This is no small task. Placebo effects can be very powerful.

If you're thinking studies of rats – or even placebos – don't tell us much about human social behavior, Rosenthal and Fode were aware of this criticism. A couple of years after publishing this now-classic study of experimenter bias in the rat laboratory, Rosenthal and Lenore Jacobson (1966) conducted a classic study of **teacher expectancies** in elementary school classrooms. They felt it would be unethical to tell teachers that any of their students were the human equivalent of maze-dull. So they only planted positive expectations in this field experiment. In particular, they administered a nontraditional IQ test in classrooms throughout a large elementary school (where Jacobson was the principal). Then they selected a handful of kids from each classroom – at random. They informed the teachers, falsely of course, that regardless of how well these students were doing now, the new IQ test showed that these gifted students were destined to "bloom" over the course of the school year. And bloom they did, especially in the younger classrooms. The results for the first graders appear in Figure 10.3. As you can see, kids who'd randomly been labeled "bloomers" showed more than twice the usual increase in IQ over the course of the school year. Teacher expectancy effects appear to be just as powerful – and just as unconscious – as experimenter expectancies.

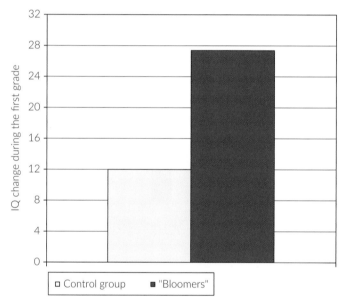

Figure 10.3 *In their study of teacher expectancies, Rosenthal and Jacobson (1966) found that first grade children selected at random, but falsely identified as intellectual "bloomers," showed larger increases in IQ over the course of a school year relative to their identical peers. This is an example of the power of the situation to shape human behavior.*

If you're wondering what experimenter bias, placebo effects or even teacher expectancies have to do with evolutionary psychology, part of the answer is that these phenomena illustrate the two core themes of social psychology. First, we don't always interpret things at face value. Instead, we often create or interpret reality in keeping with our own beliefs and expectations. Teachers expected "bloomers" to be smart, and thus they viewed them through this intellectually rosy lens. This is the social psychological theme of **constructivism**. Second, much like rats and first graders, we human beings are often putty in the hands of others. This is the social psychological theme of the **power of the situation** (Myers, 2013; Smith & Mackie, 2007). Evolutionary psychology is central to this two-part theme because each of these two themes is grounded in an important human adaptation. We're constructivists because we're constantly using our big brains to try to make sense of the world. We're highly sensitive to social situations because we've evolved to care deeply about the needs and wishes of others. This two-part evolutionary fact – that we are large brained, hypersocial creatures – lies at the very heart of social psychology.

But what is social psychology? To paraphrase Gordon Allport's (1954b) classic definition, **social psychology** is the scientific study of how other people, including imagined or remembered others, influence our thoughts, feelings, and behavior. This doesn't just include phenomena that are obviously social – like how and why we form close relationships. It also includes subtler phenomena such as why we obey authority figures, even when they have no real authority over us. As you will soon see, it also includes how simply being in the presence of another person can change our well-learned stereotypes about that person's social group.

Perhaps the most interesting thing about social psychology is that one of its core themes – the power of immediate situations to shape human behavior – might seem to stand in sharp contrast to one of the key themes of evolutionary psychology. A key theme of evolutionary psychology, of course, is that human behavior is the product of millions of years of evolutionary history. The way to resolve this apparent discrepancy between the ancient past and the immediate present is the main theme of this chapter. It is that millions of years of evolutionary history have produced a highly social organism that is genetically programmed to be powerfully shaped by other members of its species. We're strongly programmed to be both flexible and sociable. This is why you find people – and no other animals – thriving in the arctic as well as in the Amazon. In this chapter, we'll discuss how evolutionary concepts can inform social and cultural psychology. We'll also discuss how social and cultural psychology demand a nuanced, and sometimes critical, interpretation of evolutionary psychology.

Let's begin, though, with a closer look at the social psychological axiom that situations powerfully shape human behavior. How powerful are social situations, really? If we define situations broadly to include that rich set of widely shared situations known as culture, can culture overpower potent evolutionary pressures? Before we consider that important cross-cultural question, let's take a quick peek at the power of the situation within American culture.

JUST HOW POWERFUL ARE SOCIAL SITUATIONS?

Sherif's classic conformity studies

In 1935, social psychologist Muzafer Sherif published a clever study of the subtle form of social influence known as conformity. **Conformity** refers to changing one's beliefs or behavior to be consistent with the beliefs or behavior of others – even when no one asks you to do so. When you wear jeans rather than a kilt or try the kelp because Jean tried it, you are – perhaps without giving it much thought – engaging in conformity. Sherif wanted to know how powerful conformity was when people were thrown together with total strangers they knew they'd never see again. He conducted a study that presumably focused on visual perception. In various phases of the study, participants estimated how far a stationary dot of light had moved in an otherwise dark room. Because of a visual illusion called the **autokinetic effect**, most people who viewed the stationary light felt that it moved.

In phase one of the study, people took part alone and simply reported how far they felt that the light moved (in inches). The next day, though, people judged the movement of the light while sitting with two other naive participants. So now people were exposed to the answers provided by two strangers. Sherif was careful not to tell people that they needed to arrive at any kind of agreement or group answer. They were simply making the same judgments in the presence of others that they had originally made alone. In every group Sherif studied, though, people seem to have felt great pressure to conform to the judgments of the other goofballs who happened to be in the room with them. By the final group session, a nearly perfect consensus had always emerged regarding exactly how far the light moved. There was substantial variation across the groups in their estimates of how far the light moved, but the norm within a given group seemed to become a subjective reality. Even when people came back to the lab alone, as much as a year later, most people stuck close to their group's original judgment. In a follow-up study, Sherif planted stooges in the groups and instructed them to give very high movement estimates. The judgments of the stooge usually had a large effect on the group's answer. Further, these falsely inflated group norms were readily passed along to new groups of complete strangers, across multiple generations. Sherif had essentially created tiny three-person cultures of subjective movement in his lab.

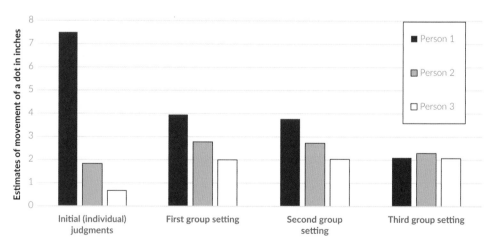

Figure 10.4 *In Sherif's (1935) conformity study, participants who made independent (solo) judgments varied widely in how much they thought a stationary dot of light moved. But when they repeated their judgments three times in the presence of two other naive participants, a group consensus emerged. In this group you can see that everyone eventually agreed that the light moved about two inches.*

Hitler as an intuitive social psychologist

When the benevolent and ingenious Muzafer Sherif began his classic studies of social influence, the malicious and ingenious Adolph Hitler had already been appointed chancellor of Germany, and he was using his intuitions about social influence to try to conquer the world (Cartwright, 1979; Smith & Mackie, 2007). Unfortunately, Hitler was an excellent intuitive social psychologist, and he masterfully manipulated entire nations (especially his own Nazi Germany) during World War II. As an example, after being appointed as German chancellor, Hitler did not immediately decide to invade Austria. Instead, he began his rule by taking very popular actions such as bringing Germany out of a terrible economic depression, annexing regions of Europe that were ethnically German, and making speeches against the limitations imposed on Germany in the Treaty of Versailles, which many Germans felt had unfairly blamed Germany for World War I. So first Hitler built up some political capital, and then he began to spend it. One horrific way in which he did this was to identify scapegoats (Jews, Gypsies, and other minorities) he could blame for Germany's past troubles. A **scapegoat** is a person or social group – usually one with very little power – who people blame for their own problems. It was only after Hitler had built up some sociopolitical clout that he was able to convince most of his countrymen that his Third Reich, including his ethnic cleansing plan, was the route to a bright future.

Arguably, Hitler came within a failed battle or two of world domination. Estimates of the total fatalities in World War II range from 50 to 85 million people, many of them innocent civilians who were killed by soldiers or concentration camp guards who merely followed orders from the mid-level managers of Hitler's carefully planned Holocaust. How could this have happened? How could a loving German father hug his wife and daughter, set off to work at Auschwitz, and then execute hundreds of his fellow Germans, just because they happened to be Jewish? After wrestling with distressing questions like this for nearly two decades after World War II, social psychologist Stanley Milgram decided to address his questions empirically. In his unique and highly controversial studies, Milgram (1963) examined the parameters of human obedience to authority. What he found shed a bright but unsettling light on the Holocaust. Powerful social situations can turn lovable, kindhearted people like me and you into callous henchmen (and henchwomen) who are willing to hurt innocent strangers.

Milgram's obedience studies

Milgram recruited American men from all walks of life to take part in "a study of memory" at Yale University. A portion of one of Milgram's fliers for his famous study appears in Figure 10.5. When recruitment for **Milgram's obedience studies** began in 1961, the total payment of $4.00 (plus carfare) was a decent reward for an hour of easy and interesting work. When participants arrived at the lab, they met a pleasant co-participant (who was actually in cahoots with the experimenter). Because of a clever ruse, real participants felt that they lucked out and would get to play the role of "teacher." It would thus be their job to teach the other participant – "the learner" – a long series of word pairs by reading the learner all the pairs (e.g., "fat–neck," "slow–train") from a list. After the training, the learner would have to repeat the second word in each word pair after the teachers read the first word from each word pair – and then offer the learner four multiple-choice answer options. As you surely know, one way in which people learn in real life is by getting punished when they make a mistake. In my family, for example, a commonly punished mistake is called playing poker. So Milgram's real participants – the teachers – must have thought little of it when they learned that they would have to deliver a brief electric shock to the learner every time he made a mistake.

Public Announcement

WE WILL PAY YOU $4.00 FOR ONE HOUR OF YOUR TIME

Persons Needed for a Study of Memory

*We will pay five hundred New Haven men to help us complete a scientific study of memory and learning. The study is being done at Yale University.

*Each person who participates will be paid $4.00 (plus 50c carfare) for approximately 1 hour's time. We need you for only one hour: there are no further obligations. You may choose the time you would like to come (evenings, weekdays, or weekends).

*No special training, education, or experience is needed. We want:

Factory workers	Businessmen	Construction workers
City employees	Clerks	Salespeople
Laborers	Professional people	White-collar workers
Barbers	Telephone workers	Others

All persons must be between the ages of 20 and 50. High school and college students cannot be used.

*If you meet these qualifications, fill out the coupon below and mail it now to Professor Stanley Milgram, Department of Psychology, Yale University, New Haven. You will be notified later of the specific time and place of the study. We reserve the right to decline any application.

*You will be paid $4.00 (plus 50c carfare) as soon as you arrive at the laboratory.

Figure 10.5 *As you can see, participants in Milgram's studies thought they were signing up for a study of memory and learning. Most of them would learn something very uncomfortable about how willing they were to obey an authority figure.*

But this study of "teaching" was actually a clever trap. First, the learner was seated in a separate room by himself. Teachers probably gave this no thought, but Milgram was putting some physical and psychological distance between teachers and victims ... err um, learners. Second, the learner was strapped firmly into a sturdy chair "to avoid excessive movement." This process was all sanitized and made very technical. For example, the teachers looked on as the experimenter applied electrode paste to the learner's skin "to avoid blisters and burns" from the electrical leads. Third, the teacher learned – after agreeing to play the role of teacher – that he would have to give *increasingly large* shocks to the learner each time the learner made a mistake. The first shock would be a "slight" punishment of 15 volts. The second would be 30 volts. With each new mistake, the teacher would have to deliver a little more shock. As you can see in Figure 10.6, the punishment for a wrong answer increased in small steps to a maximum of 450 volts. The next set of shock switches was labeled "DANGER SEVERE SHOCK" followed by a label of "XXX" for the last two switches.

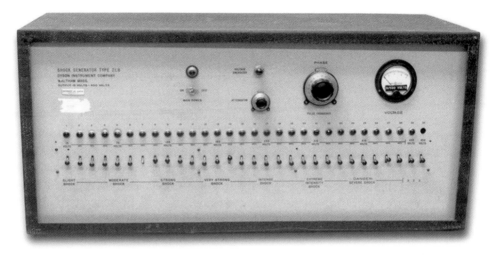

Figure 10.6 *Milgram's shock delivery machine began at only 15 volts but increased bit by bit to a maximum of 450 volts. Beginning at 360 volts, a label stated "DANGER SEVERE SHOCK." The last couple of switches were ominously labeled "X X X."*

The experiment began innocently enough, but the learner did not seem to be learning very well. He gave about three wrong answers for every correct answer. For a long time, he seemed to accept the increasingly painful shocks quite stoically. If participants delivered the 300-volt shock, however, they heard the apparently distraught learner kick on the wall and ask to be released. The learner said he refused to continue and kicked the wall again at 315 volts. But after that point, the learner went silent – offering no further anwers. Invariably, participants asked the experimenter how they should repond to this. He calmly told them that the absence of an answer was considered a wrong answer.

If participants asked to stop the study at this or any other point, the experimenter calmly and firmly said things like "Please continue" and "The experiment requires that you continue." In some versions of the study, the learner specifically complained about the pain. If participants expressed concerns about this, the experimenter stated: "Although the shocks may be painful, there is no permanent tissue damage, so please go on." It would be hard to overstate how stressed out and uncomfortable most of the teachers seem to have felt. The teachers were clearly very concerned about the learner. But in the end, 65% of Milgram's original group of 40 participants kept giving shocks all the way up to the 450-volt maximum. As Jerry and Elaine once commiserated in a classic *Seinfeld* episode: "I will *never* understand people. They're the *worst!*" Virtually everyone who first learns about the Milgram study is shocked to learn that 65% of the participants – however begrudgingly – gave the poor confederate the most extreme levels of shock possible. So, it seems fair to say that most of these 40 men seem to have checked their morality at the door to Milgram's laboratory.

Just how far would you go in this uncomfortable situation? Of course, we can't really answer that question, but we can use Milgram's original data to answer an even more important question: Just how far did everybody go? You already know that in Milgram's original (1963) study, 35% of the men disobeyed the experimenter at some point (100% – 65% = 35%). But where, exactly, did the most disobedient (and presumably most compassionate) person draw the line? It's worth noting that before the study began, the teachers always recevied a 45-volt "sample shock" from the shock machine, and suffering this very real shock was certainly no piece of cake. Did any participant refuse to give more shock than the 45 volts he himself had experienced? After feeling the painful sample shock, did at least one highly principled person refuse to deliver any shocks at all?

The answer to this question is important because it tells us about the power a situation like this one can have on virtually everyone, not just the 65% of people who aren't bold enough to stand up to injustice. The answer, by the way, is 300 volts. Yes, 300 volts. Everyone who took part in the version of Milgram's study described here gave the learner what they thought was a 300-volt shock. It wasn't until the learner began kicking the wall in protest that a brave 5 out of 40 participants courageously decided they could no longer deliver the shocks. So, even if you feel you are as brave and principled as the 5 in 40 people who disobeyed the experimenter at this point, I'd like to reiterate that everyone – including these heroes – gave the learner what they thought was a 300-volt shock. It's pretty hard for me to believe I wouldn't have done the same. Further, in case you're wondering whether people really thought these shocks were painful to the learner, they did. At the study's end, teachers were all asked: "How painful to the learner were the last few shocks that you administered to him?" The answer scale ranged from 1 (*not at all painful*) to 14 (*extremely painful*). The most common response was 14, and the mean was 13.42. Ouch!

Why are we so ridiculously obedient? Because in a hypersocial species like ours, social situations matter greatly. Everything about this potent social situation – except for the victim's plight – suggested that the thing to do was to obey an authority figure. In other primates, the "authority figure" is usually the alpha male (and/or his close allies). In chimps, for example, the alpha male is truly the boss of his troop. He has privileged access to everything from desirable foods to desirable mates. If another male challenges the alpha male's authority, there is likely to be serious bloodshed and possibly even death. Frans de Waal describes the operation of hierarchies and power principles in chimpanzee troops as "chimpanzee politics." His point is that, like people, chimps are inherently hierarchical and even political. In chimpanzee politics, however, the battles are fiercer than they are in people. In chimpanzee politics, for example, the only recounts are for missing fingers after a bloody fight. But as de Waal is also quick to remind us, the goal of the rigid social hierarchy in chimps is not to promote fighting but to minimize it. If all the members of a troop are aware of their social rank, this makes it easy to know who gets to do what and whose wishes matter more during disagreements (de Waal, 1982, 1996). Human beings, like chimps, are keenly attuned to power, authority, and social status. It's just that the cues we use are a bit more complex and flexible than those chimps use. A police officer's uniform, a doctor's white coat, a person's physical strength, and whether a person has a BMW or a PhD are all cues for authority.

It was no accident, then, that the experimenter in Milgram's original study was wearing a white lab coat. In follow-up studies, Milgram (1963) directly manipulated this simple status cue. Taking away the white lab coat greatly reduced obedience. Along similar lines, obedience to the experimenter's orders dropped a great deal when teachers had to touch the learner to deliver the shock. It's easier to harm a physically or psychologically distant victim. The principle of distance also applied to teachers and the experimenter. When the experimenter gave his orders and instructions by telephone, teachers were much more willing than usual to disobey.

In addition to offering a powerful contextual explanation for atrocities such as the Holocaust, Milgram's famous obedience studies also changed the face of how people do research in the social and medical sciences. In Milgram's day, it was usually up to researchers themselves to decide, for example, if it was OK to deceive participants or to stress them out (as Milgram's procedure obviously did). Because of critics' thoughtful reactions to this and other ethically sensitive (or abhorrent) studies, modern researchers have to convince an ethical review board – often a university **institutional review board (IRB)** – that a proposed study is ethical. The members of an IRB board are trained in the basic principles of ethics, and if they say a study is unethical, the researcher who proposed it has to go back to the drawing board (e.g., by manipulating a variable in a way that cannot easily cause psychological harm).

This does not mean that modern researchers can never use deception or stress people out. But it does mean that any risks imposed by a study must be offset by its likely payoff to society. This is known as the **risk–benefit rule** (Pelham & Blanton, 2018). For example, Jeremy Burger (2009) conducted a replication of the original Milgram study. In Burger's case, though, he went to great lengths to reduce any risk of participation. This included stopping the study when people delivered 150 volts of shock rather than 450 volts and having a clinical psychologist run the study. The clinical psychologist had a clear mandate to stop the study immediately "if he saw any signs of excessive stress." Burger observed a clear replication of Milgram's original obedience results in his 2009 replication. Obedience is alive and well.

Automatic social tuning illustrates the power of the situation

So, the idea that situations powerfully shape human behavior is a core principle of social psychology. But even in a field like social psychology, we are sometimes surprised at just how powerful situations can be. Let me share just one more example of this idea. In the past two decades, social psychologists have become increasingly interested in the study of prejudice and stereotypes. It's now well established, for example, that prejudice and stereotypes often become **automatic**. This means that prejudice often operates quickly and unconsciously, rearing its ugly head even when we wish it wouldn't. This is one reason why prejudice is hard to change. When they began an extensive program of research on stereotypes in the mid-to-late 1990s, Brian Lowery and colleagues (2001) knew very well that prejudice often operates automatically.

Based on Hardin and Higgins' (1996) **shared reality theory**, however, these researchers wondered if even well-learned prejudices might wax and wane with the social context. The essence of shared reality theory is that human beings are "strongly motivated to share their understanding of the world in general and their social world in particular" (Echterhoff et al., 2009, p. 496). Lowery et al. (2001) began their study of shared reality by replicating an effect known as **implicit prejudice**. Unlike explicit prejudice (e.g., "Black people can't be trusted"), implicit prejudice refers to gut associations. To document implicit prejudice, researchers have shown that it's easier for most people to associate Black faces (or stereotypically Black names) with negative words than with positive words. The reverse is true for White faces (or names). Thus, if you briefly flash up a stereotypically White name such as Brian or Stacey on a computer monitor, this prime (the name) should speed up a person's ability to recognize a word like "good" or "sunset," and it should slow down a person's ability to recognize a word like "bad" or "vomit."

By the turn of the 21st century, many experts believed that implicit racial prejudice was practically universal and practically impossible to change. But shared reality theory predicts that people are constantly "tuning" their attitudes, even their implicit attitudes, to be consistent with those of likable and/or powerful others with whom they happen to be interacting. To most White people, it probably seems safe to assume that a high-status Black person, such as a Black experimenter, would have positive gut associations about his own ethnic group. Whites who want to be accepted by this Black experimenter could be expected to engage in what Lowery et al. (2001) called **automatic social tuning**, an unconscious tendency toward more favorable attitudes about the social group of a person with whom you are currently interacting. Just as Sherif's participants found their perceptual attitudes becoming like those of the other judges who sat in the same room with them, White people might (automatically) find their racial attitudes becoming more like those of a handsome, personable Black experimenter.

To test this idea, Lowery et al. (2001, Study 4) simply manipulated the race of their experimenter. So, their participants took part in a study of implicit racial prejudice run by either a White or a Black experimenter. The experimenter even told participants that he was measuring implicit racial prejudice. But it would've been virtually impossible for participants to gain any conscious control over their level of implicit racial prejudice. This is because the priming stimuli (the Black or White faces) were presented so quickly – for about 1/50 of a second – that no one could see them. Specifically, a Black or White face appeared near the center of a computer screen at the beginning of each trial of the study. But each face was flashed up so briefly that no one ever reported being aware that they had seen any faces at all. For Whites, the clearest evidence of implicit prejudice would mean (a) recognizing the word "good" more quickly (in fewer milliseconds) when primed by White than by Black faces and (b) recognizing the word "bad" more quickly (again, in fewer milliseconds) when primed by Black than by White faces. As you can see in Figure 10.7, this is exactly what Lowery et al. (2001) found – when a White guy ran the study.

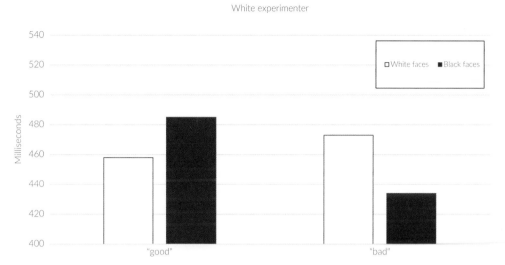

Figure 10.7 *White participants were primed with young Black or White faces. They then reported as quickly as possible whether the target words "good" or "bad" appeared shortly after the primes. White faces better primed the word "good." Black faces better primed the word "bad." Scores are response times to identify the words "good" or "bad" (in milliseconds).*

So far, Lowery et al. (2001) merely documented a variation on a pretty well-known theme. White people have more favorable gut associations about Whites than they do about Blacks. But this all changed when a Black guy showed up to run the same experiment. As you can see in Figure 10.8, the implicit prejudice effect observed for White participants disappeared when the experimenter was Black. These findings suggest that even very well-learned social beliefs are subject to the power of the situation. In Sherif's classic study, no one had a lot of experience judging dots of light in a dark room. Even Milgram's obedience study put people in a highly ambiguous setting. But Lowery et al. showed that even seemingly deep-seated associations may be subject to the power of social situations.

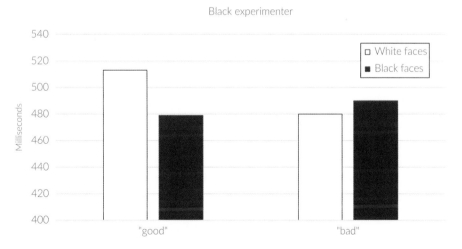

Figure 10.8 *For half of Lowery et al.'s (2001) participants, a Black rather than a White experimenter conducted the study of implicit prejudice. Notice that all hints of racial bias disappeared. In fact, there was a non-significant bias in favor of the same Black faces that had produced implicit racial prejudice when the experimenter was White.*

Can situations overshadow sex differences in sexual choosiness?

Recall that there is a lot of evidence that women are sexually choosier than men are. This sex difference shows up in cultures worldwide, and it is presumably grounded in parental investment processes. Although I argued in Chapter 4 that this sex difference is pretty robust, recall that I did mention what some consider an exception to this rule. My spin on Conley's (2011) research – which I'm guessing Conley would not endorse – was that if the person to whom one might be attracted is hot, rich, and famous enough, there's no longer anything to be choosy about, and so women become highly interested in casual sex. Heterosexual female students said they'd be just as interested in having casual sex with Johnny Depp as heterosexual male college students said they'd be in having casual sex with Angelina Jolie. Of course, it's not clear if it's fair to consider another person's level of beauty, fame, and wealth a "situation," but Conley's studies did suggest a boundary condition (target "hotness") on sexual choosiness.

Recent experiments conducted with speed daters suggest a much more ephemeral (truly situational) determinant of sexual choosiness. In case you're not familiar with speed dating, it's like taking a dozen two-hour blind dates and squeezing them down into an hour or two. To be a little more specific, **speed dating** consists of a series of rapid-fire dyadic, getting acquainted conversations with strangers who are all interested in finding dates. The way most heterosexual speed dates work is that all the women remain seated while all the men float around the room according to an assigned schedule. Each woman might thus have a dozen or more men stop by in an hour, all of them for one-on-one conversations of only four minutes. After all the rapid-fire dates are done, participants all privately indicate – to the speed date organizers – which, if any, of the people they met they would like to contact again – possibly for a real date. Matches only occur when both the man and the woman indicate to the organizers of the speed date that they are interested in recontacting each other.

Notice that the men do all the floating around in a typical speed date. The logic for this arrangement has usually been twofold. First, women have more stuff to keep track of, and so it is easier for men to do the moving about. Second, this is how it usually works on standard dates; the men do the "pursuing." Social psychologists Eli Finkel and Paul Eastwick (2009) wondered if this situation – the rule about who does the moving around the room and thus who sits and waits for "courters" – might play a role in people's sexual choosiness. So they conducted a number of speed dating sessions in which they randomly determined whether the men or the women did the moving around. When the men did all the moving, Finkel and Eastwick found that, on average, men were less choosy than women. The men gave "yeses" (yes, I'd like to see this person again) significantly more often than the women did. But when the men all sat in one place and the women all milled about the room to get to them, this countercultural norm completely wiped out the usual difference in sexual choosiness. We'll have to see how well this intriguing effect holds up to replication. But assuming it does, it appears that Finkel and Eastwick have identified an easily manipulated situation that can completely eliminate the usual sex difference in sexual choosiness. Reverse the roles and men begin to behave at least somewhat more like women, by being choosier.

Moving beyond speed dating to daily life, social role theorists such as Wendy Wood and Alice Eagly (2012) have argued that dramatic changes in sex roles at home and in the workplace beginning in the 1940s have had a huge impact on how men and women relate to one another. During World War II, for example, many women entered the workforce for the first time, and this change in roles had a huge impact on American work and family life. The development of safe and reliable methods of contraception in the early 1960s (especially the birth control pill) also had a huge impact on the ways in which men and women relate to one another sexually.

To summarize thus far, social psychologists have documented in a wide variety of ways that one of the most powerful forces driving human behavior is the behavior of the other human beings in one's immediate environment. Although this fact might seem to fly in the face of evolutionary thinking, an easy way to resolve the apparent tension between evolutionary and social psychology is to concede that, as hypersocial creatures, we evolved to be highly sensitive to the needs and wishes of others. This is especially true when we respond to those who have power over us but still true even when we respond to those whose only credentials are that they happen to be in the same room with us. If social psychologists are right that we are powerfully affected by other people, even complete strangers, then it stands to reason that we are even more powerfully affected by the entire cultures in which we live and develop. Cultures are, after all, made up of people and often in very large numbers. Cultural psychology, then, might best be considered social psychology writ large. There can be no question that human evolution ultimately made human culture possible. But this raises the intriguing question of whether culture ever trumps the evolutionary processes that created it.

THE EXTREME DIVERSITY OF HUMAN CULTURE

Culture refers to a widely shared set of beliefs, behaviors, and emotions regarding the appropriate ways in which people live, work, and relate to one another. Almost nothing escapes its grasp. To name just a few things, culture includes art, dress, diet, education, entertainment, government, language, law, music, religion, science, sports, technology, and work. If you want a shorter definition of something so rich and multifaceted, culture refers to a set of widely shared but often unwritten rules and values about how to live one's life.

A peek at Hofstede's cultural dimensions

Cultural psychologist Geert Hofstede (2001) has argued that a great deal of global variation in culture boils down to six key cultural dimensions. One dimension is masculinity vs. femininity, mentioned in Chapter 6. As you may recall, Sweden is a very feminine culture. In contrast, Japan is a very masculine culture. You can thus bet that the average Swedish person will be less competitive, and more nurturing, than the average Japanese person. And you can guess that being nurturing is also valued more strongly by the average person in Sweden than by the average person in Japan. Although everyone is obviously different, culture tells you something about the central behavioral and attitudinal tendencies of large groups of people.

According to Hofstede, and many other experts on culture, another important dimension of culture is that of **individualism** vs. **collectivism** (Markus & Kitayama, 1991). This refers to whether people focus mainly on themselves as autonomous individuals, with personal rights and unique traits, or whether people focus mainly on themselves as members of cohesive social groups that are much more important than any of their individual members. In individualistic cultures, it's usually OK to "toot your own horn." After all, in such cultures "the squeaky wheel gets the grease." In contrast, in collectivistic cultures, it's often frowned upon to draw too much attention to yourself. Instead, you should focus on being a good group member. In Japan, for example, "the nail that stands out gets pounded down."

Notice that we've only covered two of Hofstede's six cultural dimensions, and we've already run into a complexity. Whereas Japan is a more masculine culture than Sweden, Sweden is a more individualistic country than Japan. You might be tempted to stereotype Swedes as being nicer than the Japanese, but that's only true if you think being nice is all about being nurturing. If you think being nice is all about being modest, you'll have to draw the opposite conclusion. I mention this complexity, and make a specific reference to stereotypes, because one of the dangers of knowing about average differences among large groups of people is to oversimplify things and thus to begin to stereotype. Try not to stereotype. If necessary, pretend that a likable Black, Swedish experimenter is on his way over, from his fieldwork in Japan.

Hofstede has identified several other important dimensions of culture. One more example is **power distance** – "how a society handles inequality among people." In countries where there is a great deal of power distance, everyone has a place in a clearly understood hierarchy, and most people readily accept it. Of course, the extreme form of this is a culture where slavery or caste systems put some people forever at the very bottom of a social ladder. Chimps would presumably be OK with this. At the other extreme, most people from countries that are low in power distance pride themselves on being highly egalitarian, and they may take offense at the idea that some people are better than others. From a purely selfish perspective, it's surely a lot better to be a king or queen in a high power distance culture – and a lot better to be a commoner in a low power distance culture. From a global perspective, by the way, America scores on the moderately low side in power distance. According to Hofstede's analyses, at least, the U.S. is not such a bad place to be poor or low in social status. From a global perspective, though, this cultural finding isn't surprising. All else being equal, wealthy countries tend to be more egalitarian, and they usually have wider social safety nets. Based on Hofstede's cross-cultural analyses, I'd rather be poor in Austria or Denmark, for example, than be poor in the U.S.

I point out these concrete examples of Hofstede's well-studied cultural dimensions to argue that human cultures are incredibly diverse. And they are diverse in a wide variety of ways that go well beyond Hofstede's thoughtfully derived cultural dimensions. Let's consider just a few specific cultural dimensions: religiosity, honor, and human sexuality and marriage.

Cross-cultural variation in religious beliefs

Let's begin with religiosity. Over the past decade or so, Gallup polls that cover the large majority of the earth's population reveal that a global median of 84% of people (in 114 surveyed countries) say that religion plays "an important role in their daily lives" (Crabtree, 2010). We're a religious planet. But this high median value across many nations hides tremendous cross-national variation. In the world's most religious countries, like Bangladesh and Niger, more than 99% of survey respondents (yes, virtually everyone) reported being religious in Gallup's World Poll. At the other extreme, in Estonia and Sweden, only about one person in six reported being religious. If there are any "Bible belts" in these European countries, they must surely be pulled pretty tight. On top of this diversity in the simple percentage of people who report being religious, I hope it's obvious that there is also tremendous global diversity in the details of people's specific religious beliefs. From beliefs about reincarnation and resurrection to beliefs about what specific foods are acceptable for human consumption, the global diversity of specific religious beliefs is truly remarkable.

I also hope it's obvious that culturally determined religious beliefs have profound implications for human behavior, including behavior that is subject to evolutionary forces. Evolutionary psychologists have long been concerned with explaining systems of power, status, and intergroup conflict (de Waal, 1982; Sidanius & Pratto, 2000). For example, the issue of separation of church and state that is the subject of much debate in the U.S. has very little meaning in countries where virtually everyone is a devout believer. On the other hand, the question of exactly which specific religious group should wield the most political power probably gets tougher rather than easier in highly religious countries. Like other deeply held personal beliefs, religious beliefs can sometimes fuel conflict. Crabtree and Pelham (2009) found, for example, that in highly religious countries, people report observing higher than usual levels of ethnic intolerance.

But life in less religious countries is not always a bowl of cherries either. Globally speaking, there is a strong negative correlation between suicide rates and religiosity levels (Pelham & Nyiri, 2008). In countries with fewer religious believers, then, more people take their own lives. Further, this is true even after controlling statistically for confounding factors such as national wealth. Suicide rates in Kuwait, the most religious country for which suicide data were available, were less than 2 people per 100,000 per year. In contrast, in Estonia, the least religious country for which suicide data were available, suicide rates were almost 11 times higher. Suicide is an evolutionary puzzle in any nation, but it arguably becomes more puzzling as it becomes more common (but see Buss, 2008, who offers some clever solutions to this evolutionary puzzle).

You may also remember the global survey of helping behavior discussed in Chapter 9. Worldwide, more religious people are more likely to report helping others. All this being said, evolutionary theories such as terror management theory (to be covered in detail in Chapter 11) suggest a couple of reasons why some nations are more religious than others in the first place. In countries where people have more exposure to death and dying (countries with higher disease load and higher infant mortality rates), religiosity levels are higher, even after controlling for national wealth (Fincher & Thornhill, 2012). So even if culture sometimes overrides evolution, there seem to be other times when culture is heavily driven by it (Diamond, 1997; Fincher et al., 2008).

Cross-cultural variation in the salience of honor

Moving from religion to honor, there is enormous variation worldwide – and even across regions of the U.S. – in what Dov Cohen and colleagues (1996) call the "culture of honor." In an honor culture, people (especially men) are taught that their honor, like their physical possessions, must be constantly defended against threats or insults. If you want to know if your recent acquaintance CJ grew up in an honor culture, just make a tasteless joke about how slutty his mother is. The more of your teeth CJ knocks out, the more likely it is that he grew up in a culture of honor. On second thought, maybe there are safer ways to assess the culture of honor. But as I hope this thought experiment illustrates, there is dramatic cultural variation within the U.S. in the degree to which people feel they need to respond to insults to their personal (or family) honor with physical violence.

As I mentioned in Chapter 8, I grew up in an honor culture. The culture of honor is as much a part of southeastern U.S. culture as very, very sweet tea (which Northerners might confuse with maple syrup), country music, or tiny little country churches. So as a Southerner, my culturally programmed instincts are to be pleasant and highly respectful to others, especially strangers. But when a person insults me or one of my friends or family members, or tries to take something that I know is mine, my gut reaction is to want to kick this person's ass. I'm not saying that ass-kicking is a great or noble idea. I'm just reporting, with some embarrassment, on my culturally programmed gut reaction. As anyone who grew up in a non-honor culture can tell you, a much more reasonable response to an insult or a small injustice is to laugh it off or ignore it. But try to tell me this after Magic Johnson and his "All Stars" insulted me and my basketball-challenged friends back in 1996 – by instructing his personal janitor to start mopping the floor of our basketball court, while we were trying to play a friendly four-on-four basketball game in the decrepit but beloved "Men's Gym" (now known as the Student Activity Center) at UCLA. To be clear about my take on the situation, we had already been there for an hour when Magic arrived, and there were still two other open courts available. But Magic wanted the best court (center court, which I considered our court because we were there first). Furthermore, in the past, when Magic had arrived at 9 a.m. he had summarily sent us all out of the gym claiming to have reserved it. I had done the research to confirm that, in fact, he had never reserved the gym. He seems to have just felt he owned it.

So, as a believer in (or victim of) the culture of honor, I was flabbergasted when all seven of my friends responded to having their court mopped while they were trying to play on it by letting Magic walk all over them. They all quickly conceded the half-mopped court. By this time, after all, we all knew Magic had never reserved the court and had no right to it. "Teacher, you must give the court to Magic Johnson because he is a basketball legend." I still get angry to this day thinking about this. (Yes, I know he seems like a very lovable guy on TV.) To my friends, who all grew up in non-honor cultures, when a very large and very famous person tells you to leave the court, you just do it. In the past, I too had conceded the court because I believed that Magic had it reserved. This time, however, I didn't budge. My honor button had been pushed one time too many. When Magic approached me and told me to get off his court, I explained to him that he was a liar, and that I was sick of being lied to – and bullied.

Magic's response was to up the ante. He sent a guy over to talk to me who was roughly Shaquille O'Neal's size, but much more muscular. The guy got in my face (well, his chest did), looked down at me, and said: "If you know what's good for you, you need to get off Magic's court." This didn't work. Anyone who has grown up in an honor culture knows it is a badge of honor to stand up to Goliath. If he kicks your ass, that's a badge of honor. If you get lucky and kick his, you'll be in the company of people like David (as in David and Goliath). As my brother Stacy likes to put it: "If you see me and a bear in a fight, and you jump in, it oughta be to help the bear." When I just stood there looking up at Goliath defiantly, it got a little ugly. A point guard who was more my own size simply tried to shove me off the court. I'll spare you the details, but that didn't work. By this point, I suspect that Magic probably saw a looming lawsuit and asked his players to call off the assault.

With everyone watching and a powerful feeling of racial tension in the air (did I mention that I am White?), Magic walked over to me and began to explain to me – the way a father talks down to a naughty child – that I was creating an unnecessary scene. But my culture of honor button had been pushed until it was stuck: I had had enough. Before things ever got this crazy, I had already made a firm resolution not to touch anyone unless I was being assaulted, but I refused to leave the court. The tension quickly re-escalated. I finally got my honor-saving excuse to leave the court when the UCLA student employee who was in charge of the gym heard what was happening (from the basement), came to center court, and pleaded with me to leave the court. His culturally ingenious words were something like: "Dr. Pelham, we've talked about this, and we both know you are right. Magic has no right to the court. But I'm asking you to step off – so no one gets hurt." It didn't dawn on me until afterwards that "so no one gets hurt" meant "so you don't get your ass kicked, you tiny little guy who is eaten up with the culture of honor."

Cohen et al.'s (1996) research on the culture of honor suggests that my response to feeling bullied by an arrogant superstar is highly predictable. For those who grew up being taught that honor is a fragile and prized possession, ignoring threats and insults simply isn't an option. But am I the only one who feels this way? That's what Cohen et al. (1996) wanted to find out. To do so, they staged an ingenious study of culture and reactions to bullying. Magic Johnson was not available to serve as a naturally existing bully, so Cohen et al. had to create one – in their lab at the University of Michigan. In all three of their studies, they began by recruiting Northern and Southern male college students. The men all thought they'd be taking part in a study of "limited response time conditions on certain facets of human judgment." But that was just a ruse to get the Yankees and Rebels into the lab. After the men showed up and completed a short demographic survey, the experimenter sent them down a long, narrow hallway, to drop off their work at a table. But to get to the table they had to squeeze past a male confederate. The confederate always allowed the real participant to pass by to get to the table. For half the participants, the confederate also allowed the men to get right back to the other end of the hall. But for the other half of the men, the return trip wasn't so pleasant. On their way back, these men found that the confederate had opened a long file drawer that now blocked their path. As each man approached, the confederate's response was to slam the file drawer shut, bump the man in the shoulder as he passed him and call the man an "asshole." The question was how men responded to the obnoxious confederate's carefully choreographed insult.

The answer was that the Southern men responded to the insult by wanting to kick this insulting loser's ass. Across three studies that all used this same manipulation, Cohen et al. (1996) looked at a wide range of reactions to the insult. On almost all of them, the Southern men responded to the insult by really wanting to hurt somebody. In Study 1, for example, two trained raters were strategically placed in rooms where they could see each participant's face right after the obnoxious confederate insulted him. Of course, these raters were kept blind to where the participants had grown up. The raters coded the men's reactions for expressions of anger as well as amusement. As you can see in Figure 10.9, Northerners were slightly more amused than angered by the staged insult. Southerners, on the other hand, were much more angered than amused. The only thing surprising to me about this clever study is that none of the Southerners laid hands on the confederate. Perhaps the power of the immediate situation – being in a research study at a well-respected university, in the North – toned down the well-learned reactions of many of the Southern men.

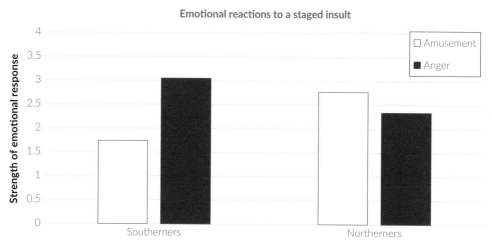

Figure 10.9 *Whereas Southern men responded to a staged insult with more anger than amusement, Northern men responded with more amusement than anger.*

In follow-up studies, Cohen et al. (1996) observed very similar cultural differences to the same staged insult when they assessed changes in testosterone levels, stress-hormone levels, or the firmness of the insulted men's handshakes – when they greeted a stranger who had not been privy to the original insult. In a third study, the researchers even staged a game of "chicken" shortly after the insult.

To set up this game, they sent each freshly insulted man down a long, narrow hallway where a large (6'3", 250 lb.) stranger walked directly at the participant. The confederate had been instructed to step aside only at the very last moment, to avoid a collision. In the control condition (in which the men had not been insulted), the Southerners lived up to their stereotypical reputations for politeness to strangers. They stepped aside at about 9 feet, whereas the Northerners did not step aside until about 6 feet. But after the insult, Southerners did not step aside until about 3 feet. The Northerners showed only a tiny response to the insult, stepping aside to let the large stranger pass at about 5 feet.

Additional research has shown that the culture of honor is a strong predictor of real-world violence. Nisbett (1993) showed, for example, that homicide rates are much higher in Southern states than in Northern states – but not right across the board. The cultural difference only occurs for homicides resulting from arguments. Nisbett also showed that the large regional difference in argument-related homicides holds up even after controlling statistically for regional differences in poverty and high temperatures, both of which are known to be good predictors of homicide rates.

More recently, Thomas Timmerman (2007) controlled for both poverty and temperature in a very different kind of study. He analyzed more than 5 million "at bats" (plate appearances) in major league baseball (MLB) games covering a 36-year period. He found that MLB pitchers from the South were more likely than MLB pitchers from the North to hit batters with a pitch. However, this seems to have been the case only after threats to a pitcher's honor. First, Southern pitchers were much more likely than Northern pitchers to hit the batter who was batting right behind someone who had just hit a home run off the pitcher. Second, Southern pitchers were more likely than Northern pitchers to hit batters in retaliation. If your pitcher had just hit one of Billy Joe's teammates with a pitch, the chances were greatly increased that Billy Joe would even the score with a "beanball" (a ball thrown to hit a batter) of his own. Hurting others who have recently hurt you (or those who have hurt someone to whom you are connected) probably has an evolutionary basis (e.g., see Azrin et al., 1967). If this is true, however, it's clear that some cultures promote and socialize this evolved tendency much more than others.

Worldwide, there appears to be dramatic variation in the strength and salience of the notion of personal (or family) honor. I say "appears to be" because, as far as I know, no studies have systematically ranked the world's countries on the culture of honor mentality. However, it's pretty well accepted that most Latino cultures are honor cultures (Vandello & Cohen, 2003). It is probably no accident, then, that many Latin American countries appear at or near the top of the world homicide rankings. According to a 2014 report by the United Nations Office on Drugs and Crime (see www.unodc.org), the five countries with the highest homicide rates on earth are all in Latin America or the Caribbean. In this distressing top five list, you'll find Honduras, Venezuela, the U.S. Virgin Islands, Belize, and El Salvador. In 2012, the average homicide rate in these five nations was just under 57 homicides per 100,000 people per year. At the other global extreme, Monaco, Lichtenstein, Singapore, Iceland, and Japan had the five lowest homicide rates in the world. The average homicide rate across these five countries in 2012 was 0.16 homicides per 100,000 people per year. The top five to bottom five ratio is about 350:1. Just how much of this variation we can account for with the culture of honor is hard to say. Pinker (2011) would probably be quick to note, for example, that corruption levels rather than a culture of honor per se might be the primary reason why so many Latin American countries have high murder rates. Whatever the reasons, the amount of cross-cultural variation in homicide rates is mindboggling.

As noted in Chapter 8, Pinker (2011) has also noted that homicide rates worldwide are declining. From a historical perspective, most nations are moving in the direction of less killing. To document changes in homicide rates in America's New England region over the past few hundred years, Pinker (2011, p. 95) was forced to use a logarithmic scale for homicides – to keep the steep downward slope in his graph from looking like the face of a cliff. In the American New England of the 1600s, homicide rates approached 100 people per 100,000 per year. By the early 1900s, that figure had dropped to roughly 1 person per 100,000 per year. And in most parts of the U.S., homicide rates are lower today than they were when your great-grandparents were young. The founding fathers had to worry a lot more than you and I do about all forms of homicide, including patricide. It seems highly unlikely that the collective American gene pool has become kinder and gentler over the past few centuries. Culture must matter.

Cross-cultural variation in sexual behavior and marriage

As you know very well by now, evolutionary psychologists care at least as much about sex as they do about violence. Culture matters here, too. Evolutionary thinkers have astutely noted that in every culture ever studied, there have always been rules and norms about sexual behavior (Wilson, 1978). That being said, it is extraordinary how much historical and cultural variation there has been about such rules. In **sexually restrictive countries**, such as many parts of Asia and the Middle East, the norms and rules about sex before marriage are so iron-handed that very few teenagers are bold enough to have premarital sex. Unsurprisingly, then, rates of teenage pregnancy in such sexually restrictive countries are pretty low. At the other extreme, in **sexually permissive countries** such as the Netherlands, many parents take it for granted that their teenagers will be sexually active, and so they focus their parental energies on ensuring that their teens engage in safe, consensual sex. Somewhat ironically, then, rates of teenage pregnancy are also low in sexually permissive countries. Somewhere between these two cultural extremes, we find **semi-restrictive countries** such as the U.S. In the U.S., the most common parental strategy for dealing with teenage sexuality seems to be wishful thinking. It is probably for this reason that American teenagers are so poorly informed about issues such as safe sex, and have such high teenage pregnancy and abortion rates (Ansuini et al., 1996; Jaccard et al., 1998). American parents just don't talk to their kids enough (or soon enough) about sex. I'm pretty sure the evolutionary pressures that promote sex among sexually mature teens do not check in with the silent parents of these sexually mature teens before promoting conception. So when my daughter becomes a teenager I'll have to decide between moving to the Netherlands and moving to

Afghanistan. Or maybe I'll bite the bullet and actually talk to her about safe sex. (I've already had many talks with my 14-year-old son, who – thankfully, I guess – is still grossed out by the very idea of sex.)

If you think modern cross-cultural variations in sexual permissiveness reflect cultural diversity, you ain't seen nothing yet. The global and historical variations in norms and laws regarding sexual behavior are astonishing. Consider Gilbert Herdt's (1981) anthropological analysis of ritualized homosexual behavior among a Papua New Guinea warrior tribe that Herdt dubbed the "Sambia." I can't possibly summarize Herdt's influential work more succinctly than did Mary Weismantel (2004, p. 497). As Weismantel put it, Herdt got social scientists' attention when he:

> described secret ceremonies in the men's house of a New Guinea tribe in which young boys were required to fellate [give oral sex to] older men. Herdt's discovery prompted much interest as an example of "homosexual rites," but … the ritual was not about sexual enjoyment. It was about reproduction. Neither male nor female children, according to Sambian beliefs, would mature into adults capable of reproduction without first orally imbibing semen. The human capacity to reproduce, as Sambia men saw it, was contained in a scarce, precious, and immortal fluid—visible as semen in men and breast milk in women—that must be physically transmitted from one generation to another, indefinitely, if human life is to continue.

If learning about these unusual Sambian sexual rituals makes you really uncomfortable, welcome to the fascinating and highly uncomfortable world of cultural anthropology. Ignoring the many complex cultural and ethical issues raised by our knowledge of this eyebrow-raising sexual ritual, knowing about how radically different Sambian culture is from any modern Western culture is both eye-opening and humbling. Human beings are incredibly flexible creatures, and the diversity in cross-cultural beliefs about sex – like the cross-cultural variation in almost everything else – is truly astonishing (see Walker et al., 2010).

Just as there are enormous historical and cross-cultural variations in the rules and norms regarding sex, there are also enormous historical and cross-cultural variations in the rules and norms about that familiar institution that makes some people want to stop having sex – at least with each other. Of course, that institution is marriage. King Solomon had many wives. Today, most Christians and Jews the world over believe in strict monogamy – or at least **serial monogamy** (having more than one spouse in your lifetime but having only one spouse at a time). In many African cultures, things are even more relaxed; men can have several wives in their lifetimes and they can even have them all at once. The practice of having multiple wives is known as **polygyny**, and I recently got a closer than usual look at it when I surveyed the students in one of my human development classes. I simply asked the students how many siblings they had. The person with the most siblings was a thoughtful and engaging 45-year-old man from Africa called Matthew. He reported having 39 siblings. When I ethnocentrically asked him how that was biologically possible, he mentioned that his father had 7 wives.

The alpha males in many mammalian species have the animal equivalents of many wives, and so evolutionary psychologists do not find it so surprising that there are still places where powerful men can have many wives. Alpha male elephant seals have very large harems that they spend a lot of time defending in pretty vicious battles. The benefit to the alpha male, of course, is producing a lot of offspring (sometimes hundreds), who are completely ignored by the alpha male but well cared for by their devoted mothers. Remember parental investment theory? But most benefits come with costs. The main cost to alpha male elephant seals, by the way, is that they have pretty short lifespans (see Clutton-Brock & Isvaran, 2007). It's dangerous at the top. Remember Caesar?

Given men's greater tendency toward sexual promiscuity, then, it would be a bit of an evolutionary puzzle to learn that there are many cultures in which people practice **polyandry**. Polyandry is the practice of having multiple husbands (although they do not all have to be named Andy). For a long time, social scientists thought polyandry was exceedingly rare. But recent research in anthropology has shown that it is much more common than we once thought. In fact, it exists in a wide variety of forms, and it exists in some form or another all over the globe. Katherine Starkweather and Raymond Hames (2012) identified 53 cultures worldwide that practice some form of true polyandry. Suffice it to say that there is healthy debate among evolutionarily inclined anthropologists (and psychologists) about whether polyandry could have possibly evolved – or whether it flies in the face of evolution. Starkweather and Hames (2012) argue not only that polyandry exists all over the globe but also that it exists in quite a few cultures resembling those in which we evolved (such as hunter-gatherer cultures). Furthermore, there do appear to be some reliable cross-cultural predictors of polyandry, and they are loosely consistent with the idea that it could have evolved.

As far as the predictors of polyandry go, it is more common than usual in cultures where there are many more marriageable men than women. Ironically, one way in which this can happen is polygyny. Some cultures that have polygyny also have polyandry. I guess in these cultures, what's fair for the goose really is considered fair for the gander. Polyandry is also more likely to exist in cultures in which male mortality rates are high, because of a war or social conflict. A second husband, I suppose, is a pretty good life insurance policy against the first. Polyandry also seems to be at least somewhat more likely in cultures in which there's a great deal of male "absenteeism." This might happen, for example, because of the prevalence of extended male hunting trips, as is true in native Canadian Inuit cultures.

In farming cultures, polyandry is also much more common in specific places – such as the Himalayan regions of Tibet, Nepal, and India – where there is very little land and the rugged land that does exist is difficult to farm. In such places, polyandry seems to control population growth while also allowing two or more men to work together to run farms that no one man could run by himself. It's probably no accident that in these "land-starved" cultures, people care deeply about keeping their plots of land in their own families. I sure wouldn't want to be a real estate agent in such places. In these cultures, it may be no accident that the most common form of polyandry is **fraternal polyandry**, in which a woman takes two or more brothers as husbands. Although it may be tough for

Westerners to accept the "yuck" factor of brothers having sex with the same woman, rearing your brother's child makes a lot more evolutionary sense than being cuckolded by an unrelated stranger. In the case of fraternal polyandry, at least, you'd be helping to care for a child that shares a quarter of your genes. The lucky child might even be handsome enough to look a lot like you.

From a purely selfish perspective, I hope it's obvious how it could be nice to have two husbands. Your chances of having someone agree to do the dishes, for example, could double – and thus go from about ½ of 1% to a full 1% (every little bit helps). But Starkweather and Hames (2012, p. 152) also make a clever argument for what may be in it for some of the men who become "junior husbands." As they put it, sometimes:

> it may be in the interest of a male with low competitive abilities to make the best of a bad situation by becoming a junior husband and having some chance of reproduction. Through time the marriage market may improve, and by working hard the junior husband may be able to demonstrate his attractiveness as a mate to another female and marry her.

All of this, with his wife's permission, I assume.

To provide just one more example of cultural diversity in the rules and norms of marriage, most Westerners say that they marry for love. Many Easterners offer much more pragmatic explanations, such as division of labor, financial stability, or reproduction. Arranged marriages are also virtually unheard of in the U.S. and Europe but still common in some parts of India, Africa, and the Middle East, although this is quickly changing as a result of globalization. Whether specific cultural practices such as polyandry or arranged marriages could have evolved is a tricky question. But one thing is clear. They exist in an organism that evolved, and at least one important route through which they may have come to exist if they did not evolve is culture. It's amazing how many ways there are to be a person.

If you feel like the point of this chapter is to take back everything else I've said in this book, let me say yet again that I don't believe sociocultural and evolutionary psychology are incompatible. The two perspectives merely represent two different windows on the complex drama of human social behavior. If human beings were not programmed by millions of years of evolution to be extremely flexible – and extremely sensitive to the needs and wishes of others – then we could safely ignore social and cultural psychology. If this sounds like a cop out, consider the clownfish. Clownfish are **sequential hermaphrodites**. Clownfish all hatch as males. They live in very hierarchical groups in which one and only one fish – the largest – becomes female. This big female bullies all the smaller males and stays atop the strict hierarchy. And she mates only with the largest male. But if this alpha female dies (or gets captured by a clueless dentist from Sydney), the male who had been second in command will now become a female, and all the other males will move up a notch in the clownfish hierarchy (Boyer, 2015). Thus clownfish are so sensitive to the situation (the absence of an alpha female) that they can undergo a situationally induced sex change. The sex of crocodilians (such as alligators) is also situationally determined. In the case of crocodilians, however, the determining factor is the temperature of the soil in which the eggs are incubated (Crews, 2003). But in both clownfish and crocodilians, this sex determination system has a firm genetic basis. Clownfish would not ever change sex if their genome did not program them to do so – and in ways that seem highly consistent with life history theory, by the way. Similarly, we would not be able to survive in both the Arctic and the tropics if we were not genetically programmed to be a highly social and a highly adaptable species. Several other primate species have rudimentary cultures, but as Mark Nielsen (2012, p. 170) put it: "*Homo sapiens* are the world's cultural species *par excellence*."

Figure 10.10 *Clownfish are sequential hermaphrodites, meaning that they all begin life as males. Then only one clownfish in a given group – the largest – becomes a female. The sex of crocodilians is also situationally determined, but based on the temperature of the incubating eggs. Like clownfish and crocodilians, people are highly sensitive to situations.*

So, in the diverse and complex social worlds we all inhabit, from Argentina to Zimbabwe, we ignore social and cultural psychology at our own peril. Getting back to a question I raised earlier in this chapter, then, does culture ever trump the evolutionary processes that helped create it? It seems obvious to me that the answer is yes, sometimes. There's an obvious, mechanistic sense in which evolution created culture. But creating something does not mean you always trump it. Geppetto created Pinocchio, after all, but this did not mean that the naughty, curious, and resourceful Pinocchio always obeyed him.

FOR FURTHER READING

» Fincher, C.L., Thornhill, R., Murray, D.R. & Schaller, M. (2008). Pathogen prevalence predicts human cross-cultural variability in individualism/collectivism. *Proceedings of the Royal Society*, 275(1640), 1279–85.

» Gneezy, U., Leonard, K.L. & List, J.A. (2009). Gender differences in competition: Evidence from a matrilineal and a patriarchal society. *Econometrica*, 77(5), 1637–64.

» Kurzban, R. & Leary, M.R. (2001). Evolutionary origins of stigmatization: The functions of social exclusion. *Psychological Bulletin*, 127(2), 187–208.

» Nielsen, M. (2012). Imitation, pretend play, and childhood: Essential elements in the evolution of human culture? *Journal of Comparative Psychology*, 126(2), 170–81.

» Richerson, R.J. & Boyd, R. (2008). Migration: An engine for social change. *Nature*, 456(7224), 877.

» Starkweather, K.E. & Hames, R. (2012). A survey of non-classical polyandry. *Human Nature*, 23(2), 149–72.

» Triandis, H.C. (1989). The self and social behavior in differing cultural contexts. *Psychological Review*, 96(3), 506–20.

SAMPLE MULTIPLE-CHOICE EXAM QUESTIONS

Here are four sample quiz questions for Chapter 10. You can find the Chapter 10 quiz at: www.macmillanihe.com/evolutionary-psychology

10.01. Milgram's studies of obedience among "teachers" in what the teachers thought was a word learning activity revealed that:

a. men were much more willing to harm incompetent learners than women were

b. the United States is a much more obedient culture than the UK or Sweden

c. the large majority of people will harm another person if an assertive experimenter orders them to do so

10.02. Which person listed below is most likely to behave as if he were the alpha male?

    a. a man who is stranded on a deserted island and does not have to answer to anyone else

    b. the CEO (chief executive officer) or founder of a major corporation

    c. both A and B are correct

10.03. Recent research in cultural and social psychology suggests that human beings evolved to:

    a. be very sensitive to social situations

    b. seek power whenever they have the opportunity

    c. stand strong against most persuasive arguments

10.04. Rates of murder that stem from arguments or insults are likely to be very high in:

    a. a masculine culture

    b. an honor culture

    c. a legally permissive culture

Answer Key: c, b, a, b.

Chapter 11
DEATH BE SOMEWHAT PROUD

TERROR MANAGEMENT THEORY

"The fear of death follows from the fear of life. A man who lives fully is prepared to die at any time."

— *Mark Twain (source unknown)*

"I don't want to become immortal through my work. I want to become immortal through not dying."

— *Woody Allen (source unknown;*
with apologies to David Buss)

In about seven billion years, something truly terrible will happen. Our sun, having exhausted all its fuel, will die. It won't be pretty. Actually, it will be kind of pretty from very far away. But that's not the point. Assuming human beings still exist, which is a huge assumption, it certainly won't be pretty to us. As the sun begins to die, it will slowly expand into a red giant that will eventually engulf the earth. So even if the Matt Groening Foundation has digitized and archived every episode of *The Simpsons*, this iconic TV show and every human memory of it will be utterly and completely destroyed. The same thing goes for every copy of *Don Quixote*, every copy of every Jay-Z music video, and every copy of, well, everything. This will make the tragic meteor strike of 66 million years ago look like a fender bender. And, yes, fenders will cease to exist, too. I'm talking about the end of everything.

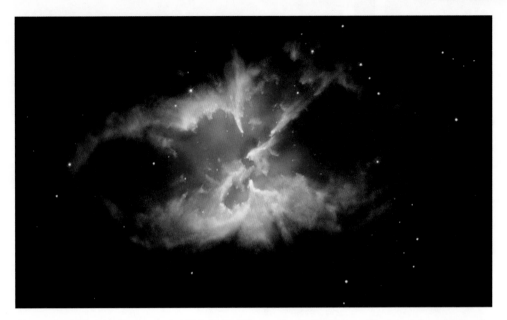

Figure 11.1 *The planetary nebula NGC 2818. When our sun dies, it too will create a beautiful and deadly nebula.*

In case this is news to you, let me assure you that it's hard to find an astronomer who disagrees with this gloomy forecast. In fact, virtually every theory of the evolution of the universe involves the eventual destruction of virtually everything. Things do get recycled in the universe, but this usually happens in places like stars. Even the best acid-free archival paper can't survive that. I sure hope life really is all about the journey because the destination sucks. If you find this a little distressing, you're practically alone. Yes, I said you are practically alone. And so am I. That's because, as far as we know, no other animal species in the 4.7-billion-year history of our planet ever contemplated its own demise, much less the demise of everything. That's right. We have a very special relationship with death. To be sure, many animals seem to know what death is, and some even seem to mourn lost family members. But we seem to be the only species who knows for sure that death is coming: "Never send to know for whom the [death] bell tolls; it tolls for thee." When my daughter Brooklyn was about two and a half, she lovingly reassured her older brother Lincoln that his dead goldfish, Monty, would be OK "as soon as he gets his medicine." It wasn't long before she came to the painful conclusion that modern goldfish medicine has its limits. Monty wasn't coming back.

LIFE SUCKS BECAUSE WE DIE

It's not clear exactly when we *Homo sapiens* first became aware of our own mortality, but it certainly wasn't yesterday, and it certainly wasn't just in a suburb of Cleveland. Although there are a few quirky languages that don't have future verb conjugations, even these languages allow their users to talk freely about the future. There cannot have been very many human cultures anywhere in which people were oblivious to the existence of aging and death. A big cost of being able to speak and understanding the concept of funerals is worrying about what the speaker will say about you at your funeral, and who will bother to come hear the eulogy. As Stephen Jay Gould (1985) put it, human beings' awareness of their own mortality is likely to be a psychologically painful byproduct of having a large brain – in much the same way that backaches are a physically painful byproduct of an otherwise highly adaptive upright posture. Because the enormous adaptive advantages conferred by large brains more than compensate for this existential thorn in the flesh, large brains have blossomed in human evolution. So we're also stuck with a thorn. The theory that examines how we deal with this evolutionary thorn is known as terror management theory.

We can't stop death, but maybe we can manage it. According to Tom Pyszczynski and colleagues (1999), the core assumption of **terror management theory** is that human beings cope with their intense fear of death by psychologically defending their positive views of themselves and their cultures. One route to making peace with death, then, is to acknowledge that you are going to die someday, but to emphasize that things much bigger than you will live on. Another common way to cope with the thought of death, for many, is to decide that whereas your physical body will die, your soul or spirit will live on in an afterlife. According to terror management theory, then, it is no accident that practically every religion ever known promotes a belief in some kind of afterlife. The assurance of something enduring, whether it is by means of resurrection, reincarnation, or movement to a higher astral plane, offers people meaning when there would otherwise be little else but anxiety and hopelessness, if not abject terror.

CULTURAL WORLDVIEWS AND THE DYNAMICS OF MORTALITY SALIENCE

I should clarify that religious beliefs are only one of many popular ways in which people defend themselves from the fear of death. Terror management theorists have studied a wide array of reassuring beliefs that they refer to as **cultural worldviews**. Cultural worldviews include self-validating beliefs as diverse as religious beliefs, a belief in the sanctity of marriage, devotion to one's government, identification with one's ethnic group or political party, the belief that the world is fair and just, and the belief that Michael Jordan was once a better basketball player than LeBron James now is. As you can plainly see, unless you are a delusional Michael Jordan fan, a cultural worldview doesn't have to be true to do its job. You may have also noticed that most of the cultural worldviews listed here are pretty traditional. In the early days of terror management theory, these were about the only kinds of cultural worldviews studied. This has changed, but before I tell you how and why, let me share an example of how terror management theorists test the **mortality salience hypothesis**. This is the idea that when we have recently been reminded of our own deaths and death is in the back of our minds, we work harder than usual to maintain, respect, and validate our cultural worldviews.

Recall that terror management theory states that our cultural worldviews act as buffers (psychological crutches) that erase or reduce the fear of death. People who've been thinking about death defend their cultural worldviews because they're trying to replace deep feelings of terror with deep feelings of meaning. Greenberg et al. (1995) tested this hypothesis by asking some people to think and write about their own physical deaths. They asked another group to think and write about a non-threatening topic, namely watching TV. After the **mortality salience manipulation** (the "reminder of death"), people moved on to what they thought the experiment was really about, which was problem-solving. The problem was, though, that the solution to the problems required people to use cherished cultural icons as tools rather than as cherished cultural icons. Specifically, people had to use a small U.S. flag to sift some sand out of a black liquid that would badly discolor any fabric that it touched. They also had to use a crucifix as a hammer. As you can see in Figure 11.2, which I've recreated from video footage of the study, the only way to filter the sand out of the black watery mixture would be to use a rubber band to attach the flag to the top of an empty jar and then use the flag as a filter. The actual problem was tougher than it looks here, by the way, because participants were not shown the solution and they were given some not-so-useful distractor items. Relative to people in the control condition, people in the mortality salience condition took longer on the problem-solving tasks, reported feeling especially tense during the tasks, and reported that the tasks were more difficult. Doing something vaguely unpatriotic or sacrilegious feels a lot worse than usual when you've recently been thinking about coffins.

Figure 11.2 *An approximation of some of the problem-solving materials used in Greenberg et al.'s (1995) terror management study. Participants who had been thinking about their own deaths were highly reluctant to use the U.S. flag to filter the sand out of the black water. Doing so would stain a cherished cultural icon.*

A much more common way in which researchers have tested the mortality salience hypothesis is to see how people respond to other people who praise or criticize their cultural worldviews. Consider this immigrant from the African nation of Eritrea. Here's Aster's immigration story (adapted from Greenberg et al., 1992a):

> The first thing that hit me when I came to this country was the incredible freedom people had. In my home country of Eritrea everything is not as good.

Here there is freedom to go to school, freedom to work, and freedom to make your own decisions. Here anyone who works hard can make their own success. In my country most people live in poverty with no chance of escape. In this country people have better chances for success than anywhere else. While there are problems in any country, America truly is a great nation and I don't regret my decision to come here.

I don't know about you, but I've got a lot of respect for this woman. I must say, though, that I'm not nearly as keen on her sister, who is also a recent immigrant from Eritrea. Here's Ayana's immigration story:

When I first came to this country from my home in Eritrea I believed it was the "land of opportunity" but I soon realized this was only true for the rich. The system here is set up for rich against the poor. All people care about here is money and trying to have more than others. There is no sympathy, no compassion. It's all one group putting down others, and nobody cares about the foreigners. The people only let foreigners have jobs like pick fruit or wash dishes because no American would do them. Americans are spoiled and lazy and want everything handed to them. America is a cold and uncaring place, unwelcome to foreigners.

Boy, is she a drag. If it's so terrible here, I'd be happy to help her raise some money for a ticket back to Eritrea. In fact, a middle seat in a leaky boat sounds perfect. As you can see, I've been thinking a lot about death lately because I'm behaving much like the ethnocentric participants in another terror management study (Simon et al., 1997). Ignoring terror management issues for the moment, I hope it's obvious that many people dislike those who criticize their countries. What's not so obvious – in the absence of terror management theory – is why mild levels of disliking should swell into disdain, distrust, and derogation when we've recently been thinking about our own deaths. Unfortunately, thinking about your own death can increase your level of racism and intolerance. Thinking about one's own death even has an effect on people's perceptions of landscapes. What do you think about the landscape photograph in Figure 11.3?

This iconic photo of the Snake River in Wyoming's Grand Teton National Park was taken by famous photographer Ansel Adams in 1942, when he was an underpaid government employee. Of course, it's objectively very beautiful. The rugged mountains and the powerful river give us a glimpse of nature untamed. There was a reason they called it the Wild West. But, come to think of it, what's so bad about taming? Would you really rather be there, in that God-forsaken wilderness, or in a pleasant and picturesque city park, where the only wolves are the ones working on Wall Street?

Sander Koole and Agnes van den Berg (2005) found that reminding participants of their own mortality influenced their relative liking for wild versus cultivated Dutch landscapes. In case you took my dismissive comments about that beautiful Ansel Adams photo seriously, it's worth noting that most people seem to think wild landscapes are more beautiful than cultivated ones. At least that was true for the entire set of Dutch landscapes used by Koole and van den Berg. My theory about this finding is that wild landscapes really are more beautiful than cultivated

Figure 11.3 *Ansel Adams took this photo of the Snake River and the Tetons. I used to think it was really beautiful, and then I remembered I'm going to die. It sucks.*

ones. But this dramatic preference for wild rather than cultivated landscapes was cut in half when death was in the back of people's minds. Koole and van den Berg argue that as beautiful as the wilderness is, it reminds us of death and our inability to control nature. In contrast, rolling farmland and cityscapes remind us of our triumph over nature. Who knows? If we can triumph over nature, maybe we can somehow triumph over death. In fact, these were not just assumptions. A different group of Dutch participants agreed with statements such as these about how nature makes us feel about death.

So terror management processes can even influence a person's taste in art. This also includes art presumably created by the talented and timeless Johnny Depp. Greenberg et al. (2010) argued that one reason why some of us adore celebrities or wish to have astronomic stars named after us is that feelings of fame, even worshipping the famous from afar, can help us cope with the fear of death. In keeping with this idea, they found that people who had been recently reminded of their own deaths not only expressed an increased interest in becoming famous but also showed an increased desire to have a star named after themselves (I guess they didn't know that stars also die). Most interesting of all, death reminders also increased people's liking for an abstract painting that had presumably been created by Johnny Depp.

Figure 11.4 *This photo of a cityscape was taken in Vancouver, British Columbia, where your author once took a very nice stroll. Now that's a beautiful landscape.*

In the three decades since terror management theorists first got people thinking about the pervasive role of death in the human psyche, the mortality salience hypothesis has fared very well. Terror management theorists have used a wide variety of mortality salience manipulations. These range from showing people images of terrible accidents or catching people on sidewalks near funeral homes to flashing up the word "death" on computer monitors, but below the threshold for conscious perception. Such manipulations have reliably produced a collective tsunami of worldview defense (see Burke et al., 2010).

MANAGING OUR TERROR SOMETIMES MAKES US NICER

Some readers may be happy to learn that managing our fear of death doesn't always take the nasty ethnocentric turns that researchers observed in many of the early studies of terror management. Terror management theory began partly as an effort to explain stereotyping and discrimination. But we now know that people who've been reminded of their own mortality defend wonderful cultural worldviews just as readily as they defend ethnocentric ones. People like me and you, who are politically liberal, become more convinced of the merits of our own liberal attitudes after a mortality salience manipulation. Oh, I'm sorry – my mistake. If liberalism isn't your cup of tea, I hope that even a Tea Party conservative like you can appreciate the value of caring. Given that the cultural value of helping others is almost universally endorsed by liberals and

Figure 11.5 *Superman may be highly allergic to kryptonite, but as long as he steers clear of it, he's not dying any time soon. Cohen et al. (2011) found that fantasies about the ability to fly increased in people who'd recently been thinking about their own deaths. This would explain Superman's market share advantage over Marvel's the Hulk or even DC's Batman and Robin. Despite their names, those last two wimps can't fly at all. They'd both be dead by now, if not for our immortal hero.*

conservatives alike, I hope you'll understand why mortality salience manipulations can sometimes increase rates of giving and helping. One of the most interesting reasons why we sometimes help others is to quell the sting of death – a finding referred to as the "Scrooge effect" (Jonas et al., 2002).

An even more heartwarming turn in recent research on death and oblivion is that mortality salience manipulations often cause people to cherish not just their cultural worldviews but the close others who live in those cultures with them. Thinking about our own mortality seems to increase our desire to develop and nurture close relationships (Mikulincer et al., 2003). I know just what you're thinking. OK, terror management processes apply to important social problems such as ethnocentrism as well as to altruism and even romantic love, including love for Johnny Depp. But do they apply to comic book-loving airline pilots? They sure do. Cohen et al. (2011) argued that the common fantasy of being able to fly can serve as a quirky worldview defense. After all, fantasizing about flying makes people feel they can transcend the usual laws of nature. And besides that, Superman is forever. Sure enough, Cohen et al. (2011) found that making people think about their own deaths increased their reported desire to be able to fly. In a second study, they showed that this effect is highly specific to flight. A mortality salience manipulation increased people's desires to fly but had no effect on people's desires to read minds.

Other predictions of terror management theory

So far, we've only scratched the surface of terror management theory. Terror management theorists have not limited themselves to the mortality salience hypothesis. They have also explored the implications of terror management theory for other important questions, such as whether having high self-esteem makes it a little less necessary to be so defensive; the answer is usually yes (see Greenberg et al., 1992b). Another interesting hypothesis from terror management theory reverses the usual causal arrow to show that threatening people's cherished cultural worldviews makes thoughts of death more accessible than usual. For example, Landau et al. (2004) described the victim of a brutal murder. Of course, this description prompted thoughts of death. But these thoughts were more nagging than usual when people learned that the victim had been a good person. Because one very popular cultural worldview is that the world is fair, threatening this cultural worldview seems to have made it harder than usual for people to shake their thoughts of death (see Hayes et al., 2010, for a review). I know of no research on this topic, but this finding could have important implications for common clinical disorders such as depression and PTSD (post-traumatic stress disorder). Do thoughts of death plague us even more fiercely than usual when the loss of a loved one seems particularly unjust? The loss of a small child or the death of a morally upright person "before her time" may be especially hard to take, in part, because it threatens our cultural worldviews.

Figure 11.6 *Not long after losing my father to a slow death from cancer, and then losing three other relatives shortly thereafter, I made this sculpture of one of my childhood heroes. In addition to being able to fly, Underdog is humble, lovable, and practically immortal. Maybe death can't be proud, but Cohen et al. (2011) sure can. They explained this kind of thing very well.*

SOME DEVILS (AND ANGELS) IN THE DETAILS OF TERROR MANAGEMENT

Before I close this chapter on terror management theory, I should make a couple of points about the details of terror management research. First, one of the most interesting things about terror management processes is that they work best when we're not watching them. After giving people a mortality salience manipulation, researchers usually distract people for a while to get them to stop thinking consciously about death. The specter of our own death has the biggest psychological impact when it's lurking just beneath the surface. There could be many reasons why this is true, but one of them is probably that some defensive processes work best when you don't know about them. Consciously deciding to fantasize about flying to reduce your fears of death – like consciously choosing to dislike someone who is critical of your country – might not be very reassuring. In fact, when I derogate people on purpose – as a conscious strategy for feeling better about myself – it's not quite as satisfying as usual. Insecurity-based self-deception is apparently a dish best served under the table (Greenberg et al., 1994; von Hippel & Trivers, 2011).

Speaking of derogation, I also have to note that there are some pretty thoughtful people who have derogated terror management theory. More than 400 empirical terror studies after its inception, terror management theory is still pretty controversial, especially within the controversial field of evolutionary psychology. Many of these controversies are beyond the scope of this book, but I will briefly note a few. Kirkpatrick and Navarrete (2006) argue that some of the basic assumptions of terror management theory are evolutionarily unlikely. They argue, for example, that the "survival instinct" that presumably fuels terror management processes is an unlikely adaptation, even in people. From this viewpoint, organisms don't have a basic "survival motive" any more than they have a basic motive to become famous or prevent climate change. Instead, they're motivated to do a long list of very specific things (like eating, having sex, and regulating one's body temperature), each of which ultimately has the consequence of promoting survival and reproductive success. Point taken. If it helps terror management theorists feel any better, other very thoughtful people have made exactly this same mistake (Pelham, 1997).

Other critics have argued that terror management processes sound more like cultural adaptations to a wide variety of deep worries – including anxiety about being separated from loved ones – rather than representing an evolved master motive. In our evolutionary history, we were typically surrounded by a handful of people to whom we had to be very deeply attached. The terror of an imagined separation from those we love may be just as important as the terror of not breathing. I'm inclined to agree with this thoughtful criticism, too. But in my view, terror management theory is more than worthy of inclusion in a book on evolutionary psychology because even if a terror management module never evolved, it is clear that evolution set the stage for terror management processes in exactly the way that Stephen Jay Gould suggested: Big brains + language = acute awareness of our own mortality.

There are also some criticisms of terror management theory I consider pretty unfair. For example, some ardent critics of terror management theory argue that terror management processes aren't real. One such argument is that terror management reduction is merely a laboratory artifact. Those who take this snarky view argue that terror management researchers have – knowingly or unknowingly – created false terror management effects in the lab. Others argue that although the terror management reduction effects observed in the lab may be real, these effects are so rarefied that they would evaporate in the real world. Yet another variation on this theme is the argument that terror management reduction processes are a Western cultural phenomenon, grounded firmly in Judeo-Christian religious beliefs.

Pelham and colleagues (in press) recently addressed criticisms such as these by examining terror management reduction processes in daily life in 16 nations across the globe. They capitalized on the fact that one good way to see what lots of people are thinking about in daily life is by using the Google Correlate research tool. This online research tool allows users to enter a specific search term and compare the weekly internet search volume for this search term since January 2004. For example, this search tool shows that year after year, Americans search Google for "mittens" in the fall and winter much more often than in the spring or summer. Predictably, Americans also search for "sunscreen" much more often in July than in December. More impressively, Google search volume across time or U.S. states also tracks public opinion very well. Thus, in states where people search things like "climate change hoax" more often, public opinion polls show that there is greater public skepticism about climate change.

Pelham and colleagues (in press) tested the idea that thinking about religion is a good way to reduce one's concerns about death. They did so by examining national week by week variation in Google search volume within each of 16 nations for 12 years. In all 16 nations, they observed that higher than usual weekly Google search volume for life-threatening illnesses in one week predicted increases in search volume for religious content in the following week. Thus, the more people searched for terms like *cancer*, *diabetes*, and *hypertension* in one week, the more they searched for terms like *God*, *Jesus*, and *prayer* the next week. This terror management reduction pattern held up even after controlling for how much people had searched for the same religious terms in the previous week. Terror management concerns thus predicted changes in how much people thought about religion from one week to the next. These effects also held up controlling for year by year variation in levels of religious search volume. Further, they held up controlling for both weekly increases in search volume associated with religious holidays (*Christmas*, *Easter*), and weekly variation in searches for a non-life-threatening illness (*sore throat*). Finally, these threat reduction effects occurred in 16 nations across the globe including such culturally diverse places as Australia, Canada, Chile, India, Ireland, Malaysia, and the Philippines. Terror management threat reduction processes seem to occur across the globe. Further, they seem to occur over periods of a week or so (as well as over the brief periods studied in the lab). Although there was a good deal of cross-cultural variation in the magnitude of this terror management effect, coping with fears of death by turning to religion seems to happen all over the globe.

Of course, there are many different interpretations of these findings. As Pelham and colleagues noted, the fact that death seems to make people think about religion says nothing about the ultimate validity of any religion. Whether existential terror fools people into accepting soothing myths or draws people closer to divine realities is up for debate. Further, the cultural robustness of these effects certainly does not mean there is a religion module, a terror management module, or "seek God because of terror" module. First of all, there are plenty of nations on earth where only a minority of people are religious. Second, there is at least a little room for debate about how robust the illness–religiosity link we observed was in the highly secular nation of Japan. It is certainly safe to say that the effect was much weaker in Japan than it was elsewhere across the globe. Nonetheless, the simple fact that this major illness–religion link was so robust would seem to say something about how much people worry about death across the globe, and how often religion beliefs may offer people a form of existential reassurance.

Finally, these online threat reduction effects do not seem to be unique to religion. Using the same Google Correlate research tool, and the same major illness terms as mortality-relevant threats, Pelham (2018c) found that the more often Americans searched the internet for *cancer, hypertension*, and *diabetes* one week, the more often they searched for politically reassuring beliefs and symbols (*founding fathers*, *American flag*) the next.

Putting all the laboratory and field studies of terror management together, I think it's fair to say that the substantial body of research on terror management theory suggests that human beings have had to learn to deal with a major bummer that is associated with having a very large brain. In my view, terror management effects are no less important if it turns out that terror management is a culturally learned solution (rather than an evolved solution) to a vexing problem, which was almost undeniably created by evolution. Until we become immortal, which I certainly plan on doing if at all possible, the psychology of death isn't likely to fade away any time soon.

FOR FURTHER READING

» Becker, E. (1973). *The denial of death*. New York: Simon & Schuster.

» Greenberg, J., Simon, L., Porteus, J., Pyszczynski, T. & Solomon, S. (1995). Evidence of a terror management function of cultural icons: The effects of mortality salience on the inappropriate use of cherished cultural symbols. *Personality and Social Psychology Bulletin*, 21(11), 1221–8.

» Von Hippel, W. & Trivers, R. (2011). The evolution and psychology of self-deception. *Behavioral and Brain Sciences*, 34(1), 1–56.

SAMPLE MULTIPLE-CHOICE EXAM QUESTIONS

Here are four sample quiz questions for Chapter 11. You can find the Chapter 11 quiz at: www.macmillanihe.com/evolutionary-psychology

11.01. Studies on terror management theory show that the tendency for people to honor, obey, or bolster their cultural worldviews is usually much stronger than usual among people who:

a. are currently thinking about their own mortality

b. were recently thinking about their own mortality but have had a few minutes to forget about the threat

c. are very old

11.02. Many evolutionary psychologists have criticized terror management theory by noting that:

a. there is probably no such thing as a "life instinct."

b. only a handful of studies have tested the basic predictions of terror management theory

c. there are cultures in which no one expresses much of a fear of death

11.03. Terror management theorists refer to widely shared and important beliefs as:

a. foundational systems

b. fountains of meaning

c. cultural worldviews

11.04. What finding in research on terror management is highly consistent with the idea that situations are very powerful – and that our important beliefs may thus change from moment to moment?

a. research on how much terror management processes vary across cultures

b. the finding that death doesn't bother people much when they have recently succeeded at a difficult task

c. research on the mortality salience hypothesis

Answer Key: b, a, c, c.

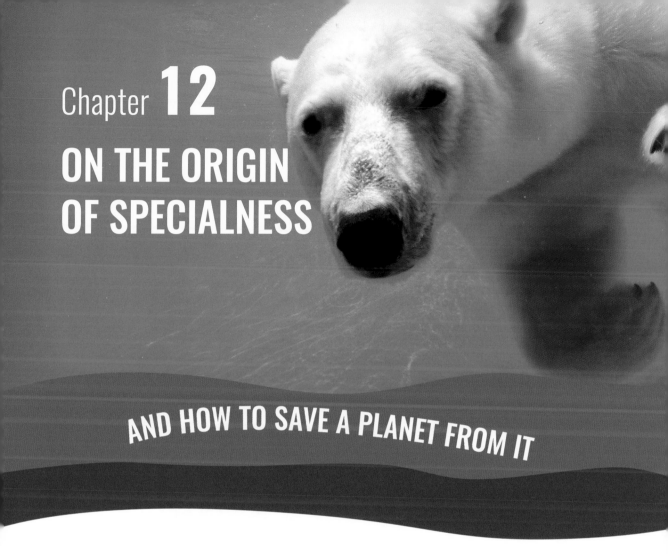

Chapter 12

ON THE ORIGIN OF SPECIALNESS

AND HOW TO SAVE A PLANET FROM IT

"This very expensive GLOBAL WARMING bullshit has got to stop. Our planet is freezing, record low temps, and our GW scientists are stuck in ice."

— *Donald Trump (2014)*

About 5,000 years ago, once people had gotten the hang of farming, living in large city-states, and trading extensively, an unknown Sumerian trader or traders invented the **cuneiform** writing system to keep track of economic transactions. Because we live in a world surrounded by numbers and written language, it is difficult for us to appreciate how incredibly ingenious it was for someone to realize that writing things down solves a myriad of problems. When Basam and Gabor got into their semi-monthly fistfight about whether Gabor owed Basam five more or six more geese to pay for a newly weaned goat, my pet theory is that it was an exasperated neighbor who finally got sick of all the fighting and thus proposed the cuneiform writing system. The cuneiform system involved making marks with a stylus in wet clay that was then dried and fired as a permanent record of economic transactions. This system initially focused almost exclusively on who had traded exactly what with whom – and in exactly what quantity. Thus, some Sumerian traders made the impressive leap of impressing important things in clay. This early cuneiform writing system was about as sophisticated as the scribbles of your four-year-old niece, but it quickly caught on because it was way better than relying exclusively on human memory for what someone said a few weeks ago.

Figure 12.1 *This bit of Sumerian "monumental archaic style cuneiform" is from just 2,600 years ago, many centuries after traders invented a much cruder version. Despite what we might imagine, writing was invented not because of a deep need for self-expression but out of pragmatic concerns for equitable social exchange.*

For example, it apparently wasn't too long before the great-great-great-grandchild of that original irate neighbor got a fantastically brilliant idea. Instead of drawing a funky duck, duck, duck, duck to represent four ducks, this brilliant person realized that four-ness itself (like two-ness and thirty seven-ness) was a concept. He or she thus created abstract characters for numbers that saved ancient Sumerians a lot of clay. I won't insult you by belaboring how much easier it is to write and verify the cuneiform version of "17 goats" than to write "goat, goat, goat, goat, goat, goat, goat, goat, goat, goat, goat, goat, goat, goat, goat, goat …" oh yeah "… goat," but I can summarize a few thousand years of human technological and scientific development by reminding you that incredibly useful concepts such as homeostasis, fractions, π (pi), and logarithms, which make possible great things such as penicillin and YouTube videos would have never come about were it not for the development of written language.

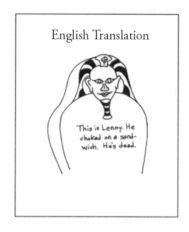

To summarize what happened over the course of the next several thousand years, suffice it to say that written language, including numbers and math, revolutionized – and sometimes limited – human scientific and technological development. For example, one of the biggest ruts that brilliant human beings ever got stuck into had to do with numbers. If you've ever given much thought to Roman numerals, it may have dawned on you that they are an inefficient pain in the butt. Who thought it was a great idea to represent 1,000 as M while representing 18 as XVIII? And why the big emphasis on 5 (V, that is) in a base-10 number system? The short answer to these questions seems to be that those who formalized Roman numbers got a little too obsessed with counting on their fingers and never fully got over it. For example, I hope it's obvious that the Roman numerals I, II, and III are stand-ins for human fingers. It's probably a lot less obvious that the Roman V (5) is a stand-in for the "V" that is made by your thumb and pointer finger when you hold up a single hand and tilt it outward a bit (sort of the way you would to give someone a "high five"). If you do this with both your hands and move your thumbs together until they cross right in front of you, you'll see that the X in Roman numerals is essentially, V + V. Once you're done making shadow puppets, I can tell you that the biggest drawback to Roman numerals is that the Roman system did not perfectly preserve place (the way we write numbers in the 1s column, 10s column, 100s column, and so on).

If you try doing subtraction, long division, or any other procedure that requires "carrying" in Roman numerals, you run into serious problems. Such problems appear to have limited sharply the development of math, and perhaps technology, in ancient Rome. I can surely say that, popes and Super Bowls aside, there's a good reason why Roman numerals have fallen by the wayside. In the much more popular Arabic (base-10) system of representing numbers, a five-digit number can never be smaller than a one-digit number because a numeral's position is much more important than its shape. A bank in New Zealand got a painful reminder of this fact in May 2009 when it accidentally deposited NZ$10,000,000 (yes, ten million) rather than NZ$10,000 (ten thousand) in the account of a couple who had applied for an overdraft. The couple quickly fled the country with the money – all three extra zeros of it. To everyone but the unscrupulous couple this mistake may seem tragic, but I can assure you that bank errors of this kind would be way more common if we had to rely on Roman numerals.

Because this is a book about evolution, and because we evolved holding firmly onto the basic mammalian plan for the pentadactyl ("five-fingered") limb discussed in Chapter 1, it's worth pointing out that our familiar base-10 number system could itself be considered a bit of evolutionary baggage. We apparently didn't improve on Roman numerals as much as we could have. The best theory for why people all over the planet use a base-10 counting system is that people all over the planet spent many millennia counting on their 10 fingers. But as most mathematicians could tell you, a base-8 number system is inherently superior to the base-10 system. I don't like playing favorites, but mathematicians have assured me that there is something special about powers of 2, and a base-8 system would be built on powers of 2 (as in $2^3 = 8$). Your computer's microprocessor, for example, is not constrained by having any fingers, and thoughtful engineers went with a binary processor for good reasons. Just as it is easier to split things in half mentally rather than splitting them into thirds or tenths, it is easier to turn switches on or off rather than turning them to one of three, or ten, different states. So, if there is a lucky 8-fingered race of intelligent aliens out there, there is a very good chance they would make fun of us for making a less serious version of the mistake made by the ancient Romans. We've apparently stuck with our quirky base-10 number system, rather than adopting a superior base-8 system because evolution happened to stick us with 10 fingers.

"Why yes, Dr. Grisham, that all goes without saying. But on the other, other, other, other, other, other, other hand ..."

TALKING + TRADING = WRITING

If you're wondering how we got from ancient Sumer to modern New Zealand and then eight-fingered aliens, the main point of this foray into the cultural evolution of written language is that modern life depends completely on written language, including numbers and mathematics. It was not until we had invented written language that we really began the series of increasingly impressive inventions that eventually allowed us to transform our planet from a bunch of deserts and rainforests to a bunch of concrete jungles, complete with the coffee shops where I hope millions of you are reading this book. I hope you can see, though, that written language was not invented in a vacuum. Human beings had to be able to talk before they could invent writing. But they also had to be extremely interested in trading before they would have any strong motivation to develop a system designed to keep track of who had traded what with whom.

I'm suggesting, then, that it's the unique combination of our facility with language and our abiding interest in social exchange that has made us the unique creatures that we are. It's not our sophisticated tool use, our abstract reasoning skills, our opposable thumbs, or our fantastic hand–eye coordination that separated us so clearly from other primates. Instead, it's that human invention called writing. We've probably had sophisticated spoken language for at least 100,000 years, and it's possible that some of our hominid ancestors had linguistic capabilities that greatly exceeded those of modern great apes. But neither *Australopithecus* nor *Homo erectus* invented written language, and we *Homo sapiens* lived very much the same way these other ancient hominids lived until we invented written language. One traditional theory about why Neanderthals died out when *Homo sapiens* survived is that these very strong, very big-brained human beings didn't have sophisticated speech. If they never got the hang of talking, we can also be sure they never got hooked on phonics. On the other hand, analyses by D'Anastasio and colleagues (2013) suggest that Neanderthals may have had spoken language after all. The micro-architecture of the hyoid bone that is crucial to careful articulation appears to be extremely similar in Neanderthals and modern humans. Even if Neanderthals did have spoken language, though, they surely didn't invent written language. And we didn't either until after the invention of agriculture and all the trading it prompted.

So, more than 90,000 years of spoken language without written language never seems to have gotten us very far. In contrast, in an evolutionary eye-blink after we invented written language, one of us painted the Sistine Chapel, several of us wrote constitutions, and many of us came to enjoy the benefits of smartphones. My point is that none of this would be true if it were not for the fact that we are both sophisticated talkers *and* skillful traders – with a deep concern for fairness. It is that precise combination, I believe, that set the stage not just for a unique human adaptation but for a unique human invention. That invention, again, was written language.

There can be little doubt that written language is an invention that piggybacked spoken language. This is why children learn to speak effortlessly but only learn to read and write with great effort. Researchers may hotly debate whether there is really a language instinct, but even most critics of this idea accept the idea that we learn spoken language very easily. In contrast, no one believes in a written language instinct. Written language has surely piggybacked spoken language. But it also seems very likely that written language climbed up there in the first place because of the human predisposition toward social exchange. There would have never been any motivation for those ancient Sumerian traders to have invented writing if they had not been engaging in so many economic transactions – and if they had not been so scrupulously preoccupied with making sure they were fair.

In addition to allowing the invention of the scientific method and thus things like planes, computers, and modern medicine, the invention of writing almost certainly facilitated the development of culture (Diamond, 1997). Together with evolution, culture is a profoundly powerful driver of human behavior. Like evolution, culture is often an invisible influence until scientists place it in their cross-hairs. One of the defining features of culture is that it involves widely shared beliefs, and there has never been a human invention that promoted information-sharing better than writing does. There could scarcely be formal religions without religious documents, for example, and the preservation of cultural rules and traditions became one of the first practical applications of language beyond its original use as a method of keeping receipts.

Are there any drawbacks of this wonderful, uniquely human invention? Every good thing, language included, comes with drawbacks. Lottery winners discover greedy cousins, doting parents discover the extremes of human exhaustion. The obvious drawbacks of written language include the fact that there would be no climate change, improvised explosive devices, or Holocausts in the absence of written language. On the other hand, you may recall that evolutionary psychologist Steven Pinker (2011) has made a very compelling case that the modern human world is far more peaceful and civilized than it has ever been. Regardless of how we define aggression, it just keeps going down. Experts such as Jared Diamond would be quick to agree that this is true by orders of magnitude when we compare modern human cultures with those of the ancient human hunter-gatherers. We are killing each other at a much lower rate than ever before.

Although we are killing each other a lot less often than we used to, we seem to have stepped up the pace quite a bit for killing the rest of the planet. I believe one of the problems with written language, and the scientific method that it has enabled, is that we have not applied it broadly enough to the modern problems that plague us most. It was not until 1879, twenty years after Darwin published his famous *On the origin of species*, that it dawned on a German guy named Wilhelm Wundt to apply the scientific method to the study of the human mind. Well over a century later, most people, including many social scientists, do not seem to realize that most of the world's major problems are behavioral – and thus partly evolutionary – rather than technological.

APPLIED EVOLUTIONARY PSYCHOLOGY: REDUCING OVERREACTIONS

Reducing overreactions to recycled water: NEWater

We are finally beginning to realize that many human problems are psychological. I would like to share a few examples of how we can use psychology, including evolutionary psychology, to make the world a better place. Recall that, in Chapter 8, I argued that emotions often trump reason. We have hardwired, evolved emotional reactions that are pretty hard to suppress. As I was writing this chapter, my aging dog Liberty tracked some of her own poo into our newly carpeted basement. I became pretty disgusted as I picked her up to carry her to the shower and found that I had managed to get some of her poo on one of my favorite sweatshirts. Human beings have a natural aversion to poo because it's chocked full of pathogens. A gene that made poo seem delicious or nutritious would have been weeded out of the gene pool a very long time ago (Cosmides & Tooby, 1997). Poo became disgusting to us, then, because it's dangerous to eat it. In fact, it's so disgusting that most people have a strong aversion to anything associated with poo. This is why recycled water has been such a hard sell in Australia.

If Australians became desperate enough for water, though, they might change their minds. Singaporeans did. Singapore is an island nation that has virtually no natural sources of fresh water. For decades, this meant that they bought a lot of their fresh water from Malaysia. Malaysians didn't exactly give it away, though. In the mid-to-late 1990s, scientists made big improvements in micro-filtering technology that finally allowed for the relatively inexpensive recycling of large volumes of water that came right from the drains of millions of consumers. This recycled water is extremely pure. Accordingly, in 1998, the Singapore Public Utilities Board (PUB), tired of feeling insecure about water, reactivated an old plan to recycle used water. As you already know, our innate disgust for poo guaranteed that the PUB faced a very serious public relations problem. They tackled this psychological problem with psychology, mostly with classical conditioning.

"So, after much debate, and by a narrow vote of 4–3, we've agreed to call it *not* 'Cheez Pee,' *not* 'Cheez Urine,' and *definitely not* 'Cheese Piss' but rather 'Cheez Whiz.'"

Does the name Pavlov ring a bell? If it does, you surely know that classical conditioning involves getting people to like things by associating these things with something that is already well loved. Pavlov's hungry puppies loved meat powder, and after Pavlov preceded meat powder just a handful of times with a buzzer, his dogs began to get excited and drool the minute they heard the buzzer.

The PUB didn't have a bunch of meat powder laying around, and so they took advantage of Singaporeans' positive associations about national celebrities. They ran ads in which celebrities endorsed a bottled form of the ultra-pure recycled water, which they called **NEWater** ("new" "water"). My proposal to call it "poo water" fell on deaf ears.

The public relations experts at PUB weren't above using a little nationalism as well as a little conditioning to sell recycled water to the public. Some of the NEWater ad campaigns capitalized on the fact that many Singaporeans felt, rightly or wrongly, that Malaysia had long been overcharging them for access to fresh water. The PUB ads thus made it a point of national pride to drink NEWater. As a part of one promotional campaign, the Singaporean prime minister at the time publicly drank from a bottle of NEWater proclaiming: "Let's drink to the nation" (Creagh, 2008). In case you forgot, human beings evolved to be extremely sensitive to unfair social exchanges (Robinson et al., 2007). The PUB's campaigns were thus using evolution to beat evolution. By 2006, three water recycling plants in Singapore were producing 20 million gallons of recycled water per day, although most of this went to uses other than drinking water. According to Singapore's PUB website, Singaporeans were getting 30% of their water from recycling in 2015. Evolution made recycled water a hard sell, but classical conditioning, intergroup rivalry, and social exchange processes have now helped sell millions of gallons of it.

Reducing overincarceration: the Len Bias story

One of the most interesting implications of evolutionary psychology is based on the idea that we evolved to live not in organized groups of millions of people but in small families and tribes in which everyone knew everyone else. For tens of thousands of years, people in a family or tribe ate the same foods, told the same stories, and spoke the same language. Jared Diamond (1992) described tribes from the Pacific island of Papua New Guinea who, until their recent exposure to modern cultures, lived only miles from other tribes but quite reasonably assumed they were the only people on earth. The hundreds of different tribes on this one mountainous island spoke hundreds of languages as different as Spanish and Chinese, and they often had radically different cultures. Even today, after decades of Western influence, the residents of the highland areas of Papua New Guinea alone speak several hundred very different languages.

Throughout the globe and throughout all but the most recent sliver of human history, this is how things were. Human groups were pretty isolated. And in these ancient human groups, assuming that your own personal experiences were very much like those of all other people usually worked just fine. Ancient people never had to worry about the regional, national, or global implications of their behavior. The implications of this basic fact of human evolutionary history are profound. In the ancient world, for example, it was probably wise to be highly distrustful of outsiders. Likewise, it was probably wise to steer clear of a neighbor who had a reputation for being stingy or aggressive. By the same token, responding to a specific threat or pathogen that had harmed your child or your neighbor as if it could harm you was probably a great idea. But what if we lived in a bizarre world in which the behavior of one unhealthy, unlucky, or unscrupulous neighbor caused people to do things that had dramatic consequences for people living in places as far away as Detroit or San Diego? That's ludicrous, right?

That's also Congress. According to former U.S. Speaker of the House Tip O'Neill, there is a very important sense in which "All politics is local." According to this idea, people vote to put representatives in national office based mainly on their own local interests, which are often incompatible with the interests of the U.S. as a whole. New Jersey voters have no interest in paying for an expensive bridge in Georgia, but they are happy to tack on a bit of "pork" to a transportation measure that would bring a bridge (and all the jobs that come with it) to their home state – or better yet their hometown. So, American voters often vote as if they lived in tribes rather than in a nation. Perhaps it's hard to blame them. No one is paying them to research the issues and make good decisions for America. But we're paying members of Congress to do so, and it's part of their job to be good stewards of the entire nation rather than just acting locally. Further, many of the mistakes made by the members of Congress, even some very well-intended mistakes, can be traced to a very strong tendency to think locally. Nothing illustrates this principle better than the tragedy of Len Bias.

I'm a college basketball fan, and I'm pretty fond of the University of Maryland Terrapins – as long as they are not playing UCLA, Texas, Georgetown, Miami, or any of my favorite SEC (Southeastern Conference) teams. Like politics, basketball is also local. It's just that I've lived in a lot of localities. Right now I live in Maryland, and this is where the sad story of Len Bias took place. Bias was a truly fantastic college basketball player. Some say he was the greatest college player who never played in the NBA. In the mid-1980s, in the greater Washington, DC area, there was no one more beloved than the quiet, modest and athletically gifted Len Bias. In his senior year at Maryland, Bias was recognized as both the ACC player of the year and a consensus All-American. In the summer of 1986, Bias was quickly selected in the first round of the NBA draft by the delighted Boston Celtics. Two days later, Bias was partying with some friends. Someone convinced him to try what must have been a great deal of cocaine. Several hours later, Bias was dead, because of cocaine-induced cardiac arrest.

In response to this local tragedy, Congress acted nationally, as if they lived in a small tribe where one of their own children had been murdered. Bias died on June 19, 1986. By the end of October, 1986, both houses of Congress had approved and Ronald Reagan had signed into law what's often called the **Len Bias law**. This law mandates very lengthy penalties for possessing even small amounts of drugs, especially crack cocaine. The law means that a first-time offender who is caught with five grams (less than 1/5 of an ounce) of crack cocaine goes to prison for a minimum of five years. Here's how Dan Baum (1997, p. 225), author of *Smoke and mirrors*, summarized Washington's response to Bias's death:

> Immediately upon returning from the July 4 recess, Tip O'Neill called an emergency meeting of the crime-related committee chairmen. Write me some goddamn legislation, he thundered. All anybody up in Boston is talking about is Len Bias. The papers are screaming for blood. We need to get out front on this now. This week. Today. The Republicans beat us to it in 1984 and I don't want

that to happen again. I want dramatic new initiatives for dealing with crack and other drugs. If we can do this fast enough, he said to the Democratic leadership arrayed around him, we can take the issue away from the White House.

In life, Len Bias was a terrific basketball player. In death, he would became the Archduke Ferdinand of the Total War on Drugs.

Other accounts of the local reaction to Len Bias's death sound more romanticized than politicized. For example, more than 11,000 residents of the greater DC area poured into a local memorial service for Bias. But, in my view, the fact that Len Bias was so adored in Washington was the biggest single catalyst for the passage of a powerful national law that has been on the books since shortly after Bias's tragic death. Ironically, though, many who were once fond of this national anti-drug law now agree that its national consequences have been disastrous. The main problem is that the law put a lot of first-time drug offenders in prison for a long time, for possessing very small amounts of drugs. Things were even worse for petty drug users or low-level street dealers who were repeat offenders. Not long after the Len Bias law was passed, many U.S. states passed "three strikes laws" that imposed extremely lengthy prison sentences (typically 25 years) for people convicted of a third felony of any kind, including marijuana possession. Things quickly took a very bad turn for American Blacks and Latinos, and this often included the female romantic partners of low-level male drug dealers, whose only crime some have described as merely dating a person who was selling drugs (see Alexander, 2012).

To be sure, liberals and conservatives have very different interpretations of the Len Bias law. However, political interpretations aside, it's hard to deny that this law played a huge role in the dramatic increase in American prison populations. As I just suggested, many social policy experts also argue that the Len Bias law had a disproportionately negative impact on Blacks and Latinos. Blacks are actually somewhat less likely than Whites to use most illegal drugs, for example, but they are much, much more likely to be incarcerated for drug-related offenses. Ignoring race altogether, this law and other laws and social policies that reached their peak under the Reagan administration (often in a bipartisan fashion) roughly tripled the proportion of Americans who were incarcerated between 1980 and 2010, at a time when national violent crime rates were meaningfully decreasing. In fact, when it comes to federal prisons, a Congressional Research Service report by Nathan James (2014) indicated an almost eightfold increase in the prison population between 1980 and about 2010 (a period when the total U.S. population increased by only 37%). Today, the U.S. makes up less than 5% of the earth's population but about 25% of the earth's prison population. Arguably, the biggest part of this huge problem is not that we put way too many people in prison. It's that we keep them there for a very, very long time. Further, once they get out, we make it hard for them to straighten up by denying them many basic rights and social services. In many states, convicted felons cannot ever vote, for example, even after serving their entire sentences (Alexander, 2012). In 10 U.S. states, those convicted of drug crimes are permanently banned from ever receiving food stamps. In contrast, people convicted of rape or murder remain fully eligible.

Even if you disagree with my interpretation of why this all happened, I hope you can see that social mistakes of this magnitude could never have happened in the Pleistocene. People lived locally and acted locally, and their responses to tragedies in their immediate environments rarely led to the overincarceration of millions of people living thousands of miles away.

So what do we do about it? I'm happy to say that we are finally doing a little bit to correct this huge mistake, although to me it feels like we're doing much too little way too late. For the record, the U.S. Congress and some U.S. states have begun cutting into the Len Bias law in the past decade. In 2012, as you may recall, both Colorado and Washington State decriminalized marijuana. By 2018, several other U.S. states and Washington DC had relaxed their laws on marijuana use or possession, but with some fears that national laws might trump these state decisions. There are still many obstacles to major changes in U.S. drug laws. The biggest obstacle is probably what some activists have dubbed the **prison-industrial complex**. In the past two decades, the percentage of inmates living in *for-profit* prisons has increased dramatically, and for-profit prisons that make more money by keeping more people in prison have lobbied state and local governments hard to stay "tough on crime." A long time ago, where my ancestors lived and worked as sharecroppers in Alabama, they had a different name for "for-profit prisons." Back then they called them plantations.

Here's how human rights activist John Whitehead (2012) summarized the modern U.S. prison situation:

> Little wonder, then, that public prisons are overcrowded. Yet while providing security, housing, food, medical care, etc., for six million Americans is a hardship for cash-strapped states, to profit-hungry corporations such as Corrections Corp of America (CCA) and GEO Group, the leaders in the partnership corrections industry, it's a $70 billion gold mine. Thus, with an eye toward increasing its bottom line, CCA has floated a proposal to prison officials in 48 states offering to buy and manage public prisons at a substantial cost savings to the states. In exchange, and here's the kicker, the prisons would have to contain at least 1,000 beds and states would have to agree to maintain a 90% occupancy rate in the privately run prisons for at least 20 years.

> The problem with this scenario, as Roger Werholtz, former Kansas secretary of corrections, recognizes is that while states may be tempted by the quick infusion of cash, they "would be obligated to maintain these (occupancy) rates and subtle pressure would be applied to make sentencing laws more severe with a clear intent to drive up the population." Unfortunately, that's exactly what has happened. Among the laws aimed at increasing the prison population and growing the profit margins of special interest corporations like CCA are three-strike laws (mandating sentences of 25 years to life for multiple felony convictions) and "truth-in-sentencing" legislation (mandating that those sentenced to prison serve most or all of their time).

I wish I had more to say about how to solve this major social problem, but I can offer a couple of suggestions. The first is to trust the evolved human tendency to be outraged by injustice and to educate yourself and others about the causes and consequences of this major social problem. In so doing, I would suggest that we all remember that our audiences, whether they include conservative Republican Ron Paul (who is just as critical of the war on drugs as I am) or your Marxist roommate Frieda (who is just as critical of Ron Paul as I am), are all likely to be more persuaded by tragic stories with a human face than they are by statistics such as the roughly 2.3 million Americans who are currently in prison, jail, or juvenile detention. There are millions of such stories, and they disproportionately belong to the economically disenfranchised, especially poor Black men and Latinos. Find these stories and share them. A great place to start in your search for such powerful personal stories is the website of Students for Sensible Drug Policy (https://ssdp.org). To find them, just do something people could have never done 10,000 years ago. Use Bing or Google. (My name is Brett, and I do not use drugs, but I support the rights of others to make their own decisions about them.)

If you are as critical as I am of private, for-profit prison corporations such as Corrections Corporation of America (rebranded in 2017 as Core Civic), another thing you can do to solve this particular sociopolitical problem is to bring the highly unethical business practices and lobbying efforts of for-profit prisons to the light of day, as I have tried to do here. If you're interested in learning even more about this issue, check out the work of human rights activists such as John Whitehead. He and others at the Rutherford Institute are working to make sure that the U.S. does not continue to hold the title of the world's most incarcerated country. If the U.S. can change its unfair incarceration policies, ethnic minorities and the poor will not be the only ones who are relieved. Taxpayers of all political stripes and from all walks of life – who do not wish to spend billions of dollars a year overincarcerating their fellow Americans – will be relieved, too. I wish I had more good news about ending a war – the U.S. war on drugs – that has at least part of its roots in human evolution. But I can at least say that knowing how any war got started is often one of the keys to ending it.

Reducing helicopter parenting

Before I address a couple of other major social problems that are grounded in human evolution, I would like to note that the war on drugs is not the only example of how our evolutionary history of living in small groups, and trusting our immediate perceptual experiences (even when they come from news footage), has set the stage for major social problems. Another major problem that seems to have evolutionary roots is the current American trend toward dramatically overprotective parenting. Just as the Len Bias story led lawmakers to intensify an irrational war on drugs, vivid newspaper stories of child abductions have led millions of American parents – known as **helicopter parents** – to become paralyzed by fear and to worry deeply about problems that – statistically speaking – are virtually nonexistent. As Steven Pinker (2011) eloquently argued, the tremendous amount of effort we put into making sure we never leave our kids alone, because of an exaggerated fear of abduction by strangers, is simply not a wise way to express our well-intended parental love and devotion. First, the risk to children of stranger abduction is much, much lower than most of us think. Second, the things we do in response to the perceived threat are often either useless or counterproductive. Here's Pinker's (2011, p. 446) summary of the real risk that an American child will be abducted these days by a stranger:

> The annual number of abductions by strangers [in America] has ranged from 200 to 300 in the 1990s to about 100 today, around half of whom are murdered. With 50 million children in the United States, that works out to an annual homicide rate of one in a million ... That's about a twentieth of the risk of drowning and a fortieth of the risk of a fatal car accident. The writer Warwick Cairns calculated that if you *wanted* your child to be kidnapped and held overnight by a stranger, you'd have to leave the child outside and unattended for 750,000 years.

Many would argue that if we save only one child by being overly vigilant about child abduction, then all the lost opportunities for children to walk five blocks to play at the park, all the milk carton alerts, all the hovering parents, and all our collective anxiety will have been worth it. But as Pinker notes, this is simply wrong. We always have to trade risks against benefits. We could all keep our kids safe at home all the time and skip that ski trip, that beach vacation, or even those years of formal schooling. But we don't do so because we're quite willing to accept some amount of risk for a desired payoff. Likewise, we could prevent a lot of head injuries across the nation by wearing our bicycle helmets during dinner, but that would be almost as ridiculous as plastering missing kids' faces all over milk cartons and fueling the fear of stranger abduction more than we help reduce it.

Pinker (2011, p. 446) points out another big problem with our public response to this perceived risk. Most of the collective measures we take don't really do anything:

> Many measures, like the milk carton wanted posters, are examples of what criminologists call crime-control theater: they advertise that something is being done without actually doing anything.

He further argues that the biggest consequence of the growing trend for parents to drive their children to school is more tragic childhood fatalities:

> More than twice as many children are hit by cars driven by parents taking their children to school as by other kinds of traffic, so when more parents drive their children to school to prevent them from getting killed by kidnappers, more children get killed.

Research by Tracy DeHart and colleagues (2006) also suggests that overprotective parents harm their children psychologically in unintended ways. They asked the primary caregivers (usually the mothers) of a large group of adult college students how they had parented these young adults when the young adults were growing up. DeHart et al. assessed three different dimensions of parenting. On the positive side, kids whose moms reported having behaved in a warm and nurturing fashion toward them ended up with high adult levels of explicit (consciously reported) and implicit (intuitive, association-based) self-esteem. Good job, mom. On the negative side, though, kids whose moms reported having engaged in **overprotective parenting** did not have higher than usual explicit self-esteem as adults. Well-intended parental hypervigilance simply bore no fruit. But it did bear at least one thorn. When it came to the implicit (indirect, unconscious) measure of self-esteem, kids whose moms reported having been overprotective reported more negative associations about themselves as young adults. At some instinctive level, they felt undermined. They thus had low implicit self-esteem.

At a much more personal level, I had a friend in high school, N.C., who was the child of a highly overprotective single dad. I had no doubts that this dad, M.C., doted on his son, but M.C. was incredibly overprotective. N.C. sometimes responded to this overprotectiveness by internalizing his dad's lack of confidence in him, as DeHart et al.'s research would suggest. But at other times, N.C. became defiant and engaged in unnecessary risk-taking. I remember one occasion when N.C.'s dad treated him like a baby in front of me and two other friends during a beach trip. N.C., who was a pretty weak swimmer, responded to being babied by swimming out into the deep ocean waters, just to defy his father. It got pretty ugly from there, but suffice it to say that if not for the help of M.C.'s loving friend Dory, N.C. would have been a goner. Like parental neglect, parental overprotectiveness can have real costs to the recipient. At some level we all know this, which is why poorly intended people (unlike well-intended parents) can sometimes capitalize on this harmful psychological process by overhelping those whose successes they wish to undermine (Gilbert & Silvera, 1996).

Reducing airport hypervigilance

Since the infamous 9/11 terror attacks, I've felt that American authorities have behaved very much like well-meaning but hypervigilant parents at airports all over America. Consider the enormous amount of time we all waste taking symbolic measures to be sure no Italian great-grandmothers make it onto a plane with explosives concealed in their comfortable Wicked Witch of the West shoes or their grannie panties. The 9/11 attacks made it a perfectly appropriate safety strategy for pilots to begin locking themselves in their cockpits during commercial flights, and to match all customers to their luggage. But the safety experts I trust have pointed out that everything else that now happens every day at hundreds of American airports – the chemical swabbing, the careful checking of IDs against easily faked boarding passes, the full-body scanners, the banning of liquids and penknives, and the demand that we remove our shoes – is simply useless.

And the human cost is very real. According to the National Air Traffic Controllers Association, Americans fly 64 million commercial flights a year. If we conservatively estimate an average of 150 people per flight, that's 9.6 billion occasions per year on which an American person flies someplace in a plane, after enduring the well-intended scrutiny of the Transportation Security Administration (TSA). If we very conservatively assume that post-9/11 TSA screening procedures cost the average airline traveler a mere extra hour per flight, this represents at least 9.6 billion American hours of lost life every year. That's time we could all be spending learning to make homemade pasta from our non-terrorist Italian great-grandmothers – or watching reruns of *The Simpsons* in our comfy Bart Simpson pajamas. If a person is lucky enough to live to be

85, he or she enjoys about 500,000 waking hours of life. Dividing the 9.6 billion hours of lost time every year by the 500,000 hours in a single very long life gives us the equivalent of 19,200 complete American lives lost (birth to death) every year. I realize this may seem like hyperbole. But in my view, just because a life is lost in bits and pieces does not mean it's not lost. Call it a really gigantic and unnecessary waste of time if you prefer, but whatever you call it, it is folly. This folly would never have happened in the Pleistocene, not only because we couldn't fly back then but also because everything we saw back then was real. It had actually happened to one of us, that is. And if it really had happened to one of us, then it was likely to be a real and serious threat.

To summarize, our Stone-Age brains respond to the tragedies we see in sensational news stories of child abductors and terrorists in exactly the same way U.S. lawmakers responded to the tragic story of Len Bias. We simply did not evolve to live in a world where we are constantly surrounded by images of tragedies that look big and immediate but in reality represent small and distant threats. Combine biases in media coverage with the evolved human tendency to be more sensitive to threats than to opportunities (the fact that "bad is stronger than good"), and you get several large-scale modern disasters. Educating ourselves and others about what threats are truly most worrisome and what threats just feel that way is the first step to saving trillions of taxpayer dollars – and billions of hours of human life lost in prisons and airports. Getting back to airports, if you want more information on exactly why our current TSA airport screening procedures are so unwise, just use your favorite internet search engine to search for "Smoke Screening Charles Mann." Mann is the author of a provocative 2011 *Vanity Fair* article that spells out the current TSA screening debacle. If you're not outraged after reading Mann's telling article, try Matt Sledge's equally eye-opening article about how members of Congress get to skip all the routine security screening. As Sledge (2014) put it:

> Members of Congress may have helped create the nightmare that is flying in America after Sept. 11, but they no longer have to endure it. Under a Transportation Security Administration 'whitelist,' lawmakers and other high-ranking government officials breeze past airport security. The TSA claims it's all about efficiency – but critics at the American Civil Liberties Union say it's undemocratic.

APPLIED EVOLUTIONARY PSYCHOLOGY: REDUCING UNDERREACTIONS

Saving lives via organ donations

Another clear example of how ancient evolutionary processes can create modern problems – and a much better example of how psychology can come to the rescue – comes from research on organ donation. According to the U.S. Department of Health and Human Services, about 29,000 Americans receive organ transplants every year. Unfortunately, however, for every four Americans who receive a transplant, one American dies waiting for one. Sadly, one of the many reasons for this shortage of organ donors appears to be terror management processes.

To sign up as an organ donor, people have to acknowledge their own mortality. As we've already learned, this is not something most people do gleefully. In fact, research on terror management and prosocial behavior reveals a sad twist. Reminding people of their own mortality normally makes people more helpful than usual. But this is no longer the case if the helping behavior could short-circuit the terror management mortality defense process. Hirschberger et al. (2008) found exactly this. Reminding people of their own mortality increased their donations to two different charities. In contrast, reminding people of their own mortality decreased the likelihood that people would donate money to organizations that promoted organ donations.

Creatures as fragile and insecure as we are seem to stop helping when doing so would remind us of our own deaths. In the case of organ donations, there is no obvious evolutionary solution to this evolutionary dilemma. But there is a behavioral economic one. Consistent with research on the **status quo bias** (the tendency to do what one has always done, even when it is highly irrational), researchers have shown that a good way to get millions of extra people to become organ donors is to make being a donor the legal default. In countries where policy-makers have made it the default to be an organ donor (known as having an **opt-out approach**), rates of being an organ donor usually approach 100%, even though it's easy for people to opt out if they wish. In contrast, in countries with an **opt-in approach** (where people have to take action to become an organ donor), organ donation rates rarely exceed 20%. As Johnson and Goldstein (2003) showed, these cross-national differences in organ donation policy translate into clear differences in how many people actually receive life-saving transplants. Applying the status quo bias to a social problem that is fueled, in part, by evolutionary processes can save lives. Biological technology makes organ transplants possible, and every year that technology gets better. But we also need social scientific technology – to make sure that what can happen does happen (see Davidai et al., 2012; Thaler & Sunstein, 2008).

Saving the earth: combating climate change

Solving major problems involving incarceration, water shortages, and organ donation are important. But solving all three problems won't do us much good if the planet is covered in water in 100 years – because of melted polar ice caps. Climate change due to human activity, especially greenhouse gas emissions, has the potential to make the earth extremely difficult to inhabit, even in the next century. We absolutely must find a solution to the impending global disaster known as "climate change." Ask most Americans, however, and you'll hear that they do not expect climate change to become a serious threat during their lifetimes (Jones, 2014).

Luckily, there are some countries where nearly everyone recognizes the reality of climate change. In Japan, South Korea, and Costa Rica, roughly 90% of the population believes human activity has caused climate change (Pelham, 2009). Further, in countries in which more people believe human activity is responsible for climate change, people behave much more responsibly. In 2009, Costa Ricans were six times as likely as Uzbekistanis to say that climate change is caused by human activity. Costa Ricans also produced about 12 times as much per capita GDP as Uzbekistanis for every gallon of fossil fuels they burned (Pelham, 2009). So, in countries where more people believe in climate change, more people are getting things done in an earth-friendly (low greenhouse gas emissions) fashion. Of course, the causal arrow can run in either direction. People who burn fewer fossil fuels might justify their efforts by concluding that climate change is a very real problem. But it seems obvious that taking responsibility for climate change is one big step on the road to fighting it. It seems even more obvious that denying the reality of climate change, as many Americans do, is a huge stumbling block to fighting it. Why work hard to fight something that isn't real?

©BWP

"Is it getting hotter down here?
Or is it just me?"

Why don't most Americans take climate change more seriously? At least some of the reasons are probably grounded in defensiveness, and some of this defensiveness is probably grounded in terror management. Tell me we are endangering future life on the planet, and instead of recycling, car-pooling, or eating less meat, I'll simply become more critical of foreigners. This big problem is compounded by several other unfortunate aspects of our evolved human nature. These include the facts that we evolved to think locally rather than globally, to respond to immediate rather than long-term rewards and dangers, and to deal with the concrete rather than the abstract (Center for Research on Environmental Decisions, 2009). As Seymour Epstein (1994) put it, we evolved to think *experientially* (intuitively) more often than *rationally* (analytically). In Figure 12.2, you can see an example of how we might activate Epstein's **experiential system** to convince people that climate change is real.

In contrast to powerful images, dry charts and abstract statistics will not usually be enough to convince us to take dramatic actions regarding a probabilistic event, no matter how dire the abstract consequences. Specific judgmental heuristics also seem to get in the way of progress. The idea of an average global temperature increase of "only a few degrees" is certainly not highly *representative* of a global

Figure 12.2 *You can see these NASA images and many more in Dina Spector's (2013)* Business Insider *article on climate change. Each reveals a visceral, before and after look at what climate change is doing to the planet.*

disaster. In fact, it more strongly resembles most people's idea of a slightly hotter than usual Fourth of July picnic. Perhaps we should remind people, in a concrete way, that the difference between thousands of square miles of glaciers and trillions of gallons of very cold sea water is often a matter of a degree or two, and a few decades.

Unfortunately, there's another judgmental heuristic that also seems to contribute to skepticism about climate change, at least for people in cooler parts of the earth. The availability heuristic also plays a big role in many people's skepticism about the reality of climate change, especially global warming. In an analysis of U.S. states and an analysis of 117 nations across the globe, Pelham (2017b) found that in places where the climate is cool, fewer people believe in global warming. This was true in the U.S., for example, even after controlling statistically for median household income, education levels, and the percentage of Republican voters per state. Archival studies of how people respond to short-term variations in the local weather and experiments in which people are primed to think about unseasonably hot or cold weather yield conceptually similar effects (e.g., see Egan & Mullin, 2012; Joireman et al., 2010). Many people only seem to believe that planet earth is getting warmer when their own neighborhood has been warm lately (or is chronically warm). So one reason the typical resident of Maine is less likely to believe in global warming than the typical resident of Maui is that the teeny speck of the globe known as Maine has a pretty low average temperature.

Of course, there is one group of people who take climate change very seriously. Poll almost any climate scientist who has no financial ties to big oil, and he or she will tell you that long-term climate change due to human activity is a virtual certainty. But only a little more than half of the American public is persuaded by this harmonious chorus of scientific opinion. Most scientists who have no special training in climate modeling fall somewhere between public opinion and expert opinion. However, there is one group of scientists who are collectively quite skeptical of climate change. According to a 2016 survey conducted by the George Mason University Center for Climate Change Communication, only 46% of U.S. TV weather reporters (meteorologists) reported that they believed climate change is mainly the result of human activity (Maibach et al., 2016). Of course, this stands in contrast to the almost unanimous modern consensus among climate change scientists that human greenhouse gas emissions are the cause of this important problem.

I hope it's clear that this is bad news for the planet. Many people consider their local weather forecasters a trustworthy source of information. One would surely hope that the scientific cousins of climate scientists would trust the climate change data. Why don't they? There are several reasons (Bagley, 2012). But the most interesting, by far, seems to be that meteorologists are very much like the professional baseball players or chess masters who have been asked to play a slightly different game. Meteorologists are specifically trained to model the extremely unpredictable world of weather, not climate. Just as it is hard to predict exactly how many boys will be born on any given day in a small hospital, it is hard to predict whether mothers-to-be will have to travel to the hospital that Tuesday in the rain. Meteorologists are in the business of reducing complete uncertainties to decent gambles on a specific day, and they find it intuitively implausible that anyone could use data vaguely resembling their own to predict anything with great precision. They need to be reminded that predicting climate change is more like predicting whether June will be warmer than May than predicting whether I should invite May and June to a picnic next Saturday.

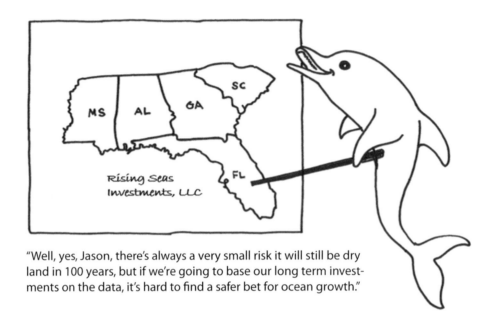

"Well, yes, Jason, there's always a very small risk it will still be dry land in 100 years, but if we're going to base our long term investments on the data, it's hard to find a safer bet for ocean growth."

Some solutions: default effects

So our brains have evolved in a wide variety of ways that conspire to make us poor stewards of a planet we are choking with carbon dioxide. Is there anything we can do to turn things around? There is. First, with a little help from informed local and national policy-makers, we can use Dick Thaler's status quo bias to promote green behaviors – especially when we combine our understanding of this bias with simple applications of learning theory (Thaler & Sunstein, 2008). The status quo bias is essentially psychological inertia: it's the tendency to do what we and others have always done in the past – which is often what takes the least effort in the present situation. In the U.S. we keep doing things like minting pennies (which cost much more to make and manage than they are worth) and electing U.S. presidents using the whacky Electoral College system (which sometimes allows the person who comes in second in the popular vote to win the U.S. presidency).

We do whacky things like these because we always have done them. Pennies made numismatic sense in 1800, or even 1900. In 1900, two pennies would purchase a first class postage stamp. But today we just don't need a coin that small. Allowing someone who comes in second to become president, or denying the residents of Washington, DC the right to be represented in Congress never made sense. But we keep doing these weird and unfair things because they have long been the status quo. In my view, another unfortunate example of the status quo bias is cutting a slice of extremely sensitive skin (the entire foreskin) from the tips of boys' penises. An even more severe version of this harmful tradition applies to female genital cutting (also known as female genital mutilation) in many traditional cultures in Africa and the Middle East. According to the World Health Organization (2018), more than 200 million girls and women alive today have endured this dangerous and unnecessary genital cutting. In practice, male circumcision is not as dangerous as female circumcision because it has been so heavily medicalized. But it is surely just as painful and just as unnecessary – unless your societal goal is reducing people's natural level of sexual pleasure, in which case either kind of circumcision is a great idea. If these forms of dangerous and unnecessary flesh-cutting had not existed for centuries, and some guy got the bright idea to start them today, I'm pretty sure we'd all think that guy was crazy. Imagine that I tried to begin a campaign to chop off people's earlobes. Earlobes are way less useful than foreskin, for example. And yes, to answer your question, I'd only allow surgeons to do it. What kind of Philistine do you think I am? How many people do you suppose would support me? We do a lot of weird and even harmful stuff simply because we (and many others) did it in the past.

Back to fixing climate change

But, if we know about the status quo bias, we can use it to make good things happen. As suggested in a 2009 report by the Center for Research on Environmental Decisions (CRED), it's often possible to use **default effects** to promote and maintain green behavior. One example of this is to set the default on copy machines to produce double-sided copies. People can switch to single-sided copies if they like, but the very large majority of people will accept the default. The CRED report indicated that by switching to the double-sided default in all their campus copiers and printers, Rutgers University saved more than a million sheets of paper in the first year of the change. Many other schools and businesses have followed this example. Many automakers are also setting new defaults to cut down on the use of fossil fuels. When I purchased a Hyundai Accent in January 2014, I was at first dismayed to see that it came without a spare tire. But carrying around all that weight in millions of cars across the country burns a lot of extra fossil fuel. My first reaction to the change was that I felt vulnerable without a spare and would soon get one. It's been four years, and I haven't gotten around to it. Besides, Hyundai makes up for this with free roadside assistance. I wouldn't be caught dead now driving a car in which I constantly lugged around a heavy spare tire.

Another solution: immediate costs and rewards

Removing even the smallest barriers to change and offering immediate rewards can also go a very long way to promoting green behavior. Many universities and businesses who noticed that people were not recycling very much reduced a common barrier to recycling by moving to "single-stream recycling" – so that people didn't have the perceived hassle of trying to figure out where to recycle what. If it all goes in one bin, there goes a very big barrier. Along similar lines, many solar power companies in Maryland offer consumers a chance to switch to solar power without having to purchase the solar systems themselves. Some companies install solar panels on consumers' roofs for free, and some do so and charge them less for power than they had paid before going green. This is next on my list of green behaviors.

The U.S. government's Car Allowance Rebate System, colloquially known as **cash for clunkers**, which began and ended in 2009, appears to have helped Americans remove about half a million gas guzzlers from U.S. roads. Moving from the carrot to the stick, however unpopular it has been, the U.S. gas guzzler tax, introduced in 1978 as part of the Energy Tax Act, may have soured a few consumers on new cars that don't meet EPA (Environmental Protection Agency) guidelines for fuel economy. I strongly suspect, though, that programs that reward people for buying green cars will have a bigger long-term impact on consumer behavior than will taxes for misbehavior. Such reward programs do not always require congressional action. As the U.S. EPA reports on its official website, Clemson and MIT now offer either discounted or preferred parking to students who can document that they drive SmartWay vehicles. Many U.S. government agencies also provide partial reimbursements to employees who use public transport rather than driving to work. As I hope you are beginning to see, if Americans are to follow the lead of many European and Latin American countries, who tend to be much greener than we are, we will have to combat climate change by taking many small actions, and sticking to them.

Speaking of sticking to things, there can be no doubt that one of the best ways to promote any positive (or negative) social behavior is to engineer a new set of social norms surrounding the behavior. People in my suburban Maryland neighborhood take great pride in filling their recycling bins higher than their trash bins. In contrast, my siblings in rural Georgia seem to have never heard of recycling. Theories such as Hardin and Higgins' (1996) shared reality theory suggest that whenever change agents or policy-makers can get a large enough group of people to engage in any kind of behavior, powerful social norms to support the behavior will quickly follow. The same basic need to belong that propels infant monkeys to cling to their mothers can propel people to recycle or engage in prosocial behavior. I can recall well living in Texas back when it was as commonplace for people to throw trash on the highway. A very successful "Don't Mess with Texas" anti-littering campaign that began in the mid-1980s – and capitalized on people's pride in their social identities – seems to have forever changed norms about littering. Campaigns against smoking in public buildings have also had a great deal of success in cities all over the U.S.

Combating climate change will be no easy battle, and for reasons I have already listed, there is still plenty of cause for alarm. However, one of the biggest rays of hope in the fight against climate change is that it's clear that climate change affects everyone. Further, non-profit organizations such as the Center for Research on Environmental Decisions serve as models to other prosocial and environmental agencies by promoting the tremendous power of applied psychology. CRED has made it its goal to use everything we know about the human heart and mind to educate policy-makers, educators, and political activists about the best ways to convince the public to pull together to save the planet.

CONCLUSIONS

The stories of NEWater, the war on drugs, organ donation, and combating climate change are but specific examples of a much broader point. Physical scientists – who have done things with written language that the ancient Sumerians could have only dreamed about – have produced a modern world that is incredibly comfortable and convenient for people like me and you. But to maintain the comforts of a few, we are destroying the planet, and we can harm each other today more easily than ever before. Although ancient physical problems such as famine and malaria still exist, they are being displaced from the top rungs in the list of world problems by psychological problems such as obesity, divorce, climate change, overincarceration, and terrorism (including our inappropriate responses to it). Physical scientists have no answers to problems such as congressional gridlock or ethnic cleansing because they do not fully understand that people are not like planets or electrons. Many human problems exist because parents, physicians, politicians and physicists have patently incorrect theories of human nature. One of the best fountainheads of better theories about human nature, I hope you now know, can be found in the wedding of psychology and evolution.

If we are to solve today's most important problems, from violence, famine, and climate change to the maltreatment of women, children, and the poor, we must not only understand how electrons flow but also how social interaction flows. We must not only understand how chemical reactions change molecules but also how social interactions change hearts and minds. We must learn as much about levity as we have about gravity. Until we tackle the most important scientific questions of all – questions of sex, cheating, death, and cheating death, to name only a few – we will not save the planet, and we will not learn to be kinder to one another or to future generations. In the grand scheme of things, we haven't been on the planet very long at all. Let's not leave any sooner than we have to, and let's be as nice as possible to each other for as long as we're here.

FOR FURTHER READING

» Alexander, M. (2012). *The new Jim Crow: Mass incarceration in the age of color-blindness.* New York: The New Press.

» Thaler, R.H. & Sunstein, C.R. (2008). *Nudge: Improving decisions about health, wealth, and happiness.* New Haven, CT: Yale University Press.

SAMPLE MULTIPLE-CHOICE EXAM QUESTIONS

Here are four sample quiz questions for Chapter 12. You can find the Chapter 12 quiz at: www.macmillanihe.com/evolutionary-psychology

12.01. According to your text, the fact that human beings are concerned with fairness and the fact that we are very good at language eventually led to the invention of:

   a. writing

   b. religion

   c. legal systems

12.02. What judgmental heuristic or bias predicts that people will base their judgments of the reality of global warming on the weather or climate in the specific place where they happen to live?

   a. the availability heuristic

   b. the consensus bias

   c. the locality bias

12.03. Writing is almost certainly a cultural invention rather than an evolved predisposition. True or false?

   a. True, and this is why it takes a lot of schooling to teach most people to write

   b. False; the fact that human beings across the globe can learn to read suggests that written language did evolve

   c. True; and this is why there seems to be a critical period in childhood for learning to read

12.04. According to your text, overblown concerns about the risks of drugs in the U.S. have contributed to:

   a. an abundance of expensive drug treatment centers that do very little to help people battle addiction

   b. a social stigma surrounding drug use that prevents many people from seeking drug treatment

   c. very high incarceration rates in the United States

Answer Key: a, a, a, c.

GLOSSARY

active genotype-environment effects – a situation in which the developing person selects environments (e.g., partners, activities) that facilitate the expression of phenotypes consistent with the person's genetic makeup. *See* the PEA model.

adaptation – the process by which organisms change over long periods in ways that promote reproductive success in specific environments. Adaptation is the way genes end up sticking around inside one or more species. Example: A gene that promotes rapid or efficient swimming in aquatic animals is likely to be passed on to future generations.

adolescence – the psychological window of life when people are getting ready to take on adult roles. Views of adolescence vary radically across cultures.

adoptive parents – parents who become the legal caretakers of genetically unrelated children. They represent an exception to the Cinderella effect because, on average, they take very good care of their genetically unrelated children.

adult romantic attachment styles – the adult romantic version of infant attachment styles. Adults who are anxiously attached, for example, often experience fear of being rejected or abandoned by their romantic partners.

aggression – in people, actions that are intended to harm others; in animals more broadly, actions that do harm others, period (e.g., battling over a mate, predation, parasitism).

allele – a variation on a specific gene. For the genes in all cells except sex (sperm and eggs) cells, people carry one allele from their dads and one allele from their moms.

alpha – the member of a social group who has the highest social rank. In many social organisms, there is a separate alpha male and alpha female, with the male having the highest status. In some species of hyena, however, females are larger than, and dominant over, males. The alpha female is thus the top dog.

altricial – a term describing organisms whose young are helpless and who thus depend on parental care to survive. Most altricial species are also slow to reach physical maturity. People are extremely altricial. Contrast with precocial.

altricial visual development – the slow process by which human beings come to see well. The development of adult levels of visual acuity takes about five years.

altruism – prosocial behavior that is also voluntary, costly to the doer, and performed without the expectation of reward.

anchoring and adjustment bias (aka **anchor and adjust heuristic**) – the tendency to stick too close to an initial starting point, including an arbitrary starting point, when revising a judgment you know to be incorrect.

anger – a basic emotional reaction to threat or harm that occurs when the threatened person feels more powerful than the person or creature who caused this emotion. In a fight-or-flight situation, anger promotes fight rather than flight.

angry aggression – *see* hostile aggression.

anxious – an insecure infant attachment style characterized by chronic worry about abandonment, especially in scary or unfamiliar situations.

appeal to nature fallacy – the erroneous tendency to think something is good because it is natural. Organic cigarettes still cause cancer. Cannibalism exists in many animals, but that doesn't make it ethical in people.

arbitrariness – in linguistics, the fact that the sounds of most words have no obvious connection to their meanings. According to linguists such as Hockett, this is one of the unique and universal features of all human languages.

archival research – research that uses naturally existing public records (e.g., homicide records, marriage records) to test a research hypothesis.

assist – in basketball, passing the ball to an open teammate who immediately takes a shot and scores. The assist is awarded to the passer. A study of NBA players showed that they engage in reciprocity by paying back recent assists.

auditory looming bias – the tendency to judge things that we hear coming toward us to be coming faster than they really are.

autokinetic effect – a visual illusion that makes a stationary dot of light in an otherwise dark room look like it is moving. Muzafer Sherif capitalized on the variability in this illusion by asking people to discuss their perceptions of the movement of a stationary light. Groups of strangers quickly converged on a consensus about how much the light moved. *See* conformity.

automatic – a term for well-learned information-processing and/or behavioral patterning that is (prototypically) fast, unconscious, mandatory, and efficient.

automatic social tuning – an unconscious tendency to adopt more favorable attitudes about the social group of a person with whom you are currently interacting. This finding supports shared reality theory.

availability heuristic – a rule of thumb that involves judging how likely something is based on how easily it comes to mind. People who use this heuristic are prone to overestimate the likelihood of highly memorable events (e.g., homicides).

avoidant – an insecure infant attachment style characterized by psychological detachment from one's primary caregiver, even in unfamiliar situations.

bell-shaped curve – *see* normally distributed.

benefits – in Hamilton's rule, this is the fitness-relevant value (survival advantage) that applies to the recipient of a helpful action; saving a niece's life is a much greater benefit to her than merely buying her lunch.

Ben Underwood – a boy who became blind as a toddler and then taught himself to "see" using echolocation. His case highlights the flexibility of human development.

better angels argument – the thesis of Pinker's book about how and why human beings have become much less aggressive over the past few centuries. Reasons for this trend include changes in the costs and benefits of aggressive behavior over time, and broadening definitions of what constitutes "us" or "we."

Big Bang – the rapid and dramatic expansion of matter that appears to have begun the evolution of the observable universe about 13.7 billion years ago.

bilateral symmetry – the physiological trait that means that if you draw a line down the center of the animal's body (head to rear), you will have produced two nearly identical (mirror image) halves. Ants, turtles, and people are all bilaterally symmetrical. Lobsters aren't quite symmetrical because one claw is much larger than the other. Sponges and anemones aren't symmetrical at all.

bogus pipeline – a technique for increasing honest responding in self-reports by convincing respondents that the researcher can determine their true attitudes physiologically, by means of an ostensible "lie detector."

bottlenecks – a dramatic reduction in population numbers for a particular species (e.g., due to predation or habitat destruction). This can have a big impact on natural selection (and thus speciation) because of reduced genetic variability in the species. An extreme bottleneck is often a precursor to extinction.

brachiating – swinging from branch to branch (e.g., in a forest canopy) by grabbing one vine with one hand, swinging, and grabbing a different branch with a free hand. Tree-dwelling primates are very good at this.

canine teeth (canines) – the four menacing, spike-shaped teeth that are common in carnivorous mammals. Saber-toothed cats had enormous canines.

canons – fundamental principles that are accepted largely on faith. The four canons of science are determinism, empiricism, parsimony, and testability.

carbon-14 dating – one of the most common forms of radiometric dating. C-14 dating relies on the fact that carbon-14 has a predictable half-life of 5,730 years.

cash for clunkers – a U.S. government program that ended in 2009 and which appears to have helped Americans remove about half a million gas guzzlers from U.S. roads.

Chase and Simon's (1973) chess master studies – the tremendous memory advantages chess masters had over college students disappeared completely when the experimenters placed pieces on a chess board at random rather than showing people images from real chess games. This supports specificity of learning.

cheater detection module – a presumably evolved, domain-specific rule for assessing cheating in what ought to be a fair social exchange.

Cinderella effect – the distressing but well-documented tendency for stepparents to neglect, abuse, and even kill stepchildren at a much higher rate than biological parents of children.

Clark and Hatfield's (1989, 2003) studies – two clever field studies that supported parental investment theory by showing that men seem to be much more willing than women to engage in casual sex with a stranger.

codominance – in contrast to dominant-recessive inheritance, a form of inheritance in which each of two differing alleles is expressed completely in organisms heterozygous for a specific trait (e.g., a homozygous red mom and a homozygous white dad might produce offspring with white and red patches).

co-evolution – cooperative evolution between two different species. This happens when each of the two species benefits from some resource provided by the other. *See also* symbiosis.

collectivism – a cultural orientation that emphasizes group wishes and social identities over individual wishes and personal identities. In collectivist cultures, the rights and wishes of individuals are downplayed in favor of maintaining and promoting the wellbeing of social groups (family or religious). *See* individualism.

competition – squaring off against the members of one's own or another species to obtain resources that promote selective fitness. This can range from fighting over a good nesting site to wrestling or butting heads over the chance to eat or mate.

competitive exclusion – the evolutionary principle that states that two species that require the same biological resources can't permanently occupy exactly the same biological niche. Normally, one species will eventually outcompete the other.

conformity – changing one's beliefs or behavior to be consistent with the beliefs or behavior of others, even when no one asks you to do so. Muzafer Sherif documented this in his studies of the autokinetic effect.

confound – a third variable or "nuisance variable" that may naturally co-occur with a presumed cause, and thus may be the real reason for any changes in an outcome of interest.

conjunction fallacy – mistakenly reporting that A *and* B can be more likely than A all by itself. People often fall prey to this logical mistake because they base probability judgments on representativeness. Remember Linda the feminist?

conservation – the recognition that things do not always undergo a real physical change when they change their appearance. In violation of this logical rule, preschoolers seem to believe that the way things *look* are the way they always *are*.

conspicuous consumption – behavior that is motivated by a desire to illustrate one's sexual fitness. This is presumably the human equivalent of the peacock's colorful tail, in that it advertises one's wealth to potential mates. *See also* sexual selection.

constructivism – the idea that a great deal of what people perceive and remember is determined by their preexisting theories and expectations.

contact hypothesis – the well-supported hypothesis that a powerful way to reduce stereotyping and discrimination is to foster equal status contact among the members of groups who have historically disliked or distrusted one another.

contingency – an aspect of life history theory that states that the way in which organisms develop often depends on (is contingent on) their early environments. In people, developing many versus few active sweat glands is an example.

convergent evolution – the independent evolution of very similar physical traits or behaviors in organisms that share no recent ancestors. This usually happens when the organisms in question did share very similar selection pressures, which the specific adaptation helped solve. Flight in insects and birds is a good example.

copy number variations – a genetic variation in which a string of several nucleotides is accidentally repeated (e.g., GG or GGG rather than G).

cosmology – the astronomical study of the origin and formation of the universe.

cost–benefit rule – in the context of aggression, the principle that animals typically engage in aggression when the most likely rewards (the benefits of so doing) are likely to exceed the most likely costs (the likely injury or damage experienced).

costs – in Hamilton's rule, this is the fitness-relevant price (the reduction in personal or reproductive fitness) paid by an organism that helps another organism.

covariation – (short for concomitant variation) the first of John Stuart Mill's three logical requirements for establishing causality. In modern statistical terms, covariation is the same as correlation.

critical periods – specific periods that are the only opportunities for something to develop normally. Imprinting in geese happens in a brief critical period.

crossing over – a genetic "shuffling" process that occurs shortly after a sperm fertilizes an egg. It means that sex chromosomes from father and mother split down the middle and then reassemble themselves in ways that mix genetic information from the two parents. This increases genetic diversity.

cuckold – a man whose wife (or sexual partner) is secretly impregnated by another man, leading the fooled man to care for a child who is not his own offspring.

cuckoldry – fathering a child with someone else's female partner, usually that person's wife.

cuckoo birds – a group of "brood parasites" who often lay their eggs in the nests of other birds, leading the duped parent(s) to incubate and then dutifully raise the cuckoo chicks.

cultural worldviews – the self-validating beliefs, such as religious beliefs, a belief in the sanctity of marriage, or devotion to one's government, that – according to terror management theory – serve as defenses against one's chronic fear of death.

culture – a widely shared set of beliefs, behavior, and emotions regarding the appropriate ways in which people live, work, play with, and relate to one another.

cuneiform – an ancient Sumerian writing system invented to keep track of economic transactions. This led to modern written language and mathematics.

default effects – a way of promoting and maintaining green behavior by capitalizing on the status quo bias. An example is setting the default on copy machines to produce double-sided copies. Few people switch to single-sided copies.

defector argument – a popular argument against altruism. This argument states that if a gene did promote unselfish behavior, many other members of the animal's group would take advantage of the do-gooders. The selfish genes that promoted this would pretty quickly "take over" in the population.

deindividuation – a state in which people don't feel personally identifiable, lose their sense of self, and thus behave more aggressively than usual. Among other things, deindividuation lowers the likely costs of aggression.

dependent variable – the variable that is measured in an experiment, under the assumption that it is a consequence of the independent variable.

determinism – one of the four canons of science. This is the assumption that the universe is orderly – that all events have meaningful, systematic causes. The goal of science is to uncover such causes.

displacement – in linguistics, the fact that language allows us to describe things that are not in front of us right now. This allows us to communicate about the distant past or future, which few other animals seem to do. Hockett argued that this is a universal feature of human languages.

dissociations – statistical disconnections between things that one might expect to be related. Dissociations are consistent with the idea of mental modularity.

dizygotic twins – "fraternal" twins; those who, like all siblings, share only half of their genes. *See* monozygotic twins, twin studies.

DNA fingerprinting – identifying a specific person by using modern genetic techniques to determine the person's exact unique genotype. Even identical twins have ever so slightly different DNA fingerprints due to unique mutations.

dominant – in genetics, the term used to describe an allele for a specific gene that is fully expressed phenotypically when it appears along with a recessive allele for the same gene.

echolocation – sensing what is in one's environment by sending out "sound waves" and detecting differences in how quickly the waves bounce back from different locations. Bats and dolphins evolved this ability. Ben Underwood was a blind prodigy who developed it on his own by making sharp clicking noises.

eliminating confounds – the third of John Stuart Mill's logical requirements for establishing causality. This boils down to making sure that no competing predictors of an effect were the real reason for the observed effect. Experiments solve the problem of confounds by holding all possible confounds constant while manipulating a single presumed cause.

emerging adulthood – a term coined by Jeffrey Arnett to characterize the extended period of adolescence (ages 18–25) that occurs today in most wealthy countries. Emerging adults are done with puberty, but they've not yet taken on adult roles.

empathic concern (empathy) – an emotional state in which you identify with a suffering person's pain (you put yourself in the other person's shoes), but you remain calm enough to take thoughtful action to help the distressed person.

empathy-altruism model – a theory of helping that states that experiencing true empathic concern for another person (putting yourself in the person's emotional shoes) often promotes true altruism.

empiricism – the scientific canon that states that the best way to figure out the nature of the world is to make careful, systematic observations.

emulative violence – the tendency to repeat aggressive actions after seeing others engage in them (aka copycat violence). *See* social learning.

epigenetic inheritance – the process by which environments sometimes determine whether specific genes are expressed at all. Although there is some controversy about how pervasive this is, conditions such as extreme stress, diet, or long-term drug ingestion seem to determine whether some genes get turned on or not.

error management theory – an evolutionary theory that states that natural selection has nudged people toward judgmental biases that promote selective fitness. For example, it might be adaptive for people to overestimate anger in a stranger's face or for women to underestimate men's claims of sexual commitment.

ethnography – a descriptive research technique often used by anthropologists. Ethnographers provide detailed descriptions of the ways of life, rules, and social norms of specific cultural groups.

eukaryotes – cells, like those found in plants and people, that have a nucleus and an endoplasmic reticulum. Most modern life forms consist of eukaryotic cells.

even a penny will help technique – a technique for increasing compliance rates for prosocial behavior by reminding would-be helpers, at the end of a request for a charitable contribution, that "even a penny will help."

evocative genotype-environment effects – a situation in which the developing person elicits (evokes) responses from others in their world that facilitate the expression of phenotypes consistent with the child's genetic makeup. *See* the PEA model.

evolution – the process by which organisms have changed and diversified over the course of earth's history. Evolution occurs when genes that promote reproductive success in a particular organism in a specific environment become more numerous than genes that provide no such advantage. *See* adaptation, natural selection.

evolutionary psychology – the interdisciplinary scientific study of how our thoughts, feelings, and behavior are influenced by evolutionary biological processes such as adaptation and natural selection.

exaptation – an adaptation that is put to a secondary or tertiary use. Feathers in birds seem to have evolved originally for thermoregulation, but they were then commandeered for flight, and then again for sexual display, at least in some species.

expected utility – economists' term for the long-run, predicted (average) effect of something probabilistic (and desirable or undesirable). It's calculated by multiplying probabilities by payoffs. The expected utility of a 5% chance of winning $100 in a gamble is $5.

experiential system – the highly intuitive judgmental system identified by Seymour Epstein, as the alternative to his rational (more thoughtful) judgment system.

experimenter bias – the presumably unconscious tendency for experimenters to create (or see) what they expect to see. A solution to this problem is keeping experimenters blind to the manipulated conditions of those they are studying.

external validity – the degree to which a research finding generalizes to a variety of ways of defining the constructs of interest, to other occasions, to other populations, and to other situations. *See* OOPS! heuristic.

extinction – the loss of a species due to the death of the last reproducing members of the species. About 99.9% of all living species that have ever existed are now extinct, although many of the genes of extinct species have survived in other species.

falsifiability – a key property of scientific discovery popularized by Karl Popper. The gist of this principle is that scientific ideas must be open to revision or dismissal based on empirical observations and/or critical analysis.

fast strategy – (aka K strategy) according to life history theory, this is a strategy for survival and reproduction that happens in harsh conditions (e.g., when food is scarce, when pathogens are common). This refers to taking greater risks, producing more offspring, first producing them at a younger age, and often dying young as a result of such a strategy.

fear – a basic emotional reaction to threat or harm that occurs when the threatened person feels he or she is less powerful than the person or creature who caused harm or threat. In a fight-or-flight situation, fear promotes flight rather than fight.

fecundity – the reproductive strategy of producing many seeds or offspring in one's lifetime. Among most animals, prey tend to have higher fecundity than predators.

feelings trump thoughts – the idea that when strong feelings (such as disgust) run counter to one's carefully reasoned thoughts, feelings will win out because they are grounded in powerful behavioral aversions that have long been adaptive.

fight-or-flight response – a physiological response to threat that includes an increase in heart rate and a dramatic reduction in digestive activity. These two physiological changes ready an organism to either attack or escape from a source of danger.

five key features of evolution – it's slow, occurring over thousands, millions, or billions of years. It's conservative; adaptations that work well are rarely discarded. It creates baggage; many useful adaptations come with drawbacks. It implies continuity; people are a lot like other mammals. It's orderly; genes program adaptive developmental patterns. Mammals are not born with their adult teeth, for example.

fixed allele – a state in which all members of a species are homozygous for a specific gene (or a single nucleotide, if applied at this much finer level). Although fixation is often viewed as a problematic lack of genetic variability, genes or nucleotides may also become fixed because they are wildly successful.

fMRI (functional magnetic resonance imaging) – a modern brain imaging technique that reveals what's happening in a living person's brain based on indirect, high-tech (and safe) measurements of blood flow to different regions of the brain. Spatial resolution (exactly where is that happening?) of fMRI is very good. Temporal resolution (exactly when did it happen?) is not as good.

founder effect – a chance effect in natural selection that occurs when only a few specific members of a species make their way to a new habitat (e.g., an island previously uninhabited by this species). This leads to effects similar to bottlenecks.

fraternal polyandry – a form of polyandry in which a woman takes two or more brothers as husbands. This approach partially reduces concerns about cuckoldry.

free-riders – members of a group who readily accept anything others offer them without repaying the favors.

free sample technique – a compliance technique that involves giving a consumer a "free" sample of a food, material good, or service, with the goal of getting the person to purchase the real thing. It presumably works because of reciprocity.

frequencies – counts, numbers of objects. Gigerenzer argued that many judgmental biases (such as those based on heuristics) disappear or get weaker when you ask people about concrete frequencies rather than abstract probabilities.

frustration–aggression hypothesis – the idea that frustration often leads to anger, which often leads to hostile aggression, especially against the perceived source of the frustration. This may be grounded in the mammalian fight-or-flight response.

gambler's fallacy – the assumption that if a random outcome has occurred several times in a row, it is less likely than usual that it will occur the next time it could occur. Note that this is roughly the opposite of the hot hand fallacy.

gene – the basic unit of inheritance, a small section of DNA that is located at a specific spot on a chromosome. Its function is to program protein synthesis, which leads to physical and psychological development.

general purpose reasoning machine – the mythical, principled, thoughtful judges and decision-makers that we all seem to think we are. In reality, human judgment and intelligence seem to be pretty circumscribed (modular, domain-specific).

genetics – the scientific study of the biological transmission of physical and behavioral traits from parents to their offspring, including how environments can influence this transmission process.

genome – all the possible genetic blueprints for a specific species, including every gene and all its possible forms (alleles). The human genome, for example, consists of 46 chromosomes and about 20,000 specific genes.

genotype – all the versions of all the specific genes possessed by a specific organism (that organism's exact genetic makeup). Contrast with phenotype.

genotype-environment correlations – the idea that genotypes and environments often support one another; as is the case, for example, when genetic relatives of a child create environments that promote or magnify the simple effects of particular genes. Genotype-environment effects may be passive, evocative, or active.

golden rule of social exchange – the social rule that if I give you something, you should give me something in return, especially if you agreed to do so. *See* reciprocity.

gradualism – the idea that speciation happens bit by bit at a relatively constant rate for most species. The data suggest that gradualism is the exception to the more usual rule of punctuated equilibrium.

graduated driver's license programs – programs adopted across the U.S. over the past couple of decades that only allow new (mostly teenage) drivers to drive under restricted conditions. Such programs have saved many lives.

grammar – the abstract rules of language use. This includes things such as verb tense, noun–verb agreement, and how to make plurals. Kids seem to learn grammar effortlessly, even if they are never explicitly taught it.

h^2 – *see* heritability coefficient.

Hamilton's rule – an evolutionary rule about inclusive fitness: all else being equal, an organism will help another organism when $rb > c$, that is, when the relatedness (r) of the organisms multiplied by the benefits (b) to the organism in need is greater than the costs (c) to the potential helper. I should thus sacrifice myself for three of my brothers because they collectively possess 150% of my genes.

haplodiploidy – an unusual aspect of sexual reproduction in some social insects (e.g., ants, bees, and wasps). Haplodiploidy means that if a queen has mated with only one male, all the members of her female worker caste will share 75% of their genes (rather than 50% like most other animal siblings) with one another.

helicopter parents – overprotective parents who "hover" over their children rather than allowing their children to experience the small to moderate risks of daily life.

heritability – the genetic transmission of properties from parents to their offspring.

heritability coefficient (h^2) – the estimate of the degree to which a physical trait or behavior is genetically (rather than environmentally) determined. Score theoretically ranges from 0 (no genetic contribution) to 1.0 (completely genetic).

heterozygous – a genotype in which the organism carries different alleles for a specific gene from its mother and its father. If dominant-recessive inheritance is at work, the organism will only express the dominant allele.

heuristics – *see* judgmental heuristics.

heuristic value – in a research context, something (e.g., a law, theory, or specific concept) that leads to specific, testable (falsifiable) research ideas.

hominid – a wide variety of bipedal (upright walking), large-brained primates, only some of whom were direct ancestors of modern human beings but all of whom had many human features. "Lucy" and the Neanderthals are two well-known species of hominid. We, too, are hominids.

homology – the tendency for animals that share a common ancestor (and thus genes) to share physical and/or psychological traits. Example: All members of the cat family have very similar skeletons and all are meat-loving carnivores, despite coming in very different sizes.

homophobia – negative attitudes and feelings about gay, lesbian, bisexual, and other gender-nontraditional people.

Homo sapiens – the fully modern humans (like you and me) who emerged about 200,000 years ago (maybe even earlier).

homozygous – a genotype in which the organism carries matching alleles for a specific gene from its mother and its father. If dominant-recessive inheritance is at work, the organism will express a recessive gene only if homozygous for that allele.

honest predictors – in sexual selection, a trait that has evolved to be highly attractive to potential mates because it accurately indicates that the organism in question possesses other desirable traits. If peacocks with prettier tails are, in fact, physically healthier, then the tail is an honest predictor of fitness.

honor culture – a culture in which people are taught that their honor, like their possessions, must be constantly defended against threats or insults.

hostile aggression – aggression performed with the goal of harming the victim – often fueled by anger and thus sometimes called "angry aggression." Contrast with instrumental aggression.

hot hand fallacy – the sometimes fallacious belief that a person who experiences success with a random event has a greater probability of immediate further success in additional attempts. The concept is often applied to sports, such as basketball. Compare with gambler's fallacy.

hot stove reflex – the rapid and instinctive withdrawal response many animals make to a painful stimulus applied to a hand, foot, paw, or leg. This reflex requires only functional limbs and an intact spinal cord (no higher brain areas needed).

Human Genome Project (HGP) – an international research project completed in 2003 that mapped out the entire human genetic blueprint.

hybridization – a possible route to speciation that occurs when two different species prove to be able to mate and produce fertile offspring. If the offspring end up with traits that increase selective or inclusive fitness in a particular environment, a new species may emerge (sometimes "absorbing" one or both of the old species).

identity fusion – "a visceral sense of oneness with the group"; Swann and Gómez's idea of merging one's personal identity intensively with that of a group to which one belongs. Spaniards who report identity fusion with their nation report that they would sacrifice their own lives to save a group of fellow (unknown) Spaniards.

implicit prejudice – a form of prejudice thought to be based on automatic associations to which people do not typically have conscious access.

imprinting – an instinctive bonding process that happens in most precocial birds right after hatching. After imprinting, ducklings or goslings will dutifully follow the large moving object (usually mom) to which they've bonded.

incest aversion (incest avoidance) – the natural repulsion that many organisms have toward mating with close genetic relatives. Incest aversion is highly adaptive because mating with a close relative dramatically increases the chances that one's offspring will suffer from rare recessive genetic defects and diseases.

including the other in the self – the psychological process of merging one's sense of self with that of another person about whom you deeply care. This orientation seems to promote altruism for the person to whom one is deeply connected.

Inclusion of Other in the Self (IOS) Scale – a pictorial scale assessing the degree to which people feel their identities overlap with those of close others.

inclusive fitness – a conception of fitness based on the number of copies of its genes ("offspring equivalents") an organism produces. This idea led to Hamilton's rule, which is highly relevant to topics such as altruism.

incomplete dominance – in contrast to dominant-recessive inheritance, a form of inheritance in which each of two competing alleles is expressed to some degree in organisms heterozygous for a specific trait (e.g., a homozygous red mom and a homozygous white dad might produce pink offspring).

independent variable – the (causal) variable that is manipulated in an experiment.

individualism – a cultural orientation that emphasizes the rights and wishes of the individual, autonomous person. In individualistic cultures, it is often acceptable to promote one's own personal agendas and to celebrate the individual self. *See* collectivism.

infant attachment style – an infant's characteristic way of relating to and depending on their primary caregiver. *See* anxious, avoidant, secure.

infection – harming another organism by invading its tissues and using the infected organism's biological resources to make copies of oneself; the amount of harm created for the host organism can range from discomfort to death.

institutional review board (IRB) – a committee of experts who review research proposals (often at universities) to ensure that proposed studies do not cause physical or psychological harm to participants. IRB members follow principles such as the risk–benefit rule in deciding what procedures researchers must follow.

instrumental aggression – aggression in which the victim is harmed only as a means to an end. Robbing a bank or taking a desirable toy from another child are examples. Contrast with hostile aggression.

internal validity – the degree to which a research finding allows you to know whether an independent variable truly caused changes in a dependent variable.

interspecific competition – competition between different species that try to exploit the same resource. Lions and hyenas, for example, often engage in this.

intraspecific competition – competition between two or more members of the same species. It is usually more common than interspecific competition.

isolation – a common route to speciation. This happens when groups of members of the same original species become geographically isolated and face very different selection pressures. Eventually the ancestors of the two groups may evolve in such different ways that they become different species. *See* speciation.

isotope – an unstable form of an atom that contains extra neutrons. Because the extra neutrons are lost from the atom at a predictable rate over thousands of years, this makes radiometric dating (such as carbon-14 dating) possible.

judgmental heuristics – quick and dirty rules of thumb for solving problems of magnitude or likelihood. *See* representativeness, availability, numerosity.

"just so" stories – a label sometimes applied to evolutionary psychology that suggests either that evolutionary hypotheses are so vague as to be unfalsifiable, or that evolutionary thinkers dream up such stories as after-the-fact descriptions rather than true scientific explanations.

kamikaze sperm – the once-popular idea that some sperm specialize not in fertilizing eggs but in attacking and destroying the sperm of one's sexual rivals. This is an interesting idea for which there proved to be no empirical support.

kin selection – costly helping behavior offered to a genetic relative. This poses no problems for evolutionary theory because relatives share many of our genes.

Lamarckian evolution – (after Jean Baptiste Lamarck) an old and incorrect theory of evolution built on the idea that parents passed on traits they acquired during their lifetimes to their offspring. Modern genetics showed that this doesn't happen.

last universal common ancestor – the last organism on earth to be a common ancestor to all of the 8.7 million species of life now alive on earth.

Len Bias law – a national law passed in 1986 that mandated lengthy penalties for possessing even small amounts of drugs, especially crack cocaine. This has led to dramatic increases in incarceration rates in the U.S. since 1986.

life history theory – a theory of evolution that emphasizes that organisms with exactly the same genes may develop different phenotypes in different environments and that there are tradeoffs in what maximizes personal or selective fitness. For example, the more offspring a pair of songbirds produces, the more likely it is that the couple will not be able to keep them all fed. Thus, robins who lay two or three eggs may have more surviving offspring than robins who lay five or six.

logical positivism – the idea that science and philosophy should be based solely on things that can be observed with absolute certainty. Many logical positivists (e.g., Karl Popper) also emphasize falsification as an approach to scientific discovery, meaning they try to disconfirm scientific ideas rather than trying to prove them true.

loss-aversion – being more sensitive to losses than to gains. For example, most people prefer a guaranteed payment of $8,000 over a 90% chance of winning $10,000.

lowball technique – getting people to agree to a great deal that subsequently becomes less wonderful. People are highly reluctant to back out on deals even once they go a little sour. Compliance experts capitalize on this tendency to honor an agreement by offering people great deals that they never intend to honor.

male warrior hypothesis – the hypothesis that, on average, men evolved to be more physically aggressive and xenophobic than women because hurting and/or distrusting outgroup members (e.g., in a war or battle) has lower costs and greater potential fitness benefits for men than for women.

masculinity vs. femininity – the cultural dimension Geert Hofstede defines (starting with masculinity) as "a preference ... for achievement, heroism, assertiveness and material rewards for success. ... Its opposite, femininity, stands for a preference for cooperation, modesty, caring for the weak and quality of life."

mate guarding – taking measures to prevent another person from "stealing" your romantic or sexual partner. This ranges from getting married or giving your partner highly pleasurable sexual experiences to engaging in threats or violence. *See also* mate hoarding, mate poaching.

mate hoarding – a reproductive strategy popular among high-ranking male members of species who live in densely packed social groups (e.g., male elephant seals). Mate hoarders try to maintain a "harem" of fertile partners and may viciously fight to maintain their reproductive monopolies.

mate poaching – trying to attract a sexual or romantic partner who you know to be in an existing relationship. *See also* mate hoarding, mate guarding.

meiosis – an aspect of sexual reproduction that means that shortly after fertilization of an egg, sex chromosomes from both parents split down the middle. Alleles from one parent may then trade places with homologous alleles from the other parent. Meiosis increases genetic diversity in offspring, which can fuel natural selection.

menarche – the appearance of a girl's first menstrual period. In the past 150 years, the age of menarche in wealthy countries has been getting younger and younger.

menopause – in people, the point, at about age 50, when women stop ovulating and thus become infertile. Menopause occurs in only a few known species, all of which are long-lived and altricial.

mental modularity – Jerry Fodor's idea that, rather than being a general purpose problem-solver, the human mind consists of many separate segments, which are specific, highly insulated, information-processing tools. *See* specificity principle.

mere ownership effect – the tendency for people who have been given an object to evaluate that object much more favorably than usual. The effect is even bigger than usual when people get to choose and touch the owned object. Can this help explain why most adoptive parents are so loving?

meta-analysis – a study of studies. An approach to research in which scientists mathematically combine the results of two or more (often very many) studies. In a meta-analysis, for example, a researcher might average the effect sizes for all known studies on a specific topic, or see if a known effect is really bigger (on average) for women than for men.

midlife crisis – a period in middle age when, recent data suggest, people often become distressed and unhappy, and begin to take risks that they were less likely to take a decade earlier. Although this pattern is far from universal, it is common enough that it is detectable in large samples and population studies (e.g., in national suicide rates by age group).

Milgram's obedience studies – Stanley Milgram's classic and ethically controversial studies of obedience, which showed that virtually everyone he studied was willing to inflict a great deal of pain on a fellow participant in a study of learning, merely because an authoritative and forceful experimenter ordered them to do so.

Miller-Urey experiment – a classic (1953) experiment that showed that adding heat and electricity to four inorganic molecules (ammonia, hydrogen, methane, and water) leads to the formation of amino acids, the building blocks of life.

modeling – *see* social learning.

modern synthesis – the version of evolutionary theory that integrates evolution and modern genetics. Darwin's original theory was limited because Darwin didn't know how natural selection could work. The modern synthesis explains this.

modules – specific, isolated mental functions that are thought to be either hardwired or easily learned because of preparedness. Modules presumably solve a specific problem of survival or reproduction. The most well-known module is the cheater detection module of social judgment.

monozygotic twins – "identical" twins; those who share virtually all their genes. In twin studies of the heritability of a trait, it's important to know whether twins share all (monozygotic) or only about half (dizygotic) of their genes.

Morganucadon – (aka Morgie) a primitive mammal about the size and shape of a chipmunk (see Figure 1.1). Morgie coexisted with the dinosaurs when they went extinct. Early mammals like Morganucadon eventually evolved into the incredibly diverse array of mammals alive today.

morning sickness – the nausea and vomiting that many women experience when pregnant. It's most common during the first trimester of a woman's pregnancy and seems to reduce the risk of birth defects based on ingested teratogens.

mortality salience hypothesis – the idea that when we have recently been reminded of our own deaths and death is in the back of our minds, we work harder than usual to maintain, respect, and validate our cultural worldviews.

mortality salience manipulation – the main manipulation in studies of terror management theory, which requires people to think about their own physical deaths. The consequence of this manipulation is that people become more interested than usual in defending their cultural worldviews.

multilevel selection theory – the theory that, under the right circumstances, groups behave almost as if they are individual organisms. If the benefits to the group of individual cooperators or altruists greatly outweigh the costs to the individual altruists, group-level selection ("survival of the fittest species" rather than "survival of the fittest genes") can presumably occur. Also known as group selection.

multiple nucleotide polymorphisms – two or more adjacent nucleotide variations that differ meaningfully across people (that is, two or more adjacent SNPs).

mutation – a genetic error (e.g., a copying error) that means that children can come to possess genetic variations that neither of their parents possessed. Although mutations are often harmful, the good ones (because they increase survival or successful reproduction) are crucial to natural selection.

mutualism – a form of cooperation in which each member of a dyad does (or allows) something that is beneficial to both parties. Unlike reciprocal altruism, mutualism requires no accounting for past or future favors.

myth of race – the erroneous and sometimes self-justifying idea that there are dramatic psychological differences between the people who have historically inhabited different regions of the earth. Genetic analyses show that we are all one race and that the differences between the so-called "races" are superficial, reflecting specific adaptations (e.g., dark skin, thinner bodies that dissipate heat) to local physical environments.

naive scientist – Fritz Heider's term for laypeople, who think like scientists, in the sense that they try to figure out the causes of other people's behavior.

natural selection – the process by which genes that promote reproductive success in a specific environment become more common in future organisms. In contrast, genes that confer reproductive disadvantages are unlikely to be passed on.

Neanderthal – a species of extinct hominid (*Homo neanderthalensis*) with brains a little larger than our own. They lived in Eurasia until about 30,000 years ago. Although Neanderthals were highly intelligent, genomic analyses suggest that they probably had limited ability to use language.

need to belong (need for connectedness) – the human motivation to be connected, physically and psychologically, to other people. This powerful need lies at the heart of a great deal of prosocial behavior, perhaps including altruism.

NEWater – a brand of recycled water produced in Singapore. Public officials in Singapore managed to overcome people's natural aversions to recycled water by getting the public to associate NEWater with Singaporean celebrities.

normally distributed – a way of describing traits or behaviors whose frequency in a population fits a bell-shaped curve, meaning that average scores are much more common than extreme scores in either direction. Height in people is normally distributed.

norm of reciprocity – the powerful social norm that we should pay back favors to those who have helped us in the past – and are allowed to pay back injuries to those who have harmed us. Both a great deal of helping behavior and a great deal of aggression may thus be grounded in the human tendency to value fairness.

nucleotides – the base pairs – typically adenine (A) paired with thymine (T) and cytosine (C) paired with guanine (G) – that make up the "rungs" in the spiral DNA ladder (DNA double helix). In other words, tiny bits of DNA.

numerosity heuristic – the judgmental bias of assessing magnitude by paying too much attention to frequency information and not enough attention to the absolute size of the individual pieces. *See* ratio-bias phenomenon.

observational learning – *see* social learning.

occasions – the second dimension of the OOPS! heuristic for assessing external validity. This one has to do with whether a research finding holds up across different times, ranging from time of day to historical and even geological times.

"ontogeny recapitulates phylogeny" – Ernst Haeckel's idea that the development of an embryo over the course of days or weeks (ontogeny) revealed what had happened in the evolutionary history of that organism (phylogeny). To Haeckel, watching embryonic development was like having an evolutionary time machine.

OOPS! heuristic – a heuristic for summarizing four issues researchers should consider when evaluating the external validity of a research finding. The four issues are operationalizations, occasions, populations, and situations.

operational definitions – ways of measuring hypothetical constructs by expressing them via concrete, observable actions or procedures.

operationalizations – the first dimension of the OOPS! heuristic for assessing external validity. This one has to do with generalizability across specific ways of defining the hypothetical constructs being studied.

opt-in approach – an approach to organ donation that requires people to take active steps to register as organ donors. Unfortunately, this approach leads to very low rates of organ donation because of the status quo bias.

opt-out approach – a strategy for promoting very high rates of organ donation by specifying that the default is to be an organ donor. People must thus take active efforts to exclude themselves from the list of organ donors if they so wish.

organogenesis – the period in early development when all the major organs begin to develop. In people, this window is about 15–60 days after conception. This is a period of great susceptibility to teratogens.

overprotective parenting – a parenting style in which parents strive to protect their children from all possible negative events and thus prevent their children from developing their own problem-solving and coping skills. *See* helicopter parenting.

overregularization – the tendency for young children to apply the rules of grammar too stringently. An example is saying: "We goed to the store yesterday." This suggests an understanding of grammatical rules rather than simple memorization.

ovulation – the cyclical release of a mature egg (or eggs) by a female mammal. In the past decade, research has shown that ovulation in people bears at least some resemblance to ovulation in other mammals. Specifically, most women are more interested than usual in sex when they are ovulating and most men are more sexually attracted than usual to women who are ovulating. Appearance cues, smell, and vocal cues all appear to be a part of this process. *See* stinky T-shirt paradigm.

palmar (grasping) reflex – the innate tendency for neonates to grab firmly onto anything you place in their palms. This reflex is probably a lot more useful to primate babies whose moms carry them on their hairy backs than it is to human babies.

Pangaea – the huge supercontinent that began drifting apart about 175–200 million years ago, and which eventually became the modern continents. *See* plate tectonics.

panspermia – the theory that either life or the chemical precursors thereof first evolved elsewhere in the universe and came to earth by means of asteroids.

paper-folding problem – a judgment task developed by Scott Plous to demonstrate the foibles of human judges. *See* anchoring and adjustment bias.

paramecia – extremely simple, single-celled organisms that have existed for at least 200 million years (single form, paramecium). Even paramecia compete with one another for food sources.

parasitism – feeding off the body or nutritional resources of a host, which is a subtle form of aggression.

parental care – costly things that parents do for their offspring. This includes things as varied as producing and incubating eggs and teaching one's offspring to make a spear. Such parental care typically reduces a parent's chances of survival while increasing the parent's personal fitness, by maximizing the production and survival of healthy offspring.

parental care motivational system – a presumably innate tendency for adult human beings to be predisposed to care for and bond with needy infants. The children of adoptive parents seem to benefit greatly from this system.

parental investment theory – the theory that if one sex makes greater biological and behavioral investments in its offspring, that sex will be sexually choosier and less promiscuous. In altricial species that engage in pair-bonding, the theory also predicts that the more highly invested sex will seek out a mate who is more likely to help them care for and nurture any offspring.

parsimony – the scientific canon that states that, all else being equal, simpler explanations are to be preferred over complex ones. Also known as "Occam's razor" and "Lloyd Morgan's canon."

passive genotype-environment effects – a situation in which parents or other family members (who share genes with a child) create worlds that facilitate the expression of phenotypes that are consistent with a child's genetic makeup. Children are passive, in that they "soak up" such environments. *See* the PEA model.

passive observational methods – techniques for studying behavior without manipulating any variables. This includes tools such as surveys and interviews, unobtrusive observations, archival research, and ethnographies. *See* the PEA model.

PEA model – a way of summarizing the positive genotype-environment correlations that exist when the worlds in which people live shape their behavior in ways that facilitate the expression of their genes.

penile plethysmograph – a device that assesses male sexual arousal by measuring increases in the diameter or total volume of the penis.

pentadactyl limb – the prototypical mammalian limb structure that includes a hand, foot, paw, or flipper with five digit bones, along with a two-boned lever that attaches nearer the digits and a single, sturdier bone that attaches nearer the trunk. This basic limb plan is shared by virtually all mammals and is thus a physical example of homology.

personal fitness – the number of viable offspring an animal produces, which is a traditional indicator of "evolutionary success." However, Hamilton proposed that a superior indicator of fitness is inclusive fitness, which focuses on how many copies of one's genes survive rather than how many kids one leaves behind.

phenotype – the actual physical properties of an organism such as its size and color, and whether and how it moves around. This stands in contrast to genotype (which does not always influence phenotype).

physical aggression – harming someone's body by biting, crushing, hitting, kicking, punching, scratching, shooting, stabbing, or otherwise harming the person. In people, men tend to be more physically aggressive than women.

physical attractiveness stereotype – the widespread assumption that physically attractive people are happier, more honest, and more sociable than their less attractive peers. Because even newborns prefer to look at more attractive faces, it appears that this stereotype probably has an evolutionary basis.

physical strength – power, the ability move heavy objects, which is associated with fighting ability. Physical strength is a surprisingly good predictor of attitudes about aggression, including a willingness to go to war over cross-national disputes.

placebo – an inert pill containing no drugs of any kind. To see if a drug works for pharmacological reasons, researchers need to see if it works better than a placebo.

plate tectonics – (aka continental drift) Wegener's once controversial but now well-established idea that giant plates on the earth's crust have been slowly drifting for millions of years on the earth's mantle. This creates mountains and earthquakes, and over many millions of years it has dramatically shaped evolution. Antarctica used to be warm, for example.

polyandry – the practice of having multiple husbands.

polydactyly – having extra fingers and/or toes. Surprisingly, in people and cats (both of whom usually have five digits on each limb), polydactyly is genetically dominant over having the usual five digits per limb.

polygyny – the practice of having multiple wives.

polymerase chain reaction (PCR) – "molecular photocopying," a genetic amplification technique that begins with a single strand of DNA and produces millions of copies of it by relying on the enzyme polymerase and a long series of cyclical temperature changes that fuel the DNA copying process.

populations – the third dimension of the OOPS! heuristic for assessing external validity. The degree to which a research finding holds up for a wide range of people or species (e.g., women as well as men, the poor as well as the wealthy, robins as well as rats).

positive test bias – the tendency to test hypotheses by paying more attention to evidence that would support the hypotheses than to evidence that would invalidate or disconfirm the hypotheses. "What do you like most about jazz?"

power distance – Hofstede's cultural dimension of "how a society handles inequality among people."

power of the situation – the social psychological axiom that a great deal of what people think, feel, and do is determined by their immediate social situation.

pragmatic reasoning schemas – learned knowledge structures that operate somewhere between the very precise level of modules and the flexible but highly taxing level of abstract thinking. Cheng and Holyoak might prefer to explain studies of cheater detection modules in terms of concepts such as "permission schemas."

precocial – a term describing organisms whose young can fend well for themselves at a very young age. Alligators, geese, and sea turtles are very precocial. Contrast with altricial.

predation – the act or process of killing another organism to make that organism (the prey) a food source. Robins and killer whales both engage in predation.

preparedness – an innate readiness to learn some things easily. Examples: It is very easy for many mammals to learn to fear snakes, it is easy for human children to acquire language, and it is easy for most predators to learn to stalk and hunt.

prevarication – lying, intentionally deceiving people or misrepresenting things. Hockett argues that this is one of the universal features of human language.

principle of contagion – the instinctive (or easily learned) assumption that things take on properties of things that they touch or resemble. This leads to an aversion to some things that are not truly harmful (such as an aversion to recycled water).

prison-industrial complex – a term in the U.S. coined to reflect the dramatic growth in *for-profit* prisons that has occurred following the Len Bias law. This includes the lobbying efforts of for-profit prisons to stay "tough on crime."

problem of induction – the dilemma that it's impossible to prove any empirical statement to be universally true. This is the case because no matter how many careful observations one has made in support of a theory or hypothesis, it is always possible that a future observation will invalidate the same theory or hypothesis.

productivity – one of Hockett's presumed universals of human language. It means that all languages allow users to create an infinite number of novel utterances and that all languages are constantly evolving.

prokaryotes – primitive, single-celled organisms that lack a nucleus and thus have no complex inner structure (and for which DNA floats about freely). Prokaryotes presumably evolved before more complex eukaryotic cells, which do have nuclei.

proliferation – the rapid production of trillions of synaptic connections between brain cells all over the brain that occurs during infancy and toddlerhood.

prosocial behavior – behavior that benefits another person, regardless of how costly it is or what motivated the behavior.

prospective studies – studies that follow people over time, with the usual goal of assessing temporal sequence.

prospect theory – a theory of human judgment based on the idea that the curve describing our psychological responses to negative stimuli is steeper than the curve describing our psychological responses to positive stimuli. This predicts greater sensitivity to losses than to gains and is probably highly adaptive.

psychology – the scientific study of how people think, feel and behave.

psychophysics – the study of how our subjective sensory experiences (e.g., sweetness, loudness) change with objective changes in the physical stimuli we are judging (e.g., sugar concentrations, the changing energy levels of a sound).

puberty – the biological changes associated with sexual maturation.

punctuated equilibria – the theory that, rather than being gradual and continuous, speciation rates are variable. Accordingly, there appear to be long periods of stability for many species, followed by occasional periods of rapid, dramatic change.

Punnett square – a 2 x 2 matrix in which the genotype (the two alleles) of one parent is expressed in the columns and the genotype of the other parent is expressed in the rows, allowing calculations of the likelihood of different phenotypes across many hypothetical pairings of the two parents.

quantitative genetics – the (highly common) type of genetic transmission that occurs when many different genes all contribute (usually some more than others) to a phenotype. In people, for example, height is influenced to at least a small degree by about 700 genes.

radiometric dating – a technique for determining the age of an ancient animal or artifact by assessing the ratio of the normal vs. isotopic forms of an atom such as carbon. The technique works because isotopes decay predictably over known periods. The less ^{14}C a biological sample contains, for example, the older it is.

random assignment – the experimental technique of placing people in different conditions in an experiment by giving every participant exactly the same chance as every other participant of being assigned to any given condition of the experiment.

ratio-bias phenomenon – the preference for gambles with a greater number of winning possibilities (e.g., 10 out of 100 rather than 1 out of 10), even when such gambles offer no true (abstract) statistical advantage. *See* numerosity heuristic.

reaction formation – Freud's term for developing a conscious attitude about something or someone that is the opposite of your own feared unconscious desires. Acting as if you dislike someone on whom you have an inappropriate crush is an example. Some researchers have argued that homophobia is another example.

realistic group conflict theory – the theory that intergroup aggression often arises because of competition for scarce, desirable resources. In a summer boys' camp, Sherif created aggression between the Rattlers and the Eagles simply by staging group competitions.

recessive – in genetics, the term used to describe an allele for a specific gene that is not expressed phenotypically at all when it appears along with a dominant allele for the same gene.

reciprocal altruism – "trading favors," prosocial behavior directed at a genetically unrelated animal who has helped you in the past. Many social animals engage in reciprocal altruism.

redback spider – a highly venomous species of Australian spider. Male redbacks often throw themselves into the mouths of the females with whom they are mating. Female redbacks usually eat the males, but the self-sacrifice helps males fertilize a greater number of eggs.

red-necked phalarope – a small species of wading water bird in which the males take on the parental duties of incubating the eggs and caring for the chicks after they hatch. Given this unusually high parental investment on the part of males, it is not surprising that male phalaropes are picky maters. The females are also much more colorful than the males, another reversal of the usual pattern for birds.

reflex – an innate (instinctive, hardwired) behavior that occurs reliably in specific situations, without any need for learning or insight. Blinking, shivering, and sneezing are permanent reflexes. In contrast, many newborn reflexes disappear with age.

relatedness – in Hamilton's rule, this is the proportion of genes shared by two organisms in question. It's better to help when relatedness is high.

relational aggression – harming someone psychologically by damaging a personal connection the person has to someone else. Both stealing a person's mate and spreading lies about a person qualify as relational aggression. In people, women and girls are at least as high in relational aggression as men and boys are.

relative deprivation – having or getting less in comparison with a salient comparison group. The term sometimes refers to the anger or dissatisfaction that results from this perceived slight. For example, a child who is at first delighted to receive a candy (sweet) may become unhappy when she sees that her sister received two such candies.

representativeness heuristic – a rule of thumb that involves judging the likelihood or magnitude of an event based on how much it resembles (is similar to) some other event. An example is judging people to be more aggressive if they wear black. Another example is thinking that frogs cause warts.

rest and digest – the opposite of a fight-or-flight response in primitive invertebrates such as hydra and mollusks. When there's no threat and there's food to be had, it's wise to engage in catabolic (growing or rebuilding) physiological activities.

risk–benefit rule – a rule for determining whether a specific research study is ethical. The likely benefits to society of the proposed research must outweigh any reasonably foreseeable risks to those who participate in the research. *See* institutional review board.

risk contact theory of warfare – the theory that warfare exists in highly intelligent, socially coordinated beings like people because it has fitness benefits. The theory includes the distressing hypothesis that, because a few men can father many children, war can have fitness advantages even when male mortality rates are high. *See* male warrior hypothesis.

rooting reflex – the tendency for newborns to turn their heads and suck when you lightly stroke their cheeks. This reflex seems to promote successful breastfeeding.

Sapir-Whorf linguistic relativity hypothesis – the idea that human thought depends heavily on language. This implies that people who speak different languages must, by necessity, think differently. Despite a great deal of looking, there has been only limited support for this idea, suggesting language has many universal features.

savant – a person who suffers from serious mental disabilities (often autism) and yet possesses incredible intellectual, musical, or artistic talents in specific domains. The sculptor Alonzo Clemens is an artistic savant.

scapegoat – a person or social group – usually one with very little power – who people blame for their own problems. Hitler used principles of social influence to make scapegoats of Jews, gypsies, and other minorities in World War II.

secure – the most common infant attachment style, which reflects an infant's feelings of trust in a primary caregiver, and thus the infant's ability to use the caregiver as a resource (a "secure base") in times of distress or uncertainty. Secure infants behave as if they know they can trust their caregivers.

segregation – physically separating oneself from those who are competing for the same resource(s). Variations on this principle occur in life forms as diverse as people and plants. Plants can often tell their own roots from those of a competitor.

selective fitness – an organism's overall chances of getting lots of its genes into the gene pool (by surviving, mating, and producing surviving offspring).

self-fulfilling prophecies – the tendency for people's expectations that something is going to happen to make that very thing happen (even if it is unwelcome).

selfish grandparent effect – the finding that the average amount of care grandparents provide to their grandchildren is directly proportional to the likelihood that they are genetically related to the grandchildren.

semi-restrictive countries – countries in which the norms and rules about sex before marriage are unclear and in which there is widespread variation in parental strategies for dealing with teenage sexuality. The U.S. is a semi-restrictive country.

sensitive periods – somewhat flexible periods in which we are predisposed to develop specific traits or capabilities more readily than at other times of life.

sequential hermaphrodite – an organism that begins life as one sex but can change (usually permanently) to the other sex. Clownfish are sequential hermaphrodites.

serial monogamy – the practice of having more than one spouse in your lifetime but having only one spouse at a time.

sexual cannibalism – the practice in many female praying mantises of eating their male mates during a sexual encounter.

sexual dimorphism – sex-linked variation in a particular species. In gorillas, for example, males are much larger and stronger than females. In many birds of prey, it is the females who are larger.

sexual jealousy – envy and possessiveness grounded in your romantic partner's real or imagined sexual or emotional infidelities. David Buss's research suggests that men are usually more jealous than women about sexual infidelity. In contrast, women are usually more jealous than men about emotional fidelity.

sexually permissive countries – countries in which most parents take it for granted that their teenagers will be sexually active. In such countries, most parents focus their energies on ensuring that their teens engage in safe, consensual sex.

sexually restrictive countries – countries in which the norms and rules about sex are so iron-handed that very few teenagers are bold enough to have premarital sex.

sexual parasitism – in tiny male anglerfish, attaching oneself to the body of a female anglerfish. Because the male and female body tissues fuse, male anglerfish rely completely on the females for everything from nutrition to locomotion.

sexual selection – the natural selection of specific physical traits or behavioral tendencies that make an organism attractive to members of the opposite sex. A peacock's colorful tail is thought to be an example.

sexual strategies theory – the theory that women and men have evolved to seek certain traits in a mate that increase their own selective fitness. Relatively speaking, women should more strongly prefer partners who are high in social status, whereas men should more strongly prefer partners who are young. Both sexes should prefer physically healthy and intelligent partners.

shared reality theory – the theory that human beings have a deep need to view the world, and the people in it, in the same fashion as other people, especially those to whom they feel psychologically close and who happen to be physically close at the moment.

single nucleotide polymorphism (SNP) – variation in just one nucleotide (e.g., guanine rather than cytosine) in a string of DNA that occurs in enough people (say 1%) to be considered meaningful genetic variation. SNPs (pronounced snips) are associated with important health outcomes such as responses to specific drugs.

situations – the fourth dimension of the OOPS! heuristic for assessing external validity. This one has to do with generalization across different situations (e.g., across formal vs. informal situations, at work vs. at play, or across cultures).

slow strategy – (aka R strategy) according to life history theory, this is a strategy for survival and reproduction that happens in resource-rich and benevolent conditions (e.g., when food is plentiful, when mortality rates are low). This refers to making longer term gambles, having fewer offspring, first producing offspring at a later age, and often living longer as a result.

smell (olfaction) – a sense that appears to play a large role in sexual interest and sexual aversion. Heterosexual men consider the body odors of women who are ovulating sexier and more pleasant than those of women who are not ovulating.

social dominance theory – an evolutionarily inspired theory of social hierarchies and intergroup relations that emphasizes the myths and social structures that maintain status differences between powerful and less powerful groups. For example, the U.S. system of basing school funding on local property taxes makes it hard for poor children to get a good education.

social exchange theories – a family of theories in sociology and social psychology that are built on the core assumption that we keep track of what others have done for us and carefully compare this with what we have done for them.

social hierarchy – a group structure in which dominant animals (those at or near the top of the social ladder) enjoy special privileges over subordinates (low ranking animals). Most primates have very clear social hierarchies.

social inequality – a state of affairs in a culture or region in which poor people have dramatically less wealth than wealthy people. Social inequality appears to be a better predictor of rates of violent crime than is median household income.

social learning – a form of operant learning in which an organism learns not by being reinforced or punished but by observing the behavior of another organism and copying behaviors that are rewarded or avoiding behaviors that are punished.

social norms – powerful but often unspoken rules about how we ought to behave in social situations. Eating pasta with a fork and refraining from playing with a stranger's hair are both social norms.

social psychology – to paraphrase Gordon Allport, this is the scientific study of how other people, including imagined or remembered others, influence our thoughts, feelings, and behavior.

socioemotional selectivity theory – a theory of lifespan development that suggests that in cultures where longevity is high, seniors place great value on experiencing positive emotions and spending time with loved ones, while placing less value than they once did on having novel experiences.

specialization – a route to speciation in which the ancestors of a species make numerous adaptions to a specific, perhaps extreme, environment. Camels evolved, for example, to be really good at coping with hot and arid conditions.

speciation – the evolution of separate species, thought to happen when dramatic changes in environment – or the availability of a large and highly variable environment – lead specific organisms to take such divergent evolutionary paths over great periods that they can no longer interbreed.

species – a group of animals that share much the same basic genome and thus can mate and produce healthy, fertile offspring. *Homo sapiens* (people) and *Pica pica* (the European magpie) are examples.

specificity principle – the idea that people who stand out as geniuses in specific areas (where they have great expertise) are no better than the average person when you assess performance in a different domain.

speed dating – a popular dating event in which participants take part in a series of multiple brief conversations with strangers who are all interested in finding dates.

spermatophore – a ball of nutrients, and sperm, that the males of some cricket species offer to females to try to entice them to mate. Females often accept the offer but only accept the sperm if the rest of the spermatophore met some minimal standards of volume and quality.

sperm competition – the battle for fertilization that sometimes happens between the sperm of different males. Ways of winning the battle include producing more and faster swimming sperm than one's rivals as well as mating more frequently.

spontaneous alternation – the finding that, after having just found food in a specific location in a laboratory maze, foraging animals such as mice and rats tend to avoid this location in the immediate future. This alternation bias is presumably highly adaptive in real-world searches, where eaten food is not magically replenished.

status quo bias – a judgmental and behavioral bias grounded in psychological inertia. It's the tendency to do what we and others have done in the past, which is often what takes the least effort in the present situation.

status-seeking – the evolutionary principle that social organisms usually recognize a dominance hierarchy (a social ranking system) and compete to make their way up in the hierarchy. Such competition sometimes leads to aggression.

stinky T-shirt paradigm – a paradigm for studying the role of smell in human mating and incest aversion – by having people rate the pleasantness, sexiness, and so on of T-shirts that were worn by people under careful conditions that allowed the shirts to pick up the wearer's natural body odors, without picking up other smells.

straw man fallacy – the approach of trying to discredit a way of thinking by attacking a weak or ridiculous version of that way of thinking.

structural violence – laws, rules, or social systems that facilitate harm in people or make it hard or impossible for them to enjoy basic human rights. Lax rules in coal mines that often lead to explosions or cave-ins are a dramatic example.

supergiant – a star with a mass 10–70 times greater than that of our own sun. Stars of this extreme mass become supernovas when they die and scatter heavy matter (like iron) throughout the universe, seeding other solar systems with heavy matter.

supernova – the dramatic explosion of a supergiant that occurs near the end of its lifespan, briefly but dramatically increasing the star's luminosity. *See* supergiant.

superordinate goals – goals that are shared by the members of two opposing groups. Creating such goals, and requiring members of both groups to work together to achieve them, can greatly reduce intergroup conflict.

superorganisms – highly cooperative and independent groups of social individuals who behave almost as if they were a single organism. Ants and the Portuguese man o' war are examples of superorganisms.

surrogate mother – an artificial mother used in Harry Harlow's studies of infant rhesus monkey attachment. The infants strongly preferred the contact comfort of a fake mom covered in terrycloth over a wire mom that provided them with milk.

surveys and interviews – a set of passive observational techniques that rely on people's self-reports of their thoughts, feelings, and behavior. Examples include public opinion polls, censuses, and structured clinical interviews.

suspicion – a state of distrust and wariness about why or whether a person has done something that increases the sophistication of people's social judgments about the person's suspicion-arousing actions.

symbiosis – an interaction or ongoing relationship between the member of two different species that yields benefits to each organism. When shrimp clean fish (and eat what they clean away) both species benefit.

synaptic pruning – the process by which the enormous number of synapses in the toddler brain is reduced to a much lower (and much more highly organized) number of synapses during normal development.

teacher expectancies – the unconscious tendency for teachers who expect specific children to perform well to treat those they expect to succeed in ways that promote their success. The classroom equivalent of experimenter bias in the lab.

temporal sequence – the second of John Stuart Mill's three logical requirements for establishing causality. Establishing temporal sequence means documenting that changes in a presumed cause happen prior to changes in a presumed consequence.

teratogen – a chemical, physical or psychological event to which a mother and developing baby are exposed that causes abnormal development.

terror management theory – the theory that human beings cope with their intense fear of death by psychologically defending their positive views of themselves and their cultures. The main way of so doing is defending one's cultural worldviews.

testability – the scientific canon that states that theories and hypotheses must be subject to confirmation or disconfirmation. A major way of making theories testable is using clear operational definitions.

Thales – an ancient Greek thinker who was arguably the world's first true scientist. Unlike the philosophers who came before him, Thales was an empiricist who strongly preferred natural rather than mystical explanations.

theory – a statement about the causal relation between two or more variables. It's typically stated in abstract terms, and it usually has some empirical support.

thermography – an objective, physiological measure of sexual arousal that works by assessing changes in the average temperature of people's genitals.

third-variable problem – a methodological problem in which some additional variable exists that may influence the dependent variable and that varies systematically along with the independent variable(s). This is a threat to internal validity. It's what John Stuart Mill worried about when he said we must eliminate all possible confounds.

tonic immobility – an instinctive response to severe threat in which animals feign death or "play possum." The response often seems to deter otherwise interested predators from killing and eating the seemingly dead animals.

tradeoff – in life history theory, the idea that many things that increase an organism's selective fitness are in direct conflict with other things that could also increase selective fitness. The more offspring a mother produces, for example, the less nutrition she can provide to any individual child.

trolley problem – a hypothetical dilemma used to study prosocial behavior. In a common version of the problem, a maniac has tied five strangers to a trolley track, the trolley's engineer is oblivious to this, and respondents have to report whether to divert the train (sacrificing a single stranger in so doing) to save the five strangers.

true experiment – a research design in which the researcher randomly assigns participants to one or more conditions, enacts a manipulation, and then assesses whether the different experimental groups behave differently.

twin studies – studies that attempt to assess the heritability of traits by assessing the phenotypic correlations (e.g., between heights or IQ scores) of monozygotic or dizygotic twins who were separated at birth. A problem with this design is that identical twins look very much alike and are thus subject to the same stereotypes.

unobtrusive observation – a passive observational research technique that involves the direct or indirect behavioral observation of people who do not know their behavior is being measured.

vampire bats – a social species of bats that engage in complex forms of reciprocal altruism by sharing blood with hungry cave-mates. Some bats also share blood with others who have recently groomed them but have not recently shared blood.

verbal aggression – hurting someone by saying bad things to or about the person. Unlike relational aggression, this doesn't always harm the victim's relationship with someone else and may be done directly to the victim. In people, women and girls are at least as high in verbal aggression as men and boys are.

vicarious learning – *see* social learning.

waist-to-hip ratio – according to Singh, this is a cue for sexual selection that has proven to be an honest predictor of female fertility. Singh's research suggests that the most attractive ratio is roughly 0.73 (corresponding roughly to "36-24-36").

Wason card task – a classic task used by Peter Wason to assess people's general ability to test causal hypotheses. Most people who are given an abstract hypothesis to test tend to err by looking for evidence that would falsely confirm the hypothesis they've been asked to evaluate.

weaning – the mammalian process of transitioning one's offspring from nursing to the consumption of solid food. In people, weaning happens much sooner than one might expect based on how altricial we are.

within-subjects design – a method in which experimenters expose the same group of people to two or more experimental conditions at different times, to see if people behave differently under the two conditions.

working models – conscious and unconscious mental representations of the self in relation to one's primary caregivers. A positive model of both self and other, for example, leads to a secure attachment style.

zooids – biologically distinct organisms that are so specialized in their cooperative functions that none of them could survive alone. Several different zooids make up the Portuguese man o' war.

REFERENCES

Abbott, R., Albach, D., Ansell, S., Arntzen, J.W., Baird, S.J. et al. (2013). Hybridization and speciation. *Journal of Evolutionary Biology*, 26(2), 229–46.

Abramson, P.R. (2017). *Screwing around with sex*. Joshua Tree, CA: Asylum 4 Renegades.

Abramson, P.R., Boggs, P., & Mason, J. (2013). Sex is blind: Some preliminary theoretical formulations. *Sexual Disabilities*, 31, 393–402.

Abramson, P.R., & Pinkerton, S. D. (2002). *With pleasure: Thoughts on the nature of human sexuality*. Oxford: Oxford University Press.

Adams, E.S., & Mesterton-Gibbons, M. (2003). Lanchester's attrition models and fights among social animals. *Behavioral Ecology*, 14, 719–23.

Adams, H.E., Wright, L.W., & Lohr, B.A. (1996). Is homophobia associated with homosexual arousal? *Journal of Abnormal Psychology*, 105, 440–5.

Adams, S. (2009). Cuckoo chicks dupe foster parents from the moment they hatch. Available at: www.telegraph.co.uk/news/earth/wildlife/4109282/Cuckoo-chicks-dupe-foster-parents-from-the-moment-they-hatch.html.

Adolph, K.E. (2000). Specificity of learning: Why infants fall over a veritable cliff. *Psychological Science*, 11, 290–5.

Ahn, W.-K., & Graham, L.M. (1999). The impact of necessity and sufficiency in the Wason four-card selection task. *Psychological Science*, 10, 237–42.

Ainsworth, M., & Bowlby, J. (1965). *Child care and the growth of love*. London: Penguin Books.

Aknin, L.B., Hamlin, J.K., & Dunn, E.W. (2012). Giving leads to happiness in young children. *PLoS ONE*, 7, e39211.

Aktipis, C.A. (2004). Know when to walk away: Contingent movement and the evolution of cooperation. *Journal of Theoretical Biology*, 231(2), 249–60.

Aktipis, C.A. (2011). Is cooperation viable in mobile organisms? Simple walk away strategy favors the evolution of cooperation in groups. *Evolution and Human Behavior*, 32, 263–76.

Alberts, S.C., Altmann, J., & Wilson, M.L. (1996). Mate guarding constrains foraging activity of male baboons. *Animal Behaviour*, 51(6), 1269–77.

Alexander, M. (2012). *The new Jim Crow: Mass incarceration in the age of color-blindness*. New York: The New Press.

Allport, G. (1954a). *The nature of prejudice*. Reading, MA: Addison-Wesley.

Allport, G.W. (1954b). The historical background of modern social psychology. In G. Lindzey (ed.) *The handbook of social psychology* (vol. 1, pp. 3–56). Cambridge, MA: Addison-Wesley.

Anderson, C.A., & Bushman, B.J. (2002). Human aggression. *Annual Review of Psychology*, 53(1), 27–51.

Anderson, K.G. (2006). How well does paternity confidence match actual paternity? *Current Anthropology*, 47, 513–20.

Anderson, N.H. (1968). Likableness ratings of 555 personality-trait words. *Journal of Personality and Social Psychology*, 9, 272–9.

Andrade, M.C. (1996). Sexual selection for male sacrifice in the Australian redback spider. *Science*, 271, 70–2.

Andrade, M.C. (2002). Risky mate search and male self-sacrifice in redback spiders. *Behavioral Ecology*, 14, 531–8.

Ansuini, C.G., Fiddler-Woite, J., & Woite, R.S. (1996). The source, accuracy, and impact of initial sexuality information on lifetime wellness. *Adolescence*, 31, 283–9.

Archie, E.A., Hollister-Smith, J.A., Poole, J.H. et al. (2007). Behavioural inbreeding avoidance in wild African elephants. *Molecular Ecology*, 16, 4138–48.

Arnett, J.J. (2003). Conceptions of the transition to adulthood among emerging adults in American ethnic groups. *New Directions in Child and Adolescent Development*, 100, 63–75.

Arnett, J.J. (2012). *Human development: A cultural approach*. Upper Saddle River, NJ: Pearson.

Aron, A., Aron E.N., & Smollan, D. (1992). Inclusion of Other in the Self Scale and the structure of interpersonal closeness. *Journal of Personality and Social Psychology*, 63, 596–612.

Aron, A., Aron, E.N., Tudor, M., & Nelson, G. (1991). Close relationships as including other in the self. *Journal of Personality and Social Psychology*, 60, 241–53.

Asimov, I. (1964). *Asimov's biographical encyclopedia of science and technology*. Garden City, NY: Doubleday.

Atran, S. (2001). A cheater–detection module? Dubious interpretations of the Wason selection task and logic. *Evolution and Cognition*, 7, 1–7.

Au, T.K.-F. (1983). Chinese and English counterfactuals: The Sapir-Whorf hypothesis revisited. *Cognition*, 15, 155–87.

Austad, S.N. (1994). Menopause: An evolutionary perspective. *Experimental Gerontology*, 29, 255–63.

Ayton, P., & Fischer, I. (2004). The gambler's fallacy and the hot-hand fallacy: Two faces of subjective randomness? *Memory and Cognition*, 32, 1369–78.

Azrin, N.H., Hutchinson, R.R., & Hake, D.F. (1967). Attack, avoidance, and escape reactions to aversive shock. *Journal of the Experimental Analysis of Behavior*, 10, 131–48.

Azrin, N.H., Rubin, H.B., & Hutchinson, R.R. (1968). Biting attack by rats in response to aversive shock. *Journal of the Experimental Analysis of Behavior*, 11, 633–9, doi: 10.1901/jeab.1968.11-633.

Bagley, K. (2012). Why don't TV meteorologists believe in climate change? Available at: www.alternet.org/story/155571/why_don%27t_tv_meteorologists_believe_in_climate_change.

Baker, R.R., & Bellis, M.A. (1993). Human sperm competition: Ejaculate adjustment by males and the function of masturbation. *Animal Behaviour*, 46, 861–85.

Balshine, S. (2012). Patterns of parental care in vertebrates. In N.J. Royle, P.T. Smiseth and M. Kölliker (eds) *The evolution of parental care* (pp. 81–100). Oxford: Oxford University Press.

Bandura, A. (1977). *Social learning theory*. Englewood Cliffs, NJ: Prentice Hall.

Bandura, A., Ross, D., & Ross, S.A. (1961). Transmission of aggression through imitation of aggressive models. *Journal of Abnormal and Social Psychology*, 63(3), 575–82.

Barber, N. (2004). *Kindness in a cruel world: The evolution of altruism.* Amherst, NY: Prometheus Books.

Barber, N. (2009). Do parents favor natural children over adopted ones? Available at: www.psychologytoday.com/us/blog/the-human-beast/200906/do-parents-favor-natural-children-over-adopted-ones.

Barkan, S.E. (2012). *Social problems: Continuity and change*. Irvington, NY: Flat World Knowledge.

Barry, K.L., Holwell, G.I., & Herberstein, M.E. (2008). Female praying mantids use sexual cannibalism as a foraging strategy to increase fecundity. *Behavioral Ecology*, 19, 710–15.

Bartholomew, K. & Shaver, P.R. (1998). Methods of assessing adult attachment. In J.A. Simpson & W.S. Rholes (eds) *Attachment theory and close relationships* (pp. 25–45). New York: Guilford Press.

Batson, C.D. (2008). Empathy-induced altruistic motivation. Address at the Inaugural Herzliya Symposium on Prosocial Motives, Emotions, and Behavior, March 24–7.

Batson, C.D., & Weeks, J.L. (1996). Mood effects of unsuccessful helping: Another test of the empathy-altruism hypothesis. *Personality and Social Psychology Bulletin*, 22, 148–57.

Batson, C.D., Duncan, B., Ackerman, P., Buckley, T., & Birch, K. (1981). Is empathic emotion a source of altruistic motivation? *Journal of Personality and Social Psychology*, 40(2), 290–302.

Baum, D. (1997). *Smoke and mirrors: The war on drugs and the politics of failure*. New York: Little, Brown.

Baumeister, R.F., & Leary, M. (1995). The need to belong: Desire for interpersonal attachments as a fundamental human motivation, *Psychological Bulletin*, 117, 497–529.

Baumeister, R.F., Bratslavsky, E., Finkenauer, C., & Vohs, K.D. (2001). Bad is stronger than good. *Review of General Psychology*, 5, 327–70.

Bear, G., & Pelham, B.W. (2018). Parental investment theory: From "right swipes" to "I do."

Becker, E. (1973). *The denial of death*. New York: Simon & Schuster.

Becker, G.S. (1968). Crime and punishment: An economic approach. *Journal of Political Economics*, 76, 169–217.

Beckett, C., Maughan, B., Rutter, M., Castle, J., Colvert, E. et al. (2006). Do the effects of early severe deprivation on cognition persist into early adolescence? Findings from the English and Romanian adoptees study. *Child Development*, 77(3), 696–711.

Beck-Johnson, L.M., Nelson, W.A., Paaijmans, K.P., Read, A.F., Thomas, M.B. et al. (2013). The effect of temperature on Anopheles mosquito population dynamics and the potential for malaria transmission, *PLoS ONE*, 8, e79276.

Beggan, J.K. (1992). On the social nature of nonsocial perception: The mere ownership effect. *Journal of Personality and Social Psychology*, 62, 229–37.

Bell, E.A., Boehnkea, P.T., Harrison, M. & Maob, W.L. (2015). Potentially biogenic carbon preserved in a 4.1 billion-year-old zircon. *Proceedings of the National Academy of Sciences*, 112, 14518–21.

Belsky, G., & Gilovich, T. (1999). *Why smart people make big money mistakes and how to correct them: Lessons from the new science of behavioral economics.* New York: Simon & Schuster.

Berkowitz, L. (1981). The concept of aggression. In P.E. Brain & D. Benton (eds) *Multidisciplinary approaches to aggression research* (pp. 3–15). Amsterdam: Elsevier/North-Holland.

Berkowitz, L. (1989). Frustration-aggression hypothesis: examination and reformulation. *Psychological Bulletin*, 106, 59–73.

Berkowitz, L. (1990). On the formation and regulation of anger and aggression: a cognitive neo-associationistic analysis. *American Psychologist*, 45, 494–503.

Bernard, H.R. (2006). *Research methods in anthropology: Qualitative and quantitative approaches* (4th edn). New York: Alta Mira Press.

Betrán, A.P., Ye, J., Moller, A.-B., Zhang, J., Gülmezoglu, A.M. et al. (2016). The increasing trend in Caesarean section rates: Global, regional and national estimates: 1990–2014. *PLoS One*, 11(2), e0148343, doi: 10.1371/journal.pone.0148343.

Bickman, I. (1974). The social power of a uniform. *Journal of Applied Social Psychology*, 4, 47–61.

Blanchard, T.C., Wilke, A., & Hayden, B.Y. (2014). Hot-hand bias in rhesus monkeys. *Journal of Experimental Psychology: Animal Learning and Cognition*, 40(3), 280–6.

Bleske-Rechek, A., Nelson, L.A., Baker, J.P., & Remiker, M.W. (2010). Evolution and the trolley problem: People save five over one unless the one is young genetically related, or a romantic partner. *Journal of Social, Evolutionary, and Cultural Psychology*, 4(3), 115–27.

Bodenhausen, G.Y. (1990). Stereotypes as judgmental heuristics: Evidence of circadian variations in discrimination. *Psychological Science*, 1, 319–22.

Boksem, M.A., Mehta, P.H., van den Bergh, B., van Son, V., Trautmann, S.T. et al. (2013). Testosterone inhibits trust but promotes reciprocity. *Psychological Science*, 24, 2306–14.

Bolter, D.R., & Zihlman, A.L. (2011). Dental development timing in captive *Panpaniscus* with comparisons to *Pan troglodytes*. *American Journal of Physical Anthropology*, 145, 647–52.

Boothe, R.G., Dobson, V., & Teller, D.Y. (1985). Postnatal development of vision in human and nonhuman primates. *Annual Review of Neuroscience*, 8, 495–545.

Boyer, S. (2015). Clown anemonefish. Florida Museum of Natural History. Retrieved on June 7, 2015 from www.flmnh.ufl.edu/.

Bro-Jorgensen, J. (2002). Overt female mate competition and preference for central males in a lekking antelope. *Proceedings of the National Academy of Sciences*, 99, 9290–3.

Brookman, F., Mullins, C., Bennett, T., & Wright, R. (2007). Gender, motivation and the accomplishment of street robbery in the United Kingdom. *British Journal of Criminology*, 47, 861–84.

Brosnan, S.F., & de Waal, F.B.M. (2002). A proximate perspective on reciprocal altruism. *Human Nature*, 13, 129–52.

Brosnan, S.F., & de Waal, F.B.M. (2003). Monkeys reject unequal pay. *Nature*, 425(6955), 297–9.

Brown, A.M., & Yamamoto, M. (1986). Visual acuity in newborn and preterm infants measured with grating acuity cards. *American Journal of Opthalmology*, 102, 245–53.

Brown, R. (1965). *Social psychology*. New York: Free Press.

Brown, R. (1986). Linguistic relativity. In S.H. Hulse (ed.) *One hundred years of psychological research in America: G. Stanley Hall and the Johns Hopkins tradition* (pp. 241–76). Baltimore: Johns Hopkins University Press.

Brown, R., & Berko, J. (1960). Word association and the acquisition of grammar. *Child Development*, 31, 1–14.

Brown, S.L., Nesse, R.M., Vinokur, A.D., & Smith, D.M. (2003). Providing social support may be more beneficial than receiving it. Results from a prospective study of mortality. *Psychological Science*, 14, 320–7.

Brueland, H. (1995). *University of Florida book of insect records: Highest lifetime fecundity* (Chapter 18). Retrieved at: www.entnemdept.ufl.edu.

Brusatte, S.L., Butler, R.J., Barrett, P. M., Carrano, M.T., Evans, D.C. et al. (2014). The extinction of the dinosaurs. *Biological Reviews*, 90(2):628–42.

Bryant, G.A., & Haselton, M.G. (2009). Vocal cues of ovulation in human females. *Biology Letters*, 5, 12–15.

Buckels, E.E., Beall, A.T., Hofer, M.K., Lin, E.Y., Zhou, Z. et al. (2015). Individual differences in activation of the parental care motivational system: Assessment, prediction, and implications. *Journal of Personality and Social Psychology*, 108(3), 497–514.

Bugental, D.B., Corpuz, R., & Samec, R. (2013) Outcomes of parental investment in high risk children. *Journal of Experimental Child Psychology*, 116(1), 59–67.

Bunch, G.B., & Zentall, T.R. (1980). Imitation of a passive avoidance response in the rat. *Bulletin of the Psychonomic Society*, 15, 73–5.

Burger, J.M. (2009). Replicating Milgram: Would people still obey today? *American Psychologist*, 64, 1–11.

Burger, J.M., Messian, N., Patel, S., del Prado, A., & Anderson, C. (2004). What a coincidence! The effects of incidental similarity on compliance. *Personality and Social Psychology Bulletin*, 30, 35–43.

Burke, B.L., Martens, A., & Faucher, E.H. (2010). Two decades of terror management theory: A meta-analysis of mortality salience research. *Personality and Social Psychology Review*, 14, 155–95.

Buss, D. (1995). *The evolution of desire: Strategies of human mating.* New York: Basic Books.

Buss, D. (2008). *Evolutionary psychology: The new science of the mind* (3rd edn). Boston: Pearson.

Buss, D.M. (2013). Sexual jealousy. *Psychological Topics*, 22, 155–82.

Buss, D.M., & Schmitt, D.P. (1993). Sexual strategies theory: An evolutionary perspective on human mating. *Psychological Review*, 100, 204–32.

Buss, D.M., Larsen, R. J., Westen, D., & Semmelroth, J. (1992). Sex differences in jealousy: Evolution, physiology, and psychology. *Psychological Science*, 3(4), 251–5.

Buss, D.M., Haselton, M.G., Shackelford, T.K., Bleske, A.L., & Wakefield, J.C. (1998). Adaptations, exaptations, and spandrels. *American Psychologist*, 53, 533–48.

Buss, D.M., Shackelford, T.K., Kirkpatrick, L.A., Chloe, J., Hasegawa, M. et al. (1999). Jealousy and beliefs about infidelity: Tests of competing hypotheses in the United States, Korea, and Japan. *Personal Relationships*, 6, 125–50.

Cahill, J.A., Stirling, I., Kistler, L., Salamzade, R., Ersmark, E. et al. (2015). Genomic evidence of geographically widespread effect of gene flow from polar bears into brown bears. *Molecular Ecology*, 24, 1205–17, doi: 10.1111/mec.13038.

Callaway, E. (2016). Elephant history rewritten by ancient genomes. *Nature*, available at: www.nature.com/news/elephant-history-rewritten-by-ancient-genomes-1.20622.

Cannon, W.B. (1914). The emergency function of the adrenal medulla in pain and the major emotions. *American Journal of Physiology*, 33, 356–72.

Carroll, J.S., Padilla-Walker, L.M., Nelson, L.J., Olson, C.D., Barry, C.M. et al. (2008). Generation XXX: Pornography acceptance and use among emerging adults. *Journal of Adolescent Research*, 23, 6–30.

Carstensen, L. L., Isaacowitz, D. M., and Charles, S. T. (1999). Taking time seriously: A theory of socioemotional selectivity. *American Psychologist*, 54, 165–81.

Carter, G.G., & Wilkinson, G.S. (2013). Food sharing in vampire bats: Reciprocal help predicts donations more than relatedness or harassment. *Proceedings of the Royal Society*, B, 280(1753), 20122573.

Cartwright, D. (1979). Contemporary social psychology in historical perspective. *Social Psychology Quarterly*, 42, 82–93.

Castro, J. (2015). Animal sex: How anglerfish do it. *Live Science*, January 6.

Center for Research on Environmental Decisions (2009). *The psychology of climate change communication: A guide for scientists, journalists, educators, political aides, and the interested public.* New York.

Charles-Sire, V., Guéguen, N., Meineri, S., Martin, A., & Bullock, A. (2013). The effect of priming with a love concept on blood donation promise. *Transfusion and Apheresis Science*, 50, 87–91.

Charlton, B.D., Frey, R., McKinnon, A.J., Fritsch, G., Fitch, W.T. et al. (2013). Koalas use a novel vocal organ to produce unusually low-pitched mating calls. *Current Biology*, 23, R1035–6, https://doi.org/10.1016/j.cub.2013.10.069.

Chase, W.G., & Simon, H.A. (1973). Perception in chess. *Cognitive Psychology*, 4, 55–81.

Cheng, P.W., & Holyoak, K.J. (1985). Pragmatic reasoning schemas. *Cognitive Psychology*, 17, 391–416.

Chincotta, D., & Underwood, G. (1996). Digit-span and articulatory suppression: A cross-linguistic comparison. *European Journal of Cognitive Psychology*, 9, 89–96.

Chomsky, N. (1986). *Knowledge of language: Its nature, origin and use.* New York: Praeger.

Chung, C., & Baldwin, A.J. (2015). The effect of Christian belief in eternal life on age related social partner choice. *Internet Journal of Geriatrics and Gerontology*, 9, 1.

Cialdini, R.B. (1993). *Influence: Science and practice* (3rd edn). New York: HarperCollins.

Cialdini, R.B., Cacioppo, J.T., Bassett, R., & Miller, J.A. (1978). Low-ball procedure for producing compliance: Commitment then cost. *Journal of Personality and Social Psychology*, 36, 463–76.

Clark, R.D., & Hatfield, E. (1989). Gender differences in receptivity to sexual offers. *Journal of Psychology and Human Sexuality*, 2, 39–55.

Clark, R.D., & Hatfield, E. (2003). Love in the afternoon. *Psychological Inquiry*, 14, 227–31.

Clutton-Brock, T.H. (1991). *The evolution of parental care.* Princeton, NJ: Princeton University Press.

Clutton-Brock, T.H., & Isvaran, K. (2007). Sex differences in ageing in natural populations of vertebrates. *Proceedings of the Royal Society*, 274, 3097–104.

Cohen, D., Nisbett, R.E., Bowdle, B.F., & Schwarz, N. (1996). Insult, aggression, and the southern culture of honor: An "experimental ethnography." *Journal of Personality and Social Psychology*, 70, 945–59.

Cohen, F., Sullivan, D., Solomon, S., Greenberg, J., & Ogilvie, D.M. (2011). Finding everland: Flight fantasies and the desire to transcend mortality. *Journal of Experimental Social Psychology*, 47(1), 88–102.

Collett, P., & Marsh, P. (1974). Patterns of public behavior: Collision avoidance on a pedestrian crossing. *Semiotica*, 12, 281–300.

Collins, N.L., & Freeney, B.C. (2004). An attachment theory perspective on closeness and intimacy. In D.J. Mashek & A. Aron (eds) *Handbook of closeness and intimacy* (pp. 163–88). Mahwah, NJ: Lawrence Erlbaum.

Conley, T. (2011). Perceived proposer personality characteristics and gender differences in acceptance of casual sex offers. *Journal of Personality and Social Psychology*, 100, 309–29.

Conselice, C.J., Wilkinson, A., Duncan, K., & Mortlock, A. (2016). The evolution of galaxy number density at z < 8 and its implications. *The Astrophysical Journal*, 830, 83.

Copi, I.M. (1978). *Introduction to logic* (5th edn). New York: Collier Macmillan.

Cosmides, L. (1989). The logic of social exchange: Has natural selection shaped how humans reason? Studies with the Wason selection task. *Cognition*, 31, 187–276.

Cosmides, L., & Tooby, J. (1997). *Evolutionary psychology: A primer.* Available at www.cep.ucsb.edu/primer.html.

Crabtree, S. (2010). Religiosity highest in world's poorest nations. Available at: http://news.gallup.com/poll/142727/religiosity-highest-world-poorest-nations.aspx.

Crabtree, S., & Pelham, B.W. (2009). More religious countries, more perceived ethnic intolerance: Picture is more complex for more religious versus less religious people. Retrieved from www.gallup.com.

Creagh, S. (2008). Treated sewage as water? They'll drink to that. *Sydney Morning Herald*. Retrieved at: www.smh.com.au/news/national.

Crews, D. (2003). Sex determination: Where environment and genetics meet. *Evolution & Development*, 5(1), 50–5.

Cullen, T.M., Fraser, D., Rybczynski, N., & Schröder-Adams, C. (2014). Early evolution of sexual dimorphism and polygyny in Pinnipedia. *Evolution*, 68, 1469–84, doi: 10.1111/evo.12360.

Daly, M. & Wilson, M. (1988a). Evolutionary social psychology and family violence, *Science*, 242(4878), 519–24.

Daly, M. & Wilson, M. (1988b). *Homicide*. New York: Routledge.

Daly, M. & Wilson, M.I. (1994). Some differential attributes of lethal assaults on small children by stepfathers versus genetic fathers. *Ethology & Sociobiology*, 15(4), 207–17.

Daly, M. & Wilson, M. (1998). *The truth about Cinderella.* London: Weidenfeld & Nicolson.

Daly, M. & Wilson, M. (2001). An assessment of some proposed exceptions to the phenomenon of nepotistic discrimination against stepchildren. *Annales Zoologici Fennici*, 38, 287–96.

Daly, M., & Wilson, M. (2008). Is the "Cinderella effect" controversial? A case study of evolution-minded research and critiques thereof. In C.B. Crawford & D. Krebs (eds) *Foundations of evolutionary psychology* (pp. 381–98). Mahwah, NJ: Erlbaum.

Daly, M., & Wilson, M. (n.d.). The "Cinderella effect": Elevated mistreatment of stepchildren in comparison to those living with genetic parents. Available at: www.cep.ucsb.edu/buller/cinderella%20effect%20facts.pdf.

D'Anastasio, R., Wroe, S., Tuniz, C., Mancini, L., Cesana, D.T. et al. (2013). Micro-biomechanics of the Kebara 2 hyoid and its implications for speech in Neanderthals. *PLoS ONE*, 8, e82261.

Darby, C.L., & Riopelle, A.J. (1959). Observational learning in the rhesus monkey. *Journal of Comparative and Physiological Psychology*, 52, 94–98.

Dar-Nimrod, I., Heine, S.J., Cheung, B.Y., & Schaller, M. (2011). Do scientific theories affect men's evaluations of sex crimes? *Aggressive Behavior*, 37, 440–9.

Darwin, C. (1859). *On the origin of species by means of natural selection.* London: J. Murray.

Darwin, C. (1872). *The expression of the emotions in man and animals.* London: J. Murray.

Davidai, S., Gilovich, T., & Ross, L.D. (2012). The meaning of default options for potential organ donors. *Proceedings of the National Academy of Sciences*, 109, 15201–5.

Davies, D. (2015). "Ghettoside" explores why murders are invisible in Los Angeles. Retrieved from www.npr.org/2015/01/26/381589023/ghettoside-explores-why-murders-are-invisible-in-los-angeles.

Dawkins, R. (1976). *The selfish gene.* Oxford: Oxford University Press.

Dawkins, R. (2006). *The God delusion.* Boston, MA: Houghton Mifflin.

Deacon, R.M., & Rawlins, J.N. (2006). T-maze alternation in the rodent. *Nature Protocols*, 1, 7–12, doi:10.1038/nprot.2006.2.

DeCasper, A.J., & Spence, M.J. (1986). Prenatal maternal speech influences newborns' perception of speech sounds. *Infant Behavior and Development*, 9, 133–50.

De Fraja, G. (2009). The origin of utility: Sexual selection and conspicuous consumption. *Journal of Economic Behavior and Organization*, 72, 51–69.

DeHart, T., Pelham, B.W., & Tennen, H. (2006). What lies beneath: Early experiences with parents and implicit self-esteem. *Journal of Experimental Social Psychology*, 42, 1–17.

DeHart, T., Pelham, B., Fiedorowicz, L., Carvallo, M., & Gabriel, S. (2011). Including others in the implicit self: Implicit evaluation of significant others. *Self and Identity*, 10, 127–35.

DeLoache, J.S., Miller, K.F., & Rosengren, K.S. (1997). The credible shrinking room: Very young children's performance with symbolic and nonsymbolic relations, *Psychological Science*, 8, 308–13.

DeNault, L.K., & McFarlane, D.A. (1995). Reciprocal altruism between male vampire bats, *Desmohs votundus. Animal Behavior*, 49, 855–6.

Denes-Raj, V., & Epstein S.J. (1994). Conflict between intuitive and rational processing: When people behave against their better judgment. *Journal of Personality and Social Psychology*, 66, 819–29.

Dennett, D.C. (1993). *Consciousness explained.* Harmondsworth: Penguin.

Depuydt, S. (2014). Arguments for and against self and non-self root recognition in plants. *Frontiers in Plant Science*, 5, 1–7, https://doi.org/10.3389/fpls.2014.00614.

Dethlefsen, L., McFall-Ngai, M., & Relman, D.A. (2007). An ecological and evolutionary perspective on human-microbe mutualism and disease. *Nature*, 449(7164), 811–18.

DeWall, C.N., MacDonald, G., Webster, G.D., Masten, C.L., Baumeister, R.F., et al. (2010). Acetaminophen reduces social pain: Behavioral and neural evidence. *Psychological Science*, 21(7), 931–7.

De Waal, F.B.M. (1982). *Chimpanzee politics: Power and sex among apes.* Baltimore: Johns Hopkins University Press.

De Waal, F.B.M. (1989). Food sharing and reciprocal obligations among chimpanzees, *Journal of Human Evolution*, 18, 433–59.

De Waal, F.B.M. (1996). *Good natured: The origins of right and wrong in humans and other animals.* Cambridge, MA: Harvard University Press.

De Waal, F.B.M. (1997a). Food transfers through mesh in brown capuchins. *Journal of Comparative Psychology*, 111, 370–8.

De Waal, F.B.M. (1997b). The chimpanzee's service economy: Food for grooming. *Evolution and Human Behavior*, 18, 375–86.

De Waal, F.M.B. (2000). Survival of the rapist. Available at: www.nytimes.com/books/00/04/02/reviews/000402.002waalt.html.

De Waal, F.B.M. (2014). *The bonobo and the atheist: In search of humanism among the primates.* New York: W.W. Norton & Co.

Dial, K.P., Jackson, B.E., & Segre, P. (2008). A fundamental avian wing-stroke provides a new perspective on the evolution of flight. *Nature*, 451(7181), 985–9.

Diamond, J. (1987). Soft sciences are often harder than hard sciences. *Discover*, 34–9.

Diamond, J. (1991). Pearl Harbor and the emperor's physiologists. *Natural History*, 100, 2–5.

Diamond, J. (1992). *The third chimpanzee: The evolution and future of the human animal.* New York: HarperCollins.

Diamond, J. (1997). *Guns, germs, and steel: The fates of human societies.* New York: W.W. Norton & Co.

Dill, J., & Anderson, C.A. (1995). Effects of justified and unjustified frustration on aggression. *Aggressive Behavior*, 21, 359–69.

Dion, K., Berscheid, E., & Walster, E. (1972). What is beautiful is good. *Journal of Personality and Social Psychology*, 24, 285–90.

Dollard, J., Doob, L.W., Miller, N.E., Mowrer, O.H., & Sears, R.R. (1939). *Frustration and aggression.* New Haven, CT: Yale University Press.

Dominguez-Bello, M.G., Costello, E.K., Contreras, M., Magris, M., Hidalgo, G. et al. (2010). Delivery mode shapes the acquisition and structure of the initial microbiota across multiple body habitats in newborns. *Proceedings of the National Academy of Sciences*, 107, 11971–5.

Duffy, M. (1993). *Occam's razor.* London: Sinclair-Stevenson.

Dunn, E.W., Aknin, L.B., & Norton, M.I. (2008). Spending money on others promotes happiness. *Science*, 319, 1687–8.

Durante, K.M., Li, N.P., & Haselton, M.G. (2008). Changes in women's choice of dress across the ovulatory cycle: Naturalistic and laboratory task-based evidence. *Personality and Social Psychology Bulletin*, 34, 1451–60.

Duval, S., & Wicklund, R.A. (1972). *A theory of objective self-awareness.* New York: Academic Press.

Eagly, A.H., Ashmore, R.D., Makhijani, M.G., & Longo, L. C. (1991). What is beautiful is good, but: A meta-analytic review of research on the physical attractiveness stereotype. *Psychological Bulletin*, 110, 109–28.

Eberhardt, J.L., Davies, P.G., Purdie-Vaughns, V.J., & Johnson, S.J. (2006). Looking deathworthy: Perceived stereotypicality of Black defendants predicts capital sentencing outcomes. *Psychological Science*, 17, 383–6.

Echterhoff, G., Higgins, E.T., & Levine, J.M. (2009). Shared reality: Experiencing commonality with others' inner states about the world. *Perspectives on Psychological Science*, 4, 496–521.

Egan, P.J., & Mullin, M. (2012). Turning personal experience into political attitudes: The effect of local weather on Americans' perceptions about global warming. *Journal of Politics*, 74, 796–809.

Eisenberger, N.I., Lieberman, M.D., & Williams, K.D. (2003). Does rejection hurt? An fMRI study of social exclusion. *Science*, 302(5643), 290–2.

Eisner, M. (2003). Long-term historical trends in violent crime. *Crime and Justice: A Review of Research*, 30, 83–142.

Ekman, P. (1972). Universal and cultural differences in facial expression of emotion. In J.R. Cole (ed.) *Nebraska Symposium on Motivation, 1971* (vol. 19, pp. 207–83). Lincoln: Nebraska University Press.

Ekman, P. (1993). Facial expression and emotion. *American Psychologist*, 48, 384–92.

Eldredge, N. (2016). *Eternal ephemera: Adaptation and the origin of species from the nineteenth century through punctuated equilibria and beyond*. New York: Columbia University Press.

Eldredge, N., & Gould, S. J. (1972). Punctuated equilibria: An alternative to phyletic gradualism. In T.J. Schopf (ed.) *Models in Paleobiology* (pp. 82–115). San Francisco, CA: Freeman Cooper & Co.

Ellis, J.A., Stebbing, M., & Harrap, S.B. (2001). Significant population variation in adult male height associated with the Y chromosome and the aromatase gene. *Journal of Clinical Endocrinology & Metabolism*, 86, 4147–50.

Ellis, N.C., & Hennelly, R.A. (1980). A bilingual word-length effect: Implications for intelligence testing and the relative ease of mental calculation in Welsh and English. *British Journal of Psychology*, 50, 449–58.

Epstein, S. (1994). Integration of the cognitive and the psychodynamic unconscious. *American Psychologist*, 49, 709–24.

Ericsson, K.A. (2002). Attaining excellence through deliberate practice: Insights from the study of expert performance. In M. Ferrari (ed.) *The pursuit of excellence in education* (pp. 21–55). Hillsdale, NJ: Erlbaum.

Ermini, L., der Sarkissian, C., Willerslev, E., & Orlando, L. (2015). Major transitions in human evolution revisited: A tribute to ancient DNA. *Journal of Human Evolution*, 79, 4–20.

Euler, H.A. (2011). Grandparents and extended kin. In C. Salmon and T.K. Shackelford (eds) *The Oxford handbook of evolutionary family psychology*. Oxford: Oxford University Press.

Everett, D.L. (2005). Cultural constraints on grammar and cognition in Pirahã: Another look at the design features of human language. *Current Anthropology*, 46(4), 621–34.

Fan, P., Manoli, D.S., Ahmed, O.M., Chen, Y., Agarwal, N. et al. (2013). Genetic and neural mechanisms that inhibit drosophila from mating with other species. *Cell*, 154, 89–102.

Farrelly, D., Clemson, P., & Guthrie, M. (2016). Are women's mate preferences for altruism also influenced by physical attractiveness? *Evolutionary Psychology*, 14(1), 1–6.

Fein, S. (1996). Effects of suspicion on attributional thinking and the correspondence bias. *Journal of Personality and Social Psychology*, 70, 1164–84.

Fennessy, J., Bidon, T., Reuss, F., Kumar, V., Elkan, P. et al. (2016). Multi-locus analyses reveal four giraffe species instead of one. *Current Biology*, 26, 2543–9. doi: 10.1016/j.cub.2016.07.036.

Fessler, D.M., & Navarrete, C.D. (2004). Third-party attitudes toward sibling incest: Evidence for Westermarck's hypotheses. *Evolution and Human Behavior*, 25, 277–94.

Festinger, L. (1957). *A theory of cognitive dissonance*. Stanford, CA: Stanford University Press.

Fiddick, L., Cosmides, L., & Tooby, J. (2000). No interpretation without representation: The role of domain-specific representations and inferences in the Wason selection task. *Cognition*, 77, 1–79.

Field, T., Gewirtz, J., Cohen, D., Garcia, R., Greenberg, R. et al. (1984). Leave takings and reunions of infants, toddlers, preschoolers, and their parents. *Child Development*, 55, 628–35.

Fincher, C.L., & Thornhill, R. (2012). Parasite-stress promotes in-group assortative sociality: The cases of strong family ties and heightened religiosity. *Behavioral and Brain Sciences*, 35, 61–79.

Fincher, C.L., Thornhill, R., Murray, D.R., & Schaller, M. (2008). Pathogen prevalence predicts human cross-cultural variability in individualism/collectivism. *Proceedings of the Royal Society*, 275(1640), 1279–85.

Finkel, E.J., & Eastwick, P.W. (2009). Arbitrary social norms influence sex differences in romantic selectivity. *Psychological Science*, 20, 1290–5.

Finn, J.A., & Gittings, T. (2003). A review of competition in north temperate dung beetle communities. *Ecological Entomology*, 1, 1–28.

Fisher, R.A. (1925). *Statistical methods for research workers*. Edinburgh: Oliver & Boyd.

Fisher, R.A. (1935). *The design of experiments*. Edinburgh: Oliver & Boyd.

Flavell, J.H. (1986). The development of children's knowledge about the appearance-reality distinction. *American Psychologist*, 41, 418–25.

Flaxman, S.M., & Sherman, P.W. (2000). Morning sickness: A mechanism for protecting mother and embryo. *Quarterly Review of Biology*, 75, 1–36.

Flynn, J.R. (1999). The discovery of IQ gains over time. *American Psychologist*, 54, 5–20.

Fodor, J.A. (1983). *Modularity of mind: An essay on faculty psychology*. Cambridge, MA: MIT Press.

Foot, P. (1967). The problem of abortion and the doctrine of the double effect. *Oxford Review*, 5, 5–15.

Ford, H. & Crowther, S. (1922). *My life and work*. Garden City, NY: Doubleday.

Fox, K. (2009). *The smell report: An overview of facts and findings*. London: SIRC, available at www.sirc.org/publik/smell.pdf.

Fox, M.W. (ed.) (1973). *Readings in ethology and comparative psychology*. Monterey, CA: Brooks/Cole/Wadsworth.

Fraley, R.C., & Shaver, P.R. (2000). Adult romantic attachment: Theoretical developments, emerging controversies, and unanswered questions. *Review of General Psychology*, 4, 132–54.

Frank, M.C., & Gilovich, T. (1988). The dark side of self- and social perception: Black uniforms and aggression in professional sports. *Journal of Personality and Social Psychology*, 54, 74–85.

Frank, M.C., Everett, D.L., Fedorenko, E., & Gibson, E. (2008). Number as a cognitive technology: Evidence from Pirahã language and cognition. *Cognition*, 108, 819–24.

Franks, N.R., & Richardson, T. (2006). Teaching in tandem-running ants. *Nature*, 439(7073), 153.

Fraser, D., & Spigel, I.M. (1971). Shock-induced threat and biting by the turtle. *Journal of the Experimental Analysis of Behavior*, 16, 349–53, doi: 10.1901/jeab.1971.16-349.

Friedrich, J.M., Glavin, D.P., Rivers, M.L., & Dworkin, J.P. (2016). Effect of a synchrotron X-ray microtomography imaging experiment on the amino acid content of a CM chondrite. *Meteorics and Planetary Science*, January, 8, doi: 10.1111/maps.12595.

Gadagkar, R. (2010). Ant, bee and wasp social evolution. In M. Breed and J. Moore (eds) *Encyclopedia of Animal Behavior* (vol. 1, pp. 73–81). Oxford: Academic Press.

Galanter, E. (1962). Contemporary psychophysics. In R. Brown, E. Galanter, E.H. Hess & G. Mandler (eds) *New directions in psychology*. New York: Holt, Rinehart, & Winston.

Galen, L.W. (2012). Does religious belief promote prosociality? A critical examination. *Psychological Bulletin*, 138(5), 876–906.

Gallup, F., & Pelham, B.W. (2009). Don't worry, be 80: Worry and stress decline with age. Retrieved from http://news.gallup.com/poll/124655/dont-worry-be-80-worry-stress-decline-age.aspx.

Gangestad, S.W., Haselton, M.G., & Buss, D.M. (2006). Evolutionary foundations of cultural variation: Evoked culture and mate preferences, *Psychological Inquiry*, 17, 75–95.

Gangestad, S.W., Thornhill, R., & Garver-Apgar, C. E. (2010). Fertility in the cycle predicts women's interest in sexual opportunism. *Evolution and Human Behavior*, 31, 400–11.

Gardner, R.A. & Gardner, B.T. (1969). Teaching sign language to a chimpanzee. *Science*, 165, 664–72.

Gause, G.F. (1934). *The struggle for existence*. Baltimore, MD: Williams & Wilkins.

Geen, R. (1998). Aggression and antisocial behavior. In D.T. Gilbert, S.S. Fiske & G. Lindzey (eds) *The handbook of social psychology* (4th edn). New York: McGraw-Hill.

Gejman, P.V., Sanders, A.R., & Duan, J. (2010). The role of genetics in the etiology of schizophrenia. *Psychiatric Clinics of North America*, 33, 35–66, doi: 10.1016/j.psc.2009.12.003.

Georgiev, A.V., Klimczuk, A.C., Traficonte, D.M., & Maestripieri, D. (2014). When violence pays: A cost-benefit analysis of aggressive behavior in animals and humans. *Evolutionary Psychology*, 11, 678–99.

Gibson, K. (2009). Differential parental investment in families with both adopted and genetic children. *Evolution and Human Behavior*, 30, 184–9.

Gibson, L.J. (2006). Woodpecker pecking: How woodpeckers avoid brain injury, *Journal of Zoology*, 270, 462–5.

Gick, M.L., & Holyoak, K.J. (1983). Schema induction and analogical transfer. *Cognitive Psychology, 15*, 1–38.

Gigerenzer, G. (2008). Why heuristics work. *Perspectives on Psychological Science*, 3, 20–9.

Gilbert, D.T. (1989). Thinking lightly about others: Automatic components of the social inference process. In J.S. Uleman & J.A. Bargh (eds) *Unintended thought* (pp. 189–211). New York: Guilford.

Gilbert, D.T., & Ebert, J.E. (2002). Decisions and revisions: The affective forecasting of changeable outcomes. *Journal of Personality and Social Psychology*, 82, 503–14.

Gilbert, D.T., & Silvera, D.H. (1996). Overhelping. *Journal of Personality and Social Psychology*, 70, 678–90.

Gill, R.J., Arce, A., Keller, L., & Hammond, R.L. (2009). Polymorphic social organization in an ant. *Proceedings of the Royal Society: Biological Sciences*, 276, 4423–31. doi: 10.1098/rspb.2009.1408.

Gilovich, T., Vallone, R., & Tversky, A. (1985). The hot hand in basketball: On the misperception of random sequences. *Cognitive Psychology*, 17, 295–314.

Gladwell, M. (2008). *Outliers: The story of success*. London: Little, Brown.

Glaser, T., Walton, D.S., & Maas, R.L. (1992). Genomic structure, evolutionary conservation and aniridia mutations in the human PAX6 gene. *Nature Genetics*, 2, 232–9.

Glenn, J. (1996). *Scientific genius: The twenty greatest minds*. New York: Crescent Books.

Gordon, P. (2004). Numerical cognition without words: Evidence from Amazonia. *Science*, 306, 496–9.

Gorrell, J.C., McAdam, A.G., Coltman, D.W., Humphries, M.M., & Boutin, S. (2010). Adopting kin enhances inclusive fitness in asocial red squirrels. *Nature Communications,* 1, 22, available at www.nature.com/articles/ncomms1022.

Gottman, J. (1994). *Why marriages succeed or fail*. New York: Simon & Schuster.

Gould, S.J. (1977). *Ontogeny and phylogeny*. Cambridge, MA: Harvard University Press.

Gould, S.J. (1984). A most ingenious paradox: When is an organism a person; when is it a colony? *Natural History*, 93, 20–30.

Gould, S.J. (1985). *The flamingo's smile: Reflections in natural history*. New York: W.W. Norton.

Gould, S.J. (1991). Exaptation: A crucial tool for evolutionary psychology. *Journal of Social Issues*, 47, 43–65.

Gould, S.J., & Eldredge, N. (1977). Punctuated equilibria: The tempo and mode of evolution reconsidered. *Paleobiology*, 3(2), 115–51.

Gould, S.J., & Vrba, E.S. (1982). Exaptation: A missing term in the science of form. *Paleobiology*, 8(1), 4–15.

Green, B.G. (1984). Thermal perception on lingual and labial skin. *Perception & Psychophysics*, 36, 209–20.

Greenberg, J., Kosloff, S., Solomon, S., Cohen, F., & Landau, M. (2010). Toward understanding the fame game: The effect of mortality salience on the appeal of fame. *Self and Identity*, 9(1), 1–18.

Greenberg, J., Pyszczynski, T., Solomon, S., Simon, L., & Breus, M. (1994). Role of consciousness and accessibility of death-related thoughts in mortality salience effects. *Journal of Personality and Social Psychology*, 67, 627–37.

Greenberg, J., Simon, L., Pyszczynski, T., Solomon, S., & Chatel, D. (1992a). Terror management and tolerance: Does mortality salience always intensify negative reactions to others who threaten one's worldview? *Journal of Personality and Social Psychology*, 63, 212–20.

Greenberg, J., Simon, L., Porteus, J., Pyszczynski, T., & Solomon, S. (1995). Evidence of a terror management function of cultural icons: The effects of mortality salience on the inappropriate use of cherished cultural symbols. *Personality and Social Psychology Bulletin*, 21(11), 1221–8.

Greenberg, J., Solomon, S., Pyszczynski, T., Rosenblatt, A., Burling, J., et al. (1992b). Assessing the terror management analysis of self-esteem: Converging evidence of an anxiety-buffering function. *Journal of Personality and Social Psychology*, 63, 913–22.

Grivell, R.M., Reilly, A.J., Oakey, H., Chan, A., & Dodd, J.M. (2012). Maternal and neonatal outcomes following induction of labor: a cohort study. *Acta Obstetricia et Gynecologica Scandinavica*, 91(20), 198–203.

Guéguen, N. (2009). Menstrual cycle phases and female receptivity to a courtship solicitation: an evaluation in a nightclub. *Evolution and Human Behavior*, 30, 351–5.

Guéguen, N., & Jacob, C. (2005). The effect of touch on tipping: An evaluation in a French bar. *International Journal of Hospitality Management*, 24, 295–9.

Guéguen, N., & Legoherel, P. (2000). Effect on tipping of barman drawing a sun on the bottom of customers' checks. *Psychological Reports*, 87, 223–6.

Guéguen, N., Meineri, S., & Stefan, J. (2012). "Say it with flowers"… to female drivers: Hitchhikers holding a bunch of flowers and driver behavior. *North American Journal of Psychology*, 14, 623–8.

Gwynne, D.T. (2001). *Katydids and bush-crickets: Reproductive behavior and evolution of the Tetiigoniidae.* Ithaca, NY: Cornell University Press.

Haeckel, E. (1874). *Anthropogenie* (4th edn). Leipzig: Wilhelm Engelmann.

Haidt, J. (1995). The emotional dog and its rational tail: A social intuitionist approach to moral judgment. *Psychological Review*, 108(4), 814–34.

Hall, M. (1833). On the reflex function of the medulla oblongata. *Philosophical Transactions of the Royal Society*, 123, 635–65.

Hamel, A., Fisch, C., Combettes, L., Dupuis-Williams, P., & Baroud, C.N. (2011). Transitions between three swimming gaits in Paramecium escape. *Proceedings of the National Academy of Sciences*, 3, 7290–5, doi: 10.1073/pnas.1016687108.

Hamilton, L., Cheng, S., & Powell, B. (2007). Adoptive parents, adaptive parents: Evaluating the importance of biological ties for parental investment. *American Sociological Review*, 72, 95–116.

Hamilton, W.D. (1964a). The genetical evolution of social behavior I. *Journal of Theoretical Biology*, 7, 1–16.

Hamilton, W.D. (1964b). The genetical evolution of social behavior II. *Journal of Theoretical Biology*, 7, 17–52.

Hardin, C.D., & Higgins, E.T. (1996). Shared reality: How social verification makes the subjective objective. In E.T. Higgins & R.M. Sorrentino (eds) *Handbook of motivation and cognition: The interpersonal context* (vol. 3, pp. 28–84). New York: Guilford.

Hardin, G. (1960). The competitive exclusion principle. *Science*, 131, 1292–7.

Hare, B., & Woods, V. (2013). *The genius of dogs: How dogs are smarter than you think.* New York: Penguin Group.

Harford, T. (2011). *Adapt: Why success always starts with failure.* London: Little, Brown.

Harlow, H.F. (1958). The nature of love. *American Psychologist*, 13, 573–86.

Harlow, H.F., Dodsworth, R.O., & Harlow, M.K. (1965). Total social isolation in monkeys. *Proceedings of the National Academy of Sciences*, 54, 90–7.

Harper, M., Wapner, R.J., Sorokin, Y., Miodovnik, M., Carpenter, M. et al. (2006). Maternal morbidity associated with multiple repeat cesarean deliveries. *Obstetrics and Gynecology*, 107, 1226–32.

Haselton, M.G., & Buss, D.M. (2000). Error management theory: A new perspective on biases in cross-sex mind reading. *Journal of Personality and Social Psychology*, 78, 81–91.

Haselton, M.G. & Funder, D. (2006). The evolution of accuracy and bias in social judgment. In M. Schaller, D.T. Kenrick, & J.A. Simpson (eds) *Evolution and social psychology* (pp. 15–37). New York: Psychology Press.

Haselton, M.G., & Gildersleeve, K. (2011). Can men detect ovulation? *Current Directions in Psychological Science*, 20, 87–92.

Haselton, M.G., Mortezaie, M., Pillsworth, E.G., Bleske-Rechek, A., & Frederick, D.A. (2007). Ovulatory shifts in human female ornamentation: Near ovulation, women dress to impress. *Hormones and Behavior*, 51, 40–5.

Hayes, J., Schimel, J., Arndt, J., & Faucher, E.H. (2010). A theoretical and empirical review of the death-thought accessibility concept in terror management research. *Psychological Bulletin*, 136, 699–739.

Heider, F. (1958). *The psychology of interpersonal relations.* New York: Psychology Press.

Herdt, G. (1981). *Guardians of the flutes: Idioms of masculinity.* Chicago: University of Chicago Press.

Hicks, D.L., & Hicks, J.H. (2014). Jealous of the Joneses: Conspicuous consumption, inequality, and crime. *Oxford Economic Papers*, 66, 1090–120.

Higgs, P.G., & Pudritz, R.E. (2009). A thermodynamic basis for prebiotic amino acid synthesis and the nature of the first genetic code. *Astrobiology*, 9, 483–90, doi:10.1089/ast.2008.0280.

Hill, K., Hurtado, A.M., & Walker, R.S. (2007). High adult mortality among Hiwi hunter-gatherers: Implications for human evolution. *Journal of Human Evolution*, 52, 443–54.

Hirschberger, G., Ein-Dor, T., & Almakias, S. (2008). The self-protective altruist: Terror management and the ambivalent nature of prosocial behavior. *Personality and Social Psychology Bulletin*, 34, 666–78.

Hockett, C.F. (1958). *A course in general linguistics*. New York: Macmillan.

Hockett, C.F. (1960). The origin of speech. *Scientific American*, 203, 88–96.

Hofstede, G. (2001). *Culture's consequences. Comparing values, behaviors, institutions, and organizations across nations* (2nd edn). Thousand Oaks, CA: Sage.

Homans, G.C. (1958). Social behavior as exchange. *American Journal of Sociology*, 63, 597–606.

Horner, V., Carter, J.D., Suchak, M., & de Waal, F.B.M. (2011). Spontaneous prosocial choice in chimpanzees. *Proceedings of the National Academy of Sciences*, 103, 13847–51.

Houston, D.C. & Copsey, J.A. (1994). Bone digestion and intestinal morphology of the bearded vulture, *Journal of Raptor Research*, 28, 73–8.

Howell, E. (2017). What is the Big Bang theory? *Space.com*, June 12, 10:47 p.m. ET.

Huang, Y., Zaas, A.K., Rao, A., Dobigeon, N., Woolf, P.J. et al. (2011). Temporal dynamics of host molecular responses differentiate symptomatic and asymptomatic influenza A Infection. *PLoS Genetics*, 7, e1002234, doi:10.1371/journal.pgen.1002234.

Huber, E., Webster, J.M., Brewer, A.A., MacLeod, D.I., Wandell, B.A. et al. (2015). A lack of experience-dependent plasticity after more than a decade of recovered sight. *Psychological Science*, 26(4), 393–401.

Humphrey, L.T., De Groote, I., Morales, J., Bartone, N. Collcutt, S. et al. (2014). Earliest evidence for caries and exploitation of starchy plant foods in Pleistocene hunter-gatherers from Morocco. *Proceedings of the National Academy of Sciences*, 111, 954–59, doi: 10.1073/pnas.1318176111.

Iron Man (2008). Film produced by Marvel Studios and distributed by Paramount Pictures.

István, U. (1999). Nicotine and other insecticidal alkaloids. In I. Yamamoto and J. Casida (eds) *Nicotinoid insecticides and the nicotinic acetylcholine receptor* (pp. 29–69). Tokyo: Springer.

Jablonski, N.G., & Chaplin, G. (2000). The evolution of human skin coloration. *Journal of Human Evolution*, 39, 57–106.

Jaccard, J., Dittus, P.J., & Gordon, V.V. (1998). Parent-adolescent congruency in reports of adolescent sexual behavior and in communications about sexual behavior. *Child Development*, 69, 247–61.

James, N. (2014). The federal prison population buildup: Overview, policy changes, issues, and options. Available at: http://fas.org/sgp/crs/misc/R42937.pdf.

Jelbert, K., Stott, I., McDonald, R.A., & Hodgson, D. (2015). Invasiveness of plants is predicted by size and fecundity in the native range. *Ecology and Evolution*, 5, 1933–43.

Johnson, E.J., & Goldstein, D.G. (2003). Do defaults save lives? *Science*, 302, 1338–9.

Johnstone, R.A. (1995). Sexual selection, honest advertisement, and the handicap principle: Reviewing the evidence. *Biological Reviews*, 70, 1–65.

Joireman, J., Truelove, H.B., & Duell, B. (2010). Effect of outdoor temperature, heat primes and anchoring on belief in global warming. *Journal of Environmental Psychology*, 30, 358–67.

Jonas, E., Schimel, J., Greenberg, J., & Pyszczynski, T. (2002). The Scrooge effect: Evidence that mortality salience increases prosocial attitudes and behavior. *Personality and Social Psychology Bulletin*, 28, 1342–53.

Jones, E.E., & Sigall, H. (1971). The bogus pipeline: A new paradigm for measuring affect and attitude. *Psychological Bulletin*, 76, 349–64.

Jones, J.M. (2014). In U.S., most do not see global warming as major threat. Retrieved from http://news.gallup.com/poll/167879/not-global-warming-serious-threat.aspx.

Jost, J.T., Banaji, M.R., & Nosek, B.A. (2004). A decade of system justification theory: Accumulated evidence of conscious and unconscious bolstering of the status quo. *Political Psychology*, 25, 881–919.

Judson, O. (2002). *Dr. Tatiana's sex advice to all creation*. New York: Metropolitan Books.

Juvonen, J., & Graham, S. (2014). Bullying in schools: The power of bullies and the plight of victims. *Annual Review of Psychology*, 65, 159–85.

Kaati, G., Bygren, L.O., & Edvinsson, S. (2002). Cardiovascular and diabetes mortality determined by nutrition during parents' and grandparents' slow growth period. *European Journal of Human Genetics*, 10, 682–8.

Kahneman, D. (2011). *Thinking, fast and slow*. New York: Farrar, Straus, & Giroux.

Kahneman, D., & Tversky, A. (1972). Subjective probability: A judgment of representativeness. *Cognitive Psychology*, 3, 430–54.

Kahneman, D., & Tversky, A. (1979). Prospect theory: An analysis of decisions under risk. *Econometrica*, 47, 263–91.

Kalinka, A.T., & Tomancak, P. (2012). The evolution of early animal embryos: conservation or divergence? *Trends in Ecology and Evolution*, 27, 385–93.

Keller, R., Davidson, L.A., & Shook, D.R. (2003). How we are shaped: The biomechanics of gastrulation. *Differentiation*, 71, 171–205.

Kellermann, A.L., & Mercy, J.A. (1992). Men, women, and murder: Gender-specific differences in rates of fatal violence and victimization. *Journal of Trauma*, 33, 1–5.

Kendler, K.S., & Baker, J.H. (2007). Genetic influences on measures of the environment: A systematic review. *Psychological Medicine*, 37, 615–26.

Kenrick, D.T. & MacFarlane, S. W. (1986). Ambient temperature and horn honking: A field study of the heat/aggression relationship. *Environment and Behavior*, 18, 179–91.

Ketelaar, T., & Au, W.T. (2003). The effects of feelings of guilt on the behaviour of uncooperative individuals in repeated social bargaining games: An affect-as-information interpretation of the role of emotion in social interaction. *Cognition and Emotion*, 17, 429–53.

Kilner, R.M., & Hinde, C.A. (2012). Parent-offspring conflict. In N.J. Royle, P.T. Smiseth and M. Kölliker (eds) *The evolution of parental care* (pp. 119–32). Oxford: Oxford University Press.

Kimmel, C.A. (2001). Overview of teratology. *Current Protocols in Toxicology*, 13, Unit 13.1.

King, K.B., & Reis, H.T. (2012). Marriage and long-term survival after coronary artery bypass grafting. *Health Psychology*, 31, 55–62.

Kipling, R. (1902). *Just so stories*. London: Macmillan.

Kirkpatrick, L., & Navarrete, C.D. (2006). Target article: 'Reports of my death anxiety have been greatly exaggerated': A critique of terror management theory from an evolutionary perspective. *Psychological Inquiry*, 17, 288–98.

Kitaoka, A. & Ashida, H. (2003). Phenomenal characteristics of the peripheral drift illusion. *Vision*, 15, 261–2.

Klayman, J., & Ha, Y.-W. (1987). Confirmation, disconfirmation, and information in hypothesis testing. *Psychological Review*, 94, 211–28.

Klein, S.B., Cosmides, L., Tooby, J., & Chance, S. (2002). Decisions and the evolution of memory: Multiple systems, multiple functions. *Psychological Review*, 109, 306–29.

Knudsen, A. (2004). Sensitive periods in the development of the brain and behavior. *Journal of Cognitive Neuroscience*, 16(8), 1412–25.

Kolbert, E. (2014). *The sixth extinction: An unnatural history*. London: Henry Holt & Co.

Koole, S.L., & van den Berg, A.E. (2005). Lost in the wilderness: Terror management, action orientation, and nature evaluation. *Journal of Personality and Social Psychology*, 88, 1014–28.

Kramer, M.S., Aboud, F., Mironova, E., Vanilovich, I., Platt, R.W. et al. (2008). Breastfeeding and child cognitive development: New evidence from a large, randomized trial. *Archives of General Psychology*, 65, 578–84.

Krebs, D.L., & Miller, D.L. (1985). Altruism and aggression. In G. Lindzey and E. Aronson (eds) *Handbook of Social Psychology* (3rd edn, pp. 1–71). New York: Random House.

Krems, J.A., Neel, R., Neuberg, S.L., Puts, D.A., & Kenrick, D.T. (2016). Women selectively guard their (desirable) mates from ovulating women. *Journal of Personality and Social Psychology*, 110, 551–73, doi: 10.1037/pspi0000044.

Kukkonen, T., Binik, Y.M., Amsel, R., & Carrier, S. (2007). Thermography as a physiological measure of sexual arousal in both men and women. *Journal of Sexual Medicine*, 4, 93–105.

Kukkonen, T., Binik, Y., Amsel, R., & Carrier, S. (2010). An evaluation of the validity of thermography as a physiological measure of sexual arousal in a nonuniversity adult sample. *Archives of Sexual Behavior*, 39, 861–73.

Kumar, P., Pandit, S.S., Steppuhn, A., & Baldwin, I.T. (2016). Natural history-driven, plant-mediated RNAi-based study reveals CYP6B46's role in a nicotine-mediated antipredator herbivore defense. *Proceedings of the National Academy of Sciences*, 111, 1245–52.

Kunstler, G.G., Falster, D., Coomes, D.A., Hui, F., Kooyman, R.M., et al. (2016). Plant functional traits have globally consistent effects on competition. *Nature*, 529(7585), 204–7.

Kurzban, R. & Leary, M.R. (2001). Evolutionary origins of stigmatization: The functions of social exclusion. *Psychological Bulletin*, 127(2), 187–208.

LaBarba, R.C. (1981). *Foundations of developmental psychology*. New York: Academic Press.

Lamb, T.D. (2011). Evolution of the eye: Scientists now have a clear vision of how our notoriously complex eye came to be. *Scientific American*, 305(1), 64–9.

Landau, M.J., Johns, M., Greenberg, J., Pyszczynski, T., Solomon, S. et al. (2004). A function of form: Terror management and structuring of the social world. *Journal of Personality and Social Psychology*, 87, 190–210.

Larrick, R.P., Timmerman, T.A., Carton, A.M., & Abrevaya, J. (2014). Temper, temperature, and temptation: Heat-related retaliation in baseball. *Psychological Science*, 22, 423–8.

Leadbeater, E., Raine, N.E., & Chittka, L. (2006). Social learning: Ants and the meaning of teaching. *Current Biology*, 16(9), R323–5.

Leat, S.J., Yadav, N.K., & Irving, E.L. (2009). Development of visual acuity and contrast sensitivity in children. *Journal of Optometry*, 2, 19–26.

Lenroot, R.K., & Giedd, J.N. (2006). Brain development in children and adolescents: Insights from anatomical magnetic resonance imaging. *Neuroscience Biobehavioral Review*, 30, 718–29.

Lewis, D.M., Russell, E.M., Al-Shawaf, L., & Buss, D.M. (2015). Lumbar curvature: A previously undiscovered standard of attractiveness. *Evolution and Human Behavior*, 36, 345–50. Available at https://labs.la.utexas.edu/buss/files/2013/02/Lumbar-EHB-2015.pdf.

Leyk, D., Gorges, W., Ridder, D., Wunderlich, M., Rüther, T. et al. (2007). Hand-grip strength of young men, women and highly trained female athletes. *European Journal of Applied Physiology*, 99, 415–21.

Lieberman, D., Pillsworth, E.G., & Haselton, M.G. (2011). Kin affiliation across the ovulatory cycle: Females avoid fathers when fertile. *Psychological Science*, 22(1), 13–18.

Lieberman, M.D. (2013). *Social: Why our brains are wired to connect*. New York: Broadway Books.

Lobel, M., Dunkel-Schetter, C., & Scrimshaw, S.C. (1992). Prenatal maternal stress and prematurity: A prospective study of socioeconomically disadvantaged women. *Health Psychology*, 11, 32–40.

Lorenz, K. (1952). *King Solomon's ring: New light on animal ways*. New York: Crowell.

Lowery, B., Hardin, C., & Sinclair, S. (2001). Social influence effects on automatic racial prejudice. *Journal of Personality and Social Psychology*, 81, 842–55.

Lydon-Rochelle, M., Holt, V.L., Martin, D.P., & Easterling, T.R. (2000). Association between method of delivery and maternal rehospitalization. *Journal of the American Medical Association*, 283, 2411–16.

Lykken, D.T. (1995). *The antisocial personalities*. Hillsdale, NJ: Erlbaum.

Ma, B., Forney, L.J., & Ravel, J. (2012). The vaginal microbiome: Rethinking health and diseases. *Annual Review of Microbiology*, 66, 371–89, doi: 10.1146/annurev-micro092611-150157.

McCloskey, R. (1941). *Make way for ducklings*. New York: Viking Press.

McDonald, M.M., Navarrete, C.D., & van Vugt, M. (2012). Evolution and the psychology of intergroup conflict: The male warrior hypothesis. *Philosophical Transactions of the Royal Society B: Biological Sciences*, 367(1589), 670–9.

McKelvie, S.J., & Schamer, L.A. (1988). Effects of night, passengers, and sex on driver behavior at stop signs. *Journal of Social Psychology*, 128, 685–90.

Mackintosh, N.J. (1974). *The psychology of animal learning*. London: Academic Press.

McKnight, A.J., & Peck, R.C. (2002). Graduated licensing: What works? *Injury Prevention*, 8 (Supplement II), 32–8.

Maibach, E., Perkins, D., Francis, Z., Myers, T., Seitter, K., et al. (2016). *A 2016 National Survey of Broadcast Meteorologists: Initial Findings*. George Mason University, Fairfax, VA: Center for Climate Change Communication.

Maner, J.K., Luce, C.L., Neuberg, S.L., Cialdini, R.B., Brown, S. et al. (2002). The effects of perspective taking on helping: Still no evidence for altruism. *Personality and Social Psychology Bulletin*, 28, 1601–10.

Mann, J., & Patterson, E.M. (2013). Tool use by aquatic animals. *Philosophical Transactions of the Royal Society*, 368, 1–11.

Mariampolski, H. (2006). *Ethnography for marketers: A guide to consumer immersion*. Thousand Oaks, CA: Sage.

Markus, H.R., & Kitayama, S. (1991). Culture and the self: Implications for cognition, emotion, and motivation. *Psychological Review*, 98, 224–53.

Marlowe, F. (2000). Paternal investment and the human mating system. *Behavioral Processes*, 51(1/3), 45–61.

Marouli, E., Graff, M., Medina-Gomez, C., Lo, K.S., Wood, A.R. et al. (2017). Rare and low-frequency coding variants alter human adult height. *Nature*, 542(7640), 186–90, doi: 10.1038/nature21039.

Marsh, A. (2017). *The fear factor: How one emotion connects altruists, psychopaths, and everyone in-between*. New York: Basic Books.

Marsh, A.A., Stoycos, S., Brethel-Haurwitz, K., Robinson, P., VanMeter, J. et al. (2014). Neural and cognitive characteristics of extraordinary altruists. *Proceedings of the National Academy of Sciences*, 111(42), 15306–14.

Matsumoto, D., & Willingham, B. (2009). Spontaneous facial expressions of emotion of congenitally and noncongenitally blind individuals. *Journal of Personality and Social Psychology*, 96, 1–10.

Mayberry, R.I., Lock, E., & Kazmi, H. (2002). Linguistic ability and early language exposure. *Nature*, 417, 38.

Mellers, B., Hertwig, R., & Kahneman, D. (2001). Do frequency representations eliminate conjunction effects? An exercise in adversarial collaboration. *Psychological Science*, 12(4), 269–75.

Meng, J., Wang, Y., & Li, C. (2011). Transitional mammalian middle ear from a new Cretaceous *Jehol eutriconodontan*. *Nature*, 472, 181–5.

Merton, R.K. (1948). The self-fulfilling prophecy. *The Antioch Review*, 8, 193–210.

Meyerowitz, E.M. (2002). Plants compared to animals: The broadest comparative study of development. *Science*, 295, 1482–5.

Michael, R.T., Gagnon, J.H., Laumann, E.O., & Kolata, G. (1995). *Sex in America: A definitive study*. New York: Warner Books.

Mikulincer, M., Florian, V., & Hirschberger, G. (2003). The existential function of close relationships: Introducing death into the science of love. *Personality and Social Psychology Review*, 7(1), 20–40.

Milgram, S. (1963). Behavioral study of obedience. *Journal of Abnormal and Social Psychology*, 67, 371–8.

Miller, G., Tybur, J.M., & Jordan, B.D. (2007). Ovulatory cycle effects on tip earnings by lap dancers: Economic evidence for human estrus? *Evolution and Human Behavior*, 28, 375–81.

Miller, S.L. (1953). A production of amino acids under possible primitive earth conditions. *Science*, 117, 528–9.

Miller, S.L., & Maner, J.K. (2010). Ovulation as a male mating prime: Subtle signs of women's fertility influence men's mating cognition and behavior. *Journal of Personality and Social Psychology*, 100, 295–308.

Miller, W.R. (2011). Tardigrades. *American Scientist*, 99(5), 384, retrieved June 6, 2017 at: www.americanscientist.org/article/tardigrades.

Mitteroecker, P., Huttegger, S.M., Fischer, B., & Pavlicev, M. (2016). Cliff-edge model of obstetric selection in humans. *Proceedings of the National Academy of Sciences*, 113, 14680–5, doi: 10.1073/pnas.1612410113.

Miya, M., Pietsch, T.W., Orr, J.W., Arnold, R. J., Satoh, T.P. et al. (2010). Evolutionary history of anglerfishes (Teleostei: Lophiiformes): A mitogenomic perspective. *BMC Evolutionary Biology*, 10, 58–85.

Miyatake, T., Katayama, K., Takeda, Y., Nakashima, A., Sugita, A. et al. (2004). Is death-feigning adaptive? Heritable variation in fitness difference of death-feigning behavior. *Proceedings of the Royal Society of London*, 271, 2293–6.

Moll, J., Krueger, F., Zahn, R., Pardini, M., de Oliveira-Souza, R. et al. (2006). Human fronto-mesolimbic networks guide decisions about charitable donation. *Proceedings of the National Academy of Sciences*, 103(42), 15623–8.

Murdock, G.P., & White, D.R. ([1969] 2006). Standard Cross-Cultural Sample. *Ethnology*, 9, 329–69.

Myers, D.G. (2008). *A friendly letter to skeptics and atheists: Musings on why God is good and faith isn't evil.* San Francisco, CA: Jossey-Bass.

Myers, D.G. (2013). *Social psychology* (11th edn). New York: McGraw-Hill.

Nairne, J.S., Thompson, S.R., & Pandeirada, J.N. (2007). Adaptive memory: Survival processing enhances retention. *Journal of Experimental Psychology: Learning, Memory, & Cognition*, 33(2), 263–73.

Natanson, L.J., & Skomal, G.B. (2015). Age and growth of the white shark, *Carcharodon carcharias*, in the western North Atlantic Ocean. *Marine and Freshwater Research*, 66, 387–98.

National Human Genome Research Institute (n.d.) All about the Human Genome Project (HGP). Available at: www.genome.gov/10001772/all-about-the--human-genome-project-hgp.

National Institutes of Health (2018). What are single nucleotide polymorphisms (SNPs)? Available at: https://ghr.nlm.nih.gov/primer/genomicresearch/snp.

Naveh-Benjamin, M., & Ayres, T.J. (1986). Digit span, reading rate, and linguistic relativity. *Quarterly Journal of Experimental Psychology*, 38A, 739–51.

Nei, M. (2013). *Mutation-driven evolution.* Oxford: Oxford University Press.

Neuberg, S.L., & Schaller, M. (2014). Evolutionary social cognition. In E. Borgida & J. Bargh (eds) *APA handbook of personality and social psychology,* vol. 1*: Attitudes and social cognition* (pp. 3–45). Washington, DC: APA.

New, J.J., & German, T.C. (2015). Spiders at the cocktail party: An ancestral threat that surmounts inattentional blindness. *Evolution and Human Behavior*, 36, 165–73.

Newman, M.E. (1997). A model of mass extinction. *Journal of Theoretical Biology*, 189, 235–52.

Nielsen, M. (2012). Imitation, pretend play, and childhood: Essential elements in the evolution of human culture? *Journal of Comparative Psychology*, 126(2), 170–81.

Nielsen, M., Moore, C., & Mohamedally, J. (2012). Young children overimitate in third-party contexts. *Journal of Experimental Child Psychology*, 112, 73–83.

Nisbett, R.E. (1993). Violence and U. S. regional culture. *American Psychologist*, 48, 441–9.

Nisbett, R.E., & Cohen, D. (1996). *Culture of honor: The psychology of violence in the South.* Boulder, CO: Westview Press.

Nyaradi, A., Li, J., Hickling, S., Foster, J., & Oddy, W.H. (2013). The role of nutrition in children's neurocognitive development, from pregnancy through childhood. *Frontiers in Human Neuroscience*, 7(97), 1–13.

Nye, B. (2014). Bill Nye debates Ken Ham. www.youtube.com/watch?v=z6kgvhG3AkI.

Odom, J.D. (2006). EPSCoR 2020: Expanding state participation in research in the 21st century – A new vision for the Experimental Program to Stimulate Competitive Research (EPSCoR). Available at: www.nsf.gov/od/iia/programs/epscor/docs/EPSCoR_2020_Workshop_Report.pdf.

O'Leary, M.A., Bloch, J.I., Flynn, J.J. et al. (2013). The placental mammal ancestor and the post-K-Pg radiation of placentals. *Science*, 339, 662–7.

Olivola, C.Y. & Todorov, A. (2010). Fooled by first impressions? Reexamining the diagnostic value of appearance-based inferences. *Journal of Experimental Social Psychology*, 46, 315–324.

Ostrov, J.M., Kamper, K.E., Hart, E.J., Godleski, S.A., & Blakely-McClure, S.J. (2014). A gender-balanced approach to the study of peer victimization and aggression subtypes in early childhood. *Development and Psychopathology*, 26, 575–87.

Ostrovsky, Y., Meyers, E., Ganesh, S., Mathur, U., & Sinha, P. (2009). Visual parsing after recovery from blindness. *Psychological Science*, 20, 1484–91.

Packer, C. (2001). Infanticide is no fallacy. *American Anthropologist*, 102, 829–31.

Pappas, S. (2012). Why woodpeckers don't get concussions. Retrieved December 29, 2016 from www.livescience.com/19586-woodpecker-skull-concussions.html.

Patel, B.H., Percivale, C., Ritson, D.J., Duffy, C.D., & Sutherland, J.D. (2015). Common origins of RNA, protein and lipid precursors in a cyanosulfidic protometabolism. *Nature Chemistry*, 7, 301–7, doi:10.1038/nchem.2202.

Payne, R.B. (2005). *The cuckoos.* Oxford: Oxford University Press.

Pelham, B.W. (1997). Human motivation has multiple roots. *Psychological Inquiry*, 8(1), 44–7.

Pelham, B.W. (2009). Views on global warming relate to energy efficiency. Available at: http://news. gallup.com/poll/117835/views-global-warming-relate-energy-efficiency.aspx.

Pelham, B.W. (2015). Intuitive evolutionary hypothesis testing. Unpublished data.

Pelham, B.W. (2017a). A life history perspective on birth and parenting strategies across the globe. In preparation.

Pelham, B.W. (2017b). Not in my back yard: Egocentrism, collectivism, and skepticism about climate change. Under review.

Pelham, B. (2018a). Birth medicalization in the U.S.: Origins and consequences. Under revision.

Pelham, B.W. (2018b). Myths and realities of the mid-life crisis. In preparation.

Pelham, B.W. (2018c). The soothing route from "cancer" to "founding fathers." In preparation.

Pelham, B.W., & Blanton, H. (2018). *Conducting research in psychology: Measuring the weight of smoke* (5th edn). Thousand Oaks, CA: SAGE.

Pelham, B.W., & Carvallo, M.R. (2015). Why Tex and Tess Carpenter build houses in Texas: Moderators of implicit egotism. *Self and Identity*, 14, 692–723.

Pelham, B.W., & Crabtree, S. (2008). Worldwide, highly religious more likely to help others. Available at: http://news.gallup.com/poll/111013/worldwide-highly-religious-more-likely-help-others.aspx.

Pelham, B.W., & Neter, E. (1995). The effect of motivation on judgment depends on the difficulty of the judgment. *Journal of Personality and Social Psychology*, 68, 581–94.

Pelham, B., & Nyiri, Z. (2008). In more religious countries, lower suicide rates. Available at: http://news.gallup.com/poll/108625/more-religious-countries-lower-suicide-rates.aspx.

Pelham, B.W., Carvallo, M., & Jones, J.T. (2005). Implicit egotism. *Current Directions in Psychological Science*, 14, 106–10.

Pelham, B.W., Sumarta, T.T., & Myaskovsky, L. (1994). The easy path from many to much: The numerosity heuristic. *Cognitive Psychology*, 26, 103–33.

Pelham, B.W., Shimizu, M., Carvallo, M.R., Arndt, J., Greenberg, J. et al. (in press). Searching for God: Weekly search volume for major illnesses in Google predicts changes in Google search volume for religious content in 16 nations. *Personality and Social Psychology Bulletin*.

Pelletier, F., & Festa-Bianchet, M. (2006). Sexual selection and social rank in bighorn rams. *Animal Behaviour*, 71, 649–55, doi:10.1016/j.anbehav.2005.07.008.

Pettigrew, T.F. (1998). Intergroup contact theory. *Annual Review of Psychology*, 49, 65–85.

Phillips, D.P., & Carstensen, L.L. (1986). Clustering of teenage suicides after television news stories about suicide. *New England Journal of Medicine*, 315(11), 685–9.

Piaget, J. (1970). *Genetic epistemology.* New York: W.W. Norton.

Pietsch, T. (2005). Dimorphism, parasitism, and sex revisited: Modes of reproduction among deep-sea ceratioid anglerfishes (Teleostei: Lophiiformes). *Ichthyology Research*, 52, 207–36, doi: 10.1007/s10228-005-0286-2.

Pigliucci, M., & Kaplan, J. (2000). The fall and rise of Dr Pangloss: Adaptationism and the Spandrels paper 20 years later. *TREE*, 15, 66–70.

Pinker, S. (1994). *The language instinct: How the mind creates language.* New York: HarperCollins.

Pinker, S. (1997). *How the mind works.* New York: W.W. Norton & Co.

Pinker, S. (2002). *The blank slate: The modern denial of human nature.* London: Allen Lane.

Pinker, S. (2011). *The better angels of our nature: Why violence has declined.* London: Penguin Books.

Pipitone, R.N., & Gallup, G.G., Jr. (2008). Women's voice attractiveness varies across the menstrual cycle. *Evolution and Human Behavior*, 29, 268–74.

Plato (1954). *The last days of Socrates* (reissue edn, ed. H. Tarrant, trans. H. Tredennick). New York: Penguin Classics.

Plous, S. (1993). *The psychology of judgment and decision making.* New York: McGraw-Hill.

Polderman, T.J., Benyamin, B., de Leeuw, C.A., Sullivan, P.F., van Bochoven, A. et al. (2015). Meta-analysis of the heritability of human traits based on fifty years of twin studies. *Nature Genetics*, 47, 702–12.

Popper, K. ([1974] 1990). *Unintended quest: An intellectual autobiography.* LaSalle, IL: Open Court.

Poulain, M. (2012). The longevity of nuns and monks: A gender gap issue investigated with new Belgian data. Presented at the 2012 Annual Conference of the Population Association of America, San Francisco, CA.

Powers, D. (2011). Japan: No surrender in World War II. Available at: www.bbc.co.uk/history/worldwars/wwtwo/japan_no_surrender_01.shtml.

Pratto, F., Sidanius, J., & Levin, S. (2006). Social dominance theory and the dynamics of intergroup relations: Taking stock and looking forward. *European Review of Social Psychology*, 17, 271–320.

Pray, L.A. (2008). DNA replication and causes of mutation. *Nature Education*, 1(1), 214. Available at: www.nature.com/scitable/nated/article?action=showContentInPopup&contentPK=409.

Prior, H., Schwarz, A., & Gunturkun, O. (2008). Mirror-induced behavior in the magpie (Pica pica): Evidence of self-recognition. *PLoS Biology*, 6, e202.

Psouni, E., Janke, A., & Garwicz, M. (2012). Impact of carnivory on human development and evolution revealed by a new unifying model of weaning in mammals. *PLoS ONE*, 7, e32452.

Pusey, A.E., & Packer, C. (1994). Infanticide in lions. In S. Parmigiani, B. Svare & F. vom Saal (eds) *Protection and abuse of young in animals and man*. London: Harwood.

Puts, D.A., Dawood, K., & Welling, L.L. (2012). Why women have orgasms: An evolutionary analysis, *Archives of Sexual Research*, 41, 1127–43.

Pyszczynski, T., Greenberg, J., & Solomon, S. (1999). A dual-process model of defense against conscious and unconscious death-related thoughts: An extension of terror management theory. *Psychological Review*, 106, 835–45.

Ramsey, C.B., Staff, R., Bryant, C., Brock, F., Kitagawa, H., et al. (2012). A complete terrestrial radiocarbon record for 11.2 to 52.8 kyr B.P. *Science*, 338(6105), 370–4.

Raup, D.M. (1986). Biological extinction in earth history. *Science*, 231(4745), 1528–33.

Reb, J., & Connolly, T. (2007). Possession, feelings of ownership and the endowment effect. *Judgment and Decision Making*, 2, 107–14.

Refinetti, R. (2005). Time for sex: Nycthemeral distribution of human sexual behavior. *Journal of Circadian Rhythms* 3(4), doi: 10.1186/1740-3391-3-4.

Reifman, A.S., Larrick, R.P., & Fein, S. (1991). Temper and temperature on the diamond: The heat-aggression relationship in Major League Baseball. *Personality and Social Psychology Bulletin*, 17, 580–5.

Rensberger, B. (1986). *How the world works: A guide to science's greatest discoveries*. New York: William Morrow.

Rietveld, C.A., Hessels, J., & van der Zwan, P. (2015). The stature of the self-employed and its relation with earnings and satisfaction. *Economics and Human Biology*, 17, 59–74.

Rikowski, A., & Grammer, K. (1999). Human body odour, symmetry and attractiveness. *Proceedings of the Royal Society of London*, 266, 869–74.

Robinson, P.H., Kurzban, R., & Jones, D. (2007). The origins of shared intuitions of justice. *Vanderbilt Law Review*, 60, 1633–88.

Roese, N.J. & Jamieson, D.W. (1993). Twenty years of bogus pipeline research: A critical review and meta-analysis. *Psychological Bulletin*, 114, 363–75.

Romanes, G.J. (1882). *Animal intelligence*. London: Kegan, Paul, Trench & Co.

Ronay, R., & von Hippel, W. (2010). The presence of an attractive woman elevates testosterone and physical risk taking in young men. *Social Psychological and Personality Science*, 1, 57–64.

Rosenthal, R., & Fode, K. (1963). The effect of experimenter bias on the performance of the albino rat. *Behavioral Science*, 8, 183–9.

Rosenthal, R., & Jacobson, L. (1966). Teachers' expectancies: Determinants of pupils' IQ gains. *Psychological Reports*, 19, 115–18.

Royle, N.J., Smiseth, P.T., & Kölliker, M. (eds) (2012). *The evolution of parental care*. Oxford: Oxford University Press.

Rozin, P., Millman, L., & Nemeroff, C. (1986). Operation of the laws of sympathetic magic in disgust and other domains. *Journal of Personality and Social Psychology*, 50, 703–12.

Rozin, P. et al. (2008). Disgust. In M. Lewis & J. Haviland (eds) *Handbook of emotions* (3rd edn, pp. 757–76). New York: Guilford.

Sailer, S. (2002). Q&A: Steven Pinker of 'Blank Slate', available at www.upi.com/QA-Steven-Pinker-of-Blank-Slate/26021035991232/.

Sandall, J., Soltani, H., Gates, S., Shennan, A., & Devane, D. (2013). Midwife-led continuity models versus other models of care for childbearing women. *The Cochrane Library*, 8, 1–107.

Sapir, E. (1921). *Language: An introduction to the study of speech*. New York: Harcourt, Brace & Co.

Sapir, E. (1929). The status of linguistics as a science. *Language*, 5, 207–14.

Sato, N., Tan, L., Tate, K., & Okada, M. (2015). Rats demonstrate helping behavior toward a soaked conspecific. *Animal Cognition*, 18(5), 1039–47.

Scaglione, J., & Scaglione, A.R. (2006). *Bully-proofing children: A practical, hands-on guide to stop bullying*. Lanham, MD: Rowman & Littlefield.

Scarr, S., & McCartney, K. (1983). How people make their own environments: A theory of genotype greater than environment effects. *Child Development*, 54, 424–35.

Schacter, D.L. (1996). *Searching for memory: The brain, the mind, and the past*. New York: Basic Books.

Schaller, G.B. (1972). *The Serengeti lion: A study of predator-prey relations*. Chicago: University of Chicago Press.

Schick, A., & Steckel, R.H. (2015). Height, human capital, and earnings: The contributions of cognitive and noncognitive ability. *Journal of Human Capital, 9*, 94–115, doi: 10.1086/679675.

Schmidt-Nielsen, K., Schmidt-Nielsen, B., Jarnum, S.A., & Houpt, T.R. (1957). Body temperature of the camel and its relation to water economy. *American Journal of Physiology*, 188, 103–12.

Schmitt, D.P. (2005). Sociosexuality from Argentina to Zimbabwe: A 48-nation study of sex, culture, and strategies of human mating. *Behavioral and Brain Sciences*, 28(2), 247–311.

Schmitt, D.P., Alcalay, L., Allik, J., Angleitner, A., Ault, L. et al. (2004). Patterns and universals of mate poaching across 53 nations: The effects of sex, culture, and personality on romantically attracting another person's partner. *Journal of Personality and Social Psychology*, 86, 560–84.

Schroder, K.E., Carey, M.P., & Vanable, P.A. (2003). Methodological challenges in research on sexual risk behavior: II. Accuracy of self-reports. *Annals of Behavioral Medicine*, 26, 104–23.

Schwartz, G.T., & Dean, C.M. (2005). Sexual dimorphism in modern human permanent teeth. *American Journal of Physical Anthropology*, 128, 312–17, doi: 10.1002/ajpa.20211.

Sela, Y., Shackelford, T.K., Pham, M.N., & Euler, H.A. (2015). Do women perform fellatio as a mate retention behavior? *Personality and Individual Differences*, 73, 61–6.

Sell, A., Eisner, M., & Ribeaud, D. (2016). Bargaining power and adolescent aggression: The role of fighting ability, coalitional strength, and mate value. *Evolution and Human Behavior*, 37, 105–16.

Sell, A., Hone, L.S., & Pound, N. (2012). The importance of physical strength to human males. *Human Nature*, 23, 30–44, doi: 10.1007/s12110-012-9131-2.

Selye, H. (1956). *The stress of life*. New York: McGraw-Hill.

Service, R.F. (2015). Researchers may have solved origin-of-life conundrum. Available at: www.sciencemag.org/news/2015/03/researchers-may-have-solved-origin-life-conundrum.

Shackelford, T.K., & Goetz, A.T. (2007). Adaptation to sperm competition in humans. *Current Directions in Psychological Science*, 16, 47–50.

Shah, C., van Gompel, M.J., Naeem, V., et al. (2010). Widespread presence of BOULE homologs among animals and conservation of their ancient reproductive function. *PLoS Genetics*, 6(7): e1001022.

Sharp, S.P., & Clutton-Brock, T.H. (2011). Competition, breeding success and ageing rates in female meerkats. *Journal of Evolutionary Biology*, 24(8), 1756–62.

Shepher, J. (1971). Mate selection among second generation kibbutz adolescents and adults: Incest avoidance and negative imprinting. *Archives of Sexual Behavior*, 1, 293–307.

Sherif, M. (1935). A study of some social factors in perception: Chapter 2. *Archives of Psychology*, 27, 17–22.

Sherif, M. (1958). Superordinate goals in the reduction of intergroup conflict. *American Journal of Sociology*, 63, 349–56.

Shimizu, H., & Okabe, M. (2007). Evolutionary origin of autonomic regulation of physiological activities in vertebrate phyla. *Journal of Comparative Physiology A*, 193, 1013–19, doi: 10.1007/s00359-007-0256-4.

Shubin, N. (2008). *Your inner fish: A journey into the 3.5-billion-year history of the human body*. New York: Pantheon Books.

Shuster, G., & Sherman, P.W. (1998). Tool use by naked mole-rats. *Animal Cognition*, 1, 71–4.

Sidanius, J., & Pratto, F. (2000). *Social dominance: An intergroup theory of social hierarchy and oppression*. Cambridge: Cambridge University Press.

Silk, J.B., Alberts, S.C., & Altmann, J. (2003) Social bonds of female baboons enhance infant survival. *Science*, 302, 1231–4.

Silke, A. (2003). Deindividuation, anonymity, and violence: Findings from Northern Ireland. *Journal of Social Psychology*, 143, 493–9.

Simon, L., Greenberg, J., Harmon-Jones, E., Solomon, S., Pyszczynski, T. et al. (1997). Terror management and cognitive experiential self-theory: Evidence that terror management occurs in the experiential system. *Journal of Personality & Social Psychology*, 72, 1132–46.

Singh, D. (1993). Adaptive significance of female physical attractiveness: Role of waist-to-hip ratio. *Journal of Personality and Social Psychology*, 65, 293–307.

Singh, D., Dixson, B.J., Jessop, T.S., Morgan, B., & Dixson, A.F. (2010). Cross-cultural consensus for waist-hip ratio and women's attractiveness. *Evolution and Human Behavior*, 31, 176–81.

Sistiaga, A., Mallol, C., Galván, B., & Summons, R.E. (2014). The Neanderthal meal: A new perspective using faecal biomarkers. *PLoS ONE*, 9, e101045.

Skinner, B.F. (1948). "Superstition" in the pigeon. *Journal of Experimental Psychology*, 38, 168–72.

Skinner, B.F. (1979). *The shaping of a behaviorist: Part two of an autobiography*. New York: Alfred A. Knopf.

Skwarecki, B. (2013). Friendly viruses protect us against bacteria. *Science News*, retrieved July 31, 2017 from www.sciencemag.org/news.

Slater, A., & Quinn P.C. (2001). Face recognition in the newborn infant. *Infant and Child Development*, 10, 21–4.

Slater, A., Bremner, G., Johnson, S.P., Sherwood, P., Hayes, R. et al. (2000). Newborn infants' preference for attractive faces: The role of internal and external facial features. *Infancy*, 1, 265–74.

Sledge, M. (2014). Congress sails past airport hell under special TSA program. Available at: www.huffingtonpost.co.uk/entry/congress-tsa-whitelist_n_5875388.

Smallwood, K. (2014). Why don't vultures get sick when eating dead things? Available at: www.todayifoundout.com/index.php/2014/10/dont-vultures-get-sick-eating-dead-things-cant.

Smith, E.R., & Mackie, D.M. (2007). *Social psychology* (3rd edn). New York: Psychology Press.

Solomon, H., Solomon, L.Z., Arnone, M., Maur, B., Reda, R. et al. (1981). Anonymity and helping. *Journal of Social Psychology*, 113(1), 37–43.

Sotherland, P.R., & Rahn, H. (1987). On the composition of bird eggs. *The Condor*, 89, 48–65.

Spector, D. (2013). Shocking before and after pictures of how climate change is destroying the earth. Available at: www.businessinsider.com/climate-change-before-and-after-photos-2013-5.

Starkweather, K.E., & Hames, R. (2012). A survey of non-classical polyandry. *Human Nature*, 23(2), 149–72.

Stearns, S. (1992). *The evolution of life histories*. Oxford: Oxford University Press.

Stefan, J., & Guéguen, N. (2014). Effect of hair ornamentation on helping. *Psychological Reports*, 114, 491–5.

Stefanucci, J.K., Proffitt, D.R., Clore, G.L., & Parekh, N. (2008). Skating down a steeper slope: Fear influences the perception of geographical slant. *Perception*, 37, 321–3.

Stevens, S.S. (1961). To honor Fechner and repeal his law. *Science*, 133, 80–6.

Stevens, S.S., Carton, A.S., & Shickman, G.M. (1958). A scale of apparent intensity of electric shock. *Journal of Experimental Psychology*, 56, 328–34.

Stockard, C.R. (1921). Developmental rate and structural expression. *American Journal of Anatomy*, 28(2), 115–27.

Stulp, G., Buunk, A.P., & Pollet, T.V. (2013). Women want taller men more than men want shorter women. *Personality and Individual Differences*, 54(8), 877–83.

Sugiyama, L., Tooby, J. & Cosmides, L. (2002). Cross-cultural evidence of cognitive adaptations for social exchange among the Shiwiar of Ecuadorian Amazonia. *Proceedings of the National Academy of Sciences*, 99, 11537–42.

Svenson, G.J., Brannoch, S.K., Rodrigues, H.M., O'Hanlon, J.C., & Wieland, F. (2016). Selection for predation, not female fecundity, explains sexual size dimorphism in the orchid mantises. *Scientific Reports*, 6, 37753, doi: 10.1038/srep37753.

Svetlova, M., Nichols, S.R., & Brownell, C.A. (2010). Toddlers' prosocial behavior: From instrumental to empathic to altruistic helping, *Child Development*, 81, 1814–27.

Swann, W.B., Jr., Gómez, Á., Buhrmester, M.D., López-Rodríguez, L., Jiménez, J. et al. (2014). Contemplating the ultimate sacrifice: Identity fusion channels pro-group affect, cognition, and moral decision making. *Journal of Personality and Social Psychology*, 106, 713–27.

Swanson, E.M., McElhinny, T.L., Dworkin, I. Weldele, M.L., Glickman, S.E. et al. (2013). Ontogeny of sexual size dimorphism in the spotted hyena (*Crocuta crocuta*). *Journal of Mammalogy*, 94, 1298–310.

Symons, D. (1979). *The evolution of human sexuality*. New York: Oxford University Press.

Thaler, R.H., & Sunstein, C.R. (2008). *Nudge: Improving decisions about health, wealth, and happiness*. New Haven, CT: Yale University Press.

Theobald, D.L. (2010). A formal test of the theory of universal common ancestry. *Nature*, 465(7295), 219–22.

Thibaut, J.W., & Kelley, H.H. (1959). *The social psychology of groups*. New York: Wiley.

Thorndike, E.L. (1911). *Animal intelligence: Experimental studies*. New York: Macmillan.

Thornhill, R., Gangestad, S.W., Miller, R., Scheyd, G., McCollough, J.K. et al. (2003). Major histocompatibility complex genes, symmetry, and body scent attractiveness in men and women. *Behavioral Ecology*, 14, 668–78.

Thornhill, R., & Palmer, C.T. (2000). *A natural history of rape: Biological bases of sexual coercion*. Cambridge, MA: MIT Press.

Timmerman, T.A. (2007). "It was a thought pitch": Personal, situational, and target influences on hit-by-pitch events across time. *Journal of Applied Psychology*, 92, 876–84.

Todorov, A., Olivola, C.Y., Dotsch, R., & Mende-Siedlecki, P. (2015). Social attributions from faces: Determinants, consequences, accuracy, and functional significance. *Annual Review of Psychology*, 66(1), 519–45.

Tomasello, M. (2005). *Constructing a language: A usage-based theory of language acquisition*. Cambridge, MA: Harvard University Press.

Tooby, J., & Cosmides, L. (1988). The evolution of war and its cognitive foundations. *Institute for Evolutionary Studies Technical Report*, 88–1.

Tosti, G., & Thorup-Kristensen, K. (2010). Using coloured roots to study root interaction and competition in intercropped legumes and non-legumes. *Journal of Plant Ecology*, 3(3), 191–9.

Triandis, H.C. (1989). The self and social behavior in differing cultural contexts. *Psychological Review*, 96(3), 506–20.

Tricomi, E., Rangel, A., Camerer, C. F., & O'Doherty, J.P. (2010). Neural evidence for inequality-averse social preferences. *Nature,* 463(7284), 1089–91.

Trivers, R.L. (1971). The evolution of reciprocal altruism. *Quarterly Review of Biology*, 46, 35–57.

Trivers, R.L. (1972). Parental investment and sexual selection. In B. Campbell (ed.) *Sexual selection and the descent of man* (pp. 136–79). Chicago, IL: Aldine.

Trump, D. (2014). 4:39 PM, 1 January, Twitter. https://twitter.com/realDonaldTrump/status/418542137899491328.

Tumulty, J., Morales, V., & Summers, K. (2014). The biparental care hypothesis for the evolution of monogamy: Experimental evidence in an amphibian. *Behavioral Ecology*, 25(2), 262–70.

Turkheimer, E., Haley, A., Waldron, M., D'Onofrio, B., & Gottesman, I.I. (2003). Socioeconomic status modifies heritability of IQ in young children. *Psychological Science*, 14, 623–8.

Tversky, A., & Kahneman, D. (1974). Judgment under uncertainty: Heuristics and biases. *Science*, 185(4157), 1124–31.

Tversky, A., & Kahneman, D. (1983). Extensional versus intuitive reasoning: The conjunction fallacy in probability judgment. *Psychological Review*, 90(4), 293–315.

Tyler, T. (2006). Restorative justice and procedural justice. *Journal of Social Issues*, 62, 305–23.

Van Baaren, R.B., Holland, R.W., Kawakami, K., & van Knippenberg, A. (2004). Mimicry and prosocial behavior. *Psychological Science*, 15, 71–4.

Van Kranendonk, M.J., Deamer, D.W., & Djokic, T. (2017). Life springs. *Scientific American*, 317(2), 28–35, doi: 10.1038/scientificamerican0817-28.

Vandello, J.A., & Cohen, D. (2003). Male honor and female fidelity: Implicit cultural scripts that perpetuate domestic violence. *Journal of Personality and Social Psychology*, 84, 997–1010.

Vassoler, F.M., White, S.L., Schmidt, H.D., Sadri-Vakili, G., & Pierce, R.C. (2013). Epigenetic inheritance of a cocaine resistance phenotype. *Nature Neuroscience*, 16, 42–7, doi: 10.1038/nn.3280.

Von Baer, K.E. (1828). *On the developmental history of animals: Observation and reflection* [original in German]. Königsberg: Bornträger.

Von Hippel, W., & Trivers, R. (2011). The evolution and psychology of self-deception. *Behavioral and Brain Sciences*, 34(1), 1–56.

Voracek, M. (2009). Comparative study of digit ratios (2D:4D and other) and novel measures of relative finger length: Testing magnitude and consistency of sex differences across samples. *Perceptual and Motor Skills*, 108, 83–93.

Wang, L., Cheung, J., Pu, F., Li, D., Zhang, M. et al. (2011). Why do woodpeckers resist head impact injury: A biomechanical investigation. *PLoS ONE*, 6, 1–6, e26490.

Walker, D.B., Walker, J.C., Cavnar, P.J. et al. (2006). Naturalistic quantification of canine olfactory sensitivity. *Applied Animal Behavior Science*, 97, 241–54.

Walker, R.S., Flinn, M.V., & Hill, K.R. (2010). Evolutionary history of partible paternity in lowland South America. *Proceedings of the National Academy of Sciences*, 107, 19195–200.

Warneken, F. (2015). Precocious prosociality: Why do children help? *Child Development Perspectives*, 9(1), 1–6.

Warneken, F., & Tomasello, M. (2006). Altruistic helping in human infants and young chimpanzees. *Science*, 311, 1301–3.

Wason, P. (1968). Reasoning about a rule. *Quarterly Journal of Experimental Psychology*, 20, 273–81.

Webb, S.J., Monk, C.S., & Nelson, C.A. (2010). Mechanisms of postnatal neurobiological development: Implications for human development. *Developmental Neurobiology*, 19, 147–71.

Wegner, D.M. (1994). Ironic processes of mental control. *Psychological Review*, 101, 34–52.

Weismantel, M. (2004). Moche sex pots: Reproduction and temporality in ancient South America. *American Anthropologist*, 106, 495–505.

Weisfeld, G.E., Czilli, T., Phillips, K.A., Gall, J.A., & Lichtman, C.M. (2003). Possible olfaction-based mechanisms in human kin recognition and inbreeding avoidance. *Journal of Experimental Child Psychology*, 85(3), 279–95.

Weiss, A., King, J.E., Inoue-Murayamad, M., Matsuzawae, T., & Oswald, A.J. (2012). Evidence for a midlife crisis in great apes consistent with the U-shape in human wellbeing. *Proceedings of the National Academy of Sciences*, 109, 19949–52.

Weiss, L., Laforsch, C., & Tollrian, R. (2012). The taste of predation and the defences of prey. In C. Bronmark & L.-A. Hansson (eds) *Chemical ecology in aquatic systems* (pp. 111–26). Oxford: Oxford University Press.

Welling, L.L., Jones, B.C., DeBruine, L.M., Smith, F.G., Feinberg, D.R. et al. (2008). Men report stronger attraction to femininity in women's faces when their testosterone levels are high. *Hormones and Behavior*, 54, 703–8.

Whitehead, J.W. (2012). Jailing Americans for profit: The rise of the prison industrial complex. Available at: www.rutherford.org/publications_resources/john_whiteheads_commentary/jailing_americans_for_profit_the_rise_of_the_prison_industrial_complex.

Whitehouse, H., McQuinn, B., Buhrmester, M. & Swann, W.B., Jr. (2014). Brothers in arms: Libyan revolutionaries bond like family. *Proceedings of the National Academy of Sciences*, 111, 50, 17783–5.

Whorf, B.L. (1956). The relation of habitual thought and behavior to language. In J.B. Carroll (ed.) *Language, thought and reality*. Cambridge, MA: MIT Press.

Wiesel, T.N., & Hubel, D.H. (1963). Single-cell responses in striate cortex of kittens deprived of vision in one eye. *Journal of Neurophysiology*, 26, 1003–17.

Wilke, A., & Barrett, H.C. (2009). The hot hand phenomenon as a cognitive adaptation to clumped resources. *Evolution and Human Behavior*, 30(3), 161–9.

Willer, R., Sharkey, A., & Frey, S. (2012). Reciprocity on the hardwood: Passing patterns among professional basketball players. *PLoS ONE*, 7(12), e49807.

Wilson, D.S., & Sober, E. (1994). Reintroducing group selection to the human behavioral sciences. *Behavioral and Brain Sciences*, 17, 585–654.

Wilson, D.S., van Vugt, M., & O'Gorman, R. (2008). Multilevel selection theory and major evolutionary transitions: Implications for psychological science. *Current Directions in Psychological Science*, 17, 6–9.

Wilson, E.O. (1975). *Sociobiology: The new synthesis*. Cambridge, MA: Harvard University Press.

Wilson, E.O. (1978). *On human nature*. Cambridge, MA: Harvard University Press.

Wilson, R.T. (1989). *Ecophysiology of the Camelidae and desert ruminants*. Berlin: Springer.

Winegard, B.M., & Deaner, R.O. (2014). Misrepresentations of evolutionary psychology in sex and gender textbooks. *Evolutionary Psychology*, 12, 474–508.

Winter, I., & Uleman, J.S. (1984). When are social judgments made? Evidence for the spontaneity of trait inferences. *Journal of Personality and Social Psychology*, 47, 237–52.

Wood, W., & Eagly, A.H. (2012). Biosocial construction of sex differences and similarities in behavior. *Advances in Experimental Social Psychology*, 46, 55–123.

World Health Organization (2018). Female genital mutilation: Fact sheet. Retrieved from www.who.int/mediacentre/factsheets/fs241/en.

Yon-Say, B., *Single Ladies*.

Yule, G.U. (1902). Mendel's laws and their probable relation to intra-racial heredity. *New Phytology*, 1, 222–38.

Zajonc, R.B. (1965). Social facilitation. *Science*, 149, 269–74.

Zajonc, R.B. (1980). Feeling and thinking: Preferences need no inferences. *American Psychologist*, 35, 151–75.

Zawitz, M.W. (1995). Guns used in crime, Bureau of Justice Statistics, NCJ-148201. Available at: www.bjs.gov/content/pub/pdf/GUIC.PDF.

Zimbardo, P.G. (1969). The human choice: Individuation, reason and order versus deindividuation, impulse and chaos. In W.J. Arnold & E. Levine (eds) *Nebraska Symposium on Motivation* (vol. 18, pp. 237–307). Lincoln, NE: University of Nebraska Press.

SUBJECT INDEX

NAME INDEX